Mussolini
and the Jews

The Institute of Jewish Affairs gratefully acknowledges the assistance of the Memorial Foundation for Jewish Culture which made the preparation and publication of this volume possible.

MUSSOLINI AND THE JEWS

German–Italian Relations
and the Jewish Question in Italy
1922–1945

MEIR MICHAELIS

Published for
THE INSTITUTE OF JEWISH AFFAIRS, LONDON
by
THE CLARENDON PRESS, OXFORD
1978

Oxford University Press, Walton Street, Oxford OX2 6DP

OXFORD   LONDON   GLASGOW   NEW YORK
TORONTO   MELBOURNE   WELLINGTON   CAPE TOWN
IBADAN   NAIROBI   DAR ES SALAAM   LUSAKA
KUALA LUMPUR   SINGAPORE   JAKARTA   HONG KONG   TOKYO
DELHI   BOMBAY   CALCUTTA   MADRAS   KARACHI

British Library Cataloguing in Publication Data
Michaelis, Meir
  Mussolini and the Jews.
    1. Jews in Italy—Persecutions 2. Fascism—Italy—History 3. Italy—Politics and government—1922–1945
  I. Title II. Institute of Jewish Affairs
  323.1'19'24043   DS135.18   78–40260

ISBN 0–19–822542–3

Typeset by CCC and printed and bound at William Clowes & Sons Limited, Beccles and London.

To the memory of
DANTE A. LATTES

PITIGLIANO 1876 –
DOLO (VENEZIA) 1965

Preface

FIFTEEN YEARS ago I made a first attempt to trace the impact of German-Italian relations on Fascist racial policy in a paper entitled 'On the Jewish Question in Fascist Italy', based on published sources only, which covered the period from the March on Rome to the enactment of the anti-Jewish laws (1922–38).[1] My main conclusion—that Mussolini's anti-Semitic legislation, though undoubtedly an Italian variant of Hitler's Nuremberg laws and a demonstration of ideological and political solidarity with the Third Reich, was not the result of *direct* German interference—has since been confirmed by Renzo De Felice (who had access to the unpublished Italian sources) and is now generally accepted.[2] At that time, however, I was not in a position either to reconstruct the complex story of *indirect* German interference or to bring the narrative up to the end of World War II, most of the relevant documents not yet being available to me. The present study, the result of ten years' research in England and Israel, is an attempt to fill the gap. It covers the whole Fascist period from the march on Rome to the fall of Fascism, including the twenty months of the German occupation, during which Hitler's Jewish affairs experts extended the 'final solution' of the Jewish problem to Mussolini's Fascist puppet Republic. It is based largely on unpublished German, Italian, English, and Hebrew records which were acquired in London, Oxford, Bonn, Freiburg im Breisgau, Munich, Rome, Milan, Jerusalem, and Rehovoth between 1962 and 1975.

While the documentation here presented and analysed does not modify the picture drawn a decade and a half ago in any essential detail, it certainly adds a new dimension to it. It shows how the character of Fascist anti-Semitic policy was shaped and

[1] M. Michaelis, 'On the Jewish Question in Fascist Italy', *Yad Vashem Studies*, IV (1960), 7–41 (also in Hebrew). See also the revised Italian version: 'I rapporti italo-tedeschi e il problema degli ebrei in Italia (1922–1938)', *Rivista di Studi Politici Internazionali*, XXVIII (Apr.–June 1961), 238–82.
[2] See R. De Felice, *Storia degli ebrei italiani sotto il fascismo*, 3rd edn., Turin, 1972, pp. 242–247.

moulded by the exigencies of the Rome–Berlin Axis from its very inception, despite the fundamental conflict of interest between the two countries and the divergence of views on Hitler's doctrine of Nordic superiority. It also throws light on Nazi–Fascist collaboration in the racial sphere. Until Mussolini's downfall in July 1943 the nature and extent of this collaboration was largely, if not exclusively, determined by the Fascists who initiated it. It was only after the Italian armistice, when Hitler decided to treat the German-occupied part of Italy as conquered territory, that the situation was drastically reversed.

This book is dedicated to the memory of Dante A. Lattes, the Nestor of Italian Zionism.

London–Oxford–Oranim–Jerusalem,   Meir Michaelis
July 1970–December 1975

Acknowledgements

I AM greatly indebted to the Institute of Jewish Affairs, London, for a generous research grant which made the writing of this book possible. For valuable bibliographical help and research facilities I would like to thank Miss Ann Abley of St. Antony's College, Oxford; Dr. Giulio Anau of the Union of Italian Jewish Communities, Rome; Mrs. Perla Baumann, the late Mr. Emanuel Brand, Mrs. Clara Guini, and Dr. Shmuel Krakowski of the Yad Vashem Institute, Jerusalem; Dr. Elizabeth E. Eppler of the Institute of Jewish Affairs, London; Dr. Boris Guriel of the Weizmann Archives, Rehovoth; Dr. Michael Heymann of the Central Zionist Archives, Jerusalem; Mr. Kenneth Hiscock of the Foreign Office Library, London; Dr. Anton Hoch and Dr. Thilo Vogelsang of the Institut für Zeitgeschichte, Munich; Mr. Ezra Kahn of the Institute of Contemporary History and Wiener Library, London; Dr. Liliana Picciotto-Fargion and the late Dr. Eloisa Ravenna of the Centro di Documentazione Ebraica Contemporanea, Milan; and Dr. Friedrich-Christian Stahl of the Militärarchiv, Freiburg im Breisgau.

To Prof. H. Booms, Dr. Milan Hauner, Prof. A. Hillgruber, Prof. H.-A. Jacobsen, Dr. Helmut Piper, and Dr. Amedeo Tagliacozzo I am grateful for their valuable help in the acquisition of unpublished records from German and Italian Archives.

Many scholars have generously allowed me to draw upon their special knowledge. Among them I must mention especially Prof. Paolo Alatri, Prof. Charles Y. Bloch, Dr. Sergio Della Pergola, Prof. Shaul Friedlander, the Hon. Margaret Lambert, the Hon. Adrian Lyttelton, Dr. Jens Petersen, Dr. E. Franco Sabatello, the late Prof. Gaetano Salvemini, Prof. Nino Valeri, and Prof. Leo Valiani.

I have benefited greatly from many discussions, both oral and written, with Michael Tagliacozzo, the foremost authority on the Holocaust in Rome.

For valuable testimonies I am indebted to various protagonists in the dramatic events, including the late Dr. Elia S. Artom, Dr. Giuseppe Bolaffio, the late Leone Carpi, the late General Emilio Faldella, Dr. Nahum Goldmann, Count Dino Grandi, the late Prof. Dante A. Lattes, Dr. Renzo Levi, General Giorgio Liuzzi, Signora Fanny G. Minerbi, the late Dr. Umberto Nahon, Alfonso Pacifici, the late General Emanuele Pugliese, the late Renzo Ravenna, Settimio Sorani, Dr. Aldo

Tagliacozzo, the late Lelio Vittorio Valobra, and the late Colonel Massimo Adolfo Vitale. Quotations of Crown Copyright material appear by permission of H.M. Stationery Office.

Finally, I wish to record my indebtedness to Dr. Mario Minerbi, my collaborator since 1959; to Prof. Arnaldo Momigliano whose support helped me over many a bad patch; and to my wife who typed and retyped the manuscript and encouraged me in every possible way.

Contents

LIST OF ABBREVIATIONS   xiii

PART I: FROM THE MARCH ON ROME TO THE SPANISH CIVIL
     WAR (1922–1936)

I   The Historical Background   3

II   Mussolini and the Jews (1922–1932)   10

III   The Rise of Hitler and the First Anti-Semitic Campaign
in Italy (1933–1934)   57

IV   Abyssinia, Spain, and the *Rapprochement* with Nazi
Germany (1935–1936)   81

PART II: FROM THE ROME–BERLIN AXIS TO THE FALL OF
     FASCISM (1936–1945)

V   From the Axis Alliance to the Munich Conference (1936–
1938)   107

VI   From the Munich Conference to the Pact of Steel (1938–
1939)   192

VII   Towards Non-Belligerency (1939)   231

VIII   From Non-Belligerency to War (1939–1940)   276

IX   War and Defeat I (1940–1943)   291

X   War and Defeat II (1943–1945)   342

XI   Epilogue   407

APPENDICES

I   The Anti-Jewish Polemics of 1933–1934   415

II   The *ras* of Cremona   418

III   Mussolini and Léon Blum   420

IV   Pius XII and the Third Reich   424

A NOTE ON THE SOURCES   427

BIBLIOGRAPHY   432

INDEX   463

Abbreviations

ACS	Archivio Centrale dello Stato Italiano, Rome
ADAP	*Akten zur Deutschen Auswärtigen Politik,* Baden-Baden
ASMEI	Archivio Storico Ministero Affari Esteri Italiano, Rome
AUCII	Archivio Unione Comunità Israelitiche Italiane, Rome
BA/K	Bundesarchiv, Coblenz
BA/MA	Bundesarchiv/Militärarchiv, Freiburg i. Br.
CDEC	Centro di Documentazione Ebraica Contemporanea, Milan
CZA	Central Zionist Archives, Jerusalem
DBFP	*Documents of British Foreign Policy,* London
DDF	*Documents diplomatiques français,* Paris
DDI	*Documenti diplomatici italiani,* Rome
DGFP	*Documents of German Foreign Policy,* London
DZA	Deutsches Zentralarchiv, Potsdam
FRUS	*Foreign Relations of the United States,* Washington
GFM	German Foreign Ministry Records, Foreign Office Library, London
IC	Italian Collection, St. Antony's College, Oxford
IFZ	Institut für Zeitgeschichte, Munich
IMT	*International Military Tribunal* (Trial of Major War Criminals), Nuremberg
ND	*Nuremberg Document*
NS/HA	NSDAP Hauptarchiv, Wiener Library, London
O.O.	*Opera Omnia di Benito Mussolini,* Florence, 1951–63
PA	Politisches Archiv, Bonn
PRO	Public Record Office, London
V.B.	*Völkischer Beobachter,* Berlin and Munich
VJZG	*Vierteljahrshefte für Zeitgeschichte,* Munich
WA	Weizmann Archives, Rehovoth
YVS	Yad Vashem Archives, Jerusalem

PART I

FROM THE MARCH ON ROME
TO THE SPANISH CIVIL WAR
(1922–1936)

I The Historical Background

DESPITE ITS small size, the Italian Jewish community is of special interest to the student of Jewish history. Firstly, because its annals span well over twenty centuries and half a dozen successive civilizations. Secondly, because the emancipation of Italian Jewry was uniquely successful. As late as 1848, there was hardly a country in Europe where the restrictions placed upon the Jews were more galling; twenty-two years later there was no part of the world where religious freedom was more real, or religious prejudice so small.[1] When Theodor Herzl visited Rome in 1904, he was told by King Victor Emmanuel III that in Italy no distinction was made between Jews and Christians; 'Jews may occupy any position, and they do. The army, the civil service, even the diplomatic corps: everything is open to them ... Jews, for us, are full-blown Italians'.[2]

The late President of Israel, Chaim Weizmann, accurately described this phenomenon when he wrote:

The community was a small one, but its members took an active part in Italian life—political, economic, artistic, scientific—and were to all intents and purposes indistinguishable from their fellow-citizens, except that they went to synagogue instead of to Mass ... It was a great experience for me to meet ancient Jewish families with a long intellectual tradition (sometimes deriving from Spain), a wide culture and an exquisite hospitality. Amid all the suffering of the last few years, there is for me a special poignancy in the destruction which has overtaken the Italian Jewish community ... 'They had given so much to Italy and so much to their own people'.[3]

All students of Italian Jewry, whether Jewish or Gentile, Fascist or anti-Fascist, are agreed that there was virtually no Jewish problem in modern Italy. The late Cecil Roth, among the foremost authorities on the subject, affirmed in his monumental

[1] For details see M. Rossi, 'Emancipation of the Jews in Italy', *Jewish Social Studies*, xv (April 1953), 113-34; R. De Felice, 'Per una storia del problema ebraico in Italia alla fine del XVIII secolo e all'inizio del XIX. La prima emancipazione (1792–1814)', in id., *Italia giacobina*, Naples, 1965, pp. 317–96.
[2] T. Herzl, *Tagebücher, iii (Gesammelte Zionistische Schriften, iv,* Tel Aviv, 1934, p. 549 (entry for 23 Jan. 1904).
[3] C. Weizmann, *Trial and Error*, London, 1949, pp. 356-7.

work *The History of the Jews of Italy* that after 1870 there was no country in either hemisphere where Jewish conditions 'were or could be better':

> It was not only that disabilities were removed, as happened elsewhere too during these momentous years, but that the Jews were accepted freely, naturally and spontaneously as members of the Italian people, on a perfect footing of equality with their neighbours . . . There was in the Italian Jew no element of the foreigner. Established in the country already for two thousand years, he was as much a native as any other component of the Italian people. So far, indeed, had the original purity of Italian 'blood' been modified in the course of the centuries that he perhaps represented the only ethnic component that had remained constant since the beginning of the Christian era. Even the newest elements in the Synagogue—the descendants of the German immigrants of the fifteenth and sixteenth centuries, or of the Marrano refugees of the seventeenth—were by now thoroughly established and acclimatized . . . Some rearguards of the ultra-Catholic party, devoid of influence, automatically maintained a spluttering guerilla warfare, but it created more amusement than friction. The new antisemitism, when it began to rear its ugly head north of the Alps towards the end of the century, had no repercussions in the country. Nor when persecution broke out in the Russian empire in the eighteen-eighties did any appreciable eddy of the fugitives who swept the English-speaking world reach this poor and imperfectly industrialized Latin land and thereby disturb the balance . . . The profession of Judaism was regarded as an amiable eccentricity rather than a social mistake.[1]

Gentile students of the phenomenon have expressed similar views. Benedetto Croce, the eminent liberal scholar, wrote in his *History of Italy from 1871 to 1915* that, fortunately, 'there was no sign of that folly (*stoltezza*) which goes by the name anti-Semitism and which consists in first strengthening by persecution the solidarity of the Jews and their separation from all other peoples, and then trying to overcome the consequences of persecution by more persecution'.[2] Antonio Gramsci, the leading theoretician of the Italian Communist Party, made the same point in his celebrated study of the Risorgimento, ascribing the absence of anti-Jewish feeling to the elimination of municipal particularism and Catholic cosmopolitanism, 'the most characteristically

[1] C. Roth, *The History of the Jews of Italy*, Philadelphia, 1946, pp. 474–5.
[2] B. Croce, *Storia d'Italia dal 1871 al 1915*, 11th edn., Bari 1956, p. 101.

Italian forms of the medieval and feudal residue'.[1] Luigi Villari, son of a noted historian and the leading Fascist propagandist in the Anglo-Saxon countries until 1940, thought that the virtual non-existence of a Jewish problem in modern Italy was primarily due to the numerical insignificance of Italian Jewry and to the absence of a Jewish proletariat:

Out of a total population of 42,000,000, only one per thousand are Jews. The immense majority of them are of the Sephardim branch exiled from Spain at the time of the *Reyes Católicos*, or later immigrants from the Levant who are themselves of Spanish origin. Very few of the Italian Jews are poor, and there are not those seething masses of Jewish proletarians which elsewhere cause so much trouble of a social and economic nature. Above all, the Italian Jews have for the most part been resident in the country for many generations, and even if they retain their old religion—to which indeed many of them are deeply attached—they have been completely absorbed into the body of the nation and regard themselves and are regarded by their neighbours as thorough Italians. Jews played an honourable part in the *Risorgimento*, and the number of Jews who fought and died for their country in the World War are considerable, as may be seen from the rolls of honour in the various synagogues.

With the establishment of the Italian Kingdom, even social discrimination against the Jews (which outlasted the legal and political disabilities) soon disappeared, 'although traces of it survived here and there':

Jews have for long been placed on a footing of equality with Christians in all fields of activity, including the army, the navy, the civil services and the professions, admitted to the best society, except in a few old-fashioned circles, and not a few have had titles of nobility conferred on them. In politics it was no handicap to be a Jew. Italy has had one Jewish Prime Minister (Luigi Luzzatti, M. M.). . . . and another, Sidney Sonnino, who, although a Christian by religion, was the son of a Jewish father (incidentally he proved one of the ablest, most patriotic and honest statesmen the country ever had). Many other Jews have held ministerial rank; one, General Ottolenghi, was Minister of War, and to-day, in the Fascist Government, the Minister of Finance, Guido Jung, is of Jewish origin, while many other Jews hold high positions in the public service.[2]

[1] A. Gramsci, *Il Risorgimento*, 6th edn., Rome, 1954, pp. 167–8.
[2] Sonnino was Prime Minister from February to May 1906 and from December 1909 to March 1910; Luzzatti from March 1910 to March 1911; Ottolenghi was War Minister in 1902–3.

The advent of Fascism, according to Villari, did not lead to any deterioration in the position of Italian Jewry. On the contrary, twelve years after the March on Rome relations between Jews and Gentiles in Italy were more harmonious than ever before: 'There was a moment after the outbreak of the Russian Revolution, many of whose leaders in the early days of Bolshevism were Jews, when certain expressions of anti-Semitism occurred in Italy as in every other country on both sides of the Atlantic. But they did not last; very few of the Italian subversive leaders were Jews, and in fact the immense majority of Italian Jews had no sympathy of any kind with Bolshevism ... Today (1934, M. M.) it is safe to say that anti-Semitism is non-existent in Italy.'[1]

In 1934 no one thought of challenging Villari's account of Italian (and Fascist) benevolence towards the Jews. Three years later, however, when an anti-Jewish campaign was already well under way in Italy, the subject was raised afresh by Sir W. McClure, a seasoned British diplomat who had spent many years in the country. McClure agreed with Villari that there had been no anti-Jewish movement worthy of the name from the unification of Italy to the second decade of the 'Fascist era'. But while it was true that ever since 1870 Jews had taken their 'full share in the national life' and had found 'few obstacles to their activities, social, professional or political', it was no less true that the Jewish issue had always cropped up in times of crisis in one way or another, even before the Bolshevik Revolution and the rise of Fascism. The prominent part played by many Jews in the Risorgimento and the alleged prominence of the Jewish element in Freemasonry aroused resentment in certain Catholic circles, and during the last two decades of the nineteenth century there was a revival of clerical anti-Semitism. A decade later, the conflict between Italy and Turkey gave rise to polemics against both the Italian Zionists (who were charged with divided loyalties) and 'international Jewry' (which was accused of opposing Italian aspirations in North Africa:)

The first anti-Semitic talk I ever heard in Italy was in connexion with the Libyan war. At that time it became an article of faith with a few people that 'International Jewry' was against Italy. Italian Jewry and

[1] L. Villari, 'Luigi Luzzatti', in *Twelve Jews*, ed. H. Bolitho, London, 1934, pp. 123–5.

Italian Freemasonry had welcomed the Young Turk movement, which, it was pointed out, had had one of its roots in the Masonic Lodge of 'Macedonia Risorta' in Salonica. The names of 'Maître' Salem and Carasso Effendi were recalled, secret links were divined between organisations in different countries. It was alleged that the 'Jewish-controlled' press was particularly hostile to Italy: 'Berliner Tageblatt', 'Frankfurter Zeitung', 'Neue Freie Presse', 'The Daily Telegraph' and Lucien Wolf in the 'Daily Graphic' were all adduced as proof of an anti-Italian Jewish combination. A number of Italians were beginning to react more strongly against Freemasonry and to find its international links in the Jewish communities.

At that time the anti-Jewish agitation was mainly conducted by a few members of the Italian Nationalist Association which had been founded in December 1910, less than a year before the Italian invasion of Libya. The outbreak of World War I gave a fresh impetus to the anti-Jewish tendencies: 'On the outbreak of the Great War, and even before, there were a good many voices in Italy which complained of the stranglehold the (German–Jewish) Banca Commerciale had acquired, and was tightening, upon Italian industry and commerce. This feeling was only partly anti-Jewish, and mainly anti-German—which reads curiously to-day. It was felt that Germany was using Jews to dominate Italy, and some people began to argue that Jews were specially useful instruments for such a purpose, as they had no real "patria" (fatherland)'.

The 'anti-national' attitude of the two Jewish Socialist leaders, Claudio Treves and Giuseppe Emanuele Modigliani, was an additional source of grievance: 'The steadfast refusal of the Italian Official Socialist Party to support the War, an attitude which differed sharply from the general attitude of Socialists in Germany, Austria, France and England, where only exceptions took a stand against the War, led to further searchings of hearts. The increasing prominence of Treves and Modigliani began to be remarked upon. It was Treves who in 1917 raised the slogan "Next winter no one must be in the trenches", and after Caporetto, when Turati (Filippo Turati, the Gentile Socialist leader, M. M.) made a patriotic declaration in the Chamber, Treves and Modigliani made no sign.'

Shortly after the war (from which the Italian people emerged in a state of dejection and bitterness), the forged *Protocols of the*

Elders of Zion began to be talked of in Italy. Two Italian translations were published in 1921, one by a Fascist publicist in close touch with Mussolini, the other by a right-wing Catholic journalist in Florence, 'and its assertions were believed by a few people, who found in this work a far-fetched explanation of the Soviet Revolution. The prominence of Jews in the Russian movement was noted, and ever since this period there has been an increasing tendency to attribute world evils to the Jewish International.'

The popular association of Jewry with Bolshevism was not the only reason why the Jews of Italy became an object of criticism and suspicion during the post-war crisis which culminated in the Fascist March on Rome. Another was the "Sionist question" (which had entered a new phase with the establishment of a British mandatory regime in Palestine). Not only did the idea of 'division of allegiance' arise. It was also maintained that a 'Sionist Palestine' was in effect an instrument of British Imperial policy, and that Italian Jews, in supporting the Jewish National Home, were potentially weakening Italy's position in the Mediterranean 'by leading to a serious alteration in the *status quo*.'

Fascism was thus tinged with anti-Jewish prejudice from the very outset. Up to now, however, the anti-Jewish polemics had had 'little importance'. Only a small minority of the Italian Jews were Zionists. And although both 'Jewish Bolshevism' and 'Jewish high finance' had been the object of attack in the Fascist press from time to time, very few Italians associated the Italian Jewish community with either of these phenomena: 'The Italian Jew was generally held to be, as he has generally shown himself to be, a "good patriot." There have been voices raised against this idea, but they have generally been voices in the wilderness.'

McClure concluded his survey affirming that Italy was still 'a long way from being anti-Semitic', and that such anti-Jewish feeling as existed in certain Fascist circles was 'purely political, not racial', racial anti-Semitism being totally out of step with Italian history and traditions.[1]

The above was written in May 1937. When, a mere fourteen

[1] PRO/F.O. 371/21182/R3585/2476/22 (McClure to Foreign Office, 11 May 1937). On pre-Fascist anti-Semitism, cf. R. Mazzetti, *L'antiebraismo nella cultura italiana dal 1700 al 1900*, Modena 1939; id., *Orientamenti antigebraici della vita e della cultura italiana*, Modena, 1939; M. Michaelis, 'Riflessioni sulla recente storia dell'Ebraismo italiano', *La Rassegna Mensile di Israel*, xliii (May–June 1977), 193–6.

months later, Mussolini embarked on a racial campaign against his Jewish subjects, it was clear to all Italians that their master had stooped to copy the German racial doctrines which he had hitherto rejected with scorn. It was a fatal step for the Fascist dictator; the beginning of that surrender of independence which led his country to disaster and himself to the gibbet in the Piazzale Loreto in Milan.

In the following pages we propose to analyse in detail the various stages by which the Fascist regime passed from anti-racialism to racial anti-Semitism on the German model, taking as our central theme the impact of German–Italian relations on the evolution of the racial question in Italy.

II   Mussolini and the Jews (1922–1932)

MUSSOLINI'S INTEREST in Jews and Judaism dates back to his Socialist youth. In 1908, at the age of twenty-five, he wrote (in an article on Nietzsche's philosophy of force): 'The inversion of moral values was the chief feat of the Jewish people. The Palestinians [*sic*] defeated their age-old enemies by destroying their codes of moral values. This was an act of spiritual vengeance in harmony with the sacerdotal temperament of the Jewish people.'[1] The article was an attack on Claudio Treves, the Jewish Socialist leader, who had defined Nietzsche's superman as a piece of adolescent symbolism and whom Mussolini was to oust from the editorship of *Avanti*, chief organ of the Italian Socialist Party, in December 1912.

But if sacerdotal Judaism was anathema to the young Socialist, so was Pan-German racialism, a phenomenon which he first encountered in 1909, during a sojourn in the Austrian Trentino. His reaction took the form of a pamphlet in which he denounced 'theoretical and practical Pan-Germanism' as an insult to the Latin race and an attempt to undermine the international solidarity of the working class.[2]

It has been suggested that jealousy of intellectually superior Jewish rivals, like Treves and Modigliani, turned Mussolini into a latent anti-Semite during his Socialist phase.[3] But while it is true that he was not above an occasional anti-Jewish sneer, it is equally true that the chief targets of his vitriolic pen were fellow Gentiles, such as Leonida Bissolati, Ivanoe Bonomi, Angelo Cabrini, and Guido Podrecca, whom he had expelled from the Party as right-wing deviationists in July 1912. Moreover, as a left-wing extremist of radically internationalist and anti-racialist views, he could not make use of anti-Semitic arguments in inner-party struggles, nor could he approve of Italian nationalists like

---

[1] *O.O.* i. 174–84.

[2] *O.O.* xxxiii. 153–213.

[3] A. Pincherle, 'In margine alla storia degle ebrei italiani', *Nuova Rivista Storica*, xlvi, (Sept.–Dec. 1962), 599–602. According to Massimo Rocca, Mussolini, when still editor of *Avanti*, spoke slightingly of Karl Marx, 'a Jew and a bourgeois in spite of himself' (*Come il fascismo divenne una dittatura*, Milan, 1952, p. 40).

Francesco Coppola who, in 1911, attacked 'international Jewry' for allegedly opposing the Libyan war.[1]

Various Jews took part in the conversion of the future Duce to interventionism and nationalism (G. Pontremoli, E. Jarach, E. Jona, C. Sarfatti). There were also five Jews among the founders of the Fighting Fasci (*fasci di combattimento*) on 23 March 1919, and another three (Gino Bolaffi, Bruno Mondolfo, and Duilio Sinigaglia) went down in history as so-called *martiri fascisti* (Fascist martyrs), having fallen in the Fascist cause before the March on Rome.[2]

According to Giuseppe Antonio Borgese, Mussolini was also strongly influenced by two Jewish women, one Russian and one Italian. Speaking of them to the anarchist Leda Rafanelli in a moment of confidence, he said: 'One is too ugly, but has a noble and generous mind'—this in reference to Angelica Balabanoff; 'the other is beautiful, but has a mind that is guileful, greedy and even sordid'—this in reference to Margherita Sarfatti.[3] When Sarfatti's son, Roberto, fell as an Alpine volunteer on the summit of the Col d'Echerle, Mussolini wrote in commemoration: 'There is, in truth, something of the religious, of the poetic and the profound in the sacrifice of these young men. The voice of their Fatherland must resound in their souls with accents and rhythms of which we know nothing ... A boy who still has scarcely obtained a minimal acquaintance with life, who has not yet "taken" anything from life, gives all: the present and the future, that which is and that which might have come to pass. This means that there must be in him that real will to renunciation which is the secret and the privilege of a great love.' This tribute to the fallen Jewish hero appeared in the *Popolo d'Italia* on 7 February 1918.

As might be expected, Mussolini's switch from Socialism to

---

[1] F. Coppola, 'Israele contro l'Italia', *L'Idea Nazionale.* 16 Nov. 1911 (letter to Charles Maurras), and 'Il mio "antisemitismo"', *L'Idea Nazionale*, 30 Nov. 1911.

[2] For the Jewish 'Fascists of the first hour' (Cesare Goldmann, Piero Jacchia, Ricardo Luzzatti, Eucardio Momigliano, Enrico Rocca) see IC/Job 160/046585–93; for the Jewish 'Fascist martyrs', cf. De Felice, *Storia degle ebrei italiani,* p. 73. An authoritative Fascist publication (*P.N.F. Pagine eroiche della rivoluzione fascista,* ed. M. di Simone, Milan, 1925) lists another three 'martyrs' with typically Jewish names: Amedeo Carpi, Aldo Milano, and Italo Tedeschi (pp. 28, 213, 221). In all probability these were Catholics of Jewish extraction, not members of the Jewish community.

[3] G.A. Borgese, *Goliath. The March of Fascism,* London, 1938, pp. 205–6; L. Rafanelli, *Una donna e Mussolini,* Milan, 1946, pp. 50–51.

interventionism gave an added impetus to his ideological crusade against Pan-Germanism and the cult of the Nordic race. On 16 February 1915, he wrote in his paper:

> For the last hundred years, the Germans have been poisoned by a constant apology of the fair-haired race, the only one capable of creating and propagating *Kultur* in a decaying Europe. The Empire was to be the instrument for this work of salvation. But the Empire, as it tries to spread, is discovering the limitations of its power. In trying to dilate, it dies . . . Germany must be crushed (*schiacciata*). And she can be crushed quickly with the help of Italy . . . The giant has created a monstrous machine—militarism—to ensure his dominion over all peoples. This machine must be smashed (*frantumata*) . . . Then, and only then, will the pillaging and murderous Germans reacquire the right of citizenship in humanity.[1]

As the war moved into its most critical stage, Mussolini's anti-Germanism began to take on an anti-Jewish note. On 11 November 1917—four days after Lenin's seizure of power and three months before the above-quoted tribute to Roberto Sarfatti—he launched a violent campaign against 'Judaeo-German' Bolshevism in the *Popolo d'Italia,* denouncing the October Revolution as the fruit of an unholy alliance between the German High Command and the 'synagogue'. Hindenburg, he claimed, did not have to march on Petrograd, since the Jew Ceorbaum (*sic*)—meaning Lenin—had captured it for him with the aid of three of his fellow Jews—Apfelbaum (Zinoviev), Rosenfeld (Kamenev), and Bronstein (Trotsky). In this connection Mussolini also accused Modigliani of delivering a 'Leninist' speech in the Italian Chamber of Deputies, including a defence of Trotsky and 'other similar scoundrels (*canaglie*) in German pay.'[2]

Twenty-one years later, when Fascist propagandists were required to furnish evidence of the Duce's anti-Semitic past, it was found inexpedient to reprint the above articles, since the identification of the 'synagogue' with—of all things—Pan-Germanism and Prussian militarism was hardly calculated to please the rulers of the Third Reich.

In 1919 Mussolini's anti-Bolshevik crusade temporarily assumed a more specifically anti-Jewish character. By 16 March

---

[1] *O.O.* vii. 203–4.
[2] *O.O.* x. 41–43, 110, 111–13, 137–9, 202.

of that year he had come to the conclusion that Lenin's regime was not 'German-Jewish', but Jewish pure and simple; on 4 June he went further, defining Bolshevism as a worldwide Jewish conspiracy against the Aryan race. Strange as it might seem, the big bankers of London and New York—Rotschild (*sic*), Warnberg (*sic*), Schyff (*sic*), and Guggenheim—were in league with the Bolsheviks, the reason being that both were equally Semitic: 'Race does not betray race ... Bolshevism is being defended by international plutocracy. That is the real truth.' Lenin's revolution was in all probability an act of 'Jewish vengeance against Christianity.' The Gentile reaction might well take the form of 'a pogrom of catastrophic proportions.'[1]

The article—a rehash of all the anti-Semitic fables current in 1919—was bound to provoke a reaction from the numerous Jews in Mussolini's entourage who, while supporting Fascism in its struggle against Bolshevism, were not prepared to be themselves the targets of anti-Bolshevik propaganda.[2] Their intervention appears to have had the desired effect, for in the following year the Duce publicly ate his own words: 'Bolshevism is not, as people believe, a Jewish phenomenon. The truth is that Bolshevism is leading to the utter ruin of the Jews of Eastern Europe ... It is easy to foresee that the collapse of Bolshevism will be followed by a pogrom of unprecedented proportions.' In Italy, Mussolini continued, no distinction was made between Jews and Gentiles; anti-Semitism was alien to the Italian people and likely to remain so. The Italian Jews, therefore, had no need of a National Home in Palestine, their 'New Zion' being 'right here, in this adorable Italy of ours which, for the rest, many of them have heroically defended with their blood.' This tribute to Jewish heroism, however, was followed by a stern warning to the Italian Zionists who were creating a problem of dual loyalties: 'Let us hope that the Italian Jews will have the sense not to stir up anti-Semitism in the only country where it has never existed.'[3]

[1] *O.O.* xiii. 168–70. Mussolini's attack provoked a sharp reply from Leone Carpi, the future leader of the Revisionist Zionists in Italy ('I "complici ebrei"', *Italia del Popolo*, 5 June 1919).

[2] On this, see De Felice, op.cit., pp. 82–3; on Mussolini's Jewish backers, cf. E. Rossi, *Padroni del vapore e fascismo*, Bari, 1966, p. 56 and V. Castronovo, *La stampa italiana dall'Unità al fascismo*, Bari, 1970, pp. 256, 257–8, 264, 266, 269.

[3] *O.O.* xv. 269–71 (19 Oct. 1920). On 8 July 1921, however, Mussolini once more alluded to the 'Semitic' character of the Bolshevik leadership, with special reference to 'Bronstein' (*O.O.* xvii. 34).

By implication this warning was also addressed to Jewish Liberals and Socialists, some of whom were then playing a prominent part in the fight against Mussolini's movement.

Having dropped political anti-Semitism (which he was not to take up again until after Hitler's rise to power), Mussolini trained his guns on Zionism which he had come to regard as a threat to Italian interests. As late as 1918 his paper had expressed warm support for Zionist aspirations,[1] but his *rapprochement* with the Vatican (which had begun to oppose Zionism immediately after the Balfour Declaration) and the growing Anglo-Italian rivalry in the Near East after World War I induced him to change his mind. On 21 June 1921 he called on the Italian Government to join the Pope in his fight against 'English' Zionism, adding, however, that anti-Zionism should not be confused with an anti-Semitism which was as alien to him as to any other Italian.[2] On 1 September he went further, lumping together Zionists and Jewish anti-Fascists as anti-national elements ('so-called Italians') in an anonymous article which aroused widespread indignation among Italian Jews, including loyal Fascists.[3] In a subsequent article (16 June 1922) he approached the problem from a strictly imperialist point of view: 'Is it in the interests of Italy to have an anglicized Palestine in the Far East [*sic*], if only through Zionism—to which, by the way, the old-established Palestinian Jews are bitterly opposed—or to have a frenchified Syria? No. The fate of the Italians in Tunisia should serve as a warning.'[4] In any evaluation of these utterances it should be borne in mind that Mussolini's objections to the Jewish National Home were shared not only by the Holy See and the Italian nationalists (who considered the Balfour Declaration a blow to both Italian and Catholic interests), but also by many Italian statesmen of the pre-

---

[1] See M. Michaelis, 'Gle ebrei italiani sotto il regime fascista VIII', *La Rassegna Mensile di Israel*, xxx, (June–July 1964), 254–6; the author of the pro-Zionist articles was presumably Agostino Lanzillo, a member of the *Pro-Israele* as well as a regular contributor to the *Popolo d'Italia*.

[2] *O.O.* xvi. 438–9.

[3] Mussolini's authorship of the anonymous article was revealed by Giovanni Preziosi after the enactment of the racial laws, most probably on the Duce's orders ('Mussolini e l'ebraismo prima della Marcia', *La Vita Italiana*, lvi, 15 Sept. 1940, 241–52). Several replies from Italian Jews are reproduced in Preziosi's article.

[4] 'Libertà alla Siria', *Il Popolo d'Italia*, 16 June 1922 (*O.O.* xviii. 244–6).

Fascist era, including two Foreign Ministers of Jewish origin, Sidney Sonnino and Carlo Schanzer.[1]

It was during this period that Mussolini first encountered the phenomenon which was to change the fate of Italian Jewry sixteen years later—German anti-Semitism. In March 1922, six months before his rise to power, he went to Berlin for a series of meetings with the leading political figures of the Weimar Republic, including Wirth, the Reich Chancellor, Rathenau, the Foreign Minister, and Stresemann, the ex-Chancellor. Of all those he met it was the Jew Rathenau—a gifted organizer, a brilliant intellectual, a political realist, and a sincere admirer of Italian culture—who made the deepest and most favourable impression on him; the two had a long and cordial talk, during which Mussolini assured the Foreign Minister that Italian Fascism had nothing in common with the Bavarian Orgesch (an organization of anti-Semitic right-wing extremists), certain superficial similarities notwithstanding.[2] It may seem strange today that Mussolini identified German anti-Semitism and right-wing reaction with the Orgesch and not with National Socialism in 1922, but there is no indication whatever that Hitler's name was known to him at the time. In an account of his visit to Berlin he referred to the swastika as the 'badge of the anti-Semites' (*distintivo degli antisemiti*), evidently unaware of the fact that it was the badge of the Hitlerites.[3] In his interviews and articles on the Weimar Republic he dealt at some length with Hitler's rivals on the extreme German Right, condemning their Pan-German ideas, rejecting their claim to the South Tyrol, and denying any intention of establishing relations with them; but nowhere did he make any mention of Hitler or his movement.[4] It is worth

[1] On the Vatican see Meinertzhagen to Curzon, 7 Oct. 1919 (*DBFP*, 1st Ser. iv. 433), M. Beilinson's report of 12 Dec. 1921 (CZA/file Z4/2136, London Office), and C. Weizmann, *Trial and Error*, pp. 353–4; on the nationalists, 'L'atteggiamento del gruppo nazionalista', *Israel* (15 June 1922); on Sonnino, *DDI*, 6ª serie i. 77, 82, 136, 165; on Schanzer, Weizmann, *Trial and Error*, pp. 353–4. See also F.E. Manuel, 'The Palestine Question in Italian Diplomacy 1917–1920', *Journal of Modern History*, xxvii (Sept. 1955), 263–80; U. Nahon, 'Gli echi della Dichiarazione Balfour in Italia e la Dichiarazione Imperiali del maggio 1918', *La Rassegna Mensile di Israel*, xxxiv (June 1968), 334–50; S.I. Minerbi, *L'Italie et la Palestine (1914–1920)*, Paris, 1970; and I. Friedman, *The Question of Palestine 1914–1918*, London, 1973, pp. 150–6.

[2] *O.O.* xviii. 99.

[3] Ibid. 97.

[4] Ibid., 98–9, 104; cf. Mussolini's preface to R. Suster, *La Germania repubblicana*, Milan, 1923, p. 7.

remembering in this connection that in March 1922 the future dictator of Germany was still only a provincial agitator, too obscure and inexperienced to make any impact on national politics, and that he had not yet dissociated himself from the virulent Pan-German campaign against Italian rule in the South Tyrol which so incensed his Italian model. It was only eight months later, after the Fascist March on Rome, that he began to attract attention in Italy by proclaiming his willingness to write off the Alto Adige in return for Italian support against France.[1]

In his dispatches from Germany Mussolini did not deal with the Jewish question, except for passing references to the anti-Semitic character of the extreme German Right. It was not until three months later, after the assassination of Rathenau, that he repaired the omission in an article dedicated to the memory of the Jewish Foreign Minister. After paying tribute to Rathenau's personality ('one of the most characteristic and interesting figures in the world of German politics') and defending his conduct ('always loyal and patriotic'), he pointed out that the late Foreign Minister's policy had recently met with increasing approval in Germany, even in right-wing circles. The Rapallo Treaty with Russia, in particular, had been unanimously welcomed. There were, however, two things which the German right-wing extremists could not forgive him. First, his loyal acceptance of the Versailles Treaty (his so-called policy of 'fulfilment'); secondly, his Semitic origin:

To the extremists on the German Right who consider themselves men of the purest Aryan stock (*di stirpe ariana purissima*) it was intolerable that a Jew should lead and represent Germany before the world. On the matter of Aryanism and Semitism there prevails in Germany a state of trouble and violence. It makes no difference that the German Jews conducted themselves with gallantry during the War; it likewise makes no difference that many of them consider themselves so completely assimilated as to constitute, under the presidency of Dr. Naumann,[2] the League of German Nationalist Jews who are determined to break with their religion and their race (when asked to lend financial support to the Jewish colonies in Palestine, the Praesidium of the League . . . replied as follows: 'We are too German and too poor to give a single *pfennig* for the rebuilding of Palestine'); nor does it make any

---

[1] See below, p. 22 and n. 2.
[2] Dr. Max Naumann, chairman of the Verein nationaldeutscher Juden.

difference that, apart from the tiny 'Mizrahi' faction in Berlin, the German Jews are 'Germans'. All that does not save them from the rancour of the Pan-Germans who cannot but detest the *Judenrepublik* of Berlin. There is no doubt that millions of Germans—especially in white and by now monarchical Bavaria—are rejoicing in private, and maybe even in public, at the assassination of Walther Rathenau . . . All the generals of the German Empire, the admirals, the diplomats, the aristocrats, the high officials of the Empire have remained unmolested. Not one of those who constituted the ruling class of the Empire has been killed . . . All the victims of political murder are men of the Left. The crime that put an end to the life of Rathenau is the 319th committed since the Armistice. . . The truth is that the Republic in Germany is at its last gasp. If France were not there to prevent it, the Wittelsbach would be back on their throne in Bavaria, and Hohenzollern would be back in Berlin.[1]

Three things are evident from the above. First, that in 1922 Mussolini still hated and feared the Pan-German militarism he had denounced as a Socialist and fought as an interventionist; second, that his dislike of Pan-Germanism extended to the Pan-German brand of anti-Semitism, his own anti-Jewish prejudices notwithstanding; and third, that while he was right about the weakness of the Republic, he was utterly wrong about the forces who were destined to overthrow it. The only people he considered capable of liquidating German democracy were the old-style conservatives, with special reference to the generals and admirals of the exiled Kaiser; nor did he doubt that the collapse of the Weimar Republic would be followed by a restoration of the monarchy. It never occurred to him that the destroyer of the *Judenrepublik* was to be a man of his own stamp, a popular demagogue and a 'Fascist' on the Italian model.

Despite Mussolini's emphatic denials, the rumours about his contacts with German right-wing extremists continued to spread. Matters came to a head in July when certain anti-Fascist papers accused him of planning a meeting with Reinhold Wulle, an anti-Semitic Reichstag deputy, who allegedly wanted to found a German 'Fascist' party (the Deutsch-Völkische Freiheitspartei) with Mussolini's assistance. The Reich Commissioner for Public Order was sufficiently alarmed to draw the attention of the Wilhelmstrasse to these accusations, adding that the Fascist

[1] *O.O.* xviii. 257.

leader had better be contacted and put on his guard against Wulle.[1] Mussolini's reaction took the form of yet another angry denial which appeared in his paper on 21 July: 'There seems to be a press agency abroad which has the task of defaming Italian Fascism. This agency has spread the news that I am in touch with a German deputy, a certain Wulle, in order to set up a Fascist movement in Germany and that I shall be going to Munich or to Berlin for this purpose. All this is a figment of the imagination (*inventato di sana pianta*). I do not know the deputy Wulle, I have never had relations of any kind with him, neither direct nor indirect, nor do I propose to have any in the future. That being so, I have no intention of going abroad for the reason alleged.'[2]

Only five days later, however, a 'Bavarian Hitlerite' (whose identity was never disclosed) arrived in Rome for a meeting with one of Mussolini's henchmen—Giovanni Preziosi, editor of the anti-Semitic review *La Vita Italiana* and future Minister of State, who was to go down in history as the dean of Italian Jew-baiters and as Hitler's *homme de confiance* in Italy. A renegade priest, Preziosi had imbibed Catholic prejudices against the Jews before the war; an expert on emigration problems, with several scholarly books to his credit, he had acquired first-hand knowledge of 'international Jewry' in America during the same period. A nationalist and an interventionist, he contributed to Italy's entry into World War I with a book on German economic penetration (the Banca Commerciale Italiana had been founded by the Deutsche Bank); subsequently, he discovered that the 'German peril' was in reality a 'Jewish peril', the German capitalists in control of the Italian economy being Jews. In August 1920, three months after his conversion to Fascism, he launched an anti-Semitic campaign in his paper, beginning with a vitriolic attack on the 'Jewish International.'[3] It was this campaign (ignored by the Fascist leadership at the time) rather than Preziosi's support for Mussolini which induced the

[1] Reich Commissioner for Public Order to Foreign Ministry, 13 July 1922 (GFM/K548/K154800).

[2] *O.O.* xviii. 305. Far from being a Fascist, Wulle was a conservative Italophobe, violently opposed to Hitler's 'betrayal' of the South Tyrol. In 1933 Hitler had him thrown into a concentration camp.

[3] *** 'L'Internazionale ebraica', *La Vita Italiana*, xvi (15 Aug. 1920), 97–109. In his second (signed) article on the subject ('Ancora l'internazionale ebraica', ibid. xvi, 15 Sept. 1920, 197–208), Preziosi denied being anti-Jewish ('Anti-Semitism is repugnant to our liberal Italian conscience').

'Bavarian' to approach him in July 1922 and to offer him an anti-Semitic article on 'The Jews, the Passion and Resurrection of Germany' which was duly accepted and published in the following month.[1]

Sixteen years later, in the heyday of the Rome-Berlin Axis, it was claimed by Lieutenant-Colonel Ulrich Fleischhauer, head of the anti-Semitic *Weltdienst*, that the 'Bavarian' was none other than Hitler himself and that his encounter with Preziosi was the first step on the path of collaboration between the two kindred movements.[2] The claim, though accepted by at least one eminent scholar,[3] is not borne out by the evidence. For one thing, the 'Bavarian' was in Rome on 26 July 1922, whereas Hitler never set foot on Italian soil until June 1934; for another, the article submitted to Preziosi is obviously the work of a devout Catholic, whereas Hitler was not only anti-Catholic but fanatically anti-Christian.[4] If the 'Bavarian' had been a political figure of any importance, or at least the bearer of an important political message, Preziosi would certainly have hastened to inform his leader, with whom he was then in constant touch (he was acting as intermediary between Mussolini and Vincenzo Riccio, Minister of Public Works in Facta's government). However, he did nothing of the sort, with the result that the Duce was still unaware of Hitler's existence two months later when the latter decided to contact him through an emissary. We are left with the impression that the meeting between Preziosi and the 'Bavarian', so far from being the first step on the road towards the 'Pact of Steel' and the 'parallel war', was a chance encounter between two outsiders, fellow Jew-baiters rather than fellow Fascists.[5]

On 17 August 1922 Hitler made his first public reference to the dramatic events in Italy, calling upon his supporters to follow

[1] Un Bavarese, 'Gli ebrei, la passione e la risurrezione della Germania. (Il pensiero di un tedesco)', *La Vita Italiana*, xx (15 Aug. 1922), 97–105.

[2] *Il Giornalissimo* (7 July 1938); G. Preziosi, *Giudaismo-bolscevismo-plutocrazia-massoneria*, 3rd edn. Milan, 1944, p. 54. Though flattered by this attribution, Prezioso was unable to confirm it.

[3] De Felice, p. 51 (repeated in *Mussolini Il fascista*, i, Turin, 1966, p. 234 n.1 and—with reservations—in *Mussolini e Hitler. I rapporti segreti 1922–1933*, Florence, 1975, p. 18 n.2).

[4] On this, see *Hitler's Table Talk 1941–44*, ed. H.R. Trevor-Roper, London, 1953, pp. 57, 59–61, 304.

[5] On Preziosi's role, see R. De Felice, 'Giovanni Preziosi e le origini del fascismo', *Rivista Storica del Socialismo*, 17 (Sept.–Dec. 1962), 493–555. For Preziosi's account of his meeting with the 'Bavarian', cf. 'Hitler', *La Vita Italiana*, xxxvii (30 Oct. 1930), 212; 'Saluto a Hitler', *La Vita Italiana*, xli (Feb. 1933), 225.

the Italian example: 'This struggle (between nationalism and internationalism), which so far Italy has been the only country to be willing to wage, must be waged by us too, and the beginning must be made in Bavaria.'[1] The vagueness of wording (there is no mention of either Mussolini or Fascism) seems to suggest that Hitler had no very precise information about the 'sister revolution'. A month later he was still equally vague: when asked about the Fascist leader by Kurt Lüdecke, his future diplomatic agent, 'he replied rather tartly that he only knew what everybody else was reading in the news reports.'[2] It is evident that there was as yet no contact between the two kindred movements, the 'Bavarian's' visit to Preziosi notwithstanding. According to Lüdecke, neither Hitler nor anyone else in the National Socialist Party had any idea what Mussolini and his movement were really like: 'How useful it might be to establish contact with him no one in our ranks knew; nor did we know whether his programme really paralleled ours in any essential.'[3] Hitler himself made the same point in a letter to Mussolini twenty years later, deploring the fact that in 1922 he had had no time to keep track of events in Italy: 'We were so engrossed in a life-and-death struggle in our own country that the world around us and its problems seemed to us to mean very little at first.'[4]

When Lüdecke suggested that it might be well to find out more about Mussolini, Hitler agreed; he also agreed that it would be wise to obtain the backing of a prominent sympathizer, General Ludendorff, evidently realizing that his own name was as yet insufficient to effect an introduction. About a week later, having gained Ludendorff's consent, Lüdecke was duly received by Mussolini in Milan; he found the leader of the Blackshirts affable and interested, but so uninformed that he had to 'begin from the beginning': 'Mussolini had never heard of Hitler. In fact, each of these men, now so constantly in the spotlight of world affairs, was then so obscure that a rational man in my place would have felt—politically speaking—like a hyphen connecting two zeros ... Not Hitler's name, but Ludendorff's had impressed the Duce.' Lüdecke did his best to enlighten his

[1] Quoted in G. Schubert, *Anfänge nationalsozialistischer Aussenpolitik*, Cologne, 1963, p. 62.
[2] K.G.W. Lüdecke, *I knew Hitler*, New York, 1937, p. 56.
[3] Ibid., p. 58.
[4] Hitler to Mussolini, 21 Oct. 1942 (GFM/F19407–12).

interlocutor, sketching a picture of conditions in Germany, explaining Hitlerism 'as an inevitable development' and stressing the importance of Hitler as a political figure. Mussolini 'listened with obvious sympathy and understanding', agreeing 'that the system created at Versailles was impossible for Germany and for all concerned.' After a political discussion, during which Mussolini gave him 'an outline of the internal drifting of Italy', Lüdecke led the conversation round to the Jewish peril: 'Touching on the issue of international finance, I found his views paralleled Hitler's. Then, pursuing the subject, I spoke of the Jews. He agreed with my facts, but was evasive about what measures they called for. While he admitted that he watched the Jews carefully, he pointed out that in Italy the Jewish question was not the problem it was in Germany. I did not know at the time that Marghareta [*sic*] Sarfatti, his devoted friend and biographer, was a Jewess, or that Aldo Finzi, one of his early followers and an important liaison man, was a converted Jew.' When Lüdecke ventured to raise the delicate question of the South Tyrol, the Duce reacted with unexpected violence: 'No discussion about that—ever! The Alto-Adige is Italian and must remain so.' In conclusion, Mussolini assured his visitor that the victory of Fascism was both inevitable and imminent ('Nous serons l'état, parce que nous le voulons!'), after which Lüdecke took his leave, convinced that in a few weeks Mussolini would either be in power or face a firing-squad.[1]

It is clear from the above that Mussolini was perfectly willing to meet German right-wing extremists, despite his categorical denials.[2] It is equally clear, however, that, for all his 'sympathy and understanding', he refused to commit himself in any way ('as a seasoned politician, he said just what he wanted to say, and no more') and that no agreements were reached.[3] Finally, it is obvious that he was determined to keep on the right side of 'international Jewry', in spite of (or perhaps because of) his belief in the power of Jewish high finance. Moreover, he was too much of an Italian to approve of the German brand of anti-

[1] Lüdecke, op.cit., pp. 68–71.
[2] It was one of Mussolini's principles to cultivate non-committal relations with all those who might 'some day' be useful to him.
[3] Lüdecke, p. 68.

Semitism which he knew to be repugnant to his fellow countrymen, including the vast majority of his fellow Fascists.

For his part, Lüdecke hastened to report to Hitler who— impressed by his envoy's account of the Fascist 'revolution' and persuaded that 'on Mussolini and his good-will might depend the reshaping of the European constellation for our benefit'—readily agreed to write off the South Tyrol in return for Italian friendship. There is no evidence that he was in any way troubled by the Duce's refusal to join him in his fight against the Jews.[1] In November—Mussolini meanwhile having marched on Rome— he informed an Italian diplomat of his decision to renounce the Alto Adige, adding that 'towards an Italy disposed to help us we have a duty of absolute loyalty.'[2] Having thus prepared the ground, he tried to re-establish contact with his Italian model in March 1923, only to meet with a flat refusal.[3] The rebuff failed to deter him, for six months later he again sent Lüdecke to Italy, this time in order to gain political and financial support for his imminent putsch. The Duce however, had by now become inaccessible: 'Mussolini, being legally prime minister of Italy, in friendly relations with the government in Berlin, could not officially take notice of the representative of a party opposing that government.' Lüdecke was passed on to 'Baron Russo', from whom, according to his own account, he received 'no help or special commitment.'[4] We are left with the impression that Mussolini did not as yet consider the Hitlerites worth the risk of diplomatic complications, despite Hitler's recognition of the Brenner frontier. The impression is reinforced by an official Italian document, a dispatch by the Italian consul in Munich, from which we learn that on the eve of Hitler's abortive putsch the Duce contemptuously referred to the National Socialists as 'buffoons', a definition in which the consul enthusiastically concurred.[5]

Unable to win over Mussolini or his entourage, Lüdecke decided to concentrate on publicity, the Italian press being 'more

[1] It is not clear from Lüdecke's account whether the subject was ever mentioned in his conversation with Hitler.

[2] A. Tedaldi to Mussolini, 17 Nov. 1922 (*DDI*, 7ᵃ serie i. 79–80).

[3] Neurath to Wilhelmstrasse, 29 Mar. 1923, (GFM/K151953–4).

[4] Lüdecke, p. 134. Giacomo Barone-Russo was Mussolini's *chef de cabinet*; Lüdecke mistook the name for an aristocratic title.

[5] Durini di Monza to Mussolini, 10 Nov. 1923 (*DDI*, 7ᵃ serie ii. 318).

accessible' than the Fascist government. In October he wrote a series of articles with a view to enlightening the Italian public on the ideas and objectives of his Führer, with special reference to the Jewish issue. He also persuaded the editors of the *Corriere Italiano*, a paper close to the Fascist dictator, to send a special correspondent to Munich for an interview with Hitler who took advantage of the occasion to denounce German irredentism in the South Tyrol and to draw the attention of the Italians to the 'Jewish-Marxist' conspiracy against the Gentile world. The Fascist response to all this, however, was far from encouraging; the Italian papers, while giving ample publicity to Hitler's and Lüdecke's views, pointedly refrained from any expression of sympathy or support.[1] German diplomats in Rome became increasingly convinced that the National Socialists were mistaken in regarding Italian Fascism as a kindred movement; the Chargé d'Affaires, von Prittwitz, informed the Wilhelmstrasse that Lüdecke's efforts to spread anti-Semitism in Fascist circles were most unlikely to meet with success, while von Neurath, the Ambassador, in a letter to Stresemann, acquitted the Duce of complicity in Hitler's ill-starred Munich *coup*.[2] Given Lüdecke's insignificance and the obvious failure of his mission, it was not considered necessary to put a stop to his activities in Italy.[3]

Having decided to reject collaboration with German 'Fascism' and anti-Semitism for the time being, Mussolini could have no possible motive for raising the Jewish problem in his country. All the same, the Fascist seizure of power (30 October 1922) evoked a certain alarm among the leaders of Italian Jewry, owing as much to the Duce's previous invectives against Jewish Bolshevism as to the general enthusiasm which the March on Rome aroused among the anti-Semitic elements abroad, especially in Germany.[4] Simultaneously, charges of anti-Semitism were levelled against

---

[1] Hitler did not know at the time that the *Corriere Italiano* was partly owned by the Jew Aldo Finzi, then Under-Secretary at the Ministry of the Interior (ACS/Carte R. Farinacci, busta 2 (1923), fasc. F. Finzi to Farinacci, 30 Oct. 1923).

[2] Prittwitz to Wilhelmstrasse, 22 Sept. 1923 (GFM/L1703/L501420–21); Neurath to Stresemann, 18 Nov. 1923 (GFM/5272H/326512–13).

[3] Köpke to Bavarian Ministry of Exterior, 21 Dec. 1923 (GFM/L1703/L501456–57).

[4] See 'Männer und Waschweiber', *V.B.*, 1 Nov. 1922; 'Nel nuovo Ministero italiano', *Israel*, 2 Nov. 1922; 'Rom und Jerusalem', *Jüdische Rundschau*, 3 Nov. 1922; R. Michels, 'Der Aufstieg des Faschismus', *Neue Zürcher Zeitung*, 29 Dec. 1922. On 3 November 1922 Hermann Esser, one of Hitler's earliest followers, announced amid rousing applause that the 'German Mussolini' was Adolf Hitler (*V.B.*, 8 Nov. 1922).

Mussolini and Fascism in the international Jewish press, and various foreign Jewish personalities came to Rome in order to find out the truth from their Italian brethren. Given Mussolini's determination to avoid a clash with 'international Jewry' at this juncture, the Fascist reaction was swift; immediately after the March on Rome a member of the Italian Government assured the Chief Rabbi of Rome, Dr. Angelo Sacerdoti, that Fascism, despite certain rumours to the contrary, was entirely free from anti-Semitic tendencies.[1] A year later (30 November 1923) the Duce in person received Dr. Sacerdoti, at the latter's urgent request, in order to repeat these assurances as publicly and as emphatically as possible: 'As Dr. Sacerdoti in the ensuing conversation drew the Hon. Mussolini's attention to the fact that the anti-Semitic Parties abroad desire in some fashion to find an accession of strength to their anti-Semitic policy in an alleged anti-Semitic attitude on the part of Italian Fascism, on which they wish to model themselves, His Excellency declared formally that the Italian Government and Italian Fascism have never had any intention of following, nor are following, an anti-Semitic policy, and further deplore that foreign anti-Semitic Parties should desire to exploit in this manner the spell which Fascism exercises in the world.'[2] According to Guido Bedarida, this public declaration was followed by a strictly confidential remark which is of particular interest in our context; 'I have refused to receive Hitler, and the Bavarian papers have accused me of being a tool of the Jews; when they hear what I am telling you now, they will say that I have myself become a Jew.'[3]

Not content with giving assurances to the Italian Jews, Mussolini also took steps to improve relations with the heads of 'international Jewry'. On 20 December 1922—less than two months after the March on Rome—he received a Zionist delegation composed of Dante Lattes, Angelo Sacerdoti, and Moshe Beilinson in order to discuss the possibility of a *modus vivendi* between Zionism and Fascism. He began by explaining to his interlocutors the reasons for his coolness towards the Jewish National Home: Zionism was a tool of British imperialism;

---

[1] 'Una nostra intervista col Dr. Sacerdoti', *Israel*, 6 Dec. 1923.
[2] 'Fascismo e antisemitismo: le rassicuranti dichiarazioni dell'on. Mussolini in un colloquio col Rabbino Maggiore di Roma', *Israel*, 6 Dec. 1923.
[3] G. Bedarida, *Ebrei d'Italia*, Leghorn, 1950, p. 10.

Zionist aims were 'Utopian'; and the participation of Italian citizens in the movement was calculated to provoke a conflict of loyalties. The delegates tried to rebut the charges, insisting that the Zionists had no intention whatever of playing the British game; that Zionist aims were by no means incompatible with the legitimate aspirations of the Arabs; that Italy stood to gain by Zionist activities in Palestine; and that the Italian Zionists were as loyal to their country as any other section of the population. The Duce thereupon relented and agreed to have a talk with the President of the World Zionist Organisation, Dr. Chaim Weizmann.[1]

Weizmann was received by Mussolini on 3 January 1923.[2] After the interview (which lasted for over an hour), he called on Sir Ronald Graham, the British Ambassador in Rome, and told him that the Duce's aversion to Zionism had anti-British rather than anti-Jewish motives. On 5 January Graham reported to the Foreign Secretary, Lord Curzon:

Signor Mussolini, in reference to the unsympathetic attitude of Italy towards Zionism, stated that the Zionists wished him to 'faire le jeu de l'Angleterre', and this he was determined not to do. He repeated this phrase more than once, and appeared to Dr. Weizmann to speak with some bitterness. He made use of the well-worn argument of Great Britain's design to split the ring of Moslem States by a Jewish Palestine, and referred to the refusal of your Lordship and M. Poincaré to allow the mandate question to be reopened to enable him to insert one or two points of importance to Italy.

Dr. Weizmann pointed out the unreasonableness of this last request in view of the fact that the approval of the previous Italian Government had been given to the present mandates. With regard to Signor Mussolini's contention that Zionism was a tool in the hands of His Majesty's Government to weaken the Moslem States for the benefit of the British Empire in the East, Dr. Weizmann, whilst denying that this was in any way the case, said that even if it were so, Italy stood to gain as much as Great Britain by a weakening of Moslem power. Signor Mussolini admitted that the Arabs had been giving him trouble in Cyrenaica and Tripoli, and implied that he had no confidence in them.

Signor Mussolini raised the question of Italy obtaining concessions in Palestine, and also securing an outlet there for emigration. Dr. Weizmann was able to show that by the terms of the Mandate itself

[1] CZA/File 24/2136.
[2] WA/Weizmann Diary, entry for 3 Jan. 1923: '"Mussolini". Meeting 9.'

there could be no policy of favouritism which would debar Italy or any other country from participating in the development of the country. To enable emigrants to live and be absorbed, a considerable outlay of capital was necessary; the Zionist organisation provided funds for its own immigrants, but the Palestine Administration was short of funds, and any scheme for importing Italian labour would have to be backed with Italian funds.

Dr. Weizmann was struck by the mediocre character of the arguments adduced by the President of the Council, and by his superficial acquaintance with the subject, although, in the circumstances, little else could be expected. In the end, Signor Mussolini consented to allow Dr. Weizmann to announce to a meeting of Jews that evening that he would have no objection to the name of an Italian Jew being put forward for appointment as a member of the Jewish agency in Palestine—the body provided by the terms of the mandate as the official channel for bringing Jewish opinion before the British Administration. Dr. Weizmann was very pleased with this concession, as being likely to have considerable influence over Italian Jews, who, like other elements in Italy since the advent of the new régime, have been adopting a non-committal attitude.

Later in the evening, one of Signor Mussolini's secretaries informed Dr. Weizmann that his Excellency had been much impressed with the conversation, and that he had ordered a memorandum on the subject to be prepared for him.[1]

The meeting between Weizmann and Mussolini was hailed as a significant step forward by *Israel*, the Italian Zionist weekly, which claimed that the talk between the two leaders had served 'to dispel the misunderstandings that had arisen with regard to the Palestine policy' of the Italian Government.[2] In reality, Weizmann was far from satisfied with the result of his visit and said so plainly in a public speech on 26 March 1923: 'To-day there is a tremendous political wave known as Fascism, which is sweeping over Italy. As an Italian movement it is no business of ours—it is the business of the Italian Government. But this wave is now breaking against the little Jewish community, and the little community, which never asserted itself, is to-day suffering from anti-Semitism.'[3] Quarter of a century later the Zionist

[1] PRO/F.O. 371/8993/p.20/E371/53/65, reproduced in D. Carpi, 'P'iluto ha-medinit shel Weizmann b'Italia ba-shanim 1923–1934', *Ha-zionut. M'assef l'toldot ha-tenuah ha-zionit v'ha-yishuv ha-yehudi b'Eretz Yisrael II*, Tel Aviv, 1971, pp. 195–6.

[2] *Israel*, 4 Jan. 1923.

[3] C. Weizmann, 'Relief and Reconstruction', *American Addresses*, New York, 1923, p. 49.

leader reiterated the attack in his memoirs, affirming that prior to the advent of Fascism Italy had been 'entirely free' of anti-Jewish bias but that a change had begun to appear 'shortly after the accession of Mussolini':

> He himself violently denied any anti-Semitic tendencies, but they were fostered by underlings like Staracci [*sic*] and Federzoni, and the whole fascist press was flavoured with anti-Semitism. From time to time articles appeared attacking Zionism and the participation of Italian Jews in the movement. The Zionists, and the Jews generally, though they did not give loud expression to their views on the subject, were known to be anti-fascist. Enzo Sereni, a member of a very distinguished family—later one of the founders of the co-operative colony Govat Brenner [*sic*]—was marked by the Italian police. A brother of his, a known Communist, was arrested and condemned to the Lipari Islands ... Later he escaped from the Lipari islands and made his way to Moscow. Other Jews were caught smuggling anti-fascist literature from France into Italy, and the position of the community became a difficult one. All these circumstances made my visits to Rome matters of some importance to the Italian Jews. They felt that my talks with the head of the government ... would help to ease the situation for them.[1]

In the light of the evidence now available it is clear that Weizmann had correctly diagnosed the latent antagonism between Fascists and Jews which was to become virulent during the following decade. Even so, his account is highly misleading and full of inaccuracies. Contrary to his assertion, no high-ranking member of the Fascist hierarchy ever attacked the Jews in public during the early years of Mussolini's rule, least of all Federzoni, the former Nationalist leader, who later opposed the Duce's anti-Jewish policy in the Fascist Grand Council on 6 October 1938. Nor is there any evidence of a specifically Jewish anti-Fascism prior to the enactment of the anti-Jewish laws.[2] There was friction between the regime and the Jews from the outset, mainly because of Fascist suspicions of Jewish 'separatism' and 'internationalism'; but until the birth of the Rome–Berlin Axis there was no attempt whatever on the part of the Fascist

[1] *Trial and Error*, pp. 454–5.
[2] Weizmann's error about Federzoni is perhaps due to the latter's opposition to Zionism (see above, p. 15 n. 1). On the absence of a specifically Jewish anti-Fascism, cf. L. Salvatorelli and G. Mira, *Storia d'Italia nel periodo fascista*, 5th edn., Turin, 1964, pp. 791–2; on the prominence of Jews in the anti-Fascist movement, E.R. Papa, *Storia di due manifesti*, Milan, 1958, pp. 97–101.

authorities to create a 'Jewish problem' in Italy. What is more, the consolidation of the dictatorship, beginning with the years 1926–7, resulted in a steady improvement of relations with the Jewish minority (recurrent crises notwithstanding) until finally even the anti-Fascist exiles ceased to accuse Mussolini of anti-Semitism. In 1923 the Duce's assurances to Weizmann and Sacerdoti, while infuriating the German Jew-baiters, had little effect on either Fascists or Jews; nine years later his philo-Semitic statements to Emil Ludwig were taken at face value by all concerned.[1]

From 1922 to 1936 (and on occasion as late as 1937) the official attitude of the Fascist Government to the Jews was summarily expressed in the phrase: 'The Jewish problem does not exist in Italy.'[2] It goes without saying that the spokesmen of Italian Jewry hastened to subscribe to the official thesis, paying tribute to the magnanimity of the supreme leadership and blaming the sporadic manifestations of anti-Semitism on 'irresponsible underlings.'[3] At first these expressions of regard for the new rulers were largely a matter of tactics; by 1932, however, even the non-Fascist Zionists had become convinced that Mussolini was as good as his word. The civil and religious rights of the Jewish minority were being scrupulously respected, the activities of the Italian Zionist Federation were being encouraged within limits (despite Mussolini's well-known aversion to Italians with 'dual loyalties'), and no Fascist leader of any importance was permitted to voice anti-Jewish sentiments in public. Even the press attacks on the Jews, while they had not ceased altogether, were becoming increasingly rare.

It was in this relaxed atmosphere that Mussolini chose to make what seemed at the time to be his definitive pronouncement on racialism and anti-Semitism in a talk with Emil Ludwig: 'Race! It is a feeling, not a reality; ninety-five per cent, at least, is a feeling. Nothing will ever make me believe that biologically pure races can be shown to exist today. Amusingly enough, not one of those who have proclaimed the nobility of the Teutonic race was himself a Teuton ... National pride has no need of the

[1] See De Felice, *Storia degli ebrei italiani*, pp. 92–102, 118–19.
[2] See, e.g., the interview granted by the then Under-Secretary for Foreign Affairs, Dino Grandi, to the *Wiener Morgenzeitung*, reported in *Israel*, 24 May 1926.
[3] Cf. 'Il Presidente Weizmann a Roma', *Israel*, 22–9 Sept. 1926.

delirium of race.' As for German anti-Semitism, the Duce agreed with his Jewish interlocutor that it was a side-tracking stunt: having lost a war, the Germans needed the Jew as a scapegoat to hit out at. Italy had no Jewish problem: 'Anti-Semitism does not exist in Italy ... The Italian Jews have always shown themselves good citizens, and they fought bravely in the war. They occupy leading positions in the universities, in the army, in the banks. Quite a few of them are generals.'[1] In June 1932 (about two months after his talks with Ludwig) Mussolini published his celebrated treatise on Fascist doctrine, in which the concept of the nation is defined in 'anti-racialist' terms: 'Not a race, nor geographically defined region, but a people, historically perpetuating itself; a multitude unified by an idea and imbued with a will to live, the will to power, self-consciousness, personality.'[2] Not content with rejecting racialism in theory, the Fascist dictator gave practical proof of his anti-racialism by making a Jew, Guido Jung, his Minister of Finance in July 1932. The appointment was an indirect rebuff to Hitler, by then the leader of the strongest political party in Germany, who was loudly proclaiming his ideological solidarity with 'the great man south of the Alps' and his desire for an alliance with him.[3] The Italian Jews could hardly fail to be impressed by the apparent antithesis between the Duce and his German disciple; on 27 October *Israel*, in an editorial devoted to the tenth anniversary of the March on Rome, emphasized the 'radical difference between the true and authentic Fascism—Italian Fascism, that is—and the pseudo-Fascist movements in other countries which ... are often using the most reactionary phobias, and especially the blind, unbridled hatred of the Jews, as a means of diverting the masses from their real problems, from the real causes of their misery, and from the real culprits.'[4]

A closer scrutiny shows how even during this first phase of Fascist rule Mussolini's attitude to the Jews was a great deal more complex than his official declarations would suggest. As we have seen, he had repeatedly made use of anti-Semitic arguments both as an interventionist and as a Fascist before the March on Rome;

[1] E. Ludwig, *Colloqui con Mussolini*, 2nd edn., Milan, 1950, pp. 71–3.
[2] *O.O.* xxxiv. 120.
[3] See, e.g., Hitler's preface to V. Meletti, *Die faschistische Revolution*, Munich, 1931, p. 7.
[4] 'Decennale', *Israel*, 27 Oct. 1932. We are informed by *avvocato* Alfonso Pacifici, the then co-editor, that he was the author of the anonymous article.

once in power, he had decided not to raise the Jewish issue, realizing as he did that anti-Semitism had no political value in Italy and that a clash with 'international Jewry' was most unlikely to benefit his regime. There is ample evidence, however, that his change of tactics did not involve any real change of heart. While admitting the 'practical' non-existence of a domestic Jewish problem, he continued to resent the manifestations of Jewish separatism in general and of Zionism in particular, as well as the opposition of religious Jews to mixed marriage. The renewed *rapprochement* with the Holy See, culminating in the Lateran pacts of 1929, gave a fresh impetus to the anti-Zionist tendencies.[1] Moreover, he continued to overestimate the power of 'international Jewry', with special reference to 'Jewish high finance', a fact which aroused in him two conflicting attitudes— of respect on the one hand and of resentment on the other. Speaking to Prince Starhemberg in June 1932, he declared: 'I have no love for the Jews, but they have great influence everywhere. It is better to leave them alone. His anti-Semitism has already brought Hitler more enemies than is necessary.'[2] This declaration, made during the honeymoon between Fascism and Jewry, embodied to perfection the Fascist dictator's attitude to the Jews during the first fourteen years of the so-called 'Fascist era'.

The Duce's ambivalent attitude was accurately reflected in his contradictory behaviour. In public he invariably struck philo-Semitic attitudes, sometimes in an exaggerated fashion.[3] In his anonymous articles, on the other hand, he gave repeated vent to his irritation against the Jews. In March 1928, after protracted negotiations with leading Zionists, he permitted the creation of the Italy–Palestine Committee; but in November of the same year he unleashed a violent press campaign against the Italian Zionists, accusing them of disloyalty to Italy. The first shot fired in this campaign was an article entitled 'Religion or Nation?' unsigned but written by Mussolini himself, which appeared in the *Popolo di Roma* of 29–30 November. The anonymous author

---

[1] Ernesto Rossi has stressed the importance of Catholic anti-Semitism in Italy (*Il manganello e l'aspersorio*, Florence, 1958, pp. 351–95: 'the Jesuits as precursors of racialism'). The fact remains, however, that it was not the Concordat but the alliance with the anti-Catholic Hitler which induced Mussolini to persecute the Jews.

[2] E.R. von Starhemberg, *Between Hitler and Mussolini*, London-New York, 1942, p. 93.

[3] See, e.g., 'Fascismo e antisemitismo', *Israel*, 12 Jan. 1928: 'Fascist anti-Semitism, or anti-Semitic Fascism, is an absurdity.'

(whose identity was revealed to the Jewish leaders by Margherita Sarfatti a day or two later) began by pointing out that practically all the leaders of international anti-Fascism, from Treves to Torrès, were 'Semites', after which he proceeded to review the unseemly manifestations of Jewish separatism which had occurred at the Zionist congress in Milan a few weeks earlier:

Italian Christians will perhaps be a little surprised and disturbed to learn that there is another people in Italy which declares itself completely apart (*perfettamente estraneo*) not only from our religious faith but also from our nation, from our people, from our history and our ideals. A guest people, that is, which stays among us like oil amid water, together but not really mixed together (*insieme ma senza confondersi*), to use the expression of the late Rabbi of Florence, Margulies . . . All the Zionists speak of a 'Jewish people', of a 'Jewish race', of 'Jewish ideals', without the least reference to the religious element . . . Now we ask the Italian Jews: Are you a religion or a nation? This question does not have the aim of creating an anti-Jewish movement but rather that of taking out of a shadowy zone a problem which exists and which it is perfectly useless to ignore any longer. From the answer we shall draw the necessary conclusions.

Mussolini's attack provoked replies from a number of Jewish Fascists (who proclaimed their unconditional devotion to the Duce and their uncompromising hostility to Zionism), from Dante Lattes (who denied that there was a conflict of loyalties), and from an anti-Semitic Gentile who called on the Fascist Government to deprive the Jews of their Italian citizenship and deport them to Palestine. On 16 December Mussolini responded with another anonymous article, entitled 'Reply to the Zionists', in which he claimed that there were three kinds of Jews in Italy: sincere Italians, insincere Italians, and Jewish nationalists. For the moment he was prepared to tolerate the activities of the Italian Zionist Federation; once a Jewish State was set up in Palestine, however, relations between Jews and Gentiles would have to be radically reviewed by the Fascist regime 'because one cannot be a citizen of two countries at one and the same time.'[1]

[1] On the Comitato Italia-Palestina, see R. Guariglia, *Ricordi (1922–1946)*, Naples, 1949, pp. 183–4; D. Carpi, 'Il problema ebraico nella politica italiana fra le due guerre mondiali', *Rivista di Studi Politici Internazionali*, xxiii (Jan.–Mar. 1961), 46–50; G. Carocci, *La politica estera dell'Italia fascista (1925–1928)*, Bari, 1969, pp. 211–13. On the anti-Zionist campaign, U. Nahon, 'Rapporto confidenziale all'Esecutivo Sionistico, giugno 1937', in *Scritti in memoria di Leone Carpi*, Jerusalem, 1967, p. 257 n. 24; id., 'La polemica antisionista del "Popolo di Roma" nel 1928', in *Scritti in memoria di Enzo Sereni*, Jerusalem, 1970, pp. 216–53; Lattes to Zionist Organisation, London, 27 Dec. 1928 (CZA/File Z4/3238/III).

Mussolini sought to exploit both foreign Jewish elements and the Italian Jewish communities abroad as instruments of his 'imperial' policy; hence the support given to the Italian Jewish colonies of the Mediterranean region, hence also the encouragement of, and assistance to, the foreign Jewish students at Italian universities.[1] At the same time, however, he showed himself deeply suspicious of 'international Jewry', which he identified with all the forces against which Fascism had risen in revolt— liberalism and democracy, Socialism, Bolshevism, and Freemasonry. According to Raffaele Guariglia, for many years the Near Eastern affairs expert of the Italian Foreign Ministry, Mussolini's dislike and distrust of the Jews was profound; even the loyal Italian Jews were suspect, Italian Jewry being part of the Jewish International as well as part of the Italian nation. Guariglia's account has been challenged by his former superior, Dino Grandi (Under-Secretary of Foreign Affairs from 1925 to 1929 and Foreign Minister from 1929 to 1932), who denied (in a letter to the writer) that Mussolini was in any way anti-Semitic during the period under review. The contradiction between these two versions is, however, more apparent than real. It is perfectly true that the Duce was never an anti-Semite in Hitler's sense of the term, not even after his conversion to racialism; but it is equally true that he was opposed to the participation of Italian citizens in the Zionist movement and distrustful of 'international Jewry.' Until the second half of 1936 these private feelings had little effect on the dictator's official attitude, given his determination to avoid an open conflict; however, they go far to explain the effortless ease with which he passed from his initial philo-Semitism and anti-racialism to racial anti-Semitism on the German model in 1938.[2]

Allusions to a specifically 'Jewish' anti-Fascism were not infrequent in the Fascist press during the early years of the regime. When the chairman of the Zionist Executive, Nahum Sokolov, came to Rome for an interview with the Duce in October 1927, a representative of the *Giornale d'Italia* questioned

---

[1] On the Italian-Jewish colonies, see A. Milano, *Storia degli ebrei italiani nel Levante*, Firenze, 1949; *DDI*, 7ª serie v, 163-4.
[2] Guariglia, op.cit., pp. 181-2; Grandi to the writer, 25 July 1972. See also Mussolini's observations on Jewish internationalism in a letter of 14 Aug. 1927 (*DDI*, 7ª serie v, 345-346).

him on the 'notorious anti-Fascism of the Jewish world.'[1] Mussolini went so far as to believe that there existed 'heads' of international Jewry and instructed Sacerdoti to organize a meeting with them for the purpose of reaching an agreement between Hitler and the Jews; the unfortunate rabbi was forced to inform him that, in fact, there were no such heads, the Jews not being organized on an international level.[2]

Mussolini was particularly desirous of maintaining good relations with the big Jewish bankers which did not prevent him at the same time from regarding Jewish high finance as opposed to Italian interests. On 17 March 1932, in a unsigned article, he took issue with international high finance in general and with Jewish high finance in particular: 'Jacob Schiff died quite a while ago, but his powerful banks remain and continue to function; and there survives, far from defeated, his principle: "The direction of world affairs and of humanity devolves on the big banks; it costs a few millions but yields enormous profits." Whence is to be deduced the close alliance between the God Jehovah, the Bible and the big Jewish–German–American Banks.'[3] Mussolini might have added that at least one of those German–Jewish bankers in America—Otto Hermann Kahn— was notoriously an ardent admirer of his, so much so that until 1938 the Fascist press chose to ignore his Jewish origin, describing him as a 'great American' rather than as an 'international Jew.'[4]

The Duce's attitude to mixed marriage furnishes another characteristic illustration of his involved state of mind. When his daughter Edda wanted to marry the son of a Jewish colonel (in 1929, the year of the Concordat), he objected violently, pointing out that 'ninety per cent of all mixed marriages end in failure' and adding that 'such a marriage, a real and proper scandal, apart from the unhappiness it would cause, could not and would

---

[1] 'Interessanti dichiarazioni di Sokolov sul Fascismo', *Israel*, 3 Nov. 1927; cf. 'Stampa non buona', *Israel*, 26 Jan. 1928.

[2] J. Draenger, *Nahoum Goldmann*, ii, Paris, 1956, p. 226; for details see below, Ch. III.

[3] 'Il regno di Geova', *Il Popolo d'Italia*, 17 Mar. 1932. The anonymous article was commonly ascribed to Mussolini himself (L. Villari, *Italian Foreign Policy under Mussolini*, New York, 1956, p. 199). In any case no one could have published such a diatribe in the Duce's paper without his explicit consent.

[4] See 'Cos'ha detto di Mussolini il banchiere Otto Kahn all "American Club" di Parigi', *Il Popolo d'Italia*, 12 Oct. 1923.

not be carried out.'[1] But when the editors of *Israel* protested against the ever-growing number of mixed marriages, they aroused the dictator's reprimand: 'The frequency of mixed marriages in Italy must be greeted with satisfaction by all who consider themselves good, sincere, and loyal (*sicuri*) Italians, as it constitutes proof of the perfect civic, political, and above all "moral" equality between all Italians, whatever their remote descent.'[2]

It has been suggested that Mussolini's attacks on Jewish Bolshevism and Jewish high finance betray the direct influence of foreign anti-Semitic literature (Italy having no anti-Semitic traditions of her own). There is ample evidence that he read such publications,[3] but it is worth remembering that equally fallacious notions were widespread in Western liberal circles. The pin-pricks against Jewish Bolshevism in Giolitti's *Stampa* (16 March 1920) are a case in point, and so is Balfour's assertion (made in a conversation with Felix Frankfurter) that European subversive movements were dominated by Jewish elements, Lenin himself being a Jew on his mother's side.[4] An even more striking example is the following altercation between Colonel F. H. Kisch of the Zionist Executive and Henry Herbert Asquith, the former British Prime Minister, to whom Judaism, Zionism, and Bolshevism were interchangeable terms (26 November 1924): 'Dined at Government House (in Jerusalem) to meet Mr. Asquith with whom I had a short conversation in the course of which he enquired as to the degree of Zionism prevalent among the Jews of Western Europe, saying he was aware that it was encouraged by the Government in Russia "where the Jews rule supreme." I pulled him up sharply saying that he had no more right to cite Trotzky as a Jew than I had to cite Lenin as a Christian. I informed him of the persecution of Zionists by the Soviet Government, at which he expressed doubting surprise.'[5] Similar

---

[1] Edvige Mussolini, *Mio fratello Benito*, Florence, 1957, pp. 122–3; cf. IC/*Segreteria particolare del Duce*/Job 109/029683/A (police report on meeting between Edda and 'young Pacifici', 15 Sept. 1929).

[2] 'Matrimoni misti e malinconie inattuali', *Il Popolo d'Italia*, 29 May 1932. Mussolini's authorship of the anonymous article was disclosed by Paolo Orano, *Gli ebrei in Italia*, Rome, 1937, p. 123.

[3] In his talks with Ludwig he mentions Gobineau, Chamberlain, Woltmann, and Lapouge (Ludwig, op.cit., p. 72).

[4] *DBFP*, 1st Ser.iv. 1276 (24 July 1919).

[5] F.H. Kisch, *Palestine Diary*, London, 1938, p. 154.

experiences have been recorded by other Zionist leaders.[1] As for 'Jewish financial power', the Duce's *idée fixe* accurately reflected the conviction prevalent in Italian political circles that the Jews were in control of economic affairs in the Western world and that their influence was generally harmful to Italian interests— a conviction by no means confined to members of the Fascist Party. The following extract from the memoirs of Daniele Varè, a professional diplomat and anything but an anti-Semite (he was named after Daniele Manin, the Jewish Risorgimento hero), may be quoted in illustration: 'During my travels abroad— which were constant—I had frequent occasion to feel, and at times to resent, the hostility of the Jewish bankers to my country, a hostility behind which lurked questions of interest and investments.'[2] Jewish leaders in touch with the Italian Government have repeatedly pointed out that complaints of this kind reflected a commonplace in Italian politics.[3]

Given the above considerations, it appears improbable that Mussolini allowed himself to be influenced by the anti-Semitic theories of his foreign admirers during the period under review. When Starhemberg informed him in July 1930 that the Austrian Heimatschutz accepted patriotic Jews as members, he expressed approval, adding that anti-Semitism, as preached by the Hitlerites, was 'unworthy of a European nation ... stupid and barbarous.' In June 1932 he went further, expressing doubts about Hitler's sanity and dismissing his racial theories as 'nonsense.'[4] As late as april 1937, having meanwhile become the Führer's ally, he reaffirmed his opposition to racialism in a talk with Schuschnigg, the Austrian Chancellor: 'It is clear that there are substantial differences between Fascism and Nazism. We are Catholics, proud of our faith and respectful of it [*sic*]. We do not accept the Nazi racial theories, still less their juridical conse- quences.'[5] In any assessment of these utterances it should be borne in mind that Hitler's racial doctrines had anti-Italian as well as anti-Jewish implications (a fact which never ceased to infuriate Mussolini); it was Hitler's teacher, Houston Stewart

[1] See *Memories. The Autobiography of Nahum Goldmann*, London, 1970, pp. 165–6.

[2] D. Varè, *The two Impostors*, London, 1949, p. 177–8.

[3] This was stressed by the late Prof. Dante A. Lattes in one of his letters to the writer (10 June 1959).

[4] von Starhemberg, op.cit., pp. 24, 92–3.

[5] R. Mosca (ed.), *L'Europa verso la catastrofe*, i, Milan, 1964, p. 186.

Chamberlain, who had branded the Italians as an inferior race, the hybrid descendants of an empire whose fall was caused by an excess of racial interbreeding.[1]

The Duce's repudiation of the racial gospel (not to mention his condemnation of anti-Semitism) was bound to antagonize the foreign Jew-baiters, most particularly the German ones, many of whom regarded him as a traitor to their cause. In 1923 Alfred Rosenberg, editor of Hitler's *Völkischer Beobachter* and future Party philosopher, deplored Mussolini's failure to come to grips with the Jewish peril;[2] in the following year he founded an anti-Semitic monthly, the *Weltkampf*, in which a good deal of space was devoted to the 'incomprehensible' manifestations of Fascist philo-Semitism. In the very first issue (June 1924) Rosenberg drew attention to the Fascist dictator's public repudiation of anti-Semitism, adding that he was unable 'to state the deeper reasons for this attitude with any degree of certainty.'[3] In the second issue he discussed the Matteotti affair, attacking the 'Jewish-controlled' *Corriere Italiano* (which had ridiculed Hitler's anti-Semitism in October 1923) and expressing the hope that Mussolini would now follow the advice of 'the consistent Fascist Farrinacci [*sic*] to rid himself of his "Jewish cohort."'[4] In September Rosenberg published an article by an Italian Fascist, Giuseppe Fredrigotti, on 'Fascism and its False Friends', in which Mussolini was criticized for accepting Jewish financial support and tolerating Jews in key positions. The article ended with the words: 'Let us hope that Mussolini will purge his movement so as to enable Fascism to complete its national mission.' In a prefatory note Rosenberg expressed cautious optimism, pointing out that the Matteotti scandal, followed by 'the rise of Fassinacci' (*sic*), might induce the dictator to reverse his stand on the Jewish

[1] In his talks with Ludwig Mussolini referred to Chamberlain's anti-Italian theories with keen resentment (op.cit., p. 72).

[2] A.R., 'Deutschland und Italien', *V.B.*, 17–18 June 1923.

[3] 'Juden als Abgeordnete in Italien', *Der Weltkampf*, i (June 1924), 40; cf. 'Italienische Merkwürdigkeiten', loc. cit. 40–1.

[4] 'Peinlicher Skandal', ibid. (July 1924), 38–9. Roberto Farinacci was the Fascist *ras* (chieftain) of Cremona and editor of *Cremona Nuova* (renamed *Il Regime Fascista* in January 1926). On 22 June 1924—twelve days after the Matteotti murder—he wrote in his paper: 'The sad Matteotti episode … has rid us of all our opponents who had surrounded the Duce and whom we used to call "the Jewish courtiers"' (quoted in H. Fornari, *Mussolini's Gadfly. Roberto Farinacci*. Nashville, 1971, p. 88).

question.[1] A less optimistic note was sounded by Adolf Dresler, the first Nazi biographer of Mussolini, who roundly denounced Fascism as a 'Jewish' movement, utterly dissimilar to anti-Jewish Hitlerism. Whoever regarded Fascism and Nazism as kindred phenomena, Dresler insisted, was an ignorant fool, if not a deliberate liar: 'Both movements, it is true, are pursuing the lofty goal of national rebirth, but Fascism was born of treason and perjury; in league with Freemasonry and Jewry, it dragged Italy into an unnecessary war, actuated solely by a thirst for imperial power ... Fascist rule began with the brutal violation of the South Tyrol where the attempt was made forcibly to turn 250,000 Germans and about 600,000 Slavs into Italians ... National Socialism is national and social, Fascism is Jewish, capitalist, and imperialist.' In analysing Fascist philo-Semitism, Dresler drew heavily on Fredrigotti's highly inaccurate account: 'An Egyptian newspaper has claimed that Mussolini is himself a Jew, an immigrant from Poland, whose real name is Mausler. Whether this is true we cannot tell ... It is certain, however, that Mussolini is a great friend of the Jews. His "right-hand man", Aldo Finzi, recently sacked because of the Matteotti affair,[2] is a Jew and so is his Minister of Agriculture, Acerbo[3] ... The Jew D'Annunzio has had honours lavished upon him (the State, for instance, has made him a "present" of a villa on Lake Garda, taken from a German family) and has finally even been ennobled as Prince of Montenevoso[4] ... The Jew Mortara was appointed Lord Chief Justice of Italy, and foreign Jews were also received with great courtesy.'[5] True, there were a few anti-Semites in the Fascist Party. Giovanni Preziosi had drawn attention to the Jewish peril in *La Vita Italiana*, and there had been attacks on the Jews in *La Fiamma Nera*, organ of the Arditi, and in *L'Impero*, a Roman daily edited by Fascist extremists. However, these were

[1] G. Fredrigotti, 'Der Faschismus und seine falschen Freunde', *Der Weltkampf*, i (Sept. 1924), 18–21.
[2] Giacomo Matteotti, the Socialist leader, was kidnapped and murdered by Fascists on 10 June 1924.
[3] Giacomo Acerbo, an aryan, was Under-Secretary at the Prime Minister's Office in 1924. In 1938 he was appointed President of the Council for Demography and Race.
[4] Far from being a Jew, D'Annunzio was not above occasional anti-Semitic sallies (M. Michaelis, 'Gli ebrei italiani sotto il regime fascista I', *La Rassegna Mensile di Israel*, xxviii (May 1962), 226–8).
[5] Mortara was appointed President of the Supreme Court before the March on Rome; he was ousted by the Fascists in 1923.

voices crying in the wilderness; their effect on Italian public
opinion, including Fascist opinion, had been altogether negligible. And since a racial consciousness was also lacking, anti-
Semitism was unlikely to take root in Italy in the foreseeable
future.[1]

Dresler's biography of the Duce appeared in the late autumn
of 1924, while Hitler was still in prison. In the following year
(the Führer having meanwhile been set at liberty) Rosenberg
launched a fresh campaign against Fascism and its 'false friends',
this time in Hitler's own paper, denouncing the 'terror regime'
in the South Tyrol and deploring Mussolini's dependence on the
'Polish Jew Toeplitz', president of the Banca Commerciale
Italiana.[2] When Count Volpi, the Governor of Tripolitania, was
appointed Minister of Finance in July 1925, Rosenberg
announced the news under the characteristic heading: 'Mussolini
capitulates! Toeplitz's man of straw Minister of Finance.' Volpi,
he explained, was a vice-president of the Banca Commerciale,
and his meteoric rise was entirely due to this fact. According to
financial circles in Rome, Volpi's appointment had assured the
stability of the lira: 'To us this means that Mussolini has
submitted to the dictatorship of Jewish high finance, handing
over the economy of the entire country to the Hebrew financier's
man of straw. The *Finanzjude* Toeplitz has thus been recognized
as the real dictator of Italy.' There was no doubt that 'Wall
Street and the City of London had a finger in this pie, threatening
Mussolini with a financial catastrophe.' In conclusion, Rosenberg
drew a parallel between Fascist Italy and the Weimar Republic,
claiming that Stresemann, too, was on the point of capitulating
to the Jews and calling on his Party comrades to redouble their
efforts in the struggle for German liberty.[3]

Strange as it may sound, Rosenberg's version of the above
events was confirmed many years later by Mussolini himself.
That, at any rate, is what Giovanni Preziosi told a German
diplomat in Rome on 1 February 1943, recounting a conversation
he had had with the Duce a few days earlier. In the course of that
conversation Mussolini informed the dean of Italian Jew-baiters

---

[1] A. Dresler, *Mussolini*, Leipzig, 1924, pp. 51–2, 58.
[2] 'Das Gewaltregiment in Südtirol', *V.B.*, 12 Dec. 1925, 'Die Freimaurerei und Italien,'
V.B., 31 Dec. 1925.
[3] 'Mussolini kapituliert! Der Strohmann von Toeplitz Finanzminister', *V.B.*, 7 July 1925.

'that after the Matteotti crisis in 1924 the only way in which he could maintain his position was by appointing Count Volpi Minister of Finance in order to propitiate the Jews.' Preziosi added that even in 1943 the 'subterranean power' of the Jews in Italy was too great for the Fascist dictator to be able to pursue an all-out anti-Semitic policy as he would like to do.[1]

There is no reason to believe that Preziosi invented the above conversation with his leader; but it is more than likely that the latter was using Preziosi in order to pull wool over the eyes of the Germans. For while it is true that the murder of Matteotti shook the Fascist regime to its foundations, compelling the Duce to resort to desperate measures in self-defence, it is equally true that the crisis was overcome on 3 January 1925, well over six months before Volpi's appointment.[2] Moreover, in a talk with his biographer, Yvon De Begnac, in 1940 Mussolini gave a very different—and much more convincing—account of the motives which had prompted him to replace Alberto de Stefani by Count Volpi fifteen years earlier.[3] It remains to add that at the very moment of his alleged surrender to Toeplitz his second-in-command in the Fascist Party was none other than Roberto Farinacci, the leading Fascist opponent of the Banca Commerciale and the hope of the German anti-Semites.[4]

Rosenberg was by no means the most violent of the 'anti-Mussolinians' in the Nazi camp; others went further, denouncing the Fascist dictator as 'simply a Jewish hireling' (*Judenknecht*), a charge frequently repeated by Hitler's rivals on the extreme German Right.[5] To the 'Socialists' in the movement, headed by Gregor and Otto Strasser, Mussolini's flirtation with the Jews was the most irritating (if not the most important) aspect of his alliance with 'reaction' and his betrayal of the workers.[6]

These attacks on the 'great man south of the Alps' greatly

[1] Minute by Doertenbach, 2 Feb. 1943 (YVS/K206733–35).
[2] On this, see A. Lyttelton, 'Fascism in Italy: The Second Wave', *Journal of Contemporary History*, i (Jan. 1966), 75–100.
[3] Y. De Begnac, *Palazzo Venezia*, Rome, 1951, p. 356; cf. R. De Felice, *Mussolini il fascista*, ii, Turin, 1968, pp. 85–90. On Toeplitz, see I. Toeplitz, *Il banchiere*, Milan, 1963.
[4] Farinacci held the post of Party Secretary from 12 February 1925 to 30 March 1926. On his campaign against Toeplitz, see Fornari, op.cit., pp. 115, 149, 178.
[5] K. Heiden, *Der Fuehrer. Hitler's Rise to Power*, London, 1967, p. 221; 'Mussolini', *Sigilla Veri*, iv, Erfurt, 1931, pp. 766–7.
[6] See R. Kühnl, *Die nationalsozialistische Linke*, Meisenheim/Glan, 1966, pp. 203–6; K.-P. Hoepke, *Die deutsche Rechte und der italienische Faschismus*, Düsseldorf, 1968, pp. 197–237.

annoyed and embarrassed Hitler who, having re-founded his
Party in February 1925, was more than ever determined to
follow in Mussolini's footsteps and to win the friendship of Fascist
Italy, regardless of the Italian attitude to the South Tyrolese and
the Jews. A good many months had to pass, however, before he
felt strong enough to impose his will on the editor of his paper,
not to mention the rest of his disunited and recalcitrant followers.
It was not until the end of 1925 that Rosenberg began to tone
down his attacks, paying reluctant tribute to the Duce's struggle
against Marxism and Freemasonry, expressing qualified approval of his social policy, and stressing the desirability of a
rapprochement with Italy.[1] Even so, the campaign against
'Mussolini and his false friends' did not cease. In February 1926
Rosenberg again reproached the Fascist leader with his failure
to rid himself of his Jewish masters, adding that 'Fascism was
now paying the penalty.'[2] In November he went further, warning
the Duce that only the victory of National Socialism could save
him from disaster: 'Mussolini, having struck down Marxism, has
had to come to terms with high finance. If he remains isolated,
international deceit will triumph again.'[3] In 1927 Rosenberg
repeated his charges in a book on *The Future of German Foreign
Policy*. After wondering whether the Italians had enough 'Aryan'
blood in their veins to make the Fascist experiment succeed and
deploring the continued presence of numerous Jews in Mussolini's
entourage, he continued: 'We do not know what Mussolini really
thinks, but the fact remains that he has officially repudiated anti-
Semitism in any shape or form ... It is likewise a fact that the
Wall Street bandit, Otto Hermann Kahn, was given a grand
reception in Rome and that the biggest Jew in Italy, the banker
Toeplitz, is more firmly in the saddle than ever before.' To be
sure, there were some encouraging signs: the suppression of
Freemasonry in Italy had infuriated the Jews all over the world,
and Mussolini's social policy had been something of a blow to
'Masonic and Jewish bankers'. An alliance with Italy was vital
for Germany, and 'all true Germans' were in duty bound to work
for it; their task, however, was not made any easier by the Duce's

[1] 'Die Sozialpolitik des Faschismus', *V.B.*, 23 Oct. 1925; A.R., 'Krisenstimmung', *V.B.*, 9
Feb. 1926.
[2] 'Der jüdisch-freimaurerische Weltkampf gegen Deutschland und Italien', *V.B.*, 13 Feb.
1926.
[3] 'Nationalsozialismus im Weltkampf', *V.B.*, 7–8 Nov. 1926.

repeated anti-German outbursts and his brutal oppression of the South Tyrolese, not to mention his public condemnation of German racial philosophy.[1]

In the ensuing years Mussolini's increasingly harsh Italianization policy in the Alto Adige and his increasingly cordial relations with 'international Jewry' confirmed Rosenberg in his scepticism about the Fascist experiment.[2] In the meantime, however, Hitler had succeeded in reasserting his authority and in imposing his pro-Italian views on his reluctant Party comrades, if not on the rest of the German Right. Rosenberg, too, was compelled to toe the line; from 1928 onwards criticism of Mussolini and Fascism became increasingly rare in Hitler's paper, and by 1932 it had ceased altogether. The sufferings of the South Tyrolese were passed over in silence, and so were the Duce's philo-Semitic statements to Emil Ludwig. The *Judenknecht* Mussolini had become a 'Roman genius', the leading statesman of his epoch, whose achievement was worthy of the highest praise and whose policy deserved unconditional support. The Fascist regime was held up as an example to the rest of mankind.[3] For his part, the Duce endorsed German revisionism (which he hoped to deflect from the Brenner to the Rhine); his newspapers displayed an ever-increasing enthusiasm for 'German Fascism', while politely ignoring Hitler's racialist aberrations.[4] For the moment neither side was interested in airing controversial issues; it was only after Hitler's advent to power that the ideological truce between the two sister movements temporarily broke down.

Hitler had launched his counter-offensive against the 'Italophobes' in his Party within a few months of his return to politics. In August 1925, while the editor of his paper was denouncing the 'oppressive Fascist regime' in the South Tyrol, he wrote the foreign policy chapter of *Mein Kampf*, in which he dismissed the anti-Italian agitation as a 'Jewish swindle': 'The reason why in

---

[1] A. Rosenberg, *Der Zukunftsweg einer deutschen Aussenpolitik*, Munich, 1927, pp. 41–6, 49, 60–1.
[2] A. Rosenberg, *Der Mythus des 20. Jahrhunderts*, Munich, 1930, pp. 81, 643; the anti-Italian passages reappeared in the 1940 edition, the Rome-Berlin Axis and the Pact of Steel notwithstanding. See also Rosenberg's *Letzte Aufzeichnungen*, Göttingen, 1955, p. 342.
[3] See, e.g., K. von Wieden, 'Was wir vom Faschismus wissen müssen', *Nationalsozialistische Monatshefte*, 3 (May 1932), 223–7.
[4] See De Felice, *Storia degli ebrei italiani*, pp. 137–8.

the last few years certain definite circles have made the "South Tyrol" question the pivotal point of German–Italian relations is obvious. *Jews and Habsburg legitimists have the greatest interest in preventing a German alliance policy which might lead some day to the resurrection of a free German fatherland. All this fuss today is not made for love of the South Tyrol—which it does not help but only harms—but for fear of a possible German–Italian understanding* . . . Especially we National Socialists must guard against being taken in tow by the Jewish-led bourgeois patriots of the word.' Elsewhere in his book Hitler deplored the base cowardice of many so-called 'national' Germans who had capitulated to the 'Jew-incited' clamour of public opinion, 'joined the general outcry' against a potential future ally, 'and senselessly helped to support the fight against a system which we Germans, precisely in this present-day situation, must feel to be the sole ray of light (*Lichtblick*) in this degenerating world.'[1]

But what of Mussolini's repudiation of anti-Semitism? What of his surrender to Jewish high finance which Rosenberg had deplored only a few weeks earlier? On this point, too, Hitler disagreed with the Party philosopher. Mussolini and Fascism, he insisted, had 'dared . . . to free themselves from the Jewish-Masonic embrace and oppose a nationalistic resistance to this international world poisoning.' The Fascist regime, therefore, could be regarded as so stablized and serving the interests of Italy so absolutely that there was no longer any reason to fear 'a really effective obstruction of political necessities by international Jewish forces'. If the Italian dictator, for whatever reasons, had so far preferred the indirect approach to the Jewish peril, it did not follow that Fascism had failed to come to grips with the problem: '*The struggle that Fascist italy is waging, though perhaps in the last analysis unconsciously (which I personally do not believe) against the three main weapons of the Jews is the best indication that the poison fangs of this supra-state power are being torn out, even though by indirect methods. The prohibition of Masonic secret societies, the persecution of the supra-national press, as well as the continuous demolition of international Marxism, and, conversely, the steady reinforcement of the Fascist state conception, will in the course of the years cause the Italian Government to*

[1] A. Hitler, *Mein Kampf*, 15th edn., Munich, 1932, pp. 709–12, 520–1.

serve the interests of the Italian people more and more, without regard for the hissing of the Jewish world hydra.'[1]

In his second book (written in 1928 and published posthumously in 1961) Hitler went to the length of asserting that the Jews had launched a worldwide campaign against Italy on the very day of the March on Rome; from that day onwards the South Tyrol issue had been puffed up for the purpose of discrediting a system which served the interests of the Italian people rather than those of world Jewry. After six years of Fascist rule Jewish influence had ceased to be a factor in Italian politics: hence the desirability of an alliance with Mussolini. However distressing the fate of the South Tyrolese (and even Hitler could not deny that they had genuine grievances), it must not be allowed to stand in the way of a *rapprochement* with the sole truly national Power in Europe. For his part, the Duce ought to facilitate such a *rapprochement* by openly encouraging his German supporters and by restraining his over-zealous underlings in the South Tyrol.[2]

Mussolini predictably failed to respond to Hitler's appeal. There was no reason why he should risk a clash with the Weimar regime (which had succeeded in restoring stability and prosperity by 1928) for the sake of a provincial agitator who had so far failed to make his mark in German politics.[3] But while refusing to side with his German disciple in public, he was not above intriguing with him in secret, given the identity of views on the South Tyrol issue and also the possibility that German Fascism might some day become a force in German political life. It was for both these reasons that the link, established before the beer hall Putsch was kept furbished throughout the period under review, even during the year of Hitler's detention in the fortress of Landsberg.[4]

In 1923 Mussolini, after his rebuff to Lüdecke, had been confirmed in his contempt for the 'Nazi buffoons' by the fiasco of

[1] Ibid., p. 721.

[2] *Hitlers zweites Buch*, ed. G. Weinberg, Stuttgart, 1961, pp. 191–209.

[3] On this, see A. Bullock, *Hitler. A Study in Tyranny*, rev. edn., Harmondsworth, 1962, pp. 135–45.

[4] For details, see A. Cassels, 'Mussolini and German Nationalism, 1922–25', *Journal of Modern History*, xxxv (June 1963), 137–57; J. Petersen, *Hitler–Mussolini. Die Entstehung der Achse Rom–Berlin 1933–1936*, Tübingen, 1973, pp. 14–18, 24–8, 41–9; and M. Michaelis, 'I rapporti tra fascismo e nazismo prima dell'avvento di Hitler al potere (1922–1933)', *Rivista Storica Italiana*, lxxxv (Sept. 1973), 544–600.

the 'March on Berlin'. Undeterred by either set-back, Hitler addressed an appeal to his Italian idol from his prison cell, assuring him of his devotion, reiterating his renunciation of the Alto Adige, and offering him the friendship of the 'Germany of tomorrow' in return for Fascist sympathy. Given his obsession with the threat to his Brenner frontier, the Duce appears to have welcomed these assurances, despite their lack of any concrete political value.[1] Even before the receipt of Hitler's message he had shown his interest in the latter's Party by granting asylum to several prominent National Socialists who had fled their country after the abortive Munich *coup*. One of these was Hermann Göring, the future Reichsmarschall; another was Hans Frank, the future Governor-General of Poland. It was Göring who transmitted Hitler's letter to Mussolini; while in Rome, he handed it to Giuseppe Bastianini, then Secretary-General of the Italian Fasci Abroad, who in turn passed it on to his chief. Bastianini was impressed by his guest whom he came to consider 'the sole political brain on the Hitlerite General Staff'; but he reacted sharply when the latter tried to enlighten him on the Jewish peril, pointing out that Jewish Fascists had played a prominent part in the fight against Bolshevism.[2] Though shocked at this rebuff, Göring was not discouraged; for he knew that not all Fascists were as insensible to the issue as Bastianini. Not long afterwards he proclaimed his conviction that an open break between Fascists and Jews was ultimately inevitable: '*No matter how often Mussolini insists that he is not fighting Jewry, the fact remains— and current events are proof of this—that Jewry is fighting him.* Anti-Semitic currents already exist in the Fascist camp itself, and they are clamouring for energetic measures against the Jews; why Mussolini has so far failed to yield to this clamour is not yet entirely clear.' Even so, Fascism and National Socialism were kindred movements, and the divergence of views on the racial problem was more apparent than real. If Mussolini really wanted to carry out the Fascist programme, he would have to declare war on the Jews whether he liked it or not; the suppression of the

---

[1] G. Bastianini, *Uomini, cose, fatti*, Milan, 1959, p. 147.
[2] Ibid., pp. 183–5. For Frank's visit to Italy see H. Frank, *Im Angesicht des Galgens*, 2nd edn., Neuhaus b. Schliersee, 1955, pp. 214–15.

Masonic lodges was a first step in this direction, and other steps were bound to follow.[1]

For the moment Göring's mission in Italy was confined to a resumption of the informal contacts initiated by Lüdecke. The Italians, while willing to keep in touch, could hardly consider supporting a movement which had just been dissolved throughout the Reich. On his release from prison, Hitler sought an immediate interview with Mussolini, but was refused; his request for a signed photograph of the Duce (submitted to the Italian Embassy in Berlin and duly forwarded to Rome) was likewise turned down.[2] As late as October 1926 a Fascist agent reported to Farinacci that the consolidation of German nationalism had been facilitated by the elimination of 'charlatans like Hitler and Ludendorf' (*sic*), adding that Fascist Italy could now look forward to a genuine alliance with the German Right.[3] By 1927, however, the time was considered ripe for a more tangible relationship with the Austrian 'charlatan'; in February of that year a Fascist German-language news-sheet began to appear at Munich, the *Nord–Süd Korrespondenz,* which was given ample publicity in Hitler's paper.[4] Concurrently, a high officer of the Fascist secret service at Merano informed a visiting 'German Fascist' (whom he mistook for a Nazi) that 'his' leader was receiving money from Mussolini in return for his loyal stand on the Alto Adige issue. Another prominent Fascist told the same visitor that, given the weakness of the Weimar regime Fascism was bound to triumph in Germany even as it had triumphed in Italy; it was on this assumption that Mussolini was subsidizing Hitler. When the German objected that aid to a sworn enemy of the Weimar Republic might jeopardize relations with Berlin, his interlocutor replied that the German Embassy 'was in the secret and would hush the matter up for political reasons'.[5] On 15 May 1928 (five days before the Reichstag elections), the diplomatic representative of the Reich at Munich, in a confidential report

---

[1] H. Göring, 'Zum deutsch-italienischen Konflikt II', *V.B.*, 6 Mar. 1926.
[2] F. Anfuso, *Da Palazzo Venezia al Lago di Garda,* Bologna, 1957, p. 16; M. Donosti (pseudonym of Mario Luciolli), *Mussolini e l'Europa,* Rome, 1945, p. 80.
[3] Biseo to Farinacci, 8 Oct. 1926 (IC/Job 330/113305–6).
[4] Haniel to Wilhelmstrasse, 28 July 1928 (BA/K/R 43 I/Italien); Carocci, op.cit., p. 196; Petersen, op.cit., p. 25.
[5] Sworn deposition of Dr. Wilhelm von Brehmer ('Bekommt Hitler italienisches Geld?', *Vossische Zeitung,* 7 May 1929; GFM/5272H/K326331–62).

to the Wilhelmstrasse, accused Italy of financing Hitler's election campaign; in a subsequent report (23 August) he submitted detailed evidence of collusion between Hitler and Mussolini in the Alto Adige.[1] Despite this collusion, however, the Duce continued to turn down Hitler's requests for a meeting and to ignore his pleas for a more lenient treatment of the South Tyrolese.[2]

In May 1929 Hitler successfully prosecuted a libel action against right-wing and left-wing opponents who had accused him of 'betraying' the South Tyrol in return for Fascist gold. While Mussolini kept a discreet silence, his newspapers came out in defence of the sister movement, dismissing the charges as base calumnies and hailing the verdict as a triumph for both Fascism and Hitlerism. The Duce's own paper took advantage of the occasion to assure its readers that Hitler, far from being the 'buffoon' his enemies made him out to be, was a political realist with sound Fascist ideas—despite his anti-Semitism which was 'undoubtedly the weak point in his programme'.[3]

In 1930 the world depression put an abrupt end to the recovery of the Weimar Republic, with the result that, almost overnight, Hitler and his Party became a major factor in German (and European) politics.[4] Mussolini was elated at the meteoric rise of German Fascism which he regarded as a victory for his own movement. As recently as 3 March 1928 he had said that Fascism was 'not an article for export'. On 27 October 1930, however— six weeks after Hitler's electoral success—he loudly contradicted himself: 'The phrase that Fascism is not an export commodity is not mine. It is too banal . . . Today I affirm that Fascism as an idea, a doctrine, a realization, is universal.' Two years later he went further, claiming that there was 'no salvation outside our principles', Fascism being the panacea for all the ills of Western

---

[1] Krebs to Wilhelmstrasse, 23 Aug. 1928 (GFM/L232/L067497–500).

[2] *DDI*, 7ª serie vi. 284; M. Toscano, *Storia diplomatica della questione dell'Alto Adige*, Bari, 1967, p. 113.

[3] 'Hitler ottiene piena vittoria', *Il Tevere*, 16 May 1929; E. Morreale, 'Come la pensa Hitler', *Il Popolo d'Italia*, 18 May 1929. Morreale's article was based on an interview with Hitler who told him that he had no intention of persecuting the Jews: 'L'antisemitismo del movimento hitleriano non ha un carattere spiccatamente combattivo' (DDI, 7ª serie vii. 414, memorandum of 8 May 1929).

[4] At the Reichstag elections 14 September 1930 Hitler polled 6,409,600 votes, winning 107 seats out of 577 as compared with 12 out of 491 at the previous elections.

civilization: 'Within ten years Europe will be Fascist or fascistized.'[1]

Universal tendencies were inherent in fascism from its very inception, but until Hitler's electoral triumph they had little effect on Fascist policy. As early as February 1921 Mussolini called for co-operation with those of like conviction in other countries; once in power, however, he insisted that the aims of Fascism were 'exclusively national' and that hence he had no concern with any foreign party of a similar character.[2] In November 1923 he said to Primo de Rivera that Fascism had universal as well as national aspects, and in April 1925 he allowed the Fascist Grand Council to discuss the possibility of a 'moral alliance' with kindred movements abroad; but in January 1926 he again dissociated himself from his 'more or less successful' foreign imitators. In December 1927 he proclaimed his conviction that the world was about to enter a 'Fascist age'; but a few weeks later he told a Romanian journalist that Fascism was 'not an export commodity' and that he resented the attempts of his German admirers to identify his movement with anti-Semitism.[3] In April 1929 Asvero Gravelli, one of Mussolini's earliest followers, founded the review *Anti-Europa* which proclaimed the need for a Fascist International; but in May 1930 the Duce assured Theodor Wolff, the editor of the *Berliner Tageblatt*, that there was 'not the faintest connection' between Italian Fascism and the self-styled Fascists beyond Italy's borders: 'I do not know any Fascism outside Italy; in fact, there is none. Italian Fascism is something quite different ... To use an expression which I dislike, Fascism is not an article for export. People said that Primo de Rivera was a Fascist in our sense, but he had nothing to do with us. When he was overthrown people said that Fascism had suffered a defeat. We are not responsible for these people abroad, even if they claim to be our sympathizers; they do not

[1] *O.O.* xxiii. 122; xxiv. 283; xxv. 147.
[2] *O.O.* xvi. 450; *DDI,* 7ª serie i. 184; cf. M.A. Ledeen, *Universal Fascism. The Theory and Practice of the Fascist International, 1928–1936,* New York, 1972; D. Veneruso, 'Il fascismo internazionale (1919–1938)', in S. Fontana (ed.), *Il fascismo e le autonomie locali,* Bologna, 1973, pp. 23–72.
[3] *O.O.* xx. 113; xxi. 293; *DDI,* 7ª serie iv. 159; *O.O.* xxxii. 79; 'Fascismo e antisemitismo', *Israel,* 12 Jan. 1928.

interest us. Italian Fascism differs from the German imitation in not being anti-Semitic.'[1]

After Hitler's success at the polls, the Fascist dictator no longer troubled to conceal his interest in the 'German imitation.' Much to the annoyance of the German Government, he instructed his underlings to encourage the setting-up of the Nazi Party cells throughout Italy and most particularly in the Alto Adige where he hoped to split and undermine the German irredentist movement with their aid.[2] Giovanni Giuriati (who had succeeded Augusto Turati as Party Secretary in October 1930) informed one of Hitler's emissaries that he would welcome co-operation between the two movements, including an exchange of confidential information.[3] The Duce himself assumed the role of Hitler's mentor; after letting him know that he was 'following the fortunes of his Party with keen interest', he began to send him regular messages through his liaison man with the German Right, Major Giuseppe Renzetti.[4] By the spring of 1932 the link between the two demagogues had become so close as to cause 'acute embarrassment' to Dino Grandi, the pro-Western Italian Foreign Minister.[5]

Oddly enough, the growing intimacy between Blackshirts and Brownshirts evoked less alarm in Jewish circles than the March on Rome had done ten years earlier. There were several reasons for this. First and foremost, the flirtation between the two sister movements coincided with the honeymoon between Fascists and Jews; Mussolini's talks with Ludwig took place at the very moment when the pro-Hitler campaign in the Fascist press was at its height. Second, it was generally held that Mussolini was the

[1] On Gravelli's plans for a Fascist International, see IC/Job 287/087731–49; on Wolff, *O.O.* xxiv. 224 and PRO/F.O. 371/14422/C3869/3869/22 (Sir Horace Rumbold to Foreign Office, 12 May 1930).

[2] GFM/L1703/L501565–804 (secret files of German Embassy, Rome): PA/AA Chef AO–13 (Akten betr. Italien/Landesgruppe italien 1932): M. Michaelis, 'I nuclei nazisti in Italia e la loro funzione nei rapporti tra fascismo e nazismo nel 1932', *Nuova Rivista Storica*, lvii (May–Aug. 1973), 422–38.

[3] NS/HA/Reel 78, Folder 1575 (unsigned and undated memorandum, seized by the Munich police during a search at the Brown House in 1932).

[4] IC/*Segreteria particolare del Duce*/Job 170/050243–50, 52–78; De Felice, *Mussolini e Hitler*, pp. 211–29, 232–41, 245–58, 291–303.

[5] GFM/2784/D140020–22 (Schubert to Wilhelmstrasse, 16 Mar. 1932); PRO/F.O. 371/15979/C2509/327/22 (Sir Ronald Graham to Foreign Office, 24 Mar. 1932). Grandi's own version (ACS/Carte Grandi/busta 1/fasc.6/sottofasc.1) appears to be coloured by a desire to gloss over his differences with his master.

only statesman capable of exercising a beneficial influence on Hitler (an illusion shared by the Duce himself). Third, it was hoped that Fascist Italy's exemplary treatment of her Jews would have a salutary effect on visiting National Socialists;[1] it is worthy of note in this connection that Hitler had toned down his attacks on the Jews since 1928—so much so that the mentor of the German Right, General Ludendorff, publicly denounced him as a traitor to the anti-Semitic cause.[2] Fourth, it was noted with relief that Mussolini, for all his 'keen interest' in the Brownshirts, continued to evade Hitler's increasingly urgent requests for a meeting.[3] It remains to add that the intermediary between the Duce and the Führer, Major Renzetti, was married to a Jewess, and so was the Italian Ambassador in Berlin, Luca Orsini Baroni; in the autumn of 1932 Orsini Baroni was succeeded by Vittorio Cerruti, a staunch opponent of Hitlerism, who likewise had a Jewish wife.[4]

But if Mussolini was unwilling to antagonize the Jews for the sake of Hitler, he was equally unwilling to alienate Hitler for the sake of the Jews. While repudiating racialism, he did not want to pass as a *Judenknecht* in the eyes of his anti-Jewish admirers; he therefore made it clear in a variety of ways that his public utterances against anti-Semitism need not be taken too seriously. For one thing, he never put a stop to the anti-Semitic activities of Preziosi and other Jew-haters on the lunatic fringe of the Fascist Party; for another, he founded an extremist Fascist paper of his own—the Roman daily *Il Tevere*, edited by Telesio Interlandi—which began to display marked anti-Semitic and

---

[1] Cf. 'Il capro espiatorio', *Israel*, 17 Dec. 1931.

[2] E. Ludendorff, *Weltkrieg droht auf deutschem Boden*, Munich, 1930, pp. 19–20. Undeterred by this attack, Hitler continued to assure all and sundry that law-abiding Jews had little to fear from his movement (*The Times*, 15 Oct. 1930; Lüdecke, p. 481). Among those taken in by Hitler's apparent moderation was Renzetti who affirmed ('Hindenburg e Hitler', *Gerarchia*, xii, Mar. 1932, 235–7) that the National Socialists discountenanced violent anti-Semitism and that they had nothing against loyal Jews; 'Nessuno ... ha l'intenzione di indire delle persecuzioni o dei pogrom ... Se si tiene conto di ciò e del fatto che nello stesso campo delle croci uncinate si riconosce che in Germania vivono molti ebrei di sentimento nazionale, onesti, si può dedurre che anche in tale questione il buon senso e la ragione avranno il sopravvento.'

[3] IC/*Segreteria particolare del Duce*/Job 170/050252–78; GFM/5257H/E315488–91.

[4] Elisabetta Cerruti, author of *Visti da vicino*, Milan, 1951. On Susanne Kochmann, Renzetti's German-Jewish wife, see Bella Fromm, *Blood and Banquets. A Berlin Social Diary*, New York–London, 1942, p. 89; J. Goebbels, *Tagebücher*, ed. Lochner, Zurich, 1948, pp. 422–3; GFM/1045/311329–30 (Abwehr, Italien).

pro-Nazi tendencies long before Hitler's rise to political eminence.[1]

Nor was this all. In February 1928 Hitler's paper began to publish a series of 'Roman letters' by Angelo Vecchio-Verderame, an agent of the Fascist Government, which were strongly tinged with anti-Semitism. In one of these letters the Jews were accused of opposing an Italo-German *rapprochement*; in another it was hinted that the Duce himself was none too fond of the chosen people, his public statements to the contrary notwithstanding.[2] In 1931 the Fascist German-language press in the Alto Adige was placed at the disposal of Hitler's propagandists; in October and November of that year the *Alpenzeitung* of Bolzano published what purported to be 'authentic information' on the Hitler-Bewegung, a panegyric on the Führer and a defence of every point in his programme, including racialism and anti-Semitism.[3] In February 1932 Hitler discussed 'questions of plutocracy and anti-Semitism' with a group of Fascist emissaries; according to Goebbels (who took part in the talk) a 'large measure of agreement' was reached.[4] Finally, on 27 January 1933—three days before Hitler's rise to power—the Duce in person told the German Ambassador that in Germany (as distinct from Italy)

---

[1] In June 1925 Italo Tavolato, one of Interlandi's collaborators, informed the Germans that the *Tevere* (founded on 27 December 1924) was 'Mussolini's personal creation' (Thomsen to Bülow, 23 June 1925, GFM/K542/K154238); the Duce himself told Nino d'Aroma in July 1937 that Interlandi was 'a personal whim' of his (N. d'Aroma, *Mussolini segreto*, Bologna, 1958, p. 126). From April 1926 onwards Rosenberg regularly drew the attention of his readers to Interlandi's attacks on the Jews; a year later he also began to praise him for his pro-Hitler stand (A. Rosenberg, 'Die Reise nach Tripolis', *V.B.*, 10 Apr. 1926; 'Die Hitlerrede und die italienische Presse', *V.B.*, 29 Apr. 1927; 'Antisemitische Erkenntnisse in Rom.!', *V.B.*, 4 May 1927; 'Sensationeller Aufsatz des faschistischen "Tevere"', *V.B.*, 19 Feb. 1930). For Interlandi's approval of Hitler's anti-Semitism, see, e.g. 'Croce uncinata', *Il Tevere*, 13 June 1931; for his close relations with Mussolini, A. Lyttelton, *The Seizure of Power. Fascism in Italy 1919–1929*, London, 1973, p. 400. Dino Grandi informs the writer that Mussolini considered Interlandi his 'mouthpiece' ('portavoce di alcune sue idee') (letter of 5 June 1972).
[2] Verderame, 'Römische Briefe', *V.B.*, 4 Feb. 1928; verderame, 'Römische Briefe 9', *V.B.*, 4 May 1928; cf. Vecchio-Verderame to Grandi, 21 May 1928 *(DDI*, 7ª serie vi. 310–11). Grandi informs the writer that he does not remember Vecchio-Verderame and that the above-quoted report probably never reached him (letter of 25 July 1972).
[3] 'Die Hitler-Bewegung. Was sie ist, und was sie will. Eine authentische Information', *Alpenzeitung*, 31 Oct. and 3 Nov. 1931.
[4] J. Goebbels, *Vom Kaiserhof zur Reichskanzlei*, 31st edn., Munich, 1941, p. 49. Goebbels noted with particular satisfaction that the Italian visitors, while denying the existence of a Jewish problem in Italy, were 'at bottom all of them anti-Semites.'

the Jews did indeed constitute a problem: 'If he were in Germany, he would presumably also be an anti-Semite.'[1]

In addition to encouraging unofficial manifestations of anti-Semitism, Mussolini also practised unofficial discrimination against the Italian Jews. From the very beginning he saw to it that members of the Jewish community did not reach positions of control either in the government or in the Party hierarchy; the only Jew to play a major role in the Fascist Party—Aldo Finzi—was baptized and married the niece of a cardinal.[2] No Jew was ever admitted to the Italian Academy, although the number of outstanding Jewish scholars was disproportionately high. Until 1938 it was pretended that the absence of Jews at the top was purely accidental; when Ludwig questioned Mussolini about the alleged exclusion of 'Semites' from the Academy, the latter replied that the allegation was 'absurd'.[3] After the enactment of the racial laws, however, it was explicitly admitted by Fascist spokesmen that the Duce had always regarded Jewish influence as harmful and that he had 'usually prevented the Jews from achieving any prominent position in the regime'.[4]

In retrospect these symptoms of latent tension may seem highly significant. At the time, however, their impact on Italian Jewry was negligible; nor is it likely that Mussolini himself attached much importance to these discreet anti-Jewish manœuvres of his (which did not disturb the prevailing harmony between the regime and the Jews and were not meant to).

Ten years after the March on Rome, Italian anti-Semitism was still only an oddity. The most vociferous of the Fascist Jew-baiters, Giovanni Preziosi, was notoriously an outsider, ignored by the Italian public, at odds with the Fascist Party, and detested by Mussolini himself.[5] Telesio Interlandi, though close to the

---

[1] Von Hassell to Wilhelmstrasse, 27 Jan. 1933 (GFM/8038H/E578094).

[2] Finzi, a member of the first Fascist Grand Council and Under-Secretary of the Interior from 1922 to 1924, served as a scapegoat after the Matteotti murder, with which, however, he had had no connection (cf. G. Salvemini, *The Fascist Dictatorship in Italy*, London, 1928, pp. 349–50). 'Aryanized' in 1938, he was expelled from the Fascist Party in November 1942 (IC/Job 114/031558). In March 1944 he was shot by the Germans at the Ardeatine Caves.

[3] Ludwig, p. 72.

[4] C. Pellizzi, *Italy*, London, 1939, p. 192.

[5] On Mussolini's aversion to Preziosi (whom he accused of 'having the evil eye'), see C. Rossi, *Mussolini com'era*, Rome, 1947, p. 260; E.F. Moellhausen, *La carta perdente*, 2nd edn., Rome, 1948, pp. 311–16; R. Rahn, *Ruheloses Leben*, Düsseldorf, 1949, p. 245; cf. also Preziosi to Mussolini, 31 Jan. 1944 (IC/Job 331/94–106).

dictator, was a minor figure, and his paper had a negligible circulation. Neither Preziosi nor Interlandi was permitted to call for anti-Jewish measures in Italy; all they could do was to denounce such abstractions as 'Jewish plutocracy' or 'Jewish high finance'. Preziosi's protector, Roberto Farinacci, was in disgrace since his dismissal from the post of Party Secretary. While sharing some of his protégé's prejudices, he had Jewish friends and collaborators; nor did he ever attack the Jews in his speeches and writings during the period under review. Moreover, he was critical of Hitler in 1932—so much so that by the end of that year he had become Rosenberg's *bête noire*.[1]

The unofficial exclusion of Jews from certain key positions affected only a very few people; the average Jew (who could no more aspire to a post in the Cabinet or to membership of the Italian Academy than the average Gentile) was not conscious of any discrimination. It is worth recalling in this connection that under Fascism the number of Jewish university teachers continued to be disproportionately high, and so did the number of Jewish generals and admirals. Nor was the Fascist Party by any means *judenrein*. Guido Jung, on being appointed Minister of Finance, became an *ex officio* member of the Fascist Grand Council. Alberto Liuzzi, a baptized Jew with an Aryan wife, attained the rank of consul-general in the Fascist militia. Margherita Sarfatti was the Duce's first official biographer as well as co-editor of his monthly review, *Gerarchia*, for which only trusted Fascists were permitted to write. Gino Arias was the chief theorist of the *Stato corporativo* and a regular contributor to both *Gerarchia* and *Il Popolo d'Italia*; another regular contributor was Carlo Foà, an eminent Jewish physiologist. Giorgio Del Vecchio was the first Fascist Rector of the University of Rome. Given this situation, very few Italian Jews disagreed with Mussolini when he made his above-quoted statement on the 'perfect civic, political, and above all "moral" equality between all Italians, whatever their remote descent'.[2]

---

[1] For Farinacci's disgrace, see De Felice, *Mussolini il fascista*, ii. 168–75, 184–6, 512–24; for his criticism of Hitler, cf. R. Farinacci, 'Fascismo e nazionalsocialismo', *La Vita Italiana*, xl (15 Sept. 1932), 249–51; 'Governare o lasciar governare', *Il Regime Fascista*, 13 Dec. 1932; for Rosenberg's reaction, cf. 'Wem nützt das, Herr Farinacci?', *V.B.*, 23 Dec. 1932. Rosenberg was supported by Interlandi ('A chi giova?', *Il Tevere*, 15–16 Dec. 1932).

[2] On the Jewish university professors, see *Vita Universitaria*. of 5 Oct. 1938; on Alberto Liuzzi, V. Teodorani (ed.), *Milizia volontaria. Armata di popolo*, Rome, 1962, p. 252; on the

In February 1929 not a few Italian Jews were alarmed at Mussolini's Concordat with the Vatican which restored Roman Catholicism to its place as the state religion. Their fears, however, were quickly dispelled. On 10 March Mussolini declared at the Party Assembly that the Jews had nothing to worry about: the agreements with the Church did not mean that 'other cults hitherto tolerated are from now on to be persecuted, suppressed, or even disturbed'. On 13 May, in his speech to the Chamber of Deputies, he was even more emphatic: 'The Jews have been in Rome ever since the time of the Kings; perhaps it was they who supplied the clothes after the rape of the Sabine women. There were fifty thousand at the time of Augustus, and they asked to weep on the corpse of Julius Caesar. They will stay here undisturbed.' He was as good as his word. Since the signing of the Concordat lessened the Duce's dependence on the goodwill of the Pope, its long-term effect on Fascist policy towards the Jews was actually positive.[1]

The agreement with the Vatican was followed by a comprehensive Law on the Jewish Communities (No. 1,731 of 30 October 1930; No. 1,279 of 24 September 1931; No. 1,561 of 19 November 1931) which gave a coherent legal status to Italian Jewry and provided an economic base for its religious and cultural activities. The Jewish population was organized in twenty-six autonomous communities, each of them invested with juristic personality and empowered to levy taxation on its members. The voluntary basis of association was abolished; membership was henceforth compulsory on all persons of Jewish birth, provided that they did not formally renounce Judaism or embrace another religion. A national federation of the communities was achieved by the constitution of a central body, the Union of Italian Jewish Communities, which henceforth represented the entire Jewish body before the government and the public. Article 36 of the new law enjoined upon the Union the

Jewish generals and admirals, E. Rubin, *140 Jewish Marshals, Generals and Admirals*, London, 1952, pp. 156–214.

[1] *O.O.* xxiv. 14, 82; D. Carpi, 'The Catholic Church and Italian Jewry under the Fascists (to the Death of Pius XI)', *Yad Vashem Studies*, iv (1960), 50. Prior to the signing of the Lateran pacts, Mussolini was worried about the effect which pro-Jewish or pro-Zionist policies might have on his 'neighbour' in Rome, as is clear both from his letter of 14 August 1927 (see above, p. 32 n. 2) and from his conversation with Victor Jacobson, Jewish Agency representative at the League of Nations, on 6 June 1927 (Jacobson to Kisch, 20 June 1927, CZA/File 1325).

duty of participating in the 'religious and social activity' of Jewry and of maintaining 'spiritual and cultural contacts' with the Jewish communities of other countries, especially with those which had ties with Italian Jewry and Italy. (Six years later these 'spiritual and cultural contacts' were to be cited by Fascist propagandists as evidence of Jewish disloyalty to Italy.) The Law on the Jewish Communities was in part a manifestation of what Mussolini called 'our ferocious totalitarian will' (meaning the Fascist urge for regimentation and centralization) and in part an attempt to make the Jewish minority a more efficient tool of Fascist 'imperial' policy. Even so, it won praise from the Jewish leaders who rightly saw in it a significant expansion of their own power.[1]

The spread of Hitlerism in Italy and its encouragement by the Fascist authorities were bound to cause uneasiness in Jewish circles. They were quickly reassured, however, by both Mussolini's condemnation of Hitler's racial theories and his evident determination not to tolerate any National Socialist meddling in Italian domestic affairs. In the early years of Fascism Hitler and his emissaries had repeatedly attempted to stir up anti-Jewish feeling in Italy, only to meet with humiliating rebuffs. By 1932 the lesson had sunk in. Heinrich Brand, Hitler's chief lieutenant in Italy, warned the Brown House (the Headquarters of the Nazi Party) that his position was delicate in the extreme; the Italians, while hoping for Hitler's victory, were not prepared to risk any complications for his sake. Brand was worried about Jewish influence and its possible effects on the official Italian attitude towards his movement. On 11 January 1932 he reported to Gregor Strasser that the misconduct of certain Party comrades in Italy had apparently been exploited by 'Jewish propaganda', with disturbing results; on 2 July he informed Rudolf Hess that 'Jewish counter-propaganda' was assuming the proportions of a regular campaign.[2] He proposed to meet the threat by adopting a policy of prudent restraint and strict non-interference in Italian politics. To be sure, even in 1932 Hitler's agents tried to foster

[1] 'La nuova legge delle Comunità', *Israel*, 20 Jan. 1931; De Felice, *Storia degli ebrei italiani*, pp. 102–9, 475–88.
[2] PA/AA/Chef Ao–13 (Akten betr. Italien/Landesgruppe Italien 1932); Brand to Strasser, 11 Jan. 1932, Bl. 4–5, Brand to Hess, 2 July 1932, Bl. 2. See also Michaelis, 'I nuclei nazisti in Italia e la loro funzione nei rapporti tra fascismo e nazismo nel 1932', 430, 432.

anti-Semitism among their fellow Germans—sometimes in a manner which embarrassed the official representatives of the Reich;[1] but they scrupulously refrained from any anti-Jewish agitation outside the German community. One of Brand's collaborators, a certain Glaser, made discreet (and apparently successful) attempts to influence the Fascist press in Hitler's favour. On the pretext of 'correcting factual inaccuracies', he rewrote the articles on National Socialism which the two leading Milanese dailies—the *Corriere della Sera* and Mussolini's own *Popolo d'Italia*—were receiving from their respective correspondents in Germany. According to Brand, the Italians were grateful to Glaser for his 'friendly co-operation'.[2] There is, however, no evidence that Glaser's propaganda had any bearing on the Jewish issue, since none of the 'corrected' articles contained any reference to the Jews.

Given the loyal attitude of the Italian authorities and the caution exercised by Hitler's representatives, the leaders of Italian Jewry soon ceased to worry about National Socialist activities in Italy. The prevailing optimism was accurately reflected in Alfonso Pacifici's above-quoted editorial on the tenth anniversary of the March on Rome.[3]

After a decade of Fascist rule, Italy was still a model of tolerance as far as treatment of her Jewish minority was concerned. Relations between the authorities and the Jews had never been better. Mussolini had by no means abandoned his prejudices; but he had come to the conclusion that Jewish internationalism, like Catholic internationalism, was a force he could handle.

The latent tension between Fascists and Jews was due less to doctrinaire anti-Semitism (which was foreign to most Italians) than to Fascism's all-embracing claim on the individual; any regime with totalitarian pretensions is bound to resent manifestations of separatism. Paradoxically, it was the Duce's very

---

[1] Report by German Consulate at Trieste to German Embassy in Rome, 26 Jan. 1932 (GFM/L1703/L501724–30).

[2] Brand to Hess, ibid.

[3] See above, p. 30 n. 2; cf. also D. Lattes, 'Eternità e universalità d'Israele', *Israel*, 14–21 Jan. 1932. To be sure, men like Sacerdoti and Lattes had no illusions about Mussolini's character, having had first-hand experience of his emotional instability, his duplicity, and insincerity; they could not, however, fail to appreciate the fact that his philo-Semitic utterances were backed by concrete actions.

success in imposing totalitarian rule which eased the tension, since it freed him from his initial preoccupation with Jewish opposition to Fascism. By 1932 he had evidently come to feel that Jews in small doses, far from constituting a threat, were a useful addition to the Italian population. In June 1932 he said to Starhemberg: 'We too have our Jews. There are many in the Fascist Party, and they are good Fascists and good Italians . . . A country with a sound system of government has no Jewish problem.'[1] He made the same point in his above-mentioned conversation with the German Ambassador. After lavishing praise on Jung (whose Jewish blood he considered to be 'an asset'), he added that for Italy it was 'not at all difficult and even quite advantageous to digest the tiny percentage of Jews'.[2] However, while recognizing the merits of his Jewish compatriots, he continued to reproach them with 'separatism' and 'dual loyalties' in his anonymous articles.

Despite the prevailing cordiality, the anti-Jewish bacilli were still unmistakably there; but it needed a drastic change in the international situation to make them virulent. As we now know, that change was not long in coming.

---

[1] von Starhemberg, p. 93.
[2] See above, p. 51 n. 3.

III   The Rise of Hitler and the First Anti-Semitic Campaign in Italy (1933–1934)

HITLER'S RISE to power (30 January 1933) was welcomed by the Duce on the assumption that it would enhance the prestige of his own movement and strengthen his position *vis-à-vis* France and Britain. His ideological pride in the victory of the sister movement was clearly reflected in a resolution passed by the Fascist Grand Council on 9 March 1933, inviting the world to recognize 'in the Fascist movement growing beyond the frontiers of Italy the affirmation of a new spirit which—directly or indirectly—is drawing inspiration and guidance from the solid complex of doctrines and institutions whereby Italy has created the modern State'. The enthusiasm of the Fascist press found its most eloquent expression in Interlandi's paper: 'Hitler, together with Fascist Italy, will create a well-defined and solid barrier of will-to-peace in distraught Europe between France, the great Western disturber of the peace, and the harried group of Eastern *provocateurs* that gravitate around France. In the name of the new order that Europe wants, we hail the advent to power of Hitler, loyal friend of Fascist Italy, admirer of Mussolini.'[1]

For the moment, however, the Duce's approval of German Fascism did not extend to the anti-Jewish and anti-Christian excesses in Germany, still less to the Führer's designs on Austria. His mixed feelings about the sister revolution are accurately reflected in a signed article, entitled 'Between two Civilizations', which appeared in the *Popolo d'Italia* on 22 August: 'Behold another great country which is creating the unitary, authoritarian, totalitarian, that is the Fascist State, *with certain accentuations which Fascism has spared itself*, having to act in a different historical milieu.'[2]

In 1933 Mussolini could not yet risk antagonizing the Western

[1] *O.O.* xxv. 200; *Il Tevere*, 10 Feb. 1933. Mussolini's enthusiasm for Hitler worried his anti-German Ambassador in London, Dino Grandi, who told Sir John Simon on 8 March that he had vainly tried to dissuade the Duce from his pro-German orientation (*DBFP*, 2nd Ser. v.57–8).
[2] *O.O.* xxvi. 44.

Powers by forming an ideological bloc with Hitler; nor could he afford to alienate Western public opinion by proclaiming his solidarity with a Jew-baiter. But if Hitler's racial mania was a source of grave embarrassment to him, so was the anti-Hitler campaign conducted by 'international Jewry'. Whatever his reservations about the Führer, he needed German support for his 'revisionist' policy; nor could he, as the self-styled head of 'universal Fascism', approve of an ideological crusade against the kindred regime in Berlin. Moreover, as a dictator with totalitarian pretensions, he could not but resent the part played in this crusade by his Jewish compatriots: while the Fascist press was exulting over the triumph of the sister movement in Germany, the representatives of Italian Jewry vied with their anti-Fascist brethren abroad in denouncing the German atrocities. It was a disturbing demonstration of Jewish internationalism which a Fascist dictatorship could hardly tolerate; at the same time, however, it was (or seemed to be) an impressive display of worldwide 'Jewish power', confirming the Fascist leader in his long-standing conviction that 'world Jewry' was indeed a force to be reckoned with in international politics.

Given his determination to keep on the right side of both Jews and Brownshirts, the Duce was anxious to bring about a reconciliation between the two. Being both a 'philo-Semite' and a Fascist, he was widely believed to be the sole Western statesman qualified for such a task. Before attempting to work out some sort of *modus vivendi* between 'international Jewry' and the Third Reich, however, he would have to establish his credentials as an impartial mediator. This he did in the only way open to him— by dissociating himself from both Hitler's crusade against Jewry and Jewry's crusade against Hitler. On the one hand, he harshly condemned German racial policy which he regarded as a piece of gratuitous folly.[1] On the other, he unleashed a veritable anti-Jewish campaign—the first in the history of modern Italy—in

---

[1] On 28 March Mussolini said to Hassell that the 'anti-German world propaganda of the Jews and Freemasons . . . showed the great power and the excellent organization of these circles' (GFM/3170/675880–82); on 30 March he told the French Ambassador, Henri de Jouvenel, 'qu'il ne fallait jamais toucher ni les Juifs, ni l'Église, car cela équivalait à tirer des coups de canon dans le vide'; on 17 April he told his *chef de cabinet* that Hitler's anti-Jewish campaign was an error which would cost the Germans dear (P. Aloisi, *Journal*, Paris, 1957, pp. 105, 109).

part of the Fascist press.[1] On 31 March 1933 he made an attempt to restrain his inept German pupil, urging him through Cerruti to call off the projected boycott of Jewish shops and to stop persecuting his Jewish subjects on racial grounds.[2] Simultaneously, however, he took the Jews to task in his newspapers for spreading 'atrocity stories' about the Third Reich. Interlandi's *Tevere* poured scorn on the Jews' lamentations concerning German racialism, declaring that Judaism was itself the 'father of racialisms.' Farinacci's *Regime Fascista* charged the Jews with dual loyalties, pointing out that Italian Jewry was part of the Jewish International as well as part of the Italian nation and calling upon the Fascist Government to restrict the number of Jews in 'sensitive' posts. The *Popolo d'Italia* took up the anti-Jewish theme in a more moderate form; in the second half of 1933 'Farinata' (Ottavio Dinale), one of Mussolini's earliest associates, published in that paper a series of articles which were the obvious reflection of the dictator's personal view on the subject. On the one hand, he deplored Hitler's racial persecutions, describing them as a sign of the 'immaturity' of National Socialism; on the other, he insisted that not only the Germans, but also the Italians had the right to take measures of defence against the 'Jewish peril'. Dinale agreed with Farinacci on the desirability of an unofficial *numerus clausus*, hinting that steps might have to be taken to prevent the Jewish element from gaining undue influence in Italy.[3]

The first anti-Jewish campaign of the Fascist press reached its culmination in March 1934 when sixteen alleged 'enemies of the

---

[1] According to Renzo De Felice (*Storia degli ebrei italiani*, pp. 122, 160), the anti-Jewish press campaign 'originated outside Mussolini's entourage', among Fascists who disapproved of the dictator's philo-Semitic policy. In the light of the evidence now available, however, it is clear that the campaign was inspired by the Duce himself. See below, Appendix I.

[2] V. Cerruti, 'Mussolini e gli ebrei', *La Stampa*, 12 Sept. 1945. Hitler flew into a rage, declaring that Mussolini, for all his political genius, knew nothing about the Jewish problem whereas he, Hitler, was the greatest living authority on the subject. Mussolini deplored Hitler's intransigence in a talk with Sir Ronald Graham, saying that it was one thing to deal sternly with Bolsheviks, 'but pressure on purely racial or religious grounds antagonised not only Jewish but also Christian opinion throughout the world' (Graham to Foreign Office, 3 Apr. 1933, PRO/F.O.371/16720/410). See also *DDF*, 1ʳᵉ série iii,556 (de Jouvenel to Paul-Boncour, 23 May 1933: ' ... persécution juive ... considérée ici comme une monstrueuse sottise').

[3] See *Il Regime Fascista*, 26 May 1933; 'Voci della stampa italiana', *Israel*, 8 June 1933; 'Interessanti rilievi del "Popolo d' Italia"', *Israel*, 14–20 Sept. 1933; 'Voci della stampa italiana', *Israel*, 19 Oct. 1933.

regime', fourteen of them Jews, were arrested at Ponte Tresa and in Turin and charged with subversive activities. The charges turned out to be largely unfounded; the trial which took place in November ended with the acquittal of all but two of the accused. All the same, the arrests were seized upon as a pretext for an unprecedented attack on Italian Jewry; the Jewish origin of the 'culprits' was thrown into relief by the entire Italian press which spoke of 'Jewish anti-Fascists in the pay of expatriates'. As Salvatorelli and Mira have rightly pointed out, 'the prominence accorded to an alleged Jewish anti-Fascism was strange and novel. It was clearly an anti-Semitic point which could not but hit home, at a moment when the relations between Fascism and Nazism were on the agenda . . . In reality, no specifically Jewish anti-Fascism could be discerned or proven in Italy either up to that time or later.'[1] The Jews predictably reacted with protestations of loyalty; and since 'Jewish anti-Fascism' was being increasingly identified with Zionism, Jews of assimilationist tendencies hastened to give vent to their patriotic zeal by setting up an appropriate weekly organ, *La Nostra Bandiera* (*Our Banner*), to mark themselves off from Zionists and other 'disloyal'

[1] *Il Tevere*, 31 Mar. 1934; Salvatorelli and Mira, *Storia d'Italia nel periodo fascista*, pp. 791–792. Salvatorelli is, however, wrong in asserting that the Jewish origin of the 'culprits' was mentioned in the official communiqué of the Stefani agency (30 Mar. 1934); the same mistake occurs in Barbara Allason's *Memorie di un'antifascista*, Florence, 1946, p. 178. In 1934 Mussolini's anti-Semitism was still strictly unofficial, given his determination to avoid an open clash with 'Jewish power'. The Counsellor of the German Embassy, in commenting on the arrests, pointed out that this was the first time a distinction had been made between Jews and non-Jews in Italy; he was unable to throw any light on the reasons for this change (Smend to Wilhelmstrasse, 5 Apr. 1934, GFM/L1027/L301081). It is clear, however, that this unprecedented display of journalistic anti-Semitism could not have occurred unless an order had emanated from the centre, i.e. from Mussolini (cf. D. Zucàro, *Lettere all'O.V.R.A. di Pitigrilli*, Florence, 1961, p. 14). One of the 'culprits', Sion Segre, tells us that he was subjected to systematic anti-Semitic abuse by the Italian police; given the lack of 'Jew-consciousness' in Italy, such a thing could not have happened without instructions from above (S. Segre Amar, 'Sopra alcune inesattezze storiche intorno alle passate vicende degli Ebrei d'Italia', *La Rassegna Mensile d'Israel*, xxvii, May 1961, 236–8). Other Jewish observers, however, were inclined to believe that Mussolini had been misled by his underlings (see, e.g., V. Jacobson to Zionist Executive, 19 July 1934, CZA/File Z4/3238 iii, based on confidential talk with Umberto Nahon, co-editor of *Israel*: 'It seems that the Head of the Government, who at first was angry with the Jews and the Zionists, is by now convinced that there was no "plot" . . . and is annoyed with those of his officials who (deliberately?) puffed up the affair, thus inducing the government to take steps and make statements which today seem utterly unjustified'). Dr. Nahum Goldmann, in a memorandum of 11 July 1934, reveals that Mussolini, while refusing to receive the representatives of Italian Jewry, assured them through one of his secretaries that he had no doubts as to their loyalty (CZA/File Z4/3238 iii).

elements.[1] For their part, the Italian Zionists courageously stood their ground, flatly refusing to yield to intimidation and pressure. When, in May 1934, Mussolini urged Dante Lattes through an intermediary (a prominent Jewish Fascist) to disband the Italian Zionist Federation, the latter replied with a determined No, and the dictator thought it wiser not to insist.[2]

In addition to harassing the Jews in his newspapers, the Duce also encouraged opposition to 'Jewish subversion' (as distinct from hatred of Jews as such) beyond the borders of Italy. In 1930 he had expressed emphatic approval when Starhemberg told him that the Austrian Heimatschutz rejected anti-Semitism as a political weapon. In 1933 he still advised foreign admirers like Dollfuss, Mosley, and Mussert not to copy the racialist aberrations of his clumsy German imitator.[3] However, given the competition between Rome and Berlin for the allegiance of foreign Fascist and rightist groups, he felt compelled to give his blessing to 'moderate' anti-Jewish currents in kindred movements abroad and to call for the adoption of 'mildly' anti-Jewish measures in Austria, urging the Austrian Chancellor to add a 'dash of anti-Semitism' (*una tinta di antisemitismo*) to his programme in order to take the wind out of the sails of the Austrian Nazis.[4] Subsequently, his advocacy of 'moderate' and 'defensive' anti-Semitism found expression in a resolution which was submitted to the international Fascist Congress at Montreux in December 1934 and unanimously approved: 'Considering that certain Jewish groups in certain places have installed themselves as in a conquered country, openly or secretly exercising an injurious influence on the material and moral interests of the homeland which gives

[1] The editor of *La Nostra Bandiera* was Ettore Ovazza, a Fascist since 1920 and a convinced anti-Zionist; see his *Sionismo bifronte*, Rome, 1935.
[2] De Felice, *Storia degli ebrei italiani*, p.158 n.l. The accuracy of De Felice's account was confirmed to the writer by Dante Lattes himself. The intermediary was Carlo Foà.
[3] In a signed statement contributed to the *Jewish Economic Forum* on 28 July 1933, Sir Oswald Mosley declared that 'Fascism is in no sense anti-Semitic, and bias for or against the Jews is completely irrelevant to the issues involved in our political creed. Anti-Semitism was never known in Fascist Italy, and Mussolini has often expressed himself in this sense. The attacks on the Jews in Germany do not rest on any Fascist principle but are a manifestation of an inherent quality in the German character.' Mussert declared as late as December 1935 that on the Jewish question the Dutch National Socialists agreed with Mussolini rather than with Hitler (H.W.J. Sannes, *Onze Joden en Duitschland's Greep naar de Wereldmacht*, Amsterdam 1946, pp. 238–9).
[4] J. Braunthal, *The Tragedy of Austria*, London, 1948, pp. 199–201, 203–5; *Geheimer Briefwechsel Mussolini–Dollfuss*, Vienna, 1949, p. 53.

them hospitality, constituting a kind of state within a state, profiting from all rights and exempting themselves from all duties; and considering that the said Jews have furnished or are furnishing by their conduct elements useful to international revolution destructive of the ideas of country and Christian civilization (this Congress) denounces the nefarious activity of these elements and pledges itself to fight against them.' This resolution (which was signed by the Italian delegate, Eugenio Coselschi, in order to please the numerous Jew-haters among the non-Italian participants) may be described as an attempt to strike a balance between explicit condemnation of 'certain Jews' and implicit condemnation of Hitler's racial persecutions. While calling for resistance to the activities of 'subversive' Jewish elements, it unequivocally rejected the idea of a 'universal hate-campaign against the Jews', maintaining a careful distinction (incompatible with racial anti-Semitism) between good and bad Jews and leaving each signatory free to deal with the Jewish problem as he saw fit.[1] Even so, the signing of an anti-Semitic document by an official spokesman of the Fascist regime was a new departure in Italian politics which could not but distress the Jews and their friends.[2]

For the moment, however, the Fascist dictator had no intention of translating the threats of his underlings into action.[3] While he was determined to impose his will on Italian Jewry and to use it as an instrument of his revisionist policy, he was equally determined to maintain (and if possible enhance) his reputation as a friend and protector of the Jews. He therefore saw to it that a balance was struck between unofficial attacks on the Jews and official moves in their favour. On 16 February 1933, having just launched his anti-Jewish offensive in the columns of the *Tevere*, he received Nahum Sokolov whom he assured of his 'cordial sympathy' for the Jews in general and the Jewish National Home

[1] 'Il Convegno di Montreux e la questione ebraica', *La Nostra Bandiera*, May 1935 (cf. also De Felice, *Storia degli ebrei italiani*, pp. 172–3 n.2. The National Socialists did not attend, having no interest in a Fascist International which they could not control (A. del Boca and M. Giovanna, *I 'figli del sole'*, Milan, 1965, pp. 62–75).

[2] One of those friends was Ezio Garibaldi, grandson of the Risorgimento hero, who denounced the resolution in the columns of *La Nostra Bandiera* (May 1935). Garibaldi was particularly incensed at the fact that the signatories had put the 'material interests' of their respective countries before the 'moral' ones.

[3] Neither Guido Jung nor any other highly placed Italian Jew was dismissed from his post during the anti-Jewish press campaign.

in particular.[1] In the ensuing months, having stepped up the anti-Jewish polemics in the Fascist press, he likewise stepped up his activities on behalf of Hitler's Jewish victims. On 24 March he voiced his disapproval of German racialism in a conversation with the British Ambassador, adding that he was 'giving strongest advice at Berlin against it'; a week later he intervened with the Führer in an attempt to avert the impending anti-Jewish boycott.[2] On 6 April he authorized the Italian Foreign Ministry to inform Federico Jarach, a leading Jewish industrialist and a friend of Farinacci's, that there was no objection to the immigration of German Jews, 'provided they did not engage in political activities harmful to Italy or Germany'; he also authorized the leaders of Italian Jewry to render assistance to their persecuted brethren.[3] On 19 April he apparently attempted to interpose a word on behalf of German Jewry in a conversation with Hitler's heir presumptive, Hermann Göring, having been urged to do so by the British Foreign Secretary.[4] On the following day he received Sacerdoti who handed him a resolution of the Council of the Union of Italian–Jewish Communities, calling for the restoration of equal rights to their German co-religionists. The Duce was most sympathetic, expressing the hope 'that the regretted situation would soon return to normal.'[5] On the same occasion, however, he demonstrated his ignorance of Jewish affairs by requesting the rabbi to put him in touch with the heads of world Jewry. On being informed that there were no such heads, he agreed to see Weizmann with a view to exploring the possibility of an 'accord' between Jewry and Hitler. The meeting between Weizmann and Mussolini took place on 26 April; but although the Duce was lavish with expressions of sympathy and support, it failed to yield any tangible result. While appreciating

[1] See *Jüdische Rundschau* (21 Feb. 1933), 71.

[2] Graham to Vansittart, 24 Mar. 1933: 'In speaking of Hitler, Signor Mussolini deplored present phase of Nazi violence and said that he was giving strongest advice at Berlin against it. But as Nazis had been fed for years past on anti-Jewish propaganda they had now, having come into power, passed for the moment out of control. He hoped situation would soon quiet down' (*DBFP*, 2nd Ser. v.105).

[3] ASMEI/Germania p. 14, 1933, sottofasc. *Antisemitismo tedesco—lo semestre 1933* (De Felice, *Storia degli ebrei italiani*, p. 151 n.4 and p. 156 n.3).

[4] Sir John Simon to Sir Ronald Graham, 10 Apr. 1933 (*DBFP*, 2nd Ser. v.137). On the failure of Göring's mission, see de Jouvenel's dispatch to Paul-Boncour, 20 Apr. 1933 (*DDF*, 1re série iii.270–1).

[5] 'I sentimenti degli ebrei d'Italia espressi al Capo del Governo da Angelo Sacerdoti', *Israel*, 27 Apr. 1933.

Mussolini's efforts on behalf of German Jewry, Weizmann had no faith in his schemes for mediation and no intention of being in any way involved in them, declaring that he saw no point in 'arguing with tigers.'[1]

The approach to Weizmann, however, was only the first of several attempts to win over 'world Jewry' to the idea of a *modus vivendi* with the Third Reich. Shortly afterwards Sacerdoti proceeded to Geneva and Paris in order to urge acceptance of Mussolini's project on the major Jewish organizations. On 10 July he reported to his master that his suggestions had met with a favourable response; after full and frank discussions, five Jewish leaders had expressed their willingness to work for a *détente* with Germany, provided Hitler agreed to restore the civil rights of their German brethren.[2] By this time, however, Mussolini had come to realize that there was no chance of dissuading the Führer from his racial policy; all he could do was to urge restraint on the Jews themselves in the hope that a softening of the anti-German agitation might create a more favourable atmosphere for mediation at a later date. With this end in view the spokesmen of Italian Jewry were ordered to abstain from public manifestations of hostility to Hitlerism, while the Italian delegates to the World Jewish Conference at Geneva (5–12 September 1933) were instructed to prevent the adoption of an extreme anti-German resolution.[3] But while the Jewish leaders were more amenable to reason than Hitler, they could not be expected to call off the anti-Hitler crusade unless the anti-Jewish measures in Germany were rescinded.

Unable to compel either Hitler or 'world Jewry' to do his bidding, the Fascist dictator resumed his diplomatic tightrope-

[1] No record of the meeting exists. Weizmann's own account of his third encounter with the Duce refers in reality to the fourth (*Trial and Error*, p. 372). There are, however, references to the third meeting in various other sources: P. Quaroni, *Valigia diplomatica*, Milan, 1956, pp. 292–5; WA/Weizmann to Mussolini, 15 June 1933 (draft) and Weizmann to Mussolini, 17 June 1933; ASMEI/Palestina p. 5, 1933, Colloquio fra il Capo del Governo e il Signor Weizmann (*sic*), memorandum by Suvich; cf. G. Cohen, 'Ra-ayon halukat Eretz Yisrael u-medina yehudit 1933–5', *Ha-Ẓionut*, iii, Tel Aviv, 1973, pp. 348–50.

[2] ASMEI/Germania, p. 14, 1933, sottofasc. *Antisemitismo tedesco—30 trimestre 1933* (reproduced in De Felice, *Storia degli ebrei italiani*, pp. 494–7). The five Jewish leaders in question were the Chief Rabbi of France, the President of the Alliance Israélite universelle, Neville Laski and Norman Bentwich of the Board of Deputies of British Jews, and Dr. V. Jacobson of the World Zionist Organisation.

[3] Cf. De Felice, *Storia degli ebrei italiani*, pp. 135–6 and the documents cited there.

walking between the two, alternately attacking and defending both; nor did he abandon his quest for a compromise formula which might enable him to arrange some sort of truce between National Socialists and Jews. On 6 October he warned the German Ambassador against underestimating the 'world power of the Jews and Freemasons, from which a tremendous offensive against the new Germany was to be expected.'[1] On 17 February 1934 he again raised the issue of German–Jewish relations with Weizmann, asking him whether he had meanwhile contacted the Germans. When the Zionist leader reminded him of his previous refusal to have any dealings with the 'tigers' in Berlin, the Duce expressed his complete agreement, adding that German barbarism was a threat to the very existence of Western civilization.[2] A few months later, however, he instructed Sacerdoti to approach another leading Jewish figure, Dr. Nahum Goldmann, who, as representative of the Comité des Délégations juives and of the planning committee for the World Jewish Congress, was in a sense the official Jewish spokesman on all Diaspora questions.[3] Sacerdoti duly invited Goldmann to Rome in the summer of 1934, but the latter refused, explaining that he considered Mussolini's project impracticable in the proposed form. He 'thought it impossible that Hitler would make any concessions in his anti-Jewish programme, and even in the highly unlikely event that he did, he would not under any circumstances restore the former rights of the German Jews'. World Jewry, however, could not be a party to any settlement that was not based on 'complete and unrestricted civil rights because such an agreement would invite all anti-Semitic regimes to curtail Jewish rights in a similar way'. Either equality of rights was total or it was not equality, and even if a compromise were possible on the

---

[1] Hassell to Wilhelmstrasse, 6 Oct. 1933 (GFM/5737/HO28755–61); as has been noted, Mussolini had warned Hassell of the 'great power and the excellent organization' of the Jews as early as 28 Mar. (see above, p.58 n. 1).

[2] WA/*Rapport sur la conversation qui a eu lieu entre S.E. Mussolini et le prof. Weizmann à Palazzo Venezia le 17 février 1934* (memorandum by Jacobson). After his talk with the Duce, Weizmann told Gino Scarpa, a Foreign Ministry official, that the time was not ripe for the establishment of a Jewish State (S.I. Minerbi, 'Gli ultimi due incontri Weizmann–Mussolini', *Storia Contemporanea*, v, Sept.–Dec. 1974, 470–1).

[3] In 1934 Goldmann also became the representative of the Jewish Agency for Palestine at Geneva, accredited to the Mandates Commission of the League of Nations. The President of the Mandates Commission was an Italian, Marquis Alberto Theodoli, notoriously hostile to Zionism (A. Theodoli, *A cavallo di due secoli*, Rome, 1950, pp. 135–8).

basis of curtailed rights, the spokesmen of Jewry 'could not possibly pay the price of jeopardizing the rights of all other Jews in the world'. Mussolini would therefore do better to intervene in Berlin on his own account, without the participation of Jewish leaders. True, even if Hitler were to soften his racial policy, world Jewry would remain hostile to him, 'but in the absence of tangible persecution its protest would become less virulent'. On all these grounds it was preferable that neither he (Goldmann) nor any other Jewish representative should be officially involved in negotiations with the Germans.[1]

Sacerdoti was 'thunderstruck' when Goldmann refused to go to Rome with him: 'It was inconceivable to him as an Italian that one could decline a summons from the Duce. Besides, he feared unpleasant consequences for himself.' Mussolini himself was 'much displeased'; shortly afterwards, however, he admitted that Goldmann's refusal had been justified.[2]

This admission was made on 13 November 1934, when Goldmann finally did call on Mussolini at the Palazzo Venezia to discuss a variety of burning Jewish issues. By that time the Duce had abandoned his schemes for resolving the German-Jewish conflict, German–Italian relations having meanwhile taken a sharp turn for the worse. Describing the interview thirty-five years later, Goldmann pointed out that Mussolini's philo-Semitic stance had been a genuine asset at the time, his inability to restrain Hitler's anti-Jewish zeal notwithstanding: 'Some six months before I saw Mussolini I was informed by a Viennese

[1] *Memories*, pp. 134–5. The meeting between Sacerdoti and Goldmann presumably took place on the eve of Mussolini's ill-starred encounter with Hitler (14–15 June 1934), which provided the Duce with another opportunity for raising the Jewish issue with his maladroit German imitator. Before taking up the problem with Hitler, he instructed Sacerdoti to question Goldmann as to 'world Jewry's' minimum conditions for ceasing to oppose the Third Reich (ibid., p. 134). From the German diplomatic documents we know that the Jewish question was in fact discussed by the two dictators (GFM/3086/617328–32; GFM/6036/E444864–66; *DGFP*, Serie C iii, 12, 18), but no details are given. According to Konrad Heiden (*Der Fuehrer*, p. 585), Mussolini tried to convince his guest that his anti-Jewish obsession was unjustified, adding that the persecution of the German Jews made it difficult even for him to be friends with the Third Reich. But while Heiden's account accurately reflects the Duce's well-known views on the subject, it is not supported by any documentary evidence. The day before Hitler's arrival in Italy Weizmann urged Mussolini through Grandi to take up the problem of the German Jews with the Führer (CZA/File Z4/17049). For a detailed analysis of the meeting between Hitler and Mussolini, see Petersen, *Hitler–Mussolini*, pp. 344–59.

[2] *Memories*, pp. 134–5.

source that Chancellor Dollfuss of Austria, who was completely under the influence of Italy, intended to introduce a change in the constitution involving the clause that guaranteed the civil rights of the Jews. Through Baron Aloisi, the Italian delegate to the League, I requested the Duce to use his influence with Dollfuss to prevent this infringement of the rights of the Austrian Jews. The Duce informed me that through Baron Sovich [*sic*] . . . he had sent a handwritten letter to Dollfuss asking him not to interfere with Jewish civil rights. My Jewish friends in Vienna later confirmed this.'[1]

When Goldmann wrote the above in 1969, he was still unaware of the fact that the Duce himself had advised Dollfuss through Suvich to add a 'dash of anti-Semitism' to his programme, only to reverse his stand a few months later. He was equally unaware of the motives which had prompted Mussolini to unleash an anti-Jewish press campaign in 1933. All he has to say on the subject is that 'in the winter of 1934, Mussolini's relations with the Italian Jews became strained because an anti-Fascist conspiracy had been discovered in Turin, and most of the conspirators had turned out to be Jewish students'; it never occurred to him that the alleged conspiracy which he himself had described as a 'very harmless' affair in July 1934—was no more than a pretext for stepping up an anti-Jewish smear campaign which had been going on ever since Hitler's accession to the chancellorship.[2]

But if Goldmann was wrong about the Duce's motives for both attacking and defending the Jews, he was right about the uses of a visit to Rome in November 1934. He could hardly have chosen a happier moment; since the assassination of Dollfuss (25 July 1934) the anti-Jewish press polemics in Italy had shown signs of fizzling out, while relations between Rome and Berlin were going from bad to worse. In this situation Mussolini—who, since Hitler's rise to power, had been consistently concerned to show the world that Italian Fascism was morally superior to 'barbarous German National Socialism'[3]—was eager to impress a spokesman of 'world Jewry' with his magnanimity and generosity. Not only

[1] Ibid., p. 154.
[2] Ibid. In his memorandum of 11 July 1934 (see above, p. 60, n. 1), Goldmann points out that the Turin 'plot' had turned out to be 'very harmless'.
[3] See below, p. 75, and p. 75 n. 3.

did he indulge in an extravagant display of verbal philo-
Semitism, denouncing as 'madness' any form of anti-Jewish
discrimination, proclaiming his faith in Zionism, ('I am a Zionist
myself'), and protesting his 'profound and enduring sympathy
for the World Jewish Congress'; he also took concrete steps to
demonstrate the value of his friendship, making promises which
he very largely kept.

The first of the problems discussed at the meeting between
Goldmann and Mussolini was the impending reversion of the
Saar to Germany. Goldmann pointed out that the question of the
Jews in the Saar was one of principle: 'If the League of Nations
approved the return of the province to Germany without
guaranteeing Jewish rights, it would appear to sanction
Germany's anti-Jewish legislation.' He added that Italy bore a
'particular responsibility' in the matter, the Italian Baron Aloisi
being chairman of the three-power commission of the Saar. The
Duce expressed emphatic agreement, declaring that he would
'force Germany to let the Saar Jews leave and take their money
with them'. He was as good as his word.[1]

Mussolini was equally responsive when Goldmann requested
his intervention on behalf of the Austrian Jews who were being
subjected to increasingly severe (if unofficial) harassment by
Dollfuss's successor, Schuschnigg. 'It is pure folly,' he exclaimed,
'for the Austrian Government, which is in an extremely weak
position, to pick a quarrel with the Jews. Do not worry. I am a
friend of the Jews. We cannot permit the Austrian Jews to be
attacked. Monsieur Schuschnigg will be here next week, sitting
in the very chair you are sitting in now, and I shall tell him I do
not want to see a Jewish problem created in Austria. Do not
worry about that any more. I shall speak to him very seriously.
You can rely on me.'[2]

The conversation then turned to the German-Jewish conflict.
After listening to Goldmann's explanations, the Duce readily
acknowledged that his scheme for a negotiated settlement with
Hitler had been unrealistic, adding that the Jews were 'a great,
indestructible people' (*un peuple grand et éternel*) who had no reason

---

[1] J. Draenger, *Nahoum Goldmann*, pp. 234–7. The Franco-German agreement on the Saar
was signed in Rome on 3 December 1934; at Italy's request a clause was inserted
permitting the Jews to leave with all their possessions.

[2] Mussolini's intervention appears to have borne fruit, since the position of Austrian
Jewry remained tolerable until Hitler's invasion of Austria.

to be afraid of 'Herr Hitler'. He then launched into a tirade against his German imitator which is worth quoting in full: 'I know Herr Hitler'. (Five months earlier the two had met for the first time in Venice). 'He is an idiot, a rascal (*vaurien*), a fanatical rascal, an insufferable talker. It is torture to listen to him. *You are much stronger than Herr Hitler. When there is no trace left of Hitler, the Jews will still be a great people. You and we*—and as he shouted these words, his interlocutor was not sure if *we* meant Italy or Fascism—'*are great historical powers. Herr Hitler is a joke (plaisanterie) that will be over in a few years.* Have no fear of him and tell your Jews to have no fear of him either.'[1]

When Goldmann objected that Hitler had 'a fleet, an army and an organized nation of seventy million people', while the Jews were dispersed and powerless, Mussolini replied that it did not matter: 'I am telling you that you are much more powerful than Herr Hitler. The main thing is that the Jews must not be afraid of him. We shall all live to see his end. *But you must create a Jewish State. I am a Zionist myself and I told Dr. Weizmann so.* You must have a real State (*un véritable État*), not the ridiculous National Home that the British have offered you. *I shall help you create a Jewish State*, but the main thing is that the Jews must have confidence in their future and not be afraid of that idiot in Berlin.'[2]

The above outburst is notable both as an extreme manifestation of Mussolini's resentment against Hitler (whom he had failed to manipulate for his own ends) and as a frank revelation of his chief motive for courting the representative of 'world Jewry'— his conviction that Jewish power, whatever its limitations, was as yet more worthy of respect than German power.[3]

[1] Our italics. All quotations are from the French original (Draenger, op. cit., pp. 214–36); for the English translation, see *Memories*, pp. 156–63.

[2] On 19 February 1934, Weizmann informed Sir Eric Drummond (who had succeeded Graham as British Ambassador in Rome) that Mussolini had discussed the partition of Palestine and the eventual establishment of a Jewish State with him (Drummond to Foreign Office, 19 Feb. 1934, PRO/F.O.371/17876/E1279/31/285). Mussolini's paper had come out in support of a Zionist State as early as September 1933 ('Saggezza', *Il Popolo d'Italia*, 8 Sept. 1933); it did so again on the very day of the last meeting between Weizmann and Mussolini ('Una soluzione', *Il Popolo d'Italia*, 17 Feb. 1934). The second article (anonymous like the first) was written by Mussolini himself (*O.O.*xxvi.171–2).

[3] Germany's growing isolation since 1933 had evidently shaken the Duce's belief in Hitler's political future (see Hassell's report of 6 October 1933, above p. 65, n. 1). Moreover, he seems to have feared that the Führer's anti-Semitic excesses would do harm to Italy's image, given the similarity between the German and Italian regimes (memorandum by Bülow of 3 May 1933, GFM/5753/HO28676).

When Mussolini had finished his tirade against Hitler, Goldmann turned to the minorities question, pointing out that Poland had announced its intention of suspending minority rights and that Polish Jewry would soon be deprived of whatever legal guarantees it still enjoyed unless the signatories of the Treaty of Versailles intervened. He added that while he was 'sure of Britain's position and almost sure of France's', he had doubts about the Italian attitude for two reasons: first, because Mussolini was 'no great friend of minority rights in general'; and second, because he was 'not opposed in principle to revision of the treaty'. Revision was a 'matter of high policy" (*du domaine de la Grande Politique*), with which the Jews did not concern themselves. But if the treaty was to be revised, radical revision would be necessary, and the Jewish question would have to be dealt with in such a way as to provide a 'firm foundation' for the existence of Jewish minorities.

Mussolini hastened to reassure his visitor, declaring that he 'fully shared' his views on the minorities question and condemning Poland's move as a 'paranoid gesture': 'Poland is trying to imitate me and play the role of a Great Power. But Poland is not a Great Power.' In any case, he would 'never permit the revision of the peace treaties to begin with a revision of minority rights'. Aloisi had issued a statement to that effect in Geneva, and the Italian Government would stick to this position. A revision of the peace treaties was an incontestable necessity; but if the Poles were to approach him on the minorities question—which they had not yet done—his reply would be a resounding No. The Jews could count on that.

Encouraged by so much benevolence, Goldmann asked the dictator to grant an audience to Sacerdoti (who had been in disgrace since the discovery of the anti-Fascist conspiracy in Turin). The Duce magnanimously replied that he would be glad to do so if Goldmann wanted him to. He was equally forthcoming when his visitor requested a final 'small favour': official publicity 'for the sake of his prestige'. Next morning the *Agenzia Stefani* carried an official report of the conversation between Goldmann and Mussolini.[1]

---

[1] Sacerdoti was present at the interview, having received Mussolini's permission to accompany Goldmann at the latter's request.

For all his affability and generosity, however, Mussolini did not entirely conceal his prejudices against 'international Jewry'. When discussing the question of Austrian Jewry, he complained about the meddling of American-Jewish groups in European affairs, calling it 'a terrible habit'. Then, when Goldmann was about to take his leave, he brought up the question of Jewish anti-Fascism: 'Can you answer a question that puzzles me? The Jews are an intelligent people, a realistic people, a very practical people. Why is it that Jews have everywhere and always been such dogged supporters (*partisans fanatiques*) of formal democracy?'

To Goldmann this was 'a very delicate point'. While anxious not to offend his powerful host, he could hardly pretend to share the latter's faith in the Fascist creed. He therefore took refuge in scholarly analysis, explaining that there was 'a historical reason': 'Oppressed peoples always tend to be revolutionary, libertarian and democratic. Democracy brought the Jews emancipation and civil equality, and they are naturally grateful for it.' The Duce agreed that this was indeed natural ('Je le comprends fort bien') ; all the same, it was clear that Jewry's attachment to the 'ideas of 1789' was an obstacle to friendship with the Fascist regime, whatever the tactical motives for co-operation on specific issues.

While hinting at some of his grievances against 'international Jewry', Mussolini scrupulously refrained from any allusion to his grudge against the Italian Zionists (who had been the chief target of his anti-Jewish press campaign since the beginning of 1934). He evidently saw no point in bringing up the subject of Jewish 'dual loyalties' at a moment when he was trying to further his designs on the Middle East by wooing the leaders of the World Zionist Organization.[1]

Goldmann was understandably pleased with the results of his mission. Even if the Duce's championship of the Jewish cause was due to purely selfish calculations, there could be no doubt about its moral and material value at a time when millions of Jews were suffering discrimination and persecution. For his part, Mussolini had every reason for welcoming an exchange of ideas with a leading Jewish figure at a moment when, having

[1] Mussolini presumably espoused the idea of a Jewish State in the hope that the partition of Palestine would enable him to gain a foothold in the Middle East at Britain's expense (Minerbi, loc. cit., pp. 476–7).

temporarily broken with Hitler, he was busy mending his fences with France and angling for popularity in the West.[1]

The meeting between Goldmann and Mussolini marked the beginning of a new phase in the dictator's relations with the Jews. In 1933 he had attempted to bring about some sort of reconciliation between Hitler and Jewry, both in order to remove a stumbling block on the path of Italo-German collaboration and to win acclaim as a benefactor of 'world Jewry' and a defender of Western civilization. As long as he had hopes of bringing Jews and National Socialists to the negotiating table, he saw to it that each move in favour of the Jews was balanced by some expression of understanding and sympathy for the German point of view. On 15 March 1933 he had deplored the 'systematic Jewish . . . world propaganda' against the Hitler regime and Fascism in a conversation with the German Ambassador. And in his above-quoted message of 31 March 1933, while urging Hitler to desist from his racialist folly, he had explicitly recognized the existence of a Jewish peril and the need to take measures of defence against it: 'Every regime has not only the right but the duty to eliminate untrustworthy elements from positions of authority.' Two days later he had gone further, informing the Germans that he was willing to assist them in combating Jewish 'atrocity propaganda' against the Third Reich if they so desired.[2] In his above-mentioned talks with Graham and Sacerdoti (24 March, 3 and 20 April) he had expressed the hope that the Führer would listen to counsels of moderation and soften his racial policy. Only two months later, however, he urged the Germans to persist in their struggle against Jewry: 'to weaken now and beat a retreat' would be 'very dangerous, precisely with respect to a power like the Jews. Certainly there had been much clumsiness and exaggeration at the beginning, but on no account must weakness be shown.'[3]

In the second half of 1933 the Duce began to change his tune,

---

[1] In his attempts to win popularity in the West, the Duce naturally made use of his loyal Jewish subjects. In October 1933 Sacerdoti, in an interview with Henri de Kérillis, solemnly asserted that anti-Semitism was so foreign to Mussolini as to be beyond his comprehension ('Fascisme et Judaïsme', *Echo de Paris*, 13 October 1933).

[2] Hassell to Wilhelmstrasse, 15 March 1933 (GFM/3154/668755–57); V. Cerruti, 'Mussolini e gli ebrei', *La Stampa*, 12 Sept. 1945; Neurath to Hitler, 2 Apr. 1933 (*IMT* xxxv.523–4).

[3] Memorandum by Hassell, 10 June 1933 (GFM/8007/E621724–6).

having come to realize that his half-hearted concessions to Hitler's racial obsession had failed to make any impression in Berlin. He was still as anxious as ever to demonstrate his good faith to the Germans by opposing the manifestations of Jewish hostility to the Third Reich;[1] simultaneously, however, his progressive disenchantment with German Fascism found expression in a series of increasingly violent utterances against the Hitler regime in general and Hitlerian racialism in particular. As early as 13 May he told the British Ambassador 'that he was doing all he could to be friendly and helpful towards Germany, but the Germans made it very difficult to be friends'. Five weeks later he made the same point in a conversation with his *chef de cabinet*, complaining that the Germans were 'like a thousand bulls in a china shop'.[2] On 12 July—a month after warning Hitler not to weaken in his fight against the Jews—he observed in a talk with Rüstü Aras, the Turkish Foreign Minister, 'that the anti-Jewish campaign in Germany was a grave error'; and on 15 August he informed the new French Ambassador, Count de Chambrun, that there could be no ideological solidarity between Fascism and National Socialism, given his opposition to Hitler's racialism and anti-Semitism.[3] On 28 September, when discussing the Austro-German situation with Sir Ronald Graham, he expressed extreme bitterness about Hitler's contemptuous disregard for Italian interests, adding that 'his own influence at Berlin was not as great as it had been and was gradually on the wane'.[4] On 4 October he gave vent to his annoyance with Hitler in a sarcastic article on the Führer's lieutenants;[5] two days later he told the German Ambassador that Hitler's anti-Semitism was

---

[1] See above, p. 64 n. 3. It is worth noting in this connection that as late as 30 June 1934, after the alleged 'Röhm revolt', Mussolini personally intervened to prevent hostile reactions in the Italian press. For all his resentment and bitterness against Hitler he was still reluctant to lose his German trump (see Hassell to Wilhelmstrasse, 12 July 1934, GFM/8032H/E577823–4).

[2] Graham to Simon, 13 May 1933 (*DBFP* 2nd Ser. v.237); Alosis, *Journal*, p. 134. On the very day of Mussolini's conversation with Graham the Wilhelmstrasse informed the German Embassy in Rome that Hans Frank was planning to come to Rome in order to enlighten the Italians on the Jewish question (GFM/5739/HO3014–5). On 2 June, however, the Embassy was advised that, given the hostile Italian reaction, Frank's visit had been postponed and had better be cancelled altogether (GFM/5739/HO30106).

[3] Aloisi, p. 138; Chambrun to Paul-Boncour, 15 Aug. 1933 (*DDF*. 1 série iv.197: 'Je n'approuve ni leurs théories sur la race, ni leurs persécutions contre les Juifs'.

[4] Graham to Vansittart, 28 Sept. 1933 (*DBFP* 2nd Ser. v.646).

[5] 'Gli "Unterführer"', *Il Popolo d'Italia*, 4 Oct. 1933 (*O.O.* xxxvi.69–70).

likely to do a great deal of harm to the Reich, forgetting that he had said the exact opposite four months earlier.[1] On 10 October, in another conversation with Graham, he indulged in a scathing denunciation of the Hitler regime: 'German policy was at the moment in the hands of two men, Hitler and Göring, one a dreamer, the other an ex-inmate of a lunatic asylum, neither of them conspicuous for reason or logic and both suffering from an inferiority complex and a bitter sense of injustice.'[2] Four days later he was 'deeply shaken' and 'violently irritated' by Hitler's sudden withdrawal from the League of Nations.[3] On 21 October he informed Graham that he 'had told Signor Suvich to warn the German Ambassador here that he had better keep out of his (Signor Mussolini's) way, as His Excellency felt that he could hardly refrain from being discourteous to Herr (von) Hassell if they meet'.[4]

From November 1933 onward the Duce's mounting indignation with Hitler gave rise to a series of journalistic outbursts against the Führer's Nordic mythology. On 3 November the *Popolo d'Italia* published the first of several attacks on German racialism, denouncing it as scientifically untenable and politically disastrous.[5] Simultaneously Giovanni Preziosi, the leading Italian anti-Semite and hitherto one of Hitler's most ardent supporters in Italy, penned a fulminating article against the doctrine of the German 'master race', denouncing German intrigues in the South Tyrol, condemning as unjust the persecution of the Jews on racial grounds, and warning the Führer to mend his ways lest the Third Reich come to an even worse end than the Kaiser's Germany.[6] On 26 May 1934 (the Italo-German quarrel over Austria having meanwhile grown increasingly bitter) Mussolini's paper again let fly at the Hitler regime, branding it as a

[1] See above, p. 72, n. 3.

[2] Graham to Wellesley, 11 Oct. 1933 (*DBFP*, 2nd Ser. v.674).

[3] See Hassell's dispatches of 14 and 20 Oct. 1933, as well as his letter to Neurath of 25 Oct. (BA/K/R43II/1465; PA/Abt. II/Polit. Beziehungen Italiens zu Deutschland/8). In 1933 it still suited Mussolini to have the German card in his hand at Geneva, despite his own contempt for the League.

[4] Graham to Simon on farewell interview with Mussolini, 21 Oct. 1933 (*DBFP* 2nd Ser. v.702).

[5] 'Non una, ma cinque', *Il Popolo d'Italia*, 3 Nov. 1933. The article was written by Ruggero Zangrandi, a friend of Mussolini's son Vittorio. Zangrandi's chief target was Hitler's theory of Nordic nobility: if this theory were correct, he argued, the Lapps would have to be honoured as the highest type of humanity.

[6] G. Preziosi, 'Attenti!', *La Vita Italiana*, xlii, (Nov. 1933), 600.

reincarnation of that evil Pan-Germanism which had been the object of the Duce's aversion since 1909: 'One hundred per cent racialism. Against everything and everyone: yesterday against Christian civilization, today against Latin civilization, tomorrow, who knows, against the civilization of the whole world . . . From the unbridled militarism of Prussia . . . to this National Socialist racialism, drunk with a stubborn bellicosity.'[1] Two months later the brutal murder of Dollfuss confirmed Mussolini in his conviction that Hitler's movement was indeed the most radical and aggressive form of that *pangermanesimo* which he had combated first as a Socialist and then as an interventionist. Sir Oswald Mosley, who arrived in Rome at the time of the murder, found the dictator 'in such a rage that none of his associates dared approach him on the subject'.[2] He was still in a rage a few days later when he discussed the matter with Starhemberg: 'It would mean the end of European civilization if this country of murderers and paederasts were to overrun Europe . . . Hitler is the murderer of Dollfuss . . . a horrible sexual degenerate, a dangerous fool . . . Fascism is a regime that is rooted in the great cultural traditions of the Italian people; Fascism recognizes the right of the individual, it recognizes religion and family. National Socialism, on the other hand, is savage barbarism . . . Murder and killing, loot and pillage and blackmail are all it can produce.' The Duce concluded by stressing 'the necessity of having done with this dangerous madman, as he called Hitler' and by proposing the speedy creation of 'a common front against the German danger': 'Hitler will arm the Germans and make war— possibly even in two or three years. I cannot stand up to him alone. We must do something, we must do something quickly.'[3]

Despite the absence of any reference to the Jews, the above diatribe throws light on the main reason for Mussolini's increasing eagerness to champion Jewish causes—his desire to impress upon Western public opinion the superiority of 'Roman' Fascism, with its 'equilibrium and Latin humanity', over the crude Teutonic imitation. If he could not win laurels as mediator between Germans and Jews, he could at least exploit Jewish grievances against Germany for his own political and propa-

---

[1] 'Teutonica', *Il Popolo d'Italia*, 26 May 1934 (*O.O.* xxvi.232–3).

[2] Sir Oswald Mosley, *My Life*, London 1968, p.359.

[3] Von Starhemberg, *Between Hitler and Mussolini*; pp. 169–71.

gandist ends. As early as December 1933 (when he had not yet abandoned all hope of arranging a truce between Hitler and Jewry), one of his lieutenants told the British Ambassador in Rome that Mussolini was 'much interested' in the Jewish problem, 'as he was now assuming the role of protector of the Jews. His attitude was perhaps inspired to some extent by his sense of rivalry with Herr Hitler', whose 'persecution of the Jews he considered both unfair and stupid'.[1] In the course of 1934 this sense of rivalry was sharpened by the increasingly bitter conflict over Austria, by German intrigues in the South Tyrol, and by a series of German press attacks on 'faithless' Italy, on 'Jew-ridden' Fascism, and on the 'inferior' Latin race;[2] hence the Duce's growing desire to gain popularity and prestige at Hitler's expense by befriending the latter's Jewish victims and by dissuading the lesser anti-Semites from following in the Führer's footsteps. The murder of Dollfuss (which caused Mussolini to mobilize troops against Hitler) inevitably gave a fresh impetus to the Fascist crusade against German racial philosophy. On 14 August 1934 Mussolini, in one of his anonymous articles, informed the Italian public that German racialism had just been condemned as unscientific by an eminent British anthropologist, Sir Grafton Elliot Smith.[3] On 29 August he pointed out in another anonymous article that Hitler himself had admitted the non-existence of a pure German race in *Mein Kampf,* adding that National Socialism was unlikely to succeed 'in making a pure-blooded "herd". According to the most favourable hypothesis ... one needs six centuries of racial marriages and not less of racial castrations.'[4] On 6 September he lashed out against the Führer's racialist folly in a public speech at Bari: 'Thirty centuries of history permit us

[1] Drummond to Simon on conversation with Marquis Alberto Theodoli, 13 Dec. 1933 (PRO/F.O.371/16932/E7823/6498/31).

[2] The most venomous critic of 'Jew-ridden' Fascism, needless to say, was Julius Streicher (see, e.g., 'Koscher-Faschismus', *Der Stürmer,* 21 Apr. 1934); cf. K. Busch, 'Bilanz einer Studienreise nach Italien', *Der Deutsche,* 25 Mar. 1934 (on the 'racial superiority of the Germans over the Italians'), which provoked a sharp reaction from Renzetti (IC/Ministero della Cultura Popolare/Job 20/009494–95); BA/K/R 43/11 1448 (Thomsen on undesirability of racialist polemics against Italy, 28 Mar. 1933); Smend to Wilhelmstrasse, 31 Aug. 1934 ('Die italienische Presse und Deutschland', GFM/5737/H028976–80). On 19 Mar. 1934 Ciano instructed Renzetti to protest against an attack on 'Jew-ridden' Fascism in Fleischhauer's *Weltdienst* (IC/Ministero della Cultura Popolare/Job 20/009528–33).

[3] 'Fallacia ariana', *Il Popolo d'Italia,* 14 Aug. 1934 (*O.O.* xxvi.298).

[4] 'Alla fonte', *Il Popolo d'Italia,* 29 Aug. 1934 (*O.O.* xxvi.309–10).

to view with sovereign pity certain doctrines held beyond the Alps by the descendants of people who were wholly illiterate at the time when Rome had Caesar, Virgil, and Augustus.'[1] He returned to the attack on 8 September, pouring scorn on German pretensions to racial superiority and suggesting that Hitler's obsession with race was perhaps due to the 'innumerable' and 'impressive' symptoms of racial degeneration in his country.[2] Finally, speaking in Milan on 6 October, he warned Germany not 'to estrange herself from Europe's historical evolution.'[3]

When Goldmann arrived in Rome five weeks later, the Laval–Mussolini *entente* was in the making and the Fascist press was indulging in an orgy of Franco–Italian brotherhood, accompanied by vitriolic attacks on the Third Reich. Once more the doctrine of the Nordic master race was handy as a target.[4] Being about to join forces with the Western democracies against Germany, Mussolini was more than ever anxious to dissociate Fascism from Hitlerism; hence the unprecedented cordiality with which he received the spokesman of 'world Jewry' in November 1934.

For all his disillusionment with Hitler, Mussolini would have preferred to avoid an alliance with Germany's enemies. Having predicted the imminence of a 'Fascist age' and having hailed the Führer's rise to power as a victory for his own movement, he could not but be unhappy about the break between Rome and Berlin (which, moreover, diminished his bargaining power *vis-à-vis* France and Britain). However, Hitler's designs on Austria and the Danube Basin left him no choice. In 1934 he needed peace in Europe in order to prepare for war in Africa; the Führer's expansionist ambitions (which he had failed to divert to the Polish Corridor and the Rhine) threatened to interfere with those preparations and Mussolini, the apostle of revisionism, was reluctantly compelled to align himself with the defenders of the

---

[1] *O.O.* xxvi.319.

[2] 'Razza e razzismo', *Il Popolo d'Italia*, 8 Sept.1934 (*O.O.* xxvi.327–8).

[3] *O.O.* xxvi.358.

[4] 'When Rosenberg, the official "thinker" of the Third Reich, inaugurated the academic year at the University of Munich with the proclamation that Europe had received her culture five times consecutively from the "Nordic epicentrum", this theory was greeted in Italy with nation-wide hilarity . . . The *Giornale d'Italia* (18.xi.34), in solemn rebuttal, stated that it did not intend to abandon the *terra firma* of history for the quicksands of pseudo-history; the heirs of Rome and of the renaissance intended to vindicate their patrimony'. (G. Salvemini, *Prelude to World War II*, London, 1953, pp. 170–1).

status quo against his maladroit German disciple. At the beginning of December he asked Cerruti when Hitler would be ready for an attack on Austria; when the Ambassador replied that it might take no more than two years, the Duce stated that the Ethiopian campaign would be over within a year, after which the Italian Army would be back at the Brenner in full force.[1] Thus it was largely fear of an Anschluss which prompted Mussolini to launch his invasion of Abyssinia in 1935; nor did it occur to him that the only one to benefit from that enterprise would be precisely 'that idiot in Berlin'.[2]

Having temporarily broken with his 'fellow Fascist' in Berlin, the Duce naturally toned down the anti-Jewish polemics in the Fascist press; by the end of 1934 Italian anti-semitism was once again confined to vague and sporadic attacks on 'international Jewry' and Jewish high finance. To all appearances Fascists and Jews were back on former terms.[3] Even so, the smear campaign against the Jews had not been entirely without effect; while the Italians had not been won over to the anti-Semitic cause, they had undoubtedly become more 'Jew-conscious' and more suspicious of the Italian Zionists—whose 'dual loyalties', be it remembered, had given rise to press attacks in Italy even before the emergence of Fascism.[4]

Nor had the Duce himself by any means abandoned his long-standing prejudices against 'international' and anti-Fascist' Jewry. He was perfectly sincere when he denounced Hitler's persecution of the Jews as both unfair and stupid; but was he any less sincere when he said to Nino d'Aroma—at the very time of his meeting with Goldmann—that he was anything but fond of the Jews and that German Jewry had only itself to thank for the enthusiasm which Hitler's anti-Jewish measures had aroused in Germany? He agreed with Weizmann and Goldmann—at any rate during the period under review—that the Jewish people

[1] V. Cerruti, 'Perché Hitler aiutò il Negus', *Il Tempo*, 20 Apr. 1959.

[2] M. Funke, *Sanktionen und Kanonen*, Düsseldorf, 1970, pp. 30–4; G. Rochat, *Militari e politici nella preparazione della campagna d'Etiopia. Studi e documenti 1932–6*, Milan, 1971, pp. 376–9; R. De Felice, *Mussolini il duce*, i, Turin, 1974, pp. 606–15.

[3] Friendly relations between Mussolini and his Jewish subjects were restored in December 1934 when the Duce again received Sacerdoti and had a cordial conversation with him (*Memories*, p. 162).

[4] See 'Italia e Turchia', *Il Corriere della Sera*, 9 Dec. 1910; 'Per la verità', *Il Vessillo Israelitico*, lxx, (15–30 Jan. 1911), 26–8; 'Gli ebrei e l'impresa italiana', *Il Corriere Israelitico*, 1 (30 Nov. 1911), 135–6.

had a right to statehood in Palestine; but he also agreed with his journalists that participation in Zionist activities was an act of disloyalty (if not a legal offence) in an Italian citizen 'of Jewish race'. It is worth recalling in this connection that the *Tevere*, his unofficial mouthpiece, switched from outright anti-Semitism to 'anti-Zionism' at the beginning of 1934—on the very eve of Mussolini's last and most cordial encounter with Weizmann.[1]

However, having once decided that the role of protector of the Jews served his purpose, the Duce threw himself into the part with his exceptional histrionic skill; nor is there any doubt that for the moment he succeeded in impressing a sizeable section of Western opinion (not excluding Jewish opinion) with his moral and intellectual superiority over Hitler, despite the anti-Jewish campaign in the Fascist press.[2] In the words of the late Gaetano Salvemini, the Duce's 'popularity reached its climax after Hitler seized power in Germany, achieving extremes of madness and cruelty such as Mussolini and his followers had never attained. To be sure, the Fascists showed no particular eagerness to help refugees from Germany. While France, for instance, sheltered 25,000 of them, Italy gave asylum to no more than 500. But the evil-doing of one's neighbour often heightens, by contrast, one's own reputation for virtue. It did so in the case of Mussolini. Even a liberal-minded man like Stefan Zweig was enthusiastic about "wunderbar Mussolini."'[3]

But while the Duce won a great deal of praise and sympathy by assuming the role of protector of the Jews, he gained little of real value, having failed either to resolve the German–Jewish conflict or to convert the Zionist leaders to a pro-Italian policy. Given his unrealistic approach to both issues, this failure was inevitable. For one thing, he fatally underestimated Hitler, whom he regarded as an immature and inept pupil, destined to

---

[1] See e.g., 'Ebrei', *Il Tevere*, 30 Jan. 1934; 'Sionismo e patriottismo ovvero: carta canta', *Il Tevere*, 15 Feb. 1934; 'Ciarle sionistiche', *Il Tevere*, 22–3 Feb. 1934.

[2] For Jewish reactions, see 'Jüdische Studenten bei Mussolini', *Jüdische Rundschau* (25 Apr. 1933), 162; 'Mussolini über Zionismus', *Jüdische Rundschau* (16 June 1933), 256.

[3] Salvemini, *Prelude to World War II*, p. 478.

[4] Until his rise to power, Hitler himself systematically encouraged this underestimation by assuming the pose of the docile disciple, eager for guidance from his master and humbly grateful for the latter's sympathy and support. Once in the saddle, however, he lost no time in making it clear that he would not stand for any tutelage from Mussolini (memorandum by Neurath, 14 Aug. 1933, GFM/3086/616849–51; *DGFP*, Serie C i.740–741).

play second fiddle to himself.[4] For another, he greatly over-estimated his own powers in trying to compete with the British for the allegiance of the Zionist movement; quite apart from their aversion to the Fascist creed, Weizmann and his colleagues could not risk jeopardizing their relations with the Western World in general and the British Commonwealth in particular for the sake of so weak and unstable an ally as Italy.[1] Lastly, he failed to realize that 'world Jewry' was not a political entity and could not be treated as such.

Even Mussolini's propagandist success, considerable though it was, turned out to be ephemeral. In temporarily going over to the Western camp, he was not abandoning any of his anti-Western principles and objectives; he was merely trying to exploit the predicament of the Western Powers for the purpose of aggression against a fellow member of the League of Nations. But if Western statesmen were willing to connive at this aggression for the sake of Fascist support against Hitler, Western public opinion was not. That being so, Fascist Italy's alliance with the Western democracies was foredoomed to failure from the start. Once the invasion of Ethiopia was launched, the anti-Hitler front collapsed and the Duce's popularity evaporated—with fatal results for the Italian people in general and for Italian Jewry in particular.

---

[1] In his last talk with Weizmann the Duce asserted that he could restrain the Arabs if they tried to make trouble in Palestine: commenting on this assertion in his dispatch of 19 Feb. 1934 (see above, p. 69, n. 2), Drummond observed that 'Signor Mussolini was inclined to over-estimate his own powers'.

IV Abyssinia, Spain, and the Rapprochement with Nazi Germany (1935–1936)

THERE IS no doubt that Italian Jewry was severely shaken by the Duce's first anti-Jewish campaign, despite its strictly unofficial character.[1] Even so, its significance was largely obscured (as Mussolini intended that it should be) by both the official condemnation of Hitler's racialist aberration and the official manifestations of Fascist benevolence towards the Jews in general and the Zionists in particular.

After the murder of Dollfuss the Jewish problem in Italy inevitably began to recede into the background, being overshadowed (if not eclipsed altogether) by the increasingly violent clash between Rome and Berlin;[2] and by the end of 1934 the Duce's Jewish subjects had reason to feel that the storm had definitely blown over. The year 1935—the thirteenth of the Fascist era—seemed to begin under favourable auspices from the Jewish point of view. On 7 January the Laval–Mussolini agreement was signed; three months later (11–14 April) Italy joined the anti-German coalition known as the 'Stresa front'.[3] The rupture between Fascism and Hitlerism appeared to be complete. At the beginning of May Mussolini told Francesco Pittalis, the Italian Consul-General at Munich, that he had by now 'burnt his boats' as far as relations with Germany were concerned; unless the Germans mended their ways, they would be crushed by the combined might of Italy, France, and England.[4] And having once decided to throw in his lot with

---

[1] On this, see the detailed analysis in De Felice, *Storia degli ebrei italiani*, pp. 150–9.

[2] Drummond to Simon, 26 July 1934: 'Never in the course of my experience have I known the press here so outspoken and violently anti-German' (*DBFP*, 2nd Ser. vi. 869); cf. also Petersen, *Hitler–Mussolini*, pp. 361–6. Hitler himself subsequently told Renzetti that he had been deeply 'shocked and hurt' by the Italian press attacks, all the more so because he had had no intention whatever of invading or annexing Austria (Renzetti to Ciano, 21 June 1935; IC/Ministero della Cultura Popolare/Job 20/009447–8).

[3] At Stresa the British, French, and Italian governments condemned German rearmament and proclaimed their determination to safeguard the peace 'in Europe' (as distinct from Africa). Mussolini not unnaturally concluded that his Western allies would not object to his African venture (Salvemini, *Prelude*, pp. 191–9; Petersen, *Hitler–Mussolini*, pp. 399–401).

[4] Aloisi, *Journal*, p. 269 (4 May 1935).

Hitler's enemies, the Fascist dictator was bound to regard the Jews as natural allies, whatever his private feelings about Jewish high finance or the Italian Zionist Federation.

Unfortunately for the Franco-Italian accords and the Stresa front, however, the Italian invasion of Ethiopia was precisely the kind of offence which the League of Nations was designed to stop; even more unfortunately, Fascist Italy had precisely the kind of economy which the League sanctions system was capable of crippling without having to resort to military measures. To be sure, the French and British leaders had no interest whatever in crippling the Italian economy. For one thing, they needed Italian support against Hitler; for another, there were no fundamental French or British interests in Ethiopia to the defence of which Ethiopian independence was essential. Unlike the dictators, however, Western statesmen had to take some account of their public opinion; nor could they openly flout the League Covenant. Faced with the mounting tide of public indignation against the Fascist aggressor, they were compelled, contrary to their convictions, to make at least a show of opposing their Italian ally. They did so by solemnly condemning the invasion of Abyssinia and by imposing economic sanctions against the invader, taking good care, however, to exclude coal and oil from the list of goods to be withheld from Italy. The results of these half-measures were predictably disastrous. While failing to restrain the evil intention, they had the effect of destroying the system of collective security, of wrecking the anti-German coalition, and of driving the Fascist dictator into the arms of his real spiritual affinity across the Brenner.[1]

Even so the Duce could not change sides overnight.[2] While taking steps to bring about a gradual *rapprochement* with Germany, he continued to play the Western card for all it was worth, extracting the maximum political and economic advantage from the secret complicity of the French and British governments. In so doing, he naturally did not fail to take due account of Jewish power and its alleged impact on Western attitudes towards his regime. In the autumn of 1935, on the eve of his African

[1] On top of being ineffective, the sanctions served to increase Mussolini's popularity in Italy (Salvatorelli and Mira, *Storia d'Italia nel periodo fascista*, pp. 863–8). For a detailed and well-documented analysis of the conflict see De Felice, *Mussolini il duce*, i. 597–757.

[2] On the obstacles to Italo-German collaboration during the period under review see below, pp. 93–5.

enterprise, he thought it expedient to deliver himself of yet another extravagantly philo-Semitic declaration, the last of the series:

Fascism does not desire that Jewry should renounce its religious traditions, its ritual usages, its national memories, or its racial peculiarities. Fascism desires only that the Jews should recognize the national ideals of Italy, accepting the discipline of national unity. In Italy no difference exists between Jews and non-Jews either in the political or the social spheres. For many years the Italian Jews have taken an active part in the political, scientific and artistic life of Italy. In a word, a Jewish question does not exist in Italy. I, at least, do not know of one. Wherever I have detected the faintest trace of anti-Semitic discrimination in the life of the State, I have at once suppressed it. Whatever the foes of Fascism may say, we are tolerant to all. Neither I nor any other exponent of the (Fascist) regime has ever expressed anti-Jewish views. In these great days for the Italian nation I declare that Italian and Jewish ideals are fully merged into one.[1]

Coming at such a moment, this attempt to identify 'Jewish ideals' with Fascism predictably failed to produce the desired effect. The organ of the German Zionists roundly denounced it as 'Italian propaganda', pointing out that the absence of a Jewish problem in Italy (which could not be ascribed to any merit of Fascism) was irrelevant to the question of Italian aggression in Africa. To be sure, the Duce had a perfect right to demand loyalty from his Jewish compatriots; he would do well to realize, however, that Palestine Jewry had an equal duty of loyalty to the

[1] Message to Jewish students in the United States, quoted in *La Nostra Bandiera*, of December 1935, p. 3. From the evidence at our disposal it is clear that Mussolini did in fact intervene to suppress manifestations of anti-Semitism on more than one occasion. In 1928, for instance, a Jewish officer, General Guido Liuzzi, was promoted to army corps commander and army commander-designate on his orders, despite the objections of certain bigoted generals (letter of General Giorgio Liuzzi to the writer, 25 Feb. 1973); on 5 Sept. 1931, he ordered the Prefect of Cremona to confiscate Farinacci's paper whenever it might contain 'open or veiled attacks' on the Banca Commerciale or its Jewish chairman, Toeplitz (IC/*Segreteria Particolare del Duce*/Job 111/030678). Mussolini's message to Jewish students in America was followed by yet another attempt to harness 'world Jewry' to the Fascist chariot. On 20 Dec. 1935 the Palazzo Chigi commissioned Eli Rubin, an Austrian Jewish publicist, to write a pamphlet on 'The Jews in Italy', a panegyric on the liberal treatment of Italian Jewry, which was to be distributed throughout the world but especially in English-speaking countries. Its object was to influence Western opinion in favour of Mussolini's African war and to secure Jewish support in London and New York for a loan of which the Duce was in urgent need. As might be expected, the result of this propaganda campaign was an utter fiasco (E. Rubin, *Mussolini: Raciste et antisemite*, Paris, 1938).

Mandatory Power, whatever his attitude towards the Jewish issue.[1] Needless to say, the Western Zionist leaders were even less impressed by the Duce's philo-Semitic rhetoric than their *Gesinnungsgenossen* in Germany who, after all, had very special motives for appreciating Mussolini's tolerance of Jews;[2] nor could Jewish opinion in Western countries be expected to be less hostile to Fascist policy in Africa than Western opinion in general.

Once the war had broken out, the Italian Government strove to neutralize Jewish hostility in Palestine and in the Western world, to enlist Jewish support for its drive against the impending sanctions,[3] and to exploit Zionist aspirations for anti-British ends. The Italian Consul-General in Jerusalem, Mariano de Angelis, was instructed to warn Moshe Shertok (later Sharett), the political secretary of the Jewish Agency, that Jewish opposition to the African war might compel Mussolini to reconsider his attitude to the Jews.[4] Concurrently, the Union of Italian Jewish Communities, on the advice and at the invitation of a high-ranking Jewish officer of the Italian Navy and in agreement with the highest political authorities of the Fascist regime, sent two emissaries (Dante Lattes and Angiolo Orvieto) to London with the aim of mobilizing Anglo-Jewish opinion against the sanctionist policy. It was to be emphasized that the sanctions were likely to drive Mussolini into the arms of Hitler, with dire consequences for Italian Jewry.[5] Given the prevailing anti-Fascist mood in Britain, the Lattes–Orvieto mission was something of an embarrassment to the leaders of Anglo-Jewry who, in the words of one of them, 'had no desire to be dragged into international disputes'.[6] Lattes and Orvieto, according to the testimony of the former, 'had talks with Weizmann, with Balfour's niece (Blanche Dugdale), with Montefiore, with a

---

[1] 'Italienische Propaganda', *Jüdische Rundschau*, (18 Oct. 1935), 1; cf. also 'Italian Propaganda in Palestine', *The Times*, 12 Oct. 1935.

[2] On Weizmann's solidarity with Britain during the Ethiopian campaign, see Foreign Office memorandum of 21 Aug. 1936 (PRO/F.O.371/19983/141–8).

[3] The sanctions went into effect on 18 Nov. 1935.

[4] D. Horowitz, *State in the Making*, New York, 1950, p. 300. The accuracy of Horowitz's account was confirmed to the writer by the late Moshe Sharett in 1959.

[5] The high-ranking Jewish officer was Umberto Pugliese (1881–1961), General of Naval Engineers; it is most unlikely that he acted on his own initiative.

[6] Statement by Professor Selig Brodetzky of the Jewish Agency Executive (Lattes to Guariglia, 12 Nov. 1935, quoted in De Felice, *Storia degli ebrei italiani*, p. 208).

correspondent of *The Times,* and with the Italian Ambassador in London, Dino Grandi. But since Jewish influence on world politics was a mere fable, like the *Protocols of the Elders of Zion,* our efforts, though warmly appreciated by Grandi and by Suvich, had no concrete result whatever, as might have been foreseen.'[1]

Even before the arrival of Lattes and Orvieto in London, Grandi had made an attempt to enlist Weizmann's support for an 'anti-sanctionist' policy in Palestine. On 31 October 1935 he informed the Palazzo Chigi that the Zionist leader had been approached by unidentified intermediaries who explained to him that the application of sanctions by the Palestine Government, in addition to being illegal, would be politically harmful to Palestine Jewry: commercial relations with Italy would suffer, and Palestine would be reduced to the status of a British colony. The intermediaries believed that Weizmann had been convinced by their arguments; they had also 'gained the impression' that he would not fail to defend the Italian point of view in his talks with British political leaders.[2] It soon became clear, however, that the impression was false; while fully alive to the advantages of good relations with Fascist Italy and anxious to avoid an open break with Mussolini, Weizmann was as unwilling to plead the Fascist cause as the leaders of British Jewry and for the very same reasons.[3]

Undeterred by these rebuffs, the Duce and his advisers persisted in their attempts to harness Zionism to the Fascist chariot. At the end of 1935 they charged Corrado Tedeschi (one of those trusted Jewish Fascists who wrote for Mussolini's *Gerarchia*) with the task of winning over prominent liberal and right-wing Zionists in Palestine. He was to point out that Italy, unlike most other countries in the world, was free from the taint of anti-Semitism; that the Fascist regime was friendly towards the Jews in general and the Jewish National Home in particular; that the Falasha Jews in Ethiopia were going to be among the beneficiaries of Italy's 'civilizing mission' in that country, given

[1] Letter to the writer (14 Aug. 1957). Guariglia, on the other hand, agreed with Grandi and Suvich that the Lattes–Orvieto mission was 'highly useful to Italy' (*Ricordi,* p. 181).
[2] For Grandi's dispatch, see De Felice, *Storia degli ebrei italiani,* p. 178.
[3] Although Weizmann's loyalty to Britain was by no means as unconditional as that of his British-born colleagues, he more than shared their conviction that the future of Jewry in general and of the Jewish National Home in particular was inseparably bound up with that of the Western democracies.

Mussolini's splendid pro-Jewish record; and that the Zionist press had a moral duty to draw the attention of its public to the above facts at a moment when Fascist Italy was the target of so much slander and abuse. As for the anti-Jewish polemics in the *Tevere* and other Fascist papers, he was to state that these in no way reflected the official Italian attitude. Finally, he was to stress the importance of Italy as a Mediterranean Power: the leaders of Palestine Jewry, whatever their political views, would be well advised to increase their bargaining power *vis-à-vis* Britain by playing the Italian trump; if they failed to do so for ideological reasons, the British would have no valid motive for appeasing the Jews at the expense of the Arab majority in Palestine.

Ironically, Tedeschi's trip to the Holy Land was arranged and financed by CAUR (Comitati d'azione per l'universalità di Roma), an organization presided over by the very Eugenio Coselschi who, as Mussolini's delegate at Montreux, had signed the above-quoted anti-Jewish resolution a year earlier. Tedeschi subsequently complained to Guariglia that Coselschi, on orders from above, had shown unwarranted coolness towards his mission, declaring that he (Coselschi) could not be in any way involved (*ingolfarsi*) in pro-Zionist activities which were apt to alienate 'the Germans and other Nordic groups'.[1] Tedeschi insisted that there was no risk whatever of alienating the Germans, adding that Zionism was a force which Italy could not afford to ignore, prejudices on both sides notwithstanding.

In Palestine Tedeschi met Meir Dizengoff, the Mayor of Tel Aviv; Ittamar Ben Avi, a leading member of Jabotinsky's Revisionist Zionist Party and editor of the Party organ, *Doar Hayom*; Dr. J. Faitlovich, the leading authority on the Falasha Jews; and Dr. Leo Kohn of the Jewish Agency. In his reports on these meetings he claimed that his arguments had made an impression not only on the Revisionists (who were well disposed towards Italy for ideological reasons) but also on the (predominantly pro-British) General Zionists. Dizengoff had put him in touch with a member of the Zionist Executive. Ben Avi had agreed to co-operate with the Fascist propaganda machine (on

---

[1] Tedeschi sent three detailed reports on his contacts with the Palestinian Zionist leaders to Guariglia, one from Tel Aviv (6 Feb. 1936), one from Jerusalem (10 Feb.), and one from Florence (12 Mar.). All three are reproduced in full in the documentary appendix of De Felice's book (pp. 512–17).

21 February a pro-Italian article had appeared in *Doar Hayom*). Kohn had made it clear that there would be no change in the pro-British orientation of the Zionist leadership, adding, however, that the Jewish Agency Executive might be willing to give publicity to Italian philo-Semitism in accordance with Tedeschi's suggestions. Subsequently there had been a useful meeting with Shertok (Sharett) and other members of the Executive. In his final report Tedeschi expressed agreement with the prevailing view that the Revisionists (who had received Italian support since 1934) were Italy's best friends in Palestine, given the affinity between the Revisionist and Fascist movements and their common aversion to Britain. He concluded by affirming that Zionism was very much a force to reckon with as well as a potential ally against Britain; the friendship of Palestine Jewry was therefore well worth cultivating, despite the prevalence of anti-Zionist prejudice in Italian political circles. If the Fascist regime were to pursue a policy of absenteeism with regard to the Jews in Palestine, Italy would inevitably be the loser, while Britain would be the sole beneficiary.[1]

Whatever the anti-Zionist prejudices in Italian political circles, the Duce had as yet no intention of pursuing such a policy with regard to the Zionist movement. Far from abandoning his hopes of using Zionist aspirations as a means of furthering his own designs on the Middle East, he went on making overtures to the Zionist leaders until the eve of the Spanish Civil War. In May 1936 Tedeschi was permitted to publish a pro-Zionist article in *Gerarchia*.[2] At the beginning of June—a month after the end of the Ethiopian campaign—Mussolini's confidant, Marquis Alberto Theodoli, advised Nahum Goldmann that his master would welcome another exchange of views with Weizmann; on 15 June Goldmann informed Ben Gurion and Weizmann that

[1] On collaboration between Revisionists and Fascists, see Wolff (Jerusalem), 7 June 1935 (YVS/L319798–806); I. Halpern, *Tekhiat ha-yama'ut ha-ivrit*, Tel Aviv 1961; L. Carpi, *Come e dove rinacque la marina d'Israele. La scuola marittima del Bethar a Civitavecchia*, Rome, 1967; De Felice, *Storia degli ebrei italiani*, pp.168–75. On the ideological differences between Revisionism and Fascism, cf. W. Laqueur, *A History of Zionism*, London, 1972, pp. 361.–5. Not a few Italians in Palestine considered it beneath the dignity of a 'Great Power' like Italy to court such unimportant people as the leaders of Palestine Jewry; see Tedeschi's final report (De Felice, ibid., p. 516). Guariglia, while praising Lattes and Orvieto, makes no mention of Tedeschi's mission in his memoirs.

[2] C. Tedeschi, 'La soluzione integrale della questione ebraica', *Gerarchia*, xiv (May 1936), 328–35.

his Italian visitor had spoken 'in most violent terms' about England, asserting that what the Jews needed was a Jewish State which England would never give them and hinting that they could obtain it through Italy.[1] In July—the very month in which the German and Italian secret services began to co-operate in Spain—Captain Dordona, the head of the Italian propaganda organization in Egypt, had a conversation with an unnamed representative of the Jewish Agency in Cairo; the Jews subsequently informed the British Colonial Office that Dordona 'was even more categorical in his statements and more blatant in his attempts to attract Jewish support to Italian aims' than Marquis Theodoli. From a note of the conversation, written on 15 July, we learn that the Italian put the following three points to his interlocutor:

1) The Jews would never get Palestine by relying on the British. A parliamentary regime was too weak and too ready to give way to opposition. The Jews should work in association with the Italians, who would not be afraid of the Arabs, and who would aim at creating a Jewish State in Palestine, while taking Iraq and Syria for themselves.

2) Captain Dordona said that while this could not be done immediately, there were at present half a million Italian soldiers in Abyssinia none of whom would return to Italy; to these would be added in due course half a million Abyssinians, who would make excellent military material. In addition to this potential army of a million men, there would be some 150,000 Italian troops in Tripoli. It was Italy's object to dominate the Mediterranean, and with these troops available, and Abyssinia as a centre, she would be in a position to take Egypt and expand still further. It would take a few years for her to consolidate her present position, but these were the lines of her policy, and Britain would not be able to stop her.

3) In the meantime, what the Italians wanted was that the Jews should settle in the Gojjam area of Abyssinia; the object of this would be on the one hand to help the Italians consolidate their position in Abyssinia, and on the other to foster Jewish sympathy for Italy. He realised that Jewish settlement in Abyssinia could not be an ultimate aim as far as the Jews were concerned. But Italy would be prepared to undertake, in return for Jewish assistance in this matter, the creation of a real Jewish State in Palestine. When the Italians had wanted land for their own purposes in Tripoli, they had not hesitated to push out the

---

[1] Goldmann to Ben Gurion, 15 June 1936 (CZA/File S25/1322); cf. the above-quoted Foreign Office memorandum of 21 Aug. 1936 (p. 84 n. 2).

existing Arab inhabitants, and the Jews need not fear that the interests of the Arabs in Palestine would be over-scrupulously protected. He concluded by suggesting that the Jews should send a delegation to Abyssinia.

Subsequently, the same gentleman saw representatives of the Egyptian Jewish community in Cairo, and made identical proposals to them.[1]

The idea of Jewish settlement in Abyssinia was to crop up again in the autumn of 1938 when the Fascist Grand Council, by order of Mussolini, decided on the adoption of anti-Jewish measures in Italy.[2]

For their part, the Zionist leaders had every reason to worry about their dependence on British friendship at a moment when Britain was preparing to appease the Arabs at the expense of the Jews. With the collapse of the anti-Hitler front, however, the Italian card had lost its political value to the Zionist movement. Realizing the futility of a further meeting with the Duce, Weizmann reacted to the latter's advances by confidentially warning the British of Italian designs in the Middle East; nor was Jewish opinion in Palestine at all responsive to the pro-Zionist intrigues of Mussolini's agents. Jewish hostility to the Fascist regime was further increased by three other factors during the period under review—Italy's financial and propagandist support for the Arab rebellion (which broke out three weeks before the entry of Italian troops into Addis Ababa); the resumption (though on a minor scale) of anti-Jewish polemics in the controlled Fascist press; and the growing intimacy between Italy and Germany.

Italian support for the Arab rebels was a reaction (natural in the circumstances) to the imposition of sanctions. The intention was exclusively anti-British; but since the main Arab grievance against the mandatory was British support for the Jewish National Home, the effect was inevitably anti-Zionist.[3]

---

[1] PRO/F.O. 371/19983/6948/106–7.

[2] Grand Council resolution of 6 Oct. 1938 (see below, Ch. VI).

[3] On Italian anti-British activities in Palestine, see the above-quoted Foreign Office memorandum of 21 Aug. 1936; on the anti-British Bari broadcasts, cf. Ciano, *1937–1938 Diario*, Bologna, 1948, pp. 99–100. On relations between Mussolini and the self-styled 'Grand Mufti', see Esco Foundation, *Palestine. A Study of Jewish, Arab and British Policies*, ii, New Haven, 1947, pp. 773–5. The Italian press generally maintained an attitude of neutrality between Arabs and Jews until the summer of 1936 (see, e.g., 'L'urto sanguinoso tra arabi ed ebrei in Palestina', *La Stampa*, 25 Apr. 1936). Even so, anti-British articles by

The renewed anti-Jewish polemics in part of the Fascist press took the form of attacks, not as yet on the 'loyal' Italian Jews fighting in Ethiopia, but on the time-honoured abstraction known as 'world Jewry' and its alleged responsibility for Anglo-French hostility to Italy. As early as 19 December 1935 the *Azione Coloniale* blamed the imposition of sanctions on the anti-Fascist intrigues of the 'Judaeo-Masonic clique' at Geneva; in the following month Preziosi solemnly informed his readers that Italy was at war with a group of Jewish bankers, while Interlandi accused Jewry of being behind any plot to damage Italy.[1] On 5 February 1936 Guido Longo castigated 'Jewish anti-Fascism' in the columns of the *Regime Fascista*, alleging the existence of a specifically Jewish 'sanctionism' and adding that the Italian Government could no longer see any reason for antagonizing the foreign Jew-baiters (who had turned out to be Italy's most reliable allies) by befriending the victims of anti-Semitic persecution.[2] In March Preziosi denounced Italy's arch-enemy, Anthony Eden, as 'international Jewry's *homme de confiance*'.[3] Finally, in August 1936 Gaetano Pistillo, one of Preziosi's collaborators, proclaimed Fascist Italy's solidarity with the Arab liberation movement in its struggle against British colonialism and Zionism. While still denying the existence of a Jewish

Arab propagandists in Italy inevitably spilled over into anti-Zionism, if not anti-Semitism (cf. S. Sciartuni, 'La politica inglese in Palestina', *La Vita Italiana*, xlvii, 15 Jan. 1936, 45–9; id., 'La dottrina fascista e il mondo arabo', *La Vita Italiana*, xlvii, 15 May 1936, 459–65). While encouraging both Arabs and Zionists to oppose Britain, Mussolini kept assuring his British friends that reports about Italian interference in Palestine were devoid of all foundation (see below, p. 97).

[1] G. Preziosi, 'Ideologismo anglo-giudaico-massonico-leghista', *La Vita Italiana*, xlvii (15 Jan. 1936), 64–5. Interlandi's attack appeared in the *Tevere* of 8 January 1936; on the same day the *Marc'Aurelio* published an offensive anti-Jewish cartoon. For Jewish reactions to these polemics see, e.g., 'Italien im Mittelmeer', *Jüdische Rundschau* (14 Jan. 1936), 3; 'Italian und die Mandatsfrage', *Jüdische Rundschau* (25 Feb. 1936), 1.

[2] G. Longo, 'Fascismo ed Ebraismo', *Il Regime Fascista*, 5 Feb. 1936: 'It is now notorious that in the present international drive against Fascist Italy, Jewry too, acting in its own capacity . . . has played a not irrelevant part.'

[3] As early as 31 May 1935 the *Tevere* had denounced Eden as a special enemy of Italy. According to a secret police report on Balbo (which was presumably submitted to Mussolini), Eden was himself of Jewish extraction, the bastard son of King George V and a 'most beautiful Jewess' (IC/*Segreteria particolare del Duce*/Job 129/035496, unsigned report of 10 Feb. 1936). On Mussolini's personal hostility to Eden see E. Mussolini, *Mio fratello Benito*, p. 147 and Aloisi, op.cit., p. 367 (7 Apr. 1936). On the meeting between Eden and Mussolini in June 1935, cf. Earl of Avon, *The Eden Memoirs. Facing the Dictators*, London, 1962, pp. 216–35; M. Toscano, 'Eden a Roma alla vigilia del conflitto italo-etiopico (con documenti inediti)', *Pagine di storia diplomatica contemporanea*, ii, Milan, 1963, pp. 133–59.

problem in Italy, he insisted that the current clash of interests between Italy and Jewry was aggravated by the antithesis between Fascist and Jewish values.[1]

The idea of a specifically Jewish 'sanctionism' was encouraged, not by Hitler (who adopted a policy of strict neutrality between Italy and the League Powers), but by the Western anti-Semites, especially in England and France, who supported the Fascist aggression against Ethiopia. One of these was Sir Oswald Mosley who stated in an interview with the *Giornale d'Italia* on 18 October 1936 that the anti-Italian propaganda drive during the Ethiopian campaign had been inspired and directed by Jews who wanted to plunge the Western world into a fratricidal war.[2] Another was Georges Batault, an anti-Semitic French writer, who made similar charges in the columns of the *Revue Hebdomadaire*; and while this propaganda had little effect on opinion in the Western democracies, it appears to have made a profound impression on Mussolini and many members of his entourage. The following extracts from the diary of Aloisi, a diplomat of the old school and a staunch opponent of Hitlerism, are worth quoting in this connection:

28 November (1935): I am very worried by an article in the *Revue Hebdomadaire*, which accuses the Freemasons of wanting war. I am thinking of launching a counter-attack.

30 November: I showed P. Tacchi Venturi[3] the articles in the *Revue Hebdomadaire* against Freemasonry and the Jews and set forth to him my views on the subject. He is completely in agreement with me. I therefore ask him for advice regarding an eventual rebuttal ... This evening, dining at the German Embassy, I also communicated to Hassell my impressions of the two articles in the *Revue Hebdomadaire*, and we together studied the Masonic action now in progress ... He, too, will take the matter up with me again after reading the articles ...

14 December: The Paris Gringoire has published the attack inspired by me on various Jewish and Masonic personalities of the League of Nations who are working against us. At 9 o'clock I went to visit H. E.

[1] G. Pistillo, 'Il problema ebraico e l'Italia', *La Vita Italiana*, xlviii (15 Aug. 1936), pp. 187–94.

[2] As early as 1 Oct. 1935 (two days before the Italian invasion of Ethiopia) Mosley condemned 'sanctionism' in an interview with Hitler's paper ('Der britische Faschismus und die Sorgen der Londoner Regierung', *V.B.*, 2 Oct. 1935).

[3] Father Pietro Tacchi Venturi, a Jesuit priest, who acted as intermediary between the Vatican and Mussolini.

Bocchini[1] to study with him the articles in the *Revue Hebdomadaire* against Freemasonry and the Jews, of which I had spoken to him. He showed much interest in my point of view and told me he had spoken in this sense to the Duce who was completely in agreement. He will read the articles tonight; on Monday he will come to make the appropriate decisions . . .

20 December: Bocchini came to see me about the idea I had submitted to him, requesting his aid in order to restrain the manœuvres of the Jews and Freemasons. He agreed with the views expressed in the *Revue Hebdomadaire*, but for the moment the enterprise is too difficult. I explained to him how I viewed the matter. He understood, and we agreed that he should talk to the Duce about it.

1 April (1936): Received Babault [*sic*], author of the well-known articles in the *Revue Hebdomadaire* against the Jews and Freemasons. Yesterday he was received by Mussolini who talked to him for fifty minutes; they found themselves in agreement on all the ideas which they exchanged. The Duce, however, kept for reading the project which Babault submitted to him and which we shall have to discuss together. He will let him have an answer tomorrow.[2]

It is evident that Mussolini firmly believed in the hostility of 'international Jewry' to his African venture and that his reaction was one of keen resentment.[3] It is equally evident that he warmly welcomed the support of Western Jew-baiters in the struggle against Jewish sanctionism. On the other hand, there is no evidence whatever that the Duce's growing animosity towards Jewry was in any way due to German influence. No trace of such influence (except of the most indirect kind) is discernible

[1] Arturo Bocchini, Italian Chief of Police from 1926 to 1940.

[2] Aloisi, pp. 326, 330, 332, 364; cf. also Hassell to Wilhelmstrasse, 2 Dec. 1935, on Mussolini's preoccupation with alleged anti-Fascist machinations of the House of Rothschild (GFM/8015/E576282–83). Batault's articles were published in the *Revue Hébdomadaire* under the title 'Qui veut la guerre?', 16 Nov. 1935, pp. 261–7 and 23 Nov. 1935, pp. 427–53; but we have found no anti-Jewish articles in *Gringoire* between Oct. 1935 and July 1936.

[3] During his visit to Libya at the beginning of 1938, the King of Italy told Balbo that Mussolini was justifiably indignant with the Jews who, 'during the war in Africa . . . ranged themselves against us in America, England, and France with unspeakable bitterness' (N. d'Aroma, *Vent'anni insieme. Vittorio Emanuele e Mussolini*, Bologna, 1957, p. 267). Mussolini himself, addressing the National Council of the Fascist Party on 25 Oct. 1938, claimed that 'during the sanctions all the (anti-Italian) manœuvres were planned by the Jews' (*O.O.* xxix. 191). Speaking to Yvon De Begnac in October 1941, he asserted that he had first become aware of Jewish hostility to Fascism when he adopted economic emergency measures on the eve of his African war (De Begnac, *Palazzo Venezia*, p. 643). He might have added that 'Jewish hostility' had had no effect whatever on his official attitude towards the Jews until he joined forces with Hitler.

in the anti-Jewish polemics which occurred in Italy during the African war; what is more, the outbursts of journalistic anti-Semitism were not infrequently coupled with pin-pricks against the Third Reich—which goes to show that they were not in any way inspired by the Germans themselves.[1] There were signs of an impending *rapprochement* between Rome and Berlin as early as the summer of 1935; but it was only a year later, when Italy became involved in the Spanish Civil War, that its effects on Italian Jewry began to be clearly felt.

Mussolini started making overtures to Hitler the moment he encountered the first alarming signs of Western opposition to his projected Ethiopian enterprise. For his part, Hitler was anxious to facilitate that enterprise, not by any means in order to strengthen Italy (which had just joined forces with the Western Powers at Stresa), but in order to weaken the watch on the Brenner, to reduce Italian influence in the Balkans, to cause a split between the Duce and his Western allies, to exploit the predicament of the Western democracies for an Anglo-German *rapprochement* at the expense of France and the Soviet Union, and—last but not least—to divert the attention of the Western world from German rearmament and from his own aggressive designs in Europe. He therefore hastened to encourage Mussolini by assuring him of his benevolent neutrality.[2] But what if the Negus were to panic in the face of superior Italian might and to agree to some compromise acceptable to the Duce? Hitler decided to forestall such an eventuality by secretly responding to an Ethiopian request for arms.[3] Finally, having successfully encouraged both Mussolini and Haile Selassie along the path of

[1] See P. Pellicano, 'La schiavitù è finita', *La Vita Italiana*, xlvii (15 Jan. 1936), 41. After denouncing the 'spiritual alliance between England and Germany', the Italophobe theories of Rosemberg (*sic*), and the pro-English intrigues of Ribbentropp (*sic*), Pellicano adds: 'It is perhaps late to say so to Germany, but everyone will understand that Hitler's struggle against the Jews is like the Spanish hero's fight with the wineskins which contained the wine from his own land.' On the anti-German tendencies in part of the Fascist press, cf. also report by R. Strunk of 5 Feb. 1936 (GFM/7196H/E529617).

[2] See Funke, *Sanktionen und Kanonen*, 45–7 and the sources cited; cf. Hassell's dispatches of 3 Oct. 1935 (GFM/8020/E577220–22) and of 16 Nov. 1935 (GFM/8020/E577298–301).

[3] This was revealed by Haile Selassie in an interview with Serge Groussard in 1959 (S. Groussard, 'L'Allemagne de Hitler fut la seule nation à secourir l'Ethiopie contre l'Italie', *Le Figaro*, 26 Mar. 1959). For additional evidence see Funke, *Sanktionen und Kanonen*, pp. 43–5.

war, he tried to encourage Britain along the path of sanctions.[1] To be sure, he did not want the sanctionist policy to succeed; a victory of the League Powers over Fascism would be a major blow to his own prestige and a major set-back for his regime. On 17 January 1936 he told Hassell that an Italian defeat would be a moral and political disaster for him: 'It would be highly undesirable if (Germany's) isolation should, as the result of a collapse of Fascism in Italy, become a moral isolation too. We must do everything to prevent the manifold opponents throughout the world of the authoritarian system of government from concentrating upon us as their sole target.'[2] Even so, he could have no motive for siding with his Italian mentor until the latter broke with his Stresa partners and withdrew his protecting hand from Austria; and since Mussolini refused to do either, there was little scope for co-operation between Duce and Führer during the African war, least of all in the racial sphere. Mussolini could not afford a clash with the Jews as long as he played the Western card and courted the Zionist leaders. Hitler, on his side, could not afford to condemn Jewish sanctionism as long as he hoped to reach an accord with the leading sanctionist Power. It was left to Julius Streicher, the notorious Gauleiter of Franconia, to voice the secret hopes of his master with regard to the racial issue in Italy. Speaking at the Sportpalast in Berlin on 4 October 1935, the day after the Italian invasion of Ethiopia, he declared that Italy was now compelled to defend herself against Jewish atrocity propaganda, even as Germany had been during the Great War: 'The Italian people, too, will recognize at the end of this struggle that there is a Jewish question. Let us leave it to the future to reveal how the Jew has had his finger in this pie.'[3]

When, on 9 May 1936, Mussolini proclaimed 'the reappearance of the Empire on the fateful hills of Rome'[4] the *rapprochement* between the two Fascist Powers was still very much in its initial stage, despite their common aversion to democracy and their

[1] In addition to proclaiming its strict neutrality and vetoing the sale of arms to either belligerent, the Reich declared an embargo on the export of oils, fats, textiles, potatoes, iron, and steel (but not of coal which after 1934 had been displacing British coal in Italy).
[2] GFM/3175H/D682389–94; see also IC/Min. Affari Esteri/Job 321/107371 (on German ideological solidarity with Italy during the Ethiopian campaign).
[3] *Berliner Tageblatt*, 5 Oct 1935. On Mussolini's fear of an Anglo-German accord at Italy's expense, see Aloisi, p. 357 (11 Mar. 1936); IC/Min. Affari Esteri/Job 321/107350–65; Funke, *Sanktionen und Kanonen*, pp. 165–7.
[4] *O.O.* xxvii. 269.

common determination to redraw the map of the world. True, there was a marked improvement in the atmosphere, most of the minor points of friction meanwhile having been eliminated. The Fascist crusade against *pangermanesimo* and *razzismo teutonico* (which had poisoned relations between Rome and Berlin until the summer of 1935) had been very largely stopped and so had the Hitlerite crusade against 'Kosher Fascism' and the 'inferior Latin race'.[1] Vittorio Cerruti, Mussolini's 'Jew-ridden' Ambassador in Berlin, had been recalled in June 1935 at Hitler's request and been replaced by Bernardo Attolico, then a supporter of Ciano's pro-German line.[2] On 9 July the Duce had received Dr. Sven von Müller, a prominent German journalist, and told him that he had abandoned the role of protector of the Jews and the Churches in Germany.[3] Personal contact between the two leaders had been resumed on the eve of the African venture when Guido Manacorda, a professor of German at Florence University and one of Mussolini's political advisers, called on Hitler to discuss the Austrian problem. After the outbreak of war, a representative of CAUR, Manlio Barilli, had had meetings with various German anti-Semites, including Adolf Ehrt (president of the Antikomintern), Adolf Dresler, and Julius Streicher. Then, starting in January 1936, the manifestations of ideological solidarity had multiplied. At the end of that month the Duce had told Roland Strunk, a German journalist close to Hitler, that there was a 'community of destiny' between Italy and Germany ('One day we shall meet whether we want it or not. But we want to! Because we must'). High Fascist dignitaries, such as Renato Ricci and Edmondo Rossoni, had gone to Berlin to pay their respects to the Führer; Hans Frank, Hitler's lawyer and by now Minister without Portfolio, had been sent to Rome to assure the

[1] Funke, *Sanktionen und Kanonen,* pp. 39, 46 and the sources cited.

[2] Cerruti's recall was requested by Göring as early as November 1933 (Aloisi, p. 160). Hitler repeated this request in his above-quoted conversation with Renzetti on 21 June 1935, after which Cerruti was transferred to Paris (J. Petersen, 'Deutschland und Italien im Sommer 1935. Der Wechsel des italienischen Botschafters in Berlin', *Geschichte in Wissenschaft und Unterricht,* xx, June 1969, 330–41). On Ciano's pro-German intrigues, see Guariglia, *Ricordi,* pp. 213, 328–9; Hassell's dispatch of 13 February 1936 (GFM/7196H/E529613–15); and M. Michaelis, 'Il conte Galeazzo Ciano di Cortellazzo quale antesignano dell'asse Roma–Berlino', *Nuova Rivista Storica,* lxi (Jan.–Apr. 1977), 116–49.

[3] BA/K/R43 II/1448/254–60: 'Er (Mussolini) steht auf dem Standpunkt, dass Juden keine Faschisten sein könnten und habe darum die Juden aus wichtigen Aemtern entfernt . . . Ihm (Mussolini) seien Kirchenfragen egal.'

Duce of Germany's sympathy in the Ethiopian enterprise and in the joint struggle against both Bolshevism and democracy; and von Hassell, the Ambassador, travelled to Milan to give an address on Cavour and Bismarck and to explain how the unification of Europe envisioned by those two statesmen flourished reincarnated in Hitler and Mussolini.[1] Beginning in the second half of February, steps had been taken to pave the way for a more tangible relationship. On 22 February Mussolini had told the German Ambassador that 'for Italy, Stresa was finally dead'. A month later he had urged Kurt von Schuschnigg, the Austrian Chancellor, to come to a prompt settlement with Hitler, making such domestic concessions as the German dictator might deem necessary.[2] On 24 March Italy had refused to sign the draft of an anti-German resolution at Geneva. On 1 April the Duce had ordered his diplomats to take a 'more markedly pro-German line'; and on the same day a secret agreement had been signed on joint action by the German and Italian police forces against those common enemies whom the Nazis explicitly (and the Fascists implicitly) identified with 'international Jewry'—Bolshevism and Freemasonry.[3] On 19 April Mussolini had declined an invitation to participate in Staff talks with his Stresa partners; and on 21 April he had informed the League Council that he could not join in sanctions against Hitler (who had broken the Locarno Treaty by reoccupying the demilitarized zone in the Rhineland on 7 March) while himself the victim of sanctions.[4] Concurrently with these pro-German moves, however, he had gone on assuring his Western allies that he was anything but a friend of Hitler's and that a resumption of the 'watch on the Brenner' was always possible, provided Anglo-

[1] On Manacorda, Strunk, Ricci, Frank, and Rossoni, see below, Ch. V; on Barilli and other emissaries sent by Coselschi, see J. Petersen, *Hitler e Mussolini. La difficile alleanza*, Bari, 1975, pp. 387–8; on Hassell's address, *Corriere della Sera*, 18 Apr. 1936.

[2] GFM/6710/E506174–81; J. Gehl, *Austria, Germany and the Anschluss, 1931–38*, London, 1963, pp. 125–6; Funke, *Sanktionen und Kanonen*, p. 141.

[3] 'Le Duce a expédié une série de télégrammes pour une orientation plus marquée vers L'Allemagne. Par l'ambassade de Berlin il renouvelle l'assurance que nous ne ferons rien contre Hitler' (Aloisi, p. 265). Police co-operation against Communism was suggested by Colonel Mario Roatta, head of Italian military intelligence, to his German colleague, Vice-Admiral Wilhelm Canaris, in September 1935 (GFM/5573/E399912–17). The Germans accepted the suggestion in November (GFM/8039H/E578219), but it was not until the end of March that Bocchini finally proceeded to Berlin ('Il sen. Bocchini a Berlino ospite della polizia tedesca', *La Tribuna*, 31 Mar. 1936).

[4] See Funke *Sanktionen und Kanonen*, p. 144 and the sources cited.

French opposition to his African enterprise was abandoned. On 27 February—five days after telling the German Ambassador that 'Stresa was finally dead'—he had informed the French Ambassador that he was 'toujours . . . dans la ligne de Stresa'; and on 4 May Grandi had advised Eden that his master 'wished to reconstitute the Stresa front as soon as possible'.[1]

Once Ethiopia had been forced under the yoke, the Duce proclaimed his willingness to rejoin the defenders of the *status quo* in return for lifting of sanctions and recognition of his African Empire. On 4 May—the day before the fall of Addis Ababa—he declared in an interview with the *Daily Mail* that his African victory 'ought to be welcome to Britain and France', since it would 'turn Italy into a satisfied Power': 'We no longer belong to the discontented proletariat among the nations. We have come over to the other side of the barricade.' He added that he had 'no other colonial aspirations' and 'no political interests' in any part of the Arab world, least of all in Palestine; it was therefore 'untrue to suggest that Italy has stirred up trouble between Arabs and Jews'.[2] On 14 May, in an interview with *Le Matin,* he expressed the hope that the imminent rise to power of Léon Blum (whom he had previously denounced as a warmonger and whom he was soon to abuse as a Jew) would not be a hindrance to the resumption of friendly relations between Rome and Paris: 'Tomorrow men will be coming to power in France who have always made a profession of serving peace. I do not wish to doubt that they will begin at first by leaving us in peace.'[3] On 21 May he let it be known through the diplomatic correspondent of the *Morning Post* that he was 'extremely anxious to be on good terms' with Britain, so much so that he was 'prepared to offer a solemn undertaking not to oppose British interests in Egypt or elsewhere'.

[1] *DDF,* 2ᵉ série i. 357; Sir Ivone Kirkpatrick, *Mussolini. Study of a Demagogue,* London, 1964, p. 318. In the second half of May Mussolini told Starhemberg that Hitler would go to war within a few years and that by then 'a great European coalition should be ready to oppose him' (von Starhemberg, *Between Hitler and Mussolini,* p. 240). In June he made similar statements to Bertrand de Jouvenel and Louis-Jean Malvy (*DDF,* 2ᵉ série ii. 432–433, 513–14; *Le Jour,* 13 Mar. 1938; De Felice, *Mussolini il duce,* i. 749–51).

[2] G. Ward Price, *I Know these Dictators,* London, 1937, p. 239.

[3] 'Intervista al "Matin"', *Il Popolo d'Italia,* 16 May 1936 (*O.O.* xxviii. 1). For Mussolini's hostility to Blum, see his 'appeal to the students of all Europe' in the *Popolo d'Italia* of 1 Feb. 1936 (*O.O.* xxvii.224) and his above-quoted conversation with Hassell of 22 Feb. (see n. 1 above): 'France was passing more and more into the hands of the Left and in the not very distant future Léon Blum would be the uncrowned king of Europe. Relations between Italy and France were consequently deteriorating steadily.'

He was equally emphatic in an interview with the Paris *Intransigeant* on 25 May, insisting that he asked 'nothing of England' and was willing 'to give her all possible assurances'. Nor did his friendship for the wicked sanctionists stop there. On 28 May he informed a correspondent of the *New York Times* that he no longer felt any rancour towards those who had set hurdles in his path; he was ready to forgive everybody (presumably including 'world Jewry') and determined to reach agreement with Britain on all outstanding issues, including Palestine and the rest of the Near East. In an interview with the *Daily Telegraph* of the same date he again insisted that the 'end of sanctions would mark the entry of Italy into the ranks of the satisfied States' and that no problem in the Mediterranean or elsewhere should be allowed to stand in the way of an Anglo-Italian *rapprochement*: 'I beg you to repeat and to make everybody understand that Fascist Italy wants peace and that she will do everything which lies in her power to preserve peace. War in Europe would be Europe's catastrophe.'[1]

On the same day Grandi made a formal call at the Foreign Office and conveyed to Eden—'Jewry's *homme de confiance*'—the assurances of his master that Italy had no designs on British interests in Palestine or elsewhere. He added that the Duce wished to resume collaboration on a Locarno basis (provided sanctions were discontinued) and that there was no question of any closer relationship between Italy and Germany.[2] British fears were not allayed by these assurances, given the growing intimacy between Rome and Berlin and the continuance of anti-British broadcasts from Radio Bari.[3] Even so, it was felt that Italy could have no interest in abetting a German dominance of Europe; and since she had neither the will nor the power to act alone in halting Hitler, the obvious course for her was to rejoin the forces of conservation in maintaining the peace of Europe.[4]

For their part, the Germans were no less distrustful of Italy

---

[1] *New York Times*, 29 May 1936; *Daily Telegraph*, 29 May 1936.

[2] *Daily Telegraph*, 29 May 1936; Kirkpatrick, op.cit., p. 318.

[3] On the continuance of the anti-British broadcasts, see the above-quoted Foreign Office memorandum of 21 Aug. 1936: '. . . the Bari station continues to lose no opportunity to transmit extracts from the foreign press . . . selected for their mendacious and violently anti-British character'.

[4] Kirkpatrick, pp. 319–20; see also Papen (Vienna) to Wilhelmstrasse, 2 July 1936, on Anglo-French belief in Italy's desire for 'European co-operation' with the Western Powers (GFM/1499/370334–36).

and no less worried about her contradictory policy than the Anglo-French. They were fully aware of the anti-German motives which had prompted the Duce to embark on his African venture in 1935; they were equally aware of the double game he had been playing throughout the Ethiopian campaign.[1] Moreover, they knew better than anyone else that Mussolini, having conquered Ethiopia without any German aid, had no obligations towards Hitler and no motive for burning his bridges with the West. They therefore feared that after victory he would patch things up with the 'Jew-ridden' democracies in accordance with his original plan. Nor were their apprehensions allayed when the Duce, without even waiting for the fall of Addis Ababa, declared Italy to be a 'satisfied' Power and threw out hints about a possible return to Stresa. Neurath was undoubtedly sincere when, on 18 May 1936, he told an American diplomat that the 'demonstrations of friendship between Germany and Italy were mere demonstrations without basis in reality' and that he could not as yet see any way to reconcile the conflicting interests of the two countries in Austria.[2] Hitler himself was by no means certain that the African war had split Italy irremediably from her former allies. As late as 12 June—three days after the appointment of the pro-German Ciano to the post of Foreign Minister—he told Hassell that a revival of the 'so-called Stresa front' was still a possibility to be reckoned with; and on 25 June the latter expressed agreement with his master, warning the Wilhelmstrasse that Italy might yet 'go over to a front directed against Germany'.[3] In the following weeks, however, there was a complete change of scene. On 11 July the Duce gave his approval to an Austro-German Agreement which made the Anschluss a foregone conclusion; and on 17 July an event occurred which finally wrecked any chance of a reconciliation between Italy and her Stresa partners—the outbreak of civil war in Spain. Mussolini's decision to intervene in that war embroiled him in yet another conflict with the 'demoplutocracies' and made

---

[1] See, e.g., Hassell to Wilhelmstrasse, 6 Feb. 1936 (GFM/5737/HO20455–60).

[2] See memorandum on conversation between Neurath and Bullitt in *Nuremberg Trial Proceedings*, pt. i, London, 1946, p. 233. On 23 May Hassell complained to Mussolini of Cerruti's anti-German intrigues in Paris (evidently countenanced by Rome), adding that Mussolini's interview with the *Daily Mail* had aroused 'some astonishment' in Germany (GFM/1946/435651–54).

[3] GFM/1946/43661–63; 1486/368481–86.

him dependent on German support. At the end of July the German and Italian secret services began to co-operate in Spain. A month later (24 August) Mussolini received the Prince of Hesse, Hitler's 'winged messenger' and son-in-law of the King of Italy, with whom he reached agreement on joint Italo-German action in the Spanish Civil War.[1] Hitler now had his Italian mentor where he wanted him.

With the reoccupation of the Rhineland (which dealt the death-blow to the French system of alliances), Germany had become *bündnisfähig* (worthy of being an ally). Hitler was now in a position to offer real help to Italy in her conflict with their common enemies. Thus, two months after Hesse's visit, the disastrous alliance known as the Rome–Berlin Axis was born.[2]

As long as Mussolini pursued a middle course between the 'Jewish democracies' and the anti-Semitic Reich, he had no motive for modifying his attitude to the Jewish issue, his resentment against the Jewish sanctionists notwithstanding.[3] Hence, while abandoning his self-appointed role as the patron of persecuted foreign Jews, he continued to reject Hitler's racial theories and to deny the existence of a Jewish question in Italy.[4] Relations between the Fascist authorities and the Union of Italian Jewish Communities remained cordial; and with the annexation of Ethiopia this cordiality was extended to the Falasha Jews.[5] The anti-Jewish polemics in the Fascist press were

[1] On co-operation between the secret services, see *Il processo Roatta: i documenti*, Rome, 1945, p. 81; on Hesse's mission, DZA/60952 (Neurath to Dieckhoff, 24 and 27 Aug. 1936) and M. Michaelis, 'La prima missione del Principe d'Assia presso Mussolini (agosto '36)', *Nuova Rivista Storica*, lv (May–Aug. 1971), 367–70.

[2] According to Mario Toscano, 'the Axis had been born in March 1936, more from the force of circumstances than as a design willed by men; when Italy had been at war in Abyssinia and in diplomatic conflict with all the democratic States, Germany had sent her troops into the Rhineland, precipitating the gravest European crisis since Versailles. Concomitant actions, unplanned by the two governments, had brought immediate reciprocal advantages and had drawn them increasingly close together' (*Le origini diplomatiche del Patto d'Acciaio*, 2nd edn., Florence, 1956, pp. 179–80). While this is an over-simplification, Hitler's reoccupation of the Rhineland created what Funke (*Sanktionen und Kanonen*, p. 177) aptly calls a 'bündnisfähige Situation.' See also Petersen, *Hitler–Mussolini*, pp. 474–7.

[3] This resentment grew with the electoral victories of the 'Jew-ridden' Front populaire (26 Apr. and 3 May 1936) and the accession to power of Léon Blum on 4 June 1936, which resulted in an immediate worsening of Franco-Italian relations (F. D. Laurens, *France and the Italo-Ethiopian Crisis 1935–1936*, The Hague, 1967, pp. 354–6).

[4] See below, Ch. V.

[5] On 19 Sept. 1936 a Jewish community was established in Addis Ababa by vice-regal decree.

confined to sporadic attacks on 'world Jewry' and Jewish high finance; no attempt whatever was made to impugn the loyalty of the Italian Jews. With the beginning of German–Italian collaboration in Spain, however, there was a marked (if strictly unofficial) change for the worse. The overtures to the Zionists ceased, and the Bari broadcasts took on an increasingly anti-Jewish tone; in French North Africa, as in Palestine, Italian propaganda now fed on the anti-Jewish feelings of the local Muslims. Simultaneously, the unofficial manifestations of anti-Semitism at home began to multiply with such rapidity as to alarm even the staunchly Fascist editors of *La Nostra Bandiera*.[1] Jewry was now once again identified with Bolshevism, the fire of the extremist Fascist papers being concentrated on the alleged Jewish instigators of the alleged Bolshevik conspiracy in Spain. In the course of August 1936 it became increasingly evident that the *rapprochement* between Rome and Berlin was about to have serious repercussions on the Duce's relations with his Jewish subjects. The polemics against the 'Jewish-Bolshevik peril' were stepped up, and a Fascist deputy, Alfredo Romanini, published a pamphlet (*Ebrei-Cristianesimo-Fascismo*) on the common bond between Fascism and Roman Catholicism and the danger Judaism held for them both. Finally, on 12 September—six weeks before Ciano's visit to Hitler—the third anti-Jewish campaign of the Fascist press was launched with an article by Roberto Farinacci, the notorious *ras* of Cremona, who thereby assumed the role of 'head of the anti-Jewish faction' in the Fascist Party.

In the ensuing years Mussolini was to state in both public and private that the conquest of Ethiopia marked the decisive turning-point in his relations with both Germans and Jews. In his speech on the Maifeld in Berlin (28 September 1937) he declared that the Rome–Berlin Axis had been 'born in the autumn of 1935'.[2] Subsequently, he affirmed that Jewish opposition to his African venture had opened his eyes to the Jewish peril and that the anti-Jewish measures adopted in 1938 were no more than a logical extension to Italy of the racial laws

---

[1] See, e.g., 'Delineata offensiva di pressioni straniere per suscitare l'antisemitismo in Italia', *La Nostra Bandiera*, 1 Aug. 1936.

[2] *O.O.* xxviii. 252.

he had previously enacted in Ethiopia.[1] In the light of the above evidence it is clear that these pronouncements were tactical expedients, devoid of historical value. To be sure, the Ethiopian campaign prepared the ground for Mussolini's subsequent conversion to racial anti-Semitism in a variety of ways. For one thing, it made him more 'Jew-conscious'. For another, it involved him in an ideological conflict with the democracies which made him increasingly conscious of his spiritual affinity with the anti-Jew in Berlin.[2] It gave rise to a violent press campaign against Bolshevism and Freemasonry as the alleged instigators of the sanctionist policy which was apt to spill over into anti-Semitism, given the time-honoured association of the word 'Jew' with both these phenomena. It also gave rise to the secret agreement between Himmler and Bocchini of 1 April 1936, which had anti-Jewish implications for the same reason.[3] It served to increase his long-standing resentment against the 'international Jewish bankers'. Last but not least, it raised the problem of miscegenation in East Africa, convincing Mussolini of the need for a 'clear, definite, omnipresent race-consciousness', without which 'empires cannot be maintained'.[4] But ominous though these developments undoubtedly were, they had little effect on the fortunes of Italian Jewry until the Duce and the Führer began to co-operate in Spain. Even then Mussolini continued to dissociate himself from Hitler's racial theories, insisting that the Fascist brand of racialism, as practised in Abyssinia, had nothing whatever to do with anti-Semitism. It was only when he became totally committed to the Axis alliance that the Fascist dictator decided to sacrifice the Jews on the altar of German–Italian friendship.

Once Italy and Germany joined forces, however, Mussolini's official philo-Semitism was bound to become something of a liability. On the eve of Ciano's departure for Germany, therefore, it was decided to smooth his path by launching an unofficial press campaign against the Jews. If Mussolini was not a Jew-baiter, neither was he a *Judenknecht*.

For his part, Hitler showed no interest whatever in the problem of Italian Jewry; at any rate there is no reference to the

---

[1] See below, Ch. V.
[2] See Funke, *Sanktionen und Kanonen*, p. 156.
[3] See below, Ch. V.
[4] *O.O.* xxix. 126.

subject in any of his recorded utterances before 1943.[1] Nor is this surprising. Ever since 1925 he had been assuring his Party comrades that Fascism was basically an anti-Jewish movement— the implication being that Mussolini's philo-Semitic utterances were a piece of tactics, designed to prevent a premature clash between the Fascist regime and 'international Jewry'. Once Italy entered into an alliance with the Third Reich, the Duce's latent anti-Semitism was bound to come out into the open—irrespective of German pressure. Hitler was therefore content to let events work for him. Less than two years were to elapse before he was shown to be right.

---

[1] On 23 June 1943—exactly one month before Mussolini's downfall—Hitler complained to Goebbels of the Duce's failure to eliminate the Jews: 'Ausserdem sind ja in Italien die Juden nich beseitigt, sondern warten nur, dass ihre Stunde wieder kommt' (IFZ/ED 83/1, *Goebbels-Kriegstagebuch* I, 14, pp. 262–3).

PART II

FROM THE ROME – BERLIN AXIS

TO THE FALL OF FASCISM

(1936–1945)

V   From the Axis Alliance to the Munich Conference (1936–1938)

AT THE eighth rally of the National Socialist Party in Nuremberg (8–14 September 1936) Hitler and his henchmen outdid themselves in pinning all the ills of the world on the Jews. In his opening speech on 9 September the German dictator placed the blame for world unrest (with special reference to the Spanish Civil War) on what he called the 'international Jewish revolutionary centre' in Moscow).[1] On the following day Goebbels summoned the Aryans of all countries to do battle against 'Jewish Bolshevism'. Europe, he claimed, had not only the right but the duty to prevent the rise of a second 'Bolshevik-Jewish' Power by force of arms:

Bourgeois Europe eludes a decision by means of the constantly repeated phrase that there must be no interference in the internal affairs of another country. But what is reality in Russia today, what is being fought out in Spain, and what seems to be developing with a baleful precision in other European states, that concerns the whole world. It is ... a matter for all statesmen of all nations who must deal with this question unless they want to accept the responsibility for plunging Europe by their own fault into the deepest crisis and destruction. Yes, the problem of Bolshevism is the problem of Europe's very survival. Here is the parting of the ways (*scheiden sich die Geister*), here one must take sides for or against ... Jewry knows the significance of the hour. In a last convulsion it seeks to mobilize all forces against Germany. It has established itself comfortably and, as it thought, safely in Russia. It provides 98 per cent [*sic*] of the newly arisen Soviet bourgeoisie, cowardly, fat, lying, scheming, intriguing, aggressive, and frivolous. The *arriviste* Jews who now have the chance to enlarge their once petty swindles to grandiose dimensions on the backs of a people of one hundred and sixty millions are the most bloodthirsty tyrants; they have no ideals but merely make the nations suffer, a true scourge of God.[2]

[1] M. Domarus (ed.), *Hitler. Reden und Proklamationen*, i: *1932–1938*, Würzburg, 1962, p. 638: 'In einer Zeit, da bürgerliche Staatsmänner von Nichteinmischung reden, betreibt eine internationale jüdische Revolutionszentrale von Moskau aus über Rundfunksender und durch tausend Geld- und Agitationskanäle die Revolutionierung dieses Kontinents.'

[2] 'Dr. Goebbels: Der Bolschewismus muss vernichtet werden, wenn Europa wieder gesunden soll!', *V.B.*, 11 Sept. 1936. Eleven years earlier, when he was a member of the National Socialist Left, Goebbels had expressed a very different view on the subject: 'Russia today is more Russian than ever. What you call Bolshevist internationalism is

Less than two weeks earlier (29–30 August) Goebbels had paid an official visit to the International Film Exhibition at Venice where he had a long talk with his Italian opposite number, Dino Alfieri.[1] It was rumoured afterwards that the two had established co-operation in a propaganda crusade against the alleged 'Bolshevik peril' and that agreement had been reached on the need of identifying Bolshevism with the Jews. Following upon the conversation between Goebbels and Alfieri an official delegation of the Fascist Party and special correspondents of the most important Italian newspapers attended the Nuremberg rally. The controlled Fascist press gave great prominence to the event, devoting whole pages to Hitler's and Goebbels's harangues against the 'Bolshevik-Jewish' plotters in Moscow.

Taking his cue from Goebbels's 'tremendous indictment', Farinacci—who, after ten years in the political wilderness, was now temporarily back in the Duce's good graces[2]—launched the third anti-Jewish campaign of the Mussolinian press with an unsigned editorial in the *Regime Fascista* of 12 September 1936. The link between anti-Semitism and foreign policy was therefore plain from the start.

After reminding his readers that Fascism was the first political movement to take up arms against the Bolshevik-Jewish peril, the *ras* of Cremona proceeded to raise the problem of Jewish dual loyalties in Italy, alleging that Italian Jewry was part of the mythical Jewish International as well as part of the Italian nation:

We must admit that in Italy the Jews who are a very small minority

---

Pan-Slavism in the clearest and most definite form ... No Tsar had ever grasped the Russian people in its depths, in its passions, in its national instincts, so firmly as Lenin ... The Bolshevist Jew has also clearly recognized the compelling necessity of a Russian National State and with timely wisdom prepared for it. Perhaps for tactical reasons, perhaps with *arrières pensées* ... The Jewish question, even among the Bolshevists, is more complicated than people think. It is improbable that the Capitalist Jew is identical with the Bolshevist Jew. Perhaps in the final analysis, but never in current practice. Perhaps they both want the same in the end: Thou shalt devour all nations. But they are too intelligent to choose the wrong spot at which to resist forces that are stronger than their huckstering instincts' (open letter to a young Communist, *V.B.,* 14 Nov. 1925).

[1] 'Dr. Goebbels in Venedig. Die Bevölkerung jubelt dem deutschen Reichsminister zu', *Der Angriff,* 30 Aug. 1936. Alfieri had succeeded Ciano as Minister of Press and Propaganda on 9 June 1936

[2] On Farinacci's role in the Fascist Party, see Appendix II.

and who have schemed in a thousand different ways to grab (*accaparrarsi*) high posts in finance, industry, and education did not offer any resistance to our revolutionary march. We must admit that they have always paid their taxes, obeyed the laws and done their duty in war as well. Unfortunately, however, they manifest a passive attitude which is apt to arouse suspicion. Why have they never said one word which would convince all Italians that they perform their duty as citizens out of love rather than out of fear or expediency? Why do they do nothing concrete to split their responsibility from that of all the other Jews in the world, the ones whose only goal is the triumph of the Jewish International? Why have they not yet risen against their co-religionists who are perpetrators of massacres, destroyers of churches, sowers of discord, audacious and evil killers of Christians? . . . There is a growing feeling that all Europe will soon be the scene of a war of religion. Are they not aware of this? We are certain that many will proclaim: we are Jewish Fascists. That is not enough. They must prove with facts to be first Fascists and then Jews.[1]

Seven days later Farinacci made it clear that by 'loyalty to Fascism' he meant loyal acceptance of friendship with the Jew-baiter, Hitler. Replying to the remonstrances of a Milanese Jew, he insisted that nothing was further from his mind than an attempt to stir up anti-Semitism in Italy. He was by no means 'prejudicially hostile' to the Jews, had 'very dear friends' among them and 'had also availed himself of their services'; nor did he deny that they were 'highly intelligent people'. All he wanted was to give his Jewish compatriots a chance of replying to the accusations brought against Jewry at Nuremberg, a chance to show the accusers that Italian Jewry (as distinct from 'all the other Jews in the world') was 'not for the Jewish International but for the Fascist regime'. Hitler's 'racialist exaggerations' were no doubt deplorable, and his persecution of the Jews had 'perhaps been excessive'. Even so, it was the duty of all Italians—including those of the Jewish faith—to join him in condemning and opposing the nefarious activities of 'world Jewry'.[2]

[1] 'Una tremenda requisitoria', *Il Regime Fascista,* 12 Sept. 1936. On the international as well as nation-wide repercussions of Farinacci's article, see, e.g. 'Antisemitische Kampagne in Italien', *Jüdische Rundschau* (30 Sept. 1936), 4 and J. Starr, 'Italy's Antisemites', *Jewish Social Studies* i (Jan. 1939), 114; on the reactions of Farinacci's Jewish shorthand-typist, Jole Foà, cf. IC/Job 122/033865.

[2] 'Perchè provocarci?', *Il Regime Fascista,* 19 Sept. 1936. In 1934 and 1935 Farinacci's paper had repeatedly denounced Hitlerism and Nordic racialism; see O. Del Buono (ed.), *Eia, Eia, Eia, Alalà!,* Milan, 1971, pp. 229–30; G. Sommi Picenardi, 'Le nuove Valchirie', *Il Regime Fascista,* 31 Jan. 1935.

Coming from a former Party Secretary and a member of the Fascist Grand Council, these attacks were bound to cause widespread uneasiness in Jewish circles. As in 1934, the Jews reacted in a variety of ways. Some thought it wisest to confine themselves to loud protestations of unconditional loyalty. Others, while proclaiming their faith in the regime and their devotion to the Duce, tried to dissuade Farinacci from his anti-Semitic folly, alleging that he had been fooled by the propagandist manœuvres of foreign Jew-haters.[1] Yet others, headed by Dante Lattes, refused to be bullied into declarations of Fascist faith, proudly reaffirming their loyalty to the Jewish people and reminding Farinacci that both Judaism and Zionism were anathema to the allegedly Jewish rulers of Bolshevik Russia.[2]

The last to enter into the fray was Felice di Leone Ravenna, one of the fathers of Italian Zionism and President of the Union of Italian Jewish Communities since 1933, who explained (in a letter published in the *Regime Fascista* of 24 September) that he had so far refrained from reacting to Farinacci's articles because he failed to understand why Italian citizens should be required to reply to the anti-Semitic tirades delivered at the Nuremberg rally. Hitler's views on the Jewish question and his treatment of the German Jews had hitherto been regarded as an internal affair of the German Reich; nor had the founder of Fascism ever felt any need to make distinctions of race or religion in Italy.

For the moment the *ras* of Cremona welcomed the protestations of unconditional loyalty to Fascism, most of all the one from his friend Federico Jarach which he was 'greatly pleased' to publish in full.[3] To those, however, who dared to object to his views on the Jewish International or the Bolshevik-Jewish peril, he replied with threats and abuse. When told that the alleged Jewish International was an anti-Semitic myth, he retorted that there was 'at Geneva a World Jewish Parliament where Italy too is well represented' and that a Spanish Communist arrested in Poland had been found in possession of 'a substantial sum of

---

[1] 'In risposta alle pubblicazioni di 'Il regime fascista'. Il patriottismo ed il fascismo degli ebrei italiani', *La Nostra Bandiera*, 16 Sept. 1936.

[2] 'In tema di bolscevismo e ebraismo', *Israel*, (24 Sept. 1936), 4.

[3] Jarach to Farinacci, *Il Regime Fascista*, 20 Sept. 1936. Commenting on the letter, Farinacci described Jarach as 'a sincere man who has given proof of Fascist faith in difficult times (*in tempo non sospetto*)'.

money' received from Polish Jews.[1] When reminded of Mussolini's excellent philo-Semitic and anti-racialist record, he replied ominously: 'It is true that the Duce has so far (*finora*) not felt any need to make distinctions of race or religion in Italy, but there are certain Italian Jews who make a point of setting themselves apart (*tengono a distinguersi*) from Italians of other faiths by participating in pro-Zionist campaigns and in meetings of the international Jewish Congress.' As has been aptly stated, Farinacci's *finora* 'was the first signal of the impending racial campaign'.[2]

Farinacci's increasingly sharp rejoinders, culminating in his vicious attack on Felice Ravenna, greatly upset the leaders of Italian Jewry, some of whom began to question the wisdom of this controversy with a prominent member of the Fascist hierarchy. Their apprehensions, however, turned out to be premature. With the successful conclusion of Ciano's mission in Germany (21–4 October 1936), the anti-Jewish polemics had served their immediate purpose and were temporarily toned down. Subsequently, the Chief Rabbi of Rome informed Neville Laski, President of the Board of Deputies of British Jews, that this tactical retreat on the part of the Duce had been due 'to the intervention with the Government of certain important Italian Jews' and also to the unfortunate repercussions which Farinacci's attacks had had 'both in the foreign Press and amongst many Jewish communities strewn over the shores and islands of the Mediterranean'.[3] In March 1937, however, with Mussolini becoming hopelessly bogged down in Spain and increasingly dependent on German support, the anti-Jewish smear campaign was resumed with redoubled vigour. At the end of that month the social, political, and religious arguments against Jewry were elaborated by one of Mussolini's biographers, Paolo Orano, in a

[1] 'Non divaghiamo!', *Il Regime Fascista*, 20 Sept. 1936.
[2] 'Fascismo ed internazionale ebraica. Una lettera del comm. Ravenna presidente della Unione delle Communità israelitiche italiane', *Il Regime Fascista*, 24 Sept. 1936; De Felice, *Storia degli ebrei italiani*, p. 208. Farinacci added that Ravenna, instead of engaging in polemics, would have done better to confine himself to a declaration of Fascist faith.
[3] Laski to Vansittart, 7 Apr. 1937 (Memorandum on the Position of the Jews of Italy and Tripoli, PRO/F.O.371/R2476/2476/22/25–32). Laski's memorandum was based on 'enquiries made from the Chief Rabbi of the Rome community (David Prato), who is a person of the greatest intelligence and obviously a man of a very great experience and judgment, certain individual members of the Jewish community and certain Press correspondents, Jewish and non-Jewish'.

book ordered by the Duce himself.[1] It is symptomatic that this book was entitled *Gli ebrei in Italia (The Jews in Italy)*, meaning that the current anti-Jewish drive, as distinct from its two predecessors, was directed explicitly against Italian Jewry rather than against the abstractions known as the Jewish International, Jewish high finance, and the Judaeo-Masonic clique. Like Farinacci, Orano (who was Rector of the University of Perugia and a Fascist deputy in 1937) rejected Hitler's racial theories, affirming that the Jews of Italy were 'Italians of the Jewish faith'. Like Farinacci, he called upon the Italian Jews to abstain from manifestations of 'separatism' (with special reference to Zionism and anti-Hitlerism) and to dissociate themselves from their anti-Fascist co-religionists abroad, lest the regime be compelled to reconsider its attitude to the Jewish question. Unlike Farinacci, however, he made a special point of attacking the Jewish Fascists, claiming that the Fascist Ettore Ovazza, for all his devotion to the Duce, was no less afflicted with a 'chosen-people-complex' than the Zionist Dante Lattes.[2]

Orano's book alarmed the Italian Jews, all the more so because the Fascist press, led by Mussolini's *Popolo d'Italia*, reviewed it in glowing terms and gave its poisonous contents wide circulation. On 7 April 1937 Laski reported to Sir Robert Vansittart, then Permanent Under-Secretary at the Foreign Office, that the last six months had been for Italian Jewry 'months of unrest and perplexity': 'Never, during the whole period of the Fascist regime, has the situation of the Jewish community, as a result of the attitude of official circles and the tone of the Press, faced so

[1] Orano, *Gli ebrei in Italia*; A Spinosa, 'Le persecuzioni razziali in Italia', *Il Ponte*, viii (July 1952), 975. In a subsequent book (*Inchiesta sulla razza*, Rome, 1939, p. 280) Orano made it clear that his attack on the Jews had been inspired by Mussolini himself. Orano had taken an interest in the Jews from 1895 onwards, alternatively praising and denouncing them. In 1914, on the eve of World War I, he had written: 'Israel is internationalist whatever else it may be, because the nations, the fatherlands, the empires, the peoples occupying definite historical seats are likewise Israel's enemies. Every Jew is in his heart of hearts fiercely opposed to our expansion in Libya. Peace for Israel, or its comfort at any rate, consists of a troubled Italy, a troubled Europe, and a troubled world . . . Hence the Italian patriotism of the Jews in Italy is always—when closely scrutinized—a burden, an effort, a pain suffered in silence, a condemnation in disguise. The Jews are patriots by compulsion, Socialists by expediency, subversive by tradition, and, in the absolute sense, the instinctive enemies of Latin history and civilization' (*Inchiesta sulla massoneria*, ed. E. Bodrero, Rome, 1925, p. 171). This outburst presents an instructive contrast to the pose of the unbiased critic which Orano chose to adopt in elaborating his views on the Jewish question in the spring of 1937.

[2] *Gli ebrei in Italia*, pp. 109–43.

many anxieties as to what the future may hold. Even during the period of sanctions there had not appeared articles such as those which have recently been published in books, such as . . . "Gli Ebrei in Italia" of Paolo Orano.' For the moment, however, Mussolini did not wish to commit himself on the Jewish issue: 'The anti-Semitic campaign of the "Regime Fascista" was not indulged in by other Italian papers . . . The Government, which often rides two horses at the same time, did not wish the campaign to assume a national character'.[1]

Even before the resumption of the anti-Jewish propaganda offensive it was thought expedient to take certain secret anti-Jewish measures with a view to facilitating co-operation between Rome and Berlin. On 23 November 1936 (exactly one month after the signing of the Italo-German protocol in Berlin) Ciano instructed all Italian Government Ministries to refrain from sending 'compatriots of the Jewish faith' to Germany on official missions.[2] A month later Mussolini—having meanwhile announced the formation of the Rome–Berlin Axis in a public speech—began to remove the Jews from Fascist journalism. We may refer to what Giorgio Pini, newly appointed editor of *Il Popolo d'Italia*, wrote in his diary on 23 December 1936: 'Today I had a long talk (with Mussolini, M. M.) lasting till 19.20. I briefly outlined to him my initial programme . . . He approved everything except the collaboration of Adriano Grego as columnist on Page One which I had planned counting on the brilliant polemical qualities of the colleague who had been my deputy on the *Giornale di Genova*. The motive of the prohibition: contingent reasons of international policy. "You must understand", he added in order to check my insistence, "what impression it would make abroad if the political polemics in Mussolini's own paper were entrusted to a Jew".'[3] For 'abroad', read 'in Germany'.

Eight days after the above conversation, the Duce gave vent to his growing resentment against Jewry in an unsigned article, asserting that the Jews had only themselves to thank for the spread of anti-Jewish feeling in Western society: 'Anti-Semitism

[1] See above, p. 111, n. 3.
[2] ACS/Min. Cultura Popolare/Gabinetto/p. 35/*Germania*, quoted in De Felice, *Storia degli ebrei italiani*, pp. 243–4.
[3] *O.O.* xxviii. 69–70; Pini, *Filo diretto*, p. 58.

is inevitable wherever Semitism emphasizes its inroads and hence its power by its show. The excessive Jew (*troppo ebreo*) begets the anti-Jew . . . and he does it frequently.' Right now the 'excessive Jews' in Paris, headed by Blum and his co-religionists in the Popular Front Government, were provoking a strong anti-Jewish reaction in France.[1] It is worthy of note that Mussolini, while denouncing the *troppi ebrei* of other countries, made no mention whatever of Italian Jewry, leaving it to his underlings to call for the Fascistization of his Jewish subjects.

Until the summer of 1937 the Fascist press continued to distinguish between 'Jewish Italians' (i.e. Fascists) and 'Italian Jews' (i.e. Zionists or anti-Fascists). While applauding Orano's strictures on the Zionists and other 'disloyal' Jewish elements, most reviewers pointedly ignored his attack on the Fascist Ovazza.[2] Mussolini himself, however, began to have second thoughts about the value of Orano's brand of 'defensive' anti-Semitism as early as March 1937. At the end of that month (concurrently with the appearance of Orano's book), he got his unofficial mouthpiece, Telesio Interlandi, to launch a racial campaign against the Jews. Two months later (31 May) he informed Pini that Orano's book was 'confused': 'The fact is that Jewish blood is always Jewish blood and does not change.'[3] On 8 June he ordered Pini to stop publishing declarations of loyalty from anti-Zionist Jews, explaining that the Jews must be combated as such, irrespective of their attitude to Zionism or Fascism. The Jewish problem was to be placed, 'not on the political or religious, but squarely on the racial plane'.[4]

Eleven days later Mussolini's conversion to racial anti-Semitism found expression in a fresh journalistic outburst against the Jews. Taking his cue from an article in *Davar*, a Milanese Jewish periodical, he denounced as hypocrites those Jews who denied the existence of a Jewish nation. The Jew who openly avowed his race, he averred, was more worthy of respect than the assimilationist who pretended to differ from the Gentiles only in the matter of religion. It was racial exclusiveness, rooted in religious contempt for the rest of mankind, which had enabled

---

[1] 'Il troppo storpia', *Il Popolo d'Italia*, 31 Dec. 1936 (*O.O.* xxviii. 98).
[2] See the articles reproduced in A. Levi, *Noi ebrei. In risposta a Paolo Orano*, Rome, 1937.
[3] Pini *Filo diretto*, p. 102.
[4] Ibid., p. 104.

Israel to preserve its identity throughout the centuries of the dispersion; the late Rabbi Margulies had put the point well when he said that the Jew 'rises on top of the other peoples like oil on water'. Judaism was 'an outstanding example of racialism which has lasted for thousands of years and . . . which arouses profound admiration'. That being so, the Jews had no right whatever to complain if other peoples likewise adopted racialism.[1]

The racial problem began to preoccupy Mussolini the moment he decided to conquer an empire. As early as 2 April 1934 Aloisi wrote in his diary: 'Called on Mussolini at 11 a.m. He has been greatly vexed by a book called *Amore nero* (*Black Love*) which has been withdrawn from circulation. It deals with a love affair between an Italian and a Negress. Inadmissible in a nation which wants to create an Empire in Africa.'[2] In the following year the need for an 'Italian race-consciousness' began to be discussed in various Fascist papers, including Mussolini's *Popolo d'Italia*.[3] During the Ethiopian campaign the Duce became increasingly obsessed with the problem. On 26 October 1935 he warned against intermarriage with Africans in a public speech; and in the following May, when told that an Italian had engaged in a friendly card-game with an African at Massaua, he reacted by decreeing a strict ban on social intercourse with natives.[4] On 11 May 1936—six days after the capture of Addis Ababa—he ordered Badoglio and Graziani to take drastic measures against the 'terrible danger' of miscegenation.[5] On 28 May Ciano, then still Minister of Press and Propaganda, informed the German press attaché that he had instructed the press to raise the racial issue: 'Have you noticed that immediately after my return (from Africa) the papers began to carry articles on the racial question in Abyssinia? . . . In dealing with this subject, we shall express ourselves in the harshest possible terms. We shall conduct a racial policy. There are only two races with a future in Europe, the German and the Italian'.[6] In the second half of 1936—Ciano

[1] 'Davar', *Il Popolo d'Italia*, 19 June 1937 (*O.O.* xxviii. 202–3); see also Pini, *Filo diretto*, p. 108.
[2] Aloisi, *Journal*, p. 185.
[3] See esp. Mussolini's (anonymous) article 'Il "dato" irrefutabile', *Il Popolo d'Italia*, 31 July 1935 (*O.O.* xxvii. 110–11): 'We Fascists recognize the existence of different races and of a racial hierarchy . . .'
[4] *O.O.* xxvii. 176; Mussolini to Badoglio, 5 May 1936, ibid. 321.
[5] *O.O.* xxviii. 263.
[6] Hassell to Wilhemstrasse, 29 May 1936 (GFM/7196H/E529616).

having meanwhile been replaced by Alfieri at the Propaganda Ministry—racialist propaganda in the Mussolinian press gradually assumed the proportions of a regular campaign. In the following year racial laws were enacted which rendered sexual intercourse between Italians and Africans a criminal offence.[1] All this, however, concerned the Jews of Italy only in their capacity as Italians, not in their capacity as Jews.

German racial theory began to find an echo in Italy as early as the autumn of 1936 when Giulio Cogni, a 28-year-old writer and composer resident in Germany, published a book, *Il razzismo*, which was a rehash, in Italian form, of Hitler's Nordic mythology. But while glorifying the fair-haired race and extolling Fascism as a manifestation of the Nordic spirit, Cogni took care to dissociate himself from German anti-Semitism, stressing the superiority of the Italian Sephardi Jew over the German Ashkenazi Jew and denying the existence of a Jewish problem in Italy: 'The hatred and expulsion of the Jews in the North originated chiefly from the fact that the two races, all too different, not only never merged but remained facing each other in a warlike attitude . . . This has never happened amongst us.' In the spring of 1937 Cogni reiterated his objections to anti-Semitism in his second book on the subject (*I valori della stirpe italiana*) which contained an appendix by Hans F. K. Günther, the leading German apostle of the Nordic gospel. Mussolini at first supported Cogni. Neville Laski wrote in his above-quoted memorandum of 7 April 1937: 'The Italian Press, significantly enough, had fairly favourable reviews and appreciations of (Cogni's) book, and I am told that papers, known for their anti-racial views, did not have the courage to criticise the pseudo-scientific theories of this new Italian racial authority.' Subsequently, however, the Duce informed Pini that he had withdrawn his protecting hand from Cogni.[2]

The first example of a specifically anti-Jewish racialism in

---

[1] Royal decree law of 19 April 1937, No. 880, converted into law on 30 December 1937, No 2,500 (L. Preti, *Impero fascista, africani ed ebrei*, Milan, 1968, p. 214).

[2] G. Cogni, *Il razzismo*, 2nd rev. edn. Milan, 1937, pp. 157–9; id., *I valori della stirpe italiana*, Milan, 1937, pp. 133–6; Pini, *Filo diretto*, p. 90. On the hostility which Cogni's version of the Nordic heresy aroused even among good Fascists see G. Cogni, 'Risposta ai detrattori', *Il Tevere*, 20 Mar. 1937; A. Tamaro, *Venti anni di storia 1922–1943*, iii, Rome, 1954, p. 278; on Vatican hostility, *L'Osservatore Romano*, 20 June 1937 (on 10 June Cogni's *Il razzismo* had been placed on the Index of Forbidden Books by the Sacred Congregation of the Holy Office).

Italy was an editorial by Interlandi in *Il Tevere* of 30 March 1937, an attack on those 'dissident mongrels'—Jews, half-Jews, quarter-Jews, and 'nominal Italians' married to Jewesses—who were opposed to Fascist racial policy because they feared that it might some day take on an anti-Jewish character. Interlandi left no doubt that these fears were by no means unfounded. The pre-eminence of Jews in the intellectual life of the Fascist State, he insisted, was a racial as well as a political threat and would have to be dealt with accordingly. In other words, racial legislation would have to be extended from Africa to Italy proper.[1]

Interlandi's racial anti-Semitism was sharply criticized by a good many other Fascists, most particularly by Ezio Garibaldi, grandson of the Risorgimento hero and editor of the review *Camicia Rossa*.[2] Ultimately, however, the controversy was cut short by Mussolini himself in favour of his unofficial mouthpiece. In April 1942 Interlandi published an account of the genesis and growth of Fascist racialism which would have done honour to an anti-Fascist comic paper:

Any racialism might be a good thing; and non-racialism also if the Man to whom all Italians have consciously and willingly sacrificed their particular right to think for themselves (*trinciar giudizî*) had judged non-racialism as advantageous to the Italian people. This, then, is the story—and we dedicate it to those who at this moment find it convenient to tread the more barren fields in search of non-existent people with whom to argue (*impossibili interlocutori*)—the story of (Italian) racialism is as follows. Several articles of racialist inspiration are published in *Il Quadrivio*.[3] The authors of these articles win the praise of the Duce. *Hence* these preliminary racial thrusts are advantageous to the country. *Il Quadrivio* and *Il Tevere* continue to write in this vein. The clarification of certain racialist principles thus accomplished is not only admitted through the medium of certain Government organs but officially approved by higher dispositions. *Hence* this is the racial propaganda advantageous to the country. Pending the rapid formation of a group

[1] T. Interlandi, 'Il meticciato dissidente', *Il Tevere*, 30 Mar. 1937; id., 'Parliamo di razzismo', *Il Quadrivio*, 4 Apr. 1937. On the Mussolinian origin of Interlandi's racialism, cf. id., *Contra Judaeos*, Rome–Milan, 1938, pp. 5–6.
[2] E. Garibaldi, 'Discorso di attualità', *Camicia Rossa*. Oct. 1938 (reprinted in *L'Italia e i problemi della pace*, 3rd edn. Rome, 1939, pp. 33–48).
[3] See, e.g., L. Chiarini, 'Il razzismo in Italia', *Il Quadrivio*, 1 Nov. 1936; G. Cogni, 'Il genio e la razza', *ibid.*, 15 Nov. 1936; H.G. and G.P., 'Perchè il problema della razza é all' ordine del giorno', *ibid.*, 17, 24, 31 Jan.; 7, 14, 21, 28 Feb.; 7, 14, 21, 28 Mar.; 4, 11, Apr. 1937.

of responsible writers agreed on the timeliness of spreading the determined racial principles which the publications just mentioned had by
now defined, a young student of racial science (Guido Landra? M. M.)
is invited to synthesize in a concise series of 'points' the programme
of 'Italian racialism.' These 'points' are elaborated seriously and
conscientiously [*sic*]; the phases through which the elaboration passed
need not be related; all that matters today is the fact that the Duce
authorized the publication (18 July 1938), that the Party (26 July)
praised its exactitude and brevity and called upon this formulation of
doctrine to determine 'further precise political action'; and that on
these doctrinal bases it was decided to found a review named *La Difesa
della Razza* ('The Defence of the Race'). *Hence,* on 5 August 1938–XVI,
the racialism advantageous to the country was that which *La Difesa
della Razza* popularized among its two hundred thousand readers.[1]

What was Nazi Germany's share in the conversion of Mussolini
to racialism? As has been noted, the Führer's mere advent to
power in 1933 was enough to bring the latent tension between
Fascists and Jews into the open, despite the Duce's unfeigned
repugnance to Hitler's racial theories and his equally unfeigned
anxiety about Western reactions to the persecution of German
Jewry. At that time, however, the Duce still considered Jewry a
more formidable force than the disarmed and isolated Reich,
with the result that he took care to strike a balance between
unofficial attacks on the Jews and official moves in their favour.
Since then there had been a drastic shift in the European balance
of power. Jewish hostility and Western moral indignation had
not prevented Hitler from scoring one diplomatic triumph after
another; by the spring of 1936 Germany had re-emerged as a
Great Power and Mussolini not unnaturally concluded that there
was less to fear from the Jews than he had originally thought. He
further concluded that German racialism, far from being the
dangerous error he had previously held it to be, was a useful
political weapon.[2] His switch from philo-Semitism and anti-
racialism to open alignment with Hitler's Aryan mythology was
hastened, as we have seen, by ill-informed resentment against

---

[1] 'Discorso alle "nuove linfe"', *La Difensa della Razza* (20 Apr. 1942), 3; on Landra's
authorship of the 'Race Manifesto' see below, p. 176.

[2] Ciano wrote on 20 Nov. 1937: 'The secret of dictatorships of the right—and their
advantage over other regimes—consists precisely in having a national formula. Italy and
Germany have found theirs. The Germans in racial ideology. We in Roman imperialism'
(*1937–1938 Diario,* p. 54).

'international Jewry'; by the emergence of a worrying racial problem in Africa; by the joint Italo-German crusade against Jewish Bolshevism; by his growing irritation at Léon Blum, the international Socialist and friend of Matteotti's, whom he was later to accuse of having driven him into Hitler's arms;[1] by his ever-increasing contempt for the 'rotten' democracies, destined (in his opinion) to suffer defeat at the hands of the 'dynamic' dictatorships;[2] by Anglo-Italian rivalry in the Eastern Mediterranean which had the effect of increasing his animosity to 'English' Zionism;[3] and—last but not least—by his failure to score an early victory over Jewish-Bolshevism in Spain which reduced him to the role of junior partner in the Axis alliance, increasing both his dependence on German support and his willingness to make ideological concessions to his erstwhile disciple north of the Alps.[4]

Nor was this all. Quite apart from his growing resentment against Jewry and his growing dependence on German goodwill, Mussolini knew full well that an ideological alliance with Hitler would automatically bring him into conflict with the Jews all over the world, despite his tolerant attitude to the Jews of Italy. Moreover, what was he to do with the Jewish generals and admirals in the Italian armed forces, with the Jewish professors at the Italian universities, with the Jewish officials in the Italian administration, and—most embarrassing of all—with the Jewish journalists in the Fascist press and the Jewish functionaries in the Fascist Party, once he decided to march with Hitler 'to the end'?

[1] On the relations between Mussolini and Léon Blum, see Appendix III.

[2] Cf. *L'Europa verso la catastrofe*, i. 81–3; Ciano, *1937–1938 Diario*, pp.12, 66, 251.

[3] See below, p. 122, n. 4, p. 123, nn. 1, 2.

[4] While Mussolini desperately desired an early victory for Franco, Hitler aimed at prolonging the civil war in the hope that attention would be drawn away from his machinations in Central Europe and that Italy would become embroiled with the democracies (F. Hossbach, *Zwischen Wehrmacht und Hitler*, 2nd edn., Göttingen, 1965, p. 187; G.L. Weinberg, *The Foreign Policy of Hitler's Germany*, Chicago and London, 1970, pp. 298–9). On 18 Dec. 1936 Hassell wrote to the Wilhelmstrasse: 'The struggle for dominant political influence in Spain lays bare the natural opposition between Italy and France; at the same time the position of Italy as a Power in the Western Mediterranean comes into competition with that of England. All the more clearly will Italy recognize the advisability of confronting the Western Powers shoulder to shoulder (*Rücken an Rücken*) with Germany' (*ADAP*, Serie D iii. 148). According to Hugh Thomas (*The Spanish Civil War*, London, 1961, p. 634), the Italian forces in Spain at their maximum, in mid-1937, numbered about 50,000; the accuracy of this figure was confirmed by the late General Emilio Faldella, Mussolini's first military attaché in Franco Spain, in a letter to Dr. M. Minerbi (14 Oct. 1972).

For despite the undeniable loyalty of the 'Jewish Italians' to their country and their regime, it could not be pretended that such loyalty would be extended by them to include the anti-Semitic Reich. Nor would Hitler ever agree to collaborate with Jews, no matter how great their devotion to the Duce and their faith in the Fascist creed.

In these circumstances the Fascist dictator felt the need for an ideology which would allow him to rid himself not only of the 'disloyal Italian Jews' (who were being eliminated anyhow), but also of the 'loyal Jewish Italians' (who had hitherto been regarded as a definite asset). This ideology was racialism. Once 'Jewish blood' had been declared to be a threat to the 'purity of the Italian race', it would be logical to combat the Jews as such, including even Jewish war heroes and Jewish 'Fascists of the first hour'.[1]

Was there a German attempt to impose the racial policy on Mussolini? The opposite thesis emerges from the ample documentation at our disposal. True, a great many attempts have been made to pin the main, if not the exclusive, responsibility for Italian racialism on Hitler. Ever since 1938 the Italian anti-Fascists have been publishing far and wide that Fascist racial legislation was no more than an example of 'scandalous German interference' and of 'Italian servitude.'[2] Some of Mussolini's accomplices have expressed similar views, including Marshal Pietro Badoglio, the Duce's Chief of Staff from 1925 to 1940 and his successor as head of the Italian government in 1943, who affirms in his memoirs that the anti-Jewish laws were not only explicitly requested by Hitler but actually 'imposed' by him.[3] But the anti-Fascist writers have never taken the trouble to prove their assertion, considering it as self-evident, while Badoglio's book is a frantic apologia, utterly devoid of historical value, as the late Gaetano Salvemini has convincingly shown.[4]

---

[1] *O.O.* xxix. 191; Interlandi, *Contra Judaeos*, p. 61; Ciano, *1937–1938 Diario*, p. 264 (6 Oct. 1938). On the impact of 'Jewish anti-Fascism' on Mussolini's conversion to racialism, see also J. Evola, *Il fascismo, Saggio di una analisi critica dal punto di vista della Destra*, Rome, 1964, pp. 88–9; De Felice *Storia degli ebrei italiani*, pp. 192–3, 239.

[2] See Pentad, *The Remaking of Italy*, Harmondsworth, 1941, p. 103; cf. also E. Momigliano, *Storia tragica e grottesca del razzismo fascista*, Milan, 1946, p. 49: 'Germany exerted pressure and Mussolini had to obey'.

[3] See P. Badoglio, *L'Italia nella seconda guerra mondiale*, Milan, 1946, p. 92.

[4] See G. Salvemini, 'Badoglio nella seconda guerra mondiale I.', *Il Ponte*, viii (Aug. 1952), 1097–1103.

In placing the blame for Mussolini's persecution of the Jews on Hitler, the Marshal was clearly actuated by a desire to explain and justify his own failure to abrogate the racial laws after the fall of Fascism. It is worthy of note in this connection that Badoglio had publicly proclaimed his enthusiasm for Fascist racial policy in 1939, if only to curry favour with his master.[1]

In 1959 Badoglio's charge against Hitler received support from another eminent protagonist in the dramatic events: Vittorio Cerruti, the former Italian Ambassador in Berlin, who gave it as his opinion (in reply to an inquiry from the United Restitution Organization) that the German dictator had made the signing of the ill-fated Steel Pact conditional on the adoption of anti-Jewish measures in Italy.[2] But while there is no reason to doubt Cerruti's good faith, his testimony is as devoid of value as the Marshal's. For one thing, he had no inside information whatever on the subject—a fact he was honest enough to admit[3]—having left Berlin three years before the extension to Italy of Hitler's racial principles. For another, the Duce broke with his Jewish subjects at a moment when the question of a military pact with Hitler was not at all on the agenda, as we shall show below.

The charge of 'direct German interference' was likewise repeated by Harry Fornari, Farinacci's biographer and himself a refugee from Fascist anti-Semitism, who claimed as recently as 1971 that Mussolini, prior to embarking on his anti-Jewish policy, 'discussed the racial problem thoroughly with Hitler'.[4] This claim, however, is based on nothing better than a misquotation from the diary of Giorgio Pini who records that the two dictators briefly touched on the racial issue in Munich at the end of September 1938 (i.e. after, and not before, the elimination of the Jews from Italian public life) and then only with reference to the incorporation of 'racially inferior' Czechs into the Greater

---

[1] Cf. *Il Diritto Razzista* (May–June 1939), 5.

[2] V. Cerruti to United Restitution Organisation (URO), 7 May 1959: 'Nach dem Besuch Mussolinis in Berlin scheint es aber [*sic*], dass Hitler die Bedingung gestellt hätte, den unglückseligen "Stahlpakt" nur dann zu unterschreiben, wenn man auch in Italien denselben Standpunkt als in Deutschland über die Rassenfrage angenommen hätte' (*Judenverfolgung in Italien, den italienisch besetzten Gebieten und in Nordafrika. Dokumentensammlung vorgelegt von der United Restitution Organization*, Frankfurt/Main, 1962, p. xvii).

[3] 'Ich kann aber nichts bestimmtes darüber sagen, weil ich keine genauen Auskünfte besitze' (ibid., p. xvii).

[4] Fornari, *Mussolini's Gadfly*, p. 181.

German Reich, not with reference to the Jews.[1] Equally unfounded is Fornari's assertion that in September 1937 Farinacci led a fifty-man delegation to the National Socialist Party rally at Nuremberg 'to absorb racist doctrines and techniques at the fountainhead'.[2] In reality the *ras* of Cremona never set foot on German soil until 5 September 1938, by which time the persecution of the Jews in Italy was already in full swing.[3]

But while Hitler has been widely (and understandably) regarded as the real author of Mussolini's laws against the Jews ever since 1938, not a few contemporary observers tended to regard Fascist anti-Semitism as to some extent an autonomous growth, underestimating rather than overestimating the impact of the Rome-Berlin Axis on the Duce's racial policy. Among these were Kurt Kornicker, the pro-Fascist Rome correspondent of the *Jüdische Rundschau*; Sir W. McClure, press attaché at the British Embassy in Rome during the period under review; Joshua Starr, one of the earliest students of Italian anti-Semitism; and Konrad Heiden, Hitler's anti-Fascist biographer. Kornicker, in a series of dispatches to his paper at the end of 1936, expressed the conviction that the growth of anti-Jewish feeling in Fascist circles was due in part to resentment at British hegemonial aspirations in the Mediterranean and in part to fear of 'Bolshevist encirclement' in Spain.[4] McClure, in his above-quoted memorandum of 11 May 1937, pointed out that the Jewish issue had always cropped up in Italy in times of crisis, even before the rise of Fascism. If the Italian Jews had now once more become an object of criticism and suspicion, this was due, firstly, to the

---

[1] Pini, *Filo diretto*, pp. 169–70 (23 Oct. 1938).

[2] Fornari, op. cit., p. 181 (the same error in De Felice, *Storia degli ebrei italiani*, p. 291). In reality the delegation was led by Dino Gardini, Vice-Secretary of the Fascist Party and Giuseppe Bastianini, Under-Secretary of Foreign Affairs, other leading members being Count Thaon di Revel and Tullio Cianetti ('Die italienische Abordnung zum Reichsparteitag in München', *V.B.*, 7 Sept. 1937; M. Magistrati, *L'Italia a Berlino*, Milan, 1956, pp. 60–1).

[3] See 'Die Delegationen Italiens und Nationalspaniens in Nürnberg', *V.B.*, 6 Sept. 1938 (Farinacci leader of 21-man Fascist Party delegation); 'Empfang der Delegation Francos und Mussolinis', *Der Angriff*, 1 Sept. 1938: 'Farinacci ist überzeugender [*sic*] Antisemit, und seiner Entsendung als Führer der italienischen Delegation zum Parteitag ist besondere Bedeutung beizumessen'; 'Göring empfängt die italienische Abordnung', *Der Angriff*, 7 Sept. 1938.

[4] K. Kornicker, 'Rivalen im Mittelmeer', *Jüdische Rundschau*, 27 Oct. 1936, p. 2; 'Italiens Aussenpolitik', *Jüdische Rundschau*, 13 Nov. 1936, 2.

popular association of Jewry with Bolshevism and, secondly, to the Zionist question, Palestine Jewry being 'in effect an instrument of British Imperial policy'. The influx of Jewish refugees from Central Europe was an additional source of friction, the incoming German Jew being 'a very different type from the long-settled Italian Jew'. It was possible that a push had been given to anti-Semitism by German influence, or German suggestion. But there were already signs of a new feeling 'before Germany and Italy embraced'. And in Italy the feeling was 'purely political, not racial': 'Italians of Jewish blood who do not belong to "the Jewish community" are found everywhere in Italy, filling every kind of position . . . They would only become part of a "Jewish problem" if racialism developed in Italy, which so far it has not done.'[1] Starr, writing after the promulgation of the racial laws (October 1938), agreed with Kornicker and McClure that Fascist anti-Semitism was to some extent a spontaneous reaction to 'English Zionism' and 'Jewish Bolshevism': 'In the late summer of 1936 . . . the various objectives of the Italian foreign policy were seen to have for once a common denominator in the Jewish issue. Particularly in the Mediterranean, with both extremities, Palestine and Spain, in flames, the recourse to anti-Jewish propaganda appeared inevitable from the standpoint of Italian imperialism. To the Islamic world Il Duce was preparing to pose as defender of the faith against Great Britain and her ally, the Jewish Agency for Palestine, while in Spain, on the other hand, it was undeniably true that thousands of Jews were enrolling in the Loyalist ranks.'[2] Finally, Heiden, in a book published in the spring of 1939, expressed the view that it was Italy's struggle in the Mediterranean which had 'led her into anti-Semitism'.[3]

After World War II similar views were advanced by Luigi Villari and by Dante L. Germino, an American scholar of Italian extraction. The former, in his above-quoted book on Mussolini's foreign policy, affirmed that 'it was chiefly the activities of international finance that actually prepared the way for racial legislation in Italy', adding that Mussolini 'had long regarded Jews as a community inspired by international considerations

[1] PRO/F.O. 371/R3585/2476/22.
[2] Starr, 'Italy's Antisemites', 114–15.
[3] K. Heiden, *One Man against Europe*, Harmondsworth, 1939, pp. 236–7.

independent of their Italian citizenship'.[1] The latter, in a study of Fascist totalitarian rule, argued that Fascist racialism was primarily an aspect of the Fascist Party's attempt to transform the Italians into an 'imperial people' and hence 'a result of the inner workings of the Fascist system' rather than 'an imitation of totally foreign developments'. Racialism fitted neatly into the 'reform of custom' which the Party Secretary, Achille Starace, had launched in 1937: 'If the Italians could be imbued with a "racial conscience", then "the sediment of the old Italy" could be scraped away from the souls of the people.' And while 'Nazi pressures on the Fascist regime were strong', it was probable 'that even without them Italian Fascism would have arrived at some form of racial doctrine'. Anti-Semitism 'provided the regime with an opportunity to heighten terroristic activities within Italy. The new reign of terror increased anxiety throughout the country; an anxious, nervous people was an energetic people [*sic*], far more useful in the building of empires than a complacent and satisfied citizenry could be.' To Starace and his associates (Germino concluded) the persecution of the Jews 'offered simply one more opportunity for the extension of Fascism's totalitarian ideology. Those who demurred were standpatters and compromisers.' They therefore pressed for a radical anti-Jewish policy, while 'the moderate group in the government' opposed it.[2]

In 1975 Germino's thesis received support from another American scholar, Michael A. Ledeen, who claimed that the emergence of official anti-Semitism in Italy was part of an attempt 'to eradicate the vestiges of earlier values and mores, to transform the Italian people from top to bottom, and to present the world with a truly new man, *homo fascistus*.' The central notion of Fascism had always been the moulding 'of a new sort of Italian'; in Mussolini's phrase, Italians had to be transformed 'from a race of slaves into a race of masters'. But—and that was

---

[1] Villari, *Italian Foreign Policy under Mussolini*, pp. 198, 199.

[2] D.L. Germino, *The Italian Fascist Party in Power. A Study in Totalitarian Rule*, Minneapolis, 1959, pp. 25–6, 27–8. For a detailed criticism of Germino's interpretation, see Michaelis, 'I rapporti italo-tedeschi e il problema degle ebrei in Italia', 279–82. A somewhat different thesis was advanced by M. van Creveld ('Beyond the Finzi-Contini Garden. Mussolini's "Fascist Rascism"', *Encounter* xlii, Feb. 1974, 42–7) who claimed that Fascist racialism was not an imitation of Nazi doctrines but rather a 'refutation thereof', i.e. a counterblast to the anti-Italian implications of Hitler's Nordic gospel. For a criticism of this thesis, see M. Michaelis, 'The "Duce" and the Jews', *Yad Vashem Studies*, xi (1976), 22.

'the crux of the issue'—there were some recalcitrant elements 'which had refused to enter into the spirit of the new Regime' and 'which insisted on clinging to the values and goals of an earlier, corrupt epoch. The Jews were the paradigm case of this recalcitrant element. Their loyalty was divided between Israel and Italy; their anti-Fascism was legendary; they clung to values thousands of years old.' Mussolini's solution of the problem, however, 'was quite unlike that practised by the Nazis'. The 'guiding idea' of his anti-Semitic policy was to 'retrain the Jews', to 'italianize' and 'fascistize' them, and then to 'reintegrate them into Fascist society'. This idea, according to Ledeen, was in line with Mussolini's 'spiritual concept' of race. As the Duce himself said to Yvon De Begnac: 'Mixed marriages are slowly eliminating the Jewish traits.' The Jews could, and would, be 'aryanized'. Why Mussolini decreed a ban on mixed marriages (even Jewish Fascists were forbidden to marry Aryan women), Ledeen did not explain.[1]

While each of these conflicting versions throws light on some minor aspect or other of Fascist anti-Judaism, none of them explains the Duce's sudden conversion to an 'Aryan-Nordic' racialism which was totally out of step with Italian traditions and which he himself had previously condemned as 'unscientific' in signed articles and public speeches. Mussolini had all sorts of grievances against the Jews but only one reason for persecuting them as a 'race'—his ill-fated alliance with a Jew-baiter. Hostility to Jewish Bolshevism and English Zionism had not prevented him from posing as a philo-Semite during the first fourteen years of Fascist rule; nor had it deterred him from courting the Zionist leaders. His resentment against the 'international Jewish bankers' (which appears to have come to a head before his *rapprochement* with Berlin) had not affected the place of the Jews in Italian life; neither had his ambition to present the world with a 'truly new man'. The imposition of totalitarian rule, far from creating a Jewish problem in Italy, had actually facilitated the establishment of cordial relations between Blackshirts and Jews. Nor was it for the sake of the Arabs that Mussolini decided to give his racial policy an 'Aryan-Nordic' direction. That the Fascist leader did not regard 'Jewish blood' as an obstacle to 'Fascistization' is clear

[1] M.A. Ledeen, 'The Evolution of Italian Fascist Antisemitism', *Jewish Social Studies,* xxxvii (Jan. 1975), 3–17.

from both his own utterances and the testimonies of his surviving collaborators; but since Hitler held the opposite view, he felt compelled to eliminate persons of Jewish race from Italian life. His statement on mixed marriages referred to baptized Jews with 'Aryan' wives, not to members of the Jewish community. The 'Aryanizations', far from being a logical application of his 'spiritual' concept of race, were a characteristic manifestation of Fascist corruption. That Italian Fascism arrived at 'some form of racial doctrine' independently of German influence is perfectly true; for the ban on miscegenation in Africa was decreed before the birth of the Axis. It is equally true, however, that this doctrine did not take on an anti-Jewish character until Italy became a pawn of the Reich. In the words of a noted German scholar, 'the starting-point of Fascist racial policy was not the hatred of the Jews but the fear of a "race of half-breeds" in the *Impero* . . . It was in this context that Mussolini declared the laws affecting Jews, and so he felt entitled to denounce all those who had spoken of foreign influences as "poor half-wits" . . . But this legislation did not deny its model, the Nuremberg laws, and it can hardly be claimed that it was much milder.'[1]

But if Mussolini's laws against the Jews were indeed an 'imitation of totally foreign developments'—an Italian variant of the Nuremberg laws—does it follow that they were forced upon him by Hitler? Since the Duce's sudden jump from philo-Semitism to anti-Semitism coincided with the consolidation of the Axis alliance, it was natural to suspect that the Germans had had a hand in it. After World War II, however, various students of Italian politics pointed out that this suspicion was not confirmed by any documentary evidence. A first attempt at a scholarly examination of the problem (based on published sources only) was made in 1960 by the writer who arrived at the unexpected conclusion that Hitler, far from trying to force his anti-Jewish obsession on Mussolini, had made a point of refraining from interference in Italian domestic matters during the period under review. The Duce's decision to break with the Jews was due, not to any irresistible foreign pressure, but to his recognition of Italy's changed alignment in Europe and more particularly to his desire to cement the Axis alliance by eliminating any strident contrast in the policy of the two Powers.

[1] E. Nolte, *Der Faschismus in seiner Epoche*, Munich, 1963, p. 294.

Similar conclusions were reached by Renzo De Felice (who had had access to the unpublished Italian records), by Sir Ivone Kirkpatrick (who, as a diplomat, had had exceptional opportunities for studying Mussolini and his affairs at close quarters for fifteen years), and by A. James Gregor, author of a scholarly work on Fascist ideology, who regarded Mussolini's imitation of the Nuremberg laws as the most shameful aspect of his attempt at the ideological *Gleichschaltung* of Italy—'all the more shameful because Hitler had never made the alliance with Italy contingent upon such espousals.'[1]

Absence of official German intervention, however, should not be confused with absence of German influence, still less with absence of German guilt. It is amply clear from our sources that the Germans tried to influence the evolution of Fascist racial thought throughout the anti-Jewish campaign which culminated in the extension of Hitler's racial principles to Italy. They did so in a variety of ways: by encouraging the Italian Jew-baiters, with particular reference to Farinacci who was awarded the Grand Cross of the Order of the German Eagle in May 1938;[2] by inciting the Fascist authorities against the German-Jewish refugees in Italy;[3] by distributing anti-Jewish literature among their Italian friends;[4] and—last but not least—by enthusiastically responding to Fascist requests for advice and guidance on the racial question.[5] It remains to add that the official policy of non-interference did not prevent certain organs of the German press from openly voicing their dissatisfaction with the Fascist attitude to the Jews. In November 1936 Goebbels's *Angriff* sternly rebuked Giulio Cogni for denying the existence of a Jewish problem in

[1] Michaelis, 'On the Jewish Question in Fascist Italy', 24–41; De Felice, *Storia degli ebrei italiani*, pp. 242–3; Kirkpatrick, *Mussolini*, p. 353; A.J. Gregor, *The Ideology of Fascism. The Rationale of Totalitarianism*, New York, 1969, p. 260. See also M. Vaussard, *Histoire de l'Italie contemporaine*, Paris, 1950, p. 257; Tamaro, op. cit., p. 305; L. Barbaro, 'Il Führer in frac', *L'Espresso* (25 Jan. 1959), 14–15.

[2] See L. Pauler to R. Farinacci, 8 May 1938 (ACS/Roberto Farinacci 1921–45/fasc. 71); cf. also H. Barth, *Romanische Köpfe*, Berlin, 1938, p. 64.

[3] See testimony of Fritz Wiedemann, Hitler's adjutant from 1935 to 1938 (8 Mar. 1955) in *Judenverfolgung in Italien*, p. xx; minute by Winkler of Auslandsorganisation der NSDAP, 7 Mar. 1938 (GFM/119/118876); minute by Ettel, Landesgruppenleiter Italien, 5 Oct. 1938 (GFM/119/119150–54).

[4] Bülow-Schwante to German Embassy in Rome, 3 Feb. 1937; note by Mollier, 11 Feb. 1937 (*Judenverfolgung in Italien*, pp. 8, 9); Mollier to Reich Propaganda Ministry, 25 Aug. 1938 (see below, p. 168 and n. 1).

[5] See above, pp. 94–95 and 114–17.

Italy.[1] In February 1937 Streicher's *Stürmer* took Farinacci to task for demanding the 'Fascistization' of Italian Jewry rather than its elimination from Italian public life. International Jewry (the paper insisted) was as much a menace to the Italians as to the rest of Gentile humanity. Fascist Italy, therefore, had the same duty to combat the Jewish peril as her German ally.[2]

In view of the above we cannot but agree with Gregor that the Italian Race Manifesto of 14 July 1938 'did document the influence of extraneous pressures that were being felt by the theoreticians of Fascism'.[3] But was this influence equally felt by the practitioners of Fascism when they decided to sacrifice their Jewish compatriots on the altar of the Rome–Berlin Axis? Mussolini himself has given us a series of contradictory answers to this question, alternately rejecting and confirming the thesis of 'direct German interference'. In 1938 he repeatedly affirmed that it was the conquest of an empire in Africa rather than the alliance with Berlin that had prompted him to introduce racial measures into Italy.[4] In April 1943, on the other hand, he told the Hungarian Prime Minister that he had had to enact certain racial laws 'because the Germans, who were incredibly intolerant and inflexible in this matter, had insisted.'[5] In July 1944 he went even further, claiming in a conversation with Ivanoe Fossani that the adoption of an anti-Jewish policy in 1938 had been due to an explicit request from Hitler.[6]

It goes without saying that neither of these conflicting versions can be taken at its face value. In 1938 Mussolini, stung to the quick by the Pope's taunt that he was imitating Germany, had been anxious to demonstrate the 'originality' of his racial legislation. Five years later, however, faced with the utter bankruptcy of his pro-German policy, he had found it expedient to place the blame for his racialist folly on his ally; and in 1944,

[1] We have not succeeded in tracing this article (entitled 'Rassismus—italienisch gesehen'); the relevant passages are, however, quoted in 'Eine italienische Rassentheorie', *Jüdische Rundschau* (24 Nov. 1936), 2.
[2] 'Mussolini und die Judenfrage', *Der Stürmer*, No. 9, Feb. 1937; cf. also 'Jüdische Lügenmanöver. Juden in Italien geben eine Erklärung gegen den Bolschewismus ab', *Der Stürmer*, No. 18, Apr. 1937.
[3] Gregor, op. cit., p. 261.
[4] *O.O.* xxix pp. 125–6, 146.
[5] N.(M.) Kállay, *Hungarian Premier. A Personal Account of a Nation's Struggle in the Second World War*, London and New York, 1954, p. 159.
[6] I. Fossani, 'Diario di Salò', *La Repubblica d'Italia*, 25 Sept. 1947.

with defeat and ruin staring him in the face, he had repeated the charge against Hitler in a more explicit manner. In neither case had he been actuated by a desire to tell the truth for its own sake. Hence, if we are to unravel the mystery of his sudden conversion to 'Aryan-Nordic' racialism, we shall do well not to rely on his testimony, but to re-examine the history of the Axis alliance in the light of the additional evidence now in our possession.

As has been noted, contacts between Rome and Berlin were resumed on the eve of the African war when Hitler received Manacorda. At that time, however, relations between the two countries were still so strained that neither side could have any interest in raising delicate domestic issues; this also applies to the contacts established by Coselschi's emissaries with a variety of German political figures, to Ricci's visit to Berlin at the end of January 1936 (which was given a strictly non-political complexion), and to Manacorda's second and third meetings with the Führer. It is hardly surprising, therefore, that the relevant records should make no mention whatever of the Jews.[1]

On the other hand Mussolini, in his above-quoted conversation with Strunk (31 January 1936), made what appears to be an oblique reference to the race problem, saying: 'It was only trifles that stood in the way of friendship between ourselves and Germany'. One of those trifles was Hitler's Nordic gospel. But while insisting that such minor issues would not be allowed to interfere with historical necessities, the Duce made it clear to his visitor that Italy could not change sides overnight. In other words, the divergence of views on the racial gospel and other 'trifles' was likely to continue for some time to come.[2]

Bocchini's visit to Himmler (30 March – 1 April 1936) marked the beginning of ideological co-operation between the two kindred regimes; for the moment, however, this co-operation did not extend to the Jewish peril, Fascist resentment at Jewish sanctionism notwithstanding. The attempts by Himmler and his associates to raise the Jewish problem on that occasion met with

[1] On Manacorda, see GFM/4680H/E224876–89; BA/K/R 43/II/1447; E. Robertson, 'Zur Wiederbesetzung des Rheinlandes 1936', *VJZG* 10 (Apr. 1962), 205; on Coselschi's emissaries (Barilli, Insabato, Alighieri, and Salvotti), ACS/Min. Cultura Popolare/busta 324/sottofasc. Movimento fascista in Germania; busta 325/sottofasc. Antikomintern; BA/K/250–18–15/1; on Ricci, GFM/3175H/D682434–35; BA/K/Reichskanzlei/R 43/II/1449.
[2] GFM/7196H/E529621.

polite rebuffs; and the secret police agreement of 1 April made no mention whatever of the Jews, nor is there any evidence of joint Italo-German police action against Jews as such before the adoption of anti-Jewish measures in Italy.[1]

Three days after the signing of the Himmler–Bocchini agreement Mussolini raised the Jewish issue with Hans Frank, reaffirming his opposition to the German brand of racialism: 'Here I have neither anti-Semitism nor conflict with the Church. On this point, too, we differ from you. The Jews are few in number and absolutely loyal citizens, even Fascists.' The Italian King was even more outspoken: 'There are unfortunately things about your Führer which I do not understand—his anti-Semitism, for instance. What purpose is that supposed to serve? There are no more exemplary citizens in Italy than the Jews. Why should things be different in Germany?'[2] Frank does not tell us what reply, if any, he made to these remonstrances. It is obvious, however, that in this early phase of the German-Italian *rapprochement* he could not in any way have meddled with so strictly domestic a question as that of the Italian Jews.

On 30 April 1936 Hitler received Edmondo Rossoni, Mussolini's Minister of Agriculture, with whom he had a 'non-political' conversation. As might be expected, neither the Führer nor his visitor made any allusion to the Jews.[3]

The racialist controversy was, however, touched upon by Edda Ciano in the course of an informal chat with Hitler at the beginning of June. According to Paul Schmidt, the chief interpreter of the Wilhelmstrasse, the Duce's daughter remonstrated with her host concerning his racial policy, saying: 'But

---

[1] GFM/1104/319096–100 (6 April 1936). According to Bocchini's account, Himmler and his collaborators repeatedly pressed for joint action against the Jewish peril, only to be told that there was no Jewish problem in Italy: 'La Delegazione italiana fece presente che la questione ebraica in Italia ha altre caratteristiche sia per l'entità della massa, che è irrilevante rispetto alla popolazione del Regno, e sia perché l'infiltrazione nelle istituzioni del Regime e dello Stato è scarsissima', (De Felice, *Storia degli ebrei italiani*, pp. 244–5, 533–540).

[2] Frank, *Im Angesicht des Galgens*, pp. 222, 224.

[3] GFM/5739/H030426. On 29 April Rossoni had a talk with his opposite number, R. Walther Darré, which was likewise devoid of political significance (GFM/5739/H0304424–5). Funke (*Sanktionen und Kanonen*, pp. 163–4) evidently overestimates the importance of Rossoni's mission.

you can't punish a man for having a Jewish grandmother.'[1] Whether she made this remonstrance with the approval of her father we do not know; the fact remains, however, that in June 1936 the above utterance still reflected the official Fascist view on the subject.

Edda Ciano's departure for Berlin was followed by the appointment of her pro-German husband, Galeazzo, to the post of Foreign Minister on 9 June 1936. Ciano had 'no love' for the Jews whom he accused of fomenting the 'anti-German current in Italy'; but unlike some other Germanophiles in Mussolini's entourage he took no part in the anti-Jewish campaign which was to culminate in the enactment of the racial laws in 1938. Ciano's advocacy of an alliance with Hitler was based on the unrealistic assumption that Italy would be an equal partner, free to differ from her ally on domestic issues; he was therefore intolerant of German interference and averse to the adoption of anti-Jewish measures on the German model. Nor is there any evidence that the Jewish problem was ever touched upon in his conversations with the German leaders.[2]

On 3 August 1936 Hitler received Dino Alfieri, Ciano's successor as Minister of Press and Propaganda, who had arrived in Berlin two days previously to attend the Olympic Games. But although Alfieri was the leading supporter of Ciano's pro-German line in the Italian Cabinet, the meeting was confined to an exchange of trivialities (including a vague reference to the 'common tasks' of the two countries); no serious problem was so much as hinted at, least of all that of the Jews.[3]

---

[1] P. Schmidt, *Statist auf diplomatischer Bühne*, Bonn, 1952, p. 579; cf. M. Magistrati, 'La Germania e l'impresa italiana di Etiopia', *Rivista di Studi Politici Internazionali*, xvii (Oct.–Dec. 1950), 603. Schmidt does not tell us during which of her repeated visits Edda Ciano made the above-quoted remark; it is perfectly clear, however, that it was during the first, the other two having taken place in 1942 and 1943 respectively, after her father had made Hitler's racial principles his own. On the political significance of Edda's visit, see Hassell's report of 29 May 1936 (GFM/7196H/E529616). In her memoirs, Edda Ciano expresses qualified approval of Fascist racial policy, adding that she was 'delighted to be an Aryan' (*My Truth*, London, 1977, p. 149).

[2] See below, pp. 140–41, 143. On Ciano's temporary Germanophilia, see General H. Fischer, German military attaché in Rome (BA/MA/ H27/13/12 June 1936); Anfuso, *Da Palazzo Venezia al Lago di Garda*, p. 36. Hassell (who disliked and distrusted Ciano) informed Berlin on 18 June 1936, that the 'reorientation of Italy's policy towards Germany has played a part in the change of Foreign Ministers' (GFM/7197/E529654–56).

[3] Memorandum by Meissner (GFM/3236H/D700758–62).

On the other hand, we cannot rule out the possibility that the above-mentioned meeting between Goebbels and Alfieri at Venice (29–30 August) did have some sort of bearing on the Jewish issue, since Farinacci launched his crusade against the Jewish–Bolshevik peril less than two weeks later and was duly encouraged by Alfieri on Mussolini's orders. Even so, it is most unlikely that the two Ministers reached an agreement on a joint propaganda drive against the Jews (as was widely believed at the time); for Massimo Magistrati (who accompanied Goebbels to Venice and was present at the talks) tells us that the meeting was 'devoid of political significance'.[1]

It has been suggested that the seven-man Fascist Party delegation which arrived at Nuremberg on 8 September 1936 was composed of Jew-baiters who had been invited by the Germans precisely because of their anti-Semitic views.[2] In reality, the delegates were little-known Party officials, none of whom was to play a significant part in the racialist campaign. On 10 September the delegation was joined by Piero Parini, the Director-General of Italians Abroad, who had publicly criticized German racial policy as recently as the spring of 1935.[3]

When Hans Frank again went to Rome for a meeting with the Duce on 23 September 1936, a German–Italian front had already formed in Spain, and Farinacci's campaign against the Jewish–Bolshevik peril was in full swing. For the moment, however, Fascist anti-Semitism was still strictly unofficial.[4] Hence Mussolini, while denouncing Communism and democracy in harsh terms, prudently refrained from any allusion to the 'Jewishness' of these phenomena; nor did he make any reference to the Jewish origin of his *bête noire*, Léon Blum. It was only when Frank questioned him on the Fascist attitude to religion that he took the opportunity of alluding to the racial character of the Jewish

---

[1] Alfieri to Farinacci, 6 Oct. 1936, IC/Job 42/026569; M. Magistrati, *Il prologo del dramma. Berlino 1934–1937*, Milan, 1971, pp. 119–21.

[2] De Felice, *Storia degli ebrei italiani*, pp. 210–11.

[3] The delegation was headed by a certain Perusiono, member of the Fascist party Directorate, the other members being Professor Marpicati of the Fascist Academy, the *federale* of Milan (Parcuti) the *federale* of Genoa (Molfino), the *federale* of Pescara (Bianca), the deputy Bazilo, and the President of the Confederation of Industrial Workers, Cianetti ('Die faschistische Abordnung beim Reichsparteitag', *V.B.*, 9 Sept. 1936). For Parini's declaration see De Felice, *Storia degli ebrei italiani*, p. 167 n. 2.

[4] K. Kornicker, 'Antisemitische Kampagne in Italien', *Jüdische Rundschau*, (30 Sept. 1936), 4.

question, evidently in order to please his guest: 'Minister Frank
... wishes to know how Italy has succeeded in normalizing her
relations with the Church, while in Germany the question
bristles with difficulties. The Duce replies that the fight against
religion, whether Catholic or Protestant (not against the Jews
since in that case it is a question of race) is useless because
religion is as intangible as mist.'[1] It is symptomatic that it was
Mussolini who brought up the racial issue, not his German
interlocutor; and it is worthy of note that on the morrow of the
above conversation Farinacci warned Felice Ravenna that the
Duce might well feel the need to make 'distinctions of race or
religion' in Italy unless the Jews mended their ways.

Hard on the heels of Frank's visit to the Duce, Filippo Anfuso,
Ciano's *chef de cabinet,* went to Nuremberg for a secret meeting
with the Führer (to whom he was introduced by the Prince of
Hesse). According to Anfuso's detailed account, Hitler held forth
at great length on the community of destiny between the two
Fascist Powers, on their common enmity to Great Britain, on the
need for an alliance between them, and, finally, on his admiration
for the Duce. Apart from a brief and vague reference to Austria,
however, he did not allude to any controversial subject, least of
all to the divergence of views on the race problem.[2]

A month before Ciano's departure for Germany the German
and Italian governments began to exchange views about the
agreements to be reached on that occasion, hoping to straighten
out all differences of opinion beforehand. But while a great
many controversial problems were raised in the course of these
preliminary negotiations, none of the relevant records makes
any reference to the Jews.[3]

No mention was made of the Jews in Ciano's talks with the
German leaders (21–4 October), except for a passing reference
to 'the Jews who govern France'. Nor is there any allusion to the
Jewish question in the secret Italo-German protocol which was
signed by Ciano and Neurath on 23 October.[4]

[1] *L'Europa verso la catastrofe,* i. 84.
[2] Anfuso, op. cit., pp. 18–21.
[3] GFM348/III/201759–863/2; *L'Europa verso la catastrofe,* i. 86–8; DGFP, Serie C v. 1027–9, 1041–5, 1061–2, 1063, 1072–3, 1074–5, 1079–81, 1082–3, 1086–90, 1100–1, 1108, 1120–2, 1122–3, 1123–4.
[4] *L'Europa verso la catastrofe,* i. 105: 'Of France the Führer spoke ... only superficially and with slight contempt. Some abuse of the Jews who govern her and nothing further.' For the secret protocol, see ibid., pp. 90–3 and GFM/2871/963570–88.

After the birth of the Axis it was judged expedient to relax the anti-Jewish campaign in Italy. At the end of October Count De Vecchi, Minister of Education and Quadrumvir of the March on Rome, paid an official visit to the Rabbinical College at Rhodes. On 13 November a high Italian official assured a representative of the Jewish Telegraph Agency that there would be no change in the Fascist attitude to the Jews. And on 12 January 1937—ten days after the Anglo-Italian 'Gentlemen's Agreement'—the *Popolo di Roma* published an article in praise of the Jewish National Home which was widely quoted in the Zionist press.[1]

On 15 January 1937 Baron Troilo de Salvotti, a representative of CAUR and a friend of Farinacci's and Preziosi's, published an article on the Jewish question in *Wille und Macht*, the organ of the Hitler Youth, in which he reviewed the recent manifestations of anti-Semitism in the Fascist press. But while harshly criticizing Jewry, he stressed the difference between the 'international Jews' abroad and the 'Jewish Italians' at home, paying tribute to the loyalty of the latter: 'In Italy, too, the Jewish problem is not only on the agenda but on its way to a solution. It is difficult to foresee, however, when this solution will take place, since Fascist anti-Semitism is primarily directed against international Jewry; on the other hand there seems to be no need for special measures against the Italian Jews, both because of their numerical insignificance and because of the services that many of them have rendered to Fascism.'[2]

On 23 January 1937 Hermann Göring (who had come to Rome on an exploratory mission) told Mussolini that the 'strong influence of Freemasons and Jews in the British Empire' was an obstacle to Anglo-German collaboration. The Duce was presumably pleased with this remark, given his fear of an Anglo-German *rapprochement* at Italy's expense. But neither he nor Göring made any allusion to the Jewish problem in Italy or to the need for joint Italo-German action against the Jewish peril.[3]

In the second half of February 1937 Tullio Cianetti, President of the Confederation of Industrial Workers and a member of the

---

[1] 'S.E. il Ministro De Vecchi visita il Collegio Rabbinico di Rodi', *Israel*, 29 Oct. 1936; 'Italien und die Judenfrage', *Jüdische Rundschau* (17 Nov. 1936), 1; 'Neues aus Italien', *ibid.* (15 Jan. 1937), 2.

[2] T. de Salvotti, 'Das faschistische Italien und die Juden', *Wille und Macht*, (15 Jan. 1937), 25–8.

[3] *L'Europa verso la catastrofe*, i. 148.

Fascist Grand Council, went to Nuremberg for a meeting with the notorious Streicher.[1] On 21 February the Egyptian paper *Ahram* carried the news that Cianetti, while in Germany, had attacked the Jews in a public speech, calling for German–Italian co-operation in the fight against the Jewish peril. There is, however, no reference to Cianetti's alleged statement in any German or Italian source available to us; nor did his mission yield any concrete results as far as the common struggle against Jewry was concerned. It is worth noting in this connection that immediately after Cianetti's visit Streicher once more complained of Fascist Italy's failure to come to grips with the Jewish problem.[2]

From the spring to the autumn of 1937 Mussolini, while egging on his anti-Semitic underlings, repeatedly went out of his way to demonstrate his independence of any German influence in Jewish matters. At the end of his ten-day visit to Libya (12–21 March), in the course of which he was presented with the Sword of Islam, he assured the Jews of Tripoli that his government would 'always respect their traditions and religious feelings'.[3] The Fascist press hailed these words as a manifestation of 'truly Roman tolerance' and 'spiritual superiority'—a thinly veiled allusion to the difference between 'civilized' Fascism and 'barbarous' Nazism.[4]

On 25 March (three days after his return to Rome) Mussolini, in a talk with the German Ambassador, once more gave vent to his irritation against Blum who, he claimed, would have been overthrown long ago 'if international Jewry had not kept him in the saddle'.[5] Five days later he had Interlandi launch a campaign against the Jewish race in the columns of *Il Tevere*. But on 22 April he reaffirmed his opposition to German racialism in his above-quoted talk with Schuschnigg: 'It is clear that there are substantial differences between Fascism and Nazism. We are

[1] Julius Streicher, the Gauleiter of Franconia, gained worldwide notoriety in the 1930s with his anti-Semitic weekly *Der Stürmer*.
[2] See above, p. 128 n. 2. On the meeting between Streicher and Cianetti, cf. 'Worüber die Juden sich ärgern', *Der Stürmer*, No. 15, Apr. 1937; see also Magistrati, *L'Italia a Berlino*, pp. 197–9. Since Mussolini told the Germans as late as the end of September 1937 that there was no Jewish problem in Italy (see below, p. 139), he could hardly have authorized Cianetti to express the opposite opinion to Streicher over eight months earlier.
[3] See 'Le popolazioni ebraiche della Libia partecipano entusiaste alle trionfali accoglienze al Capo del Governo', *Israel*, 25 Mar. 1937.
[4] M. Biancale, 'Il Duce nel Suk ebreo', *Il Popolo di Roma*, 19 Mar. 1937.
[5] Hassell to Wilhelmstrasse, 25 Mar. 1937 (GFM/1500/370443–44).

Catholics, full of pride and respect for our religion. We do not admit the racial theories, still less their juridical consequences.'[1] On 3 May he made the same point in a conversation with the German Foreign Minister: 'As far as Nazi collaboration in the Schuschnigg Government is concerned, the Duce says that he has advised Schuschnigg to accept representation of the Nationalist parties. He emphasizes, however, that there must be a difference in system between Austria and Germany, since it would be impossible in Austria to adopt an anti-Catholic or too markedly anti-Semitic attitude.'[2]

On 4 May Nahum Goldmann was received by Ciano who assured him that Italy was not hostile to Zionism and that the anti-Jewish polemics in certain papers in no way reflected the official Fascist attitude.[3] On 21 May similar assurances were given by the Under-Secretary of the Interior, Guido Buffarini Guidi, in a conversation with Federico Jarach (who had succeeded the late Felice Ravenna as President of the Union of Italian-Jewish Communities), Guido Zevi (Vice-President of the Union), and Dante Lattes. The recent press attacks, Buffarini insisted, were of no importance whatsoever; neither was the book by Orano, a man 'devoid of authority'.[4]

On 3 June Ciano, in the course of a 'long and cordial talk' with the Chief Rabbi of Rome (David Prato), again affirmed that there was no change in the official attitude to the Jews, the manifestations of journalistic anti-Semitism notwithstanding; he added that 'his best friends were Jews' and that he had no objection to the continuance of Zionist activities in Italy. A day later, however, Giorgio Pini told Jarach that the anti-Jewish campaign was 'desired and directed by the Head of the Government in person'; and on 7 June this piece of confidential information was duly passed on to the Zionist Executive by the co-editor of *Israel*, Dr. Umberto Nahon.[5]

Less than three weeks after Pini's alarming revelation (and

---

[1] See above, p. 35, n. 5.

[2] *L'Europa verso la catastrofe*, i. 192.

[3] Nahon, 'Rapporto confidenziale all'Esecutivo Sionistico', *Scritti in memoria di Leone Carpi*, pp. 264–5; see also 'Il Ministro Ciano riceve il Dr. Goldmann', *Israel*, 6 May 1937 and De Felice, *Storia degli ebrei italiani*, pp. 184–5. Dr Goldmann informs the writer (8 Nov. 1973) that he has nothing to add to Nahon's account.

[4] Nahon, 'Rapporto confidenziale all'Esecutivo Sionistico', pp. 272–3.

[5] Ibid., pp. 273–5; cf. also 'Il Ministro Ciano riceve Rabbi Prato', *Israel*, 4–11 June 1937.

only a day or two after the appearance of his above-quoted article in defence of racial anti-Semitism), the Duce once more judged it expedient to reassure the Jews: speaking to Generoso Pope, a prominent Italo-American journalist, he declared that he would never make distinctions of race or religion in Italy; the Jews would 'be treated like all other Italians as long as they respect the laws'.[1] On 25 June Ciano made a similar statement to William Phillips, the American Ambassador in Rome.[2]

Not content with reassuring the Jews and their foreign friends, Mussolini also reassured those of his collaborators who objected to the adoption of racial measures on political or economic grounds. When Felice Guarneri, his Minister of Trade and Currency, warned him of the damaging repercussions which an anti-Jewish policy was likely to have in the economic and financial sphere, he replied that there was no need to worry since he had no intention whatever of importing Hitler's racial theories into Italy.[3]

Moreover, in accordance with his usual tactics, the Duce allowed his underlings considerable latitude in the treatment of the racial question; while Farinacci, Preziosi, and Interlandi were calling for drastic steps against the Jews, other Fascist publicists—including Rino Alessi (editor of *Il Piccolo*), Nicolò Castellino (President of the Federation of Newspaper Editors), and Ezio Garibaldi—continued to deny the existence of a Jewish problem in Italy.[4] Even some of the Fascist Jew-baiters—such as Preziosi's associate, Julius Evola—were openly critical of Hitler's racial theories, describing them as unscientific and deploring their anti-Italian implications.[5]

Whatever Mussolini's motives for playing this double game, the effect was to sow confusion among friends and foes alike. On

---

[1] 'Generoso Pope returns', *New York Times* (25 June 1937), 10.

[2] W. Phillips, *Ventures in Diplomacy*, London, 155, p. 120; Phillips to Hull, 29 July 1938 (*FRUS 1938*, ii. 587).

[3] F. Guarneri, *Battaglie economiche*, ii, Milan, 1953, p. 372.

[4] De Felice, *Storia degli ebrei italiani*, pp. 257–8.

[5] J. Evola, 'Italia e Germania: che cosa ci divide, che cosa ci unisce', *La Vita Italiana*, xlix, (15 May 1937), 563–4. Evola had been in touch with Alfred Rosenberg long before Hitler's rise to power (Gravelli to Mussolini, 30 Oct. 1930, IC/*Segreteria particolare del Duce*/Job 287/87723); but while applauding Hitler's persecution of the Jews, he was openly critical of his racial theories. On Evola's 'Roman racialism', see Evola, *Il fascismo*, pp. 95–9; id., *Il cammino del Cinabro*, 2nd edn., Milan, 1972, pp. 147–58. For German opposition to Evola's racial theories, see below, Ch. IX.

11 May 1937 the British Embassy in Rome informed the Foreign Office that there was no need to worry about the anti-Jewish polemics in the Italian press: 'You will see that there are straws in the wind, but in Italy the Jewish community have not, we think, much to fear. We do not believe that Mussolini is the type of man to indulge in a Jew hunt, even to please the Germans ... The Jews in Tripoli have obviously had rather a bad spin, but even so we do not think that the Jewish communities are likely to be seriously oppressed.'[1] No less ill informed was the Rome correspondent of Hitler's paper, Dr. Philipp Hildebrandt, who affirmed as late as 31 August that the Duce's approach to the Jewish question was 'almost diametrically opposed' to the Führer's: while Nazism combated the Jews on racial grounds, Fascism not only rejected the German racial theories but called for the complete assimilation of Italian Jewry, reproaching the Zionists with their separatism and opposition to intermarriage.[2] As we have seen, Mussolini had decided as long ago as 31 May (if not earlier) to place the Jewish problem 'squarely on the racial plane'; it is evident from the above article that three months later the Germans were still unaware of this decision, despite the increasingly violent manifestations of racial anti-Semitism in the columns of *Il Tevere, Il Quadrivio,* and *La Vita Italiana.*[3]

During his official visit to Germany (25–9 September 1937) Mussolini told a German acquaintance (a diplomat he had been in touch with both before and after 1933) that Hitler's persecution of the Jews and the Churches was a source of embarrassment to him, adding that he would have preferred to deal with a less extremist German regime.[4] On 28 September he made the same point (though in more guarded terms) in the course of a lengthy conversation with the Head of Protocol, Vicco von Bülow-Schwante, declaring that the Fascist brand of racialism had nothing whatever to do with anti-Semitism: 'Mussolini inquired in detail about the development of the Jewish question prior to

[1] See above, p. 123 n. 1 (Embassy's comment on McClure's memorandum).
[2] P. Hildebrandt, 'Die Juden im modernen Italien', *V.B.,* 31 Aug. 1937.
[3] Both Preziosi and Interlandi violently attacked Orano's 'defensive' anti-Semitism (Arthos, 'Fra coloro che son sospesi. Gli Ebrei in Italia e il vero problema ebraico'. *La Vita Italiana,* xlix, June 1937, 659–68; G. Preziosi, 'I veri termini della quistione ebraica', *La Vita Italiana,* l, July 1937, 97–8; Interlandi, *Contra Judaeos,* pp. 75–9).
[4] Hoepke, *Die deutsche Rechte und der italienische Faschismus,* p. 259.

and after the seizure of power and about its present status. He said that with 70,000 [*sic*] Jews in Italy this question constituted no problem for him. But the racial question of white and black was now coming into the foreground for him. I gave him a detailed account of the Jewish question. Concluding this topic, he told me that after long surveillance of the mail in Africa he had fortunately discovered only three cases in which Italian women had forgotten themselves. He had them beaten up as a deterrent example and then sent them to a concentration camp for five years.'[1]

Only a few hours after the above conversation, however, Mussolini told a huge German crowd on the Maifeld that Nazism and Fascism had the same enemies (presumably including 'world Jewry', if not the 'Jewish Italians'), that he was determined to march with Hitler 'to the end', and that henceforth one hundred and fifteen million souls—seventy million Germans and forty-five million Italians—would be 'indissolubly united'.[2] In the words of an acute observer, 'he was manifestly intoxicated by the spectacle of so much power and fascinated by the man who was plainly resolved to wield it. Here was an ally whom it would be profitable to join and whom it would be dangerous to cross.'[3] From that moment Mussolini fell under the influence of his erstwhile disciple. He returned to Rome determined to 'prussianize' the Italians and to redeem Italy's reputation as a faithless nation.[4]

The seed sown on the Maifeld was not long in ripening. When Hitler's Ambassador in London, Joachim von Ribbentrop, arrived in Rome for the signing of the Anti-Comintern Pact on 6 November the Duce took the opportunity of assuring him (without the slightest provocation from the German side) that he was no longer worried about the alleged power of the Jews and their decadent Western backers: 'When Freemasonry was suppressed violent reactions were threatened. But none were forthcoming; just as they are not forthcoming now when we are conducting a very determined and increasingly intense anti-Semitic campaign directed by the Hon. Farinacci, a man of some

[1] Minute by Bülow-Schwante, 2 Oct. 1937 (ADAP, Serie D i, 4).
[2] *O.O.* xxviii. 251–3.
[3] Kirkpatrick, op. cit., p. 335.
[4] Ciano, *1937–1938 Diario*, pp. 23, 46, 52, 211; Anfuso, p. 114; E. Faldella, *L'Italia e la seconda guerra mondiale*, 2nd edn., Bologna, 1960, pp. 21, 22, 42.

popularity in Italy, who already has two organs of the press in Rome—the *Tevere* and the *Quadrivio*—and a large number of followers particularly in the university world.'[1]

On 3 December Ciano wrote in his diary: 'The Jews are flooding me with insulting anonymous letters, accusing me of having promised Hitler to persecute them. It is not true. The Germans have never mentioned this subject to us. Nor do I believe that we ought to unleash an anti-Semitic campaign in Italy. The problem does not exist here. There are not many Jews and, with some exceptions, there is no harm in them. And then the Jews should never be persecuted as such. That produces solidarity among Jews all over the world. There are so many other pretexts for attacking them. But, I repeat, the problem does not exist here. And perhaps in small doses Jews are necessary to society, just as leaven is necessary to bread.'[2] From the evidence cited above we may deduce without a shadow of doubt that this time Ciano was not lying.

On 29 December Ciano reaffirmed his opposition to the adoption of anti-Jewish measures in a talk with the dean of Italian Jew-baiters: 'Conversation with Preziosi (Giovanni). He wanted my support in co-ordinating the anti-Semitic campaign, but I refused. I have no love for the Jews, but I can see no case for action of this kind in Italy. At least not for the present.'[3]

In January 1938 Mussolini took a first step towards the *Gleichschaltung* of Italy with the introduction of the Prussian goose-step which was adopted by the Italian armed forces under the title of the *passo romano*. Ciano did not object. In the following month, however, he urged his master not to imitate the German method of dealing with the Jews: 'February 6 . . . A long conversation with the Duce . . . We also talked about the Jewish problem. I expressed myself in favour of a solution which will not raise a problem that fortunately does not exist here. The Duce is of the same opinion [*sic*]. He will pour water on the flames, though not enough to suppress the thing altogether.'[4] Thus up to 6 February 1938 there is no allusion to any pressure from Germany.

[1] *L'Europa verso la catastrofe*, i. 240.
[2] Ciano, *1937–1938 Diario*, 61–2.
[3] Ibid., p. 78.
[4] Ibid., p. 107.

A week later Ciano tried to allay the fears of Mussolini's one-time Egeria, Margherita Sarfatti: 'February 13. Signora Sarfatti ... talked to me about the Jewish question with obvious anxiety and was pleased to learn my moderate views on the subject. In any case she already knew about the project of making a public announcement of a reassuring kind (*in senso tranquillizzante*) in the near future.'[1]

The public announcement (*Informazione Diplomatica* No. 14, written by the Duce and published by the Foreign Ministry) was in fact made three days later but turned out to be a good deal less reassuring than Ciano's above observations would suggest. Even so, no trace of German influence is discernible in it:

The recent polemics in the press have been such as to arouse the impression in certain foreign circles that the Fascist Government is on the point of initiating an anti-Semitic policy. Responsible circles in Rome are in a position to affirm that such impressions are completely erroneous and consider that these polemics are mainly due to the fact that the currents of international anti-Fascism are regularly directed by Jewish elements. The responsible circles in Rome are of the opinion that the universal Jewish problem will be solved in one way only: by the creation in some part of the world, not in Palestine, of a Jewish State, a State in the full sense of the word, in a position to represent and safeguard the entire Jewish masses scattered in various lands, through the normal diplomatic and consular channels. Although there are Jews in Italy too, it does not necessarily follow that there exists a specific Italian Jewish problem; while in other countries there are millions of Jews, in Italy there are only between 50,000 and 60,000 out of a total population of 44 million. The Fascist Government has never thought, nor is thinking, of adopting political, economic, or moral measures against the Jews as such, except, clearly, in cases involving elements hostile to the regime. Moreover, the Fascist Government is determinedly opposed to any pressure whatsoever, direct or indirect, to promote religious apostasy or artificial assimilation. The law which regulates and controls the life of the Jewish communities had given good results and will remain unchanged.

The sting, however, was in the tail of the document:

The Fascist Government nevertheless reserves the right to keep a watch upon the activities of Jews recently arrived in our country and to see to it that the share of the Jews in the national life should not be

[1] Ibid., pp. 111–12.

disproportionate to the intrinsic merits of the individual and the numerical importance of their community.[1]

A clear position is here taken up against Zionism but not against the Jews as such. Salvatorelli put the point well when he wrote: 'The note had a certain ambiguity and a sickly sweet flavour; it was reassuring and at the same time disquieting. The final passage established a premise from which a series of consequences restrictive to the equality of rights between Jews and other citizens could be derived.'[2]

Mussolini himself, speaking to Ciano on 15 February, described the above pronouncement as a 'masterpiece of anti-Semitic propaganda'.[3] His continuing independence of German influence, however, was clearly reflected in both his advocacy of Jewish statehood (to which the Germans were violently opposed) and the absence of any reference to the Jewish race. In any case, this is not yet the style of a man who is yielding to foreign pressure but of one who can freely choose his own path.

Ironically, the publication of *Informazione Diplomatica* No. 14 coincided with a crisis in German–Italian relations which was to last until the very eve of Hitler's return visit to Italy. On 12 February the Austrian Chancellor had been enticed to Berchtesgaden where he was bullied into signing an agreement which virtually spelt the end of his country's independence. The Italians were alarmed. On 16 February (the very day on which Mussolini's anti-Semitic 'masterpiece' was published) Ciano urged Ambassador Grandi to 'give a touch of the accelerator to the London negotiations': 'Tomorrow, should the Anschluss be an accomplished fact, should Greater Germany by then press on our frontiers with the weight of its whole seventy million, it would become increasingly difficult for us to reach an agreement or even talk with the English, since it would be impossible to prevent the whole world interpreting our policy of rapprochement with London as a journey to Canossa under German pressure.' On 18 February Ciano noted in his diary that his master 'was in a mood of irritation with the Germans . . . over the manner in which they have acted in the Austrian business. In

---

[1] Cf. *Il Giornale d'Italia*, 17 Feb. 1938; on Mussolini's authorship, see Ciano *1937–1938 Diario*, p. 113.

[2] Salvatorelli and Mira, *Storia d'Italia nel periodo fascista*, p. 980.

[3] Ciano, *1937–1938 Diario*, p. 113.

the first place they ought to have given us warning—but not a word. And then, if, instead of halting at the position they have reached, they should want to go on to a real, proper Anschluss, a general situation would be created entirely different to that in which the Axis was formed, and it would become necessary to re-examine the whole position.'[1]

After the annexation of Austria (13 March) Mussolini made the best of a bad job and shouted down Italian doubts by loudly proclaiming the value and strength of the Axis: 'The two nations whose unification has been parallel in time and method, united as they are by an analogous conception of the politics of living, can march forward together to give our tormented continent a new equilibrium.'[2] Several entries in Ciano's diary, however, betoken different feelings: the event was 'far from pleasant' for Italy (13 March), the country was 'pretty severely shaken' (15 March), and a flood of letters, protesting against the Anschluss, poured into the Palazzo Venezia and the Palazzo Chigi (17 March). The anti-Jewish excesses of the Germans in Austria were an additional source of embarrassment: '21 March . . . I have telegraphed to Germany to ask for a measure of clemency for Neumann, the great Viennese Jewish scientist, who has been thrown into prison by the Germans at the age of nearly eighty. His release would be a humane gesture which will cost little and produce very favourable reactions. I hope the Nazis are not being too heavy-handed in Vienna and in Austria in general.' On the following day, however, Ciano complained that he was being asked 'from too many quarters to intervene in favour of people arrested in Vienna by the Nazis'; he would have to restrict his intervention, both 'in order not to assume a governess attitude' and 'in order not to cheapen our recommendations which would cease to have any effect if they were too widely spread'. And on 24 March he informed the American Ambassador that Italy, as a Fascist regime and an ally of Germany, could not co-operate in the proposed establishment of an international committee to facilitate the emigration of political refugees from Austria and Germany: 'While promising to take the matter up with Mussolini, Ciano nevertheless expressed the opinion very definitely that Italy could not be represented on

[1] Ibid., p. 115.
[2] Speech in the Chamber of Deputies, 16 Mar. 1938 (*O.O.* xxix. 71).

any such body and pointed out that in view of the similarity of the two regimes political refugees from Germany would be hostile to the Fascist state as well . . . Italy could not participate in any move to care for the enemies of Fascism or Nazism.'[1]

In the course of April both Mussolini and Ciano were increasingly disturbed by the outbreak of irredentist propaganda in the South Tyrol which followed the appearance of German troops on the Brenner: '3 April . . . In the South Tyrol propaganda of a kind which we cannot tolerate is continuing . . . I advised the Duce to talk to the Führer about it. The anti-German current in Italy, fomented by the Catholics, the Masons, and the Jews, is strong and becoming steadily stronger. If the Germans behave imprudently in the South Tyrol, the Axis may at any moment be blown sky-high.'[2] On 16 April a new Anglo-Italian agreement—the so-called 'Easter Pact'—was signed in Rome which covered all questions at issue between the two countries, from Gibraltar to Bab-el-Mandeb and from Palestine to Kenya; simultaneously, conversations were begun with the French. Berlin was predictably displeased. On 17 April Ciano noted in his diary that with the Germans 'one always has to be laying the ghost of Stresa. They are so afraid of it that they are tempted to see it rise everywhere.' He added that in the South Tyrol things were going from bad to worse which, on the eve of the Führer's visit was serious. On the following day he gave vent to his irritation in even stronger terms: 'These Germans are indeed going too far—and not only in Europe . . . But is it really a physical necessity for these Teutons to exasperate the whole human race until it forms a coalition against them? They must take care—that might happen once again, and this time the retribution would be much more serious than it was in 1919.' Mussolini himself was equally worked up against his partner in 'dynamics': '21 April . . . The Duce . . . intends, quite rightly, to seal the frontiers with Germany hermetically.' '23 April . . . The Duce showed me a very recent Leipzig publication, in which the

---

[1] Ciano, *1937–1938 Diario*, pp. 132, 133, 134, 137–8; Plessen to Wilhelmstrasse, 12 Mar. 1938 (ADAP, Serie D i. 476); Phillips to Hull, 24 Mar. 1938 (*FRUS 1938*, i. 741). Commenting on his conversation with the Ambassador in his diary, Ciano wrote: 'Phillips was surprised at my reply. He sees the proposal in a humanitarian light, I only in a political. The abyss of incomprehension between us and the Americans is growing steadily deeper' (ibid., p. 139).

[2] Ciano, *1937–1938 Diario*, p. 150; cf. also Magistrati, *L'Italia a Berlino*, pp. 162–7.

question of the South Tyrol is agitated again and offensive language is used about the Italian mountain population. He was indignant. "These Germans", he said, "will compel me to swallow the bitterest pill of my life. I mean the French pill".'[1]

A few hours after the above outburst Mussolini received a prominent Jew—Leslie Hore-Belisha, the British Secretary of State for War. Nine months earlier (22 July 1937) he had urged Hore-Belisha through Grandi to work for an Anglo-Italian *détente* in the Mediterranean, proposing an agreement between the British and Italian General Staffs which would provide Italy with a 'line of retreat from the "Germanic menace" ' and pave the way for a 're-establishment of the Stresa front'. This time he was more prudent, confining himself to a discussion of military matters and an emphatic assurance that he would carry out the Easter Pact 'in letter and in spirit'. After the interview, however, Hore-Belisha had a chance of discussing the 'German menace' with Ciano: 'I asked him whether, and if so when, he thought the Germans would try to take Trieste. He answered that Trieste was an Italian city and not a discussable question. I observed that the Germans did not always pause to discuss. He said he was more afraid of the Upper Adige where the population was German. He was obviously apprehensive of the German intentions.' Other Italians told the British Minister that 'the prospective visit of Hitler was most unpopular, and that there was even a fear of hissing and hostile demonstrations'. Even so, the preparations for the Hitler visit were 'on a grand scale' and the principal streets in Rome and Naples were 'all studded with pillars and posts, adorned with swastikas'.[2]

On the following day the Duce informed his son-in-law that he had clarified his ideas on the South Tyrol question: 'If the Germans behave well and are obedient Italian subjects, I shall be able to encourage their culture and their language. If, on the other hand, they hope to move the frontier post one single yard, they must learn that it cannot be done without the most bitter war, in which I shall combine the whole world into a coalition against Germanism. And we shall crush Germany for at least

---

[1] Ciano, *1937–1938 Diario*, pp. 158–60, 162–3. On the Easter Pact, see Salvatorelli and Mira, op. cit., pp. 974–5; Kirkpatrick, pp. 342–3.

[2] See R.J. Minney, *The Private Papers of Hore-Belisha*, London, 1960, pp. 101–3, 107–19; cf. also Ciano *1937–1938 Diario*, pp. 157, 163–4.

two centuries.'[1] Thus, nine days before Hitler's arrival in Rome, Mussolini was still talking like the Germanophobe he had been twenty years earlier.

But times had changed. As Ciano had pointed out to the Yugoslav Minister on the very day of the Anschluss, German friendship was by now a 'fatality' for Rome—'oppressive perhaps, but very real'.[2] Whatever Mussolini's misgivings about the German brand of Fascism, he could not realize his Mediterranean ambitions except in association with Hitler; nor could he risk being isolated between the 'dynamic' Reich and the 'static' democracies. Hence, in the words of one of his henchmen, his occasional anti-German outbursts were no more than 'ineffectual babblings, destined to reach the ears of none outside the circle of his immediate colleagues'.[3]

Being resolved to go on with the Axis alliance, the Duce could not permit any abatement of the anti-Jewish campaign on the eve of the Führer's visit. But being equally resolved not to make irreversible decisions in advance of events, he was most anxious to put off the final rupture with Jewry as long as possible. Nor was the continuing friction between Rome and Berlin the only reason why Fascist spokesmen went on reassuring the Jews and their friends until the very last moment; other reasons were the need to prepare Italian public opinion (which had so far reacted negatively to the anti-Semitic crusade), the desire to avoid a premature clash with the Holy See (the Pope having publicly denounced Hitler's racial doctrines), and the fear of damaging repercussions in all countries where the Jews had political, cultural, or economic influence.[4]

Hitler arrived in Rome on 3 May—'in the midst of general hostility', as Ciano was to note in his diary four days later. The official minutes of his talks with Mussolini are no longer available (having been so badly damaged during the war as to be completely illegible); but we can state with assurance that neither the Germans nor the Italians made any attempt to raise

[1] Ciano, *1937–1938 Diario*, p. 164.
[2] Ibid., p. 132.
[3] D. Alfieri, *Due dittatori di fronte*, Milan, 1948, p. 155.
[4] On this, see N. Laski's above-quoted memorandum of 7 April (pp. 2–4) and De Felice, *Storia degli ebrei italiani*, pp. 273–4; for the Pope's condemnation of German racialism, cf. especially his encyclical *Mit brennender Sorge* of 14 March 1937 (G. Lewy, *The Catholic Church and Nazi Germany*, New York–Toronto, 1964, pp. 156–9).

the Jewish problem on that occasion. The four participants who have written on the subject—Schmidt and Kordt, Anfuso and Ciano—are at one in affirming that no serious question was treated by Mussolini during the six days of Hitler's sojourn in Italy; and the testimonies of these four eyewitnesses are fully borne out by all the published and unpublished German records at our disposal.[1] When Ribbentrop offered Ciano a pact of military assistance, the latter responded with a counter-draft which the Secretary of State at the Wilhelmstrasse correctly described as resembling 'a peace treaty with an enemy rather than a pact of loyalty with a friend'—a plain rejection of the German proposal which infuriated Hitler's Foreign Minister.[2] And when Hitler himself broached the subject of Czechoslovakia with the Duce, the latter assured him of benevolent Italian neutrality in case of a Czech–German conflict which, however, he did not regard as probable. There was not a word about the Jews.[3]

It is evident that in May 1938 the Duce was still afraid of an armed clash with the Western Powers (for which he knew his country to be totally unprepared) and that hence, while lavishing expressions of friendship and solidarity on his German guest, he was still anxious to retain some sort of liberty of action.

It is true, however, that on the eve of Hitler's visit large numbers of German detectives and policemen were brought to Italy to protect their Führer from possible attempts at assassination and that security measures were also taken against German–Jewish refugees on that occasion. William Phillips, the American Ambassador to Rome, testifies on this matter as follows:

No chances were taken on the possibility of any hostile demonstrations. I learned that all German Jews in Rome, Naples and Florence, the

[1] Schmidt, op. cit., pp. 386–7; E. Kordt, *Wahn und Wirklichkeit*, Stuttgart, 1947, pp. 105–106; Anfuso, pp. 55–65; Ciano, *1937–1938 Diario*, pp. 167–70; 'Material zur Führerreise Rom', GFM/348/II/201482–758; ADAP, Serie D i. 893–900. For a detailed analysis of Hitler's visit, see E. Wiskemann, *The Rome–Berlin Axis*, 3rd edn., London, 1969, pp. 133–144.

[2] See E. von Weizsäcker, *Erinnerungen*, Munich, 1950, pp. 158–9; cf. also Toscano, *Le origini diplomatiche del Patto d'Acciaio*, pp. 13–19 and D.C. Watt, 'An Earlier Model for the Pact of Steel. The Draft Treaties Exchanged between Germany and Italy during Hitler's Visit to Rome in May 1938', *International Affairs*, 33 (Apr. 1957), 185–97.

[3] Minute by Weizsäcker, 12 May 1938 (ADAP, Serie D i. 899–900). Mussolini told his guest that in case of war he would remain 'under arms' (*Gewehr bei Fuss*)—a clear sign that his independence was still intact.

three cities that Hitler would visit, had been arrested and would remain confined until Hitler had left Italy. Some were in prison and some had been taken to buildings outside of the city where they were closely guarded. In Florence, five German Jewish children between fifteen and seventeen were taken from school and placed in custody. With no confidence in Italian police efficiency, the Germans assumed charge of Italian police headquarters and inaugurated their own police protection. An Italian lady told me that she had asked certain information of a street police officer in Italian uniform, and after a blank stare, had been answered in guttural German: *Sprechen Sie Deutsch?*.[1]

It would, however, be a grave error to deduce from the above that in May 1938 Italy was already 'in the hands of the Germans'. We have quite a few other examples of such measures which have become an accepted international procedure. When, at the end of 1943, the Big Three met at the British Legation in Teheran, there was a similar instance of 'foreign interference': 'The Soviet Political Police, the NKVD, insisted on searching the British Legation from top to bottom, looking behind every door and under every cushion, before Stalin appeared; about fifty armed Russian policemen, under their own General, posted themselves near all the doors and windows. The American Security men were also much in evidence. Everything, however, passed off agreeably. Stalin, arriving under heavy guard, was in the best of tempers, and the President, from his wheeled chair, beamed on us all in pleasure and good will.'[2]

This irruption of Russian and American policemen into British territory is certainly no proof that Britain had become a vassal of the two aforesaid Powers in 1943; and precisely the same conclusion must be drawn in respect of Fascist Italy in May 1938.

Moreover, the security measures adopted on the occasion of Hitler's visit were exclusively directed against foreign Jews; the Italian Jews remained unmolested. There were Jewish officers who took part in the goose-stepping parade which was held on 4 May in Hitler's honour;[3] and there were Jewish Fascists who considered it their duty to applaud the Duce's anti-Semitic ally.

[1] Op. cit., pp. 111–12. According to Walter Schellenberg, the SS officer in charge of the security measures, over six thousand suspects were arrested (*The Schellenberg Memoirs*, London, 1956, p. 53).

[2] W.S. Churchill, *Closing the Ring, The Second World War*, v, Boston, 1951, p. 384.

[3] YWS/Testimony of General Giorgio Liuzzi (8 Feb. 1960).

Barbara Allason records the case of a 'very rich and most Fascist' Jewish lady at Turin who took pride in the fact that her son had gone to Rome to pay his respects to the Führer.[1]

On 8 May—a day before Hitler's return to Germany— Roberto Farinacci was awarded the Grand Cross of the Order of the German Eagle. The award was undoubtedly meant to encourage the Jew-baiters in the Fascist Party; but it is clear from all the relevant records that the Germans attached no political importance to it.[2]

At the beginning of June Farinacci was appointed Minister of State—a sure sign that relations between the Duce and his Jewish subjects were about to take a turn for the worse. The appointment was universally (and correctly) regarded as a friendly gesture towards the Reich; but no one has ever suggested that it was made at the request of the Germans. Nor was the *ras* of Cremona entrusted with any public function beyond the congenial one of heading the Fascist delegation which was to attend the National Socialist Party rally at Nuremberg in September.

Simultaneously, Dr. Walter Gross, head of the Racial Policy Office of the National Socialist Party (*Rassenpolitisches Amt der NSDAP*), arrived in Milan for a meeting with the Prefect Antonio Le Pera, soon to become his opposite number in Italy. It is hardly surprising that this visit (which was reported in the *Popolo d'Italia* on 3 June) should have been adduced to prove 'German interference' in Italian racial policy. In reality, however, the meeting had been requested, not by the Germans, but by Mussolini who informed the German visitor through Le Pera that he wanted detailed and up-to-date information on German racial policy, with special reference to its 'qualitative' aspect (meaning the measures taken to raise the biological value of the German population). Le Pera told Gross that he would like to pay an unofficial visit to Germany in the autumn in order to make a first-hand study of German racial doctrines and techniques; he added, however, that official Italo–German co-operation in racial matters was not considered desirable, being likely to have unfavourable political repercussions. Subsequently, the projected visit to Germany had to be cancelled because the Duce had quite unexpectedly embarked on a 'far-reaching' racial

[1] *Memorie do un'antifascista*, pp. 248–9.
[2] See above, pp. 107, 114–17.

policy without waiting for the German 'experts' to enlighten Le Pera on Hitler's biological principles. There is no doubt that Gross and his collaborators were pleased to respond to Mussolini's invitation and eager to lend a hand in the preparation of the imminent racial legislation; but it would be ridiculous to deduce that German officials of the third or fourth rank could have brought pressure to bear on the Fascist dictator. And while it is probable that the Jewish issue was touched upon in the course of the talks between Gross and Le Pera, there is no mention of it in any of the relevant records.[1]

German pressure or not, in the following weeks the Duce was still at pains to reassure the Western friends of the Jews. On 15 June (exactly one month before the publication of the Italian 'Race Manifesto') Fulvio Suvich, Italian Ambassador to Washington since 1936, called on the American Under-Secretary of State to protest against the charges of racial and religious intolerance which were being levelled against Italy by certain American newspapers:

The Italian Ambassador . . . said that because of the number of Italians in the United States and the fact that there had never been any serious disagreement between Italy and this country and no historical memories of hostility in the past, it was hard for him to understand why so large a proportion of the press in the United States and so large a section of American public opinion was so bitterly hostile to the Italian Government. He said he could fully understand the reasons for the hostility to Germany because of their persecution of the Jews, of the members of other religious faiths and the minorities in general, but he explained that the situation in Italy was quite different. He said no step had ever been taken in Italy against the Jews because the Jewish problem in Italy did not exist. He said there were not more than forty thousand Jews in Italy at the outside and of this number many . . . today were prominent citizens, highly regarded and occupying important positions under the state. He said before he himself entered public life he had been closely associated in Trieste with prominent Jews and that he had never seen any prejudice of any kind on the part of the Italians against the Jews as such. He said he could not, therefore, comprehend, in view of the attitude taken by the Italian Government toward the Catholic Church and toward the Jews in Italy why there

[1] Undated memorandum by Dr. Rudolf Frercks, member of the Rassenpolitisches Amt and editor of the *Rassenpolitische Auslandskorrespondenz* (see above, pp. 114–17). Gross was accompanied by two of his collaborators, Heissmeyer and Gütt.

should be an attempt on the part of so great a proportion of the press here to make out that the Italian Government was persecuting religious or racial minorities in that country.

Replying to Suvich's remonstrances, the American Under-Secretary of State pointed out that 'the very close relationship which existed between Italy and Germany and the fact that governmental systems not unlike in structure, however unlike they might be in methods or in details, existed in the two countries, created very naturally the popular impression that the domestic policies pursued in Germany with regard to racial minorities were favourably regarded or supported by the Italian Government'.[1]

While the Germanophobe Suvich was thus trying to dissociate Fascism from National Socialism, the Duce decided to take the first of a series of measures designed to align his country with Germany's anti-Jewish policy. In the second half of June he decreed a ban on the participation of Italian Jews in international congresses; Jewish scholars who had been chosen to represent Italy at such congresses were ordered to stay at home. For the moment, however, the ban was strictly unofficial; the Germans were no more aware of it than the Italian public.[2] It is worthy of note in this connection that on 19 June Ribbentrop renewed his offer of a military pact with Italy and that Mussolini, though in favour, once more failed to respond, telling Ciano on 27 June that he needed time to prepare public opinion.[3]

In the following month, however, the mounting tension between Italy and the Western Powers induced the Fascist dictator to throw caution to the wind—at any rate as far as the Jewish issue was concerned. On 4 July he delivered a violently anti-Western speech at Aprilia. A day later his son-in-law found him 'more and more decidedly and openly anti-French'; and on 10 June he explained to Ciano that the projected anti-Jewish measures would serve to widen the gulf between Italy and the democracies and to toughen the soft-hearted Italians. In the words of the latter:

The position with London is getting more and more complicated.

[1] Memorandum by Sumner Welles, 15 June 1938 (*FRUS 1938*, ii. 582–3).
[2] Cf. De Felice, *Storia degli ebrei italiani*, pp. 274–5; there is no reference to this ban in any of the German records at our disposal (see below, pp. 161–79).
[3] Ciano, *1937–1938 Diario*, p. 195; cf. also Toscano, op. cit., pp. 24–30.

This—in the Duce's opinion—serves to divert towards the Axis the sympathies of the enervated and defeatist bourgeois class which, after the pact of 16 April, hoped for peace through an understanding with the Western democracies. Mussolini is very angry with this section of the bourgeoisie, always ready to let its trousers down. He talks of a third wave, to be set in motion in October, with the support above all of the masses, workers and peasants . . . A first hint of the turn of the screw will be given by a bonfire of Jewish, pro-Masonic and pro-French literature. Jewish writers and journalists will be banned from all activity . . . Henceforth the revolution must impinge upon the habits of the Italians. They must learn to be less 'sympathetic' in order to become hard, relentless, and hateful—in fact, masters.[1]

Events now began to move fast. On 14 July Ciano wrote in his diary: 'The Duce announced to me that the *Giornale d'Italia* is to publish a "statement" on the racial question. It purports to be written by a group of scholars under the aegis of the Ministry of Popular Culture. But he tells me that in fact he drafted almost the whole thing himself.' And on 15 July: 'On the racial question the Duce told me that he is going to get the Secretary of the Party to summon the "scholars" and announce to them the official attitude of the regime towards the problem. An attitude which signifies, not persecution, but discrimination.'[2] Thus, twenty months after the commencement of the third anti-Jewish campaign of the Fascist press, Mussolini at last threw off the mask and openly took up a position against the Italian Jews.

The statement, called the 'Manifesto of the Race', consisted of ten 'scientific' propositions (promptly christened by the man in the street 'the Ten Commandments of the Axis'), each of which was accompanied by a brief commentary and which may be summarized as follows: (1) different human races exist; (2) a difference exists between the great and the lesser races; (3) the concept of race is a purely biological one; (4) the population of Italy is of Aryan origin and its civilization is Aryan; (5) there has been no change in the racial composition of the Italian people in the past thousand years (i.e. since the Lombard invasions); (6) a pure 'Italian race' exists; (7) it is time for the

[1] *O.O.* xxix. 120–1; Ciano, *1937–1938 Diario*, p. 207.
[2] Ciano, *1937–1938 Diario*, pp. 209–10; cf. also Pini, *Filo diretto*, p. 158. Four and a half years later Mussolini was to deny his authorship of the 'Race Manifesto', describing it as a piece of pseudo-scientific rubbish, written by 'several lecturers and journalists' (B. Spampanato, *Contromemoriale*, ii, Rome, 1951, pp. 131–2).

Italians frankly to proclaim themselves racialists and to give their racialism an Aryan-Nordic direction; (8) a clear distinction must be made between the European (Western) Mediterranean races on the one hand and Orientals and Africans on the other; (9) Jews do not belong to the Italian race and are therefore unassimilable; (10) the purely European physical and psychological characteristics of the Italian race must not be altered in any way; hence, while intermarriage with foreigners of Aryan blood is admissible in principle, intermarriage with non-Aryans is not.[1]

Despite the ritual assertion that the Fascist concept of race was 'essentially Italian' in character and that there was no intention of 'introducing the German racial theories into Italy', no one had any doubts about the German origin of Mussolini's racialist decalogue. The ordinary people in Italy, according to an acute Western observer, received it with 'resentful shame', chiefly owing to the fact that their leader had 'stooped to copy the example of German neo-barbarism'.[2] Pope Pius XI publicly branded it as a 'disgraceful imitation' of Hitler's Nordic mythology, adding that it ran directly counter to the noblest traditions of that Roman Empire which the Fascists had hitherto professed themselves so anxious to restore.[3] The King of Italy voiced similar views in private, expressing astonishment at the fact that his Prime Minister should have seen fit 'to import these racial fashions from Berlin into Italy'.[4] The Germans, for their part, hailed the "Manifesto of the Race" as a manifestation of Axis solidarity and a triumph of National Socialist *Weltanschauung*; Hitler's own paper described it as a 'revolutionary act of universal significance', calculated to pave the way for the 'most profound community of ideas' which had ever existed between two peoples: in giving his racial gospel an Aryan-

---

[1] For the full text of the document, see De Felice, *Storia degli ebrei italiani*, pp. 541–2.

[2] D.A. Binchy, *Church and State in Fascist Italy*, Oxford, 1941 and 1970, p. 614.

[3] Address to the students of the College of Propaganda, 28 July 1938 (*Civiltà Cattolica*, 29 July 1938, 373).

[4] D'Aroma, *Vent'anni insieme*, p. 275: 'It passes my comprehension how a great man like him can import these racial fashions from Berlin into Italy. Yet he must understand that if he falls into the German rut, he will range against himself the Church, the bourgeoisie, and the army high command.'

Nordic direction, the Duce had dealt the death-blow to the anti-German concept of 'Latinity'.[1]

Mussolini himself left no doubt that his racial policy aimed above all at strengthening his ties with Berlin and poisoning relations with the 'demoplutocracies'. In a talk with Ciano on 17 July he declared that 'the revolution in manners, particularly in relation to racial problems' was meant to increase the hatred of Western democrats for Italy. And a day later he told the Hungarian statesmen Imrédy and Kánya that a 'total solidarity of regime' existed between Italy and Germany, that he might sign a military pact with the Germans 'very shortly', and that he would side with Hitler in the event of a general war.[2]

But while anxious to demonstrate his unconditional loyalty to the Axis, Mussolini was equally anxious to demonstrate the 'originality' of his racial theories. All the resources of Fascist propaganda were deployed in a vain attempt to convince the Italians that Fascism had been a 'racialist' movement from its very inception. On 24 July the American Ambassador wrote in a dispatch to the State Department: 'For several days the Italian newspapers have printed editorials on the racial question endeavoring to prove that the racial principle has always been a basic doctrine of the Fascist regime and demonstrating that the strength of a nation is lost when its racial purity is weakened through the introduction of other racial strains.'[3] The Duce himself reacted to the charge of imitating Hitler in language whose very violence was the clearest evidence of his inability to refute it. Addressing a group of Fascist federal secretaries at Forlì on 30 July (two days after the Pope's above-quoted attack), he declared that it was 'simply absurd to say that Fascism had imitated anyone or anything'. He spoke even more plainly at Trieste on 18 September, denouncing as 'poor half-wits' (*poveri deficenti*) all those who, like the Pope and the King, had accused him of following the German lead.[4]

The Germans, visibly embarrassed by this controversy, hastened to come to Mussolini's aid. Himmler's organ, *Das Schwarze Korps*, magnanimously assured the Italians that their

---

[1] 'Ein revolutionärer Akt von weltgeschichtlicher Bedeutung. Italien bekennt sich zum Rassengedanken', *V.B.*, 15 July 1938.

[2] Ciano, *1937–1938 Diario*, p. 211; *L'Europa verso la catastrofe*, i. 378–9.

[3] Phillips to Hull, 24 July 1938 (*FRUS 1938*, ii. 584).

[4] *O.O.* xxix. 126, 146.

leader's racial 'philosophy' was indeed an original Italian creation, a logical development of Fascist doctrine, and that the Jewish problem in Italy was a strictly domestic Italian affair in which Germans had no business to interfere.[1] A few of the Führer's associates, however, were tactless enough to remind the Duce in public or in private that he had in fact copied the German racial theories, his angry denials notwithstanding. One of these was Julius Streicher who, in the columns of the *Stürmer*, recalled Mussolini's past utterances against racialism and anti-Semitism, adding that until recently Fascism had preferred to march 'with rather than against the Jews'. Another was Hermann Esser, one of Hitler's earliest followers, who openly boasted of the fact that Italy was following the German example. A third was Joachim von Ribbentrop, Hitler's Foreign Minister, who told the Ambassador, Attolico, on 10 January 1940 that 'Italian anti-Semitism, after all, was merely a consequence of National Socialist anti-Semitism'.[2] The Duce himself was to admit the truth of these charges a few years later, confessing to one of his loyal followers that the 'Manifesto of the Race' was indeed a rehash of German racial 'science'—'a ponderous German treatise translated into bad Italian'.[3]

But if Italian racialism was in fact a consequence of the Axis alliance and an imitation of the German model, does it necessarily follow that it was adopted at the request of the Germans? Before answering this question, we shall do well to analyse the Nazi method of interference in the domestic affairs of other European countries. Thanks to a series of studies completed in recent years on the German responsibility for the persecution of the Jews in these countries we are now in a position to throw light on this problem.[4]

[1] 'Italiens Bekenntnis zur Rasse', *Das Schwarze Korps*, 28 July 1938; 'Italien und der Papst. Rassismus in Italien', *Das Schwarze Korps*, 11 Aug. 1938. See also A. Dresler, 'Die Rassenfrage in Italien', *Der Weltkampf*, 15 (Sept. 1938), 395–401; 'Die Fortführung der Rassenfrage in Italien', *ibid.* (Oct. 1938), 439–46; 'Der neue Stand der Judenfrage in Italien', *ibid.*, (Nov. 1938), 484–7.

[2] J. Streicher, 'Kriegserklärung des Faschismus. Der Schicksalsweg des italienischen Volkes', *Der Stürmer*, No. 33, Aug. 1938; H. Esser, *Die jüdische Weltpest*, rev. edn., Munich, 1939, p. 226; *DGFP*, Serie D viii. 638.

[3] Spampanato, op. cit., pp. 131–2.

[4] See e.g., H. Hecker (ed.), *Praktische Fragen des Entschädigungsrechts–Judenverfolgungen im Ausland*, Hamburg, 1958; M. Münz, *Die Verantwortlichkeit für die Judenverfolgungen im Ausland während der nationalsozialistischen Herrschaft*, Frankfurt/Main, 1958; *Gutachten des Instituts für Zeitgeschichte*, i–ii, Stuttgart, 1958 and 1966; United Restitution Organization, *Dokumente über Methoden der Judenverfolgung im Ausland*, Frankfurt/Main, 1959.

Down to the autumn of 1938 Hitler and his henchmen proclaimed the principle of non-interference in the internal affairs of other countries, confining themselves to indirect interference through the German minorities abroad and through the local pro-German opposition groups, such as Codreanu's Iron Guard in Romania, Szálasi's Arrow Cross movement in Hungary, Mussert's National Socialist Party in Holland, and Mosley's Union of Fascists in Britain. This method was evidently not applicable to the Italian dictatorship where no open opposition was possible. Even the very few Jew-baiters in the Fascist Party—Farinacci, Preziosi, and Interlandi—could not conduct campaigns in favour of the Germans or against the Jews without the Duce's prior sanction. If the Germans exercised influence on the evolution of Fascist racial policy, this was mainly due to the fact that Mussolini himself requested their advice and guidance and that he encouraged his underlings to establish close contacts with their opposite numbers in the Third Reich.[1]

It was only after their triumph at Munich (29–30 September 1938) that the Germans felt themselves sufficiently strong to go over to a policy of direct interference. At a secret conference on 12 November Hitler's heir presumptive, the then Field-Marshal Göring, delivered himself of the following statement: 'If the Third Reich should be involved in an international conflict in the foreseeable future, it is clear that we too in Germany will first and foremost settle accounts with the Jews on the largest possible scale. Moreover, the Führer will finally go over to direct action in foreign policy as well, appealing to those countries which have already raised the Jewish question.'[2] From these words, spoken before high officials of the National Socialist regime, it emerges unambiguously that down to November 1938 Hitler had *not* passed to direct action as referred to above; and the declarations of Hitler's 'Crown Prince' are corroborated by all the published and unpublished evidence at our disposal, including the records of the Reich Foreign Ministry and the memoirs of German and Italian diplomats. On 24 November (twelve days after Göring's

---

[1] On National Socialist activities abroad, see H.-A. Jacobsen, *Nationalsozialistische Aussenpolitik 1933–1938*, Frankfurt/Main–Berlin, 1968, esp. pp. 495–597; on contacts between Fascist and National Socialist Party leaders, cf. Magistrati, *L'Italia a Berlino*, pp. 180–1.

[2] *ND*/1816-PS (*IMT* xxviii. 538–9).

above statement) Hitler admitted to the South African Minister of Defence, Oswald Pirow, that he was 'exporting anti-Semitism'; on 16 January 1939 he told Count Csáky, the Hungarian Minister of Foreign Affairs, that he would support any country which initiated the struggle against Jewry; and on 21 January he expressed himself in the same sense to the Czech Foreign Minister, Chvalkovsky, adding that he could not guarantee the frontiers of any State which refused to eliminate the Jews.[1] On 30 January he declared in a speech to the Reichstag that in the event of another war he would annihilate European Jewry (presumably including Italian Jewry): 'If the international Jewish financiers in and outside Europe should succeed in plunging the nations once more into a world war, then the result will not be the Bolshevization of the earth, and thus the victory of Jewry, but the annihilation of the Jewish race in Europe!'[2] Finally, on 2 February the German Minister in Bucharest informed the Romanian Foreign Minister, Gafencu, that the adoption of anti-Jewish measures in Romania would have a beneficial effect on the relations between the two countries.[3] We may note that at this stage German pressure takes the form of 'friendly suggestions' and not of threats (except in the case of Czechoslovakia which had been reduced to vassalage by January 1939). In effect the Romanian Government enacted the first anti-Jewish law only on 9 July 1940, despite growing German interference and the strong local anti-Semitism dating back to a time prior to the emergence of Hitlerism in Germany.[4] The question therefore arises: if the anti-Semitic Romanians could wait until July 1940, how can it possibly be argued that the Italians, lacking any domestic Jewish problem, could have been requested (let alone forced) to adopt the first anti-Jewish law by 3 August 1938—almost half a year before Hitler had raised the issue even with small and weak States much more dependent on

[1] For Hitler–Pirow conversation see *ADAP*, Serie D iv. 295; for Hitler–Csáky meeting, ibid. v. 305; for Hitler–Chvalkovsky meeting, ibid. iv. 170 and *Le Livre jaune français*, Paris, 1939, p. 61. Cf. also H. Bodensieck, 'Prag und die jüdische Frage nach München', *VJZG* 9 (July 1961), 249–61.

[2] M. Domarus, *Hitler. Reden und Proklamationen*, ii: *1939–1945*, Würzburg, 1963, p. 1058; Hitler made similar statements on 30 Jan. 1941 and on 30 Jan. 1942 (ibid., pp. 1663, 1828–9).

[3] *ADAP*, Serie D v. 316–17.

[4] Law for the exclusion of Jews from public employ (M. Broszat, 'Das Dritte Reich und die rumänische Judenpolitik', *Gutachten des Instituts für Zeitgeschichte*, i. 115).

him than Mussolini's 'Roman Empire'? On this subject it is well to remember that the Führer—in contrast to many of his lieutenants—always overestimated Fascist Italy, considering her a Great Power in whose internal affairs it was not permissible to interfere as it was in those of the smaller countries.[1] The entire ample documentation in this field, in fact, contains not the least hint of German interference in Italy's domestic Jewish question during the period under review; this applies most particularly to the memoirs of the Italian diplomats in Berlin and of the German diplomats in Rome who invariably speak of 'imitation', never of 'pressure' or 'interference'. Count Massimo Magistrati, Ciano's brother-in-law and Counsellor of the Italian Embassy in Berlin from 1936 to 1940, explicitly affirms that Mussolini's decision to persecute the Jews was 'absolutely unnecessary' and solely due to his itch to emulate Hitler and his exaggerated sense of ideological solidarity with the Reich.[2] Ulrich von Hassell, German Ambassador in Rome until February 1938, tells us that after the Anschluss Mussolini no longer saw any possibility of checking German expansion with the aid of the Western Powers; unable to oppose his erstwhile pupil, he decided to follow him, even to the extent of aping the racial folly he had previously condemned.[3] And the accuracy of this interpretation seems to be confirmed by Mussolini's repeated statements to the effect that it was better to accept than to oppose the inevitable.[4] Finally, General Enno von Rintelen, German military attaché in Rome from 1936 to 1939 and head of the German military mission in Italy from 1940 to 1943, expresses surprise at the fact that so proud a dictator as the Duce should have stooped to copy German racial doctrines which he knew to be alien and repugnant to his people.[5]

As we have seen, Mussolini had declined the offer of a military pact with Berlin in May and June 1938. The offer was renewed at Munich on 30 September and again in Rome on 28 October, but the Duce persisted in his refusal. On 30 September Ciano wrote in his diary: 'Ribbentrop has handed me a project for a

---

[1] According to Goebbels, Hitler realized only after the débâcle of 25 July 1943, 'that Italy never was a Power, is no 'Power today and will not be Power in the future' (*Tagebücher*, p. 435).
[2] Magistrati, *L'Italia a Berlino*, p. 196.
[3] U. von Hassell, *Vom anderen Deutschland*, Zürich, 1946, p. 27.
[4] *O.O.* xxix. 70; Anfuso, pp. 68, 69.
[5] E. von Rintelen, *Mussolini als Bundesgenosse*, Tübingen–Stuttgart, 1951, p. 46.

tripartite alliance between Italy, Germany, and Japan ... No doubt we will study it quite calmly and, perhaps, put it aside for some time.' And on 28 October: 'Ribbentrop has in fact come about the triple military alliance ... I gave him to understand that we still have other problems to solve and perhaps other conceptions of the future organization of international life ... Why open the door to rumour by a pact the only consequence of which would be to draw upon us the odium of aggression?' Mussolini agreed with Ciano 'upon the necessity for postponing to a future date the commitment of an alliance which would be most unpopular in Italy, not least on account of the resentment against Germany felt by the great Catholic masses'. He repeated his objections on 13 November, declaring that, if the Catholics in Germany should 'meet with the same fate as the Jews, the Axis might fail to stand the strain'.[1] In other words, the Fascist dictator embarked on his anti-Jewish policy at the very moment when he rejected the German proposal for closer ties between Rome and Berlin.

We are in possession of a highly revealing German document, a memorandum on Fascist policy towards the Jews, written in May 1943 by Sturmbannführer (SS Major) Dr. Carltheo Zeitschel, who served as adviser on Jewish affairs to the German Embassy in Paris during World War II. This document clearly reflects the hesitation of the Germans to meddle with the Jewish problem in Italy not only in 1938 (when Mussolini still enjoyed a semblance of independence) but as late as 1943 (when he had been reduced to satellite status):

Paris, May 24, 1943 ... During the period of my activity in Tunis, thanks to the courtesy of *Obersturmbannführer* (SS Lieutenant-Colonel) Rauff, I regularly received the reports of the Chief of Police and of the SD (the SS Security Service). I know, therefore, that the fact which has caused most anxiety here in France over the Jewish question is the mass flight of the more influential Jews into the Italian zone where they have found complete safety. As in recent weeks the German papers, most particularly the *V.B. (Völkischer Beobachter)* have been conducting an intense anti-Semitic propaganda campaign, I took advantage of the opportunity during my stay in Rome to discuss this

---

[1] Ciano, *1937–1938 Diario*, pp. 254, 279, 291–2; *L'Europa verso la catastrofe*, i. 414–16; cf. also Toscano, pp. 46–63.

problem with all the interested services. The following are the conclusions I have been able to draw:

1) *The German Embassy* in Rome has for years had the strictest orders from Berlin not to do anything which could in any way disturb the friendly relations between Italy and Germany. It seems, therefore, that it would be inconceivable for the German Embassy in Rome even to raise so delicate a question as that of the Jews in Italy. My cautious enquiries elicited replies in this sense from the political directors of the Embassy.

2) *The Italian Government* is not interested in the Jewish question because such a problem is practically non-existent in Italy. We cannot expect any assistance from this quarter.

3) *The Italian Army.* According to the information of *Obersturmbann-führer* Dollmann (Eugen Dollmann, Himmler's representative in Rome), there are still Jews and innumerable half-Jews serving with the forces as officers. In my opinion we cannot resort to the Italian Army for any action whatever against the Jews.

4) *The Fascist Party* has recently been reorganized, but the attitude of the new Party Secretary[1] and the functionaries nominated by him is not yet clear. It is known that the Fascist Party has not been very active until now, but it is probable that to demonstrate its activism it will take up the Jewish question which incidentally would be possible only if there were an urgent and precise order to this effect from the Duce in person.

5) *The conversations* with *Obersturmbannführer* Dollmann and his representative, Captain Wenner, demonstrate that the SD is encountering difficulties in handling this problem in Italy on its own initiative, since it can hardly reach the Duce himself, while the subordinate services show no special interest in the Jewish question, such as would make us hope that they might consider it favourably. In consequence Dr. Dollmann suggests that I submit a most urgent report to the Chief of the Security Police and the SD in Paris, *Standartenführer* (SS Colonel) Dr. Knochen, requesting as soon as possible a clear and urgent exposé to the *Reichsführer* of the SS (Himmler), whose visit to Rome is expected in about three weeks. Dr. Dollmann hopes that due to the exposé which the *Reichsführer* will make personally to the Duce, this question may be reconsidered with successful results.[2]

Indirect confirmation of the foregoing may be found in a statement by the Ambassador, von Mackensen (15 February 1943) to the effect that 'the driving force behind the (racial)

---

[1] Aldo Vidussoni had been replaced by Carlo Scorza on 17 April 1943.
[2] See L. Poliakov and J. Sabille, *Jews under the Italian Occupation*, Paris, 1955, pp. 191–2.

measures of the Fascist Government' was 'the well-known Italian pioneer (*Vorkämpfer*) of anti-Semitism', Giovanni Preziosi, who had just been appointed Minister of State in recognition of his services to the anti-Jewish cause. Mackensen adds that, given the Duce's unwillingness to take drastic action against the Jews, Preziosi saw no possibility of eliminating Jewish influence in Italy.[1] It is evident that in the fourth year of World War II the German Ambassador still regarded the problem of Italian Jewry as a strictly domestic issue to which he and his collaborators were extraneous.

By 1943 it was possible for Zeitschel and Dollmann to hope that Himmler might persuade the Italian dictator to take anti-Jewish measures on 'security grounds'. But what about 1938 when there was as yet no war and no formal alliance between the two Fascist Powers? The answer to this question may be found in a series of unpublished German documents on the beginnings of Italian racial policy, covering the period from 15 July to 19 October 1938. They include a detailed analysis of the 'Race Manifesto' by Johann von Plessen, Counsellor at the German Embassy in Rome (23 July 1938); a 29-page memorandum on the evolution of the racial question in Italy by Dr. Hans Mollier, the German press attaché (25 August); a report by Felix Ritter von Strautz, Secretary of Legation at the Embassy, on the anti-Jewish decree laws passed by the Council of Ministers at the beginning of September (5 September); a lengthy dispatch from the Ambassador, von Mackensen, on the anti-Jewish resolutions adopted by the Fascist Grand Council on 6 October (18 October); and an undated memorandum by Dr. Rudolf Frercks of the Rassenpolitisches Amt on his contacts with the men in charge of Fascist racial policy (10–19 October), including Le Pera, Guido Landra (the real author of the Race Manifesto), and Dino Alfieri, the Minister of Popular Culture.[2]

Plessen's dispatch of 23 July began with the statement that Mussolini's declaration of war on the Jews had come as a complete surprise to all concerned (obviously including the Germans) and that the names of the scholars who had allegedly written the 'Manifesto of the Race' were still unknown. It is evident that in 1938 the German diplomats in Rome were no

---

[1] Mackensen to Wilhemstrasse, 15 Feb. 1943 (YVS/K206729–30).
[2] 'Fascismus und Rassenfrage', GFM/2172/471261–338.

more in the Duce's confidence than their Western colleagues as far as Italian racial policy was concerned.

Plessen did not know whether Mussolini himself had taken a hand in the drafting of the racial decalogue; all he could say with assurance was that the document had been written and published on the dictator's orders and that the Party Secretary had given it his official blessing within twenty-four hours of its appearance.

In his analysis of the Manifesto, Plessen displayed an astonishing lack of critical sense and an equally astonishing ignorance of the facts. He thought there was more than a grain of truth in the contention of Mussolini's propagandists that the Italian brand of racialism was an original Fascist creation and a logical development of the Fascist creed. Fascism, he claimed, had begun to purge the administration and the economy of Jewish elements shortly after the March on Rome; the pronouncement of the anonymous 'scholars', therefore, was essentially an attempt to provide a theoretical basis for the struggle against Jewish influence which had been going on for the last sixteen years. Anti-Semitism, however, was only one aspect of Fascist racial doctrine and by no means the most important; the main aim of the new racial movement was the creation of a higher racial type, capable of running and defending an empire.

Plessen could not but admit that Mussolini's Aryan-Nordic gospel was somewhat unoriginal and that it was absurd to speak of a 'pure Italian race'. Even so, he considered the 'Race Manifesto' a genuine piece of scholarship and a serious attempt to adjust the racial idea to Italian conditions; its publication, he thought, was in a sense a 'revolutionary deed', likely to have far-reaching consequences in a country where race-consciousness had hitherto been lacking.

The 'originality' of the Manifesto, in Plessen's view, lay partly in its emphasis on the 'purely biological' character of the Fascist race concept which reflected Mussolini's desire to avoid philosophical or religious controversies. This desire was shared by certain pro-Fascist clerics (who had seized upon this proposition as evidence that Italian racialism differed profoundly from its German counterpart) but unfortunately not by the head of the Catholic Church who had publicly attacked the racialist decalogue within twenty-four hours of its publication, stigmatizing its doctrine as amounting to 'regular apostasy'.[1]

It is inconceivable that Plessen should have deliberately exaggerated the 'originality' of Mussolini's Aryan myth in a secret report to the Wilhelmstrasse. It is all the more puzzling that he should have presented Fascist racialism as a purely Italian phenomenon and a purely domestic Italian issue, ignoring the impact of the Axis alliance on the Duce's conversion to anti-Semitism, not to mention the well-known facts about his philo-Semitic and anti-racialist past. What matters in our context, however, is not the accuracy or otherwise of Plessen's analysis but the light it throws on the problem of German 'interference' in the Italian Jewish question.

Mollier, in his memorandum of 25 August 1938, approached the subject of Italian racialism from a different angle. He began by pointing out that until six weeks ago there had been no such thing as a Fascist point of view on the racial problem; there had been a very few racialists and a great many anti-racialists in the Fascist Party, with Italian public opinion overwhelmingly in favour of the latter. The Italian Government, while permitting both sides to air their views, had carefully refrained from committing itself. Then, all of a sudden, racialism had been declared to be not only a basic ingredient of Fascist doctrine but the 'foundation and corner-stone' of the Italian State. The 'Race Manifesto' of 14 July therefore marked a major turning-point in the history of Fascist theory and practice, the end of one period and the beginning of another.

What was the reason for this abrupt change of front? Mollier did not know and had no wish to indulge in idle speculation on the subject. But if the Duce's motives were still obscure, the political implications of his break with the Jews were obvious. It was a pro-German and anti-Western move, a manifestation of Axis solidarity and a slap in the face for the Western

---

[1] Plessen to Wilhelmstrasse, 23 July 1938 (GFM/2172/471263–68); for the Pope's speech of 15 July, cf. Bergen to Wilhelmstrasse, 19 July 1938 (GFM/2172/471262). On the racialist controversy between Church and State, see A. Spinosa, 'Le persecuzioni razziali in Italia II', *Il Ponte*, viii. (Aug. 1952), 1078–96; Rossi, *Il manganello e l'aspersorio*, pp. 269–90; A. Martini, *Studi sulla questione romana e la Conciliazione*, Rome, 1963, pp. 175–214; A. Pellicani, *Il Papa di tutti. La Chiesa cattolica, il fascismo e il razzismo 1929–1945*, Milan, 1964, pp. 101–15; Binchy, op. cit., pp. 605–32; G. Buffarini Guidi, *La vera verità. I documenti dell'archivio segreto del ministro degli Interni Guido Buffarini Guidi dal 1938 al 1945*, Milan, 1970, pp. 24–38.

democracies. In the past Mussolini had attached great importance to good relations with international Jewry; if he now
threw down the gauntlet to the Jews, it could mean only one
thing—he no longer saw any alternative to the present political
constellation, with the Rome–Berlin Axis on one side of the
barricade and the Western 'plutocracies' (the backers of the
Jews) on the other. The adoption of anti-Jewish measures, then,
was Mussolini's way of telling the world that he was resolved to
march with Hitler to the end, the Easter Pact and the recent
negotiations with Paris notwithstanding.

In addition to being a pledge of loyalty to the Axis (Mollier
continued), Fascist racial policy was also a highly significant
manifestation of ideological solidarity with the Third Reich,
adding a new dimension to the spiritual affinity between
Fascism and National Socialism. This triumph of 'Adolf Hitler's
basic idea' in another country was likely to benefit Germany in
a variety of ways. First and foremost, it would put an end to the
moral isolation in which the Reich had hitherto found itself as
the sole anti-Semitic Power in the Western world. Secondly, it
would give an added impetus to the anti-Jewish tendencies in
all countries where the problem of the Jews was on the agenda.
Thirdly, it would have the effect of enriching German racial
thought.

Was there any truth in Mussolini's assertion that Fascism had
been a 'racialist' movement from its very inception? The
answer to this question, Mollier thought, depended on one's
definition of the term 'racialism'. It was perfectly true that the
Fascist leader had always been preoccupied with the demographic problem; and it was equally true that he had adopted
racial measures in Africa before his *rapprochement* with Berlin.
On the other hand, he had always ignored the central theme of
German racial philosophy—the antithesis between the Aryan
and Jewish races and the need for preserving the purity of
Aryan blood. His sudden declaration of war on the Jews was
not a logical consequence of his population policy or his ban on
miscegenation, but a somewhat precipitate attempt to bring his
domestic policy into line with Italy's changed alignment in
Europe; the doctrinal basis of his anti-Jewish crusade was
German racial theory, despite his indignant denials. To be sure,
there had always been an anti-Jewish faction in the Fascist

Party. Farinacci had drawn attention to the Jewish peril long before Hitler's rise to power; Preziosi had clamoured for anti-Jewish measures ever since the March on Rome, and Interlandi had begun to propagate racialism on the German model shortly after the African war. These men, together with their associates, now constituted the 'general staff' of the racialist movement in Italy. But 'highly meritorious' though the work of these 'pioneers' undoubtedly was, their influence on Mussolini was limited and the impact of their propaganda on Italian public opinion had so far been slight. The prominence they now enjoyed was due, not to their intrinsic importance, but to a shift in the international situation and more particularly to their master's propagandist interest in demonstrating the priority of Fascist anti-Semitism over its German counterpart.

Having thus disposed of the Fascist claim to 'originality' in the field of racial policy, Mollier proceeded to trace the evolution of the racial question in Italy from 14 July to 25 August. With the appearance of the 'Race Manifesto' racialism 'in the true sense of the word'—racial anti-Semitism on the German pattern, that is—had become an integral part of official Fascist doctrine. A mere four days later (18 July) Le Pera's department of demography at the Ministry of the Interior had been transformed into a Directorate-General of Race and Demography—a sure sign that the practical corollaries of the racialist decalogue were at hand. On 22 July the forthcoming publication of a racialist weekly magazine—Interlandi's *La Difesa della Razza*—had been announced in the press. On 25 July the Party Secretary had received the alleged authors of the 'Race Manifesto' (including scholars with a notoriously anti-racialist past) and expressed his appreciation to them, affirming that their pronouncement was the logical culmination of 'sixteen years of Fascist racial policy' as well as the point of departure for 'further precise action'. On 28 July Pope Pius XI, evidently unimpressed by Starace's claim to Fascist 'priority' in the sphere of racial policy, had publicly accused Mussolini of aping the Germans, thereby provoking a crisis between Church and State; the Duce's reaction had been predictably swift and sharp. On 3 August the Ministry of Education had prohibited the admission of foreign Jews, even of those domiciled in Italy, to Italian schools of all grades.

Finally, on 5 August, the official Fascist attitude to the race problem had been defined in a note (*Informazione Diplomatica* No. 18) which plainly reflected the conflicting pressures to which Mussolini was subject at this juncture. It deplored the misinterpretations to which Fascist racial policy had allegedly given rise; repeated the 'bold assertion' that Fascism had been a racialist movement since 1919 and that it was the conquest of an empire rather than the alliance with Germany which had rendered the race question acute in Italy; once more denied that the Italian Government had any intention of persecuting the Jews 'as such'; claimed that the anti-Jewish measures were a purely defensive reaction to the disproportionate influence of the Jews in Italy on the one hand and the notorious collusion between 'Jewry, Bolshevism, and Freemasonry' on the other; accused the Jews of being the worst racialists in the world; and ended by declaring that 'the time was ripe for Italian racialism' which would henceforth constitute the 'fundamental basis' of the Italian State. This communiqué in a sense marked 'the end of the first phase' of Fascist racial policy.

About five days after the appearance of the 'Race Manifesto' (Mollier continued) the Fascist press had launched a large-scale racialist campaign with the twofold purpose of winning over the Italian public (which had so far been neither race-conscious nor 'Jew-conscious') and of rebutting the charges of 'imitation' and 'subservience' that were being levelled at Mussolini both at home and abroad. Most of Mussolini's journalists, however, were woefully unprepared for the task assigned to them, despite the detailed instructions received from the Ministry of Popular Culture. Their approach to the unfamiliar subject was often confused and contradictory; and much of what they wrote could only be described as 'arrant nonsense' (*blühender Unsinn*). Even so, this 'tremendous propaganda wave' had undoubtedly achieved its main purpose—that of drawing nation-wide attention to a problem which the vast majority of the Italian people had hitherto ignored.

The racialist controversy between Church and State (Mollier thought) was likely to be kept within bounds, both sides being equally reluctant to wreck the Conciliation of 1929. It was worthy of note in this connection that even staunchly anti-

Semitic and anti-clerical Fascists were averse to a *Kulturkampf* on the German model.

Turning to the main subject of his report—the elimination of the Jews from Italian public life—Mollier pointed out that 'for a wide variety of reasons' the Fascist Government had so far deemed it advisable to act with a minimum of publicity. Although an anti-Jewish purge had been initiated shortly after the appearance of the 'Race Manifesto', no anti-Jewish law had as yet been promulgated and only a single anti-Jewish measure—the decree forbidding the entry of foreign Jews into Italian schools—had been announced in the Fascist press. It was known, however, that a certain number of Jews had been ousted from the civil service and the universities, that a number of high-ranking Jewish officers had been expelled from the Fascist militia, and that an Aryan militia officer, on applying for permission to marry a Jewess, had been summarily dismissed. It was also known that as of 1 October 1938 all Jews would be excluded from the teaching profession. On the other hand, it was not yet clear whether the Jews had been eliminated from the Fascist Party (a fortnight ago the Jewish *federale* of Bari had still been in office), whether Jewish officers in the regular army had been retired, whether Jewish diplomats had been struck off the diplomatic list, and what plans (if any) there were for purging the professions and the economy.

How far did Mussolini intend to press his anti-Jewish campaign? Any answer to this question was necessarily conjectural. For the moment he evidently did not wish to rush matters (Interlandi had just been ordered to tone down his attacks on individual Jews). It was unlikely, however, that he would confine himself to defensive measures against 'disproportionate' Jewish influence, as claimed in *Informazione Diplomatica* No. 18. The machinery of persecution, once in motion, could not be stopped; the anti-Jewish measures already taken were bound to provoke a hostile reaction from Jewry which in turn would compel the Fascist dictator to go on with his anti-Jewish purge until the total elimination of the Jews from Italian public life had been achieved. That being so, it was safe to prognosticate that the Fascist machine would 'very soon' be *judenrein*, irrespective of German influence or pressure.

Even so (Mollier warned), there were obstacles to a radical

solution of the Jewish problem in Italy which it would not be easy to overcome. The most serious of these were lack of scientific preparation (because of the suddenness of Italy's switch from anti-racialism to racialism) and lack of reliable statistical data (because of the prevailing confusion between race and religion). Nor was the 'Italian mentality' (meaning the Fascist belief in the priority of action over doctrine) calculated to facilitate matters. In the short run, action without doctrinal formulation might well be effective; in the long run, however, the success of Fascist racial policy would depend on a thorough clarification of the scientific problems involved, including that of the *Judenmischlinge* (half- and quarter-Jews) which had so far not even been raised.

But whatever the limitations of Fascist racial theory and practice, it would be folly to engage in polemics or assume a governess attitude. The German press had done well, therefore, to applaud the Italian action without reservation and to defend Mussolini against the charge of imitation, well founded though it was. As for 'positive assistance', the clandestine dissemination of anti-Semitic material should now be stepped up; open interference in Italian domestic matters, however, should carefully be avoided.

In conclusion, Mollier once more raised the question of Mussolini's motives. What had prompted the Duce to break with the Jews at this particular juncture? No one knew. Various rumours were floating around, the accuracy of which it was impossible to verify. But whatever the truth, one thing was certain—Italy's conversion to racial anti-Semitism was an ideological victory for National Socialism. One of Adolf Hitler's 'most fundamental ideas' had fallen on fertile soil.[1]

[1] Mollier to Reich Ministry of Propaganda, 25 Aug. 1938 (GFM/2172/471269–97). Mollier's observations on his own share in the racial campaign are revealing: 'For obvious reasons, my own work in Rome has been restricted to a small but reliable circle, mainly comprising representatives of the University Students' Organisation . . . Even so, I would now ask for an *increased supply of anti-Semitic material,* since I have the possibility of distributing it in a suitable manner, without attracting attention' (Mollier's italics). At the beginning of September Mollier forwarded to the Propaganda Ministry a detailed report on the anti-Jewish purge in Trieste (dated 1 September); it contained an enclosure which appears to be the German translation of a secret Italian document (GFM/2172/471298–307). On 14 September 1938 a certain Dr. Johannsen of the *Aufklärungs-Ausschuss Hamburg–Bremen* submitted to the Wilhelmstrasse an unsigned report on the 'racial problem in Italy' by a secret agent in Rome, dated 9 September, which adds little to Mollier's account (GFM/2172/471314–19).

On 25 August 1938 Mollier and his colleagues were still of the opinion that Mussolini was anxious to postpone legislative action against the Jews as long as possible.[1] Only one week was to elapse, however, before they were shown to be wrong. On 1 September the Italian Council of Ministers approved the following decree law pertaining to foreign Jews in Italy, Libya, and the Aegean Islands:

On the proposal of the Duce and the Minister of the Interior it is resolved to regulate in the following manner the status of foreigners of the Jewish race who have taken up residence in Italy, Libya or in the Aegean possessions subsequent to the Great War, namely January 1, 1919, including also such persons (and their number is insignificant) who have in the meanwhile acquired Italian citizenship.

Article I. From the date of publication of the present decree law foreign Jews are forbidden to fix their permanent residence in the Kingdom, in Libya, and in the Aegean possessions.

Article II. For the purposes of the present decree law any person if he is born of parents both of whom are of the Jewish race shall be considered a Jew even though he may profess a religion other than the Jewish.

Article III. The admission of foreign Jews to Italian citizenship subsequent to January 1, 1919 is to all intents and purposes considered revoked.

Article IV. Foreigners of the Jewish race who at the date of publication of the present decree law are within the Kingdom, Libya, and the Aegean possessions and who began their sojourn therein subsequent to January 1, 1919, must leave the territory of the Kingdom, Libya, and the Aegean possessions within six months from the date of publication of the present decree law. Those who shall have failed to conform to this obligation within the aforesaid period shall be expelled from the Kingdom in accordance with article 150 of the codified text of the Public Security laws after the application of penalties established by law.[2]

On 2 September the Council of Ministers approved a decree law excluding all persons of the Jewish race from the teaching profession in general and barring such persons from admission to all schools and institutions of learning recognized by the State; a transitional exception was made in the cases of those

[1] GFM/2172/471285: 'For a variety of reasons, the Italian State will refrain as far as possible from the precise formulation of its objectives and from the publication of legal measures (against the Jews) . . .'

[2] T. Staderini, *Legislazione per la difesa della razza*, 3rd edn., Rome, 1940, pp. 16–17.

previously enrolled in the universities who were permitted to continue their studies.[1]

While the 'soft-hearted' Italians were shocked at the harshness of these measures, the Germans considered them insufficiently drastic, deploring in particular the Duce's failure to come to grips with the problem of the 'half-breeds'. On 5 September F. von Strautz, Secretary of Legation at the German Embassy in Rome, informed the Wilhelmstrasse that Fascist racial policy, for all its apparent severity, was unlikely to achieve its objective. The Italian public, to be sure, regarded the race laws as a 'crushing blow' to the Jews; the opposite view, however, had been expressed by a well-informed senior government official who pointed out that practically every Italian Jew had some Aryan blood in his veins and that hence the anti-Jewish decrees would largely fail in their purpose unless a different definition of the term 'Jew' was adopted. According to the same source, the original draft submitted by the Ministry of the Interior— the least 'Jew-ridden' of all Italian ministries—had in fact contained a more comprehensive definition; the Council of Ministers had, however, decided to reject it at the insistence of Giuseppe Bottai, the Minister of Education, who was himself a Jew on his mother's side.

Whether and to what extent the apprehensions voiced by the Italian informant were justified (Strautz continued) remained to be seen. But if it was really intended to treat all persons of mixed blood as 'Aryans', the result might well be disastrous: 'Italy would not be liberated from Jewry, and those Jews who succeeded in furnishing proof of Aryan ancestry . . . would band together more determinedly than before and form an anti-Aryan defensive front. In the opinion of the above-mentioned informant, it was feared, especially at the Foreign Ministry, that Jews remaining at their posts after the promulgation of the racial laws . . . would exercise a great deal of influence. Foreign Ministry officials of pure Italian race would in all probability be employed in the diplomatic service, while the number of Jews at the Ministry itself, and hence their influence (on appointments, for instance), would steadily increase'.[2]

---

[1] Ibid., pp. 22–7.

[2] Strautz to Wilhelmstrasse, 5 Sept. 1938 (GFM/2172/471308–13). Strautz pointed out that the council of Ministers had been at pains to present the anti-Jewish measures as an

Strautz and his unnamed Italian informant were not the only people in Rome to worry about the correct definition of the word 'Jew'. On 8 September the German diplomat received a letter from Le Pera, the newly appointed Director-General of Race and Demography, urgently requesting the text of the Nuremberg laws and the regulations governing their implementation. On 26 September Mackensen informed the Wilhelmstrasse that Le Pera had again approached the German Embassy, asking for statistical data on intermarriage between Gentiles and Jews (including *jüdische Mischlinge*) in the Reich, these data being urgently required in connection with the forthcoming session of the Fascist Grand Council, scheduled to take place at the beginning of October. Needless to say, the Germans were only too pleased to comply with these requests.[1]

The Grand Council convened on 6 October and adopted a series of resolutions on the racial question, of which the following is a summary:

1. *Need for anti-Jewish measures.* Measures against the Jewish race are a logical consequence of the racial policy pursued by Fascism ever since the March on Rome and a logical extension to Italy proper of the ban on miscegenation imposed in Africa after the Ethiopian campaign. The Jewish problem is no more than the domestic aspect of a general racial problem, rendered acute by the conquest of an empire.

2. *Mixed marriages.* (a) Italians may not marry members of the Hamitic, Semitic, or other non-Aryan races; (b) government and public employees, civil and military, may not marry foreign women, no matter what their race; (c) permission from the Ministry of the Interior must be obtained for the marriage of Italians, male or female, even with Aryan foreigners; (d) measures against Italian citizens lowering the prestige of the race in the Empire will be made more severe.

3. *Expulsion of foreign Jews.* Apart from controversial cases to be determined by a commission of the Ministry of the Interior, foreign Jews who are over 65 years of age or who have married an Italian prior to 1 October 1938, shall not be expelled.

aspect of Fascist demographic and social policy. It was, however, unlikely that intelligent Italians were taken in by this: 'Dass diese These in Wirklichkeit nicht zutrifft, weiss der mit den Zusammenhängen vertraute Italiener wohl ebenso wie wir.'
[1] See *Judenverfolgung in Italien*, pp. 12–13. Needless to say, the Germans were only too pleased to comply with Le Pera's requests.

4. *Definition of the Jewish race.* The following are considered to be of the Jewish race: (a) persons born of two Jewish parents; (b) persons born of Jewish fathers and foreign (Aryan) mothers; (c) persons born of mixed marriages who profess the Jewish religion (but not those who as of 1 October 1938 profess another religion).

5. *Exemption from discrimination.* Except as regards teachers of all grades, no discrimination on the grounds of race will be made against Jews of Italian citizenship belonging to the families of: (a) men who died, who served as volunteers, or who received military decorations in the World War or in the Libyan, Ethiopian, or Spanish wars; (b) men who were killed or wounded in the Fascist cause or who enrolled in the Fascist Party in the years from 1919 to 1922 or during the second half of 1924 (i.e. after the Matteotti murder) or who were members of d'Annunzio's Fiume Legions; (c) persons having unusual merits, to be verified by a special commission.

6. *Status of other Italian Jews.* Pending further legislation regarding the acquisition of Italian citizenship, Jews not included in (5) may not (a) be members of the Fascist Party; (b) own or manage firms employing 100 or more persons; (c) own more than 50 hectares of land; (d) perform military service in time of peace or war. The professional activities of such Jews will be governed by subsequent laws.

7. *General provisions.* (a) Jews dismissed from public positions shall be entitled to the usual pension rights; (b) any form of pressure upon the Jews to cause them to recant shall be severely repressed; (c) no change shall be made as regards freedom of worship and the activity of the Jewish communities under existing legislation; (d) the institution of both elementary and secondary schools for Jews shall be permitted.

8. *Jewish immigration to Ethiopia.* It may be decided to permit 'controlled immigration' of European Jews into certain districts of Ethiopia in order among other things to divert Jewish immigration away from Palestine. This possibility as well as the other conditions to be established for the Jews will, however, depend on the attitude of Jewry in general towards Fascist Italy. In this connection the Grand Council recalls that international Jewry has been 'unanimously hostile' to Fascism and that all anti-Fascist forces 'are directed by Jewish elements'.[1]

[1] See De Felice, *Storia degli ebrei italiani*, pp. 291–9, 553–61.

While the Italians regarded the above resolutions as fresh evidence of the Duce's deplorable subservience to Hitler, the Germans felt that Mussolini had not gone far enough in copying the Nuremberg laws. Commenting on the decisions of the Grand Council in a lengthy dispatch to the Wilhelmstrasse (18 October), Mackensen affirmed that the anti-Jewish cause had 'undoubtedly suffered a severe set-back'. At first the Fascists had apparently intended to follow the German example as far as the definition of the Jewish race was concerned (an oblique reference to Le Pera's requests for information on German racial policy); in the end, however, the Grand Council had decided to accept as 'fellow Aryans' those of the *Judenmischlinge* who professed a religion other than the Jewish. In Germany all half- and quarter-Jews had been excluded from the body of the nation, irrespective of their religious beliefs; in Italy, on the other hand, persons born of mixed marriages 'had the choice between two different worlds' (which meant that elements hostile to the Axis would continue to play a not insignificant part in Italian public affairs).

But whatever one's reservations about the Duce's approach to the racial problem (Mackensen insisted), there was no denying the fact that it was based on a 'profound grasp of the Italian mentality'. Mussolini knew that his people had so far found it hard to swallow his anti-Jewish measures because they ran counter to the anti-racialist teaching of the Catholic Church which was in 'very close touch' with the Italian masses and whose hold over the mind of the nation had hardly been weakened by sixteen years of Fascist rule. If the Italians had 'more or less revolted' against the racial legislation, it was largely because the persecution of the Jews on racial grounds affronted their Christian sense. Compassion with the Jews played 'a very large part' in the Italian attitude towards racialism (as Mackensen knew from personal experience), and it went 'very much deeper' than sympathy for 'decent Jews' in Germany. However much Mussolini might deplore this sentimental humanitarianism of his subjects, he was forced to take account of it and to give an appearance of complying with it. But the determining factor in his refusal to solve the problem of baptized 'half-breeds' on German lines was perhaps his awareness of the average Italian's profound attachment to the family and his jealousy for its integrity. (Here Mackensen might have added that Fascism, for reasons of its own, had joined with the Church in proclaiming the sanctity and indissolubility of family ties and in repudiating divorce.) A radical solution of the *Mischlingsproblem* would have wrecked innumerable Catholic marriages and aroused more antagonism than could easily be handled.

Baptized half- and quarter-Jews were not the only beneficiaries of Mussolini's 'mildness'. In his speech at Trieste on 18 September the Duce had declared that the Italian Jews who had 'undoubted military or civil merits *vis-à-vis* Italy and the regime' would meet with 'understanding and justice' and that ultimately the world would perhaps be amazed at his 'generosity' unless 'the Semites at home and abroad and their improvised and unexpected friends' compelled him to change his mind. In accordance with this declaration, the Grand Council had decided on 'very far-reaching exemptions' (*sic*) in favour of the loyal 'Jewish Italians'. Fascist 'generosity' was equally evident in the Grand Council's observations on the possibility of Jewish immigration into Abyssinia. It was perfectly clear that this offer would have 'no far-reaching practical consequences', since Ethiopia was unfit for the absorption of white labour. What mattered to the Fascists, however, was 'the generous gesture as such', the desire to show the world that Italian racial policy signified, not persecution, but merely separation. In addition, this offer of a haven of refuge for homeless Jews was an attempt to win sympathy in the Arab world, most particularly in Palestine, where the Arabs would undoubtedly welcome any move calculated to relax the pressure upon their country.

But while anxious to impress the world with his 'generosity' (Mackensen concluded), the Duce was firmly resolved to eliminate from the national body all persons considered to be Jews for the purposes of the racial laws (including those of the 'half-breeds' who had failed to dissociate themselves from the Jewish nation and religion). The policy of separation was being 'strictly enforced in all walks of life', despite the widespread opposition it had aroused.[1]

---

[1] Mackensen to Wilhelmstrasse, 18 Oct. 1938 (GFM/2172/471320–27). While stressing the unpopularity of the anti-Semitic measures, Mackensen was apparently unaware of the fact that Mussolini's racial policy had met with opposition at the Grand Council meeting of 6 Oct. (see above, pp. 116–17, 123).

Although Mackensen refrained from drawing any inferences at the end of his report, the implications of his analysis were clear: Mussolini had gone as far in copying the Nuremberg laws as conditions permitted and should not be reproached for refusing to go further; his 'mildness', far from being a sign of weakness, was a piece of clever tactics, designed to disarm criticism at home and abroad and to provide him with a blackmailing weapon against the Jews and their Western sympathizers.

Unlike Mollier, Mackensen made no mention whatever of German influence on Italian racial policy or of the need for 'positive assistance' to the Italian Jew-baiters. The subject was, however, raised afresh by Dr. Rudolf Frercks of the Rassenpolitisches Amt der NSDAP who had arrived in Rome on 10 October for an unofficial exchange of views with the Italian 'racial experts', most particularly with Le Pera and Landra, from whom he hoped to obtain first-hand information on the evolution of the racial question in Italy.[1] In an eight-page memorandum on the results of his mission, written after his return to Germany, Frercks pointed out that the Italians, faced with a host of unfamiliar racial problems, were eager for German advice and guidance, despite the official insistence on the 'originality' of Italian racial thought. That being so, it should be possible for Germany to influence the course of Fascist racial policy without in any way appearing to meddle in Italian domestic affairs.

At the beginning of June Le Pera had told Gross that an 'official exchange of views on the racial question' was undesirable for political reasons; now he told Frercks that his previous objections to close co-operation had been rendered invalid by the Duce's sudden and unexpected declaration of war on the Jews. (At the time of the meeting between Gross and Le Pera the adoption of anti-Jewish measures had not been considered imminent; a few weeks later, for reasons unknown to his entourage, Mussolini had abruptly changed his mind.) When asked whether he was still interested in the projected visit to Germany, Le Pera replied that in view of recent developments he no longer regarded the matter as urgent; he would, however,

[1] See *Judenverfolgung in Italien*, pp. 14–15.

like to go at some later date, possibly in the spring of 1939. In the meantime he would welcome an exchange of information on the German-Jewish emigrants in Italy, many of whom were now trying to pass themselves off as 'German Christians'. (In this connection Le Pera pointed out that, as Director-General of Race and Demography at the Ministry of the Interior, he was charged with the administrative implementation of the racial legislation.)

With Guido Landra (a youngster of twenty-five who had just been appointed head of the Ufficio studi sulla razza at the Ministry of Popular Culture), Frercks discussed a wide variety of topics, including the genesis and growth of Italian racialism, Mussolini's presumable motives in breaking with the Jews (about which Landra was no better informed than Le Pera), ways and means of establishing co-operation between the 'racial experts' of the two countries, and—last but not least—the opposition of certain highly placed Fascists to the anti-Semitic policy. Landra began by pointing out that, as assistant lecturer in anthropology at the University of Rome, he had repeatedly written memorandums on the need for an active racial policy; after Hitler's return visit to Italy he had found an ally in Interlandi (who was 'personally close to the Duce'), with the result that he had been commissioned to draft a statement on Fascist racial principles. (Subsequently, Frercks was informed by Landra's collaborators and by Cogni that the 'Race Manifesto' had in fact been written by Landra and that the alleged co-authors had done no more than append their signatures to the document on Starace's orders.) Although Mussolini himself had 'recognized the importance of the racial question for years', it was not clear why he had declared war on the Jews at this particular juncture. It was probable, however, that he had judged the time ripe for a racial gesture which would convince both the Germans and the Anglo-French of his unshakable loyalty to the Axis. It was also possible that he intended to use racial ideology as an instrument of his expansionist policy; according to Interlandi, he was apparently planning to 'liberate' the Italians in Southern France and Tunisia, even as Hitler had 'liberated' the Austrians and the Sudeten Germans. When Frercks asked Landra why Cogni was not among the signatories of the 'Race Manifesto', the latter replied that Cogni's excessive glorification of the Nordic race had been widely resented in Italy and that hence his participation had not been considered desirable. From this reply Frercks drew the conclusion that the 'Race Manifesto' had been written 'with a view to demonstrating the originality and scientific soundness of the Italian approach to the racial question'.

Both Frercks and Landra were inclined to think that German influence had played a not inconsiderable part in Italy's conversion to racial anti-Semitism. The conversations between members of the Rassenpolitisches Amt and 'leading Italian personalities' had presumably 'helped to clear up misunderstandings' and so had a forty-page report by Marchese Giustiniani, the former cultural attaché at the Italian Embassy in Berlin, which, according to Landra, was 'very objective and favourable to the German point of view'.

After his second talk with Landra, Frercks was asked to call on Landra's chief, Alfieri. The main reason for this invitation turned out to be a recent Munich publication in which it was claimed that the population of Southern and Central Italy had 'a strong admixture of Negro blood'. Alfieri left no doubt that he took a grave view of this insult to the 'Italian race' (which had aroused resentment 'in the highest Italian circles'). Frercks replied, with some embarrassment, that the publication in question did not reflect the official German view and would 'very shortly disappear'. Mollified by this assurance, the Minister declared that he was anxious for 'further co-operation in the field of racial science', after which he proceeded to explain to Frercks the premisses and aims of Fascist racial policy.[1]

Frercks hastened to inform Himmler (who happened to be in Rome on a visit), with the result that the offending publication was immediately withdrawn from circulation. He then had another meeting with Landra and his collaborators. The Italians, evidently pleased with the German response to their complaint, showed their appreciation by allowing Frercks to read a secret document in which the Duce expressed his approval of Alfieri's suggestions for an exchange of views on questions of racial policy. They also gave him a copy of a circular by Alfieri, addressed to the leading Italian journalists and to the publishers of all Italian periodicals, in which the official Fascist approach to the racial

[1] For the official part of the conversation, see 'Minister Alfieri über das italienische Rassenproblem', *V.B.*, 25 Oct. 1938.

issue was summed up as follows: (1) anti-Jewish propaganda should not be allowed to degenerate into vulgar abuse; (2) there was to be no 'persecution' of Jews, only discrimination; (3) the Jewish aspect of the racial problem should not be overstressed, there being plenty of other threats to the purity of the 'Italian race'; (4) the prime function of the racial movement was the creation of a 'Roman' race-consciousness, the Italians being the physical as well as the spiritual descendants of the ancient Romans; (5) no allusion should ever be made to the alleged antithesis between *romanità* and *germanesimo*, the Germans being 'fellow Aryans' as well as Italy's allies. These directives (Frercks argued) plainly reflected Mussolini's desire to avoid what he believed to be the 'weaknesses and errors' of German racialism.

As for co-operation between German and Italian 'racial experts', Landra suggested a comprehensive exchange of views on all matters of common interest, adding that he would like 'the largest possible number of his collaborators' to absorb German racial doctrines and techniques at the fountain-head. He also submitted a plan for the setting-up of an Italo–German Academy of Racial Science. Finally, he called for an end to racialist polemics between the two countries, with particular reference to German attacks on the 'inferior' Latins.

The leading opponents of racialism within the Fascist ruling clan, according to Landra, were the Minister of Education, Bottai (believed to be the son of a Jewish mother), and the Under-Secretary of the Interior, Buffarini (believed to be under the influence of a Jewish lady friend). The leading 'pillars of the racial idea', in Landra's opinion, were Starace, Alfieri, and Ciano; Farinacci was not worth mentioning.[1]

Frercks concluded his report by stressing the political significance of Italy's conversion to anti-Semitism (which had put an end to Germany's isolation in the sphere of racial policy),

---

[1] While thus denouncing as 'enemies of the racial question' two Fascist hierarchs who had outdone each other in anti-Jewish zeal at the Grand Council meeting of 6 October, Landra made no mention of those who had raised objections to the projected racial policy on that occasion—Acerbo, Balbo, De Bono, De Stefani, and Federzoni. On this, see Ciano, *1937–1938 Diario*, p. 264; L. Federzoni, *Italia di ieri per la storia di domani*, Milan, 1967, pp. 160–1; G. Acerbo, *Fra due plotoni di esecuzione. Avvenimenti e problemi dell'epoca fascista*, Bologna, 1968, p. 284; De Felice, *Storia degli ebrei italiani*, pp. 295–6. On Balbo's philo-Semitism (with particular reference to his friendship with the Jewish Mayor of Ferrara, Renzo Ravenna), cf. also YVS/Testimony of General Ivo Levi, Apr. 1960.

by warning against tactless meddling in Italian domestic affairs, and by calling for a positive response to Italian requests for advice and guidance.[1]

While differing on such issues as the 'originality' of Mussolini's racial gospel and the effectiveness of his racial laws, the German observers in Rome were at one in assuming that the decision to introduce anti-Jewish measures into Italy was entirely the Duce's and that he was at no time under pressure from their Führer.

Hitler was not in the habit of endangering his relations with a useful ally because of the Jewish question. He was determined to impose his anti-Jewish obsession upon the whole of Europe, but not before it was utterly at his mercy.[2] In 1938 he faced the risk of a war with Britain, France, Russia, and Czechoslovakia; he had no allies except Italy, and even the Rome–Berlin Axis did not constitute a formal alliance. In this situation it was obviously out of the question to anger Mussolini—a dictator very sensitive of his prestige—by intervening in the internal affairs of Italy.[3] It is worth recalling in this connection that Hitler never imposed his anti-Semitic policy on Finland, not even during World War II, when the country was occupied by 120,000 German troops.[4] And it is equally worth recalling that Mussolini's Italy was, in Hitler's eyes, 'not just like any other state': 'Hitler had declared (already in *Mein Kampf*) his "fervent admiration" for the great man in the South whom he regarded, in many ways, as his teacher, showing him the sort of deep respect which the *petit bourgeois* (that Hitler was) will always feel for feudal authority; and since the situation produced its own momentum of dependence, he may well have been pleased not

---

[1] GFM/2172/471328–38.

[2] It was only after Hitler's victory over France that Himmler's organ, *Das Schwarze Korps*, openly proclaimed the intention of imposing anti-Semitism on the rest of Europe: 'Just as for Germany herself the Jewish problem will be solved only with the expulsion of the last Jew, so the rest of Europe should know that the German peace to be expected by them must be a peace without Jews' (8 Aug. 1940). About three years later Johann von Leers, one of Goebbels's associates, went so far as to proclaim Germany's right to invade any country that refused to eliminate the Jews (*Die Verbrechernatur der Juden*, Berlin, 1944, p. 8).

[3] As late as the spring of 1938 it was possible for a prominent German journalist to write that the Jewish problem was 'hardly urgent' for Italy, given the numerical insignificance of Italian Jewry (G. Wirsing, *Engländer, Juden, Araber in Palästina*, Jena, 1938, p. 259).

[4] See *The Kersten Memoirs 1940–1945*, London, 1956, pp. 144–5; J. Wulf, 'Juden in Finnland', *Aus Politik und Zeitgeschichte*, B 16/59, (15 Apr. 1959), 164–8.

to have to apply too much pressure. His behaviour was often a cross between calculation and obsession; here it was a compound of calculation and adulation . . . No doubt Mussolini could have been forced, but in fact, unlike the minor satellites, he was not. He was able to practise the rank opportunism on which most power politicians hope to thrive.'[1]

For the rest, Mussolini was definitely hostile to the Jews from the autumn of 1936 (if not earlier) and had no need of any incitement by Hitler. The following extracts from Ciano's diary throw light on his state of mind:

'6 September (1937): The Duce let fly at America, country of niggers and Jews, the forces which disintegrate civilization. He wants to write a book: Europe in 2000. The races playing an important role will be the Italians, the Germans, the Russians, and the Japanese. The other peoples will be destroyed by the acid of Jewish corrosion.' (It is good to know that after all the speeches about Jewish Bolshevism Russia was not among the nations to be destroyed by the 'acid of Jewish corrosion'.)

'4 June (1938): The Duce is angry with Farinacci, the leader of the anti-Semitic faction, for having himself a Jewish secretary [*sic*], Jole Foà. This is the kind of thing which foreigners see as proof of a lack of seriousness in many Italians.' (For 'foreigners', read 'Germans'.)

Farinacci tried to defend the woman, pointing out that she was a veteran Fascist and adding that it was beneath his dignity to persecute a helpless female ('hated by her co-religionists because she is working for me'). But Mussolini was adamant: 'Tell Farinacci that it is in his interest to rid himself of Miss Foà. If this leaked out in Germany, he would undoubtedly greatly lose face. One cannot pose as the paladin of anti-Semitism and keep a Jewish secretary hanging around.'[2]

'25 July (1938): . . . Lord Perth came to ask for lenient treatment of the journalist Cremona who had been expelled. The reason for his expulsion was that Cremona, in conversation with other journalists, said that Mussolini cannot press his anti-

---

[1] C.C. Aronsfeld, editor of *Patterns of Prejudice*, in a memorandum on 'Germany and Fascist Italy's Race Laws', addressed to the writer (17 Aug. 1972).

[2] Fornari, p. 185; Farinacci to Mussolini, 6 June 1938 IC/*Segreteria particolare del Duce*/Job 122/034066–69.

Semitic campaign too far because in the past he received money from the Jews and even from a Jewess, the Sarfatti. *Inde ira.*'[1]

'30 July (1938): Following the Pope's speech, violently critical of racialism, I summoned the Nuncio and gave him a warning—if the Vatican continues on this path, a clash is inevitable because since the conquest of the Empire the Duce regards the racial question as fundamental. It is the lack of racial preparedness of the Italians which caused the Amhara insurrection.' (In defending the racial policy of which he had previously disapproved, Ciano naturally had to pretend that it was the conquest of an empire and not the *rapprochement* with Berlin which had induced his master to turn against the Jews.)

'8 August (1938): The Duce is very worked up (*molto montato*) about the racial question and very angry with Catholic Action. He has ordered that all Jews are to be struck off our diplomatic list. I am to begin by recalling them to Rome. He attacked the Pope violently. "I do not underestimate his strength", he said, "but he must not underestimate mine either. 1931 should have taught him. A sign from me would be enough to unleash all the anticlericalism of the Italian people which has found it hard (*ha dovuto faticare non poco*) to swallow a Jewish God".'

'22 August (1938): ... It seems that the Pope made another disagreeable speech yesterday about exaggerated nationalism and racialism. The Duce has summond Father Tacchi Venturi for this evening and proposes to deliver an ultimatum to him. "Contrary to what is believed", he said to me, "I am a patient man. But I must not be made to lose my patience, or I react by making a desert".'

'30 August (1938): ... The Duce ... also announced to me a project he has for turning Migiurtinia (the northernmost portion of Italian Somaliland, M. M.) into a concession for international Jewry. He says the country has important natural resources which the Jews could exploit. Among others there is the shark fishery "which has the great advantage that, to begin with, many Jews would get eaten".'

'4 September (1938): The Duce was very worked up about the Jews. He hinted at measures which he intends to get the

[1] Paul Cremona, Rome correspondent of the *Christian Science Monitor*. Mollier, in his above-quoted memorandum of 25 August, dealt at length with Cremona's expulsion but was unable to throw any light on the reasons for it.

next Grand Council to adopt and which will, taken together, constitute the Charter of the Race . . . The Duce went on to say: "The fight against these powerful forces, as many consider them to be, serves to give the Italians a backbone. It also serves to show that certain mountains are no more than blisters".' (By September 1938 it had evidently become clear to Mussolini that the Jews were not the 'Great Power' he had imagined them to be.)

'5 September (1938): Borelli (editor of the *Corriere della Sera,* M. M.) tells me that there is an oppressive atmosphere in Milan. The anti-Semitic measures and the demographic measures have hit too many people to be popular. But the Duce, when he believes it to be necessary, has the courage to be unpopular.'

'5 November (1938): . . . The Party has had orders from the Duce to intensify the anti-Semitic campaign.'

'12 November (1938): I found the Duce more worked up than ever about the Jews. He approves unconditionally the reprisals [*sic*] carried out by the Nazis. He says that in their position he would have gone even further . . . He proposes to enact a measure which will make Jews born in Italy in future stateless.'

It is known that the savage pogrom of November 1938 caused uneasiness even among Hitler's closest collaborators; according to von Hassell, 'most of those responsible' deplored it in private, including Göring, Himmler, and Hess.[1]

'28 November (1938): I found the Duce in a state of indignation against the King. Three times in the course of their conversation this morning the King said to him that he feels an "infinite pity for the Jews". He cited cases of persecution, among them that of General Pugliese, an old man of eighty [*sic*], loaded with medals and wounds, who has been deprived of his housekeeper.[2] The Duce said that there are 20,000 spineless people in Italy who are moved by the fate of the Jews. The King replied that he is one of them.'[3]

---

[1] Von Hassell, op. cit., pp. 31, 35, 43.

[2] General Emanuele Pugliese, the most highly decorated officer in the Italian army, was only sixty-four in 1938, having been born on 11 April 1874. He died in 1967. On him, see M. Michaelis, 'Il General Pugliese e la difesa di Roma', *La Rassegna Mensile di Israel,* xxviii. (June–July 1962), 262–83.

[3] Ciano, *1937–1938 Diario,* pp. 13, 186, 215–17, 223, 227, 230–1, 286, 291, 300. In any evaluation of Mussolini's anti-Jewish outbursts, account should be taken of the fact that he was 'in an abnormally excitable, irritable state' in 1938: 'He knew that in the

But it would be a mistake to deduce from the above that in 1938 Mussolini was an anti-Semite in the same sense that Hitler was. The Führer loathed the Jews more than anything else in the world, regarding them as evil incarnate, while the Duce inveighed against them no more than he did against innumerable others—the great democracies and his German allies, Hitler and Franco, Eden and Roosevelt, the King and the Fascist hierarchs, and, last not least, against the Italian people itself. For Hitler, racialism was the foundation and corner-stone of his whole being, whereas for Mussolini it was little more than a tactical move caused by a shift in the European balance of power. And even if he was much incensed at the Jews in 1938, this did not prevent him subsequently from sabotaging his own racial laws and, at times, from aiding and defending its victims against German bestiality. It remains to add that even after his conversion to racialism Mussolini continued to dislike and despise the Italian Jew-baiters, most particularly Farinacci and Preziosi.[1]

Needless to say, even in 1938 the Fascist dictator played his usual double and triple game. Speaking to Ciano at the Grand Council meeting of 6 October, he revealed himself as intransigent: 'The exemptions for loyal Jews (*discriminazioni*) mean nothing. The important thing is to raise the problem. Anti-Semitism has now been inoculated into the blood of the Italians. It will continue to circulate and to develop of its own accord. So, even if I am conciliatory tonight, I shall be very stern (*durissimo*) when I prepare the laws.'[2] But when his sister Edvige remonstrated with him, criticizing his racial policy, he replied that 'in Italy racialism and anti-Semitism were being made to appear as politically important as they are unimportant in their real substance':

The racial purity of this people, over which have passed so many invasions and which has absorbed so many races from the four points of the compass, and the Semitic peril in a nation like ours where high

European race Hitler was pulling away from him, and the effort to maintain an outward confidence and serenity was imposing a severe strain on his nervous system' (Kirkpatrick, p. 356).
[1] For Farinacci, see Fornari, pp. 173–4; for Preziosi, A. Tamaro, *Due anni di storia*, ii, Rome, 1948, p. 370; for Interlandi, C. Rossi, *Trentatre vicende mussoliniane*, Milan, 1958, pp. 405–6.
[2] Ciano *1937–1938 Diario*, p. 264.

finance, even if it is manipulated by Jews, cannot but become something Catholic (I know, by the way, that you and other members of your family are helping the Jews, and I am not displeased but think that thereby you can show the utter elasticity of our racial laws)—are clearly absurd fables (*fandonie*) which should be left for certain fanatics (*zelatori*) to write. But if circumstances had brought me to a Rome–Moscow Axis, instead of a Rome–Berlin Axis, I would perhaps have dressed up the Italian workers, who are so taken up with their jobs, just as promptly and with a detachment which the racialists might call Mediterranean, with the equally absurd fable of Stakhanovite ethics and the happiness they are supposed to bring. And in this case, too, it would have been a question of a showy but cheap token payment.[1]

Mussolini made similar statements to other people. Count Alessandro Casati, an ex-senator and a former Minister of Education, repeats as certain the following utterance of the Duce's: 'I still think that the Jewish problem is non-existent! Race? It makes me laugh. But there are reasons of state which I have to obey.'[2]

We already know these 'reasons of state': Mussolini's desire to demonstrate his 'total solidarity' with his German ally (who had doubted Italian loyalty ever since the 'betrayal' of 1914), his contempt for the 'decadent' democracies, and, last but not least, his growing contempt for the 'soft-hearted' Italians who had achieved less in sixteen years than the Germans in six. Ciano wrote on 27 October 1937: 'The alliance between the two countries is based above all on the identity of political regime which determines a common destiny. *Simul stabunt, simul cadent.*'[3] And on 17 July 1938: 'The Duce . . . also talked about the revolution in manners, particularly in relation to racial problems. He is studying a measure which will forbid the marriage of Italians with persons of other races, including Jews. "All this", he said, "will increase the hatred of foreigners for Italy. Good. I will do anything I can to sever relations (*voltare sempre di più le spalle*) with France and England—nothing can come from that quarter except *pourriture.*'[4] The Duce himself, in a secret address to the National Council of the Fascist Party (25

---

[1] Edvige Mussolini, op. cit., p. 175.
[2] Camilla Cederna, 'Il romanzo del '39', *L'Espresso*, (5 July 1959), 13; cf. also P. Monelli, *Mussolini piccolo borghese*, Milan, 1954, p. 235.
[3] Ciano *1937–1938 Diario*, p. 41.
[4] Ibid., p. 211.

October 1938), declared that the Italians—and in particular the 'defeatist' Italian bourgeoisie—must be dealt 'blows in the stomach' (*cazzotti nello stomaco*): 'The first blow was the introduction of the goose step (*passo romano di parata*) ... Another little blow was the abolition of "lei" (the polite form of address, M. M.) ... Another blow in the stomach has been the racial question ... It is necessary to react against the compassion (*pietismo*) with the poor Jew.'[1]

It has occasionally been argued that Mussolini's switch from philo-Semitism and anti-racialism to racial anti-Semitism was prompted, not only by the growing exigencies of the Rome–Berlin Axis but also by his desire to pose as 'Protector of Islam'. But although this theory appears to be supported both by a remark in the above-quoted conversation between the King and Balbo and by a public utterance of Farinacci's,[2] it will not stand up to the fact that Fascist racialism implied discrimination against Arabs as well as Jews. It was certainly not for the sake of the Arabs that the Duce decreed a ban on intermarriage with 'Semites' and gave an Aryan-Nordic direction to his racial gospel. Ciano wrote on 26 October 1938: 'At the Grand Council last night there was a lively debate on Balbo's proposal to grant full citizenship to the Arabs. It is easy to recognize here a flat contradiction of our racial policy. The real Fascists, like Farinacci, Starace, and Alfieri, did not hesitate to oppose the proposal. Nor did I. The project has been shelved and will be presented again in a very different garb.'[3]

It has sometimes been suggested that the economic motive was at least a contributory factor in Mussolini's decision to turn against the Jews. But the total wealth of the fifty thousand odd Jews in Italy was scarcely large enough to be tempting. It was, moreover, for a large part in fixed assets which were just as useful to the Duce in Jewish as in other hands. What the Fascists required was not illiquid Italian property, not even Italian cash,

---

[1] *O.O.* xxix. 188–91.
[2] The King said to Balbo: 'Mussolini ... is jealous—I think—because German anti-Semitism has proved so very congenial to the Arab nations of the Mediterranean Levant' (d'Aroma, op. cit., p. 267). Farinacci told Gunter d'Alquen, the editor of Himmler's paper, that the anti-Jewish laws had had a beneficial effect on Italy's relations with the Arabs ('Unterredung mit Farinacci', *Das Schwarze Korps*, 15 Sept. 1938).
[3] Ciano, *1937–1938 Diario*, p. 277.

but foreign currencies; and since the Fascist Government already controlled all foreign securities, no additional advantage in that direction was to be obtained from the sequestration of Jewish property. Indeed, it was widely believed by the end of 1938 that there had been a considerable leakage through the smuggling of currency and that hence the anti-Jewish measures had already resulted in a net loss of foreign resources.[1]

It was repeatedly affirmed by official spokesmen of the Fascist regime in the second half of 1938 that Italian racialism was largely a reaction to the alleged mass immigration of Jews from Central and Eastern Europe. On 28 July Ciano told the American Ambassador that 'while there had been only 40 to 50 thousand Italian Jews, there was now an illegal and surreptitious infiltration of Jews from Romania, Austria, and other parts of Europe which the Italian Government was powerless to prevent by ordinary means [*sic*]'. If this situation was left unremedied, 'Italy would within 5 years find itself harbouring at least half a million foreign Jews [*sic*]. Accordingly the Italian Government was resolved to discourage this immigration by making it clear to the Jews that Italy does not want them.'[2] And on 5 November Suvich informed the American Under-Secretary of State that, 'while three years ago there had been only approximately forty thousand Jews in Italy, the number had now increased as the result of the emigration of refugees from Germany to almost one hundred thousand [*sic*]; that the greater part of these Jews were persons of the professional classes with some means of their own; that they had obtained in the short time they had been in Italy a considerable advantage over the Italians exercising the same professions [*sic*], and that this situation had caused a great deal of agitation.'[3] Why it should have been impossible to put a stop to this alleged competition without resorting to racial discrimination against the Jewish officers in the Italian armed forces and the Jewish 'Fascists of the first hour', Suvich naturally failed to explain.

Oddly enough, these propaganda stories about a 'Jewish invasion' were taken at face value by a good many foreign

---

[1] Cf. memorandum on position of the Jews in Italy by Sir Andrew McFadyean, 25 Jan. 1939 (PRO/F.O.371/23799/R751/10/22). Sir Andrew was Joint Treasurer of the British Liberal Party in 1939.

[2] Phillips to Hull, 29 July 1938 (*FRUS 1938*, ii, p. 587).

[3] Memorandum by Sumner Welles, 5 Nov. 1938 (*FRUS, 1938*, ii. 597).

observers, including Mollier who affirmed (in his memorandum of 25 August) that one of the 'underlying causes' of Mussolini's sudden break with the Jews was the 'steady increase in the number of Jewish refugees in Italy'.[1] The fact remains, however, that the special Jewish census of August 1938 returned no more than 10,173 Jews of foreign nationality, 1,424 of whom were born in Italy.[2] That the influx of Jewish immigrants from Germany gave rise to a certain amount of local friction is evident from a wide variety of sources; but it is equally evident that this friction was not the reason for the adoption of racial measures against the 'Jewish Italians'.[3]

It has repeatedly been claimed that the Fascist dictator was under pressure from the pro-German extremists in his entourage. It is, however, abundantly clear from all the published and unpublished records at our disposal that Mussolini himself was the head of the pro-German faction in the Fascist Party and the moving spirit behind the racial campaign. There was not a single Italian anti-Semite whom he did not encourage between 1936 and 1938. He received Cogni and authorized him to publish a book in defence of Hitler's Nordic heresy. He egged on Farinacci, urging him to concentrate his attacks on 'the eternal collusion between Jewry and Communism' and rebuking him for 'keeping a Jewish secretary hanging around'. In February 1937 he received Preziosi, who then switched from 'defensive anti-Judaism' to racial anti-Semitism. He inspired Interlandi's crusade against the 'dissident mongrels', a fact of which the latter was to boast publicly in September 1938. He also encouraged Julius Evola, the apostle of 'Roman' racialism, ordering the

---

[1] The same opinion was expressed in the unsigned memorandum of 9 Sept. 1938 (see above, p. 168, n.1).

[2] ACS/Rilevazione sugli ebrei del 22 agosto 1938/Min Int./Dir. Gen Demografia e Razza/cart, 14/fasc. 47; see also R. Bachi, 'The Demographic Development of Italian Jewry from the Seventeenth Century', *The Jewish Journal of Sociology*, iv (Dec. 1962), 173; S. Della Pergola, *Ha-demografia shel yehudei Italia,* Jerusalem, 1972, p. 398; and F.E. Sabatello, *Ha-megamot ha-hevratiot v'ha-mikzoiot shel yehudei Italia 1870–1970,* Jerusalem, 1972, pp. 40, 60. When Mollier deplored the lack of statistical data in his report of 25 Aug., he was still unaware of the fact that a Jewish census on a racial basis had been completed three days earlier.

[3] McClure, in his above-quoted memorandum of 11 May 1937, dismisses the friction caused by the competition of foreign Jews as 'only a small matter'; the King of Italy appears to have taken a more serious view (d'Aroma, p. 267). Orano, in his book on Italian Jewry, devotes less than two pages out of 221 to the problem of Jewish refugees from Germany (op. cit., pp. 210–11).

editor of his paper to accept contributions from him.[1] Fornari asserts that the adoption of racial measures in Italy was largely due to Farinacci, but this assertion is not borne out by his own account of Farinacci's role in the racial campaign.[2] Germino contends that the driving force behind the anti-Jewish crusade was Starace, but the opposite thesis emerges from the very source he cites in support of his contention—Ciano's early diary.[3] Germino further affirms that racialism became official policy only after a 'prolonged and intense struggle' between Party extremists and government moderates at the Grand Council, but all the evidence points the other way. For one thing, the anti-Jewish purge was launched in the second half of July, whereas the Grand Council did not discuss the subject until 6 October. For another, most of the 'racialists' within the Fascist ruling clan were not 'Party extremists' at all but sycophants and time-servers—including such notorious Germanophobes as Bottai and Volpi.[4] Finally, the Grand Council was not a forum for decision, as Germino seems to assume, but an instrument for the endorsement of the Leader. Ciano wrote on 4 September: 'The Duce . . . hinted at measures which he intends to get the next Grand Council to adopt and which will, taken together, constitute the Charter of the Race. Actually the Charter has already been drawn up by the hand of the Duce. The Grand Council will do no more than sanction it with its deliberations.'[5]

[1] In addition to the sources quoted above, see also Gentizon's report in *Le Temps* of 24 Feb. 1937 (on Mussolini–Preziosi meeting); Pini, *Filo diretto*, pp. 189–190 (on Evola).

[2] Fornari admits that it was 'through political opportunism rather than conviction' that Farinacci became the Julius Streicher of Italy (p. 176), that he more than shared Mussolini's doubts about the scientific soundness of the 'Race Manifesto' (p. 185), and that the Duce generally paid little heed to his advice unless it happened to coincide with his own ideas (pp. 165–6).

[3] Ciano, *1937–1938 Diario*, p. 215: 'Commotion over Starace's communiqué (actually written by the Duce) on the Jewish question'.

[4] Bottai, after loudly beating the anti-Jewish drum at the Grand Council session of 6 October, called on Aldo R. Ascoli, Vice-President of the Union of Italian Jewish Communities, and told him that he deplored the anti-Jewish measures which had been adopted 'for reasons of foreign policy' (AUCII 1938/Ministeri/sottofasc. Min. Educ. Naz.). Buffarini admitted to the Bishop of Trieste on 20 December that the racial policy was a mistake which it was now too late to rectify—'fatto le scivolone, non sapevano ormai come far macchina indietro' (G. Botteri and F. Carniel, 'I sopravvissuti', *Trieste*, 31, May–June 1959, 15; A. Santin, *Trieste 1943–1945*, Udine 1963, p. 28 n. 4). For Volpi's Germanophobia, see Ciano, *1937–1938 Diario*, pp. 126, 191–2.

[5] Ciano, *1937–1938 Diario*, p. 230. As early as 13 October 1925 Mussolini had defined his attitude to the role of the Grand Council as follows: 'My orders are not voted on but are accepted and acted upon without any chatter. The Grand Council is not a small

It remains to add that at the Grand Council meeting of 6 October minor concessions were made to the 'government moderates' (Balbo, De Bono, De Stefani, and Federzoni) who raised objections to the proposed anti-Jewish measures.[1]

As has been noted, Mussolini did not believe in the imminence of a Czech–German conflict at the time of Hitler's visit to Italy. Less than two weeks later, however, there was a European scurry over Czech mobilization against Germany; and on 26 May the Duce declared to Ciano that, if war broke out, he would 'immediately enter the struggle on the side of the Germans.'[2] In the following months it became increasingly evident that the Führer was aiming, not at regional autonomy for the Sudeten Germans, but at the disintegration of Czechoslovakia. On 19 August the Italian assistant military attaché reported from Berlin that a conflict was expected for the end of September; and on 20 August Ciano noted in his diary that 'the crisis of the Czech question' appeared to be at hand, adding that in that eventuality there would be no alternative for Italy 'but to fall in beside Germany immediately, with all our resources'.[3] Given this possibility of being involved in a general war (for which he knew his country to be unprepared), the Fascist dictator decided to advertise his solidarity with Germany in order to put pressure on the Czechs and their Western allies. On the one hand, he proclaimed his intention of marching with Hitler to the end (in the hope that he would not be called upon to honour his pledge); on the other, he launched an anti-Jewish purge on the German model in order to convince the Anglo-French that he had burnt his boats. Discussing the Jewish question with his son Vittorio about this time, he declared that the Jews were a potential Fifth Column which it was his duty to eliminate from Italian public life: 'La nostra posizione politico-militare non ci permette di

parliament; never, I repeat never, is there any question of voting in it' (letter to Farinacci, IC/Job 53/026546).
[1] De Felice, *Storia degli ebrei italiani,* pp. 295–6. Germino is wrong in applying the term 'government moderates' to the opponents of Mussolini's racialism, since all of them had been removed from the government long before 1938—De Stefani in 1925, Federzoni in 1928, Balbo in 1933, Acerbo and De Bono in 1935.
[2] Ciano, *1937–1938 Diario,* p. 180.
[3] Ibid., pp. 221–2.

tenere nel nostro seno eventuali sabotatori dello sforzo che sta compiendo il popolo italiano'.[1]

This brings us to the last point which can throw light on the subject of German 'interference' in Italian racial policy. From Ciano's early diary and from other sources in our possession it is now clear that throughout the entire Czech–German crisis there was no collaboration whatever between the two allies. The Italians, on the contrary, were kept in the dark as to any German initiative, despite the outward manifestations of Axis solidarity. In the words of a gifted Italian diplomat who was a member of Ciano's entourage during this period: 'Nothing was known in Rome of Germany's intentions . . . except what the radio and the newspapers told the whole world. When Hitler or Goebbels spoke, the Italian Minister of Foreign Affairs stood listening anxiously before the radio-set like any private citizen and had the more important passages translated to him, while awaiting the complete translation made by the Ministry of Popular Culture.'[2] Ciano himself records in his diary that his attempts to obtain information on Germany's plans were uniformly unsuccessful and that his master was greatly disturbed by Hitler's refusal to declare his intentions.[3] This explains why the Germans were not yet in a position to raise the Jewish issue with their Italian allies. In World War II they demanded the adoption of anti-Jewish measures on 'security grounds' (for example, the request of the German High Command to eliminate all Jews from the allied forces), which they could not have done in 1938 when they had not yet divulged their intention of unleashing the conflict.[4]

It is now generally recognized that the pro-German speeches which Mussolini delivered in September 1938 had been neither requested nor expected by the Germans.[5] Equally unrequested and unexpected was the Duce's sudden declaration of war on the Jews.

[1] V. Mussolini, *Vita con mio padre*, Milan, 1957, p. 93. See also Wiskemann, op. cit., p. 145: 'Mussolini's series of speeches in Venetia in September 1938, in which he spoke of the Italian Jews, was part of the Axis campaign against the Czechs. It was not for the first time in the history of Bohemia that Czech and Jew had found themselves thrown into alliance against Germanism.'

[2] Donosti, *Mussolini e l'Europa*, p. 113.

[3] Ciano, *1937–1938 Diario*, pp. 225, 229, 231.

[4] Münz, op. cit., pp. 178, 232.

[5] See, e.g., Salvatorelli and Mira, p. 987.

In his Proclamation read at the opening of the Nuremberg Party rally on 6 September 1938, Hitler himself announced to the world that his admired teacher Mussolini had arrived at racial anti-Semitism quite independently of Germany:

I think that I must at his point announce, on my own behalf and on that of all of you, our deep and heart-felt happiness in the fact that another great European World Power [*sic*] has, through its own experiences, by its own decision and along its own paths arrived at the same conception as ourselves and with a resolution worthy of admiration has drawn from this conception the most far-reaching consequences. However much the course and the development of the Fascist and National Socialist revolutions appear to be conditioned by their own obvious individual needs, however independent of each other these two historic upheavals have been in their origin and evolution, it is none the less fortunate (*glückhaft*) for us all that in every great vital question of this time we have found a common attitude of the spirit, a common temper, which in this world of unreason and destruction brings us, simply as men, ever more closely together.[1]

It was then thought, very naturally, that this was one of the German dictator's many lying declarations and that the Fascist imitation had been explicitly requested by him, if not imposed. Now, however, in the light of the ample evidence analysed above, we are forced to conclude that for once the arch-liar Hitler was telling the truth.

---

[1] *Reden des Führers am Parteitag Grossdeutschland 1938*, Munich, 1938, p. 26.

From the Munich Conference to the
Pact of Steel (1938–1939)

OF THE four statesmen who met at Munich on 29–30 September, 1938, only the Duce had any reason for unalloyed satisfaction. The Führer, though he had ostensibly gained his point, was furious with the British for having spoiled his entry into Prague. Daladier had betrayed his ally; and both he and Chamberlain had manifestly made a craven surrender to the threat of force. Mussolini, on the other hand, was enjoying the best of both worlds. In addition to earning Hitler's gratitude for his blustering support of Germany's case, he had also earned the thanks of the Western appeasers for having restrained his partner in 'dynamics'. His bluff had not been called, and now he was being acclaimed as the man who had saved the peace. In his own country his popularity rose to new heights, despite the widespread disgust which his anti-Jewish policy had aroused. As he himself was to put it in a secret speech a few weeks later, Munich meant that for the first time since 1861 Italy had played a 'predominant and decisive part' in an event of world importance[1]

Italy's 'triumph' at the Munich Conference aroused in Mussolini contradictory reactions which were to affect the course of Fascist racial policy in a variety of ways. On the one hand, it served to increase his disdain for the 'Jew-ridden' democracies and to confirm him in his conviction that war between the Axis and the Western Powers was unavoidable in the long run; on the other, it reawakened his sense of superiority vis-à-vis Hitler (whom he had prevented from setting fire to the European powder barrel) and hence his desire to preserve the ascendancy won in Munich. In the words of Mario Toscano: 'At Munich Mussolini ... in appearance more than in reality—for his proposals had been furnished by the Germans—had come out as arbitrator and mediator, though as one decidedly partial to the Germans; who in the end had aimed at obtaining even more. An alliance with Hitler, concluded immediately after Munich, would obviously have made Mussolini lose the advantage he had

---

[1] Speech to the National Council of the Fascist Party, 25 Oct. 1938 (O.O. xxix. 192).

gained *vis-à-vis* France and Britain which he could not desire. Nor could he wish to encourage new Nazi enterprises; he feared their bearing and repercussions on Italian interests, especially in the Danube Basin'. Moreover, for all his braggadocio, he dreaded the idea of a major war.[1]

Given the above considerations, the Duce agreed with his son-in-law on the necessity for 'keeping both doors open'. Hence, while loudly proclaiming his 'total' solidarity with Hitler, he took steps to improve relations with London. On 30 September he told Chamberlain at Munich that he meant to withdraw ten thousand Italian 'volunteers' from Spain in order to facilitate 'a speedy implementation of our Pact of April 16'. On 2 October he ordered Ciano to open negotiations with the British Ambassador; and on the following day Ciano spoke to Perth on the lines agreed with his master, warning him that failure to bring the agreement into effect would compel Italy to strengthen her ties with the Reich. On 6 October Perth informed Ciano that Chamberlain, while agreeing 'in principle', asked for a 'short breathing space' in order to make his peace with Parliament on the issue (which involved British *de jure* recognition of Mussolini's African conquests). On 27 October Ciano noted in his diary that the projected triple alliance with Berlin and Tokyo had better be put into cold storage, 'particularly as Perth has secretly informed me of the British decision to implement the April Pact as from the middle of November'; and a day later both he and Mussolini firmly declined Ribbentrop's renewed offer of an outright military pact, affirming that the time was not ripe for so far-reaching a commitment. Finally, on 16 November, the Easter Pact was brought into force, Perth having presented to Ciano new credentials addressed to the 'King Emperor'.[2]

Paradoxically, the *rapprochement* between Rome and London had the effect of aggravating rather than ameliorating the situation of Italian Jewry. For the longer Mussolini continued to fight shy of a formal treaty with his German ally, the more he felt the need to reassure him, both by minimizing the significance of the Easter Pact and by stepping up his campaign against the Jews. Nor was fear of Hitler's and Ribbentrop's displeasure the

---

[1] Toscano, *Le origini diplomatiche del Patto d'Acciaio*, p. 58.
[2] Ciano, *1937–1938 Diario*, pp. 253–4, 260–1, 263, 279, 281, 293; *L'Europa verso la catastrofe*, i. 411–17; *DBFP, 3rd Ser.* iii. 320–1, 325–7, 342.

only reason for the Duce's increasing intransigence in regard to the Jewish issue. Other reasons were his well-founded conviction that the British, after their disastrous defeat at Munich, would not allow the Jewish question to stand in the way of their appeasement policy; his territorial claims against France (raised at the very moment when he was courting Britain) which forced him back into his old position of dependence on German support; and—last but not least—his growing irritation at the widespread disapproval which his persecution of the Jews had aroused among the 'soft-hearted' Italians, including many good Fascists.[1]

For all his demonstrative intransigence, however, Mussolini was still disinclined to burn his boats and still anxious to impress Western opinion with his moral and political superiority over Hitler. He did this by giving maximum publicity to the above-mentioned manifestations of Fascist 'generosity'; by ordering his diplomats and consuls abroad (except those in the Arab countries) to minimize the anti-Jewish aspect of Fascist racial policy;[2] by taking steps to prevent the treatment of foreign Jews resident in Italy from becoming a source of friction with the Western Powers;[3] by making minor concessions to those Jewish converts to Catholicism who were considered 'non-Aryans' for the purposes of the racial laws;[4] by encouraging his 'racial experts' to engage in polemics with the German apostles of 'Nordic superiority';[5] and—most important of all—by calling for the creation of a sovereign Jewish State (to which the Germans violently objected) and by hinting at the possibility of 'controlled'

---

[1] For Mussolini's growing intransigence, see Ciano, *1937–1938 Diario*, pp. 286–7, 300, 307; for the anti-French campaign, cf. Toscano, *Le origini diplomatiche*, pp. 84–94 and A. François-Poncet, *Au Palais Farnèse. Souvenirs d'une ambassade à Rome*, Paris, 1961, pp. 20–23; for the unpopularity of the racial measures even among Fascists, G. Preziosi, 'Botta e risposta', *La Vita Italiana*, lii (Nov. 15 1938), 665; Perth to Halifax, 27 Dec. 1938 (*DBFP*, 3rd Ser. iii. 497); Villari, *Italian Foreign Policy under Mussolini*, p. 202; De Felice, *Storia degli ebrei italiani*, 304–11, 378–9.

[2] ASMEI/Italia/p.57/1938 (Ciano to all diplomatic and consular missions, 26 July 1938); *FRUS 1938*, ii. p. 584–5 (memorandum by Hull, 26 July 1938).

[3] See below, p. 207.

[4] For details, see Binchy, *Church and State*, pp. 627–8.

[5] See, e.g., G. Landra, 'Die wissenschaftliche und politische Begründung der Rassenfrage in Italien' *Nationalsozialistische Monatshefte*, 10 (Apr. 1939), 298; L. Franzi, *Fase attuale del razzismo tedesco*, Rome, 1939, p. 15. It is worth noting in this connection that so notorious an opponent of German racialism as Giacomo Acerbo was chosen by Mussolini to head the Higher Council for Demography and Race (Consiglio superiore della Demografia e Razza) which was set up in September 1938.

Jewish immigration into certain districts of Ethiopia.[1] Nor was his search for a Jewish settlement area in Africa a mere tactical gesture, as Mackensen seems to imply in his above-quoted dispatch of 18 October; he was genuinely desirous of making some contribution to the solution of the refugee problem, if only in order to gain prestige. As has been noted, he told Ciano on 30 August that he was planning to turn Migiurtinia into a 'concession for international Jewry'; five days later he talked of Jubaland 'which offers better conditions for life and work'. About the same time the Duke of Aosta, Viceroy of Italian East Africa, instructed one of his officers to find an 'earthly paradise' (*sic*) for homeless Jews in Ethiopia, explaining that his master was anxious to assist the British in diverting Jewish immigration away from Palestine. On 5 December the officer reported that he had found a suitable area in the southern portion of the country; the report was duly submitted to Mussolini who transmitted a copy to the British Government.[2]

Mussolini's plans for founding a 'Jewish concentration colony' in some part of his new Roman Empire aroused interest in the American State Department which was then exploring conditions in various countries with a view to opening new doors to Jewish immigration. On 7 December President Roosevelt, evidently encouraged by the Duce's success as mediator and peacemaker at Munich, addressed to him the following appeal for co-operation in the solution of the refugee problem:

My dear Signor Mussolini: The decisive action which you took last September, which was so powerful a factor in assuring the avoidance of hostilities, is recognized everywhere as an historic service to the cause of world peace. The results of your efforts have provided a practical demonstration that even grave international crises can be resolved by negotiation without resort to armed force.

It is with this recollection in mind that I write to you today.

The problem of finding new homes for the masses of individuals of many faiths who are no longer permitted to reside freely in their native lands and are obliged through force of circumstances to find refuge abroad is one of immediate urgency. Both for those governments which desire to bring about the emigration of such individuals, as well as for

[1] For German objections to a Jewish State, see Schumberg's memorandum of 25 January 1939 (*ADAP*, Serie D v. 784) and A. Rosenberg, *Müssen weltanschauliche Kämpfe staatliche Feindschaften ergben?* Munich 1939, pp. 13–15.

[2] 'Un progetto di Mussolini, una sede per gli Ebrei di Etiopia', *Israel*, 4 June 1970.

those governments whose peoples feel it their duty and their desire to help so far as they may be able in the task of resettlement, the problem presented is one of grave complexity. Unless there is effective international collaboration, the prospect of a successful solution is not hopeful. And unless a solution based on justice and humanity can be found, and found promptly, I fear that international relations will be further embittered, and the cause of peace still further prejudiced.

I have, of course, given earnest thought to this matter and certain projects have occurred to me in which the United States could well collaborate. I am requesting Ambassador Phillips to ask an audience of you as soon as may be convenient to you after his return to Rome, and to submit these thoughts to your consideration, and to discuss them with you.

It would give me genuine pleasure to feel that you and I were working together along constructive lines toward a solution of this problem, and that thereby we might be contributing toward a happier and a more peaceful world.

The points raised in the President's letter were elaborated in a memorandum from which the following is worth quoting:

If a general plan can be found sufficiently ample in scope, and practical in character, which in his judgment holds out assurance that the problem which has arisen will be solved in consonance with justice and humanity, the President stands ready to request of the Congress of the United States that it agree to assume an appropriate share of the cost.

In searching the areas which would appear to lend themselves to resettlement, President Roosevelt has been particularly struck with the appropriateness of the Plateau, a small portion of which lies in the southwestern section of Ethiopia, and the greater portion in areas lying to the south of Ethiopia. It has occurred to him that the Chief of the Italian Government may believe that adequately financed colonization of refugee families in this area would be in accord with plans which the Italian Government may have formulated for the development and economic reconstruction of Ethiopia.

If the Chief of the Government should see merit in this plan and should care to make it his own and urge other states holding sections of this Plateau to do likewise, the President of the United States would be prepared to give the proposal as a part of a general plan his public support.

Of great importance is the German attitude on this question ... If any co-ordinated plans are to be carried out, the German Government will necessarily have to furnish full information as to probable emigration, and furthermore, some method must be agreed upon through which emigrants will not be forced to leave Germany as paupers. In this connection, it is understood in the United States that the main obstacle from the German point of view to the elaboration of such a plan lies in the difficulty of procuring foreign exchange in sufficient quantities to allow the emigrants to have cash in hand. The President has suggested that this difficulty might be met at least in part by permitting refugee emigrants to spend their German marks within Germany to a sufficient extent to provide themselves with supplies indispensable for their resettlement, as for instance, farm implements, clothing, and other requisites. If the German Government would permit emigrants from Germany to take from that country such articles for their use, up to a sufficient per capita value, the exchange difficulty would, of course, be greatly lessened.

It is the earnest hope of the President of the United States that the Chief of the Italian government will favor this suggestion and, in such event, will further it in such manner as he may deem appropriate.[1]

Phillips did not succeed in delivering Roosevelt's message until nearly four weeks later, by which time relations between Italy and the Western Powers had taken a sharp turn for the worse. The Italian claims against France had provoked a violent reaction from Paris, with the result that Mussolini decided to waive his previous reservations regarding the time for concluding the suggested alliance with Berlin and Tokyo. On 23 December Ciano noted in his diary that it was now his master's intention 'to adhere to the triangular pact of assistance, as proposed by Ribbentrop'. On 2 January 1939—the day before the meeting between Mussolini and Phillips—he notified Ribbentrop of Italy's acceptance, while the Duce himself warned the Holy See

---

[1] *FRUS 1938*, i. 858–60. On 30 December 1938 Welles instructed Phillips to make the following changes in the last two paragraphs of the above memorandum: 'The Chief of the Government has undoubtedly heard that Dr. Schacht, during his recent visit to London, established a formal contact with the Director of the Inter-governmental Committee (on Refugees) and put forward certain proposals of a specific character relating to the organisation of emigration from Germany over a specific period of years and to the financing of this emigration. At the initiative of the German Government, the Director (Rublee) now plans to visit Berlin early in the New Year for the purpose of continuing the discussions. An essential point of the financial discussions will be the difficulty of procuring foreign exchange in sufficient quantities to allow the immigrants to have cash in hand ... It is the earnest hope of the President of the United States that he may count upon the friendly interest of the Chief of the Italian Government in a general and satisfactory solution of this international problem' (ibid., p. 886). On Schacht's negotiations with Rublee (aimed at blackmailing Jewry into providing foreign currency for German rearmament), see *ADAP*, Serie D v. 767–9, 774–80.

that he would not tolerate any opposition to his racial policy.[1] It is hardly surprising, therefore, that Phillips should have found the Italian dictator in a distinctly unaccommodating frame of mind. Recording the interview in his memoirs many years later, the Ambassador wrote:

On 3 January 1939, I presented to the Duce a letter from the President together with a memorandum suggesting that the plateau region in southern Ethiopia and Kenya might be made available for Jewish colonization. The Duce said that this suggestion was impracticable, that this particular region in Ethiopia was inhabited by a people who were wholly unsympathetic to the Jews and that he had already offered a far better region north-west of Addis Ababa, a proposal which the Jews had not received favourably. Thereupon he opened a map of Ethiopia, examined the suggested plateau and showed me vaguely the area to which he referred.

I asked for permission to speak with frankness. He was aware, I said, 'of the strained relations between the United States and Germany. This unfortunate situation is partly the result of the methods which have been and are continuing to be employed by the German Government in forcing Jews to leave the country. These methods have greatly shocked public opinion in America.'

Here the Duce interrupted me with a tirade against the Jews. In his opinion, there would not be 'a Jew left in Germany. Other countries (and he mentioned in particular Rumania and Hungary) are confronted with the same problem and are finding it necessary to rid themselves of their Jewish elements. There is no room for Jews in Europe, and eventually they will all have to go.'

I reminded him that this forced emigration from Europe had created an international problem with which we in the United States were vitally concerned. It was not a question solely for those states from which the emigrants departed, but it was also a question of finding them a suitable home.

In reply, Mussolini mentioned Russia or 'vast tracts of unoccupied land in North America' which he considered more suitable than the congested areas of Europe. I explained the work of the London Committee[2] and asked him whether he would join with other leaders and states in trying to find a solution. Finally he agreed to do so and I

[1] Ciano, *1937–1938 Diario*, p. 313; id., *Diario*, i: *1939–1940*, 6th edn., Milan, 1950, pp. 11–14; *L'Europa verso la catastrofe*, ii. 12–15.

[2] The Inter-Governmental Committee on Political Refugees in London, instituted by the ill-starred Evian Conference on Refugees (6–15 July 1938); cf. *FRUS 1938*, i. 740–886 and M. Wischnitzer, *To Dwell in Safety. The Story of Jewish Migration since 1800*, Philadelphia, 1948, pp. 200–6, Laqueur, *A History of Zionism*, pp. 507–8.

expressed the hope that he would find some occasion to ally himself publicly with the movement. But when I asked whether he could intervene with the German Government, he replied, 'The continual public condemnation of Germany's actions has immensely stiffened the German attitude and actually has increased Germany's determination to deal drastically with the situation'. He thought that very little could be done with the German authorities unless there was a cessation of these attacks.

I interjected, 'In view of the widespread disgust in America with Germany's action, it is impossible to alter the attitude of Americans.' During the entire discussion, Count Ciano remained standing and offered no comment or suggestion. He might as well have worn a livery!

This conversation produced no results, for Mussolini, to my knowledge, never allied himself with the London Committee. He had evidently caught from Hitler the anti-Jewish fever, probably in order to keep in Hitler's good graces.[1]

On the following day Ciano informed the German Ambassador about the American proposals. He began by pointing out that Roosevelt's message, though drafted on 7 December, had not been delivered until 3 January because the Duce had deliberately kept Phillips waiting. He then gave Mackensen copies of Roosevelt's letter and memorandum to read. When the latter had finished reading, he told him (according to Mackensen's account) that Mussolini had 'at once answered the (American) Ambassador somewhat as follows':

Italian racial legislation which had its origin in certain needs was a *noli me tangere* (in this connection Ciano added in conversation with me that here they wanted shortly to give the screw an even sharper turn). He would not dream of making as much as a square inch of Ethiopian territory available for Jewish settlement [*sic*]. Nor had he any intention of interfering in our internal affairs in any way, all the less so since he entirely approved of our anti-Jewish legislation which he found explicable if for no other reason than because of what the Jews had done to our people in the post-war years.

As things stood today, the complete separation (Ciano used the term 'divorce') of the Aryan from the non-Aryan world was in full swing and was making progress every day in other countries as well, such as Hungary, Romania, etc. The moment had come when the whole of Europe was closing its doors to the Jews (*sich den Juden verschliesse*).

[1] Phillips *Ventures in Diplomacy*, pp. 120–2.

Personally he was by no means unsympathetic to the idea of setting up a separate Jewish State; it was not in Africa, however, that such a State would be established. In his opinion there were three countries which would be perfectly capable of absorbing Jewish emigrants. In the first place there was Russia, but as far as he knew, the Jews showed no inclination whatever to take up residence there. In the second place there was Brazil where there also existed certain difficulties, but finally there was the United States which, after all, entertained such lively sympathy for the Jews. At the moment they had 120 million inhabitants but, compared for instance with the population density of Italy, they could in his opinion accommodate 1,400 millions[*sic*]. Surely, territory suitable in every respect could be found there.

Mussolini had, as Ciano told me, clothed his somewhat humorously tinged statement in friendly terms, out of regard for the Ambassador whom he finds not unlikeable; but he now regarded the whole matter as closed. He considered it new proof of the Americans' characteristic lack of political sense and, after the Ambassador had taken his leave, made some very entertaining observations to Ciano about this strange conversation.[1]

It would be rash to conclude from the above that Mussolini, having decided to sign a military pact with Hitler, was no longer willing to make some positive contribution to the solution of the refugee problem. Despite Ciano's assertion to the contrary, there is little doubt that he would have been pleased to win applause in the Western world and earn the thanks of both Jews and Arabs by placing some part of his African Empire at the disposal of Hitler's Jewish victims. Once he embraced the Führer's racial gospel, however, the Jews were bound to react negatively to his offer of an 'earthly paradise' in Ethiopia. Nor was there anything he could do about Hitler's refusal to co-operate with the London

[1] Mackensen to Wilhelmstrasse, 4 Jan. 1939 (*ADAP*, Serie D iv. 478–9. While Ciano's version of the meeting between Mussolini and Phillips is obviously coloured by a desire to curry favour with the Germans, it tallies in substance with the Ambassador's. That Mussolini referred to the need for racial laws in Italy (a subject Roosevelt had studiously refrained from mentioning) is not improbable since Phillips's attack on German racial policy implied a condemnation of the Fascist imitation; that he poked fun at Roosevelt's message is equally credible, given his well-known contempt for the sentimental humanitarianism of Western statesmen. In his diary Ciano tells us that it was Mackensen himself who ridiculed the American proposals and made 'some sharp comments on American lack of political sense' (*Diario*, i. 15); but the two versions are not mutually exclusive.

Committee, given his total lack of influence on his erstwhile disciple.[1]

The Duce's negative response to Roosevelt's letter did not deter the British appeasers, Chamberlain and Halifax, from making a similar appeal eight days later, during an official visit to Rome.[2] Like the American President, the British Premier had been impressed by Mussolini's performance at the Munich Conference and thought that he could be applied to, as in September 1938, to bring his Axis partner to a more accommodating frame of mind. Neither Chamberlain nor his Foreign Secretary expected to detach Italy from Germany; both of them hoped, however, that Western support would give the Duce greater power of manœuvre and freedom to resume what they called 'the classic Italian role of balancing between Germany and the Western Powers'.[3] As late as 20 March 1939 Chamberlain told his Cabinet that the Italian dictator 'was probably the only person who could put the brake on Herr Hitler'.[4]

It was in the context of these illusions that Chamberlain raised the refugee problem with Mussolini on 11 January 1939. In Ciano's minute of the conversation the relevant passage reads as follows:

Chamberlain asks the Duce if he has any proposals or suggestions to advance on the question of refugees. The Duce, referring to the problem of Jewish refugees, informs Mr. Chamberlain of the message received by him recently from Roosevelt, as well as of his replies to the American Ambassador which were later confirmed in a letter sent direct to the President of the United States. Mr. Chamberlain agrees with the conclusions reached by the Duce and with the solution proposed by him [*sic*]. He says, however, that meanwhile it would be necessary to reach an agreement to facilitate the emigration of the Jews from Germany. But it is clear that no State will wish to take these Jews unless the

[1] Being resolved to 'export anti-Semitism' (see above, p. 157), Hitler could have no interest in Western schemes for the orderly emigration and resettlement of Jews; on Germany's use of anti-Semitism as a political weapon, cf. Schumburg's memorandum 25 January 1939 (see above, p. 195 n. 1).

[2] The visit lasted from 11 to 14 January 1939. Chamberlain's preoccupation with the refugee issue was due in part to genuine moral indignation and in part to the fact that Hitler's anti-Jewish excesses had the effect of increasing still further the widespread opposition to his appeasement policy; see D. Dilks (ed.), *The Diaries of Sir Alexander Cadogan 1938–1945*, London, 1971, p. 132 and Dirksen to Wilhelmstrasse, 17 Nov. 1938 and 3 Jan. 1939 (*ADAP*, Serie D iv. 288–90, 309–14).

[3] Halifax to Phipps (Paris), 1 Nov. 1938 (*DBFP*, 3rd Ser. iii. 253).

[4] PRO/Cab.23/98, p. 84.

German Government agrees to make some sacrifice by permitting them to bring out with them a sum of money, even a modest one, with which to establish themselves. The Duce states that he agrees with Mr. Chamberlain and, for his part, considers that the German Government, since it intends to solve the Jewish problem in a totalitarian manner, will be able to make some sacrifice in order to further the total exodus of the Jewish masses from Germany territory. However, one must not demand too heavy sacrifices from the German people which has suffered greatly because of the Jews, particularly in the period immediately after the war.[1]

The brevity and vagueness of Ciano's account clearly reflects his lack of interest in the subject.[2] According to the more detailed British record of the conversation (which makes no mention of Roosevelt's *démarche*), the Duce made a show of being responsive to Chamberlain's request for co-operation, even to the extent of promising to use his (non-existent) influence with the Führer:

The Prime Minister asked (Mussolini) if he would say anything about the refugee problem. The Duce said that the Jewish refugee problem was not a local one, but one of general application. It was already not a problem in Germany only, and he thought probably it would be bound to arise in many other countries, including the United Kingdom. At this point he broke into a broad smile and said that that was his opinion. The best permanent solution would be the establishment of an independent Sovereign Jewish State which would not require that all Jews should live in it, since, as subjects of such a State, they would have their status and their official representation in whatever country they lived, like other people. To find a place for such a State, one must look to the countries that had large areas of territory such as the United States of America, Soviet Russia or Brazil. He said, with some indication of irony, that it might be some time before such a solution was practicable, but it must be regarded as a long-term aim. The Foreign Secretary (Halifax) then inquired whether it would not be possible to persuade the German Government to make some effort to facilitate the departure of the Jews from Germany by allowing them to take some money out with them. Signor Mussolini thought it would be so possible, but that it would not be of much use to ask for a great deal as the

---

[1] *L'Europa verso la catastrofe*, ii. 16–17. On 17 January Attolico handed to Weizsäcker a true copy of Ciano's minute which was duly passed on to Ribbentrop and Hitler (GFM/2441/514643–49).
[2] After the conversation Ciano wrote in his diary: 'The matters which were discussed were not highly important, and both parties betrayed their mental reservations ... Effective contact has not been made' (*Diario*, i. 20).

Germans had suffered great hardships and had become very poor in consequence of the actions of the Jews [*sic*]. He thought, however, that they were quite determined to get rid of them and would be very ready to do anything they could that would expedite their departure, provided a large-scale plan could be formulated. He himself would be prepared to use any influence he might have in that direction. The Prime Minister asked how the Duce contemplated that the next step should be taken; would it not be for Mr. Rublee of the International Commission to approach the German Government in the first instance? The Duce agreed, especially as this was an international affair which could not be solved by any one State alone.[1]

Mussolini concluded by affirming that 'the reactions of British public opinion on the subject of what was after all a matter of internal policy in Germany' had merely served to aggravate the situation.[2]

On the following day the Duce hinted at his mixed feelings about the German racial theories he had just imported into Italy. Speaking to Sir Alexander Cadogan, Permanent Under-Secretary of State at the Foreign Office, he admitted that there was no such thing as an Aryan race, adding that 'only 20% of Germans were fair-haired'. On 13 January the Jewish issue was again touched upon in an informal talk between Mussolini, Chamberlain, and Ciano: 'We spoke of the Jewish question, and it was interesting to note that Chamberlain did not know the number of Jews in England. He thought there were perhaps 60,000; the Duce said they were in excess of 200,000. Chamberlain is very much concerned with the problem, fearing as he does that any further Jewish immigration into England would increase the anti-Semitism which already exists in many parts of the country.'[3]

On his return to London, Chamberlain informed his Cabinet that the Italian dictator was a charming host and a man of peace, his demonstrative loyalty to Hitler notwithstanding. As regards refugees, 'Signor Mussolini had not been very specific but he had not been unsympathetic and had expressed his willingness to

---

[1] Mussolini's views on the Jewish question in Germany appear to have been based on those expressed by Roberto Suster in his above-quoted book on the Weimar Republic (*La Germania repubblicana*, pp. 189–202,) for which the Duce wrote the preface.

[2] *DBFP*, 3rd Ser. iii. 519–20. There is no mention of Mussolini's promise to use 'any influence he might have' with Hitler in any German or Italian document available to us; Mackensen's reports of 12 and 13 January (GFM/33/25312–20), based on information supplied by Ciano, do not contain any reference to the Jews.

[3] *Diaries of Sir Alexander Cadogan*, p. 137; Ciano, *Diario*, i. 22.

help'. The Cabinet were duly impressed and congratulated the Prime Minister on the 'success' of his mission.[1]

In reality, however, the visit was not only unproductive but harmful, not least from the Jewish point of view; for it confirmed Mussolini in his contempt for the appeasers and his determination to throw in his lot with Hitler. Ciano wrote in his diary that Chamberlain's fear of Germany was an excellent reason for signing the proposed triple alliance.[2] Nor did the Duce keep his promise to intercede with Hitler on behalf of Jewish refugees from Germany.

While the British appeasers looked to Mussolini for help in reaching a settlement with the Axis Powers (including a 'just' solution of the refugee problem), Jewish leaders in Britain and America were trying to find ways and means of alleviating the lot of their brethren in Italy. On the eve of the talks between Chamberlain and Mussolini Sir Andrew McFadyean, a prominent Liberal and a former private secretary to Stanley Baldwin, proceeded to Italy at the request of the Board of Deputies of British Jews and the American Joint Distribution Committee to investigate the position of the Italian Jews and refugees under the new racial laws. He spent ten days in Milan and Rome where he discussed the problem 'with a score of different people, Jewish and non-Jewish, engaged in business, law and academic pursuits'. He was also in touch with the British Embassy but refrained from contacting Italian officials. On his return to England, he submitted a seven-page report to Neville Laski, six copies of which were sent to the Foreign Office.[3]

The first part of Sir Andrew's memorandum was devoted to a 'diagnosis of the malady'. He began by pointing out that Italian racialism, though obviously of German origin, was in a sense *sui generis*;

[1] Cabinet meeting of 18 Jan. 1939 (PRO/Cab.23/97, pp. 4–11). Chamberlain was 'convinced that Signor Mussolini and Herr Hitler could not be very sympathetic to each other, and that, although they had some interests in common, their interests were not identical. Further, he rather doubted whether Signor Mussolini was aware of Herr Hitler's plans. Accordingly, he had on several occasions given Mussolini a chance to express his real feelings of Herr Hitler. He had never taken the opportunity offered to him, but he had remained throughout absolutely loyal' to Herr Hitler. The Prime Minister said that at the time he had been somewhat disappointed at this attitude, but on reflection he thought that it reflected credit on Signor Mussolini's character.'
[2] Ciano, *Diario*, i. 21.
[3] N. Laski to Sir Robert Vansittart, 30 Jan. 1939 (see above, p. 186 n. 1).

Anti-semitism is a disease which runs a well-marked course, and the symptoms present a very consistent picture. The character of the infection varies, however, and it is plainly of importance to attempt some diagnosis of the cause in a particular case if one is concerned to inquire into the possibility and nature of a cure ... Now the case of Italy is peculiar in that, in spite of anti-semitic policy and legislation, anti-semitism outside a restricted Government circle is non-existent ... True, there are individuals who are profiting personally by the dismissal of Jewish officials, functionaries and employees, and it would be asking too much of human nature to expect such individuals to regard the policy which directly benefits them with whole-hearted abhorrence. It must be true also that propaganda on lines which are being slavishly copied from Germany must in course of time, if it is sufficiently prolonged, have some effect on ignorant minds. The fact remains that at the moment it would be difficult to hear anything outside official circles in defence of the official policy. It is notorious that Italian Jews ... were almost completely assimilated—so much so that I was constantly hearing of individuals whose Jewish origin had remained unsuspected by their closest associates for thirty years until a few months ago. It is currently stated that the anti-Jewish measures met with serious opposition in the Government itself, particularly from Balbo.[1]

What was the Duce's motive in pursuing a policy which met with opposition in the highest Fascist circles, was unpopular in the country, and served to bring Italy into contempt among decent nations? Those to whom Sir Andrew put this question invariably replied that only one man in Italy was in a position to enlighten him, namely Mussolini himself. There seemed, however, to be a universal conviction that the Fascist dictator had given his promise to Hitler.

Various rumours of varying degrees of verisimilitude were floating around. The economic motive was sometimes suggested but without much conviction. The Duce was said to have received from German sources documents so incriminating the Jews that their publication would have resulted in a spontaneous persecution compared with which the official policy was benign; other stories were that Mussolini was vulnerable to blackmail (the Germans having found documents in Vienna which

---

[1] As pointed out above, Balbo had ceased to be a member of the government in 1933; in 1939 he was Governor-General of Libya. Oddly enough, there is no reference to Balbo's well-known Germanophobia and philo-Semitism in any of the German records at our disposal.

betrayed his disloyalty to the Axis) and that Hitler had made the conclusion of a military pact between the two countries conditional on the removal of Jewish officers from the Italian forces. But the simplest explanation was that Mussolini wished to display in some striking fashion his complete solidarity with Germany, even though the proof he chose to give was widely regarded as a demonstration of his complete dependence on Hitler.[1]

But whatever the motives which had impelled the Italian leader to break with the Jews, it was abundantly clear that they were political in character, part and parcel of his international policy; from which the quite simple conclusion emerged that it would be idle to hope for any marked alleviation in Jewish conditions as long as Italy remained faithful to the Axis alliance: 'Whether Mussolini desires, and whether, if so, he could effect, a change of friendships is a matter of prophecy and nothing else, but no one could suppose that a change will come quickly.'

Having diagnosed the disease and drawn the obvious inference, Sir Andrew proceeded to analyse the problem of the foreign Jews domiciled in Italy whom he divided into three sub-classes: (1) ex-Germans and ex-Austrians; (2) Romanians and Poles; (3) Jews of other nationalities, including British and Americans. The ex-Germans and ex-Austrians (who had now to face a second or in some cases even a third exile) were the most to be pitied. They had lost their German citizenship, and the German authorities would hardly consent to receive them again across the frontiers 'unless for purely sadistic reasons'. Worse still, many of them were receiving orders to leave Italy in advance of 12 March 1939, the date fixed by law. The Poles and Romanians were only better off in that, if they could return to their own countries, they had no reason to expect excessive brutality. In fact, however, Poland and Romania were refusing to readmit them, even where they had done nothing to lose their Polish or Romanian nationality.

The best these unhappy refugees could look forward to was imprisonment in March. By the circulation of rumours and of threats the Italian Government was doing its best to drive them abroad through illicit channels; Shanghai and suicide were both

[1] Sir Andrew's speculations about Mussolini's motives are of value as showing that the Germans and the British were equally ill informed on the subject.

taking their toll. On all grounds the case of the ex-Germans was the most tragic and the most urgent. They presumably fell within the ambit of the London Committee and were (Sir Andrew thought) entitled to at least as much consideration as the Jews who had not yet escaped from Germany. As for the Poles and Romanians, some pressure might be brought to bear on their countries of origin 'to induce them to fulfil their obvious duty and readmit their own nationals'.

As for the handful of British and American Jews, Sir Andrew was given to understand that their fate 'need not cause any serious anxiety': 'It will depend on the strength of the representations which their diplomatic representatives can make in Rome, and it is probable that if publicity is not given to the matter, so that no question of principle is openly raised, the Italian Government will be found accommodating.'

Foreign Jews married to Italians had so far been treated as Aryans and suffered no hardship. The fifty thousand Italian Jews, on the other hand, had been dealt a crushing blow. Those to whom Sir Andrew talked 'were like people stupefied by a bad dream from which they had not yet awakened', and it was difficult to form an opinion as to what they had to expect if there was no major change of policy. Large numbers had applied for 'discrimination' in their favour, but no one could tell on what basis 'discrimination' would be made; meanwhile war-widows and war-orphans were being deprived of their means of livelihood. Many people, both Jew and Gentile, expected Mussolini to follow the German example step by step until there was nothing to choose between the fate of the German Jew and that of his Italian co-religionist. It was widely feared that the Bonds which were to be given to the Jews in exchange for their property, and which they would be unable to turn into cash at any time, would be accorded lower and lower rates of interest; in any case lira Bonds could hardly be regarded as a good investment of capital. Sooner or later, therefore, such Italian Jews as did not obtain discrimination would be clamouring for a means of escape and hence had to be regarded as part of the Jewish problem; the mere sense of outrage would impel large numbers to leave Italy as and when opportunity offered.

If the above analysis was correct, it followed that there was nothing which British Jewry could do directly to produce any sensible improvement in the situation: 'The origin of the malady being political, the cure must be political and therefore effected, if at all, by Government action. Those with whom I talked were unanimous in deprecating any campaign ... by foreign Jews. Their attitude was partly humanitarian; they did not desire innocent Italians at home or abroad to suffer for the sins of the Italian Government. It was partly dictated by fear and a natural apprehension that in a game of reprisals the more unscrupulous party will always win, and the Italian Jew therefore only suffer all the more; this consideration was, of course, particularly present to the minds of those who are hoping for discrimination.'

If private initiative was ruled out, what about the chances of successful government action? There was a general hope that President Roosevelt's personal interest might secure some alleviations. It was also hoped that Chamberlain's intervention might be beneficial, particularly if his talks with Mussolini were 'productive of fruitful results in a wider field'. The feeling after his visit was that the situation remained unchanged. Mussolini had, however, promised him to co-operate in the solution of the German problem; and while the nature of the co-operation was left undefined, Sir Andrew gained the impression that the Duce would indeed be willing to help if (but only if) the London Committee could present evidence that it had formulated a constructive long-term plan for emigration and resettlement. It appeared to Sir Andrew that nothing would satisfy the requirements of such a long-term plan 'except the provision of adequate territory to receive many hundreds of thousands, and even millions, of Jews from Europe over a term of years'.

If the Evian Conference could show that it was grappling with the problem on some such lines, the Italian Government would be ready to co-operate by slowing down its anti-Jewish measures 'to the extent necessary to permit of an orderly solution of difficulties'. Sir Andrew was advised that, if real progress was achieved, either the vice-chairman or the chairman of the London Committee should go to Rome and take up the matter personally with the Italian authorities.

As for Jewish immigration into Ethiopia, Mussolini had not been lying when he told Phillips that the Jews had rejected his offer of an 'earthly paradise' in that country. While Sir Andrew was in Italy, there was something like consternation at a rumour that Roosevelt's suggestion had included the settlement of Ethiopia and that the subject had also been mentioned in the talks between Chamberlain and Mussolini. There could scarcely be one Jew in Italy who would consent of his own free will to settle in Italian East Africa. In the first place there would be a natural reluctance to be used by the Facists to develop territory which the rest of the world regarded as ill-gotten gains. In the second place, and more importantly, Italian Jews would not leave Italy to remain under Italian sovereignty, with the expectation that if they were successful in the new home they would be exposed to renewed persecution. Sir Andrew was informed on good authority 'that any suggestion regarding Ethiopia might be regarded as dead. It was indeed suggested that Mussolini omitted Ethiopia from the regions to which the new legislation applied with the idea that he was conferring a favour on the Jews, and that, finding that they did not regard it in the same light, he was perfectly prepared to drop the subject'.

From the above Sir Andrew drew the 'regrettably negative' inference that the only action of any importance which Jews outside Italy could take was to use all their influence with their own governments to secure a 'constructive long-term plan'— in the hope that more time might be available and that, if war was avoided, there might even be a reversal of Italian foreign policy.[1]

Sir Andrew concluded by warning against half-measures which were likely to do more harm than good:

I believe, and I stated it frankly when in Italy, that the kind of partial solution represented by continued infiltration into this country, France, Holland and the United States should no longer be followed and is indeed to be deprecated. It is of no use to any Jew to help to create an anti-semitic problem in countries which are at present uninfected. There can be little doubt that one of Herr Hitler's objects is to innoculate [*sic*] country after country with the virus of anti-semitism and create civil unrest throughout Europe from which he hopes to gain.

If, therefore, only a general solution is possible, it is a mistake to

[1] It was widely believed in British political circles at the time that Mussolini, for all his demonstrative loyalty to Hitler, was worried about the German menace and anxious to retain some liberty of action; see, e.g., Cadogan's memorandum of 14 Oct. 1938 (PRO/F.O. 371/21659/22) and Perth to Halifax, 27 Dec. 1938 (*DBFP,* 3rd Ser. iii. 498). While this belief was well founded, British observers generally failed to realize that the Duce was no better informed about Hitler's schemes than Chamberlain or Daladier and that he had no influence whatever on the German dictator (see L.B. Namier, 'Ciano's Early Diary', *Europe in Decay,* London, 1950, p. 118).

think too closely of the problem in Italy or Germany divorced from other countries. Anything which is done for the half million odd Jews in Italy and Germany will create a demand in Poland, Romania and Hungary and raise a problem which must be roughly five times as great in its dimensions. Above all, nothing should be done in the German and Italian cases which makes the export of Jews a profitable operation for the economies of the exporting countries. Putting all moral questions aside—and it is not moral to pay a blackmailer—financial sacrifices made by the outside world which might satisfy Germany and Italy would become intolerable when extended to cover all Central European Jewry. A general solution, the execution of which would necessarily be spread over many years, should be possible [*sic*], but if not, hard as the saying is, there is at least one Gentile who is sincerely convinced that nothing more should be attempted, except perhaps the minimum of humanitarian relief and that the time has already come when the Jews in Totalitarian States must be regarded as hostages whom it is impossible to ransom, or kidnapped persons for whom blood money cannot be provided without increasing the appetite of their captors to a degree which can never be satisfied.

The Foreign Office agreed with these 'regrettably negative' conclusions and informed Laski that there was nothing in Sir Andrew's report that they would 'seriously wish to contest'. They were, however, inclined to think that the racial laws would not be too harshly applied, the Italians being a more easy-going people than the barbaric Germans. Whether Mussolini would co-operate with the London Committee in accordance with his promise was a matter of conjecture. So far all he had done was to make matters worse by creating a refugee problem in his own country; nor was he likely to quarrel with his ally for the sake of the German Jews.[1]

In the ensuing weeks it become increasingly clear that there would be no 'constructive long-term plan' for resettlement and no Italian co-operation in the solution of the German Problem. But if Mussolini, for the reasons stated, was unable to provide territory and unwilling to intercede with Hitler, could he not at least be prevailed upon to adopt a more lenient attitude towards the Jewish refugees in Italy? On 14 February 1939 Myron Taylor, Vice-Chairman of the London Committee, telegraphed the following appeal to the American State Department.

[1] Foreign Office minute of 6 Feb. 1939 (see above, p. 186 n. 1).

There has been pressure on me from many sources since the Italian decrees relating to Jews were issued to make an appeal to Mussolini to postpone the date when the decrees will go into effect. With the President's approval I should like to go to Rome from Florence and, with the assistance and collaboration of Ambassador Phillips, attempt to make this apeal.

Jewish organizations with which I am in confidential contact are preparing a detailed memorandum on the situation which I can leave with Mussolini.

My best informed friend in Italian matters, who was with me on Friday (February 10), expressed the belief that I should present the memorandum and then orally attempt to persuade Mussolini to relax the pressure on the Jews and to postpone action from March 12.

Please inform me whether you perceive any objection to this plan, to which I hope you will give your sympathetic consideration.[1]

Two days later representatives of the Italian Refugee Committee called on Phillips, the Ambassador, and discussed with him 'the approaching crisis for all foreign Jews in Italy who will not have been able to leave Italy before March 12'. The Ambassador hastened to inform the Secretary of State, pointing out that in view of the assurances received from Mussolini on 3 January, he might be in a position to make some helpful approach. On 18 February Hull replied as follows:

Myron Taylor, who will reach Florence early next week, wishes to take up with Mussolini the possibility of delay beyond March 12 in the application of the Italian Decrees. We have advised him that we perceive no objection but suggested that he consult you before making definite plans.

Mr Taylor's *démarche*, however, will be personal and unofficial as the Intergovernmental Committee's mandate does not include negotiations on behalf of involuntary emigrants from any country other than Germany.[2]

As might be expected the Duce refused flatly to receive the representative of so notoriously anti-German and anti-Fascist a body as the Inter-Governmental Committee on Political Refugees in London. On 27 February Phillips informed Hull that he had been unable to secure an audience for Taylor, adding, however, that there were still grounds for guarded optimism: 'It is possible

---

[1] Johnson (London) to Hull, 14 Feb. 1939 (*FRUS 1939*, ii. 649–50).
[2] Phillips to Hull, 16 Feb. 1939 (ibid. 651–2); Hull to Phillips, 18 Feb. 1939 (ibid. 652).

that Mussolini may be intending to postpone the provisions set for March 12 with regard to the forced departure of foreigners of Jewish extraction until a later date and that his refusal to receive Taylor was in order not to give the impression of taking such action under pressure. Mr Taylor agrees that in the circumstances it will be best to avoid all publicity and do nothing further until perhaps March 7th or 8th when, if you see no objection, you might instruct me to seek an interview with Ciano with a view to having the time limit extended'.[1]

The Ambassador's optimism was soon shown to be justified. On 8 March a representative of the Jewish Refugee Committee advised the American Embassy in Rome that, according to information received from the Ministry of the Interior, foreign Jews who had requested authorization to remain in Italy after 12 March would be permitted to do so. On 10 March Phillips had an interview with Ciano who confirmed the good news, adding that there would be no round-up or imprisonment of any foreign Jews in Italy on 12 March; even the refugees from Germany could stay. The Ambassador was left with the definite impression that 'the decision had been reached to relax the anti-Jewish campaign'.[2]

Having thus given proof of his magnanimity, the Duce hastened to reassure his German ally. On 15 March (the very day Hitler invaded Czechoslovakia) the Fascist press carried the following announcement regarding foreign Jews in Italy:

The 12th instant marked the expiration of the period established by Article 24 of the law relating to the defence of the race for the departure from the Kingdom of foreign Jews who initiated their sojourn in Italy after 1 January 1919.[3] Before this date many foreign Jews left the Kingdom of their own accord; the others with the exception of those authorized to stay under the provisions of Article 25, will gradually leave the Kingdom within the next few days. It is presumed, therefore, that with the exception of special cases for reasons of health or family conditions all foreign Jews residing in Italy subsequent to 1 January 1919 will leave the Kingdom within a brief period.[4]

---

[1] Phillips to Hull, 27 Feb. 1939 (ibid. 653).
[2] Phillips to Hull, 8 and 10 Mar. 1939 (ibid. 653–4).
[3] Royal Decree Law No. 1728 of 17 Nov. 1938 (Provisions for the Defence of the Italian Race), reproduced in De Felice, *Storia degli ebrei italiani,* pp. 362–6.
[4] *Il Tevere,* 15 Mar. 1939; Phillips to Hull, 15 Mar. 1939 (*FRUS 1939,* ii. 654).

In view of the apparent divergence between the above announcement and the previous information received from the Italian Foreign Minister, Phillips had a further interview with Ciano who assured him definitely that his statement of 10 March 'held good so far as concerns the time permitted foreign Jews to leave Italy';[1] subsequently, it was learnt that for once the Fascist Government had been as good as its word.

The Jews and their friends had won a minor battle; but Phillips was mistaken in assuming that this concession to Western opinion marked the beginning of a change for the better. Having decided to strengthen his ties with Berlin, Mussolini could not permit any abatement of the anti-Jewish drive, except for occasional humane gestures which cost him little and were in no way inconsistent with his ultimate objective, a *judenrein* Italy. Given his belief in German military superiority, he was undoubtedly sincere when he told Phillips on 3 January that there was 'no room for Jews in Europe' and that 'eventually' they would all have to go. (The word 'eventually' reflected his erroneous assumption that he could postpone the inevitable clash with the Western Powers until his country was ready for war.)

As we have seen, the Duce had decided on 23 December to adhere to the proffered triangular pact of assistance. On 1 January he ordered Ciano to notify Berlin of his acceptance, adding that he wished the pact to be signed before the end of the month. On 4 January Attolico informed Rome that the German Foreign Minister favoured 28 January as the date for signing the treaty. When the Japanese unexpectedly raised objections, Mussolini lost patience and began to press for a bilateral pact within the participation of Japan, affirming that 'such an alliance would alone be sufficient to meet the array of Anglo-French forces and at the same time would not appear to be anti-English [*sic*] or anti-American'.[2] Given this eagerness for an immediate military alignment with Berlin, there was no room for any marked alleviation in Jewish conditions, whatever the Duce's private views on the subject.

Hitler, for his part, lost no time in making it clear that he considered the common struggle against Jewry an essential aspect of the Axis alliance. In his Reichstag speech of 30 January

[1] Phillips to Hull, 17 Mar. 1939 (ibid. 654).
[2] Ciano, *Diario*, i. 36 (8 Feb. 1939).

he warned the democracies that any attack on his friend Mussolini would mean war with the Reich: 'Let no one in the world make any mistake as to the resolve which National Socialist Germany has made as far as this friend is concerned. It can only serve the cause of peace if it is clearly understood that a war waged against the Italy of today will, once it is launched and regardless of its motives, call Germany to the side of her friend.' On the same occasion he reminded his hearers that by now the solidarity of the two regimes (on which 'the salvation of Europe from its threatened destruction by Bolshevism' depended) extended to the Jewish issue: 'The time when the non-Jewish nations were incapable of conducting propaganda campaigns (*die Zeit der propagandistischen Wehrlosigkeit der nichtjüdischen Völker*) is at an end. National Socialist Germany and Fascist Italy have institutions which enable them when necessary to enlighten the world about the nature of a problem of which many nations are instinctively conscious but which they have not yet clearly thought out.' As for the solution of the refugee question, the Western Jew-lovers had no right to demand financial sacrifices from the Axis Powers when they themselves had no intention of lifting a finger for the Jews: 'It is a shameful spectacle to see how the whole democratic world is oozing sympathy for the poor tormented Jewish people but remains hard-hearted and obdurate when it comes to helping them—which is surely, in view of its attitude, an obvious duty. The arguments that are brought up as an excuse for not helping them (*Nichthilfe*) actually speak for us Germans and Italians.'[1]

On the following day Ciano noted in his diary that the Führer's speech had 'produced the best impression everywhere' (*sic*) and that even the Duce was 'very well satisfied with it'—so much so that he had his son-in-law telephone Ribbentrop to tell him 'that the words uttered làst night have given a great deal of joy and satisfaction to all the Italian people'.[2] On 4 February the Fascist leader explained the reasons for his pro-German orientation in a speech to the Fascist Grand Council which had been drafted to guide the Party hierarchs in Italian foreign policy 'for a short or for a long, even very long, term':

[1] Domarus, *Hitler, Reden und Proklamationen*, ii. 1056–8, 1062.
[2] Ciano, *Diario*, i. 30–1 (31 Jan. 1939).

The premiss from which I argue is the following: States are more or less independent according to their maritime position ... Italy is bordered by an inland sea which communicates with the ocean through the Suez Canal—an artificial means of communication which is easily blocked even by accident—and by the Straits of Gibraltar, dominated by British guns. Italy has in fact no free access to the oceans. She is really a prisoner in the Mediterranean, and the more populous and powerful she becomes, the more she will suffer from her imprisonment. The bars of this prison are Corsica, Tunisia, Malta, and Cyprus; its sentinels are Gibraltar and Suez.

From this situation Mussolini drew two conclusions: 'First, the task of Italian policy which has not and never can have as objectives continental European territory except Albania [*sic*] is ... to break the prison bars. Second, once this has been accomplished, Italian policy can have only one watchword: the March to the Ocean. Which Ocean? The Indian Ocean linking across the Sudan and Libya to Ethiopia; or the Atlantic Ocean across French North Africa? In the first, as in the second, hypothesis we find ourselves face to face with Anglo-French opposition. To brave the solution of such a problem without having secured our backs on the Continent would be absurd. The policy of the Rome–Berlin Axis therefore answers the historical necessity of a fundamental order. The same applies to our conduct in the Spanish civil war.'

After Munich it had been alleged both at home and abroad that 'once again the Axis had functioned exclusively in favour of Germany'. The Fascist reaction to this 'unfounded' allegation had been to raise territorial claims against France in order to make it clear to all concerned that the alliance between the two kindred regimes had Italian as well as German objectives. Close ties with the Reich would enable Italy to press these claims with a chance of success. Nor was there any reason to doubt the Führer's loyalty after his public promise of unconditional military support.

Apart from its ideological significance, then, the purpose of the pro-German policy was to cover and secure the continental position of Italy by treaty with the greatest European Power and free her to pursue her 'vital interests' in the Mediterranean and in Africa. But the Duce's ultimate success in achieving his imperial objectives might well depend on his ability to prevent his Axis partner from dragging him into a major war before Italy was in a condition to fight. The Czech crisis was a warning.

In his speech of 30 January Hitler had affirmed that Italy's armed forces, like Germany's, were 'equal to the severest military requirements'. Mussolini, in his address to the Grand Council, was realistic enough to paint a less rosy picture:

Are we today, in February 1939, in 'ideal' conditions to wage war? No State is ever in 'ideal' conditions to wage war if by this you mean to imply the mathematical assurance of victory . . . But there is no doubt that our preparations will be better in a few years' time. To be more precise: a) when we have renewed all our artillery (1941–42); b) when we have in service eight battleships and perhaps double the existing number of submarines (1941–42); c) when the Empire is completely pacified, self-sufficient, and capable of providing us with a native army; d) when we have realized at least fifty per cent of our autarkic plans; e) when we have held at the end of 1942 the Exhibition which should reinforce our reserves (of foreign currency); f) when we have repatriated the largest possible number of Italians from France; these 600,000 to 700,000 Italians resident in France constitute a very grave problem indeed.[1]

It was only from 1943 onwards that a war unleashed by the Axis Powers would have the greatest prospects of victory. Until then the Duce would go on playing the congenial role of mediator and peacemaker between the two rival ideological blocs, despite his ever-increasing disdain for the 'rotten' democracies and his ever-increasing eagerness for an outright military pact with the Reich.

An immediate military alignment with Berlin (Mussolini thought) would not only provide him with an excellent means of pressure against the Anglo-French; it would also enable him to put the brake on his Axis partner. So far the Führer had always acted independently of him and with scant regard for Italian interests. A formal alliance would compel him to consult his Italian colleague before making a move, thus enabling the latter to restrain his warlike initiatives.

It is against the background of these conflicting motives and mistaken assumptions about allies and enemies that the evolution of Fascist racial policy in the first half of 1939 must be understood.

[1] IC/*Segreteria particolare del Duce*/Job 1/000039–46; *O.O.* xxix. 230. For a detailed analysis of the speech cf. F.W. Deakin, *The Brutal Friendship*, London, 1962, pp. 5–8.

If the Axis was to be converted into a written agreement without delay, it would be imperative to accelerate the process of ideological *Gleichschaltung*, of which the anti-Jewish campaign was an essential part. And if Italy was to find her place in a German-dominated Europe, all Jews—including the 'exempted' ones—would eventually have to be expelled, despite the Duce's emphatic assurance that Fascist racialism signified 'not persecution, but discrimination'. But if the Fascist leader was to go on winning laurels as a peacemaker for another three years, he would have to take some account of the indignation which Hitler's anti-Jewish excesses had aroused in the Western world. Hence Ciano's declaration to Mackensen that his master had no intention of interceding with Hitler on behalf of the German Jews and that in Italy the screw would soon be given 'an even sharper turn'. But hence also Mussolini's desire for a 'constructive' solution of the Jewish problem, his refusal to imitate the German method of 'exporting anti-Semitism', and his willingness to humour the Americans over the refugee issue in Italy.

In the second half of February Mussolini redoubled his efforts to bring about a bilateral pact with the Germans; and by 10 March agreement seemed to be within reach, Hitler having accepted the Duce's proposals for Staff talks as a first step towards a military alliance.[1] A few days later, however, the German dictator entered Prague, annulling with one stroke the Munich and Vienna treaties of which his Fascist partner claimed paternity. It was the end of Mussolini's presumed ascendancy at Munich. On 14 March Ciano wrote in his diary: 'The Axis functions only in favour of one of its parts which tends to preponderate (*diviene di un peso troppo preponderante*) and acts entirely on its own initiative, with little regard for us.'[2]

Hitler's action aroused the utmost indignation in Italy. Reports poured into the Palazzo Venezia, from the police and from Fascist Party offices, emphasizing the anti-German sentiments of the people, without distinction of region or social class. Telegrams from the Italian missions abroad spoke of universal disgust at Germany's brutal annexation of Bohemia.[3] From Berlin Attolico

---

[1] Ciano, *Diario*, i. 52–3 (10 Mar. 1939).
[2] Ibid. 54.
[3] Donosti, *Mussolini e l'Europa*, pp. 150–5; Magistrati, *L'Italia a Berlino*, pp. 317–21; von Hassell, *Vom anderen Deutschland*, p. 54.

sounded a warning note, emphasizing the need of a 'basic clarification': was there equality of rights and obligations between the Axis Powers, and what did Germany make of the elementary duty of informing and consulting her ally? Was Italy to be excluded from the Balkans, with 'only *the waters of the Mediterranean* reserved to her'? If the two countries were to make common cause, it was essential that the rights and duties of each party should be clearly defined and that Hitler should categorically declare his intentions. Only then would there be any point in beginning to discuss a treaty of alliance.[1]

Mussolini himself, according to Ciano, was 'profoundly shaken' by the German *coup*: 'Even at the time of the Anschluss he had shown greater indifference'. He was shocked at the breach of Hitler's assurance that he did not wish to annex a single Czech. He had credited his partner with sincerity on this issue;[2] but after Prague, could any weight be attached to those German promises which more directly concerned Italy? He was also afraid that the Croats might proclaim their independence and place themselves under German protection. In such an event, he told Ciano, he would either have to fire the first shot against Germany or be overthrown by his own followers, since 'no one would tolerate the sight of a swastika in the Adriatic'. On 17 March Ciano warned Mackensen that the Duce, while fully agreeing with Hitler on the Czech issue (*sic*), could not tolerate any German intervention in Croatian affairs. If an attempt were made to change the *status quo* in Yugoslavia, 'the Axis would be broken'. On 19 March Mussolini ordered a concentration of forces on the Venetian border and informed the Prince Regent of Yugoslavia that he had 'called a halt to German action'. On the same day he agreed with Ciano that it was now impossible to present to the Italian people the idea of an alliance with Germany: 'The very stones would cry out against it'. In his bewilderment he considered the advisability of delaying the projected dispatch of troops to Libya and of coming to an agreement with France through London. The Duce's anger was, however, tempered by the calculation that Hitler was now too

[1] Attolico to Ciano, 18 Mar. 1939, quoted in Toscano, *Le origini diplomatiche*, pp. 165–6.

[2] Donosti, op. cit., p. 150; Pini, *Filo diretto*, pp. 169–70; *O.O.* xxix. 193.

powerful to oppose and that it was best to be on the winning side.[1]

Although Mussolini pretended to approve of Hitler's move, the Germans were well aware of the consternation and anxiety which their action in Czechoslovakia had caused in Rome. On 24 March Mackensen informed the Wilhelmstrasse that Italian discontent was due in part to the German practice of presenting Italy with a *fait accompli* and in part to the fear that in the end the old Habsburg Empire, this time under the swastika flag, would reappear on the Adriatic—'something which Italy could hardly tolerate'.[2] Three weeks later Reinhard Heydrich, Himmler's deputy, submitted to Ribbentrop a report on the widespread and violent anti-Axis feeling within the Fascist ruling clan, based on a long private talk between one of his confidential agents and an 'important representative of Italy's cultural and political interests'.

According to the unnamed Italian, it was the view of 'the widest Italian political circles' that Mussolini's Axis policy had been a dismal failure. It was 'commonly said' that the trouble began with the Anschluss of Austria to the Reich, as a result of which Italy had lost an important key position in European politics. The Italians were now faced with the unpalatable fact that Hitler had strengthened his position in Europe to a degree far exceeding what they, from their point of view, could consider tolerable. They had the feeling that they were fast being excluded from the Danube Basin and the Balkans by their ally who appeared to have 'little or no regard for Italy' and was acting 'in complete independence' of her. Nor was German support of Mussolini's Mediterranean policy as whole-hearted as had been hoped.[3]

Given the general dissatisfaction with the Duce's pro-German line (the Italian concluded), two alternatives for the shaping of Italy's future foreign policy were being discussed in responsible circles. According to one school of thought, Rome should

---

[1] Ciano, *Diario*, i. 56–60 (15–19 Mar. 1939).
[2] Memorandum by Mackensen, 24 Mar. 1939 (*ADAP*, Serie D vi. 85–9).
[3] The Germans did not conceal their irritation at Mussolini's anti-French campaign which was to some extent an anti-German move (i.e. an attempt to forestall a *détente* between Berlin and Paris); on 20 March 1939 Hitler made it clear to Attolico that he did not wish to be dragged into a French-Italian war (Guariglia, *Ricordi*, p. 374; *ADAP*, Serie D vi. 47–51).

gradually loosen the bonds with Berlin; for while Hitler had hitherto been esteemed as a powerful friend, he must by now 'be feared as too powerful'. And while such a change of front might lay Italy open to a charge of disloyalty, it would 'be universally and most readily accepted . . . by the Italian people', in addition to which it would probably enable Mussolini to obtain from Paris and London the concessions in the Mediterranean indispensable for his country's future development. According to the second school of thought, the Duce should once again play in grand style the role of mediator between the opposing blocs. As Europe's arbitrator and peacemaker he might well succeed not only in saving Italy from the horrors of war, but also in obtaining concessions from both camps. Germany, it was thought, would not be unwilling to meet Italy half-way if thereby 'hostilities of an unprecedented magnitude' could be avoided; the Western Powers 'would be guided by similar ideas'. Moreover, this alternative would have 'the positive advantage of rehabilitating Mussolini in the eyes of the Italians after the disillusionment over his recent Axis policy'.[1]

If the Fascist dictator had accepted either of the above alternatives, his anti-Semitic policy would have lost its point. But Mussolini was the prisoner of his 'dynamic' ideology. How was he to break the bars of his Mediterranean prison and 'march to the Ocean' without German backing? And how could he risk a break with Berlin before he had mended his fences with London and Paris? Hitler's Prague *coup* 'worried and humiliated' him; but if he was to find compensation, it must be within the framework of the Axis, not outside it. Moreover, Western attempts to constitute a 'democratic bloc' against aggression hardened the Duce in favour of the Germans: 'The title itself identifies our destinies with those of Germany'.[2] On 20 March he told Ciano that Italy could not play 'the prostitute' by changing her policy;[3] on the following day he informed the Grand Council that the Czechs had only themselves to thank for the loss of their independence, having failed to free themselves 'from the

---

[1] Heydrich to Ribbentrop, 14 Apr. 1939 (*ADAP*, Serie D vi. 200–2); copies of the report were sent to Göring, Lammers, Bormann, and Himmler.

[2] Ciano, *Diario*, i. 62 (21 Mar. 1939).

[3] Ibid.

influence of Jews, Freemasons, Democrats, and Bolsheviks';[1] and on 26 March, in a speech to the Fascist militia, he again emphasized the complete solidarity between the two Axis Powers, with special reference to their common struggle against 'subversive Oriental theories'.[2] The Germans, for their part, hastened to reassure the Italian dictator, solemnly recognizing 'exclusive Italian rights in the Mediterranean, in the Adriatic and in adjacent zones' and renewing their promise of unconditional military support.[3]

On 28 March the gloom induced by the rape of Prague was lightened by the happy news that Madrid had fallen to Franco's forces. On 1 April the Spanish Civil War came to an end; and on the same day the Duce wrote to Chamberlain (in reply to the latter's appeal for an Italian move to allay 'present tension') that he could not act as a general peacemaker 'before Italy's rights have been recognized': Italy was still primarily an aggrieved Power, and her grievances were the tap-root of her policy.[4]

The victory in Spain was the event Mussolini had been waiting for in order to pay Hitler back in his own coin and recover some of his lost prestige. On Good Friday 7 April, Italian troops landed in Albania. According to Ciano, the Albanian venture was primarily an anti-German move, 'designed to block further German expansion in the Balkans'.[5] Even so, it had the effect of widening the rift between Italy and the Western Powers and hence of increasing Mussolini's dependence on Hitler.[6] The Germans were predictably delighted. While London protested, Berlin conveyed its congratulations on the success of the enterprise; and Ribbentrop magnanimously told Attolico that 'any Italian victory represented an accession of strength to the

---

[1] Memorandum by Mackensen, 24 Mar. 1939 (see above, p. 219 n. 2); for a somewhat different version of Mussolini's speech, cf. G. Bottai, *Vent'anni e un giorno*, Milan, 1949, pp. 124–6.
[2] *O.O.* xxix. 249–53.
[3] Ciano, *Diario*, i. 62 (21 Mar. 1939); *ADAP*, Serie D vi. 47–51, 52–3.
[4] Chamberlain to Mussolini, 20 Mar. 1939, (*DBFP*, 3rd Ser. iv. 402–3); Mussolini to Chamberlain, 1 Apr. 1939 (ibid. 572–4).
[5] Ciano to Guariglia and to Grandi, 4 Apr. 1939 (Toscano, *Le origini diplomatiche*, p. 223); Guariglia, op. cit., pp. 388–9; Anfuso, *Da Palazzo Venezia al Lago di Garda*, p. 95; F. Jacomoni di San Savino, *La politica dell'Italia in Albania*, Bologna, 1965, p. 330.
[6] For details see Toscano, *Le origini diplomatiche*, pp. 225–30.

Axis'. The stage was now set for a resumption of the negotiations which had been interrupted by events in Central Europe.[1]

On 5 and 6 April Staff talks took place between General Wilhelm Keitel, Chief of the German High Command, and General Alberto Pariani, the Italian Under-Secretary for War. Keitel declared in the name of his master that Germany would be 'at Italy's side in the event of war'; Pariani replied that the Axis was 'the most indestructible thing there is'. But no attempt was made to discuss operational plans or a concerted conduct of a European war. Keitel did not so much as hint at the fact that on 3 April Hitler had ordered his soldiers to draw up plans for the liquidation of Poland; Pariani said nothing about the Albanian enterprise which was to begin within a few hours. Each side was equally concerned to deceive the other, and there was no indication that either party expected shortly to be engaged in joint military action.[2]

On 14 April Hitler's Crown Prince, Hermann Göring, arrived in Rome for talks with Mussolini and Ciano. He congratulated the Duce on his Albanian triumph; assured him of Germany's *désintéressement* in Yugoslavia; recognized the need of both Axis Powers for a period of peace in which to complete their armaments; warned against a premature Italian attack on France; and claimed that the Führer, while determined to solve the Polish problem, 'was not planning anything against Poland' (*sic*). Ciano made some interesting observations on Italian aid to the Palestine Arabs: 'Direct supplies of arms were too risky; Italy was therefore giving them money, and they had so far always succeeded in buying arms through Greek middlemen with the help of the funds thus received.' Both sides laid great emphasis on Axis solidarity and on the inevitability of a conflict with the Western democracies; but no attempt was made to fix objectives or establish spheres of influence. The result of the talks

---

[1] Ciano, *diario*, i. 73 (5 Apr. 1939).

[2] For a detailed analysis see Toscano, *Le origini diplomatiche*, pp. 204–22. Keitel's reticence reflected Hitler's personal distrust of the Italian Court and of Italian high society: 'In the Führer's view a certain degree of caution was necessary because of the lack of security occasioned in the unreliable Italian court circles by their connections abroad and in the Francophile elements of high society (*Oberschicht*). And while it was to be made unmistakably clear that 'the one would march alongside the other, come what may' and that we would help each other without stint, caution should be observed over giving figures' (memorandum by Neubauer, *ADAP*, Serie D vi. 932); cf. also GFM/8195/E582758-62 (Keitel on Italian armed forces).

was to reinforce Mussolini's illusion that he could restrain Hitler by means of a military pact.[1]

Ciano was, however, disturbed by the contemptuous tone of Göring's remarks about Warsaw; it reminded him unpleasantly 'of the tone used at other times about Austria and Czechoslovakia'. His fears were by no means allayed when, on 20 April, Attolico reported from Berlin that he regarded German action against Poland as imminent. Ciano now requested an early meeting with Ribbentrop; the latter replied that he was willing to come to Italy between 6 and 8 May and that he would bring with him a draft of the projected dual alliance. On 4 May Attolico informed Rome that the Legal Department of the Wilhelmstrasse had been instructed to prepare the draft of a bilateral agreement; and on the same day Mussolini completed a memorandum for communication to the Germans in which he reiterated the views expressed in his speech of 4 February: war between the Axis and the Western Powers was unavoidable, but it had better be postponed until 1943 when a military effort would have 'its best chance of success'.[2]

On 6 May the two Foreign ministers of the Axis met in Milan. For the first (and last) time Ciano found his German colleague 'in a pleasantly calm state of mind'. Not only did Ribbentrop agree on the need for postponing the inevitable war; he even went so far as to claim that Berlin required a longer period of peace than Rome—'not less than four or five years'. To give verisimilitude to this assurance, he added that in regard to Warsaw his master was 'determined to follow the path of conciliation'; his programme was 'not to take the first step', but 'to allow the matter to mature', while remaining ready to react sharply if the Poles passed over to the offensive.[3]

For all his misgivings, Ciano was impressed by this unprecedented display of moderation. So was Mussolini who that night had the truly original idea of having the pact announced before its terms were settled and telephoned accordingly to his son-in-law. Ribbentrop (who still hankered after the inclusion of Japan) demurred; but Hitler, when reached by telephone, gave his

---

[1] *ADAP*, Serie D vi. 207–11, 215–19; Toscano, *Le origini diplomatiche*, pp. 230–46.

[2] Ciano, *Diario* i. 82, 83, 87–8, 94; Toscano, *Le origini diplomatiche*, pp. 250–1, 273–4, 278–282.

[3] *L'Europa verso la catastrofe*, ii. 53–8; *ADAP*, Serie D vi. 372–4; *Le origini diplomatiche*, pp. 301–6 (on the differences between the two versions).

immediate approval. The Führer had obtained exactly what he wanted: the exclusion of Japan would facilitate the projected *rapprochement* with Russia, while the timely announcement of an Italo-German alliance might scare the Western Powers and thus enable him to isolate Poland before attacking her. The Duce, for his part, considered the announcement an excellent means of diplomatic pressure on France as well as a means of dispelling the discontent that had been manifested at the Grand Council after the occupation of Prague.[1]

On 7 May a joint statement was issued to the effect that the talks between Ciano and Ribbentrop had once more established the 'perfect identity of views between the two Governments' and that it had been decided to convert the Axis into a political and military treaty. On 12 May the German draft was handed to Attolico; it was virtually identical with that which the Italians had rejected the previous year. In the preamble the unbreakable bond between the two kindred regimes was duly emphasized:

The German and the Italian peoples, closely bound to each other by the deep affinity of their ways of life (*Weltanschauung*) and the complete solidarity of their interests [*sic*], are resolved in future to stand guard side by side and with united forces over their eternal rights to life and over the maintenance of peace [*sic*].

Article II of the projected treaty imposed on each ally the obligation to consult, but Article III gave the German dictator the escape clause he required:

Should it happen that, contrary to the wishes and hopes of the High Contracting Parties, one of them was involved in war-like complications with another Power or with other Powers, the other High Contracting Party will immediately come to its aid as an ally and support it with all its military forces on land, at sea and in the air.

In a secret annexe special provisions were made for co-operation in matters of press and propoganda, presumably including anti-Jewish propaganda.[2]

Commenting on this astounding document in a telegram to Ciano on 12 May, Attolico pointed out that the Brenner frontier was nowhere mentioned; that the customary formula about 'unprovoked aggression' had been dropped, enjoining the most

---

[1] Ciano, *Diario*, i. 94–6; Toscano, *Le origini diplomatiche*, pp. 308–10.
[2] Toscano, *Le origini diplomatiche*, pp. 309, 329–32; *ADAP*, Serie D vi. 464–9.

absolute solidarity, offensive as well as defensive; and that the expression 'eternal rights to life' lent itself 'to the most varied alarmist interpretations'. He suggested that at least in the title a defensive character should be ascribed to the treaty and that quinquennial periods of revision should be fixed. He might have added that the automatism of support very largely stultified the consultation clause; for although Article III was formally applicable to both countries, its improvident latitude was bound to work in favour of Germany, given the immense military superiority of the Germans.[1]

On 13 May Ciano noted in his diary that the proposed pact was 'real and proper dynamite'. Even so, only two modifications were made at the Duce's request: the first reduced the indefinite duration of the treaty to a period of ten years, while the second provided for a reference to the inviolability of the Brenner frontier in the preamble. In all other respects the German draft was accepted without demur. After having insisted on the need for at least three years of peace and preparation, Mussolini now left it to Hitler to start war whenever and wherever he chose, with Italy bound to range herself by his side with all her resources.[2]

On 20 May Ciano left for Berlin, and two days later he and Ribbentrop solemnly signed the instrument which Mussolini shortly afterwards christened the 'Pact of Steel'. The speeches which followed the signature of the alliance threw a revealing light on the divergence of views between the two Axis partners. While Ciano stressed the peaceful aims of the accord, his German colleague emphasized the military character of the obligations and the irrevocability of the ties beween the two Fascist regimes: 'In the future, whatever happens, the two nations will march together, always ready to extend a hand to a friend, but firmly resolved to guarantee and ensure their vital rights together'.[3] In the words of Mario Toscano, 'events had been allowed to reach such a point that it was no longer possible to cure the ambiguities in Italo-German relations. Hitler had no interest in clarifying

---

[1] Toscano, *Le origini diplomatiche*, pp. 333–5; L. B. Namier, '"The Pact of Steel": A Study in Levity', *Europe in Decay*, p. 143; *ADAP*, Serie D vi. 397–9.
[2] Ciano, *Diario*, i. 99; Toscano, *Le origini diplomatiche*, pp. 348–9.
[3] *Il Giornale d'Italia*, 23 May 1939; Toscano, *L'origini diplomatiche*, pp. 353–4.

them, while Mussolini feared the consequences of a clarification in depth'.[1]

On 23 May, the very day after the conclusion of the Steel Pact, the German dictator held a war council at the Reich Chancellery, in the course of which he announced his decision 'to attack Poland at the first suitable opportunity'; he added that secrecy was 'the decisive prerequisite for success' and that hence 'our objectives must be kept secret from both Italy and Japan'.[2]

In the following week the Duce at long last bethought himself of establishing the exact bearing of the pact he had concluded with such haste. On 31 May he dispatched General Ugo Cavallero to Berlin with a memorandum for Hitler in which he repeated his well-known views on the inevitability of war, on the desirability of a *détente* between the Reich and the Holy See, and on the need for not less than three years of peace and preparation. The rest of the document (including a paragraph about undermining the internal unity of enemy States by means of anti-Semitic, pacifist, or separatist movements) was window-dressing; what Mussolini sought was the Führer's official acceptance of his timetable which would have made it the basis for directives to be prepared by the German and Italian General Staffs. Hitler evaded the issue by 'warmly thanking' the Italian dictator for his note and by expressing 'general agreement' with its argument, adding that he would like to talk over matters personally with the Duce at some unspecified later date. In Rome this vague reply was read as consent, both because of Ribbentrop's previous assurances and because the request for a meeting seemed to imply that there was no immediate danger of an armed clash. Another two months were to elapse before it dawned upon Mussolini that he had given his Axis partner *carte blanche* to unleash World War II.[3]

Western reactions to the conclusion of the Steel Pact were mixed. On the one hand, it was hoped that the written agreement would strengthen Mussolini's position *vis-à-vis* Hitler and enable him to moderate the latter's designs; on the other, it was feared that the 'completeness of Italy's identification in policy and arms

[1] Toscano, *Le origini diplomatiche*, p. 181.
[2] *ND*/L-079, reproduced in *ADAP*, Serie D vi. 477–83.
[3] *DDI*, 8ᵃ Serie xii. 49–51; *ADAP*, Serie D vi. 605–6; Toscano, *Le origini diplomatiche*, pp. 362–74; Wiskemann, *The Rome–Berlin Axis*, p. 181.

with Germany' would deprive the Fascist leader of all liberty of action and reduce him 'to political vassalage and economic inferiority'.[1] Phillips reported to Roosevelt that the Duce was desperately afraid of war—so much so that 'we may hope for his calming influence upon Hitler'. But whether this influence would have 'the desired effect ... at any critical moment is something no one can guess'. The Pact of Steel was an aggressive document, 'making it appear that (the) Italian armed forces were ready to support Hitler's every whim'. For the moment, however, there was 'throughout Italy no activity in sight which would give the impression of intensive preparation for war'.[2]

Jewish reactions to the ill-starred pact were accurately summed up in an article on 'A Year of Racialism in Italy' by Eduard David Kleinlerer who had been Rome correspondent of the Jewish Telegraphic Agency until his expulsion in July 1938.[3] Italian Jewry (he pointed out) had hoped until recently 'that the racial legislation would be enforced only mildly, but the conclusion of the military alliance between Germany and Italy destroyed any illusions they may have held. Italian Jews, the only element which witnessed the rise and fall of the Roman Empire, approached the second year of the racial policy with increased fears for their future in the country where they have lived for centuries.'

Given the German origin of Mussolini's racial gospel, the Italo-German accord could hardly fail to arouse alarm and despondency in Jewish circles. In retrospect it is clear, however, that the Pact of Steel was a symptom rather than a factor in European politics; nor did it have any marked impact on the evolution of the racial question in Italy. There was a community of destiny between the two regimes and their leaders but no community of interests between the two peoples and no identity of views on any concrete issue, least of all on the racial issue; behind the façade of 'Axis solidarity' (which the Pact of Steel was meant to reinforce) the two allies were pursuing diametrically

[1] Loraine to Halifax, 23 May 1939 (*DBFP*, 3rd Ser. v. 654–5).
[2] Phillips, op. cit., pp. 125–6.
[3] E.D. Kleinlerer, 'A Year of Racialism in Italy', *Contemporary Jewish Record*, ii (July–Aug. 1939), 30–43; on Kleinlerer's expulsion, cf. memorandum by Welles of 26 July 1938 (*FRUS 1938*, ii. 586) and Mollier's report of 25 Aug. 1938 (see above, p. 168 n. 1).

opposed policies.[1] It was hardly a coincidence that in May 1939—the very month in which the alliance was signed—Mussolini permitted himself to make a series of philo-Semitic statements to his biographer, very much in contrast with some of his earlier utterances on the subject: Italy's adherence to the racialist camp (he now claimed) was little more than a 'formality'; the anti-Jewish outbursts of the Fascist press did not reflect his personal opinion and had no effect whatever on his policy; the racial measures had been necessary for reasons of state, but the 'Jewish Italians' were innocent victims; and while international Jewry was indeed anti-Fascist, he could not but pay tribute to the patriotism of three eminent Italian Jews, Luigi Luzzatti, Sidney Sonnino, and Giorgio Del Vecchio.[2] On the same occasion the Duce recalled his past collaboration with Nahum Goldmann and his past championship of the Jewish cause.[3]

Contacts between the 'racial experts' of the two Axis Powers were confined to non-committal exchanges of information;

[1] Grigore Gafencu, the Romanian foreign Minister, who visited Mussolini on 1 May 1939, was struck by the 'profound dissimilarity between the foreign policies of Rome and Berlin—a dissimilarity of which the Italian leaders, for all their boastings, were perfectly well aware and which created in them an incurable uneasiness as the moment approached for the inevitable written pact. In vain had Mussolini put the emphasis on "force" in his speeches; he was too much of a Mediterranean to ignore the value of "moderation" (*mesure*). His concern was always to be on the side of the strongest Power and never to have to face it alone. The company of his opponents was as indispensable to him as the support of his partner. He needed to cultivate his enmities as carefully as he cultivated his alliances, in the hope that he might always play the part of mediator. These intentions of Mussolini clearly ran counter (*contrecarraient*) to Hitler's plans. The German wanted complete success and shrank from nothing; war was the simplest way of obtaining the full measure of totalitarian demands. The Italian wanted limited successes—the only ones which could assure him his share of the profit. The battle he wanted to wage ought to be fought out in conferences. Of the two Axis partners, the one wanted to overturn the equilibrium of the world to his profit, while the other hoped to save this same equilibrium to his profit. This clash of interests and wills could not be long continued. The weaker of the two would have to give way to the arguments of the stronger' (G. Gafencu, *Derniers jours de l'Europe. Un Voyage diplomatique en 1939*, Paris, 1946, pp. 185–6. For the myth of 'Axis solidarity' see also D.C. Watt, 'The Rome–Berlin Axis, 1936–1940. Myth and Reality', *Review of Politics*, xxii (Oct. 1960), 519–43; F. D'Amoja, *La politica estera dell' impero*, pp. 186–7; Petersen, *Hitler–Mussolini*, pp. 185, 498.

[2] Giorgio Del Vecchio, an ardent Fascist and for many years Rector of the University of Rome, was dismissed from his post in October 1938 along with ninety-six other Jewish university teachers; see his letter to the *Popolo di Roma* of 11–12 December 1928 (on Fascism as the 'civil religion' of the 'Jewish Italians') and his book *Una nuova persecuzione di un perseguitato; documenti*, Rome, 1945.

[3] De Begnac, *Palazzo Venezia*, pp. 641–2.

Alfieri's and Landra's suggestions for concerted action were duly submitted to Gross, but there was no follow-up of any kind. In December 1938 Landra went to Germany for a return visit. He was received by leading German personages, including Rosenberg, Himmler, and Hess, and had an exchange of views with Gross; but no agreements were reached, and no co-operation was established. And when Gross alluded to the past divergence of views on the racial issue, Landra reacted sharply, insisting that Fascism had been a racialist movement from its very inception. On 24 February 1939, in a lecture on Fascist racialism at Berlin University, Landra openly challenged the doctrine of Nordic superiority, affirming that the dark-haired Italian was as much a *Herrenmensch* as the fair-haired German. On the same occasion he claimed that, thanks to the recent anti-Jewish measures, there was no longer any Jewish problem in Italy—the implication being that there was no longer any need for advice and guidance from the *Rassenpolitisches Amt*.[1] For the moment, however, the apostles of the blond master-race were not to be provoked. Commenting of Landra's lecture, Rosenberg paid tribute to the 'originality' of Italian racial theory and practice, adding that the adoption of anti-Jewish laws in Italy had taken the German 'racial experts' by surprise.[2] In the following month, at a meeting of German and Italian jurists in Vienna, a resolution was passed to the effect that the Jewish problem was a domestic affair which each Axis partner should tackle in his own way.[3]

Kleinlerer's article on Fascist racial policy was written in July 1939, a year after the publication of the 'Race Manifesto', and

---

[1] M. Magistrati to Ministry of Popular Culture and Ministry of Foreign Affairs on Landra's mission, 23 Dec. 1938 (*ASMEI/Germania/p.47/1938,* reproduced in De Felice, *Storia degli ebrei italiani,* pp. 581–2); Landra, 'Die wissenschaftliche und politische Begründung der Rassenfrage in Italien', 298, 305. On 20 December 1938 Landra and Gross signed a vague and non-committal declaration on co-operation in matters of racial policy which was approved by Hitler (Hess to Rassenpolitisches Amt, 11 Mar. 1939). On 26 February 1939 Landra, in a letter to Gross, submitted a series of practical proposals, including the founding of an Italian–German Society for the Study of Racial Problems; in reply Gross suggested the setting-up of an Italo-German Racial Academy on 9 May. The German counter-proposal was left unanswered, Landra having meanwhile been replaced by Sabato Visco who was opposed to the projected co-operation (undated memorandum by Vollmer, PA/Inl.1/Partei/Italien/ Baron Julius Evola/1941–1942).

[2] Landra, op. cit., 296 (prefatory note by Rosenberg).

[3] *Il Diritto Razzista* (May–June 1939), 139–40; G. Preziosi, 'Per la serietà degli studi italiani sulla razza', *La Vita Italiana,* lvi (15 Aug. 1940), 141 (Acerbo on lack of co-operation between German and Italian 'racial experts').

published in the following month; by the time it appeared in print both Rome and Berlin had come to discount the value of the Steel Pact which had been signed less than three months earlier, and a new chapter in Italian–Jewish relations had begun. The Italian dictator was still committed to the policy of the Rome–Berlin Axis; but the Italian brand of anti-Semitism was to remain *sui generis* until the end.

By THE time the ill-starred Pact of Steel was signed, relations between the Axis Powers and the Western democracies had undergone a drastic change. Both London and Paris had abandoned appeasement with a vengeance, and the theme of the 'peace front' against Fascist aggression had become the major refrain of Chamberlain's policy. On 31 March—sixteen days after Hitler's Prague *coup*—Britain and France had thrown down the gage to the German dictator in the form of a guarantee to Poland; on 13 April—six days after Mussolini's invasion of Albania—they had given similar guarantees to Greece and Romania. On 14 April President Roosevelt had addressed a message to Mussolini and Hitler, urging them to give assurances against aggression to no less than thirty countries, including Palestine. On the following day negotiations had been opened between the Western Powers and the Soviet Union; and on 12 May—ten days before the conclusion of the Italo-German alliance—an Anglo-Turkish agreement had been announced in the British House of Commons which pledged both countries to effective co-operation involving all mutual aid and assistance in the event of aggression leading to war in the Mediterranean area.[1]

The Duce's reaction to this sudden change of course took the form of angry remonstrances and bellicose threats. On 11 May, at a dinner in honour of Prince Paul of Yugoslavia, he vented his irritation on the diplomatic representative of 'Jew-ridden' America. A few days later Phillips reported to Roosevelt:

Mussolini is not in a pleasant state of mind with regard to America. At a dinner the other evening at the palace . . . he opened the conversation by asking me why we 'interfered' in European affairs when we knew so little about them, although he admitted at the same time that Italians knew very little about American affairs. I gave him the best answers that I could with regard to our hundred and one ties with Europe, and

---

[1] For details, see L. B. Namier, *Diplomatic Prelude 1938–1939*, London, 1948, pp. 71–210; F. S. Northedge, *The Troubled Giant. Britain among the Great Powers 1916–1939*, London, 1966, pp. 549–83. On Mussolini's failure to grasp the significance of this switch from appeasement to resistance, cf. Toscano, *Le origini diplomatiche*, p. 310.

our wish and that of the country to see European problems settled by peaceful negotiation. He annoyed me by remarking that the United States was run by Jews, and I gave it back to him straight that he was entirely mistaken in this respect and that it was a very unfortunate mistake to make . . .[1]

Mussolini's irritation grew when he learnt on the following day that Daladier had made a violently anti-Italian speech and Turkey was joining the 'peace front'. On 15 May he had Ciano inform the Polish Ambassador that in the event of a German–Polish war Italy would stand by her Axis partner. The conclusion of the Pact of Steel on 22 May had the effect of further increasing his intransigence towards the 'Jew-ridden' democracies. On 27 May, when Sir Percy Loraine, the new British Ambassador, paid his initial call, he took advantage of the occasion to show that he would have no further truck with the Western Powers. Ciano wrote in his diary:

The Duce, who is ordinarily courteous and engaging, was very stern; his face became absolutely impenetrable . . . He began by asserting that in view of the manifest British policy of encirclement it was necessary to ask, as he was now asking, whether any tangible value was left in the Pact of 16 April. Percy Loraine was not expecting this blow; he blushed and struggled for words . . . The Duce countered harshly in an argumentative tone; he declared that British policy was leading the whole of Europe into war . . . The Duce made a brief and cutting comment on the Anglo-Russian alliance [*sic*], and then the conversation was brusquely ended . . . His leave-taking was icy.[2]

On 31 May Mussolini told Ciano that he had 'no intention of easing relations with France'.[3] In the following weeks he continued to assure all and sundry that Italy would march with Germany in every conceivable circumstance. On 7 July, when Sir Percy Loraine brought him a message from Chamberlain calling attention to the dangers ahead and urging him to put the brake on his partner in 'dynamics', he was glad to take the

---

[1] Phillips, *Ventures in Diplomacy*, pp. 125–6. On 17 May, Ciano wrote in his diary: 'The American Ambassador . . . is resentful, particularly because Mussolini said that America is in the hands of the Jews. He wanted to deny this but used very weak arguments' (*Diano*, i. 101).

[2] *Diano*, i. 106–7; as usual, Ciano hastened to inform the German Ambassador (Mackensen to Wilhelmstrasse, 31 May 1939, *ADAP*, Serie D vi, 510). For Loraine's version, see Loraine to Halifax, 28 May 1939 (*DBFP*, 3rd Ser. v, 703–4, 704–6).

[3] Ciano, *Diano*, i. 109.

opportunity of giving the British envoy a dusty answer. According to Ciano, he debated the message 'point by point' and concluded by saying twice: 'Tell Chamberlain that if England is ready to fight in defence of Poland, Italy will take up arms with her ally Germany.'[1] On 22 July he ordered Magistrati to inform Ribbentrop that he was ready to support Hitler's every whim: 'Whenever Germany finds it necessary to mobilize at midnight, we shall mobilize at five to twelve.'[2] And as late as 21 August—eleven days before the outbreak of World War II—he 'confirmed his decision to go along with the Germans'.[3]

Oddly enough, Mussolini's resentment against the 'Jew-ridden' West had little, if any, effect on the evolution of his anti-Jewish policy during the period under review. There were various reasons for this. First, his pact with Hitler did not lead to any concrete co-operation between the two Axis countries, least of all in the field of racial legislation. Second, he was still hoping for a repetition of his Munich success, his aggressive threats against the Western Powers notwithstanding; several months were to elapse before he realized that the Führer was not interested in mediation. Last but not least, he had to reckon with a wide variety of domestic obstacles to a radical solution of the Jewish problem, the most important being the frequency of intermarriage between Jews and Gentiles in Italy. The 'complete divorce of the Aryan from the non-Aryan world' envisaged by Ciano in his above-quoted conversation with Mackensen was hardly a practical proposition in a country where well over 40 per cent of all married Jews had Aryan spouses.[4]

At the end of 1938 the Directorate-General of Race and Demography put the number of mixed couples in Italy at 7,457, including 4,478 Jews with Aryan wives and 2,979 Aryans with

---

[1] Ibid. 131; Ciano immediately informed Mackensen, stressing his master's unconditional solidarity with Hitler (Mackensen to Wilhelmstrasse, 7 July 1939, *ADAP*, Serie D vi, 730–2; GFM/472/228610). According to Loraine (whose version tallies in substance with Ciano's), Mussolini admitted that 'Danzig was not worth a world war'; in speaking of Poland, he alluded to the large number of Jews in that country (Loraine to Halifax, 7 July 1939, *DBFP*, 3rd Ser. vi, 289–90).

[2] Magistrati, *L'Italia a Berlino*, p. 383.

[3] Ciano, *Diario*, 146; 'Oggi . . . Mussolini ha confermato la sua decisione di marciare con i tedeschi'.

[4] In 1938, 43·7 out of every 100 married Jews had Aryan partners (ACS/Rivelazione sugli ebrei del 22 agosto 1938/Min. Int./Dir. Gen. Demografia e Razza (1938–43)/cart. 14/fasc. 17); see also S. Della Pergola, *Jewish and Mixed Marriages in Milan 1901–1968*, Jerusalem, 1972, p. 111.

Jewish wives. Of these couples 2,446 were childless; the remaining 5,011 had a total of 9,247 children, well over 7,000 of whom were considered Aryans for the purposes of racial legislation, having been brought up as Catholics.[1] Paradoxically, the anti-Jewish campaign launched in July 1938 had had the effect of aggravating the issue, hundreds of pending mixed marriages having been hastily concluded before the law for the defence of the Italian race was passed.[2]

The problem of the mixed couples had begun to preoccupy the Fascist leaders in the immediate aftermath of Munich. On 11 November 1938 Ciano noted in his diary: 'I rang up Buffarini to call his attention to the case of the Jew with an Aryan wife. I think that such a gesture of detachment from the Jewish nation and religion should be rewarded with special treatment (*discriminato*). If the family nucleus is to be protected, the father must not be placed in a position of inferiority with respect to his children.'[3]

On 2 July 1939 Buffarini himself made the same point in a memorandum addressed to the Duce, calling for the restoration of equal rights to all those Jewish husbands of Gentile women who had embraced the Catholic faith before 1 October 1938. If the policy of legal and moral segregation hitherto pursued were persisted in (he warned), a great many Catholic marriages would be wrecked and a great many Aryan women and children would be permanently alienated from the Fascist regime. In Germany thousands of mixed marriages had ended in divorce as a result of the Nuremberg laws. In Hungary, on the other hand, all baptised Jews with Gentile spouses had been 'aryanized' in order to prevent similar tragedies. Buffarini concluded by affirming that Italy would do well to follow the Hungarian rather than the German example and by appealing to the 'Duce's profound sense of justice'.[4]

While the problem of Jewish males with Aryan wives was a

---

[1] Cited in De Felice, *Storia degli ebrei italiani*, p. 16.
[2] Kleinlerer, 'A Year of Racialism in Italy', 34.
[3] Ciano, *1937–1938 Diario*, pp. 290–1.
[4] ACS/Min. Int./Dir. Gen. Demografia e Razza (1938–1943)/b.2/fasc. 10/cart. Famiglie miste (reproduced in Buffarini Guidi, *La vera verità*, pp. 35–6); cf. Maglione to Borgongini Duca, 7 Aug. 1939, in P. Blet, R. A. Graham, A. Martini, B. Schneider (eds.), *Actes et documents du Saint Siège relatifs à la Seconde Guerre Mondiale*, vi: *Le Saint Siège et les victimes de la Gurre mars 1939–décembre 1940*, Vatican City, 1972, pp. 119–20 (on 'Aryanization' of baptized Jews).

permanent source of worry to the Fascist authorities, that of the Aryan males with Jewish wives was studiously ignored until the Germans raised it in 1943.[1] True, as early as March 1937 Interlandi had called for measures against 'nominal Italians married to Jewesses' in his above-quoted attack on the 'dissident mongrels'. But although this article had undoubtedly been written with Mussolini's approval, the Duce began to have second thoughts on the subject the moment he decided to pass from propaganda to legislative action. Nor is this surprising. For whereas in Hitler's Germany Aryans with Jewish wives were almost bound to be enemies of the regime, the opposite was true in Mussolini's Italy where intermarriage between Jews and Gentiles was particularly common in Fascist and pro-Fascist circles. Not a few of the 'nominal Italians married to Jewesses' were among the Duce's most prominent supporters, including senior officials and army officers, eminent scholars, high-ranking diplomats, and highly placed members of the Party hierarchy. Several of these 'Jew-tainted' Gentiles were playing a not insignificant part in German–Italian relations, including Giuseppe Renzetti, the one-time intermediary between the Duce and the Führer, who served as Italian Consul-General in Berlin from 1936 to 1941, and Leonardo Vitetti, the Director-General of Political Affairs at the Italian Foreign Ministry, who was repeatedly involved in negotiations with the German leaders. The dismissal of all those loyal Aryans would have aroused more antagonism than Mussolini could easily afford at a moment of mounting international tension; so would racial measures against their Jewish spouses in a country where the marriage tie was considered indissoluble. The Germans, for their part, joined with the Fascist Government in ignoring the delicate issue; it was only on the eve of Mussolini's downfall that they began to worry about the continued presence of 'Jew-tainted Aryans' at all levels of the Fascist machine.

In addition to creating large pockets of discontent and disaffection in Italian society, the problem of the mixed couples also gave rise to a conflict with the Holy See which was to bedevil relations between Church and State until the collapse of the Fascist regime. Up to November 1938 the racialist controversy between the Duce and the Pope had not quitted the realm of

[1] See below, Epilogue.

theory. The first anti-Jewish measures had been carefully designed to avoid giving the Vatican any formal ground for complaint. For example, the scholastic legislation which prohibited the reception of Jewish pupils 'in all grades of schools, public and private, attended by Italians', contained the following significant qualification: 'Neverthless, the inscription of pupils of Jewish race who profess the Catholic religion is permitted in primary and secondary schools dependent on the ecclesiastical authorities.'[1] The details of the other anti-Jewish laws had shown a similar anxiety to avoid quarrels in the domain of practice, and Catholic sympathizers with Fascism had been hopeful that the conflict between the Holy See and the government would remain one of principle only. Their hopes were, however, rudely shattered when, on 10 November 1938, the law for the defence of the Italian race was passed by the Fascist Council of Ministers, despite two last-minute attempts by Pius XI to avert such a breach of the Concordat.[2]

The anti-Catholic character of the new law was evident from its very first article: 'The marriage of an Italian citizen of Aryan race with a person belonging to another race is prohibited; any marriage solemnized in defiance of this prohibition is null and void.' In practice, this amounted to a veto on all marriages between Italians and Jews (including unbaptized half- and quarter-Jews) by refusing to grant such marriages validity at Civil Law. One of the most important provisions of the Concordat of 1929, however, was precisely that which invested with civil consequences any marriage celebrated according to the rules of Canon Law, provided that the officiating priest complied with certain formalities, such as reading aloud the relevant articles of the Civil Code and forwarding a certificate of the ceremony to the local public official for registration within five days.[3] What would be the position under the new law if an Italian and a Jew were thus united in a 'concordatory' marriage. Two separate

---

[1] Decree of 2 Sept. 1938; quoted from the *testo unico* embodied in Royal Decree Law No. 1779 of 15 Nov. 1938, art 3.

[2] On hearing of the proposed legislation, the Pope took the unusual step of addressing two personal letters, one to the Duce (4 November) and the other to the King (5 November). The letter to Mussolini was left unanswered; the King replied on 7 November, expressing the hope that the matters at issue would be speedily settled. On 9 November Tacchi Venturi wrote to Mussolini, imploring him to refrain from violating the Concordat (De Felice, *Storia degli ebrei italiani*, pp. 550–2).

[3] Binchy, *Church and State*, pp. 393–4, 628–9.

cases had to be considered. No friction between Church and State was likely to develop where a marriage between a Catholic and an unbaptized Jew was concerned, such a union being *prima facie* void at Canon Law. The other alternative, however, opened up an issue of the utmost gravity. The definition of a Jew contained in article 8 of the Royal Decree Law No. 1728 included 'any person both of whose parents were of the Jewish race, although he or she belongs to a different religion', as well as the child of a Jewish and a foreign parent. Accordingly, the new ban also applied to any marriage where the non-Aryan partner might be a baptized Catholic, whether of recent or lifelong standing. Such a marriage was perfectly valid at Canon Law; any priest who refused to perform the ceremony would expose himself to severe canonical penalties. The new Decree Law, however, deprived it of all civil validity, in flagrant violation of article 34 of the Concordat which recognized 'the sacrament of matrimony administered according to Canon Law as valid for civil purposes'. It went even further: it forbade the celebrant of any such marriage, under penalty of a heavy fine, to carry out any of the formalities normally used in concordatory marriages. In other words, the ceremony was to be of purely religious significance, no civil effects whatever attaching to it, and the officiating priest who helped the parties to claim their rights under the Concordat laid himself open to severe punishment. Mussolini's legal experts sought to justify the measure by pointing out that even already under the Concordat not every canonical marriage was invested with civil effects: for instance, where there were obstacles at Civil Law to the union. Why, then, should the State not be at liberty to extend these obstacles to cover so-called 'racial incompatibilities' if the Duce so desired? But on the basis of this argument Mussolini had the right to fix unilaterally the limits within which he would recognize canonical marriage, without any reference to the Pope. If this were accepted, then article 34 of the agreement would not be worth the paper it was written on. Pius XI therefore had no alternative but to denounce the new law forthwith as a flagrant breach of the Concordat, an international instrument whose terms could not be modified save with the assent of both parties. On 13 November 1938 the Holy See lodged an official protest through the ordinary diplomatic channels. A day later the

Vatican organ deplored the Italian Government's action: 'Today that which was the subject of a bilateral agreement has been broken by one side; the *vulnus* inflicted on the Concordat is unmistakable.'[1] On 23 December it was claimed in the *Catholic Herald* that Royal Decree Law No. 1728 had been modified in accordance with the Holy Father's request, the offending article having been allowed to lapse. On the very next day, however, the Pope himself made it clear in his Christmas Allocution that no progress whatever had been achieved, speaking of the 'grave anxiety caused to the Head of Catholicism and guardian of morality by the ... wound inflicted on our Concordat'.[2] Subsequently, it was rumoured that the same subject figured prominently in the address which Pius XI was to have delivered in the tenth anniversary of the Conciliation (11 February 1939)—a day after death had silenced his voice. On 29 April 1939 it was suggested in the *Tablet*, a leading English Catholic paper, that Pope Pius XII, as a result of the wide concessions made to the Fascist Government in the matter of Catholic Action, would be able to 'obtain in return some guarantees regarding the limits governing racialism in Italy'. But a week later the announcement of the Steel Pact dealt the death-blow to all hopes of a compromise.

The problem of the non-Aryan Catholics was further aggravated by the unprecedented number of applications for baptism by members of the Jewish faith. Kleinlerer reported in July 1939:

In a country where intermarriage between Jews and Christians assumed extensive proportions as a result of assimilation and the absence of social exclusiveness, the absolute prohibition of mixed marriages was felt very keenly ... (But while) the marriage clause proved a hard measure, the race definition was less stringent than the German one. Because of the loophole of conversion which it provided, even Jews who formerly were active in Jewish religious and communal life succumbed to the lure of baptism. The conversion of Dr. Pio Tagliacozzo, former president of the Jewish community in Rome, and of members of his family, as well as the baptism of other Jews distinguished in economic, industrial and social life produced a profound impression. In the beginning, the conversions were in most cases due to the desire to place

[1] 'A proposito d'un decreto legge', *L'Osservatore Romano*, 14–15 Nov. 1938.
[2] Quoted in Binchy, op cit., p. 630.

the children in Catholic schools because of their exclusion from Italian schools. Later, many of these conversions were due to the desire to escape the severity of the law regarding transfer of property and the limitation of economic activities. All in all, according to official statistics published in June 1939, more than 4,000 Jews, or approximately one-tenth of the total Jewish population, were baptised since Italy's embarking upon the racialist course. There are indications that this movement of escape through the Catholic church is bound to continue and even increase. Since most of such conversions are due to motives of escape rather than spiritual conviction, the growth of a new type of Marranos, people who are nominally Catholic but still adhere secretly to Judaism, is envisaged and has been already noted. An example of practical advantage of such conversions can be seen in the recent granting by Brazil of 3,000 visas to German-Jewish converts through the intervention of the Pope.[1]

The 'new Marranos' were a source of grave embarrassment to the Catholic hierarchy as well as a source of friction between Church and State. In the words of an eminent Catholic scholar:

There were ... certain limits beyond which the Church could not carry its sympathy for the individual victims of the anti-Semite laws without stultifying its own mission ... While there have been at all times illustrious converts from Jewry who have subsequently enriched the intellectual forces of the Church, the fact remained that in general the percentage of Jewish converts, in Italy as elsewhere, has been very small. For example in the year 1936, out of 12,500 Jews resident in Rome there were only 46 conversions,[2] and it is safe to assume that the average was no higher in the rest of Italy. Now, on the other hand, the parish priests were besieged by applicants for baptism, many of them doubtless anxious to avail themselves of the loop-hole provided in the anti-Semitic legislation which excluded from the definition of Jew any person born of one Jewish and one Italian parent, provided that he or she belonged to 'another religion than the Jewish' before October 1, 1938.[3] It is hardly surprising that this stream of applications, most of them undoubtedly arising from motives which had little to do with religion, caused great concern to the ecclesiastical authorities. Special regulations were therefore issued by the bishops of several dioceses ordering their clergy to examine each case very carefully before admitting to baptism. Nevertheless, if we may believe the very doubtful

[1] Kleinlerer, loc. cit. 34–5; cf. Borgongini Duca to Maglione, 15 May 1939, in *Actes et documents du Saint Siège*, vi. 87 (on permission for baptized Jews to attend Catholic schools).
[2] *La Civiltà Cattolica* (19 June 1937), 509.
[3] Not a few persons of pure Jewish stock, while debarred from using this exemption, applied for baptism in order to secure the protection of the Church.

testimony of Farinacci, thousands of conversions were accepted during the last quarter of 1938, and in many cases the certificate of baptism was antedated, 'a criminal offence', as the Cremona *ras* was careful to point out ... Threatening to publish names if necessary, he alleged that at least 5,000 Jews [*sic*] had been admitted to baptism in the last three months of 1938.[1]

Since Catholic intervention in the racial issue has been the subject of considerable controversy, it may be useful at this stage to examine the nature and extent of ecclesiastical resistance to the Fascist brand of racialism, with special reference to its impact on German–Italian relations.

Farinacci and other Fascist extremists accused the Church of adopting a 'pro-Jewish' attitude, in 'strident contradiction' with its anti-Jewish past. In an interview accorded to Himmler's paper on 15 September 1938 the *ras* of Cremona ridiculed the Pope's attacks on the 'Race Manifesto', describing them as ineffectual attempts to stir up anti-Axis feeling in Italy: 'When the Pope speaks about politics, our people do not listen to him; they listen all the more to the Duce ... Whatever the Pope may say against the Rome–Berlin Axis, the people remain loyal to it because your Führer and our Duce are loyal to it. Religious questions may be the business of the Pope, but political ones are the exclusive province of the Duce. The Pope is wrong in pretending that racialism is a religious problem; for Italy it is a matter of political principle as well as a practical necessity ... The Germans are mistaken in assuming that the Catholic Church agrees with the Pope on each and every issue. We know that on the racial question the clergy are split into two camps and that the Pope is powerless to do anything about it.'[2] Speaking at the Institute of Fascist Culture in Milan on 7 November 1938, Farinacci expressed surprise at the fact that the Holy Father should have joined forces with the 'avowed enemies of the Church'—Communists, Freemasons, and Democrats—in order to combat 'Catholic' Fascism. Mussolini's racial legislation, after all, was no more than a logical application of Catholic principles and a logical continuation of the anti-Jewish policy pursued by former Popes, Jew-hatred being a fundamental precept of

---

[1] Binchy, pp. 626–7; *Il Regime Fascista*, 7 and 19 Jan. 1939; Borgongini Duca to Maglione, 19 Apr. 1939, in *Actes et documents du Saint Siège*, vi. 79–80 (trouble with baptized Jews).
[2] 'Unterredung mit Farinacci', *Das Schwarze Korps*, 15 Sept. 1938.

Christian doctrine.[1] Meanwhile Farinacci's paper kept up a continuous barrage against the 'Judaeophile' Vatican, the 'ally of Communists, Masons, Jews, and Protestants', and other Fascist organs followed suit.[2] As late as July 1939 Interlandi's *Quadrivio* published a bitter attack on the 'prejudiced hostility and incurable lack of comprehension' shown by the Holy See and the Catholic press on the racial question, although no article on the subject had appeared in any Italian Catholic paper since the death of Pius XI.[3]

Critics of Vatican policy—Socialists and Liberals, Protestants and Jews—generally maintain that too much fuss has been made about the Pope's rhetorical outbursts against Mussolini's racialist heresy. Gaetano Salvemini and Giorgio La Piana accused the Holy See of pursuing 'ultra philo-Fascist' policies right up to the fall of Fascism in 1943, adding that, but for the *vulnus* inflicted on the Concordat, there might never have been any racialist controversy between Church and State in Italy.[4] La Piana further asserted that Pius XI—the keynote of whose pontificate was the 'crusade against Communism'—had 'looked with favour' on the *rapprochement* between Rome and Berlin, 'perhaps in the hope that under Mussolini's influence Hitler would become more manageable'.[5] The Anglican Bishop of Durham affirmed—on the eve of the racialist controversy—that the Roman Church was 'tied hand and foot' to the Fascist tyranny and hence incapable of opposing its policies.[6] Ernesto Rossi branded the Jesuits (whose anti-Jewish views were believed to reflect the trend of thought in high Vatican circles) as the 'precursors of racialism'; Richard A. Webster, an American student of Italian Catholicism, made the same point in more guarded terms.[7] Daniel Carpi, an Israeli scholar of Italian origin, reproached the

[1] R. Farinacci, 'La Chiesa e gli ebrei', *Realtà storiche*, Cremona, 1939, pp. 86–7.
[2] See, e.g., 'Lezione di cattalicesimo ai cattolici', *Il Regime Fascista*, 28 Aug. 1938; 'La questione giudaica in Europa esaminata da "La Civilta Cattolica"', *La Vita Italiana*, lii (15 Sept. 1938), 279–316; B. Damiani, 'I giudei nel pensiero cattolico', *Il Tevere*, 15 Nov. 1938; J. Streicher, 'Il Vaticano e gli ebrei', *Il Regime Fascista*, 21 Jan. 1939.
[3] G. Sottochiesa 'La Chiesa, gli ebrei e la razza', *Il Quadrivio*, 23 July 1939.
[4] G. Salvemini and G. La Piana, *What to do with Italy*, New York, 1943, pp. 90–3.
[5] G. La Piana, 'The Political Heritage of Pius XII', *Foreign Affairs*, xviii (Apr. 1940), 498–499.
[6] *The Church Times*, 1 Apr. 1938 (quoted in Binchy, p. 669).
[7] E. Rossi, *Il manganello e l'aspersorio*, pp. 351–93; R. A. Webster, *The Cross and the Fasces. Christian Democracy and Fascism in Italy*, Stanford, 1960, pp. 124–6.

Church with its failure to show 'a unified or consistent stand' on the Jewish issue: 'Only extreme spiritual courage and humane feeling could create new standards for an evaluation of the problem . . . But there is, unfortunately, no evidence that in the period under review . . . the leaders of the Church in Italy succeeded in overcoming the traditional hatred for the Jews which they inherited from their mentors, the church fathers.'[1] Guenter Lewy, a German-Jewish scholar domiciled in the United States, complained that Pius XI 'seems to have limited his concern to Catholic non-Aryans' and that his encyclical against racialism 'neither mentioned nor criticized anti-Semitism *per se*'.[2] Pius XII (elected Pope on 2 March 1939) has been the target of even harsher criticism. Antonio Spinosa charged him with moral cowardice, claiming that his silence on the Jewish issue had the effect of encouraging the persecutors.[3] Carpi affirmed that his elevation to the papacy gave a fresh impetus to the anti-Semitic tendencies within the Catholic camp.[4] Another Israeli scholar, Czech-born Shaul Friedlander, argued that Pius XII's pro-German sentiments, coupled with his obsessive fear of Bolshevism, blinded him to the magnitude of the German danger, with unfortunate results for Hitler's Jewish victims.[5] Paolo Alatri, an Italian-Jewish scholar of repute, went even further, alleging that the new Pontiff 'trusted' Hitler as late as July 1939 and that he aimed at bringing about an anti-Communist alliance between Berlin and the Vatican City.[6] All critics are agreed that the Church had no objection whatever to a 'moderate' anti-Jewish policy in Italy, as distinct from racial persecutions on the German model.[7]

The official spokesmen of Jewry, both in Italy and elsewhere, have generally taken a much more favourable view of Vatican

[1] Carpi, 'The Catholic Church and Italian Jewry under the Fascists (to the Death of Pius XI)', 55–6.

[2] Lewy, *The Catholic Church and Nazi Germany*, pp. 296–7.

[3] Spinosa, 'Le persecuzioni razzaiali in Italia II', 1085. This charge was subsequently dramatized by Rolf Hochhuth in his controversial play *Der Stellvertreter*, Hamburg, 1963.

[4] Carpi, loc. cit. 54–5; similarly, R. De Felice, 'La Chiesa cattolica e il problema ebraico durante gli anni dell'antisemitismo fascista', *La Rassegna Mensile di Israel*, xxiii (Jan. 1957), 23–35.

[5] S. Friedlander, *Pie XII et le IIIᵉ Reich. Documents*, Paris, 1964, p. 219.

[6] P. Alatri, 'Un tentativo di mediazione tra Hitler e Pio XI', *Ulisse*, iv (autumn 1953), 147; cf. *DDI*, 8ᵃ serie xii 484 (Pignatti to Ciano, 22 July 1939).

[7] See, e.g., Webster, op. cit., p. 126; Lewry, op. cit., pp. 297–8; for documentary evidence, cf. De Felice, *Storia degli ebrei italiani*, pp. 286–8, 547–9.

policy, sometimes to the point of exaggerating the significance of Catholic pronouncements against the myths of race and blood. As late as the spring of 1937, when the third anti-Jewish campaign of the Fascist press was aleady in full swing, leading Italian Jews told Neville Laski that 'the strong attitude of the Vatican against what it deems to be racial heresy and the efforts of the Fascist Government to further good relations with the Vatican will do much to hinder the affirmation and diffusion of racial ideology in Italy'.[1] Even when it became clear that 'Axis solidarity' was more important to Mussolini than friendship with the Holy See, many Jews continued to derive comfort from the Church's uncompromising stand against the 'grave and gross error' of racialism. In July 1939 Israel Cohen, a prominent English Zionist, expressed admiration for the Pope's 'valiant and outspoken antagonism' to Fascist racial policy.[2] Six years later, millions of Jews meanwhile having perished in the Holocaust, a similar tribute was paid by Cecil Roth, the leading English authority on the history of Italian Jewry.[3]

Catholic apologists reproach the critics of Vatican policy with failure to grasp the 'profound conflict of principle' between the Church and the Fascist regime, caused by Fascism's all-embracing claim on the individual: 'Of all theories of government which have hitherto appeared in history that of the totalitarian and ethical State is perhaps the most fundamentally opposed to Christianity.'[4] As for Farinacci's attempt to equate Christian anti-Judaism with racialism, it was 'hardly necessary to insist on the dishonesty of the parallel, in which Farinacci himself probably believed as little as his Catholic adversaries'. It was true that the Jews had been subjected to repressive legislation in the former Papal States; and it was equally true that a few misguided clerics had welcomed Mussolini's conversion to anti-Semitism, Catholics being 'no more immune than others from fashionable currents of thought'. But all the anti-Jewish provisions of former

---

[1] See above, p. 111 n. 3.

[2] I. Cohen, 'The Jews in Italy', *Political Quarterly* (July–Sept. 1939), 418.

[3] Roth, *The History of the Jews in Italy*, p. 533; for further Jewish tributes, see P. E. Lapide, *The Last Three Popes and the Jews*, London, 1967, pp. 115–16, 225–9; for a more critical appraisal, cf. A. L. Kubovy, 'The Silence of Pope Pius XII and the Beginnings of the "Jewish Document"', *Yad Vashem Studies*, XI (1967), 7–25.

[4] Binchy, p. 335 (cf. also pp. 330–1, 351, 514); P. Scoppola, *La chiesa e il fascismo: documenti e interpretazioni*, 3rd edn., Bari, 1976, pp. 129, 264–70.

papal governments had dealt with the defence of religion, 'not in the name of the racialist principle as understood and applied to-day, but of a purely religious principle'.[1] As for the Catholic admirers of the 'Race Manifesto', Farinacci himself was forced to admit that most of them had ceased to attack the Jews when Pius XI announced his 'Judaic leanings'.[2] The Jesuits had been conducting a virulent anti-Jewish campaign since the end of the nineteenth century; but when Farinacci claimed them as allies against the Jewish race, the Jesuit organ reacted sharply, insisting that its attitude towards Jewry had always been based on the Christian principles of 'justice and charity', never on the racial principles imported from Hitler's Germany.[3]

Catholic writers do not deny that Vatican protests against the Fascist race laws centred on the violation of the Concordat: 'Legislative measures designed to restrict or abolish the partici-pation of Jews in the political and social life of the country would not of themselves have called for authoritative pronouncement by the head of the Church; however much he might deplore the harshness of such measures, he could not condemn them formally provided they did not impinge on the rights of the Church itself.' Even so, the Holy Father 'made no secret of his compassion for the innocent victims of the anti-Jewish persecution'; nor did he shrink from explicitly condemning 'hatred of the people once chosen by God'.[4] What is more, the lead given by the Pope and the Italian hierarchy was 'enthusiastically followed' by the Catholic masses. In the words of D. A. Binchy:

Naturally the utmost caution was necessary, for any open criticism of the new policy by the ordinary Catholic would have involved, at the very least, withdrawal of the Party *tessera*, and every Italian bread-

[1] Scoppola, pp. 607, 609–10; cf. *L'Osservatore Romano*, 7 Sept. 1938.
[2] Scoppola, p. 610; *Il Regime Fascista*, 27 Aug. 1938.
[3] E. Rosa, 'La questione giudaica e "La Civilta Cattolica"', *La Civiltà Cattolica* (1 Oct. 1938), 3–16. Undismayed by this rejoinder, Farinacci insisted that the former articles expressed the real views of the Jesuit organ (*Il Regime Fascista*, 4 Oct. 1938; cf. also *Il Regime Fascista* of 5 and 14 Jan. 1939).
[4] Binchy, pp. 615–16. As early as 25 March 1928 the Holy Office condemned 'the hatred that commonly goes by the name of anti-Semitism' (ibid., p. 610). On 7 September 1938 Pius XI himself told a group of Belgian pilgrims that Christians could not 'take part in anti-Semitism', being 'spiritually Semites' (*La Croix*, 17 Sept. 1938); and while this statement was omitted by all the Italian papers, including the Vatican organ, from their account of the Pope's address, it received enormous publicity throughout the Western world. On Pius XI's secret efforts to aid persecuted Jews, see A. Giovanetti, 'Pio XI e un appello', *L'Osservatore Romano*, 26 Jan. 1961.

winner knew only too well the economic consequences of expulsion. Yet, working privately or even anonymously, many Catholic individuals and groups fought a secret battle against the racialist measures, and Jews have borne testimony to the steadfastness with which the Church opposed persecution. In many towns clandestine leaflets were distributed among the population, telling them that 'Catholics must be philo-Semites'[1] . . . The vigilant eye of Farinacci raked the parochial and diocesan bulletins in search of 'treasonable' exhortations to show charity to the Jews, and the results of his investigations were featured daily in the columns of his newspaper. But the practical exercise of charity he and the other Party leaders were powerless to prevent, for the innate kindliness of the average Italian rose triumphant over all threats and admonitions. Prudence may have compelled the observance of the letter of the anti-Jewish laws, but their spirit has never been observed and is not observed to-day. The cruel measures designed to segregate Italian Jews from the social and economic life of their fellow-countrymen have been mitigated as far as possible by the pity and consideration shown by Italians of all classes to the victims of the persecution; and more than one Jew of my acquaintance has borne grateful tribute to the influence of the Catholic clergy which in many districts was strong enough to secure the complete failure in practice of the policy of segregation.[2]

As for the alleged identity between the foreign policies of Fascism and the Holy See, Catholic apologists maintain that the 'history of the Vatican's relations with foreign Powers . . . affords no real evidence in support of this'. When the Lateran Pacts were signed in 1929, there was no lack of prophets to forecast a 'totalitarian alliance' between the Pope and the Duce directed against 'democracy' and 'progress'. When Pius XI died ten years later, the same prophets hastened to acclaim him as 'the champion of freedom against the totalitarian Powers'. Far from being 'tied hand and foot' to the Fascist tyranny, the Church had succeeded in retaining its 'unique position of freedom from control by the totalitarian machine'; nor was it a coincidence that the 'principal duels' between the Pope and the Duce all took place after and not before Reconciliation. True, the need for maintaining correct relations with the Quirinal made the Holy

---

[1] Cohen, 'The Jews in Italy', 418.

[2] Binchy, pp. 625–6. This passage was written in November 1939; in his preface to the 1970 edition Binchy admitted that he had exaggerated the resistance of the Vatican and underestimated that of the lower clergy (p.v). On the strength of Catholic resistance, see also De Felice, *Storia degli ebrei italiani*, p. 309–10.

See 'very careful not to offend Italian susceptibilities'; but while refraining from open polemics on international problems, the Pope never shrank from pursuing policies which ran directly counter to those of the Fascist regime. Mussolini's conflict with the 'Jew-ridden' West did not prevent the Curia from maintaining the friendliest relations with London and Paris; Fascist attacks on the 'super-Jew' Roosevelt did not deter the Holy Father from adopting an 'exceptionally cordial attitude' towards him which found frequent expression in tributes to his efforts for international peace and high praise for the principles on which he sought to base it. Naturally there were issues (such as Austrian independence and the crusade against Bolshevism in Spain) on which Fascist and papal policies coincided; but such coincidences, like those between Fascist and Catholic theory, were 'entirely fortuitous' and liable to terminate at a moment's notice if the Duce suddenly decided to set another course. 'Jewish sanctionism' was undoubtedly anathema to the Vatican; but this was due, not to sympathy for Fascism or hostility to Jews, but to the well-founded fear that sanctions would drive Italy into the arms of Hitler. The Rome–Berlin Axis was 'abhorrent' to the Holy See from every point of view. There was first the danger that Catholic Italy would be infected by the blatantly anti-Catholic tenets of Nazism. Then, too, the alliance of the two Fascist dictators greatly increased the chances of a major war, 'always a supreme disaster for the Catholic Church and more particularly for a Pope who had chosen for the motto of his pontificate *Pax Christi in regno Christi*'. Lastly, the Vatican clearly foresaw that the surrender of Catholic Austria—'the last bastion of Catholicism in the Germanies'—would be part of the price with which Mussolini would buy the friendship of Hitler. By the end of 1938 all these fears had been realized. The Pact of Steel, concluded at the very height of Hitler's campaign against the church, completed the rupture between Curia and Quirinal, and by June 1939 papal policy 'was almost completely parallel with that of the Western democracies'.[1]

Mussolini's conversion to racialism (the apologists add) was a

[1] Binchy, pp. 95–6, 529, 635–7, 657–8, 663, 665–6, 707; on Vatican opposition to the Rome–Berlin Axis, cf. F. Charles-Roux, *Huit ans au Vatican 1932–1940*, Paris, 1947, pp. 161–4. For Catholic criticism of 'Jewish sanctionism', see Martini, *Studi sulla questione romana e la Conciliazione*, p. 178.

particularly grievous blow to those Italian prelates who had hitherto been favourable to the regime. Over a number of years Catholic admirers of the Duce had been constantly pointing out that Fascism, unlike Hitlerism, rejected the anti-Christian myths of race and blood. Their embarrassment was all the greater, therefore, when the 'hateful doctine' was suddenly emblazoned on the Fascist banners in July 1938. To make matters worse, the advent of *razzismo* as a political dogma in Italy coincided with a demonstration of Catholic universalism which had been largely sponsored by Pius XI himself: the erection of indigenous hierarchies in all the principal missionary lands.[1]

The silence of Pius XII in the face of crime (the apologists argue) was due, not to 'un-Christian cowardice', but to Christian prudence; he refrained from public protests on the well-founded assumption that papal caution and circumspection were more likely to benefit the Jews than papal clamour. His 'fundamental principle' was to save lives—i.e. to give concrete aid to persecuted Jews without, however, permitting himself to engage in polemics which were liable to exasperate the German rulers and to end up by unleashing their bestiality. For the rest, his 'eminently cautious' policy, 'pedestrian and unheroic' though it seemed even to loyal Catholics, paid dividends: the Holy See emerged from World War II with enhanced strength and prestige, to play a dominant part in the new democratic Italy.[2]

In evaluating these conflicting interpretations of the racialist controversy between Church and State in Italy, we shall do well to bear in mind three basic facts.

First, the Catholic brand of anti-Judaism had ceased to be a factor in Italian politics long before the March on Rome. The anti-Jewish tirades of the Jesuits did not worry the Jews (so acute an observer as the late Dante Lattes described them as 'innocuous' in a letter to the writer). Nor is there any evidence that the

[1] Binchy, p. 342.
[2] R. Leiber, 'Pio XII e gli ebrei di Roma 1943–1944', *La Civiltà Cattolica* (4 Mar. 1961), 449–58; Binchy, pp. vi–vii; C. Seton-Watson, *Italy from Liberalism to Fascism 1870–1925*, London, 1967, p. 706. It is only fair to add that Pius XII's silence has been deplored by eminent Catholics; on 11 June 1940 Cardinal Eugène Tisserant wrote to Cardinal E. Suhard: 'I fear that history will reproach the Holy See with having practised a policy of selfish convenience and not much else' (BA/K/R43 II/1440a). But whatever our views on the Pope's performance as a guardian of the moral law, the fact remains that a great many Jewish lives were saved by the Church (De Felice, *Storia degli ebrei italiani*, pp. 466–467).

Vatican ever objected to Mussolini's 'pro-Jewish' policy during the first fourteen years of Fascist rule. When Italy went over to the anti-Jewish camp, it was precisely the most pro-Fascist prelates who echoed the Pope's condemnation in uncompromising terms.[1]

Second, the racialist controversy between Church and State was primarily a quarrel over foreign policy. The breach of the Concordat, though ostensibly the point at issue, was neither the main cause of the conflict nor the main subject of the dispute; the cleavage between the Pope and the Duce over Germany had become evident long before the latter's conversion to racialism.[2] Prior to his ill-starred alliance with Hitler, Mussolini had enjoyed clerical approbation on a scale unprecedented in modern Italian history; and when he exploited that approbation in the cause of Fascist aggrandizement, the Church from Pius XI downwards acquiesced, giving its blessing to the conquest of Ethiopia and to

---

[1] Farinacci's above-quoted speech of 7 November 1938 provoked a notable reply from the Archbishop of Milan, Cardinal Ildefonso Schuster, who had hailed Mussolini's invasion of Ethiopia as a 'Christian crusade' in 1935. Speaking in his cathedral on 13 November, Schuster vehemently attacked the 'heresy born in Germany and now insinuating itself almost everywhere'. After stressing the effect of such teaching in Germany where 'in the name of this myth of the twentieth century, the children of Abraham are banished from the land', he prayed 'that the genius of the Italian stock and the wisdom of our Government may co-operate with the Divine grace in keeping far from our country this new Nordic heresy' (*Osservatore Romano*, 18 Nov. 1938). Other pro-Fascist prelates spoke in similar strain, including the Archbishop of Bologna and the Patriarch of Venice (*Osservatore Romano*, 30 Dec. 1938 and 19 Jan. 1939). On 22 November 1938 Goebbels's *Angriff* denounced Schuster's sermon as part of an attempt to destroy the Rome–Berlin Axis. Alfieri protested, imploring his German colleague to refrain from giving unnecessary publicity to such insignificant manifestations of clerical opposition (*Storia degli ebrei italiani*, p. 313).

[2] In March 1937 the Ministry of Popular Culture forbade all Italian newspapers to publish more than a garbled summary of the encyclical *Mit brennender Sorge*; as the Vatican organ observed on 24 March, The Fascist press preferred to feature a typically scurrilous reply to the encyclical which had appeared in the *Völkischer Beobachter*. Nine months later the Pope's denunciation of Hitler's anti-Catholic excesses in his Christmas Allocution was similarly expurgated. The Anschluss gave rise to violent polemics beween the Vatican organ and Farinacci's paper (see, e.g., 'Surtout pas trop de zèle', *L'Osservatore Romano*, 16 March 1938 and 'Mea Culpa', *Il Regime Fascista*, 13 Apr. 1938). During the German–Czech crises the *Osservatore Romano* openly expressed its sympathy with the Czechs—so much so that Farinacci accused the Holy See of actively supporting the Beneš Government, 'the embodiment of Masonic paganism' (*Il Regime Fascista*, 24 Sept. 1938). All the manifestations of 'Axis solidarity' were studiously ignored by the Vatican organ, Mussolini's official journey to Germany was dismissed in a few lines, while Hitler's return visit was not mentioned at all.

the crusade against Bolshevism in Spain.[1] The forging of the Rome–Berlin Axis, however, destroyed the assumptions on which this acquiescence was based. Italy ceased to be a prop of Catholicism, and the Church had no choice but to disengage itself from the Fascist regime. There was no open rupture, neither side being willing to push disagreement to a point which endangered the Concordat; even so, it was clear by the time the Steel Pact was signed that the idyll between Vatican and Quirinal was at an end. Italian Catholics, sensing the new coolness between the Holy See and Italy, began drawing apart from Fascism.[2]

Third, Vatican opposition to the Axis alliance accurately reflected the views of most Italians, high-ranking members of the Fascist hierarchy included; for on this point papal policy happened to coincide with the true interests of the Italian nation. Mussolini's surrender of Austria, his imitation of Hitler's racial folly, and his apparent support of German action in Prague had led to what one of his Ministers termed 'the breach between the people and the regime' (*frattura tra paese e regime*); the clash between Church and State served to widen that breach.[3] And while papal intervention in the racial issue was limited by considerations of 'Christian prudence', its impact on public opinion at home and abroad was considerable.[4]

[1] Seton-Watson, op. cit., p. 705; D. Mack Smith, *Italy. A Modern History,* 2nd edn., Ann Arbor and London, 1969, p. 443. On ecclesiastical support for Mussolini's African war, cf. also Binchy, pp. 643–51, 671–4, 677–9.

[2] In the words of R. A. Webster: 'The idyll between the Church and Italy ended with the change in Italian foreign policy . . . The turning point came in the spring of 1938 when the Germans annexed Austria, putting an end to the alliance between Italy, Austria and Hungary. Instead of leading the minor Catholic states, Italy herself was being swept into the German system . . . In the course of 1938 it became clear that Fascism would draw its future sustenance from German National Socialist doctrine rather than from Catholic tradition . . . The introduction of racial lore and segregation into Italy was more serious than its farcical circumstances might suggest: to the cult of the national state Fascism now joined the far more overtly pagan cult of race . . . Even the death of Pius XI and the election of a new pope did not notably improve relations between the Church and the Regime. Though Pius XII (Pacelli) was smoother and more diplomatically expert than his predecessor, he too was horrified by the Germans . . . Italian Catholics . . . shared in the general divorce between the Regime and the Italian people which became final during the disastrous years of World War II' (*The Cross and the Fasces,* pp. 113–16). On Pius XII's attitude towards the Third Reich, see Appendix IV.

[3] Guarneri, *Battaglie economiche,* ii. 364–93; Perth to Halifax, 37 Dec. 1938 (*DBFP,* 3rd Ser. iii. 497).

[4] Lapide, op. cit., pp. 115–16, 122–3; A. C. Jemolo, *Chiesa e Stato in Italia negli ultimi cento anni,* 4th edn., Turin, 1955, pp. 669–70.

Critics of Vatican policy are right in affirming that modern anti-Semitism would have been inconceivable without centuries of Christian Jew-hatred, whatever the differences between the two; that the Roman Church, being authoritarian in structure, tends to sympathize with authoritarian regimes; that the *rapprochement* between Church and State gave rise to the spread of a hybrid clerico-Fascist ideology; that the Catholic clergy were split into two camps on the Jewish issue; and that for all but the final few years the Holy See must be numbered among the collaborators of Fascism, not the resisters.[1] But—and this is what matters in our context—they are wrong in belittling papal opposition to the Rome–Berlin Axis and Catholic resistance to Fascist racial policy. Nor do the records bear out the contention that fear of Bolshevism blinded either Pius XI or Pius XII to the magnitude of the German danger.[2]

Pius XI's public attacks on Fascist racialism inevitably led to a stiffening of the Fascist attitude; for Mussolini could not afford to show any weakness at a moment when he was about to link his fortunes with those of anti-Semitic Germany. The Grand Council resolutions of 6 October 1938 were followed by a spate of anti-Jewish laws and regulations which, in the words of the foremost English authority on Italian Jewry, 'reduced the position of the Italian Jews to that of pariahs, on a lower level in many respects than in the darkest days of the Ghetto period'.[3] In March 1939 even the 'exempted' Jews were expelled from the Fascist party[4]; and by the time the Steel Pact was signed it seemed to many observers that the legal position of the Duce's Jewish subjects was little better than that of their co-religionists in Germany.

---

[1] On the Christian roots of modern anti-Semitism, see Lewy, pp. 268–70; on Catholic authoritarianism and clerico-Fascism, Binchy, p. 329 and Lyttelton, *The Seizure of Power*, p. 421; on opposition to Pius XI's anti-racialist stand in Vatican circles, Farinacci to Mussolini, 3 Aug. 1938 (IC/Job 122/033900-08).

[2] Bergen to Neurath, 4 Jan. 1936: 'The Pope ... most definitely rejected the German contention that Germany had saved the Roman Catholic Church from Bolshevism ... Germany's object was to destroy the Catholic Church' (GFM/8111/E579722-29). Pacelli made the same point in a letter to Bergen on 30 April 1937 (*ADAP Serie D i. 780*). Throughout the Russo-German war Pius XII refused to condemn Stalin or support Hitler, despite his conviction that 'in the long run' Communism was more dangerous than National Socialism (R. Leiber, 'Der Papst und die Verfolgung der Juden', *Summa iniuria oder Durfte der Papst schweigen?*, ed. F. J. Raddatz, Hamburg, 1963, pp. 103–4).

[3] Roth, op. cit., p. 528.

[4] 'Foglio di disposizioni', P.N.F., No. 1275 (quoted in De Felice, *Storia degli ebrei italiani*, p. 300).

For all his racialist intransigence, however, Mussolini was profoundly unhappy about the conflict with the Church which threatened to undermine national unity at a time of grave international crisis; he was understandably relieved, therefore, when Pius XII, on ascending to the papal throne, called a truce in the racialist controversy, assuring Ciano that he would follow a 'more conciliatory' policy than his predecessor.[1] On 16 May 1939, ten days after the announcement of the Steel Pact, Diego von Bergen, German Ambassador to the Holy See, pointed out that the new Pontiff desired to go down in history as a 'bringer of peace to the world' and that the 'most important points in his programme' were 'the settlement of the differences with Italy' and 'peace with Germany':

Before the death of Pius XI relations between the Curia and the Italian Government suffered a rapidly increasing deterioration. The crisis, then often feared, can at the moment be regarded as lifted. The reduction (*Abbau*) of differences is proceeding swiftly at present, thanks to the high degree of goodwill shown by both sides; by the Duce because of his desire to have the whole of Italy, including the clergy, unitedly behind him in critical times . . . An early normalization of our relations with the Curia is earnestly hoped for by the Italians. Friends of many years' standing have told me bluntly that the German–Vatican tension is felt to be a heavy strain on the Axis and that the blame for veering towards France, not *per se* desired by the Pope, must be laid upon Germany. The Pope has given me to understand most emphatically . . . his 'ardent desire' for the restoration of friendly relations with Germany . . . This desire is shared by numerous Italian clergy in Rome of both the higher and lower orders.

Much to the Pontiff's chagrin, however, there had been no response to his advances: 'The death of Pius XI had been followed by a noticeable *détente* in the Vatican with regard to Germany which led in part to high hopes for an impending *rapprochement.* Recently a reaction has made itself felt. The Pope felt "hurt" at the absence of a German response to his desire for peace, expressed "sincerely and with full conviction"; he was being driven more and more to the assumption that . . . official Germany did not really seek peace with the Church and the Holy See.'

Bergen had no doubt that the Pope's declarations were 'meant

[1] Ciano, *Diario*, i. 59 (18 Mar. 1939).

sincerely'. Even so (he warned), Pius XII was no less intransigent in matters of doctrine (including racial doctrine) than his temperamental predecessor: 'The Pope recently declared emphatically that in the interests of concluding peace with Germany he would be prepared for far-reaching concessions, provided the vital interests of the Church and principles of dogma were not endangered ... The Pope ... is, however, a difficult and tenacious negotiator who, in the course of the negotiations, is in the habit of continually enlarging the scope of his demands.' The Ambassador concluded by affirming that a settlement with the Curia was 'desirable and expedient on grounds of foreign policy'—an obvious allusion to Mussolini's unconcealed annoyance at the anti-Catholic excesses in Germany.[1]

After the signing of the Steel Pact it seemed for a moment as if the Duce's appeal for a *détente* between Germany and the Holy See had at long last fallen on fertile soil. On 24 May 1939 Ciano noted in his diary: 'Himmler talked at length about relations with the Church. They like the new Pope [*sic*] and believe that a *modus vivendi* is possible. I encouraged him along these lines, saying that an agreement between the Reich and the Vatican would make the Axis more popular.'[2] About the same time Ribbentrop instructed Bergen to inform the new Pontiff that his desire for an accord was fully shared by the German Government. Bergen reported on 9 June:

The Pope was ... so delighted at the possibility of paving the way for friendly relations between us and the Curia that he prolonged our conversation again and again ... I spoke on the following lines: The Pope's utterances ... had given us the impression and aroused the hope that a new epoch had dawned for German–Vatican relations [*sic*]. In your opinion it was quite possible for Church and State to dwell peacefully together within the same confines [*sic*]; should the Vatican's endeavours be thus directed, you would be favourably disposed towards them. In response to your request for proposals, I had characterized as of prime importance the elimination of the present mutual mistrust and the gradual creation of confidence. The *détente*, which was already perceptible, would have to be promoted and a press truce could contribute considerably to this. Once the atmosphere had been cleared, a private non-committal exchange of views might perhaps first be

---

[1] *ADAP*, Serie D vi. 428–30; cf. Bergen to Weizsäcker, 20 May 1939 (GFM/2196/473577–79).
[2] Ciano, *Diario*, i. 104.

entered upon and this, if favourable, could be followed by more detailed talks and possible negotiations. You had authorized these suggestions in principle but attached decisive importance to secrecy; indiscretions could set everything back by five to ten years.

In reply the Pope requested Bergen to inform Ribbentrop that he would 'always be ready to work for friendly relations with Germany, a country very dear to him'. As for secrecy, Berlin could rely on the discretion of the Curia. For the rest, he would welcome it if, 'pending the final general settlement' (*sic*), further 'harsh measures' against the Church in Germany and Austria could be avoided: 'The Pope, like yourself, apparently had in mind some kind of truce (*Burgfrieden*) for the interim period'. For all his eagerness to please his German interlocutor, Pius XII did not refrain from hinting at his profound anxiety about Hitler's aggressive policy: 'The Pope expressed concern about the international situation without, however, going into details.'[1]

Whatever Hitler's motives in authorizing the above overture, it soon became evident that he had no intention of curbing the anti-Catholic zeal of his underlings. On 5 July the Cardinal Secretary of State told Count Pignatti, the Italian Ambassador to the Holy See, that relations between the Reich and the Vatican had once again taken a turn for the worse, in view of the continuing persecution of the Church in Germany and the resumption of slanderous attacks on the clergy in the controlled German press. He added that the Holy Father could not remain silent in the face of such outrages; unless there was a drastic change for the better in the near future, he would have to take a public stand.[2] On 22 July Pignatti reported to Ciano that the breach between the Pope and the Führer was rapidly becoming irreparable; even the most pro-German prelates were by now abandoning all hope of an accord with the Reich. He had therefore urged Bergen to make another approach to the Pontiff before it was too late.[3]

Despite these warnings, however, Pius XII refused to break his self-imposed silence. His reaction to the anti-Catholic excesses in

[1] *ADAP* Serie D vi. 575–6.
[2] Pignatti to Ciano, 5 July 1939 (*DDI*, 8ª serie xii. 360–1.)
[3] Ibid. 484. Pignatti assured Bergen that the Pope still had confidence in Hitler and Ribbentrop, but Pius XII himself, in a conversation with the British Minister to the Holy See, made it clear that the opposite was true (Osborne to Halifax, 27 Aug. 1939, *DBFP*, 3rd Ser. vii. 308).

Germany took the form, not of a public stand against the Hitler regime, but of 'unofficial' polemics against the Rome–Berlin Axis in the Vatican organ, with special reference to the Fascist imitation of Hitler's racial heresy. Mussolini was predictably furious. On 20 July Ciano wrote in his diary: 'By order of the Duce I have presented an ultimatum to the Nuncio for the *Osservatore Romano*. Either it will cease its subtle propaganda against the Axis or we shall have to prohibit its circulation in Italy. It has become the official organ of the anti-Fascists.'[1] Subsequently, it was revealed that an assistant editor of the Vatican paper had been arrested on charges of plotting against the regime.[2] Mussolini and Ciano had another ground for complaint on 4 August when Pius XII showed his contempt for the racial gospel by receiving a prominent victim of the anti-Jewish persecution, Professor Giorgio Del Vecchio.[3]

The evolution of the racial question in Italy between May and August 1939 accurately mirrors the conflicting emotions and pressures to which the Duce was subject at this juncture. Of the three anti-Jewish laws enacted during this period two (No. 1054 of 29 June 1939 and No. 1055 of 13 July 1939) were a logical extension of the racial measures previously adopted, while the third (No. 1024, also of 13 July) made complete and utter nonsense of the racial principles which had been declared to be the 'fundamental basis' of the Italian State a year earlier. Law No. 1054 banned persons of the Jewish race from journalistic activity and forbade them to act as notaries; it also prohibited Jews from co-operating with Aryan colleagues in any way and from attending on non-Jews in a professional capacity. Law No. 1055 provided that clauses in wills restricting inheritance to persons of the Jewish faith were invalid; in addition it authorized the children of a Jewish father and a Gentile mother to adopt the latter's family name, and Aryans to relinquish appellations generally considered Jewish.[4]

While the above decrees were presumably pleasing to the Germans (being an obvious imitation of the Nuremberg laws), the opposite was true of Law No. 1024 which empowered

---

[1] Ciano, *Diario*, i. 132.

[2] The 'plotter' was Guido Gonella (*Il Regime Fascista*, 5 Oct. 1939).

[3] 'Italy', *Contemporary Jewish Record*, ii (Sept.–Oct. 1939), 92.

[4] Staderini, *Legislazione per la difera della razza*, pp. 139–42.

Mussolini to 'aryanize' any member of the Jewish race he chose, irrespective of services rendered to Italy or Fascism.[1] In practice this meant two things—that Jews with no claim to 'exemption' might be favoured above war veterans and early Fascists; and that persons of pure Jewish stock might receive preferential treatment over half- and quarter-Jews, not to mention converts to Catholicism with Aryan wives. The Duce subsequently told his biographer that the chief beneficiaries of Law No. 1024 were a few 'great-hearted' Jewish Italians with especially meritorious military records, including a brilliant naval engineer and a hero of the Spanish Civil War.[2]

As might be expected, Fascist officialdom found in the new law a convenient means of illicit enrichment. A lucrative traffic soon sprang up, a large bribe being the recognized way to secure a certificate of exemption from the application of the racial code. Among those involved in the racket were a number of high Fascist dignitaries, including Buffarini, the Under-Secretary of the Interior, who, according to the Italian Chief of Police, was 'at the bottom of all the filthy doings (*porcherie*) in Italy'.[3] It remains to add that some persons of Jewish origin applied for 'Aryanization' on the plea that their mothers or grandmothers had committed adultery with a Gentile.[4]

While the 'Aryanization' traffic benefited only a handful of wealthy Jews and a few corrupt Fascist bosses, the 'exemptions' laid down by the Fascist Grand Council brought advantages (however limited) to a very much larger number, given the high percentage of Italian Jews with Fascist or national merits. According to the secret Jewish census of 22 August 1938, no less than 3,502 Jewish families (out of a total of 15,000) were entitled to exemption from some of the provisions of the race laws, including 406 families of those killed in action, 721 families of war volunteers, 1,597 families of those with decorations for military valour, three families of 'Fascist martyrs', 724 families of veteran Fascists (i.e. those who had joined the Party either

[1] Ibid., pp. 136–8.
[2] De Begnac, *Palazzo Venezia*, p. 643. The naval engineer was General Umberto Pugliese (who was brought secretly out of retirement in November 1940 to advise on the retrieving of the warships sunk at Taranto); the hero of the Spanish Civil War was Lieutenant Bruno Jesi.
[3] Ciano, *Diario*, ii: 1941–1943, p. 158.
[4] Roth, p. 529.

before the March on Rome or during the Matteotti crisis), and 51 families of 'legionaries' who had participated in D'Annunzio's Fiume *coup*. In addition there were 834 Jews with exceptional political, cultural, or economic merits.[1] What the 'exemptions' would amount to in practice remained unclear—all the more so since the unconditional ejection of all Jews from the Fascist Party in March 1939 implied exclusion from the normal channels of earning a livelihood. In July 1939 Kleinlerer reported that 'some' deserving Italian Jews had been awarded 'exemption certificates', freeing them from the obligation to declare their immovable property, though not from various other disabilities. As for the others, it was hoped that they might eventually be 'excluded from the rigours of the racial legislation', if a 'lenient course in the execution of this legislation' was followed. Unfortunately, the conclusion of the Steel Pact had made the adoption of such a course less likely. The only positive factor in the situation (Kleinlerer concluded) was the pro-Jewish attitude of the Italian masses which manifested itself in a wide variety of ways, 'from personal expressions of sympathy to intervention, protection, and financial assistance to needy individual Jews', and which extended to 'all classes of Italian society, including the official followers of Fascism'.[2]

In the following months it became increasingly evident that the 'exemptions', like the 'Aryanizations', were meant to open the way for special treatment of those who could pay for it.[3] For the rest, Fascist racial policy continued to reflect Mussolini's contradictory attitude to the Jewish question as well as the conflicting motives of his servile and corrupt underlings. The following chronicle of the anti-Jewish persecution throws light on the evolution of the racial question in Italy during the period under review.

On 11 May—five days after the announcement of the Pact of Steel—Buffarini, addressing the Chamber of Fasces and Corporations, declared that the anti-Jewish measures were dictated by 'biological, political, and even religious necessity'. On 19 May Farinacci, writing in *Il Regime Fascista*, called upon the

---

[1] ACS/Rilevazione sugli ebrei del 22 agosto 1938/Min. Int./Dir. Gen. Demografia e Razza (1938–43)/cart.14/fasc.47

[2] Kleinlerer, 'A Year of Racialism in Italy', 36–7.

[3] Fornari, *Mussolini's Gadfly*, pp. 188–9.

spokesmen of Italian Jewry to demonstrate their loyalty by denying foreign reports of anti-Semitic persecution in Italy; on the same day the Catholic University of Milan published *Razza e Nazione,* an anti-racialist book by a leading German Catholic.[1] On 31 May a Jewish refugee who had failed to comply with an expulsion order was deported to Germany, but other refugees were left unmolested. On 1 June the Italian Cabinet approved a series of anti-Jewish measures;[2] on the same day *Il Resto del Carlino,* a Bolognese Fascist daily, demanded that Jews be compelled to relinquish appellations identical with Italian place-names, such as Milano, Ravenna, or Viterbo. On 2 June the senate approved a decree imposing restrictions upon the activities of Jewish professionals; simultaneously it was revealed that 4,000 Jews had embraced Christianity in order to escape some of the consequences of Fascist legislation.[3] On 11 June four Jews in Genoa were fined one hundred lire each and sent to prison for five to fifteen days for failure to register as members of the Jewish race; on 20 June eleven Jews in Trieste were sentenced to eight days imprisonment for the same offence. On 23 June twenty-six German and Czech Jews were arrested in Genoa on a charge of smuggling Jewish funds out of Italy; two days later the Union of Italian Jewish Communities appealed to the government not to deprive the Jews of their means of livelihood.[4] On 26 June Fascist vandals at Bologna defaced a synagogue and several Jewish communal buildings with swastikas; on the same day slogans denouncing anti-Semitism were chalked on a number of houses in Turin. On 27 June it was learnt that 224 enterprises had been registered by Jews in Rome in accordance with Royal Decree Law No. 126 which provided for the transfer of Jewish-owned enterprises with more than 100 employees to 'Aryan hands'.[5] On 30 June it was reported that Zionist activities had been banned in Turin, Leghorn, and Florence. It remains to add that

[1] The Rector of the Catholic University, Padre Agostino Gemelli, was a notorious anti-Semite; but even he could not stomach Hitler's Nordic paganism. During World War II he secretly aided persecuted Jews (F. Monicelli, 'Un Frate in Paradiso', *Paese Sera,* 18 July 1959; 'Padre Gemelli e gli ebrei', *Epoca,* 29 Nov. 1959).
[2] These measures were converted into law on 13 July 1939 (see above, p. 254 and n. 4).
[3] This decree was converted into law on 29 June 1939 (see above, p. 254 and n. 4).
[4] Memorandum submitted to the Ministry of the Interior.
[5] Royal Decree Law No. 126 did not apply if an Italian Jew donated his real property to his Aryan wife, to descendants who were not considered to be of the Jewish race, or to Christian institutions having educational or charitable purposes.

throughout this period Jewish refugees from Central and Eastern Europe continued to arrive in Italy.[1]

In July the Fascist rulers continued to strike a balance between demonstrative intransigence and minor concessions to pro-Jewish opinion at home and abroad. On 5 July prison terms and fines were imposed on twenty-four Jews in Milan for failure to register as members of the Jewish race; on the following day it was revealed that the number of Jews converted to Christianity since July 1938 had risen to 4,500. On 8 July the Ministry of the Interior issued an order forbidding state-controlled firms to employ or grant contracts to Jews; on 16 July the Ministry of Education, headed by the 'half-breed' Bottai, ordered Jewish university students to be segregated during examinations. On 27 July, on the other hand, the Duce demonstrated his magnanimity by permitting the entry of foreign Jews for a six-month stay provided they were economically self-sufficient.[2]

In August the mounting tension between the Axis and the Western democracies gave a fresh impetus to the anti-Jewish tendencies, with special reference to the refugee problem. On 2 August it was announced that the regulations curbing Jewish professional activity would become effective on 1 February 1940, and that Jews with Aryan names would be compelled to resume Jewish ones. On 6 August the importance of racialist propaganda was stressed in the annual report of the National Institute of Fascist Culture; on the same day it was disclosed that 700 Jewish refugees had entered Italy during July. On 8 August a Genoese Jewish war veteran (who had been blinded in action) returned his medals to the Duce in protest against the anti-Jewish laws; on the following day it was learnt that hundreds of foreign Jews, permitted to remain after the expulsion deadline of 12 March, had now been ordered to leave the country. On 14 August the King's visit to Turin gave rise to a demonstration against Fascist racial legislation which led to the arrest of several demonstrators; four days later it was reported that steps were being taken to curb the influx of Jewish refugees from Germany. On 22 August a stop was put to the activities of Jewish refugee-aid bodies in order to discourage the entry of Jews with insufficient funds; and

---

[1] 'Italy', *Contemporary Jewish Record*, ii (July–Aug. 1939), 115–16.
[2] The influx of Jewish refugees from Central and Eastern Europe continued throughout the period under review.

on 27 August a Zionist agricultural centre near Padova had to close down on orders from the Fascist authorities. On 28 August the situation took another turn for the worse when the government ordered the S.S. *Galilea, en route* for Palestine with 300 'legal' immigrants on board, to return to Italy.[1] Four days later, however, there was a complete change of scene when Hitler invaded Poland and Mussolini switched from a policy of 'total solidarity' with Berlin to one of neutrality or, as he chose to put it, of 'non-belligerency'.

It now remains to trace the developments which led to this abrupt (if temporary) reversal of Fascist foreign policy and to assess their repercussions on the evolution of the racial question in Italy.[2]

On 24 May Ciano returned to Rome, blissfully unaware of the fact that Hitler had announced his intention of attacking Poland 'at the first suitable opportunity' a day earlier. On 25 May he called on the King who warned him that Germans would soon 'reveal themselves as the great rascals they really are'.[3] In the ensuing weeks the Duce and his Foreign minister were busily engaged in the trivia of 'dynamic' Fascist diplomacy. Mussolini was considering the fomentation of a Croat revolt and the proclamation of an independent Croat State in confederation with Rome.[4] There were delicate and difficult negotiations in Berlin over the South Tyrol, in the course of which the Germans reluctantly agreed to a population transfer.[5] Mussolini was also concerned to bring Japan, Spain, and Hungary into the Steel Pact, being justifiably anxious not to remain alone in the boat with Hitler. In all these transactions he behaved as if he had plenty of time, believing as he did that the Führer would follow the path of conciliation in regard to Poland.[6]

In the first half of June Ramon Serrano Suñer, Franco's devoutly Catholic brother-in-law, paid a long visit to Italy; but

[1] 'Italy', *Contemporary Jewish Record*, ii (Sept.–Oct. 1939), 92–3; in evaluating these anti-Jewish measures we should bear in mind that Mussolini was desperately anxious to keep on the right side of Hitler until the outbreak of war, despite his growing determination to stay out of the impending conflict.

[2] For a detailed reconstruction of these developments, see F. Siebert, *Italiens Weg in den Zweiten Weltkrieg*, Frankfurt/Main.–Bonn, 1962, pp. 188–356.

[3] Ciano, *Diario*, i. 105.

[4] Ibid. 106 (entry for 26 May 1939).

[5] Siebert, op. cit., pp. 228–36.

[6] Ciano, *Diario*, i. 109 (entry for 31 May 1939).

while expressing warm regard for Fascism and its leader, he made no secret of his unhappiness about the anti-Catholic excesses in Germany. Moreover, he bluntly warned his host that Spain was not in a fit state to wage a war and that hence the military pact proposed by Mussolini would be premature.[1] On 9 July Ciano went to Madrid and found the Spanish dictator civil and friendly but reserved about anti-Catholic Germany and firmly resolved to stay out of the impending conflict between the Axis and the Western democracies: 'Franco considers that a period of peace of at least five years is necessary, and even this figure seems to many observers optimistic.'[2] On 19 July Ciano returned to Rome with empty hands. Hitler, by now engaged in secret negotiations with Moscow, was opposed to a military alliance with Japan; the accession of Hungary without Spain or Japan would be of little value. Mussolini's plans for enlarging the scope of the Steel Pact had collapsed almost as soon as they were made; and he was left alone with Hitler to face the storm about to break over his head.

The first signal was hoisted on 17 June when Goebbels delivered a violently anti-Polish speech at Danzig, accusing Warsaw of aggression against the city and reaffirming the German claim to its return.[3] This was the language which had previously been levelled at Vienna and Prague; and it aroused alarm throughout the capitals of Europe but not in Rome where Mussolini and Ciano continued to bask in the illusion that Germany had agreed to a long period of peace. Attolico, however, did not share the optimism of his superiors and at once called on the Secretary of State from whom he requested a clear statement of Hitler's intentions. Weizsäcker replied that there had been 'no new development' in the Polish question and that his master 'did not appear to have taken any decision for an immediate solution' of the Danzig problem.[4] On 6 July Attolico saw Ribbentrop who told him that there would be no war over Danzig unless 'Polish provocations' compelled the Führer to react.[5]

[1] Ibid. 111–12 (entries for 5, 6, and 7 June 1939).
[2] *L'Europe verso la catastrofe*, ii. 67.
[3] H. Heiber (ed.), *Goebbels-Reden*, i. Düsseldorf, 1971, pp. 333–7.
[4] Magistrati, *L'Italia a Berlino*, p. 369.
[5] Attolico to Ciano 7 July 1939 (*DDI*, 8ª serie xii. 378–81; minute by Ribbentrop, 8 July 1939 (*ADAP*, Serie D vi. 740–1).

Unimpressed by these assurances, Attolico continued to warn his Minister 'of the imminence of a new and perhaps fatal crisis', affirming that the Germans were preparing 'to strike at Danzig by the 14th of August'.[1] But the Duce remained optimistic and so did his son-in-law. On 5 July Ciano noted in his diary that the 'Danzig storm' seemed to have blown over; fifteen days later, on being apprised of German troop movements 'on a vast scale', he found it hard to believe that this could happen 'without our knowing it, indeed after so many protestations of peace by our Axis comrades'. On 22 July he considered that Attolico had 'lost his head'; and as late as 28 July, after a conversation with his master, he wrote: 'This Ambassador has done good work, but he now allows himself to be taken in by the war panic'.[2] Mussolini himself told the editor of *Il Messagero*, an important Fascist daily, that between July and the end of September certain 'minor changes' might be made in the map of Europe but that none of these would generate war.[3]

While Mussolini and Ciano continued to put their trust in Ribbentrop's pacific assurances, Hitler was making active preparations for an early war. By 15 June he had the army's plan for operations in Poland. On 22 June—exactly one month before Ciano accused Attolico of having 'lost his head'—the German High Command presented a detailed timetable for the attack, for which reserves were to be called up on the pretext of autumn manœuvres. On the following day Göring presided over a meeting of the Reich Defence Council attended by thirty-five Ministers, generals, and officials; the main items on the agenda were all connected with Hitler's decision to draft seven million men in the mobilization for war. Two further meetings of the Council were held in July. Finally, on 27 July the order was drafted for the occupation of Danzig, only the date being left blank for the Führer to write in.[4]

Though unaware of these alarming developments, the Duce

[1] Ciano, *Diario*, i. 132–3 (entries for 19, 20, and 21 July 1939). Magistrati was more optimistic than the Ambassador, confirming Ciano in his suspicion that Attolico was a panic-monger (ibid. 132, entry for 21 July 1939).

[2] Ibid. 130, 133, 135–6. Attolico's warnings were based on confidential information furnished by Weizsäcker (C. J. Burckhardt, *Meine Danziger Mission 1937–1939*, Munich 1960, pp. 305–9; von Weizsäcker, *Erinnerungen*, pp. 202, 243–4.)

[3] Phillips to Hull, 6 July 1939 (*Ventures in Diplomacy*, p. 127).

[4] See *ND*/C-142, *ND*/C-126, *ND*/3787-PS, *ND*/C-30 (quoted in Bullock, *Hitler. A Study in Tyranny*, p. 152).

was worried about the mounting tension over Danzig and anxious to put the brake on his Axis partner. He therefore decided to launch a proposal for an international peace conference with a view to restraining the Führer and blackmailing the democracies without risk of war. On 22 July he discussed his project with Ciano and Magistrati. Why, he asked them, should not the Axis Powers, accused as they always were of desiring war, sponsor a practical peace plan, such as a conference between Italy, Germany, France, Britain, Poland, and Spain? Mussolini knew that the Germans would dislike the idea of another Munich and might even accuse him of wishing to default on his obligations. He therefore instructed Magistrati to inform Ribbentrop that there was no question of Italy backing out of the alliance: 'If Germany has to mobilize, Italy will do so likewise and *at the same time.*'[1] On the other hand, there were excellent tactical grounds for postponing the inevitable conflict with the Western Powers. A war of nerves suited the Axis better; a conference would provide a popular way of handing Danzig over to Germany; if the democracies refused to confer, they would put themselves in the wrong; and according to the information at his disposal, Poland and her Western allies were in earnest and intended to fight. Mussolini concluded by making it plain that he would not move without Germany's prior agreement.[2]

Three days later Attolico and Magistrati called on Hitler's Foreign Minister at Fuschl, near Salzburg, in order to secure his assent to the Duce's project. Ribbentrop's reaction was predictably negative. The Führer, he claimed, agreed with Mussolini that a general conflagration was undesirable and would avoid any course of action which might lead to international complications. But a conference, far from improving the position of the Fascist powers, would merely encourage the others along the path of intransigence and expose the Axis to the attacks of the 'Jewish-Masonic' press. Ribbentrop prefaced many of his utterances with the words: 'I will tell you very frankly'. His frankness, however, did not extend to informing his guests of the

---

[1] Minute by Magistrati, 24 July 1939 (*DDI*, 8ᵃ serie xii. 497–500). Our italics.
[2] Information supplied by Magistrati to Miss E. Wiskemann (*The Rome–Berlin Axis*, p. 189); cf. Magistrati, *L'Italia a Berlino*, pp. 379–82.

Führer's plans for the invasion of Poland or to revealing at this stage what was on foot between Berlin and Moscow.

Foiled in their main objective, Attolico and Magistrati suggested an early meeting between the Duce and the Führer on the Brenner frontier; but Ribbentrop countered with the specious arguments that it would be unwise to provoke speculation in the enemy camp. He concluded by reminding the Italians that he had merely been expressing his personal opinions: 'Only the Führer could give a responsible answer to the communication from the head of the Italian Government'.[1] A few days later it was learnt in Rome that Hitler fully shared the 'personal views' of his Foreign Minister.[2]

The sole result of the meeting at Fuschl was to deepen the misunderstanding on which the Axis alliance was based. Mussolini's promise of unconditional support misled Hitler into thinking that he could drag Italy into war whenever he liked, despite the consultation clause in the Steel Pact; while Ribbentrop's pacific assurances confirmed Mussolini and Ciano in their conviction that Attolico was a panic-monger.[3]

At the beginning of August, however, it began to dawn on the Italian leaders that something dramatic was in the offing. The following entries in Ciano's diary are significant. On 2 August: '*The insistence of Attolico keeps me wondering.*' On 3 August: 'Massimo (Magistrati) writes a private letter from which it appears that he is in disagreement with the Ambassador as to the danger of an approaching crisis ... Roatta, the new military attaché, on the other hand, informs us of concentrations of forces and movements on the Polish border. Who is right?' On 4 August: 'Attolico's alarmist bombardment continues. *The situation seems obscure to me ... the moment has come when we must really know how matters stand.*' Ciano (who had hitherto deprecated Mussolini's conference plan on the assumption that the West would capitulate) was by now thoroughly alarmed. On 6 August he discussed the position with his master: 'We agree in feeling that we must find some way out. By following the Germans we shall go to war in the most unfavourable conditions for the Axis and especially for Italy.

[1] Minute by Brücklmeier, 25 July 1939 (*ADAP*, Serie D vi. 829–31); Attolico to Ciano, 26 July 1939, (*DDI*, 8ᵃ serie xii. 517–22); Magistrati, *L'Italia a Berlino*, pp. 384–8.
[2] Ciano, *Diario*, i. 136 (entries for 28 and 31 July 1939).
[3] Cf. Siebert, pp. 220–3.

Our gold reserves are reduced to almost nothing, as well as our stocks of metals, and we are far from having completed our economic and military preparations. If the crisis comes, we shall fight if only to save our "honour". But we must avoid war.'[1]

Ciano proposed an early meeting with Ribbentrop. The Duce agreed and once more prepared for his son-in-law a memorandum, designed to convince the Germans that it would be folly to embark on war at this juncture. In 1939 (he argued) the Axis would have no more than an even chance of victory, whereas in three years the odds would be four to one. He reverted to the idea of another Munich and Ciano warmly endorsed it: 'Never has the Duce spoken of the need for peace with so much warmth and without reserve. I agree with him one hundred per cent.'[2]

The fateful meeting took place at Salzburg on 11 August. For the first time the Reich Foreign Minister showed his hand, bluntly informing his Italian colleague that action against Poland was imminent. He admitted that in previous conversations he had always emphasized the need for a long period of peace; but in the meantime a new situation had arisen which was bound to precipitate events. When asked for details of Germany's military plans, he blandly replied that he could not give particulars 'because all decisions were still locked in the Führer's impenetrable bosom'. And when Ciano pleaded for a peaceful gesture, he objected on the ground that the Axis could not afford to show any weakness, adding that the conflict would be localized and that even in the event of its becoming general the victory of Germany was 'one hundred per cent certain'. Commenting on this conversation in his diary, Ciano wrote: 'I am becoming aware of how little we are worth in the opinion of the Germans.'[3]

On the following day Ciano and his entourage (which included the 'Jew-tainted' Vitetti) went to Berchtesgaden for a meeting with the Führer. Hitler was more civil than Ribbentrop but equally implacable in his decision. In an interminable monologue he described for Ciano's benefit the strength of Germany's military position, the weakness of her enemies, the grounds on

[1] Ciano, *Diario*, i. 136–8; Roatta to Carboni, 2 Aug 1939 (*DDI*, 8ª serie xii. 566–8); Roatta to Mussolini, 3 Aug. 1939 (ibid., p. 572). Roatta's warnings were based on information provided by his friend Admiral Canaris (Magistrati, *L'Italia a Berlino*, p. 392).

[2] Ciano, *Diario*, i. 139 (entry for 10 Aug. 1939).

[3] *L'Europa verso la catastrofe*, ii. 78–81; Ciano, *Diario*, i. 140.

which he must destroy Poland ('a threat . . . in the rear of the Axis'), and his certainty that he could localize the war. As for Danzig, no compromise was possible, the population transfer in the South Tyrol having been justified on the plea that the East and North-East were the German sphere of interest. As a special bait to Italy he advised the Duce to liquidate Yugoslavia 'as soon as possible'.

In reply Ciano set out with a wealth of detail Italy's lack of preparation for war, complaining that, despite the Steel Pact, Germany had neither consulted nor informed her partner. But Hitler brushed all this aside with the observation that German action against Poland would not provoke a general conflict and that in consequence he would not have to ask for Italian help "according to the existing obligation'.[1] As a last expedient Ciano ventilated the idea of issuing a joint statement calling for a peaceful settlement of the disputes which were troubling the life of Europe. Hitler reluctantly agreed to consider this suggestion, after which he restated his determination to crush Poland and his conviction that the war would be localized.

When the conversation was resumed on 13 August Hitler was even more categorical than before. He disposed of the Duce's conference plan, ranted against the democracies ('misers on their heaps of gold'), and stressed the need for solving the Polish problem 'in a totalitarian manner', adding that the last date for the opening of hostilities was the end of August. He concluded with a discourse on 'Axis solidarity': 'He was . . . fortunate to live at a time in which, apart from himself, there was one other statesman who would stand out as great and unique in history; that he could be this man's friend was for him a matter of great personal satisfaction, and if the hour of common battle struck, he would always be found on the side of the Duce.'[2]

Ciano was not taken in. 'I return to Rome', he wrote in his diary, 'completely disgusted with the Germans, with their leader, with their way of doing things. They have betrayed us and lied to us. Now they are dragging us into an adventure which we do

---

[1] *L'Europa verso la catastrofe*, ii. 86; no equivalent passage is to be found in the German minute.
[2] *Ibid.* 82–8; *ADAP*, Serie D vii. 32–40, 43–6.

not want ... I think that our hands are free, and I propose that we act accordingly.'[1]

But the Duce was in two minds. At first he agreed with Ciano; then he said that 'honour' compelled him to march with Germany and that he wanted his share of the booty. In the ensuing days he continued to vacillate between sudden decisions to stand by Hitler and the prudent impulse to evade, and eventually escape from, the clutches of the 'Pact of Steel'. Ciano's diary throws light on his volatile mood:

On 14 August: 'I find Mussolini worried ... I submit to him documents which prove the bad faith of the Germans on the Polish question. The alliance was based on premisses which they now deny; they are traitors, and we must not have any scruples in ditching them. But Mussolini still has many scruples.' On 15 August: 'The Duce ... is convinced that we must not march blindly with Germany, but he makes one reservation: he wants time to prepare the break.' On 16 August: 'Mussolini, impelled by his idea of honour, might ... reaffirm his decision to go along with the Germans. He wanted to do it two days ago, and it was difficult to restrain him.' On 17 August: '(Mussolini) wanted Attolico to confirm to Ribbentrop that, in spite of everything, Italy will march with Germany ... I fought like a lion against this idea and succeeded in making the Duce modify these instructions.' On 18 August: 'A talk with the Duce in the morning; his usual shifting feelings. He still thinks it possible that the democracies will not march and that Germany might do good business cheaply, from which business he does not want to be excluded. Then, too, he fears Hitler's rage. He believes that a denunciation of the pact ... might induce Hitler to abandon the Polish question in order to square accounts with Italy.'

On 19 August Ciano went across to Albania. In his absence, Mussolini veered round once more. On 20 August: 'The Duce ... made an about-face. He wants to support Germany at any cost ... In the meantime the English have made an appeal to the Duce to settle the controversy peacefully. Conference between Mussolini, myself, and Attolico. This is the substance: It is already too late to go back on the Germans. If this were to happen, the press of the whole world say that Italy is cowardly

---

[1] Ciano, *Diario*, i. 141 (entry for 13 Aug. 1939).

. . . I use the British communication as a pretext to obtain a delay in any decision until to-morrow morning.'

On 21 August Mussolini reaffirmed his decision to march with Hitler. Ciano reacted violently: 'I went to Salzburg in order to adopt a common line of action. I found myself face to face with a *Diktat.* The Germans, not ourselves, have betrayed the alliance in which we were to have been partners and not servants. Tear up the pact. Throw it in Hitler's face, and Europe will recognize in you the natural leader of the anti-German crusade.' It was decided to invite Ribbentrop to the Brenner Pass and to warn him that Italy would not intervene if the conflict was provoked by an attack on Poland. The evening, however, brought a dramatic change in the situation: Ribbentrop informed Ciano that 'he was to leave later for Moscow to sign a political pact with the Soviet Government'. Ciano reported to his master, and it was agreed to call off the projected meeting. 'There is no doubt', Ciano wrote on 22 August, 'the Germans have struck a master-blow. The European situation is upset.'[1]

For a moment it seemed to the Italians that Hitler's master-stroke had placed Germany on the winning side and that hence they had better reaffirm their loyalty to the Steel Pact. It soon became clear, however, that the democracies had no intention of yielding. On 23 August Ciano warned Hitler's Minister of Finance that 'despite the great diplomatic success of the Russian Pact he considered the situation to be very grave'. On the same day Mussolini authorized Ciano to present to the British a plan for the preliminary cession of Danzig to Germany, followed by 'negotiations and a great peace conference'. It was an utterly unrealistic proposal; the Duce himself appears to have realized as much, for a few hours later he relapsed into belligerence.[2]

While Mussolini continued to be torn between fear of war and fear of seeming afraid, Hitler was preparing for action. On 22 August he told his military advisers that there were two 'personal factors' on which he based his decision to strike at once: his own personality and that of the Duce. Mussolini's existence was decisive: 'If something happens to him, Italy's loyalty to the alliance will no longer be certain.' The Anglo-French were weak

[1] Ibid. 141–7; Magistrati, *L'Italia a Berlino,* pp. 421–3.
[2] Schwerin von Krosigk to Ribbentrop, 23 Aug. 1939 (*ADAP,* Serie D vii. 204–5); Ciano, *Diario,* i. 147–8.

and would probably do nothing; Russia was no longer an enemy: 'The way is open for the soldier, now that I have made the political preparations.'[1]

A day later, however, Chamberlain warned Hitler that Britain would stand by Poland, whatever the nature of the Russo-German Pact. The Führer replied that Germany, if attacked, would be found prepared. Ciano noted in his diary: 'Another hope is gone.'

On 24 August Ciano called on the King whom he found in a state of open hostility towards the Germans. On 25 August he learnt that in his absence the Duce had swung back to his most belligerent mood: 'I make use of the King's opinions in order to dissuade him, and I succeed in having him approve a communication to Hitler announcing our non-intervention for the time being . . . I was very happy over this result.' But Ciano's happiness did not last long, for within a short time Mussolini had changed his mind again: 'He fears the bitter judgement of the Germans and wants to intervene at once . . . I submit and go back to the Palazzo Chigi where consternation takes the place of the harmony that had reigned before.' In the afternoon there was another change of scene. Mackensen arrived at the Palazzo Venezia with a long and ambiguous message from Hitler. It began with a tardy explanation of the negotiations in Moscow and ended with a hint at the imminence of war and an appeal for Italy's 'understanding', without specifically asking for Italian military assistance: 'I can assure you, Duce, that in a similar situation I would have complete understanding for Italy.'[2]

Once again Mussolini was torn in two directions. First he assured Mackensen that he stood beside Germany 'unconditionally and with all his resources'.[3] Then, after the Ambassador's departure, he was persuaded by Ciano to send his ally a temporizing answer. After expressing his 'complete approval' of the pact with Stalin and assuring Hitler that he 'fully understood' the German attitude towards Poland, he came to the less agreeable part of his communication: 'If Germany attacks Poland and the latter's allies open a counter-attack against

[1] *ADAP*, Serie D vii. 167–72; *DBFP*, 3rd Ser. vii. 258–60; W. Baumgart, 'Zur Ansprache Hitlers vor den Führern der Wehrmacht am 22 August 1939', *VJZG* 16 (Apr. 1968), 120–49.
[2] *ADAP*, Serie D vii. 176–83, 235–6; Ciano, *Diario*, i. 147–9.
[3] Mackensen to Wilhelmstrasse, 25 Aug. 1939 (*ADAP*, Serie D vii. 245).

Germany, I inform you in advance that it will be opportune for me not to take the initiative in military operations in view of the *present* state of Italian war preparations . . . Our intervention can, however, take place at once if Germany delivers to us immediately the military supplies and the raw materials to resist the attack which the French and English would . . . direct against us.'[1]

Mussolini's letter was telephoned to Attolico at about 5 p.m. and delivered to Hitler an hour later. It could not have arrived at a worse moment, for Britain had just concluded a mutual assistance pact with Poland and, according to Paul Schmidt, it struck the Führer like a bombshell. Abruptly dismissing the Duce's Ambassador, he declared: 'The Italians are behaving just as they did in 1914.'[2] He then ordered Keitel to postpone the attack on Poland, after which he dispatched another letter to Mussolini, asking him what arms and raw materials he required and within what time in order to meet the attack which the Western Powers were likely to launch against his country. He concluded by cordially thanking the Duce for the military measures already taken by Italy. There was no recrimination, no note even of irritation or disappointment.[3]

Mussolini's reply was such as to rule out any hope of Italian intervention. After helping to draw up the list of Italy's needs, Ciano wrote: 'It's enough to kill a bull—if a bull could read it.'[4] On 26 August Hitler drafted a third letter to his brother dictator which was telephoned to Rome at about 3 p.m. He informed the Duce that some of the Italian demands could be met, but not before the outbreak of hostilities. Italy's decision, however, could not alter his own: 'As neither France nor Britain can achieve any decisive successes in the West, and as Germany, thanks to the agreement with Russia, will have all her forces free in the East after the defeat of Poland . . . I do not shrink from solving the

---

[1] *Hitler e Mussolini, Lettere e documenti,* Milan–Rome, 1946, pp. 10–11.
[2] Schmidt, *Statist auf diplomatischer Bühne,* pp. 453–4; Schmidt adds that there were 'angry words about Italy—but not about Mussolini'. Hitler put the blame for the Italian 'betrayal' on the King (IFZ/F34/1-2/Erinnerungen General von Vormanns I/00039).
[3] Hitler to Mussolini, 25 Aug. 1939 (*ADAP,* Serie D vii. 242).
[4] Mussolini to Hitler, 26 Aug. 1939 (*Hitler e Mussolini,* pp. 12–14); Ciano, *Diario,* i. 149–150. (IFZ/F34/1-2/Erinnerungen, General von Vormanns I/00032–33).

Eastern question even at the risk of complications in the West.'[1] Again there was no recrimination.

The Duce was almost beside himself at the poor figure he was obliged to cut before his more robust partner. In his reply (which was telephoned to Berlin at 6.42 p.m.) he expressed deep regret at being unable to intervene: 'I leave it to you to imagine my state of mind at being compelled by forces beyond my control not to afford you real solidarity at the moment of action.' Disclaiming any taint of pacifism, he concluded with a despairing appeal for a peaceful settlement: 'I venture to insist anew . . . on the advantage of a political solution which I regard as still possible.'[2]

Hitler had now become resigned to being left in the lurch by his Italian partner. In his answer (which was delivered by Mackensen on 27 August at 9 a.m.) he did not bother to refer to Mussolini's plea for negotiations, reaffirming instead his resolve to go to war, whatever the attitude of Italy or the Western Powers. At the same time he made an effort to spare the Duce's susceptibility: 'I have received your communication on your final attitude. I respect the reasons and motives which led you to take this decision. Indeed in certain circumstances it can neverthless work out well. In my opinion, however, the prerequisite is that, at least until the outbreak of war, the world should have no idea of the attitude Italy intends to adopt. I therefore cordially beg you to support my struggle psychologically with your press or by other means. I would also ask you . . . by demonstrative military measures at least to compel Britain and France to tie down certain of their forces or at all events to leave them in uncertainty.' Hitler concluded by asking for Italian labour and by thanking his ally 'for all the efforts you have made for the common cause'.[3]

Mussolini replied at 4.30 p.m., assuring the Führer that the world would not hear of his decision until after the beginning of hostilities. After a somewhat boastful account of his military measures, he also promised to place his propaganda machine at Germany's disposal and to send as much Italian labour as he could spare. Finally, he expressed his desire to keep in close touch

---

[1] *ADAP*, Serie D viii, 262–3.

[2] *Hitler e Mussolini*, pp. 15–16; Ciano, *Diario*, i. 150.

[3] *ADAP*, Serie D vii. 289–90.

in order to co-ordinate the policy of the two countries, evidently not realizing that nothing was further from Hitler's mind than any close co-operation with Italy.[1]

Ciano was justifiably pleased with his master's decision. 'Italy', he wrote, 'is saved from a great tragedy, that very tragedy which is about to fall on the German people.'[2] Mussolini, on the other hand, was profoundly unhappy. His reason told him that he had done well to disengage his country 'honourably' from the Germans, but he rebelled with every fibre of his being against inaction in the hour of battle. On 28 August Ciano recorded that the Duce was now 'quite calm, as he always is after he has made a decision. He does not want to utter the word "neutrality", but it is this frame of mind that he has definitely reached.' A day later, however, Mussolini was again restless: 'Certain articles in the English press which speak of the need for Italian neutrality have had a bad effect on him. Meanwhile he sets down a series of military and civilian measures which in my opinion need not be taken at this time.' On 30 August Mussolini was convinced that the Germans were about to strike:

> Naturally the idea of a neutrality imposed on us weighs more and more upon him. Not being able to wage war, he makes all the necessary preparations, so that in case of a peaceful solution he may be able to say that he would have waged it. Calls to arms, black-outs, requisitions, closing of cafés and amusement places ... All this carries with it two grave dangers: one, external, since it would cause London and Paris to believe that we are preparing to attack and hence induce them to take the initiative in moving against us; the other, internal, because it will alarm the population which is more and more openly anti-German and opposed to war.[3]

On 31 August two final efforts were made in Rome to stave off the conflagration. At 11 a.m. Ciano informed Halifax that the Duce could intervene with Hitler only if he were in a position to bring a 'fat prize': Danzig. (Less than twenty-four hours before

[1] *Hitler e Mussolini*, pp. 17–18. As a matter of fact, the British had been aware of the profound divergence of views between Rome and Berlin for some time; see Loraine to Halifax, 18 Aug. 1939 (*DBFP*, 3rd Ser. vii. 55–61), Halifax to Chamberlain, 19 Aug. 1939 (PRO/F. O. 800/316 (Halifax Papers)). On 20 August Loraine informed Halifax that Mussolini was unlikely 'to endorse Herr Hitler's policy of attacking and destroying Poland' (*DBFP*, 3rd Ser. vii. 84).

[2] Ciano, *Diario*, i. 150.

[3] Ibid. 152–4.

the outbreak of World War II Mussolini still failed to realize that Hitler's objective was the dismemberment of Poland.) Halifax replied that the proposal was unacceptable. Undeterred by this rebuff, Mussolini revived his suggestion of an international conference for the purpose of reviewing the contentious clauses of the Treaty of Versailles. At 12.30 a.m. Ciano communicated the conference plan to the French and British Ambassadors. Halifax undertook to submit this proposal to Chamberlain, but the day passed without any answer; and at 8.20 p.m. the telephone central office in Rome informed the Palazzo Chigi that London had cut its communications with Italy. Ciano was alarmed: 'Here, then, are the consequences of the measures taken in the last few days, or better, the consequences of too much publicity about the meagre results of the too many measures taken in the last few days.'[1]

The Duce, on being apprised of the British step, likewise took fright. His bellicose gestures had created a situation in which he might be attacked at any moment by the Western Powers. This was a risk he could not face and, despite his categorical undertaking to Hitler, he authorized Ciano to inform the British Ambassador that same evening of his decision to stay out of the conflict.[2]

On 1 September the Germans invaded Poland. Thereupon Mussolini telephoned personally to Attolico, urging him 'to entreat Hitler to send him a telegram releasing him from the obligations of the alliance'. According to Ciano, he did not 'want to pass as a traitor (*fedifrago*) in the eyes of the German people, nor in the eyes of the Italian people who, to tell the truth, do not show too many scruples'.[3]

In the expectation of favours to come, Hitler hastened to comply with his ally's request. At 10 a.m. Mackensen delivered the following reply (which the German press was not allowed to publish): 'I am convinced that I can carry out the task assigned to us with the armed forces of Germany. I therefore believe that in these circumstances I shall not need Italian military aid.'[4]

[1] Ibid. 154–6; cf. Siebert, pp. 325–33.
[2] Ciano, *Diario*, i. 155; Loraine to Halifax, 31 Aug. 1939, 11 p.m. (*DBFP*, 3rd Ser. vii. 459: 'Italy will not fight against either England or France').
[3] Ciano, *Diario*, i. 156.
[4] *ADAP*, Serie D vii. 402. Hitler concluded by thanking Mussolini 'for everything which you will do in future for the common cause of Fascism and National Socialism'.

Mussolini had succeeded in freeing his country from the trap of the Steel Pact with Hitler's approval. At 4.30 p.m. the Fascist Cabinet issued a statement informing the world that Italy would not take the initiative in military operations. But although this statement won him applause both at home and abroad, it brought no peace to the dictator's soul. He was deeply ashamed of his unheroic posture and tortured by the thought that he might be missing a chance of 'doing good business cheaply'. According to Bottai, he was also irritated at the unfeigned enthusiasm with which his Ministers greeted his decision to stay out of the conflict. Worst of all, Italy was now for the first time excluded from the councils of Europe.[1]

On 2 September the Duce made one last effort to escape the ignominy of neutrality, launching a proposal for another Munich. The British, however, dug in their toes, insisting on the withdrawal of Hitler's forces from Poland. At that even Mussolini gave up, and Ciano noted in his diary that the 'last note of hope' had died.[2]

On 3 September Britain and France declared war on Germany. That evening at 8.51 p.m. Hitler dispatched his last message to his brother dictator. After thanking him for his last attempt at mediation and reaffirming his faith in ultimate victory, he went on to remind the Duce of the indissoluble link between the two kindred regimes: 'I also believe that, even if we now march down separate paths, destiny will yet bind us one to the other. If National Socialist Germany were to be destroyed by the Western democracies, Fascist Italy would also face a hard future; I personally was always aware that the futures of our two regimes were bound up and I know that you, Duce, are of exactly the same opinion.'[3]

According to Ciano, Hitler's letter had the effect of lashing his master into renewed bellicosity: 'The Duce expressed full solidarity with Germany, and this is what he really feels . . . The idea of joining the Germans attracts him.'[4] According to Mackensen, Mussolini would not hear of 'separate paths', insisting that 'agreement was complete as to the road and the

---

[1] *O.O.* xxix. 309–11; Bottai, *Vent'anni e un giorno, p. 134; Ciano, Diario,* i. 156–7.

[2] Ciano, *Diario,* i. 156–8; Siebert, pp. 337–42.

[3] *ADAP*, Serie D vii. 448–9.

[4] Ciano, *Diario,* i. 158.

goal'. Although the wretched condition of the Italian armed forces compelled him to stand aside for the moment, the Axis alliance remained the foundation and corner-stone of his foreign policy, and he had done 'everything especially in the military field, that the Führer now wished him to do'.[1]

Two major conclusions emerge from the above analysis. First, Mussolini's switch from unconditional support of Hitler to non-belligerency implied no change of friendships, still less a change of heart. While Ciano wanted to 'ditch' the Germans, the Duce remained firmly resolved to join them at the earliest opportunity. That being so, there could be no reversal of the anti-Jewish policy and no marked alleviation in Jewish conditions, despite the clash of interests between the two Axis Powers.

Second, Hitler was no less anxious than his Italian partner to maintain the façade of 'Axis solidarity'. Though bitter about the 'second Italian betrayal' (for which he blamed not the Duce but the King), he still attached great importance to Italian friendship and remained determined to draw Italy into the war at some later date. Hence the conciliatory tone of his letters to Mussolini throughout the period of tension between Rome and Berlin. Hence also his continued reluctance to meddle in Italian domestic affairs, accurately reflected in his refusal to criticize or pass judgement on the Fascist half-measures against the Jews and in the lack of co-operation between the 'racial experts' of the two countries.

As has been noted, Hitler's representatives in Rome had repeatedly warned Berlin between August and October 1938 that Fascist racial policy was unlikely to achieve its proclaimed goal. The subsequent evolution of the racial question in Italy—the 'exemptions' and 'Aryanizations', coupled with Catholic and popular opposition to the Fascist brand of anti-Semitism—could not but confirm them in their conviction that Mussolini's anti-Jewish laws were little more than a smokescreen, under cover of which the Fascist authorities continued to aid and protect the Jews. Hitler's 'racial experts' were extremely distrustful of the men who were charged with the implementation of Fascist racial legislation, most particularly of the cynical and corrupt Buffarini who, in the words of one German observer, looked 'like a Jewish

---

[1] Mackensen to Wilhelmstrasse, 4 Sept. 1939 (*ADAP*, Serie D xiii. 1–2).

cattle-dealer'.[1] There is, however, no evidence that Hitler himself in any way shared their worries or that he ever read their reports. As late as 25 July 1943—the day of Mussolini's downfall—he was still unaware of Buffarini's existence.[2]

---

[1] Jandl to Bürkner, 22 Jan. 1944 (Deakin, *Brutal Friendship*, pp. 622–3). Buffarini himself ascribed his Semitic appearance to Etruscan origin (Moellhausen, *La carta perdente*, p. 318). On Buffarini's opposition to the anti-Semitic extremism of Preziosi and Farinacci, see *Actes et documents du Saint Siège*, vii, p. 82 (Cardinal Maglione on conversation with Buffarini, 10 Nov. 1942).

[2] On 25 July 1943 the following conversation took place between Walther Hewel, Ribbentrop's liaison officer at the Reich Chancellery, and Hitler: Hewel: 'Among others, Buffarini is said to be with (Mussolini).' Hitler: 'Who's that?' Hewel: 'Buffarini is a Fascist' (*Hitlers Lagebesprechungen. Die Protokollfragmente seiner militärischen Konferenzen 1942–1945*, ed. H. Heiber, Stuttgart, 1962, pp. 305–6).

VIII   From Non-Belligerency to War (1939–1940)

MUSSOLINI'S PROCLAMATION of non-belligerency was greeted with relief by the whole Italian people, including the leading Fascist hierarchs. With the exception of Farinacci, all the Duce's principal lieutenants supported the Foreign Minister's anti-German stand. On 13 September Ciano wrote in his diary: 'Germanophiles can be counted on the fingers of one hand. They are objects of scorn. The *Tevere*, an ultra-German paper, is called in Rome "The Rhinegold".'[1] On 8 October a 'highly placed Italian' made the same point in a confidential talk with Dr. Weizmann in Paris, affirming that there 'was now a strong reaction against Germany in high Fascist circles'.[2]

Mussolini himself, however, continued to be in two minds. On the one hand, he was annoyed with his Axis partner for unleashing a major war before Italy was in a condition to fight.[3] On the other, he was angry with the 'soft-hearted' Italians for applauding his policy of non-intervention. On 23 September his irritation found expression in a violent outburst against Jews, Freemasons, and other enemies of Fascism who were allegedly trying to undermine the morale of the Italian people.[4]

In addition to inveighing against 'subversive' Jewish elements, the Duce ordered the expulsion of foreign Jews from Italy, only

---

[1] Acerbo, *Fra due plotoni di esecuzione*, pp. 422–3; Ciano, *Diario*, i. 156, 160, 164. On the policy of non-belligerency, see E. Serra, 'I rapporti italo-tedeschi durante la non belligeranza dell'Italia', *Rassegna di Politica e di Storia*, I (Jan. 1955), pp. 8–14; G. André, 'La politica estera del governo fascista durante la seconda guerra mondiale', in *L'Italia fra tedeschi e alleati*, Bologna, 1973, pp. 115–22; H. Cliadakis, 'Neutrality and War in Italian Policy 1939–1940', *Journal of Contemporary History*, 9 (July 1974), 171–90; D. Mack Smith, *Mussolini's Roman Empire*, London–New York, 1976, pp. 190–201.

[2] Dr. Weizmann's report on his visits to France and Switzerland, 8 to 17 October 1939, Weizmann to R. A. Butler, 19 Oct. 1939 (PRO/F.O.371/22949/7670/168–69).

[3] Ibid. 168: 'Mussolini was at present in the throes of a crisis. When war became imminent, he had been much annoyed that it was Hitler who had achieved the distinction of becoming "Public Enemy No. 1" of the whole world, whereas he, Mussolini, found himself completely out of the picture.'

[4] Speech to the Fascist hierarchy of Bologna (*O.O.* xxix. 311–13); the Germans were predictably pleased (Teucci to Attolico on conversation with Göring, 14 Oct. 1939, *DDI*. 9a serie i. 475).

to change his mind on receipt of an appeal from the American Ambassador. Phillips's account is worth quoting in detail:

The hostilities inevitably precipitated another crisis with the Jews.[1] Over three thousand Jewish refugees from Poland and Germany had fled to Italy. Under a new decree these people were now obliged to leave the country by the end of the month or be deported to Germany. This meant for them the horrors of the Jewish concentration camps in German-occupied Poland where typhoid had already broken out. Representatives of the Italian Jewish Relief Committee made a strong plea for my help in preventing their deportation, and although they were not American citizens I decided to see what I could do for them at the Foreign Office. I explained to Ciano their desperate situation, pointing out that they were not a charge upon the Italian Government but that ten or fifteen thousand dollars a month for their support came from the United States in addition to funds which were being raised in Italy. Many of them were waiting to go to Palestine and possibly some visas for the United States might be available. I hoped, therefore, that their forced departure for Germany could be delayed. Ciano replied that the problem did not come within his department but that in humanitarian matters we were all concerned. He asked me to send him a memorandum of the subject matter by that evening, and this I did.

The following day I was asked to be at the Foreign Office at twelve o'clock. I found that Ciano was at the Palazzo Venezia, but Anfuso took me into his office where I spoke with Ciano by telephone. He was beside the Duce and gave me the good news that the refugees 'could stay' . . . I came away feeling greatly elated, although notices had already gone out to these poor unfortunates that they must return to Germany, as a result of which two recipients had already committed suicide. But it struck me as extraordinary that Mussolini should apparently change his mind on receipt of a two-page appeal from me. Granted that my plea may conceivably have aroused and fortified a latent humanitarianism in him, and habitually he was totally unmoved by such considerations, none the less his action, welcome though it was, remains a mystery to me.

In reality there was nothing mysterious about the Duce's apparent change of mind. He had, after all, humoured the Americans over the refugee issue in March when he was about to link his fortunes with those of Greater Germany. There was no reason why he should be less accommodating in September when

[1] On 4 September 1939 the Italian authorities began mass arrests of foreign Jews in Northern Italy (*Contemporary Jewish Record*, ii, Nov.–Dec. 1939, 67).

both Rome and Berlin had come to discount the value of the Pact of Steel.

When Phillips conveyed the news to the Jewish Relief Committee, 'they were overcome with gratitude'. But the Palazzo Chigi insisted on no publicity: 'Their stated view was that if it became known throughout Europe that the refugees could remain, Italy would be flooded by hordes of others. To me it seemed more than probable that the government had Germany in mind, for a sympathetic attitude on the part of Mussolini toward Jewish refugees from Germany might well have infuriated Hitler.'[1]

In the ensuing weeks it became increasingly evident that the mounting public indignation against Germany had infected the Duce himself. On 8 October Weizmann was told by his Italian informant that, in the view of high Fascist circles, Italy would remain neutral until the end of the war. Ten days later Phillips reported to Roosevelt that 'a complete change of policy' appeared to have occurred in Italy which day by day was beginning to manifest itself in various ways:

For weeks there has been no mention in the Press of the Rome–Berlin axis or alliance; a recent visit of Himmler to Rome has been carefully kept secret, whereas formerly every appearance of important Germans was widely publicized; the openly expressed dislike of the Berlin–Moscow deal, its dangerous consequences to the Balkans . . . While the government is not ready to declare its neutrality and the officially inspired Press still maintains its pro-German tendencies in order not to incur German hostility, I believe that Italy will avoid at all cost any trouble with the Allies . . . Mussolini is feeling his way inch by inch. He must realize that the popularity of his régime has fallen, that should the Allies succeed in overthrowing Nazism, Fascism is endangered; that should Germany win the war, Italy would become a vassal state; and that should Communism enter the Balkans, there would be difficulty in keeping it out of Italy. He is, in fact, surrounded by dangers and may be assumed to be 'sitting uncomfortable'.[2]

At first the Duce looked for escape from his predicament in an

---

[1] Phillips, *Ventures in Diplomacy*, pp. 134–5.

[2] Ibid., pp. 137–8. On 1 September the press had been ordered to abandon 'the motif of English responsibility, even in the headlines'; on 14 September it was instructed to refrain from commenting on the international situation; on 21 September it was told to express sympathy for Germany, but without engaging in polemics against the Western Powers (*Ordini alla stampa*, ed. C. Matteini, Rome, 1945, pp. 67–70).

early compromise peace. When he realized that the prosecution of the war was inevitable, he allowed himself for a time to be possessed by anti-German sentiment. His irritation was aggravated by renewed friction over the South Tyrol, by the Russo-German partition of Poland, by the charges of treachery levelled at Italy in German political circles, and—last but not least—by Stalin's invasion of Finland which provoked a sharp reaction in the Fascist press, followed by anti-Russian demonstrations throughout Italy.[1]

On 31 October Mussolini dismissed two leading Germanophiles, Alfieri and Starace, a sign that Ciano and his policy of neutrality were now in the ascendant.[2] In November he ordered into operation an earlier plan to seal the frontiers with Germany which involved building what he hoped would be impregnable fortifications along Italy's entire northern border; these defences against a German invasion continued to be built until 1942. On 20 November he tried to create trouble between Berlin and Moscow by advising the Czechs to side with the Communists. On 2 December he told Mackensen that, as far as he was concerned, 'Bolshevism remained enemy number one'. On 7 December he had the Fascist Grand Council ratify his decision to withhold military support from his Axis partner; and on 16 December he had Ciano deliver a speech in the Chamber which was hailed in Italy as the 'funeral of the Axis'. On 26 December, having learnt of Hitler's plans for the invasion of Holland and Belgium, he ordered Ciano to warn the Dutch and Belgian diplomatic representatives, explaining that he now desired a German defeat.[3] Finally, on 3 January 1940 he addressed a letter to his Axis ally which, in the words of his foremost British biographer, 'marked the culmination of the anti-German sentiment which permeated Italy'.[4] After assuming full responsibility for Ciano's anti-German speech and pointing out that the Russo-German Pact had had 'painful repercussions in Spain', he went on to

[1] Siebert, *Italiens Weg*, pp. 357–75; on friction over the South Tyrol, see Ciano, *Diario*, i. 189 (entry for 21 Nov. 1939); on anti-Italian resentment in Germany, cf. also ibid. 231–2 (entry for 4 Mar. 1940), *DDI*. 9a serie iii. 90–6, and Himmler to Bocchini, 28 Sept. 1939 (GFM/100/65439–42, on anti-Italian incidents in Germany).

[2] On 3 November Ciano noted in his diary that the new Ministry was called, *sotto voce*, the 'Ciano Cabinet' (*Diario*, i. 185).

[3] Ibid. 189, 195, 198–9, 201–2; Faldella, *L'Italia e la seconda guerra mondiale*, pp. 136–7; IC/Job 121/033841; *ADAP*. Serie D viii. 374–6.

[4] Kirkpatrick, *Mussolini*, p. 419.

accuse the Führer of betraying his racial principles: 'But I who was born a revolutionary and have not changed my way of thinking tell you that you . . . cannot abandon the anti-Semitic and anti-Bolshevik banner which you have been flying for twenty years and for which so many of your comrades have died; you cannot renounce your gospel in which the German people have blindly believed . . . The solution of your *Lebensraum* problem is in Russia and nowhere else.'

Russia, Mussolini insisted, was 'alien to Europe', the mass of her population being 'Slavonic and Asiatic', and Germany's task was in essence to defend Europe from Asia: 'In olden times the element of cohesion was furnished by the people of the Baltic; today, by the Jews. That explains everything . . . The day when we shall have demolished Bolshevism we shall have kept faith with our two Revolutions.'

Turning to the question of German-occupied Poland, the Duce roundly condemned Hitler's atrocities against the Aryan Poles, adding that a distinction should be made between the Jews and the 'genuinely Polish population': 'A people which has . . . fought courageously, deserves a treatment which does not give occasion for hostile speculations. It is my conviction that the creation of a modest, disarmed Poland which is exclusively Polish, liberated from the Jews—for whom I fully approve your project of gathering them all in a large ghetto in Lublin—can no longer constitute any threat to the Greater German Reich. If this were done, it would . . . deprive the great democracies of any justification for continuing the war.'

As for the war itself, Mussolini feared that Germany, even if aided by Italy, could not bring Britain and France to their knees. Moreover, 'Jew-ridden' America would not permit a total defeat of the democracies. That being so, it was better to seek a compromise than 'to risk all, including the regime' in trying to destroy them.[1]

While the above letter represented the high-water mark of Italy's independence towards Germany, it would be wrong to conclude that Mussolini had been won over to Ciano's anti-German line. Ciano himself admitted as much when he wrote in his diary on 31 December: 'I would be willing to fight against

[1] *ADAP*, Serie D viii. 474–7; *DDI*, 9e serie iii. 19–22; cf. André, op. cit., pp. 118–19.

Germany but not at her side. This is my point of view. Mussolini's point of view is exactly the opposite.'[1]

Hitler, for his part, continued to have complete confidence in his ally.[2] But he resented the Duce's attempt to use 'Jewish Bolshevism' as a stick with which to beat the anti-Semitic Reich and so did his Foreign Minister. On 10 January, in a talk with Attolico, Ribbentrop expressed surprise at the sharp anti-Bolshevik tone of Mussolini's letter: 'Some time ago Mussolini himself had recommended bringing about an easing of German–Russian relations, and that was exactly what Germany had done . . . For my own information, in case the Führer should ask, I would be grateful to (Attolico) for enlightening me on whether the Duce thought it possible that Germany would open her gates wide to Bolshevism and recall the Jewish emigrants. Italian anti-Semitism had, after all, only been a consequence of National Socialist anti-Semitism. Ambassador Attolico explained that of course the Duce assumed no such thing.'[3]

On 8 March Hitler himself, in a lengthy reply to Mussolini's letter, justified his pact with Moscow on the plea that Stalin was a Russian nationalist who had rid the Soviet system of its 'Jewish' and Marxist character.[4] Two days later Ribbentrop made the same point in the course of a conversation with Mussolini at the Palazzo Venezia, assuring his host that Stalin had renounced the Jewish idea of world revolution and that Jewish influence in the Kremlin was a thing of the past: 'With the removal of Litvinov, all the Jews have left the controlling positions.'[5] And on 18 March the Führer, discussing the Soviet–German Pact with the Duce at the Brenner Pass, reaffirmed his conviction that Russia, too, was 'undergoing a far-reaching evolution' and that the path Stalin had taken seemed 'to lead to a sort of Slav-Muscovite

---

[1] Ciano, *Diario*, i. 205.
[2] On 23 November 1939 Hitler assured his generals that the Duce still favoured war at the side of Germany: 'Much depends on Italy, above all on Mussolini, whose death can alter everything . . . As long as the Duce lives, so long can it be calculated that Italy will seize every opportunity to reach her imperialist goals. However, it is too much to ask of Italy that she should join in the battle before Germany has seized the offensive in the West' (*ND*/PS-789).
[3] Memorandum by Ribbentrop, 10 Jan. 1940 (*ADAP*, Serie D viii. 500); Attolico to Ciano, 10 Jan. 1940 (*DDI*, 9a serie iii. 56).
[4] *ADAP*, Serie D viii. 689.
[5] Ibid. 697.

nationalism and to be a move away from Bolshevism of a Jewish-international character'.[1]

As might be expected, the temporary rift between the two Axis partners gave rise to renewed manifestations of Fascist 'benevolence' towards the Jews, despite Mussolini's continuing commitment to the Axis alliance and his continuing resolve to make Italy *judenrein* at some unspecified later date. On 21 September 1939 it was reported that the anti-Jewish measures were being quietly relaxed. (On the very same day, however, Fascist vandals in Trieste patriotically smashed the statue of Italo Svevo, the famous Jewish poet.) On 18 October it was learnt that the Duce had approved plans for the settlement of 15,000 Jews in the Lake Tana region of Ethiopia—a fresh attempt at a 'constructive' contribution to the solution of the refugee problem which, needless to say, produced no practical result. On 20 October it was disclosed that Balbo, in a letter to a Boston friend, had admitted 'widespread opposition' to racialism. On 23 October it was officially announced that 2,801 Jews had been exempted from some of the provisions of the racial laws (8,461 applications were still pending). And on 24 November Lieutenant Bruno Jesi, a Jewish war hero, was presented with a Gold Medal, the highest Italian decoration for valour.[2]

The reconstruction of the Italian Cabinet on 31 October had the effect of accentuating the 'pro-Jewish' trend within the Fascist ruling clan, given Ciano's new-found interest in 'humanitarian matters'. As has been noted, Phillips had been told in early September that Italy did not wish to be 'flooded by hordes of Jewish immigrants'; after the 'changing of the guard', however, the Italian Embassy in Berlin was instructed to show the utmost liberality in the issue of visas to Hitler's Jewish victims, the Fascist racial laws notwithstanding.[3] In some cases Mussolini personally intervened in favour of persecuted foreign Jews. When, shortly after the fall of Poland, the Polish-born wife of an Italian Jew requested his assistance on behalf of her aged

[1] *L'Europa verso la catastrofe*, ii. 190; *ADAP*, Serie D ix. 6.

[2] *Contemporary Jewish Record*, ii. (Nov.–Dec. 1939), 67; ibid. iii (Jan.–Feb. 1940), 63; for Balbo's letter, cf. also *Boston Jewish Advocate*, 20 Oct. 1939. On Balbo's successful intervention on behalf of the Libyan Jews, see De Felice, *Storia degli ebrei italiani*, pp. 368–371.

[3] L. Simoni (pseudonym of Michele Lanza), *Berlino, Ambasciata d'Italia 1939–1943*, Rome, 1946, p. 25.

parents, then trapped in German-occupied Warsaw, the Duce replied through Bocchini that he would order his diplomats to do their best. He was as good as his word.[1]

Mussolini's resentment against his ally also found expression in renewed polemics against the German racial theories. At the end of December, when relations between the two Axis Powers had reached their lowest ebb, he requested Giacomo Acerbo—the leading Fascist opponent of the 'Race Manifesto'—to expound his views on the racial problem in a public lecture. The lecture was duly delivered in Florence on 27 January 1940 and attended by high Fascist dignitaries, including the new Party Secretary and several members of the Italian Cabinet. Subsequently, Acerbo elaborated his arguments against Hitler's Nordic heresy in a book called *The Foundations of Fascist Racial Doctrine* which was published by the Ministry of Popular Culture on Mussolini's orders.[2]

In accordance with his usual tactics, however, the Duce encouraged the Jew-baiters as well as the Jew-lovers, the Germanophiles as well as the Germanophobes. While most Fascist publicists ignored the racial question during this period, the pro-German radicals kept up a continuous barrage against the Jews and their Western backers. On 15 September Emilio Canevari announced in the columns of *La Vita Italiana* that the 'Jewish war' had broken out; in the same issue Preziosi 'exposed' the alleged machinations of the 'Jewish warmongers'. On 7 October Farinacci's paper informed its readers that Britain and France were in the hands of 'Jews warring for domination'; and eleven days later it accused international Jewry of having caused the war. On 22 October *Il Resto del Carlino* reproached Leslie Hore-Belisha, Britain's Jewish Minister of War, with his 'atavistic' Jewish hatred of Germany. On 15 November Preziosi called attention to the 'Jewish Fifth Column' in Trieste; and in the following month he brought out a pamphlet on the alleged war guilt of the Jews. Finally, on 23 January 1940 Farinacci affirmed in a nation-wide radio speech that there was no change

---

[1] Undated testimony of Mrs. Fanny Minerbi (1960); for Italian aid to Polish Jews, see also Luciana Frassati, *Il destino passa per Varsavia*, Bologna 1949, pp. 80–6.

[2] Acerbo, *Fra due plotoni di esecuzione*, pp. 297–8.

in the Fascist attitude to the Jews and no abatement of the anti-Jewish measures.[1]

In addition to lashing out at the Jews in public, the *ras* of Cremona urged his master in private to adopt a more pro-German and anti-Jewish line. On 13 September, in a thirteen-page letter to the Duce, he complained that the word 'Axis' had disappeared from the Fascist vocabulary, that many officials felt authorized to consider the pact with Germany a 'dead issue', that the press had been instructed not to play up the German successes in Poland, and that all the pro-Western 'imbeciles' in Italy wanted to join forces with 'the anti-Fascist exiles and the Jews'. After stating his conviction that Germany's victory would be swift and decisive, he went on to ask Mussolini to allow at least some of the Fascist papers to take a more friendly attitude towards the Reich, to let it be known, at least unofficially, that 'the Italians do not intend to follow the path of treason and violate their commitments' and to 'punish severely those who talk ... against the Axis'.[2] On 7 December, at the above-mentioned meeting of the Fascist Grand Council, Farinacci proposed that Italy enter the war on the side of her Axis partner, adding that failure to do so might induce Hitler to repeat the accusation of 'treason' levelled at Italy by the Austrian Emperor in 1915.[3] And on 5 February 1940 he warned his chief against the 'honorary Jews' within the Fascist ruling clan, hinting at the possibility of a conspiracy between them.[4]

Until the end of 1939 Farinacci's pleas had little effect. But the turn of the tide came in January, not long after the dispatch of Mussolini's unkind letter to Hitler. Two factors contributed to the Duce's change of heart—reports of an impending German offensive in the West (which had the effect of reviving his ardour

[1] E. Canevari, 'La guerra giudaica', *La Vita Italiana*, liv (15 September 1939), 269–74; G. Preziosi, 'La responsabilità delle "guerre ebree"', ibid. 343–4; id., 'Attenzione agli ebrei in casa nostra! (da Trieste)', ibid. (15 Nov. 1939), 590; G. Preziosi, *Come il giudaismo ha preparato la guerra*, 2nd edn., Rome, 1940; 'Italy', *Contemporary Jewish Record*, iii (Mar.–Apr. 1940), 178; cf. also A. Trizzino, 'Il caso Belisha', *La Difesa della Razza* (20 Jan. 1940), 6–10; P. Pellicano, 'Il mistero di Hore Belisha', *La Vita Italiana*, lv (15 Feb. 1940), 128–37. The Jewish leaders repeatedly protested against the press attacks to the Fascist authorities (see, e.g., AUCII/1939/Ministeri/Min.Int./Dir. gen. Demografia e Razza, conversation Ascoli–Le Pera, 16 Sept. 1939).
[2] *IC/Segreteria particolare del Duce/*Job 114/031590–92.
[3] Acerbo, *Fra due plotoni di esecuzione*, pp. 422–3.
[4] *IC/Segreteria particolare del Duce/*Job 53/026408/2. The 'honorary Jews' were Balbo, De Bono, De Vecchi, and Federzoni.

for war) and growing irritation over the British naval blockade (which he viewed as an attempt to strangle Italy economically). On 17 January Ettore Muti, the Party Secretary, attacked the Western Powers in a public speech, stressing Fascism's uncompromising hostility to democracy and the 'bourgeois' outlook.[1] On 18 January Sir Percy Loraine, in a talk with Ciano, expressed his concern at the Duce's attitude; François-Poncet did the same a day later. On 23 January Mussolini told his Ministers that France and Britain 'could no longer win the war', adding that Italy would have to take up arms with her German ally. On 31 January Sir Percy again 'hinted at the apprehension aroused by the personal attitude of the Duce'; and on the following day Mussolini delivered a violently anti-Western speech, ending with the affirmation that the Italians were yearning to fight 'that fight which is bound to come'.[2] On 8 February the Duce had Ciano inform Loraine of his decision to turn down British requests for military supplies; and on the same day he told the Prince of Hesse that he would be pleased to meet Hitler on the Brenner, adding that he meant to take his place at Germany's side as soon as this would be 'a help rather than a hindrance'. On 20 February he reiterated 'his firm hostility to the democracies and his idea of waging a war parallel to that of Germany'. On 26 February he gave an 'icy' reception to Roosevelt's emissary, Sumner Welles. On 1 March the British infuriated him by announcing that as from that day German coal would be seized on the high seas as an article of contraband; and on 2 March he himself dictated the concluding phrase of the Italian note of protest which was 'harsh and threatening'. On 7 March he angrily told Ciano that the British would be 'inexorably beaten'. On 11 March he assured an astonished Ribbentrop that Italy would enter the war at the proper moment and fight on the side of Germany; and on 18 March he informed Hitler that he intended to march alongside the Reich 'because the honour and the interests of Italy demand her intervention in the war'. Finally, on 31 March he outlined his military plans in a memorandum to the King, reaffirming his intention of waging 'a war parallel to that of Germany to achieve our objectives . . . liberty on the seas, a window on the Ocean'.[3]

[1] Muti's speech was actually written by Mussolini himself (see Ciano, *Diario*, i. 215).

[2] Ibid. 215, 219–20. The press was forbidden to publish Mussolini's speech.

[3] Ibid. 221–2, 226–8, 230, 233, 235–6, 239; *ADAP*, Serie D viii. 706–14; ix. 1–12; *O.O.* xxix. 364–7.

Mussolini's switch from neutrality to 'pre-belligerency' was inevitably reflected in renewed manifestations of official hostility to the Jews. On 10 January Virginio Gayda, editor of *Il Giornale d'Italia* and mouthpiece of the Palazzo Chigi, denied that there had been any abatement of the anti-Jewish campaign in Italy;[1] on 15 January Guido Landra requested Gross through a German friend to supply him with 'basic material' on the educational aspects of German racial policy;[2] on 17 January the Party Secretary called for an intensification of Fascist racial principles; and on 4 February Gayda, in an article on the racial question, stressed the complete solidarity between Rome and Berlin, with special reference to the common fight against Jewry.[3] Five days later matters took a sharp turn for the worse when Bocchini sent for Dante Almansi, the newly elected President of the Union of Italian Jewish Communities, and informed him on Mussolini's orders that, for reasons of high policy, the Jews would have to leave Italy. On 16 February Bocchini again sent for Almansi and told him that there was no time to lose—the Jews would have to start leaving at once, at the rate of ten a day.[4] On 29 February Farinacci lectured at the University of Naples on the theme, 'How Israel Prepared the War'; other Fascist journalists followed suit, blaming the Jews for the European conflict in general and the British naval blockade in particular.[5] Finally, on 22 March an official spokesman intimated that it was the Duce's intention to rid Italy of all Jews—including the 'exempted' ones—within eleven years.[6]

While the Fascist press lashed out at the 'Jewish warmongers' abroad, the Fascist authorities stepped up the measures against the Jewish minority at home. On 19 January it was learnt that fifteen Jews had been jailed in Turin for failing to register their enterprises and another two in Florence for being associated with firms having a capital above the 20,000 lire level permitted by law; on 25 January it was reported that the government had

[1] This in reply to an article by Geneviève Tabouis in the Paris daily *L'Œuvre*.
[2] Ehrich (Rome) to Gross, 15 Jan. 1940 (GFM/119/119292).
[3] V. Gayda, 'Razzismo italiano', *Il Giornale d'Italia*, 4 Feb. 1940.
[4] D. Almansi, 'La progettata espulsione', *Israel*, 18 Oct. 1945; see also 'Dante Almansi, President of the Union of Italian Jewish Communities, November 13, 1939 to October 1, 1944. Notes prepared by his son, Renato J. Almansi, M.D.', New York, 1971, pp. 31–4 (unpublished manuscript, kindly furnished to the writer by Dr. Amedeo Tagliacozzo).
[5] See De Felice, *Storia degli ebrei italiani*, p. 374.
[6] 'Italy', *Contemporary Jewish Record*, iii (May–June 1940), 296.

seized five million lire left by the late David Almagià to Jewish charities in Rome; on the following day it was disclosed that the Ministry of the Interior had issued an order barring Jews from renting furnished rooms to Italians; on 13 February it was revealed that a Jewish agricultural school near Pisa had been closed down on orders from above and that forty-four Jews had been stricken from the roll of Italian auditors; on 16 February *Il Popolo d'Italia* published a list of seventy-nine Jewish lawyers who had been banned from practice; on 28 February it was officially announced that further restrictive measures would become effective on 1 March; by 9 March, according to a Czech paper, a hundred and nine Jewish physicians and seventy-five Jewish lawyers had been dropped from the professional register; a day later a Rome dispatch gave the number of physicians dropped at one hundred and thirty-one; and on 1 April it was learnt that twenty Jews had been indicted for the 'crime' of employing Aryan housemaids.[1]

Hitler's invasion of Denmark and Norway—which was featured by the Fascist press with dictated enthusiasm[2]—gave a fresh impetus to the anti-Jewish drive. On 12 April it was learnt that persons of Jewish race were no longer entitled to the government marriage loans extended to needy couples; on 14 April it was disclosed that the Ministry of the Interior was 'aryanizing' the titles of about fifty cultural and charitable foundations which commemorated Jewish munificence; and on 2 May police officials refused renewal of licences to Jewish-owned cafés, bars, and jewellers' shops. With Hitler's invasion of the Low Countries on 10 May, Jewish conditions deteriorated still further. On 19 May Jewish scholars were forbidden to work in libraries and archives; on the same day it was reported that Jewish refugees from Poland, awaiting boats at Trieste, had been threatened with expulsion within thirty days;[3] on 22 May all

---

[1] 'Italy', ibid. (Mar.–Apr. 1940), 178–9; ibid. (May–June 1940), 296–7.

[2] On being informed of Hitler's latest act of aggression, Mussolini declared that he would 'give orders to the press and to the Italian people to applaud this German action without reservation' (Ciano, *Diario*, i. 249, entry for 9 Apr. 1940).

[3] On 30 September 1939 Magistrati had informed the Wilhelmstrasse that Jewish refugees holding immigration certificates would be allowed to embark at Trieste for Palestine, the British having agreed to co-operate (GFM/119/119182). On 10 January 1940 Patrick Scrivener, First Secretary of the British Embassy in Rome, had advised the Palazzo Chigi that the refugees would be permitted to proceed to Palestine, provided they arrived in Italy in time to pass the British control before their ship sailed

foreign Jews, including those on their way to the United States, were barred from entry into the Kingdom (in spite of which Jewish refugees from Germany and German-occupied countries continued to arrive in Italy); on 4 June, with war at the gates, the Ministry of the Interior requested all prefects to keep an eye on 'subversive' Jewish elements and to submit lists of Jewish anti-Fascists; and when some of the prefects replied that there were no 'dangerous' Jews in their provinces, the Ministry ordered them (6 June) to re-examine the matter and to adopt a more vigilant attitude.[1]

The constant press agitation could not fail to be exploited by Fascist gunmen; and at the beginning of May anti-Jewish excesses broke out at Trieste and even in Rome where, however, the police intervened before there were any serious developments.[2]

The Holy See signified its opposition to Fascist policy by denouncing racialism and totalitarianism; by showing practical sympathy to Jewish scholars who had been ousted from Italian universities; by encouraging both the German Resistance and the anti-Axis elements within the Fascist ruling clan; and—last but not least—by conducting a vigorous anti-interventionist campaign in the columns of the *Osservatore Romano.* On 20 October 1939 Pius XII, in his first encyclical to the bishops of the world, condemned the 'Godless State' and deplored 'the forgetfulness of that law of human solidarity and charity which is dictated and imposed by our common origin and by the equality of rational nature in all men, to whatever people they belong';[3] on 21 December he violently attacked Germany in a conversation with King Victor Emmanuel III;[4] and a few days later he conferred on Ciano, the leading Fascist opponent of the

(PRO/F.O.371/25238/737/38/48). On 10 February Rabbi David Prato, in a talk with Scrivener, had requested British assistance on behalf of Jewish refugees from German-occupied Poland but in vain (PRO/F.O.371/25239/2633/38/48). On 20 May the Italian Embassy in Berlin was ordered to stop issuing visas to refugees from Poland (Simoni, op. cit., p. 113).

[1] 'Italy', *Contemporary Jewish Record,* iii (July–Aug. 1940), 419; De Felice, *Storia degli ebrei italiani,* pp. 362–3.

[2] 'Italy', loc. cit. 419.

[3] Quoted in La Piana, 'The Political Heritage of Pius XII', 501.

[4] Ciano, *Diario,* i. 200.

Axis alliance, the Order of the Golden Spur.[1] On 26 January it was learnt that Jewish scholars excluded from Italian universities had been invited to attend a congress held by the Pontifical Academy of Sciences; and on 1 March it was reported that Roberto Almagià (an eminent Jewish geographer who had been expelled from the University of Rome in October 1938) had found employment in the Vatican library.[2] Italy's switch from neutrality to interventionism caused the Holy See to redouble its efforts in favour of peace. On 18 February the Pontiff urged Marshal Enrico Caviglia, victor of the battle of Vittorio Veneto, to warn Mussolini against a military adventure for which his army was unprepared; on 24 April he addressed a solemn peace appeal to the Duce; on 6 May he informed the King of the Belgians that a German attack on the Low Countries was imminent; and when the attack took place four days later, he sent telegrams of sympathy to the heads of the three invaded States.[3] At the same time the Vatican organ stepped up its campaign against intervention, with the result that its circulation rose by leaps and bounds. The Fascist reaction was predictably sharp. On 10 April Alfieri, then Italian Ambassador to the Holy See, warned the Cardinal Secretary of State that his master could not tolerate the 'pacifist' sermons which were being preached by Catholic priests 'in too many parts of Italy'; on 30 April Farinacci's paper branded the *Osservatore Romano* as a 'slave of Italy's enemies and manifestly a mouthpiece of the Jews'; and on 12 May Mussolini himself denounced the papacy as a 'cancer which gnaws at our national life', adding that he was ready to 'knock out' the Pope. On the same day a protest against Vatican policy was lodged through the ordinary diplomatic channels; and the Fascist Party was mobilized to beat up those who sold or bought the Vatican paper. On 16 May Ciano noted an increasing uneasiness in the Vatican 'on account of the daily incidents

[1] Ibid. 202. Cardinal Maglione sent a telegram praising Ciano's work in favour of the 'most noble cause of peace'. On Vatican involvement in the contacts between the German Resistance and the British government, see P. Ludlow, 'Dokumentation. Papst Pius XII, die britische Regierung und die deutsche Opposition im Winter 1939/1940', *VJZG* 22 (July 1974), 299–341; J. Müller, *Bis zur letzten Konsequenz. Ein Leben für Frieden und Freiheit*, Munich, 1975, p. 140.

[2] 'Italy', *Contemporary Jewish Record,* iii (May–June 1940), 297.

[3] E. Caviglia, *Diario (1925–1945)*, Rome, 1952, p. 232; *O.O.*xxix. 438–9; G. Bianchi, *25 luglio. Crollo di un regime*, Milan, 1963, p. 155; Lewy, *The Catholic Church and Nazi Germany*, p. 246.

caused . . . by interference with the sale of the *Osservatore Romano*';
and on 19 May Alfieri (who had meanwhile been transferred to
Berlin) told an official of the Wilhelmstrasse that Mussolini was
angry with the Holy See, 'not only because of its attitude towards
Italy but also, and most particularly, about that towards
Germany'. Finally, on Italy's entry into the war (10 June) the
Duce threatened to forbid the sale of the *Osservatore Romano* unless
its editor agreed to publish the military communiqués of the Axis
Powers only—whereupon the paper resolved to publish no
military reports at all.[1]

On 3 December 1939 Mussolini had told Ciano that he would
go to war in 1942, 'as our obligations demand'. Hitler's military
successes in the spring and summer of 1940, however, compelled
him to revise his timetable. After the German invasion of
Denmark and Norway he brought the date forward to the spring
of 1941; and after the invasion of the Low Countries he
proclaimed his intention of declaring war 'within a month'.
Finally, on 29 May (Holland and Belgium meanwhile having
capitulated) he told his military advisers that after 5 June any
day might be good.[2]

On 10 June the Duce announced from the balcony of the
Palazzo Venezia that Italy was entering the lists against the
'plutocratic and reactionary democracies of the West', in
accordance with her obligation under the Pact of Steel: 'At a
memorable meeting in Berlin I said that, according to the laws
of Fascist morality, when one has a friend, one marches with him
to the very end. We have done this and will do this with
Germany, with her people, with her splendid armed forces.'[3]

---

[1] Bianchi, op. cit., p. 146; Ciano, op. cit., pp. 263, 266; Alfieri, *Due dittatori di fronte*, p. 22;
C. M. Cianfarra, *The Vatican and the War*, New York, 1945, pp. 226–8; *ADAP*, Serie D lx.
309; Lewy, op. cit., p. 248.
[2] Ciano, op. cit., pp. 193, 252, 264; *Hitler e Mussolini*, pp. 43–7.
[3] *O.O.* xxix. 403–4.

ITALY'S ENTRY into the war filled the cup of bitterness for her
Jews to overflowing. It was obvious that their interests, their
hopes, and their future were bound up with the defeat of the
Reich. Hence, for the first time in their long history, they found
themselves, in a moment of patriotic excitement, in opposition to
the declared interests of the people at large; though they were,
indeed, amply justified by events, and millions of Italian Gentiles,
including highly placed Fascists, shared their aversion to the
Axis alliance. For all his boasting, the Duce now became little
more than a reluctant vassal of the Austrian whom he had once
regarded as his protégé.

As one of the first apparent results, the Fascist extremists now
began to clamour for the immediate liquidation of the Italian
Jewish population. Farinacci's paper wrote on 25 June: 'It is
time to make an end of the Jews! They who will never again
have the honour to bear arms are today only preoccupied with
making money by the shovelful at the expense of the fighters and
of embattled Italy. Can we go on like this? These are the traitors
to the Motherland, the eternal agitators, those who have caused
the war knowing they would not have to fight.'[1] Why the 'alien'
Jews should be regarded as traitors to a country not theirs, the
paper failed to explain.

While the Fascist press grew increasingly shrill and menacing,
the Fascist authorities took a series of measures against both
native and foreign Jews. On 14 June all Jewish bank accounts
were blocked, and stocks owned by non-Aryans were ordered to
be registered. On the same day the police began to arrest and
intern Jews of foreign origin (including those who had lost their
Italian citizenship through the introduction of the race laws) as
well as Italian Jews considered 'politically dangerous' (including
Socialists, Freemasons, Zionists, and 'defeatists'). On 16 June all
alien organizations (except those of a philanthropic character)
were compelled to close down. Jews were expelled from the
islands of Sicily and Sardinia, on the grounds that these were
important military bases; later on they were also excluded from

[1] 'Occhio agli ebrei', *Il Regime Fascista*, 25 June 1940.

mountain and seaside areas in the fortified zones. Given their notorious hostility to the Axis, it was considered wise to prevent them from hearing or spreading news from abroad, and in consequence all the radio sets in their possession were confiscated. By September 1940 fifteen internment camps had been set up, the largest being that of Ferramonti Tarsia near Cosenza in Southern Italy; and on the fourth of the same month it was decided to intern all 'enemy aliens', with the result that hundreds of detention camps and internment centres had to be established all over the Italian Peninsula. On 5 September it was learnt that 1,650 out of the 3,000 Jewish refugees in Italy had been taken into custody.[1]

While Jews of foreign birth were being interned, fresh curbs were imposed on the native ones. In August the licences of the Jewish pedlars (who constituted the basis of Roman Jewry) were withdrawn, only to be renewed in the following January. In October the Jewish antique-dealers, too, were deprived of their licences. Other new restrictions excluded persons of Jewish race from the publicity services of hotels, from all commercial agencies, from selling textbooks, from acting as brokers, from any activity which might bring them into contact with the customs officers, and from participating in the scrap-iron business; by the end of the year it was estimated that no less than half of Italy's Jews had lost their means of earning a livelihood.[2]

With the Italian military débâcle in Libya (December 1940) relations between the Duce and his Jewish subjects took yet another turn for the worse. The Mussolinian press promptly put the blame for the Italian set-back on the Jews; and when, on 17 December, anti-British demonstrations broke out in Trieste, Milan, and Genoa, they soon took on an anti-Jewish colouring, since Jews were available for attack and Britons were not. At Trieste the offices of the community were raided and a number of prominent Jews arrested on a charge of spreading anti-Fascist propaganda. Libyan Jewry likewise came under fire, some of the native Jews having made common cause with Italophobe Arab

[1] 'Italy', *Contemporary Jewish Record*, iii, p. 419; ibid. (Nov.–Dec. 1940), 637; De Felice, *Storia degli ebrei italiani*, pp. 363–4.

[2] 'Italy', loc. cit. (Nov.–Dec. 1940), 637; see also Roth, *The History of the Jews of Italy*, pp. 537–8. At the request of the Jewish leaders the licences of the Jewish pedlars were temporarily renewed in order to enable Aryan manufacturers to get rid of merchandise on hand (De Felice, *Storia degli ebrei italiani*, p. 415 n.1).

elements during the Italian retreat from Cyrenaica. When the Axis forces temporarily reoccupied the lost territories, harsh measures were taken against real or alleged Jewish 'Fifth Columnists' on Mussolini's orders. Some were executed, others jailed, and well over 3,000 interned for 'security reasons'; finally, on 9 October 1942 the racial laws of November 1938 were extended to Jews of Libyan citizenship. Fortunately, the British victories of 1942–3 were so sweeping and so swift that deliverance came before irreparable harm was done.[1]

On 6 May 1942, five days after the meeting between Hitler and Mussolini at Klessheim Castle, the Ministry of the Interior ordered the mobilization of all Jews between the ages of eighteen and fifty-five (including the 'exempted' ones) for forced labour. The order was, however, carried out in a rather casual fashion. A more drastic step was taken seven months later when Jews residing in Turin, Milan, and Genoa were shipped to the South Tyrol and their possessions confiscated, allegedly for distribution among bombed-out Aryans.[2]

In addition to legal measures, there were illegal acts of violence. In Rome, Ancona, and Leghorn a number of Jews were beaten up or forced to drink castor oil. At Trieste (a notorious hotbed of extremism) the local followers of Farinacci and Preziosi instigated a rash of anti-Jewish incidents in 1941 and 1942, culminating in an attack on the synagogue and the offices of the Jewish Relief Committee. In Florence young fanatics distributed leaflets branding the Jews as spies and traitors and calling for their physical liquidation; the same happened in Ferrara (where the Scuola Tedesca was destroyed on 21 September 1941) and in Turin (where Fascist hoodlums tried to set fire to the synagogue on 14 October of the same year). It remains to add that neither the government nor the Party chiefs were in any way involved in these acts of vandalism.[3]

Disciplinary measures were taken against Party members who

[1] 'Italy', loc. cit. iv (Feb. 1941), 65; G. Gorla, *L'Italia nella seconda guerra mondiale*, Milan, 1959, p. 286; URO, *Judenverfolgung in Italien*, pp. 106–10; De Felice, *Storia degli ebrei italiani*, pp. 370–1.

[2] 'Italy', loc. cit. vi (Feb. 1943), 73; De Felice, *Storia degli ebrei italiani*, pp. 364–7.

[3] De Felice, *Storia degli ebrei italiani*, pp. 388–92; Silva Gherardi Bon, *La persecuzione antiebraica a Trieste (1938–1945)*, Udine, 1972, pp. 131–58; cf. also R. B(onfiglioli), 'Gli ebrei a Ferrara dal fascismo alla liberazione', *Competizione democratica* (25 Apr. 1955), 16–17.

maintained personal ties with Jews or gave vent to unseemly manifestations of *pietismo* (compassion for the oppressed); between November 1938 and July 1943 well over a thousand *pietisti* were expelled from the Fascist Party and deprived of their jobs, while others were publicly reprimanded. On 30 March 1942 it was revealed that a number of senior civil servants had been dismissed for expressing sympathy with the Jews; on 4 January 1943 it was learnt that the mayors of Florence and Padua had been deposed, and several officials in Turin cashiered, for their lack of alacrity in carrying out the racial measures; and on 28 May it was announced that the Party *tessera* of another prominent *pietista*, Senator Luigi Messedaglia, had been withdrawn by order of the Party Secretary.[1] In addition to meting out punishment to 'Jew-lovers', the Party heads called for a spiritual mobilization against the Jewish peril; as late as 15 June 1943, six weeks before the fall of Fascism, the *federali* were ordered to step up the propaganda war against Jewry (the Jewish problem being 'more than ever on the agenda'), to give maximum publicity to Preziosi's *Vita Italiana*, and to submit reports on their anti-Jewish activities.[2]

Behind the façade of racialist intransigence, however, the Duce and his henchmen continued to play their usual double game. As the war progressed, it became increasingly evident that the two Axis partners were pursuing diametrically opposed policies towards the Jews, the alleged common struggle against the Jewish peril notwithstanding. Italy's entry into the war, far from leading to closer co-operation between Rome and Berlin, merely served to aggravate the profound conflict of interest between them and to accentuate the previous contradictions in Fascist racial policy.

Mussolini's intervention against the Western Powers in June 1940, like his war of nerves against France in November 1938 and his invasion of Albania in April 1939, was in part an anti-German move, his aim being to secure sufficient gains for Italy to counterbalance total German supremacy in Europe.[3] A token campaign on the Western Alpine border (he thought) would

[1] *Contemporary Jewish Record*, v (June 1942), 312; ibid. vi (Apr. 1943), 180; ibid. (Aug. 1943), 406; De Felice, *Storia degli ebrei italiani*, p. 378.
[2] Circular from Alfredo Cucco, Vice-Secretary of the Fascist Party, to all federal secretaries (facsimile in Bianchi, *25 luglio*, between pp. 294–5).
[3] Alfieri, *Due dittatori di fronte*, pp. 36–51; Deakin, *Brutal Friendship*, pp. 11–16.

bring him to the conference table with the French and enable him to settle, at least in part, the Italian claims to French territory; a token operation against Egypt would entitle him to take his seat at the armistice with the British which, it was assumed, would rapidly follow the fall of France. As late as August Marshal Badoglio, the Duce's principal military adviser, was still hoping for a quick end to the war through a direct assault on the British Isles.[1]

In May 1939 Mussolini had deluded himself that the Pact of Steel was an alliance between equals. By June 1940 he had come to realize that he was Hitler's junior partner (if the term 'partner' can be at all applied to the role he was to play). But he sought to blur this sad fact, and to claim an illusory parity with the Führer, by concocting the theory of the 'parallel' war, meaning a war which would be waged separately by the two allies, each in his own sphere of influence. The German army chiefs (who attached little, if any, importance to Italy and were reluctant to impart their military secrets to the Italian High Command) saw no reason to object to this arrangement. As a result, there was little genuine consultation, less joint planning, and no common policy; each ally did his best to keep the other in ignorance of his own plans and intentions. The first misunderstanding occurred immediately after Italy's entry into the war when the German dictator was surprised and disillusioned at Mussolini's failure to make any move on the French Alpine front.[2]

The Italian token attack on the Alpine border did not begin until 20 June—three days after the French had asked for an armistice. Thus it was that on 18 June an embarrassed and humiliated Mussolini travelled empty-handed to Munich in order to discuss with Hitler the terms to be imposed upon France. The Führer gave him a very warm welcome but rejected his claims to French territory, explaining that he could not agree to demands which might drive the French Government into the arms of the British. There was a fundamental conflict of interest between the two partners—while Mussolini was eager to become the heir of the French Empire and to secure the mastery of the

---

[1] Mussolini himself told Ciano as late as 18 August 'that we shall have victory and peace by the end of next month' (*Diario*, i. 301).

[2] Von Rintelen, *Mussolini als Bundesgenosse*, p. 89; id., 'Mussolinis Parallelkrieg im Jahre 1940', *Wehrwissenschaftliche Rundschau*, 12 (Jan. 1962), 16–38.

Mediterranean, Hitler was anxious to reach some agreement on his own terms with the democracies so as to free his hands in the West before turning against Russia.[1]

In early July the Duce offered to Hitler an Italian expeditionary force against Britain; it was politely declined. In August he began talking of surprise attacks on Yugoslavia and Greece; but Berlin would not have it. On 17 August Ribbentrop summoned Alfieri and told him sternly that any plan to invade Yugoslavia must be abandoned and that any action against Greece would be unwelcome in Germany. As Ciano put it, it was 'a complete order to halt all along the line'.[2]

On 4 October there was a meeting between the Axis leaders at the Brenner Pass. On this occasion the Duce demonstrated his independence by proudly rejecting his ally's offer of German armoured units for the Libyan front. According to Ciano, Hitler 'put at least some of his cards on the table and talked to us about his plans for the future'; but he did not so much as hint at the arrangements he had already made for German troops to enter Romania a few days later. The news of this *coup* enraged Mussolini, the more so because Berlin had just 'ordered' him to make no move in the Balkans. 'Hitler', he said to Ciano, 'always faces me with a *fait accompli.* This time I am going to pay him back in his own coin: he will find out from the papers that I have occupied Greece. In this way equilibrium will be re-established.'[3]

The attack on Greece was launched on 28 October; by 5 November it had collapsed and the initiative had passed to the Greeks. Hitler, having himself established the practice of acting without notice, could hardly make an outright complaint. But he gave vent to his concern in a letter to the Duce on 20 November, pointing out that the Italian fiasco would entail grave psychological and military consequences. On 11 November the tale of disaster restarted when the British launched a devastating blow against the Italian fleet in Taranto Harbour. On 4 December the

[1] Ciano, *Diario*, i. 279–81; *L'Europa verso la catastrofe*, ii. 204–7.

[2] *ADAP*, Serie D x. 23, 123–9, 408–10; cf. Simoni, *Berlino. Ambasciata d'Italia*, pp. 161–3 and Ciano, *Diario*, i. 300.

[3] *DDI*, 9a serie v. 655–8; *ADAP*, Serie D xi. 245–59; Ciano, *Diario*, i. 312, 314 (entries for 4 and 12 Oct. 1940). Hitler's adjutant, Major Gerhard Engel, records in his diary that the Italian attack on Greece infuriated the Führer (A. Hillgruber, *Hitlers Strategie*, Frankfurt/Main, 1965, p. 286). M. van Creveld's attempt to explain away Engel's testimony (*Hitler's Strategy 1940–1941. The Balkan Clue*, Cambridge, 1973, pp. 48–9) is unconvincing.

Greeks broke through the Italian lines; Mussolini was shaken and thought of asking for a truce through Berlin. On 6 December a letter from Hitler brought comfort and reassurance: the Germans regarded the Greek affair as no more than an episode 'in the great picture in which the prospects are good'. Three days later, however, the Duce suffered a further grievous blow when the British launched a surprise attack in Egypt which led to the headlong retreat of the Italian forces back across Libya.[1]

Faced with disaster on all fronts, Mussolini had no choice but to turn to his Axis partner for help. In December he addressed to Hitler two urgent appeals for military and material aid which marked the end of the 'parallel' war and paved the way for the German occupation of his country. From now on hordes of German experts (and secret agents posing as such) swarmed into Italy and began to interfere in every aspect of Italian affairs. On 30 December an Italian diplomat in Berlin gloomily noted in his diary that the Greek campaign had cost Italy her independence.[2]

In June Mussolini had joined Hitler on the assumption that the war was all but over. Since then, however, everything had gone wrong. Britain had not been brought to her knees; Spain and Vichy France had refused to join the Axis; Russia was adopting an increasingly hostile attitude, while America was giving Britain increasingly effective support. Italy, after a series of humiliating military reverses, was faced with the total loss of her African Empire; worse still, she had lost all liberty of action and was now, if she wished to survive as a Fascist regime, at Germany's mercy.

Hitler's run of victory in 1941, far from reinforcing Axis solidarity, merely served to exacerbate the tension between the two allies and to throw the conflict of interest between them into sharper relief. German intervention in the Balkans and North Africa saved the Italians from defeat; but it brought the Germans into areas which had hitherto been recognized as Italy's sphere of influence. Hitler's invasion of Russia precluded any major German military effort in the Mediterranean theatre, with the result that the Italian possessions in Africa fell piecemeal into British hands.

---

[1] *ADAP*, Serie D xi. 535–9, 666–7; Faldella, *L'Italia e la seconda guerra mondiale*, pp. 292–314; G. Gigli, *La seconda guerra mondiale*, 2nd edn., Bari, 1964, pp. 159–207.
[2] *ADAP*, Serie D xi. 682–7, 760–2; Simoni, op. cit., pp. 186–8, 190–4.

The conflict of ambitions between the two Axis Powers was particularly evident in a region which is of special interest in our context—the Near East. While Berlin was anxious to win over the Arabs and ready to back their claim to independence and unity, Rome objected to a public promise on the ground that the Arab struggle for liberation, once unleashed, was bound to take on an anti-Italian character. And since Hitler had recognized the Arab area as an Italian preserve, Ribbentrop and his advisers were unable to impose their views on the subject until it was too late.[1] On 23 October 1940 the Italians broadcast a vague and non-committal declaration of sympathy with the Arab cause which contained no reference to the Jews; and on 27 October 1941 Mussolini expressed his willingness to issue a public statement on Arab independence at some unspecified later date. It was not until 28 April 1942, when Italy had been reduced to near-vassalage, that the Fascist Government agreed to the setting-up of a pan-Arab Empire and the abolition of the Jewish National Home in Palestine—and then only in a strictly private letter from Ciano to the self-styled 'Grand Mufti' of Jerusalem.[2] The Arabs, for their part, made no secret of their distrust and dislike of the Italians and their opposition to the Fascist brand of imperialism.[3]

In 1942 the Axis forces once more passed to the attack; and a last gleam came to Mussolini in June of that year when Rommel was expected to reach the Nile Delta. On 29 June the Duce went to Africa for the occasion but returned rebuffed by Rommel and

[1] *ADAP*, Serie D x. 425–6; 65–6, 689–92; xii. 193–200, 284. Hitler had recognized the Mediterranean as an Italian preserve in a conversation with Ciano on 7 July 1940 (*L'Europa verso la catastrofe*, ii. 211); subsequently, however, Ribbentrop told a member of his entourage that the Italians would have to be ousted from the Arabic-speaking world sooner or later (F. Grobba, *Männer und Mächte im Orient; 25 Jahre diplomatische Tätigkeit im Orient*, Göttingen, 1967, p. 214).

[2] E. Rossi, *Documenti sulle origini e gli sviluppi della questione araba 1875–1944*, Rome, 1944, p. 225; M. Khadduri, *Independent Iraq 1932–1958*, 2nd edn., London–New York–Karachi, 1960, pp. 186–7, 239–41; *ADAP*, Serie D xiii. 576. As late as 7 January 1943 an official of the Wilhelmstrasse complained that Italian opposition made it impossible to give the Mufti adequate support (GFM/132/123787).

[3] On 5 July 1940 Naji Shawkat, Iraqi Minister of Justice, told the German Ambassador in Ankara that 'just as the Arab national movement had fought Anglo-French imperialism, so it would have to oppose Italian imperialism' (Papen to Wilhelmstrasse, 6 July 1940, *ADAP*, Serie D x. 117–19); on Arab hostility to Italy, see also note by Grobba, 30 Sept. 1940 (YVS/481604/1269 B4), note by von Hentig, 21 Feb. 1941 (YVS/482052–26/1269 B4), and report by German Embassy (Rome), 6 Aug. 1942 (YVS/261123/GM2258/4).

fate. Hitler's Marshal did not pay him a visit during the three weeks and more he spent there and failed to advance. Early in November followed the collapse of the Libyan front and the Allied landings in Morocco and Algeria. Mussolini's doom was approaching.[1]

The lengthening of the war and the increasingly serious military reverses inevitably revealed the artificiality of an alliance based, not on common interests, but on ideological affinity. In Italian eyes there could be no justification of the Steel Pact other than the quick achievement of historic Italian aims in the Adriatic, the Mediterranean, and Africa, as the appendix of a German victory over the Western democracies. Hence, when the tide of war turned against the Axis Powers in the autumn of 1942, public opposition to the German alliance came into the open, and cracks began to appear inside the Fascist ruling class. The general dislike and distrust of the Germans were accentuated by continued friction between the Italian civilian population and the ever-increasing number of German troops who were apt to behave as conquering invaders.[2]

Mussolini, for his part, was by now enveloped in a blanket of fatalism and resigned to following in Hitler's wake, whatever the consequences for his country and his regime. But as Italian fortunes declined and Italian dependence on Germany grew, he gave vent to a series of increasingly violent outbursts of anti-German sentiment. As early as 30 May 1941 he blamed the Germans for his reverses in Africa ('They should . . . remember that through them we have lost an Empire'). On 31 May he told Ciano that he was 'sick and tired of being rung for' by Hitler. On 10 June—the first anniversary of Italy's entry into the war—he lashed out at German meddling in Croatia ('It is of no importance that the Germans recognize our rights in Croatia on paper when in practice they take everything and leave us only a little heap of bones'). On 30 June he claimed that the Germans were 'getting ready to annex the South Tyrol', adding that 'he would resist this with armed force'. Six days later, on being informed of 'the resumption of German irredentist activities in the South Tyrol', he predicted 'an unavoidable conflict arising between Italy and Germany' and wondered whether an English victory would not

[1] Faldella, op. cit., pp. 451–500.
[2] For a detailed analysis, see Deakin, op. cit., pp. 29–123.

be preferable to a German one. On 13 July, having received another report on 'Germany's real decision to annex the South Tyrol no later than after the war', he decided to warn Hitler that an event of this kind would constitute 'the collapse of the (Fascist) regime'. On 20 July he again predicted 'an unavoidable crisis' between the two Axis countries ('We must place thousands of guns along the rivers of the Venetian region because it is from there that the Germans will launch their invasion of Italy'). On 25 September he was shocked at a report on the maltreatment of Italian labourers in Germany who were not only being beaten but set upon by trained watchdogs; and on the following day he said angrily that such things were bound to produce a lasting hatred in his heart ('I will not permit the sons of a race which has given to humanity Caesar, Dante and Michelangelo to be devoured by the bloodhounds of the Huns'). On 13 October he received news that a German had called him 'our Gauleiter for Italy'. On the same occasion he admitted to Ciano that Italy had by now been reduced to near-vassalage: 'The conquered States will be colonies. The associated States will be confederated provinces. Among these the most important is Italy. We have to accept these conditions because any attempt to rebel would result in our being reduced from the position of a confederated province to the worse one of a colony. Even if they should ask for Trieste tomorrow as part of the German *Lebensraum*, we would have to bow our heads.'

On 15 October Mussolini denounced German plans for reducing the rest of Europe to servitude ('The German people are dangerous because they dream collectively. But history teaches that all attempts to unify Europe under a single rule have failed'). On 12 January 1942 he protested to Rintelen against the conduct of Hitler's soldiers in Italy, 'especially the N.C.O.s who are presumptuous, quarrelsome, and drunken'; and on the following day he criticized Hitler for his mishandling of the Russian campaign, calling him a 'jackass' (*bestione*) and accusing him of falsifying his communiqués. On 25 January he again gave vent to his indignation at the conduct of the Germans in Italy, having learnt that a German officer, speaking with Berlin, had called the Italians 'macaroni' and expressed the hope that Italy, too, would become an occupied country. On 20 February he complained of Germany's failure to carry out her economic commitments to Italy ('Among the cemeteries I shall some day build the most important of all, one in which to bury German promises'). On 22 February he was shocked at a report from Prague to the effect that Heydrich, the deputy Reich Protector, was treating Italians, if not worse than the Czechs, certainly not much better. On 24 July he told Ciano that the Italian people were now 'wondering which of the two masters is to be preferred, the English or the Germans'. On 8 October he deplored the excesses of Hitler's underlings in the occupied territories ('if we lose this war, it will be because of the political stupidity of the Germans'). On 6 November he asked Ciano if he was keeping his diary up to date; and when the latter answered in the affirmative, he said that it would 'serve to prove how the Germans, in both military and political fields, have always acted without his knowledge'. Finally, on 8 February 1943, when Ciano told him that he could 'document all the treacheries perpetrated against us by the Germans, one after another', the dictator 'listened in silence and almost agreed with me'.[1]

Mussolini was particularly incensed at the increasingly open racial discrimination against Italian nationals in Germany. On 5 September 1941 Mackensen informed the Wilhelmstrasse that the Duce had been 'most painfully affected' by a confidential report to the effect that the Kreisleiter of Recklinghausen, Goldbeck, had signed the following circular on the problem of interbreeding between members of various nations: 'A mixture is undesirable in any case, but the mixture of the blood of a German girl with a foreigner of kindred blood, such as workers from occupied territories (Norwegians, Danes, etc.) and even enemy nationals (Englishmen) is preferable to mixture with foreigners of alien blood (the Italians are to be included in this category).'[2]

On 13 September Alfieri protested to Ribbentrop, insisting that the disparagement of the Italian race implied in German opposition to intermarriage was incompatible with 'the comradeship-in-arms between the two Axis Powers'. On 27 September he submitted a formal statement of complaint to Weizsäcker; and on 12 November Cosmelli, Counsellor of the Italian Embassy

[1] Ciano, *Diario*, ii. 33, 43, 50, 56, 59, 61–2, 64–5, 72–3, 113, 118, 129, 185, 202–3, 214, 240–51; cf. also Alfieri, op. cit. pp. 162–73, 227–9.
[2] *ADAP*, Serie D xiii. 370–1.

in Berlin, handed a similar statement to Weizsäcker's deputy, Woermann. The Nazis, however, were adamant. Dr. Gross of the Rassenpolitisches Amt bluntly told Alfieri that mixed marriages were undesirable and should be discouraged as far as possible'; and on 18 November Ribbentrop informed Woermann that he was of the same opinion.[1] It was a bitter pill for the Fascist dictator; but, having put himself and his country in thrall to Hitler, he could not refuse to swallow it.

Unable to vent his spleen on his German master, the Duce directed his ill humour at his generals (on whom he pinned responsibility for defeat), at the monarchy (which he accused of acting as a brake on his regime), at the Church (which he denounced as a 'disintegrating' force), and—last but not least—at the Italian middle classes which he considered to be 'cowardly and despicable'.[2] Unlike his propagandists, however, he never put the blame for his plight on the Jews. True, his tirades against Christianity sometimes took on an anti-Jewish colouring; in December 1941, for instance, he said to Ciano that Christmas reminded him 'only of the birth of a Jew who gave to the world debilitating and devitalizing theories'.[3] But as relations with Berlin continued to deteriorate, his references to his Jewish subjects became increasingly philo-Semitic. In September 1940 he told his biographer that his attitude to the racial question was one of 'extreme moderation'; that racial fanaticism was 'repugnant' to him; that there were no 'superior' or 'inferior' races; and that an admixture of Jewish blood could do no harm to anyone.[4] In October 1941 he went further, praising Balbo for his courageous stand in favour of the Jews, deploring the anti-Semitic excesses of his journalists (for which he alone was responsible), paying tribute to the loyalty of the 'Jewish Italians' (whose attachment to Italy had not been shaken by persecution), and predicting that the Jewish problem would be solved by intermarriage in the not too distant future. On the same occasion he claimed that he was 'doing his best' to aid Jewish emigrants and that he would 'aryanize' Dante Almansi, the President of the

---

[1] Ibid. 395–9; GFM/1517/372726–27; 1517/372953–55; 1517/372970; cf. also memorandum by Weber, 17 Jan. 1942 (*ADAP*, Serie E i. 256).
[2] Ciano, *Diario*, i. 265, 279, 300; ii. 102–3, 185, 212–13.
[3] Ibid. ii. 102 (entry for 22 Dec. 1941).
[4] De Begnac, *Palazzo Venezia*, p. 642.

Union of Jewish Communities, with whom he was 'in continuous touch'.[1]

Given his fear of Hitler and his ever-increasing dependence on him, Mussolini could not permit any mitigation of the anti-Jewish campaign. But he could, and did, refuse to imitate the barbarities to which the Jews were being submitted in Germany and German-occupied territory. The ancient Ghettos were still recognizable in many places in Italy, but the Jews were not confined to them. The memory of the Jewish badge was not quite dead among the descendants of those who had worn it, but this was almost the only part of Europe under Axis control where the yellow patch was not made obligatory. The Fascist press applauded Hitler's anti-Jewish crusade, but Italian Jews resident in Germany or German-occupied areas continued to enjoy the protection of Mussolini's diplomatic and consular representatives. When Jews were sent off to forced labour, there were sometimes demonstrations of sympathy at the railway stations; and although well over 15,000 persons of Jewish birth were liable for labour service, only about 2,000 were ever called up. Conditions in the internment camps were far from ideal, but the internees were not maltreated, nor were there periodical jail-clearances to swell the columns on their way to the gas chambers in Poland. And while the racial laws were carried out in an increasingly rigorous spirit (of 8,171 requests for 'exemption' no less than 5,685 were rejected or ignored), a great many loop-holes were found to enable Jews to evade their application. It remains to add that Jewish refugees continued to enter Italy throughout the period under review, with the connivance of the Fascist authorities.[2]

The contrast between the German and Italian approaches to the racial question was particularly striking in the conquered

---

[1] Ibid., p. 643; Renato J. Almansi, in his above-quoted notes on his father's activities, denounces Mussolini's statement to De Begnac 'as one of his usual verbal exhibitionistic exercises': 'Incidentally, my father had no contact with Mussolini ... The above conversation and Mussolini's hare-brained ideas found no practical expression of any sort' (*Dante Almansi*, p. 33).

[2] Poliakov and Sabille, *Jews under the Italian Occupation*, pp. 58–61; URO, *Judenverfolgung in Italien*, pp. 79–80; *Relazione sull'opera svolta dal Ministero degli Affari Esteri per la tutela delle communità ebraiche (1938–1943)*, Rome, n.d., pp. 6–8, 10–18, 23–8; 'Italy', *Contemporary Jewish Record*, v (Aug. 1942), 426; De Felice, *Storia degli ebrei italiani*, 361–2, 365–6; I. Kalk, 'I campi di concentramento italiani per ebrei profughi: Ferramonti Tarsia (Calabria)', *Gli Ebrei in Italia durante il fascismo*, i, Turin, 1961, pp. 63–71; YVS/JM/2792/1/Demografia e Razza/1938–1943. On the *sciamanno* (the Jewish badge worn in the age of the Ghetto), see Roth, op. cit., pp. 360–1.

countries. Wherever the German army marched in, the Jews were rounded up and deported to Hitler's death camps; wherever the Italian army appeared, they remained unmolested, at any rate until Italy's surrender to the Allied Powers in September 1943. When, in the early summer of 1941, Ante Pavelić's Croat Fascists began to massacre Serbs and Jews, the Italians at once intervened to put a stop to these atrocities.[1] And when, in the summer of 1942, the Germans signed an agreement with Pavelić's government, under which all Jews living in Croatia would be deported to Poland as 'workers', the spontaneous rescue operations of the Italian soldiery were transformed into a regular diplomatic action. As early as December 1941 Martin Luther, Under-Secretary of State at the Wilhelmstrasse, had warned Ribbentrop of Italian opposition to the 'final solution' of the Jewish problem.[2] And on 24 July 1942 he informed him that the Italian authorities were offering determined resistance to the anti-Jewish measures of the Croatian Government: 'The question of the Italian attitude to the measures . . . is extremely acute, in view of the preparations going on at present for the resettlement [*sic*] of the Jews. So far as the Croatian side is concerned, they . . . consider of special importance the deportation of the 4,000 to 5,000 Jews in the second zone which is occupied by the Italians . . . Their deportation can, however, only be effected with the assistance of the Germans because difficulties are expected from the Italian side. We have concrete evidence of the resistance put up by the Italian authorities to the anti-Jewish measures of the Croatian Government . . . Besides, the Italian chief of staff at Mostar has declared that he cannot give his approval to the resettlement of the Jews, all inhabitants of Mostar having received assurances of equal treatment.' This attitude was all the more worrying because 'everyone knows that the subversive activity of the Jews is . . . the most dangerous source of disturbances'.[3]

Ribbentrop decided to take up the matter with Rome. On 17 August Prince Otto von Bismark, Mackensen's second-in-command, submitted a request for joint action against Croatian Jewry to Ciano's *chef de cabinet*; and on 25 August Mackensen

---

[1] Poliakov and Sabille, op. cit., p. 132.
[2] Luther to Ribbentrop, 4 Dec. 1941 (URO, *Judenverfolgung in Italien*, pp. 38–9).
[3] Ibid., p. 50.

himself informed the Wilhelmstrasse that the Duce had given his consent.[1] It soon became clear, however, that the Italians were playing a double game. On 16 October Siegfried Kasche, Hitler's envoy in Croatia, reported that General Roatta, the Italian military commander, flatly refused to hand over the Jews of the second zone to the German army and that Count Pietro Marqui, the Croatian affairs expert of the Palazzo Chigi, was married to a *Volljüdin* (a pure-blooded Jewess). In a further report, dated 20 October, Kasche gave it as his opinion that the Italians were pursuing a deliberate policy of obstruction; either the Embassy in Rome had been misled as to Mussolini's decision, or else the Duce's orders had been disregarded by his subordinates, some of whom had apparently been influenced by Vatican opposition to the German brand of anti-Semitism.[2]

In February 1943 Ribbentrop, in the course of a meeting with Mussolini at the Palazzo Venezia, renewed his request for the expulsion of the Jews from the Italian zone in Croatia. Once again the Duce gave his consent. Subsequently, it was learnt, however, that the Italians had concentrated all the Jews in one camp, set up on the island of Arbe, in order to protect them from any danger that might follow on a change in the line of demarcation between the German and Italian occupation zones.[3]

Italian resistance to the 'final solution' was equally evident in France. As early as July 1942 Otto Abetz, Hitler's Ambassador to the Vichy Government, had complained of the obstructionist attitude adopted by the Italian authorities, describing it as a blow to Axis unity.[4] The full tide of obstruction, however, did not come until December of that year, after the Allied landings in North Africa and the occupation of the French Free Zone by German and Italian troops. On 4 December the Fascist Government became party to a German order expelling all Jews from French coastal and frontier areas. Unlike their Axis allies, however, the Italians interpreted this order as applying to French nationals only, not to Italian and other foreign Jews whom they considered to be under their protection. Conse-

[1] Poliakov and Sabille, pp. 136–7; URO, *Judenverfolgung in Italien*, p. 71.
[2] URO, *Judenverfolgung in Italien*, pp. 97–9; for Roatta's account, cf. 'Memoria circa l'azione della 2a armata nel territorio jugoslavo sina all'inizio del 1943' (YVS/JM/2840/Italia, Francia, Croazia/1939–1943).
[3] Poliakov and Sabille, pp. 148–9.
[4] Abetz to Wilhelmstrasse, 2 July 1942 (URO, *Judenverfolgung in Italien*, p. 47).

quently, on 30 December the Italian Armistice Commission lodged a formal protest with the French Government concerning an order issued by Ribière, the Prefect of Alpes-Maritimes, which banished all non-Aryans to the German zone.[1] The Germans were predictably furious. On 13 January 1943 Standartenführer Knochen sounded the alarm in a telegram to Heinrich Müller, the Chief of the Gestapo, imploring him to take up the matter with Himmler and to see to it that a stop was put to the Italian policy of obstruction: 'Although the number of Italian Jews (in France) is comparatively small, the privileges accorded to them have been a constant source of serious difficulty because it is impossible to understand why our Axis partner should refuse to align himself with us on the Jewish question.'[2]

On 2 February Knochen forwarded to Müller a secret report from Ribière which described in detail how the Italians in the Department Alpes-Maritimes had 'prevented the enforcement of all anti-Jewish measures which have been ordered by the French Government'.[3] On 12 February, after a conversation with Eichmann in Paris, he returned to the attack:

The best of harmony prevails between the Italian troops and the Jewish population. The Italians live in the homes of the Jews. The Jews invite them out and pay for them. The German and Italian conceptions seem here to be completely at variance. We are informed on the French side that Jewish influence has already given birth to pacifist and Communist rot in the minds of the Italian soldiers, even creating a pro-American tendency. These Jewish intermediaries also see to it that good relations are established between the Italian soldiers and the French population. They say that the French and the Italians, both Latin peoples, understand each other much better than the French and the Germans or the Germans and the Italians. They work according to a system— strong criticism of the German–Italian relationship on the one hand, preparation for a Franco–Italian understanding on the other. They endeavour at the same time to distort the way of thinking of the entire population, on the pretext that in the event of an American attack the Italians will not defend themselves because ... the Americans will at last bring them peace ... If the anti-Jewish measures throughout France are to succeed, they must also be applied in the Italian zone. Otherwise the influx of Jews into this zone—an influx which is only in

[1] Poliakov and Sabille, pp. 22–4.
[2] URO, *Judenverfolgung in Italien*, p. 125.
[3] Poliakov and Sabille, p. 56.

its initial stage—will assume formidable dimensions, and the result will be mere half-measures.[1]

Worse was to come. On 22 February Knochen informed Müller that the Italian military authorities had compelled the Police Chief of Lyon to annul an order for the arrest of several hundred Jews who were to have been sent to Auschwitz 'for labour service'. The French who were notoriously reluctant to tackle the Jewish question had been confirmed in their resistance by the measures of the Italian authorities. Above all, it was utterly intolerable that the final solution of the Jewish question should be rendered more difficult by an ally who had proclaimed his adherence to the racial gospel.[2]

Three days later Ribbentrop raised the matter with the Duce in person, urging him to check the pro-Jewish zeal of his underlings in France. He was, he said, 'well aware that Italian military circles, and sometimes the German army itself, lacked a proper understanding of the Jewish question. That was the only possible explanation of the order by the Italian High Command to annul the anti-Jewish measures which the French authorities had taken in the Italian zone at Germany's request. The Duce denied the accuracy of the information, ascribing it to the desire of the French to sow discord between Germany and Italy.' The Reich Foreign Minister concluded by affirming that the Jews in the occupied territories were 'more dangerous than English agents'.[3]

On 6 March Obersturmführer (SS Lieutenant) Heinz Röthke, in a letter to Eichmann, recapitulated all the unfulfilled Italian promises, adding that the Italian Fourth Army had used force to free Jews arrested by the French police at Annecy.[4] On 18 March Mackensen protested to Mussolini, expressing surprise at the fact that the Italian army should hamper the French authorities instead of supporting them. Once again the Duce pretended to be in agreement, apologizing for the 'sentimental humanitarianism' of his generals and assuring the Ambassador that there would be no further interference with the action of the French

[1] Ibid., pp. 60–3.
[2] Ibid., pp. 185–7; cf. Chief of Security Police and SD to Wilhelmstrasse, 25 Feb. 1943 (GFM/5602H/E401508–12).
[3] *ND*/D-734 (URO, *Judenverfolgung in Italien*, pp. 163–4).
[4] IFZ/RF 1230.

police: 'If his generals had interfered in this question, it was because they could not, with their different intellectual formation, comprehend its full significance. It was not a matter of bad will but the logical conclusion of their way of thinking. As a matter of fact, we ought to be pleased that there was a French government in existence which was prepared to carry out the (anti-Jewish) measures. It was absurd to interfere with their action. His generals seemed to have forgotten that they were not in France as an occupying force; they had come only to assist us [*sic*]. The measures taken by the French police were none of their business . . . The necessary instructions . . . would therefore be issued to General Ambrosio this very day, giving a completely free hand to the French police in this matter.'[1]

Mackensen was duly impressed by the 'Duce's clear and unambiguous stand'; that at any rate is what he told his superiors in Berlin. Two days later, however, he was (or pretended to be) shocked to learn from Bastianini that the Fascist dictator had changed his mind, having been persuaded by Ambrosio that the French police were not to be trusted. When he pointed out that the failure of the French police had been mainly due to the interference of the Italian military authorities, Bastianini replied 'that these were a few exceptional cases which were in no way typical of the situation as a whole'. The main cause of the trouble was the natural reluctance of the French to carry out a policy imposed by the Rome–Berlin Axis; that was why the Duce had decided to entrust the solution of the Jewish problem in Italian-occupied France to a high-ranking Italian police officer, Inspector-General Guido Lospinoso, 'whom he knew personally as a most energetic man'. And when Mackensen expressed the fear that the Italian generals would prevent Lospinoso from taking drastic action, Bastianini assured him that Mussolini's orders to the commander of the Fourth Army were 'clear and precise': any member of the armed forces who tried to protect the Jews would be 'called to account'.[2]

The Germans were not taken in. On 27 March Heinrich Müller arrived in Rome on Himmler's orders to take up the matter with Carmine Senise, the Italian Chief of Police, who

---

[1] *ND*/NG 2242 (URO, *Judenverfolgung in Italien*, pp. 163–4).
[2] *ND*/NG 2242 (ibid., pp. 166–7). According to Bastianini, Mackensen was not altogether enthusiastic about his master's anti-Jewish policy (*Uomini, cose, fatti*, pp. 86–8).

solemnly informed him that Lospinoso had proceeded to France 'in order to solve the Jewish problems there on German lines and in the closest collaboration with the German police'.[1] On 5 April, however, Knochen reported to Müller that Lospinoso had so far failed to contact him; and on 6 April he telegraphed to Schellenberg and Eichmann that the influx of Jews into the Italian zone was continuing and that Lospinoso's adviser on Jewish affairs was none other than the Jew Angelo Donati, 'head of a powerful financial group of Italian Jews' and a former Director of the Banque France-Italie. On 9 April Müller informed Knochen that he had asked Senise through the German police attaché in Rome to send Lospinoso to Berlin or to Paris. But there was no response, and on 24 May Knochen wrote to Müller that Lospinoso remained 'undiscoverable'; he enclosed copies of three letters from General Carlo Avarna di Gualtieri, the senior representative of the Italian High Command in Vichy, to the French authorities, from which the following is worth quoting: 'The Italian High Command requests the French Government to annul the arrests and internments of the Jews whose place of residence is in the zone occupied by us.'[2]

As Axis fortunes declined and anti-Axis feeling in Italy grew, Italian resistance to the 'final solution' continued to stiffen. On 23 June, in a telegram to Kaltenbrunner and Müller, Knochen complained of Lospinoso's continuing refusal to establish contact with him, adding that Italian sabotage, 'was endangering the application of the measures against the Jews'.[3] And on 21 July— four days before Mussolini's downfall—Röthke made the same point in a memorandum on 'the present state of the Jewish question in France': 'The attitude of the Italians is and was incomprehensible. The Italian military authorities and the Italian police protect the Jews by every means in their power. The Italian zone of influence, particularly in the Côte d'Azur, has become the Promised Land for the Jews in France. In the last few months there has been a mass exodus of Jews from our occupation zone into the Italian zone. The escape of the Jews is facilitated by the existence of thousands of flight-routes, the assistance given them by the French population and the

[1] URO, *Judenverfolgung in Italien*, p. 168.
[2] Poliakov and Sabille, pp. 74–5, 79, 84–8; URO, *Judenverfolgung in Italien*, p. 169.
[3] URO, *Judenverfolgung in Italien*, pp. 182–3.

sympathy of the authorities, false identity cards and also by the size of the area which makes it impossible to seal off the zones of influence hermetically.' Although about twenty reports on this subject had been sent to the Reich Main Security Office, there had so far been no sign of any change in the Italian attitude. The continued friction over the Jewish issue made it very difficult to maintain the façade of Axis solidarity 'because the French and the diplomatic representatives of other countries skilfully exploit this difference in the treatment of the Jews by Germany and Italy". Röthke was particularly incensed at the fact that the Italians had transferred about a thousand Jews from the Côte d'Azur to the spas in the Departments of Isère and Savoie where they had 'been placed in the best hotels'.[1]

In a subsequent report, written after the fall of Fascism, Röthke pointed out that the driving force behind the Italian policy of obstruction had been Lospinoso's right-hand man, Angelo Donati. Ever since the entry of Italian troops into France, this Jew had 'been active in securing all sorts of ameliorations' for his fellow Jews in the Italian zone of influence; his task had been facilitated by the fact that he was 'on the best of terms' with a number of high-ranking Italian officers. In the spring of 1943 he had entered into contact with Lospinoso who made him 'the official Italian expert for Jewish questions in the Italian zone of occupation': 'Confidential agents reported to us many times that the rare measures taken by the Italian authorities against certain Jews were carried out according to the directives given by Donati; for instance, the transfer of about 2,000 Jews from the Côte d'Azur to the hotels in the health resort Mégève.' It had been planned to kidnap Donati and bring him to Marseilles; but the plan had not been carried out, owing to the reluctance of the German authorities to offend the susceptibilities of their Italian allies. Donati had thus been able to go on with his game of twisting the Gestapo's tail right up to the Italian surrender.[2]

On 22 July Röthke learnt from Hauptscharführer (SS Staff Sergeant) Bauer in Marseilles that Donati had left for Rome to plead the cause of his fellow Jews in Italian-occupied France

[1] Poliakov and Sabille, pp. 104–6.
[2] Röthke to Reich Main Security Office, 26 Sept. 1943 (Poliakov and Sabille, pp. 125–6); on Donati, see 'Una perdita dolorosa, Angelo Donati', *Israel*, 12 Jan. 1961; on Lospinoso, V. Statera, 'L'ex questore Lospinoso ci racconta come aiutò quarantamila israeliti', *La Stampa*, 5 Apr. 1961.

(Mussolini having agreed to hand the Italian zone over to the Germans, retaining only Nice where the Gestapo would take over Lospinoso's Commissariat for Jewish Affairs). Meanwhile the Jews continued to conduct themselves 'in the same provocative way as before', while the Italian officers were not ashamed to 'show themselves openly in the company of Jewesses'.[1] Mussolini's 'resignation' on 25 July and the formation of a new Italian Government under Marshal Pietro Badoglio gave a fresh impetus to the Italian policy of obstruction. On 18 August Lospinoso informed the Gestapo in Marseilles that, in view of the change of government in Rome, he no longer considered himself bound by the accord previously reached between the German and Italian authorities. On 28 August it was decided at an inter-ministerial meeting in Rome to permit the entry of Jewish refugees into Italian territory; and on 4 September Röthke, in a report on 'preparations for applying the anti-Jewish measures in the Italian zone of occupation', warned his superiors that it would be hard to identify members of the Jewish race in Italian-occupied France, the Italians having forbidden the stamping of Jewish identity and ration cards with the word 'Jew'. When, on 8 September, Eisenhower announced the terms of the Italian armistice, the Germans were at long last free to extend the 'final solution' to the Jews in the former Italian zone; but in the absence of effective help from the French police, they were unable to achieve the projected mass round-up.[2]

Greece was another country under Axis rule where the Jews benefited from the 'Latin humanity' of the Italian occupation authority right up to the armistice of 8 September. Hitler, unwilling to engage his forces too deeply in an area of minor importance and anxious to satisfy at least some of Mussolini's ambitions, left his Axis ally in possession of the entire territory constituting Old Greece, including Athens, the Ionian Islands, and Rhodes; Germany retained control over a narrow strip of Thrace bordering on Turkey, the port of Salonica, and Crete, while Bulgaria received most of Thrace and Macedonia. The Jews in the German and Bulgarian zones of influence were subjected to systematic persecution, followed by deportation to

[1] Poliakov and Sabille, pp. 112–13.
[2] Ibid., pp. 38, 114, 119–22; G. Reitlinger, *The Final Solution. The Attempt to Exterminate the Jews of Europe 1939–1945*, rev. edn., London, 1968, p. 347.

the death camps in Poland; those in the Italian zone, on the other hand, lived in complete safety until the Italian surrender. The Jewish population in this zone, at first relatively small (about 900 families), kept increasing as a result of the continuous influx of Jewish refugees arriving illegally from the areas under German and Bulgarian occupation.[1]

Until the autumn of 1942 the Germans made no attempt to put a stop to this state of affairs. In the words of General Carlo Geloso, commander of the Italian Eleventh Army in Greece: 'The racial question was discussed in connection with the Jews in Greece at the beginning of the occupation (in the spring of 1941), but the German authorities confined themselves to hints and made no categorical demands.' Ciano, for his part, touched upon the issue in his correspondence with the Italian Minister in Athens, Pellegrino Ghigi, but gave him no instructions; all he did was to inform him of Hitler's decision to bring about a 'radical solution' of the Jewish problem.[2] On 25 October 1942, when the anti-Jewish terror in Salonica was at its height, Ghigi was told by his German colleague, Günther Altenburg, that the Italian authorities ought to enforce the wearing of the Jewish badge in their zone; Rome, however, flatly refused to countenance such a revival of medieval barbarity, and the Germans let the matter drop.[3]

It was not until the spring of 1943, when the mass deportations to the death camps were in full swing, that the Germans began to press for drastic steps against the Jews in the Italian zone; even then, German pressure took the form of discreet suggestions and not of threats. The German commander in Greece, General Alexander Löhr, raised the matter in the course of a talk with Geloso, inviting him to follow the German example. The latter replied that 'he could not undertake actions of this kind without a precise order from his government; no such order having been received, it was impossible for him to follow the Germans along this path, all the more so because they had acted without any

[1] Poliakov and Sabille, pp. 153–60; *Relazione sull'opera svolta dal Ministero degle Affari Esteri*, pp. 42–59.
[2] Poliakov and Sabille, p. 154; General C. Geloso, "Due anni in Grecia al Comando dell'll Armata" (YVS/JM/2840).
[3] Altenburg to Wilhelmstrasse, 25 Oct. 1942; Luther to Altenburg, 28 Oct. 1942; Altenburg to Wilhelmstrasse, 30 Oct. 1942; Altenburg to Wilhelmstrasse, 6 Nov. 1942 (URO, *Judenverfolgung in Italien*, pp. 113–16).

prior accord and without even notifying the Italians'. A similar answer was given by Geloso's chief of staff, General Tripiccione, to another German officer. Geloso was of course fully aware of the atrocities that were being perpetrated in Salonica at that moment; in his report to the Palazzo Chigi he referred to mass deportations of Jews 'in overcrowded trains, forty persons per cattle truck'.[1]

When asked by Rome whether there was any need for security measures against the Jews in Italian-occupied Greece, both Geloso and Ghigi replied in the negative: 'The Jews in our zone have never given us any trouble. None of them has been involved in espionage or in any activity on behalf of the enemy.'[2]

Not content with protecting the Jews in their own zone of occupation, the Italians did their best to help those in the German-occupied areas. In addition to requesting and obtaining the exemption of the Italian Jews in Salonica from the anti-Jewish measures, they tacitly offered sanctuary to all those non-Italian Jews who managed to make their way into Italian-occupied territory. The Italian consular authorities in the German zone gave the broadest possible interpretation to the term 'Italian subject', issuing certificates of Italian nationality to Jewish women with Greek husbands and to their children (who were described as 'minors', though some of them were over thirty). The remotest kinship to an Italian citizen was considered a sufficient reason for a certificate of Italian nationality, and so was an Italian-sounding name. In many case such certificates were issued to non-Aryans whose only claim to them was the fact that they were in danger of being arrested by the Gestapo. According to a Jewish eye-witness, a list of about twenty names of 'Italian subjects' was sent to the Gestapo for confirmation every day. The Germans naturally saw through the Italian Consul's game but affixed their stamp to his lists for the sake of the Axis partnership.[3]

The Italian army was equally helpful. Italian officers went to the German zone and swore that certain Jewish women were their wives. Jews who presented themselves at the Italian

[1] Poliakov and Sabille, p. 155; Geloso, op. cit.
[2] Poliakov and Sabille, p. 159; Geloso, op. cit.
[3] Poliakov and Sabille, pp. 155–7; M. Molho (ed.), *Communauté israélite de Thessalonique. In Memoriam. Hommage aux victimes juives des Nazis en Grèce*, 2nd edn., Thessalonica, 1973, pp. 139–42, 165–83.

Command in Larissa at once received permits to go to Athens by military train, in addition to which they were given a supply of food for the journey from the military stores. In the words of a Jewish eyewitness: 'Italian officers, *even the highest*, as well as ordinary privates, did all they could to save and protect Jews.'[1]

The Germans did not react until February 1943 when Eichmann lodged a complaint with the Wilhelmstrasse on Kaltenbrunner's orders, pointing out that the Italian practice of naturalizing 'Jews of various nationalities' was endangering the implementation of the anti-Jewish policy in Greece; he suggested that Rome be asked to withdraw its protecting hand from non-Aryans who had acquired Italian citizenship after 1 July 1942, the day on which the German commander in Salonica had decreed the mobilization of Jews for forced labour. On 15 February Berlin instructed the German Embassy in Rome to take up the matter with the Palazzo Chigi; and on the following day Mackensen advised the Wilhelmstrasse that Bismark had made representations to Blasco d'Ajeta, Ciano's *chef de cabinet*, who promised to order an investigation.[2] On 22 February d'Ajeta informed Bismark that Eichmann's charges were unfounded, not a single Jew having been naturalized by any Italian consular officer in Greece (*sic*). A day later Ribbentrop requested the Reichsführung SS to submit documentary evidence of Italian opposition to the 'final solution'; the evidence was duly furnished on 25 February, the day of Ribbentrop's arrival in Rome. Commenting on Kaltenbrunner's complaints, an official of the Wilhelmstrasse pointed out that General Geloso had consistently refused to associate himself with the anti-Jewish policy pursued by the German authorities in Greece; Mackensen and Altenburg had done their best to bring about some sort of co-operation in racial matters, but so far their efforts had 'produced no practical result'.[3]

On 25 February Ribbentrop handed to the Duce a letter from

---

[1] *Communauté israélite*, pp. 139–42 (testimony of Prof. Levy Tazartes).

[2] Eichmann to Rademacher, 2 Feb. 1943 (GFM/5602H/E401533–34); Bergmann to Embassy Rome, 15 Feb. 1943 (GFM/5602H/E401531–32); Mackensen to Wilhelmstrasse, 16 Feb. 1943 (GFM/5602H/E401530).

[3] Mackensen to Wilhelmstrasse, 22 Feb. 1943 (GFM/5602H/E401528); Sonnleithner to Reichsführung SS (Wolff), 23 Feb. 1943 (GFM/5602H/E401523); Steg to Bergmann, 24 Feb. 1943 (GFM/5602H/E401522); Bergmann to Sonnleithner, 24 Feb. 1943 (GFM/5602H/E401519–21); Hahn to Eichmann, 25 Feb. 1943 (URO, *Judenverfolgung in Italien*, p. 154).

Hitler which contained a lengthy passage on the Jewish peril.[1]
On 13 March the Palazzo Chigi, in response to a further German
démarche, informed Mackensen that the Fascist Government had
decided on a series of measures against the Jews in Italian-
occupied Greece which, it was hoped, would satisfy Berlin: (1)
Jews of Italian nationality would be subjected to the same
treatment as those in Italy proper; politically dangerous elements
would be interned or deported to Italy; (2) Jews of Greek
nationality would be interned in camps on the Ionian Islands or
in Italy; (3) Jewish subjects of friendly or neutral countries
would be requested to leave Greece; if they failed to comply with
this request, they would either be deported to their countries of
origin or be interned in camps on the Ionian Islands or in Italy.[2]
Unimpressed by these assurances, Ribbentrop ordered his
underlings on 16 March to find out whether the measures decided
on by Rome were indeed being implemented and if so, whether
they were considered adequate by the Reichsführung SS. He was
advised that Himmler's Jewish affairs experts did not believe in
Italian promises; nor did they consider internment on the Ionian
Islands or in Italy an adequate substitute for deportation to the
East.[3] In the ensuing weeks it became increasingly evident that
the Italian authorities in Greece had no intention whatever of
carrying out the alleged decisions of their government; far from
taking measures against the Jews in their own occupation zone,
they stepped up their attempts to aid and protect those under
German rule. On 20 April Röthke learnt from one of Abetz's
collaborators that the Italian Consul-General in Paris had
intervened in favour of Ines Hasson, a Greek Jewess of Italian
origin.[4] On 22 April the Italian Embassy in Berlin requested the
Reich Foreign Ministry to recognize as 'Italians' certain Greek
Jews who played an important part in the economic life of
Salonica, adding that it was for the Italian authorities—and for
them alone—to decide who was an Italian citizen.[5] On 15 May
the Embassy made another *démarche*, demanding the release of

---

[1] Hitler to Mussolini, 16 Feb. 1943 (*Hitler e Mussolini*, p. 219).
[2] *ND*/NG 5051 (URO, *Judenverfolgung in Italien*, p. 161).
[3] Sonnleithner to Bergmann, 16 Mar. 1943 (*ND*/NG 5051; ibid., p. 162); Bergmann to
Ribbentrop, 19 Mar. 1943 (*ND*/NG 5051; ibid., p. 165).
[4] Gossmann to Röthke, 20 Apr. 1943; Röthke to Gossman, 22 Apr. 1943 (URO,
Judenverfolgung in Italien, pp. 171–2). Röthke's answer was a flat refusal.
[5] Wagner to Steengracht, 29 Apr. 1943 (URO, *Judenverfolgung in Italien*, pp. 173–5).

twenty-three Greek Jews who had been deported to the East.[1] And on 18 May an official of the Wilhelmstrasse reported that Weizsäcker's successor as Secretary of State, Steengracht, had agreed to recognize as 'Italians' all Greek Jews who had been given certificates of Italian nationality.[2] On 8 June another Foreign Ministry official requested Himmler, then about to leave for Rome, to remind the Duce of the assurances given on 13 March; but there was no follow-up.[3] It was not until the second half of October—over six weeks after the Italian collapse—that the Germans extended the 'final solution' to the former Italian zone in Greece.[4]

The Italo-German quarrel over the racial issue was particularly bitter in French North Africa where the 'Aryanization' policy adopted by the Vichy Government at Germany's request affected thousands of Italian Jews. On 2 September 1942 Alfieri handed a note of protest to the Wilhelmstrasse, from which the following is worth quoting:

In Tunisia there are about 5,000 Italian citizens of Jewish race, including numerous owners of enterprises which are to be liquidated or transferred to persons of Aryan race. These liquidations and transfers pose a grave threat to the economic position of Italy in Tunisia, a position which the French authorities have tried to undermine for many years and which Italy is particularly anxious to safeguard at the present moment. Negotiations are at present in progress between the Italian and French governments; the latter have, however, argued that they are obliged to apply the regulations in question as soon as possible, 'in view of the pressure that is being brought to bear by the German Government . . .' . . . The Italian Government wishes to point out that it would be most grateful to the government of the Reich if the latter could be good enough to instruct the responsible authorities to delay rather than accelerate the application of the racial laws in North Africa, at any rate for the moment . . .[5]

Alfieri's note was passed on to Abetz who reacted sharply, insisting that the 'Aryanization' of Italian enterprises was a

---

[1] Wagner to Steengracht, 18 May 1943 (ibid., pp. 177–9). Wagner pointed out that the Italians regarded the said Jews as their protégés (*Schutzbefohlene*).

[2] Ibid.

[3] Memorandum by Thadden, 8 June 1943 (YVS/E420976–78).

[4] Memorandum by Wagner, 22 Oct. 1943 (URO, *Judenverfolgung in Italien*, pp. 195–6); cf. R. Hilberg, *The Destruction of the European Jews*, 2nd edn., Chicago, 1967, pp. 442–53 and Reitlinger, op. cit., pp. 398–408.

[5] URO, *Judenverfolgung in Italien*, p. 73.

political necessity and urging the Wilhelmstrasse to press for Italian co-operation in the implementation of the racial policy in North Africa. But Ribbentrop and his aides were not prepared to stake relations with Rome on a question of extending German racial dogma to the Italian sphere of influence; and on 22 October Luther noted that Abetz had been ordered to stop interfering. On 25 November, after yet another *démarche* by the Italian Embassy in Berlin, Woermann proposed that the German Command in Tunisia be instructed not to take any measures against Jews of Italian nationality without the prior consent of the Italian Consul-General; and in a note of 4 December he added that the Italian request 'should be complied with as far as it is compatible with military necessities'.[1] Four months and three days later Tunis was delivered by Allied troops, and the racial laws were repealed.

Another bone of contention was the continued presence of 'privileged' Italian Jews in Germany and German-occupied territory. Rome insisted that, for the purposes of foreign relations, Jews of Italian citizenship should be regarded as 'Italians'. The Germans considered such an attitude to be incompatible both with Fascist racial philosophy and with 'Axis solidarity'. Until the second half of 1942 the German leaders pretended to ignore the delicate issue. Then, on 18 August, Ribbentrop had Mackensen inform the Palazzo Chigi that, in Germany's view, Italian Jews resident in the occupied areas should either be repatriated or sent to the East 'for labour service'. The Italians replied that it was for them—and for them alone—to decide on the treatment of Italian citizens. For the moment the Germans were not to be provoked. On 19 September Luther noted that Jews of Italian nationality had been exempted from all discriminatory measures 'in deference to Italian wishes'.[2] And on 24 September he informed Weizsäcker that the problem of the Italian Jews would have to be dealt with at the highest level: 'This question will have to be clarified in a conversation either between the Führer and the Duce or between the Reich Foreign

[1] Abetz to Wilhelmstrasse, 12 Sept. 1942; memorandum by Woermann, 25 Nov. 1942; Woermann to Schnurre, 4 Dec. 1942 (GFM/5602H/E401599–608); cf. also Luther to Ribbentrop, 22 Oct. 1942 (GFM/5602H/401599–608).
[2] Luther to Ribbentrop, 19 Sept. 1942 (*ND*/NG 5123, URO, *Judenverfolgung in Italien*, pp. 81–2); Mackensen to Wilhelmstrasse, 11 Oct. 1942 (GFM/5602H/E401595–96).

Minister and Count Ciano.'[1] On 22 October, in a memorandum on 'Italy and the Jewish Question', Luther pointed out that Italy's failure to tackle the Jewish problem and her systematic opposition to German racial policy were creating an increasingly intolerable situation. To be sure, the number of Italian Jews in the German sphere of influence was small (there were less than 200 in Germany proper and about 500 in Paris), but the matter was important 'on grounds of principle': 'The continued presence of such groups of foreign Jews who consider themselves privileged and misbehave accordingly imposes a constant strain on the German population and constitutes a factor of internal subversion. It is also an inadmissible demonstration of the fact that in a matter of such importance the Axis is not pursuing a common policy which in turn gives rise to criticism of the German measures. Moreover, the special status granted to Jews of foreign nationality is creating an atmosphere unfavourable to our policy in the Western territories under Axis occupation.'

The racial laws enacted by the Fascist Government in 1938 (Luther added) had never been properly enforced, let alone followed up. On the contrary, there was an unmistakable tendency to avoid drastic measures, reflected in the retention of Jews in economic key positions, the Italianization of Jewish names, and the naturalization of foreign Jews. In the rest of Europe and in North Africa, the Italians were trying to use the economic power of their Jewish nationals as an instrument of Fascist policy, evidently not realizing that Jewry was an implacable enemy of Fascism and that Jewish capital the world over was 'one of the most important weapons employed against us'. As a result of this approach, the Italians were now protecting the Jews of Tunisia against the French, while in Romania and elsewhere Jews continued to be in control of Italian firms.

Given the delicacy of this issue, Luther felt that it should be taken up at the very highest level, possibly in a personal talk between the two leaders. He concluded by formulating three demands: (1) Italian Jews resident in Germany or German-occupied areas should either be repatriated or subjected to the same treatment as all other Jews under German rule; (2) Rome should demonstrate its solidarity with Berlin by adopting laws and measures parallel to those in force in Germany; (3) Italy

[1] Note by Luther, 24 Sept. 1942 (*ND*/PS 3688, URO, *Judenverfolgung in Italien*, p. 85).

should encourage third countries along the path of anti-Semitism, preferably in concert with the Reich.[1]

The German leaders, however, were still reluctant to put pressure on their principal ally. While Jews were being rounded up and deported all over Europe, those of Italian citizenship continued to enjoy complete immunity. In the end, Berlin decided on a compromise: There would be no meddling in Italian domestic affairs, but Italian Jews under German rule would be deprived of their privileged status. On 13 January 1943 Ribbentrop advised Mackensen, in reply to a dispatch from the latter, that Germany, while deploring Italy's failure to solve her Jewish problem on German lines, did not propose to impose her views on her partner. She could not, however, go on permitting the Italians to impose their views in the German sphere of influence: 'Given the difference between the German and Italian conceptions, it seems necessary to us to arrive at a clear-cut solution of the problem in the areas under German occupation. We cannot possibly allow the Italian view to prevail in our own country and in the areas under our control. I therefore ask you to inform Count Ciano *by word of mouth* ... that, out of special regard for the allied Italian Government [*sic*], we shall permit Jews of Italian nationality to stay in the areas under our rule until 31 March 1943. After that date, we shall have to claim freedom of action.' Ribbentrop concluded by urging the Ambassador to draw the attention of the Italians to the grave security problems which the presence of Jews was creating in the countries under Axis occupation: 'It is precisely the economically influential Jews who are the most dangerous. You should give the Italians a few examples from our own experience and emphasize that Jewry as a whole is the worst enemy of both Germany and Italy ... In our eyes Jews of Italian citizenship are as much Jews as all the others and must hence be included in our anti-Jewish measures.'[2]

Three days later Mackensen called on Ciano in order to notify him of his Minister's decision; but whereas Ribbentrop had demanded the removal of the Italian Jews from all areas under German control, the Ambassador only spoke of 'Jews in the occupied Western territories'. Ciano replied that he 'personally

---

[1] Luther to Ribbentrop, 22 Oct. 1942 (see above, p. 317 n. 1).
[2] Ribbentrop to Embassy Rome, 13 Jan. 1943 (GFM/132/123802–4). Our italics.

understood' the German point of view and was 'agreeable in principle', adding, however, that this was an issue which affected a great many other departments and would raise a host of problems. He thought that Mackensen had better submit a memorandum on the subject, but the latter refused to do so, having been ordered to confine himself to a verbal communication.[1]

On 27 January d'Ajeta advised Bismark that his government had decided to repatriate its Jewish subjects in France, Belgium, and Holland, adding that the question of procedure was being cleared up by the competent authorities; and on the following day Berlin informed its diplomatic representatives in Paris, Brussels, The Hague, and Prague that the Italians had yielded to German pressure. On 4 February d'Ajeta handed to Bismark a note to the effect that the Italian Jews resident in Germany, Czechoslovakia, and the German-occupied areas in the West were being sent home and that the Italian diplomatic and consular authorities had been ordered to complete the operation by 31 March.[2]

Emboldened by this apparent compliance, Berlin decided to step up the pressure. On 17 February Mackensen was asked to inform the Palazzo Chigi that as of 1 April Italian Jews resident in Poland, the Baltic countries, and the German-occupied Eastern areas would be subjected to the same measures as other Jews under German rule. This time, however, the Italians protested, insisting on the need for an extension of the deadline. On 22 February Mackensen urged his superiors to agree to a postponement until 20 April; on 24 February an official of the Wilhelmstrasse replied that no action would be taken before the end of April; and on 27 February the Italian Embassy in Berlin, in a note addressed to the Wilhelmstrasse, pointed out that there were very few Italian consular officers in Eastern Europe and that hence the repatriation of the Italian Jews in question could

---

[1] Mackensen to Wilhelmstrasse, 16 Jan. 1943 (GFM/132/123817); the reasons for the discrepancy between Ribbentrop's instructions to Mackensen and the latter's communication are not clear. For Ciano's opposition to the 'final solution', see Poliakov and Sabille, pp. 54, 96; for his mixed feelings about the Jews, cf. Frassati, *Il destino passa per Varsavia*, p. 29.

[2] Bismarck to Wilhelmstrasse, 27 Jan. 1943 (GFM/5602H/E401558); circular by Hahn, 28 Jan. 1943, (GFM/5602H/E401556); Mackensen to Wilhelmstrasse, 5 Feb. 1943 (GFM/5602H/E401540–41).

not possibly be completed in the short space of six to eight weeks. The Germans, unwilling to push disagreement to a point which endangered 'Axis friendship', assured their allies that they would be flexible on the time-limit; the Italians thereupon submitted requests for postponement, not only in Eastern Europe, but in other parts of Europe as well, with the result that 'privileged' Italian Jews continued to reside in all areas under German jurisdiction until after the fall of Fascism. In the end, however, Himmler and his collaborators lost patience. On 5 July Eichmann informed the Wilhelmstrasse, presumably on Kaltenbrunner's orders, that the SS was opposed to any further extension of the deadline. Rome should therefore be notified that as of 3 August Italian citizens of Jewish race would be included in the anti-Jewish measures; 'special cases' would only be considered up to 1 August.[1] Whether Eichmann's request was ever passed on to the Palazzo Chigi we cannot tell; all we can say is that a handful of Italian Jews in German-occupied territory continued to enjoy immunity right up to the Italian surrender.

In addition to intervening on behalf of their own Jewish nationals, the Italian diplomatic and consular representative in Eastern Europe tried to aid and protect non-Italian Jews until they themselves were arrested or expelled.[2] The Italian troops in Poland likewise gave a good deal of help. According to Jewish eyewitnesses, they showed their sympathy with the local Jews in a wide variety of ways, supplying them with cash and food, providing them with work, and hiding them in their barracks; in some cases they even helped them to escape to Hungary, Switzerland, or Italy.[3] What particularly infuriated the Germans was the fact that a few Italian soldiers co-operated with the Jewish resistance movement; on 30 June 1943 the commander of the German Police in Galicia reported to his direct superior in

---

[1] Bergmann to Embassy Rome, 18 Feb. 1943; Mackensen to Wilhelmstrasse, 22 Feb. 1943 (URO, *Judenverfolgung in Italien*, pp. 149, 151); Bergmann to Embassy Rome, 24 Feb. 1943 (GFM/E401524); note by Italian Embassy Berlin, 27 Feb. 1943, in reply to German verbal note of 17 Feb. (GFM/5602H/E401492–93).

[2] See Frassati, op. cit., pp. 92–5.

[3] Testimony of Sulamit Kacyzna (YVS/o–3/642); M. Hermann, 'M'getto L'vov l'khel hashikhrur ha-italki', *Yedioth Beth Lokhmei ha-Gettaoth* (Apr. 1957), 1–2; E. Brand, 'Parashat yakhasam shel ha-italkim klapei ha-yehudim b'artzoth ha-kibbush', *Yedioth Yad Vashem* (May 1960), 16–17.

Warsaw that certain members of the Italian armed forces had sold arms and ammunition to Jewish partisans.[1]

As might be expected, Italian opposition to Hitler's anti-Jewish policy did not escape the notice of Western observers. At the beginning of February 1943 the German Embassy in Rome drew d'Ajeta's attention to an article on 'Jews' Badges in France' which had appeared in the London *Times* on 21 January and which is worth quoting in full:

Before the German troops in some French departments were relieved by Italians, Vichy, at the instigation of Berlin, instructed the prefects of all departments to force all domiciled Jews whenever appearing in public always to wear the prescribed yellow badge letter J as elsewhere under German domination. Last week in the Italian-occupied departments of Savoie, Haute-Savoie, Basses-Alpes, Alpes-Maritimes and Var, the Italian commanding Generals notified the prefects that it was irreconcilable with the dignity of the Italian army that in territories occupied by Italians Jews should be compelled to appear in public with this stigmatising badge, and consequently notified the prefects that Vichy's orders were to be cancelled. When the embarrassed prefects asked Vichy what they were to do, they were told to comply with the Italian instructions.[2]

On 4 February Rudolf Schleier, Minister at the German Embassy in Paris, informed Berlin that the report in *The Times* was inaccurate for the simple reason that the Vichy Government had refused to promulgate an ordinance for the introduction of the yellow star.[3] On 12 February Knochen made the same point in his above-quoted report to Heinrich Müller, adding, however, that the divergence of views between the two allies was being skilfully exploited by the Germanphobe French.[4] In the following months the Germans grew increasingly alarmed at the impact which Italian resistance to the 'final solution' was having on opinion in third countries. At the end of May Röthke, in a note on 'The Jewish Question in Southern France', referred to the 'treasonable propaganda' which was exploiting 'this difference between the conceptions of the German and Italian governments in the matter of solving the Jewish problem'. Its theme was the

[1] Katzmann to Krüger, 30 June 1943 (*ND*/018-L; *IMT* xxxviii. 391–410).
[2] 'Jews' Badges in France. Vichy Order Cancelled by Italians', *The Times*, 21 Jan. 1943; cf. also PRO/F0371/36015/2955/52/17 (undated Foreign Office minute, 1943).
[3] Schleier to Wilhelmstrasse, 4 Feb. 1943 (GFM/5602H/E401546).
[4] See above, p. 307 and p. 307 n. 1.

contrast between the barbarous inhumanity of the Germans and the humane and Christian attitude of the Italians, based on the teaching of the Roman Catholic Church.[1]

After the abortive meeting between Hitler and Mussolini at Salzburg (7–10 April 1943), the Germans also began to worry about the continued presence of 'Jew-tainted' Gentiles at all levels of the Fascist machine. At the beginning of May an agent of the *Abwehr* (the counter-intelligence branch of the German High Command) in Rome sent a report on 'suspicious elements at the last Führer–Duce conversation' to Berlin which ran as follows: 'Among those present at the last Führer–Duce conversation was the Director-General of the Italian Foreign Ministry, Vitetti. Vitetti's wife is an American Jewess who is closely related to some of the Standard Oil Company people. She receives ten thousand dollars a month in Switzerland where she spends a considerable part of her time. Vitetti himself is known to be a loyal supporter of Federzoni.'[2]

Commenting on this item of information in a letter to Steengracht, an official of the Wilhelmstrasse observed that it was 'of particular interest inasmuch as we know from the absolutely reliable sources at our disposal that the American Minister in Berne, for example, is continually sending reports on the most intimate affairs of Germany and Italy to Washington which, as he himself admits, are based on information received from a leading Italian personality'.[3] On 24 June the Rome office of the *Abwehr* sent a detailed report on the 'Ciano group' to Berlin in which the Duce's son-in-law was accused of conducting an anti-German campaign with the help of 'Jew-tainted Aryans' and other traitors whom he had appointed to key posts in the Italian Foreign Ministry:

It is well known that Count Ciano, currently Ambassador to the Holy See, makes no secret of his sympathies for England and his hostility to Germany and that his whole large group of supporters is very active in all spheres, most particularly in the financial sphere . . . We enclose an authentic list of the highest officials of the Italian Foreign Ministry who owe their positions to Count Ciano . . . and all of whom have foreign wives, not a few of them of enemy nationality. All these people are

[1] Poliakov and Sabille, p. 96.
[2] GFM/7650H/E547015.
[3] Grote to Steengracht, 2 June 1943 (GFM/7650H/E547014).

serving Count Ciano, not the Italian Government, and all of them maintain constant contacts with enemy countries via the neutral States on the pretext of keeping in touch with the families of their wives. It is certain that this is the real and almost the only organization of traitors which exists in Italy.

The enclosed list contained the names of fifty-seven Foreign Ministry officials, by no means all of them of high rank, seven of whom—Pietrabissa, Pietromarchi, Renzetti, Rocco, Rossi-Longhi, Sapuppo, and Vitetti—were married to Jewesses or alleged Jewesses.[1] Whether Berlin ever demanded the removal of Vitetti and other suspects listed in the *Abwehr* report is not clear from the sources at our disposal. All we can say with assurance is that the Germans were seriously worried and that Ribbentrop, in his above-mentioned talk with Mussolini, hinted at the need for racial laws on the German model, in spite of which all the 'Jew-tainted Aryans' remained at their posts.[2]

The Italo–German differences over the racial issue were aggravated still further by an increasingly violent dispute over the doctrine of Nordic superiority. As has been noted, Landra had attacked this doctrine in his lecture at Berlin University on 24 February 1939. A year later, during the period of non-belligerency, the possibility of co-operation in racial matters had been discussed at a meeting held by the German–Italian Cultural Committee in Rome, and agreement had been reached on the need for an exchange of information on subjects of common interest and the desirability of regular contacts between the 'racial experts' of the two countries.[3] After Italy's entry into the war, Dr. Gross (who had not participated in the discussion) expressed the view that co-operation ought to be confined to purely scientific issues, since debates over questions of racial doctrine were likely to give rise to ideological conflicts which had better be avoided for political reasons.[4]

The Italian declaration of war also marked the beginning of angry polemics between Preziosi and Acerbo which were to have considerable repercussions in Germany. In July 1940

[1] GFM/1045/311328–30.
[2] URO, *Judenverfolgung in Italien*, p. 156. After the Italian armistice Ribbentrop ordered the German Embassy in Rome to have Vitetti arrested and sent to a concentration camp (Ribbentrop to Rahn, 29 Sept. 1943, GFM/132/123419–20).
[3] Visco to Hoppenstedt, 6 Mar. 1940 (URO, *Judenverfolgung in Italien*, p. 28).
[4] Gross to Wilhelmstrasse, 31 July 1940 (ibid., p. 29).

Preziosi published a virulent attack on Acerbo's *Fondamenti della dottrina fascista della razza* in his paper, denouncing it as a piece of anti-Axis propaganda and adding that it had caused serious concern in Berlin. Preziosi's article won applause from Interlandi (who reproduced it in *Il Tevere* of 16–17 July) and from Farinacci (who, in a letter to *La Vita Italiana,* poked fun at Acerbo's scholarship); it also provoked a lengthy reply from Acerbo himself (who, while defending his 'heretical' theses, angrily denied being an enemy of Germany or a friend of the Jews). In the following month Preziosi returned to the charge, insisting on the need for *Gleichschaltung* in the racial sphere and for unconditional loyalty to the Axis.[1]

On 24 August the German Embassy in Rome informed Berlin that Acerbo had expressed the desire to lecture on problems of racial policy in Germany in order to explain his views to the academic world and clear up the 'misunderstandings' to which Preziosi's and Interlandi's attacks had presumably given rise.[2] The Wilhelmstrasse thereupon consulted a leading apostle of the Nordic gospel, Eugen Fischer, Professor of Eugenics at Berlin University and Director of the Kaiser Wilhelm Institute of Anthropology, who had been invited to deliver a series of lectures on race and heredity at the University of Rome. Fischer replied that Acerbo's pamphlet was not merely a vicious diatribe against the German concept of blood and race but an outrageous insult to the German people. It was shocking that such a scurrilous libel should have been brought out by the Fascist Ministry of Popular Culture. On 10 November Fischer gave vent to his indignation in a letter to Bernhard Rust, the Italophobe Reich Minister of Education and Science:

True, scientific theories are a matter of controversy, but it does not follow that (Acerbo) has a right to make insulting remarks about German ideas and about the German people. He refers to the setting-up of the Gothic and Lombard States as barbarian invasions. He describes the Teutons of that time as bearers of archaic cultures, shepherds and hunters. In his view they were not conquering peoples but undisciplined gangs whose aim was not the creation of States but

[1] G. Preziosi, 'Per la serietà degli studi razziali italiani (Dedicato al camerata Giacomo Acerbo)', *La Vita Italiana,* lvi (15 July 1940), 73–5; id., 'Per la serietà degli studi italiani sulla razza', ibid. (15 Aug. 1940), 135–46 (containing Farinacci's letter and Acerbo's reply); cf. also *Il Regime Fascista,* 17 July 1940.
[2] Spakler to Pfleiderer, 24 Aug. 1940 (GFM/2191/472804–5).

only pillage and plunder . . . The descendants of the Goths, he claims, have been absorbed into the lowest strata of the Italian population . . . The whole tenor of the book is anti-racialist. With truly Jewish skill everything is twisted in such a way as to make it appear that the concept of race is no more than a piece of scientific sophistry (*Gelehrtenspitzfindigkeit*); the concept of the Aryan is . . . literally torn to shreds, all that remains is a term that serves as a pretext for separating the Jewish minority from the . . . national organism.

Unless the Italian Government dissociated itself from Acerbo's racial theories (Fischer concluded), he would prefer to cancel his projected visit to Rome.[1]

Dr. Gross, who had likewise been consulted by the Foreign Ministry, replied on 9 December that he fully agreed with Fischer's appraisal. Quite apart from the political objections raised by Preziosi and his associates, Acerbo's book had 'made a disastrous impression on German academic circles, given his complete and utter ignorance of the real problems involved'. A lecture by Acerbo in Germany would inevitably provoke hostile reactions from German scholars and give rise to ideological controversies which had better be avoided 'for reasons of over-all policy'. That being so, the only possible answer to Acerbo's request for an invitation was a 'polite refusal'.[2]

The Wilhelmstrasse readily accepted the verdict of the 'experts'; and on 13 December Walther Wüster, the German Consul-General in Rome, was instructed to transmit a 'polite refusal' to Acerbo.[3] For the moment the storm seemed to have blown over. In May 1941, however, the controversy flared up again when the *Alpendienst* at Innsbruck notified Berlin that Acerbo's book had been praised by a reviewer in *Italia che scrive* who described it as the work of an 'eminent politician', written by order of the Duce himself. On 20 May the Wilhelmstrasse asked the German Embassy in Rome whether Acerbo's attack on the German racial theories reflected the official Fascist view on the issue; and on 8 July Plessen transmitted a detailed reply from Dr. Eckart Peterich, a German scholar resident in Florence, who claimed that Acerbo (an 'influential politician', a 'highly

[1] Fischer to Rust, 10 Nov. 1940 (GFM/2191/472816–17); on Rust's Italophobia, cf. Simoni, p. 255.
[2] Gross to Rademacher, 9 Dec. 1940 (GFM/2191/472818–19).
[3] Rademacher to Wüster, 13 Dec. 1940 (GFM/2191/472820).

respected writer', and a former Minister of Agriculture) was indeed the official Fascist spokesman on the racial question and that his book accurately expressed both the prevailing aversion to the Nordic gospel and the desire of the Fascist leadership to bring its racial doctrines into harmony with the teaching of the Church.[1]

Mackensen, alarmed at the mounting tension over the racial issue, did his best to pour water on the flames. On 7 November (the Ministry of Popular Culture just having forbidden the dissemination of a German pamphlet on the Jewish question in Italy) he warned his superiors against tactless meddling in Italian domestic affairs.[2] And on 3 January 1942 he assured the Wilhelmstrasse that, contrary to Dr. Peterich's assertion, Acerbo was a man of no importance and that his pronouncements on the German concept of race in no way reflected the official Fascist attitude on the subject. For the rest, lectures by German scholars at Rome University were intended to promote the cause of German–Italian friendship; it would therefore be a grave mistake to send a man like Eugen Fischer who had no command of the Italian language and no understanding of the Italian mentality.[3]

Mussolini, for his part, prudently refrained from intervening in the controversy; but it is clear from all the sources at our disposal that he more than shared Acerbo's aversion to the Nordic gospel.[4] And while Acerbo ceased to write on the racial question after Italy's entry into the war, other Fascist scribes continued to denounce the Nordic heresy throughout the period under review.[5] It remains to add that in February 1943 the Duce showed his appreciation of Acerbo by appointing him Minister of Finance.

---

[1] *Alpendienst*, 8 May 1941, on review by Pericle Ducati in *Italia che scrive* (Mar. 1941), 81–83; Rademacher to Embassy Rome, 20 May 1941 (GFM/2191/472825–27); memorandum by Peterich, 24 June 1941; Plessen to Wilhelmstrasse, 8 July 1941 (GFM/2191/472829–36).

[2] GFM/2191/472837/2–39.

[3] GFM/2191/472843–44.

[4] See, e.g. Ciano, *Diario*, ii. 175 (entry for 25 June 1942); Spampanato, *Contromemoriale*, ii. 132.

[5] See, e.g., E. Leoni, *Mistica del razzismo fascista*, Padova, 1941, p. 27; A. Capasso, *Idee chiare sul razzismo*, Rome, 1942, pp. 35–6; V. Mazzei, *Razza e nazione*, Rome, 1942. Mazzei's thinly veiled polemics against the Fascist imitation of German anti-Semitism provoked a sharp reaction from the Italian Jew-baiters (*Il Tevere*, 11 Sept. 1942; J. Evola, 'In alto mare', *La Vita Italiana*, lx, 15 Nov. 1942, 470–81).

During the war years Mussolini's aversion to the Nordic gospel found expression in his support for the apostle of 'Roman' racialism, Baron Julius Evola. In September 1941 he praised Evola's book *Sintesi della dottrina della razza* (an exposition of the 'spiritual' concept of race), describing it as a counterblast to the 'materialistic' doctrine of blood and soil; he also encouraged the Baron to propagate his ideas in Germany, authorizing him to bring out a German version of his book (to be called *Synthesis of 'Fascist' Racial Doctrine*) and approving his plans for founding a bilingual racial review (to be entitled *Spirit and Blood*). Evola thereupon sent a detailed memorandum on his project to the leading 'racial experts' in Germany, including Rosenberg and Gross.[1]

The Germans, on their side, were at first well disposed towards Evola, given his close friendship with Preziosi and his open hostility to the Catholic Church; and in May 1941 they invited him to address the German–Italian Society in Berlin on 'Fascist Italy's Aryan–Roman decision', meaning Mussolini's sudden jump from anti-racialism to racialism in 1938.[2] On 9 October 1941 an official of the Wilhelmstrasse pointed out that Evola was being encouraged by the competent German authorities 'because he has shown understanding of the German point of view and because his "School of Fascist Mysticism" at Milan provides him with an organizational platform for influencing the Fascist Party'. Evola's plan for bringing out a bilingual racial review was particularly welcome because it would 'increase German influence in the field of racial policy in Italy and give us a chance of creating a counterweight to the Catholic concept within Fascism. In any case it will enable us to prevent the "School of Fascist Mysticism" from falling into the hands of the Catholic Church.' It was also worth noting that Evola had been received by the Duce and that his erstwhile rivals, Visco and Landra, were now singing his praises and referring to him as the 'coming man'.[3]

[1] J. C. Evola, 'Mussolini e il razzismo', *Il Meridiano d'Italia*, 16, 23, and 30 Dec. 1951; id., *Il cammino del Cinabro*, pp. 147–58; Evola to Rademacher, 22 Dec. 1941 (PA/Inl.I/Partei/Italien/Baron Julius Evola/1941–1942).

[2] Hoppe to Rademacher, 30 June 1941 (PA/ibid.). According to Hoppe, the Italian diplomats in Berlin were unenthusiastic about Evola's lecture, while the Germans considered it to be 'noteworthy' (*beachtenswert*).

[3] Rademacher to Luther, 9 Oct. 1941 (ibid.).

In the ensuing months, however, the Germans began to have second thoughts about the apostle of the 'Roman' race. In an undated German memorandum on co-operation between the 'racial experts' of the two countries (which from internal evidence must have been written at the end of 1941 or the beginning of 1942) we read that Evola's nebulous 'spiritualism' (completely at variance with the 'scientific' German approach) could hardly serve as a basis of a common racial policy; nor was it clear whether the Baron was indeed the official Fascist spokesman on the racial question.[1] To make matters worse, Evola published an openly anti-German article in Farinacci's paper on 16 November 1941, deploring the 'anti-Roman' implications of the Nordic gospel, accusing the German 'racial experts' of 'muddled thinking and mental aberrations', and denouncing Hitler's idol, Richard Wagner, as a falsifier of the Nordic mythology.[2] The Wilhelmstrasse reacted by having Gross convey an unofficial rebuke to the apostle of the 'Roman' race and by asking Bismarck to inquire of d'Ajeta whether Evola's project of a bilingual review enjoyed the support of the Duce and the Fascist Party; Mackensen replied that both Ciano and Pavolini had expressed a 'definitely negative' view of Evola's activities in Germany, adding that the Baron had meanwhile been ordered to return to Italy at once and that his journalistic project was most unlikely to receive the government's sanction.[3]

The Germans were not alone in attacking Evola's 'Roman' mythology. On 20 April 1942 Interlandi poured scorn on the Baron's 'nebulous spiritualism' in the columns of *La Difesa della Razza*—a sure sign that the Duce was about to withdraw his protecting hand from Evola.[4] And on 9 June an official of the Wilhelmstrasse notified Gross that Mussolini had turned down Evola's project, having been warned by Father Tacchi-Venturi that official support for 'Roman paganism' might give rise to a conflict between Church and State. Finally, on 23 November,

---

[1] Undated memorandum by Vollmer (ibid., see above, p. 229 n. 1).
[2] J. Evola, 'Sul contributo della romanità per la nuova Germania', *Il Regime Fascista*, 16 Nov. 1941.
[3] Rademacher to Luther, 15 Jan. 1942 (PA/ibid.); Mackensen to Wilhelmstrasse, 26 Feb. 1942 (GFM/2191/472842).
[4] See above, p. 117 n. 3; cf. also G. Landra, 'Razzismo biologico e scientismo. Per la scienza e contro i melanconici assertori di un nebuloso spiritualismo', *La Difesa della Razza* (5 Nov. 1942), 9–11.

Evola admitted the failure of his mission in a plaintive letter to Gross, deploring the Germans' refusal to co-operate.[1]

On 9 September 1942 the German view on 'Roman' racialism was summed up by a member of the Racial Policy Office who branded Evola's *Sintesi* as yet another Italian diatribe against the 'Nordic barbarians', as an unconscious attempt to apply the anti-racialist principles of the Catholic Church to the racial problem, as a 'clever improvisation' devoid of scholarly value, and as a striking illustration of 'the low spiritual level of modern Italy, due to racial decline'. He concluded by affirming that there was no point in 'encouraging the dissemination of this publication in Italy unless we want Fascist racial doctrine to remain inferior to our own in clarity and precision'.[2]

As we have seen, Mussolini had declared war on the Jews in 1938 in order to eliminate any strident contrast in the policy of the two Axis Powers. Four years later it was obvious to all concerned that the contrast was more strident than ever before.

The military reverses of the Axis in 1942 and 1943 had the effect of increasing Italy's dependence on German support. But they also had the effect of increasing Mussolini's determination to resist German encroachments on Italian sovereignty, with particular reference to German meddling in the areas under Italian occupation;[3] and it is in the context of this resistance that his opposition to the 'final solution' has to be assessed. D'Ajeta put the point well when he told Plessen on 11 October 1942 that the Duce could not permit foreigners to discriminate between his subjects; nor could he tolerate attempts on the part of the French to use racialism as a means of undermining Italy's position in Africa. And while he fully understood the need for security measures, he would never agree to the deportation of Italian citizens to the East.[4]

When, on 25 February 1943, Ribbentrop pressed for drastic measures against Jews in the areas under Italian control,

[1] Rademacher to Gross, 9 June 1942; Evola to Gross, 23 Nov. 1942 (PA/ibid.).
[2] Memorandum by Hüttig, 9 Sept. 1942 (PA/ibid.).
[3] After his meeting with Hitler at Feltre (19 July 1943) Mussolini said to one of his intimates: 'The Germans . . . want henceforward effective command of the whole Italian front, including the internal one. And this is a condition which neither the Italian people, nor the King, nor yours truly could accept' (Tamaro, *Venti anni di storia*, iii. 475).
[4] Mackensen to Wilhelmstrasse, 11 Oct. 1942 (GFM/5602H/E401595–96); cf. also Italian Foreign Office minute of 10 Oct. 1942 (GFM/5602H/E401592–94) and German note of 20 Oct. 1942 (GFM/5602H/E401589–91).

Mussolini dared not contradict him. Immediately afterwards, however, he allowed himself to be persuaded by his underlings that Italy could not be a party to Germany's crimes against the Jewish people. The following account by Colonel Carlà, an Italian staff officer in Croatia, throws light on his state of mind:

The Commander (of the Italian Second Army), His Excellency Robotti, was summoned to Rome with His Excellency Pirzio Biroli, Governor of Montenegro, in order to discuss this problem (the Jews) . . . The Head of the Government said: 'Minister Ribbentrop who has been in Rome for three days has been pressing me in every way to secure at any price the expulsion of the Yugoslav Jews. I tried to drag the matter out (*tergiversare*), but he insisted. To get rid of him I had to give my consent . . .' His Excellency Robotti . . . remarked that such an order would have painful repercussions among the Yugoslav population . . . The Head of the Government allowed himself to be persuaded and finally declared: 'True, I was compelled to consent to the expulsion, but you all think of whatever excuses you please, so as not to hand over even one single Jew. Say that we have no means of transport to take them to Trieste and that transport by land is impossible.' His Excellency Robotti was happy with this decision. In fact, not a single Jew interned in our camps was ever handed over to the Germans or the Croats.[1]

When, after Mackensen's above-mentioned *démarche* of 18 March, Bastianini urged the Duce not to withdraw his protecting hand from the Jews in Italian-occupied France, the latter readily agreed, despite the assurances just given to Hitler's Ambassador.[2]

On 5 April 1943 the question of Italian resistance to the 'final solution' was raised afresh in the course of a conversation between Mussolini and the Hungarian Prime Minister, Nicholas (Miklós) Kállay, from which the following is worth quoting:

The third point that I (Kállay) wanted to raise with Mussolini was the Jewish question and its implications regarding Hungarian Jews in Italy . . . I could not help being interested in the attitude of Italy in this matter because of its inevitable effect on my position in Hungary. Anti-Jewish measures were now beginning in Italy too [*sic*]. I could not understand why this was necessary. The number of Jews was so small— hardly 60,000—that not even the political or economic reasons which were used, for instance, by Hungarian anti-Semites could be invoked

[1] Poliakov and Sabille, pp. 147–8 (Italian text in id., *Gli ebrei sotto l'occupazione italiana*, Milan, 1956, pp. 152–3).
[2] Bastianini, op. cit., pp. 86–8 (Bastianini's intervention had been requested by Pope Pius XII).

. . . It was quite incomprehensible to me that, while little Hungary did not tolerate outside interference in this matter, while we refused to be swept away by the tide and while I was able to resist deplorably strong internal pressure and categorically to refuse German demands, he, Mussolini, in the total absence of popular anti-Semitism in Italy, should have given in to Nazi Germany. I repeatedly said that I had taken it for granted that he would stand by me in this question—and now I found myself alone among all the leaders of the Axis powers. The official spokesman and the press of Rumania, Slovakia, Bulgaria and Croatia were openly inciting the Germans against Hungary as 'the last haven of the Jews'; even in Poland and Bohemia not a finger was raised in defence of the Jews. Finally, I asked Mussolini most emphatically that there should be no discrimination against Hungarian Jews in Italy and that they should be given the same treatment as other Hungarian subjects. If a state had the right—however questionable it was—to discriminate between its own subjects, in no circumstances could it claim the same right against aliens living on its territory.

In reply the Duce admitted that there was no Jewish problem and no anti-Jewish feeling in Italy, the number and the position of the Italian Jews being 'insignificant':

He had had to take certain measures because the Germans, who were incredibly intolerant and inflexible in this matter, had insisted [*sic*]. He could afford concessions precisely because the problem was so unimportant in Italy. He appreciated and approved of my policy on this question, and he recommended that I persevere in it and congratulated me on having withstood all Germany's pressure and threats. He accepted my views on non-discrimination towards Jews of Hungarian citizenship in Italy. He did not know the exact position in this respect, but, so far as Hungarian Jews were concerned, he would act in accordance with my wishes.[1]

But whatever the Duce's private feelings about German policy in general and the 'final solution' of the Jewish problem in particular, there is no doubt that he remained committed to the Axis alliance right up to the day of his downfall. When, on 20 January 1943, Ciano hinted at the need for a separate peace, he replied 'that the Germans would hold tenaciously'; and on the following day he reaffirmed his decision 'to march with Germany to the end'. On 5 May, addressing a vast crowd of supporters from the balcony of the Palazzo Venezia, he claimed

---

[1] Kállay, *Hungarian Premier*, pp. 151–2, 159.

that the 'bloody sacrifices of these hard times' would be 'recompensed by victory'; on 19 June he declared at a Cabinet meeting that Italy had 'only one alternative: to conquer or fall at the side of Germany'; and on 16 July he told a group of Fascist hierarchs that he would rather go down fighting than surrender to the Anglo-Americans. On 19 July, after a talk with Hitler at Feltre, he said to his entourage that he was not prepared 'to obliterate at a single stroke twenty years of Fascism'; and on 22 July he assured Grandi that the war was about to be won because within a few days the Germans would 'launch a weapon which will transform the situation'.[1] At the Grand Council session of 24–5 July he affirmed against his better knowledge that German aid to Italy had been 'generous and substantial'; on the same occasion he reproached Alfieri, his Ambassador in Berlin, for wishing to break loose from Germany. Finally, on 26 July—the day after his 'resignation'—he congratulated his successor, Marshal Badoglio, on his decision 'to continue the war together with our allies, as the honour and the interests of the country require at this time'.[2]

Given his continuing commitment to his Axis ally, Mussolini could not back out of the 'common struggle against Jewry'; nor could he openly voice his objections to the German method of solving the Jewish problem. And while he was willing to propitiate the 'Jew-lovers' in his entourage, he was equally willing to propitiate the Jew-baiters. When, in December 1942, Farinacci complained to him of the relative comfort in which 'confined' foreign Jews were allowed to live at Asti in Piedmont, he replied through his private secretary that those Jews would soon be removed to detention camps in Central Italy.[3] And when, in the following month, Preziosi drew his attention to the failure of Fascist racial policy, calling for harsh measures on the German model, he expressed his complete agreement, adding, however, that he did not as yet feel equal to breaking the 'subterranean power' of the Jews. Preziosi subsequently informed a German diplomat in Rome that the Duce not only approved of his crusade against Jewry but aided and encouraged him in every possible way. It remains to add that Mussolini repeatedly

[1] Ciano, *Diario*, ii. 243–4; *O.O.* xxxi. 178; Bianchi, *25 Luglio*, pp. 401–4.
[2] *O.O.* xxxiv. 347–8, 358–9; Alfieri, pp. 335–6.
[3] De Cesare to Farinacci, 2 Jan. 1943 (IC/*Segreteria particolare del Duce*/Job 114/031575).

made use of anti-Semitic arguments in his correspondence with Hitler; in a letter of 8 March 1943, for instance, he referred to Judaism as a 'disease to be cured by fire and the sword'.[1]

The German leaders, for their part, prudently refrained from raising the racial problem with Mussolini until the deteriorating war situation rendered a solution of Italo–German differences a matter of urgency. Even then, they continued to conceal their true intentions from their Italian allies, pretending that all they were aiming at was the 'resettlement' of the Jews and their mobilization for 'labour service'. On 11 October 1942 Himmler assured the Fascist dictator that the racial measures adopted by the Third Reich were perfectly humane and rational: 'I told the Duce that we had put politically dangerous Jews into concentration camps; the other Jews had been drafted for road-building in the East . . . The oldest Jews were being accommodated in Homes for the Aged in Berlin, Munich, and Vienna. The other old Jews had been sent to the little town of Theresienstadt, a kind of Ghetto for Aged Jews, where they received their pensions and emoluments and where they could do as they liked . . .'[2] Mussolini was not taken in by Himmler's attempt at concealment, having learnt the truth about the 'resettlement' of the Jews from Prince Otto von Bismarck, the indiscreet Counsellor of the German Embassy in Rome, nearly two months earlier.[3] But he was comprehensibly unwilling to antagonize his powerful guest for the sake of the Jews.

In the light of the evidence now available, it is clear that to Hitler the destruction of European Jewry was primarily an end in itself; it is equally clear, however, that by the end of 1942 the German leaders were genuinely worried about the (real or alleged) anti-Axis activities of the 'Jewish Fifth Column' in Italy

[1] Note by Doertenbach, 2 Feb. 1943 (YVS/K206733–35); *Hitler e Mussolini*, p. 145; Simoni, p. 323 (entry for 13 Mar. 1943).
[2] H. Krausnick, 'Himmler über seinen Besuch bei Mussolini vom 11.–14. Oktober 1942', *VJZG* 4 (Oct. 1956), 423–6.
[3] On 17 August 1942 Bismarck revealed to the Palazzo Chigi what 'resettlement' in the East entailed; on 21 August the Palazzo Chigi informed Mussolini (D. Carpi, 'Ma'asseh ha-hatzalah shel yehudim b'ezor ha-kibbush ha-italki b'Kroatia', in *Nissiyonot u-f'ulot hatzalah b'tekufat ha-shoah*, ed. Y. Gutman, Jerusalem, 1976, p. 419). In May 1943 Wilhelm Kube, General Commissioner for White Ruthenia, told a visiting Fascist delegation in Minsk that the Jews were being exterminated in gas chambers (YVS/K206919); on Kube's reservations about the 'final solution', see H. Heiber, 'Aus den Akten des Gauleiters Kube', *VJZG* 4 (Jan. 1956), 67–92.

and the Italian-occupied territories. On 13 December Goebbels wrote in his diary:

The Italians are extremely lax in the treatment of the Jews. They protect the Italian Jews both in Tunis and in occupied France and will not permit their being drafted for work or compelled to wear the Star of David. This shows once again that Fascism does not really dare to get down to fundamentals but is very superficial regarding problems of vital importance (*in wichtigsten Problemen an der Oberfläche haften bleibt*). The Jewish question is causing us a lot of trouble. Everywhere, even among our allies, the Jews have friends to help them (*Hilfsmannschaften*) which is a proof that they are still playing an important role even in the Axis camp. All the more they are shorn of power (*entmachtet*) within Germany herself.[1]

On 29 January 1943 Himmler, in a letter to Ribbentrop, drew attention to the grave security problems which Italian resistance to the 'final solution' was creating throughout the territories under Axis control: 'As for Jews of foreign nationality, I want ... Italian and other foreign nationals of Jewish race to be removed from the Italian-occupied area in France. The Jews in this area are the element of resistance and the authors of the Communist propaganda which is particularly dangerous for the Italian troops. Moreover, the continued presence of the Jews in the Italian sphere of influence provides many circles in France and in the rest of Europe with a pretext for playing down the Jewish question, it being argued that not even our Axis partner Italy sees eye to eye with us on the Jewish issue.'[2]

Hitler himself, while still reposing full confidence in the person of the Duce, was alarmed at the reports on Jewish subversion and espionage in the areas under Italian occupation. That at any rate is what Ribbentrop told the International Military Tribunal at Nuremberg on 2 April 1946, in reply to a question on his above-mentioned meeting with Mussolini of 25 February 1943:

This document (memorandum on meeting between Ribbentrop and Mussolini on February 25, 1943) refers to the fact that a large-scale espionage organization had been uncovered in France. The Führer ... told me to speak to Mussolini and see to it that in cases of Jews involved in these acts of sabotage and espionage the Italian government or the army did not intervene (to protect the culprits) ... I now

[1] Goebbels, *Tagebücher*, pp. 222–3.
[2] GFM/5602H/E40158–12.

recollect very well that at the time I discussed the matter with Mussolini and begged him to adopt suitable measures since the Jews were furnishing all the information to the British and American Intelligence Services. At least that was the information which the Führer was constantly receiving ... I spoke to Mussolini at that time because the Führer was of the opinion that we had to establish a clear situation.[1]

There is some evidence that Hitler's and Ribbentrop's growing concern about the 'Jewish Fifth Column' in Italy was at least partly due to confidential information furnished by the Italian Jew-baiters. In November 1942 one of Preziosi's associates submitted to the Germans a report to the effect that the Jews at Trieste controlled or owned about 400 joint-stock companies and other enterprises and that their total wealth amounted to over $4\frac{1}{2}$ billion lire. On 14 February 1943 this document was passed on to Ribbentrop who quoted it in his talk with Mussolini eleven days later.[2] On 1 February Preziosi himself told a member of the German Embassy in Rome that the *de facto* head of the Fascist Party, Vice-Secretary Mario Farnesi, was a notorious 'Jew-lover' and a 'pliant tool of the influential Jewish wire-pullers at Trieste', that both the Ministry of the Interior and the High Command were firmly opposed to drastic measures against the Jews, and that in a country like Italy 'even a Mussolini was not in a position to eliminate Jewish influence'. On 15 February Mackensen, commenting on the above utterances in a dispatch to the Wilhelmstrasse, gave it as his opinion that Preziosi's assessment of Fascist racial policy was substantially accurate.[3] And on 23 June Hitler himself, in the course of an intimate talk with Goebbels, deplored the Duce's failure to tackle the Jewish problem in a radical manner. In Germany the Jews had been liquidated; even if the Reich were to lose the war, they would not be the beneficiaries. In Italy, on the other hand, where they had merely been subjected to mild discrimination, they were now preparing to stage a come-back. There would (Hitler thought) be no problem if Mussolini were still 'young and

---

[1] *IMT* x. 406–7; cf. also U. Cavallero, *Comando supremo. Diario 1940–43 del capo di S.M.G.*, Bologna, 1948, p. 437 (entry for 16 Jan. 1943).
[2] E. von Druffel (Trieste) to Wilhelmstrasse, 23 Nov. 1942; Bergmann to Ribbentrop, 14 Feb. 1943 (GFM/5602H/E401581–86, 87–88); URO, *Judenverfolgung in Italien*, p. 156; cf. also Gherardi Bon, op. cit., pp. 167–74.
[3] *YVS*/K206733–35, 29–30. On Farnesi's philo-Semitism, cf. Mackensen to Wilhelmstrasse, 30 July 1943 (GFM/133/I/72646).

resilient'; unfortunately, however, the Fascist leader was by now an 'old and worn-out man' who was fast losing control of the situation.[1]

Five weeks before the above conversation, the Führer had begun to lay plans for the contingency of a second Italian 'betrayal' which were to have dire consequences for the Italian people in general and the Italian Jews in particular. Under the code names 'Alaric' and 'Konstantin' measures had been prepared for the occupation of the Italian peninsula and the assumption of Italy's military responsibilities in the South of France and in the Balkans. Transport arrangements had been made for three SS divisions to be moved, if necessary, to the Italian Alpine border and for the transfer of armoured divisions from the East. Army Group West in France had offered two armoured and six infantry divisions for the operation, in addition to which two parachute divisions were to be alerted in the event of Italy's withdrawal from the war to control the central Alpine passes. It was calculated that the move to Northern and Central Italy would take eight to ten days. On 28 July—three days after the fall of Fascism—'Alaric' and 'Konstantin' were given final shape as Operation 'Axis', the execution of which was entrusted to Mussolini's *bête noire*, the Italophobe Field-Marshal Rommel.[2]

Hitler's prime concern in the Mediterranean theatre was to keep the war as far away as possible from the borders of Germany. Alfieri put the point well when he wrote: 'Germany ... proposes to preserve her forces intact, to build up new ones and put off as long as possible any eventual assault on the territory of the Reich. *This is why she considers friendly and occupied countries as bastions of the German fortress. Italy constitutes in effect just one of these bastions.*'[3] Given this approach, Mussolini was right in affirming that there could be no separate peace with Hitler's consent.[4]

While the Germans were drawing up plans for the occupation of Italy, the Italians were preparing to break loose from the

---

[1] *IFZ/ED 83/1*, Goebbels-Kriegstagebuch I, 14, pp. 262–3 (see above, p. 103 n. 1).

[2] J. Schröder, *Italiens Kriegsaustritt 1943. Die deutschen Gegenmassnahmen im italienischen Raum: Fall 'Alarich' und 'Achse'*, Göttingen, 1969, pp. 176–95, 215–20.

[3] Alfieri, pp. 298–9.

[4] At Feltre Mussolini said to his entourage: 'It's so easy to talk about a separate peace. But what would be Hitler's attitude? Do you really believe that he would allow us to retain our liberty of action?' (ibid., p. 315).

German alliance. On 15 May—two days after the surrender of the Axis forces in North Africa—the King of Italy drafted three memorandums setting forth his views on the state of the war and concluding with the words: 'We must keep in close touch with Hungary, Romania, and Bulgaria who have little love for the Germans. We must not forget to make every possible gesture of courtesy to the rulers of England and America. We must think very seriously of the possible need to detach Italy's fate from that of Germany whose internal collapse might come without warning (*improvviso*), as happened to Imperial Germany in 1918.'[1]

On 3 June the King received Grandi in audience and told him that he was resolved to put an end to the Fascist dictatorship at the 'opportune moment'. He added that Grandi and his friends should help him 'to obtain the constitutional means', i.e. a vote in the Chamber or in the Grand Council. In the meantime he would wait on events.[2]

He did not have long to wait. On 11 June the fortified island of Pantelleria with a garrison of 12,000 men surrendered to the Anglo-Americans without a struggle. Two days later Lampedusa fell; and on the night of 9 July the Allies landed in Sicily where the astonished British troops beheld, painted on the walls of houses, the inscriptions *Viva Stevens*; *Viva il Colonnello Stevens*.[3] It was evident that the Italian people were sick of the 'Fascist war' and that Mussolini's soldiers were no longer willing to fight and die for the Greater German Reich.

On 14 July General Ambrosio, in a 'Note to the Duce', described the fate of Sicily as 'sealed', adding that the Italian army (which had been virtually destroyed in Greece, Russia, and Africa) was in no state to parry an invasion of metropolitan territory. He concluded by saying that, if it proved impossible to prevent the constitution of an Allied second front, it would be up to the government to consider 'whether it would not be expedient to spare the country further sorrow and ruin and to anticipate the end of the struggle'. On the following day Ambrosio returned to the attack, telling Mussolini that the war was lost and that Italy could not 'accept the use of her territory, with no hope of

---

[1] Facsimile in Tamaro, *Due anni di storia*, i. 15.

[2] Bianchi, op. cit., pp. 384–7.

[3] Colonel H. Stevens was the celebrated broadcaster in the BBC Italian Service.

salvation, as the outer defence of the Reich'. That being so, the Duce should seek an exit from the war without delay, preferably with the Führer's assent.[1]

While Mussolini's generals were calling for the opening of negotiations with the Allies, Hitler's military advisers were pressing for German control of Italy under the nominal authority of the Duce. On 15 July General Jodl stressed the need for the setting-up of a 'strict and unified Axis command' and the placing of German commanders 'at all important points in the Mediterranean area'; and two days later the Führer himself declared that unless it proved possible to effect a 'radical change' in Italy, there would be no point in sending further troops to the Italian front.[2] But disgusted though he was with the performance of his ally, Hitler feared to take drastic action lest this should drive the Italians into open revolt.

On 16 July Farinacci, in the course of a meeting between Mussolini and a group of worried Fascist hierarchs, persuaded the dictator to summon the Grand Council, thus unwittingly setting the stage for the palace revolution which was to put an end to the Fascist regime nine days later.[3]

On 19 July the two leaders met at Feltre. In a last effort to push his failing ally back on the rails, the Führer talked for hours on end; but he refrained from raising the question of a unified Axis command, nor did he make any mention of the Jewish peril in Italy. The Duce, for his part, hardly ever opened his mouth, except in order to reaffirm his loyalty to the Pact of Steel ('Ours is a common cause, Führer'). After the meeting he told his entourage that there had been no need to bring up the question of a separate peace since Hitler had 'promised "faithfully" to send all the assistance we ask for'. It was now evident to the plotters that Mussolini would never take Italy out of the war on his own account, no matter how disastrous the situation.[4]

On the very day of the meeting at Feltre Himmler informed

---

[1] F.-K. von Plehwe, *Schicksalsstunden in Rom. Ende eines Bündnisses*, Berlin, 1967, pp. 65–8; Tamaro, *Due anni di storia*, i. 186.

[2] W. Hubatsch (ed.), *Kriegstagebuch des Oberkommandos der Wehrmacht*, iii/2: 1943, Frankfurt/Main, 1963, pp. 789–90, 798–9.

[3] Fornari, *Mussolini's Gadfly*, pp. 194–5; cf. Bottai, *Vent' anni e un giorno*, p. 277.

[4] *Kriegstagebuch des Oberkommandos der Wehrmacht*, iii. 805–7; BA/MA/III M/1000/39–50/Kriegstagebuch Seekriegsleitung, 19 July 1943, p. 382; PA/RAM 34/43/Schmidt-Niederschriften; *Hitler e Mussolini*, pp. 165–90; *O.O.* xxxiv. 342; Alfieri, p. 317; cf. also Deakin, pp. 399–418.

Martin Bormann, Hitler's secretary, that a *coup d'état* was being planned in Rome with the aim of installing an anti-German government under Marshal Badoglio, but that Italian circles loyal to the Axis had organized a counter-movement, led by Riccardi, Ricci, Farinacci, Preziosi, and others, which aimed at 'setting up a War Cabinet for the purpose of conducting a determined anti-Masonic, anti-Jewish, and pro-German policy, the radical elimination of traitors of every kind, the reconstruction of the Fascist Grand Council in permanent session, and the creation of a unified military command for the Axis forces. They seek German support for putting the Duce completely in the picture, with the aim of the immediate granting of full powers to Riccardi or one of his above-named collaborators.'[1]

Immediately after the Feltre meeting Italian discontent with the Pact of Steel and with the Duce as its representative came to a head. But Hitler and his henchmen made no particular preparations to meet a crisis, having been advised by their Ambassador in Rome that Farinacci, the leading pro-German and the leading specialist in crisis situations, had forced a meeting of the Grand Council in order to introduce the sweeping reforms required to invigorate the Italian war effort.[2] On 25 July—the very day of Mussolini's downfall—Goebbels noted in his diary:

In the course of the day we received confidential information to the effect that a certain change (*Umschwung*) was taking place in Italian domestic politics. Led by Farinacci, the Old Guard Fascists have requested the Duce to call a meeting of the Fascist Grand Council. At this meeting, according to Mackensen, the Duce is to be asked to initiate more energetic policies. He is to be persuaded to get rid of the burden of holding so many offices so that he may regain his initiative and strength for guiding the over-all policies and the war effort of Italy . . . Farinacci is not only an energetic man but also a pronounced friend of Germany. We can depend on him blindly.[3]

Misled by Mackensen, the German leaders allowed events to take their course; indeed it was decided that the preliminary alert for operations 'Alaric' and 'Konstantin' should be called

[1] Brandt to Wagner, 19 July 1943 (GFM/133/I/72411–12).
[2] Mackensen to Wilhelmstrasse, 22 and 24 July 1945 (GFM/133/I/72420–24, 72435–36).
[3] Goebbels, *Tagebücher*, p. 367. The last two sentences (which are missing from the German original) have been quoted from the English translation (*The Goebbels Diaries*, ed. L. P. Lochner, New York, 1948, p. 460).

off. The complacency of Berlin was fully shared by the Duce who (despite warnings from Farinacci and many others) was confident of his own ability to handle the situation and placed implicit trust in the chief plotter, Victor Emmanuel III.[1]

The way was thus left free to the conspirators (if the term may be applied to men of widely divergent views, some of whom had no clear idea of what they intended to achieve). In the words of Anfuso, 'each character donned his mask and came on to the stage'.[2] At the Grand Council meeting of 24–5 July the pro-German Farinacci vied with his anti-German rivals, led by Grandi and Bottai, in denouncing Mussolini's policies and his conduct of the war. Grandi's motion (which called for the revival of all the existing organs of government and the resumption by the King of the command of the armed forces) was approved by nineteen members, with seven others voting against it and one abstaining. On the following afternoon the Duce was dismissed by the King and placed under arrest. Badoglio formed a caretaker government of senior officers and civilian technicians; the Fascist Party was dissolved and the Fascist militia incorporated into the army. Farinacci and Preziosi fled to Germany where they were received by the Führer; Buffarini, Le Pera, and Interlandi were arrested and imprisoned.[3]

---

[1] Schröder, op. cit., pp. 215–16; Mackensen to Wilhelmstrasse, 24 July 1943 (GFM/133/I/72433–34); Bianchi, p. 656.

[2] Anfuso, *Da Palazza Venezia al Lago di Garda*, p. 282.

[3] On the Grand Council meeting and the fall of Fascism, see Deakin, pp. 439–85; Bianchi, pp. 644–733; C. Scorza, *La notte del Gran Consiglio*, 2nd edn., Milan, 1969; on Farinacci, GFM/133/I/72461 (Mackensen to Wilhelmstrasse, 26 July 1943); Fornari, op. cit., pp. 205–8; on Preziosi, GFM/133/I/72644 (Mackensen to Wilhelmstrasse, 30 July 1943); F. Bellotti, *La repubblica di Mussolini. 26 luglio 1943–25 aprile 1945*, Milan, 1947, pp. 7–22; on Le Pera, A. Strazzera-Perniciani, *Umanità ed eroismo nella vita segreta di Regina Coeli—Roma 1943–1944*, Rome, 1959, pp. 22, 25; on Buffarini and Interlandi, GFM/133/II/72127 (Rahn to Wilhelmstrasse, 13 Sept. 1943); E. Dollmann, *Roma nazista*, Milan, 1951, p. 261; G. Pini and D. Susmel, *Mussolini. L'uomo e l'opera* (Firenze, 1963), iv. 301.

WITH THE overthrow of the Fascist regime Italian racial policy had lost its point. But Marshal Badoglio, having made a public pretence of continuing the war at Germany's side, was understandably reluctant to antagonize his 'ally' by repealing the anti-Jewish laws. As he put it in his memoirs three years later: 'It was not possible at that moment to abrogate publicly all the racial laws without coming into violent conflict with the Germans or, to be more precise, with Hitler. He had not only inspired this legislation, he had actually forced it on Mussolini [*sic*] who only a few months earlier had declared in the Senate that there was no Jewish problem in Italy. I sent for representative Jews and told them that, though it was not possible at the moment to revoke the laws, they would not be carried out.'[1] The spokesmen of Italian Jewry, for their part, confined themselves to expressing the 'well-founded hope' that the new rulers, having put an end to the Fascist tyranny, would cancel the anti-Jewish decrees 'in due course'. They had to wait until 20 January 1944, by which time the greater part of Italy was under German control.[2]

While the racial measures against the Italian Jews were only slightly relaxed, the policy of aiding and protecting foreign Jews under Italian jurisdiction was stepped up. At the beginning of August Angelo Donati opened negotiations with the Badoglio Government and the Allied diplomatic representatives at the Vatican in order to make possible the evacuation of Jewish refugees to North Africa. On 24 August Sir Francis Osborne, the British Minister to the Holy See, reported to the Foreign Office:

I have had several visits from an Italian Jew, Donati . . . who has been doing excellent work at considerable personal risk and expense on behalf of refugee Jews (mostly Yugoslavs, but also Poles, Germans, Austrians, Czechs, etc.) in Italy and more particularly that part of Southern France the occupation of which is now being turned over

[1] Badoglio, *L'Italia nella seconda guerra mondiale*, p. 92; for a critical analysis of Badoglio's highly misleading account, see De Felice, *Storia degli ebrei italiani*, pp. 428–30.
[2] AUCII/1943/Abolizione decreti razziali/Memorandum of 30 Aug. 1943; *Gazzetta Ufficiale*, 9 Feb. 1944.

from the Italians to the Germans. There are already some 14,000 in Italy. He now hopes to arrange for entry into Italy *in transit* of some 15,000 others from the South of France who will otherwise be seized by the Germans and transported to ... certain death. The italian [*sic*] authorities have shown great humanity and goodwill but in the present circumstances their financial, food and accommodation resources do not permit of the absorption in Italy of these 15,000. Donati therefore urges that arrangements should be made for their shipment at the earliest possible moment to Algeria, Tunis and Moroccon [*sic*], at least for temporary reception ... Donati says that ample dollar funds are available for their settlement, but owing to exchange difficulties funds cannot be transferred to Italy. It is believed that Italy could supply shipping if we could supply fuel. If possible, it would also be desirable to remove from Italy the 14,000 foreign Jews already here ... Please give the proposal your urgent and sympathetic consideration.[1]

In a subsequent telegram Osborne pointed out that, according to Donati, four Italian liners (which had been used for the repatriation of Italians from East Africa and could take 9,000 people per voyage) were now available for the transport of Jewish refugees:

Donati says that the costs of 5,500 dollars per day of the voyage ... *plus* fuel and lubricants, war risk insurance and the expenses of food for the passengers could all be paid by the American Jewish organisation, but that the oil and lubricants would have to be supplied by the British and American Governments ... The four ships in question are now ready to undertake the three trips necessary to convey the some 30,000 (Jewish refugees) to North Africa. But the British and American Governments should expedite the arrangements as far as possible so as to make use of the ships while they are available.[2]

Donati himself tells us that the new Italian Government 'agreed to admit to Italy the number of Jews who could feasibly be evacuated to North Africa' and that the British and American governments 'had no objection in principle to his solution'. He adds that at the above-mentioned inter-ministerial meeting of 28 August (which was presided over by Badoglio himself) 'every assurance was given that the possibilities for carrying out this operation existed'—this on the erroneous assumption that the final break with Germany could be postponed until October.

[1] PRO/F.O.371/12671/49/48.
[2] Ibid.

Donati thereupon opened negotiations for chartering the four ships which were to take the Jews to North Africa; and on 8 September, after a talk with Ivanoe Bonomi (who was to succeed Badoglio as Prime Minister in June 1944), he left Rome for Nice in order to organize the departure of the Jews to Italy. On the very same day, however, the premature announcement of the Italian surrender dealt the death-blow to his evacuation scheme.[1]

On the following day (the Germans having meanwhile taken over the Italian zone in the South of France) Osborne sent yet another vain appeal to his superiors in London: 'I have been asked to draw your attention urgently to the situation of refugee Jews in Dalmatia (5,000) Greece (at least 15,000) Albania (1,000) and Istria and Venetia (7,000) in the event of replacement of Italian by German troops. In the first three cases communications with Italy would almost certainly be cut. In the last case German control of Italian territory is apparently contemplated. No suggestion is offered by Donati . . . but need of provision for their protection is advanced . . . The number of Jewish refugees in the South of France is now given as 15,000/20,000.'[2]

By the time Osborne's telegram reached the Foreign Office (10 September), neither the Italians nor the Allies were any longer in a position to provide for the protection of the Jews. The King and Badoglio had fled to Brindisi, Rome had capitulated to Field-Marshal Kesselring's forces, Trieste had been occupied by units of Rommel's Army Group B, and nearly all Italian troops in Yugoslavia, Greece, and the Aegean Islands had surrendered to their former ally. On the following day, 11 September, Kesselring declared all Italian territory, including Rome, to be a theatre of war under German military control; and on 13 September Hitler signed blanket instructions for Albert Speer, his Minister of Armaments, concerning the 'safeguarding' of the Italian war industry. Italy, in Mussolini's above-quoted phrase, had now been 'reduced from the position of a confederated province to the worse one of a colony', with fatal results for the Italian Jews.[3]

In assessing the impact of the German occupation on the

---

[1] Poliakov and Sabille, *Jews under the Italian Occupation*, pp. 40–2.
[2] See above, p. 343 n. 1.
[3] Deakin, *Brutal Friendship*, pp. 530–3; Schröder, *Italiens Kriegsaustritt*, pp. 283–313; G. Janssen, *Das Ministerium Speer*, Frankfurt/Main–Berlin, 1968, pp. 250–2.

Jewish tragedy in Italy, we shall do well to bear in mind three basic facts.

First, the geographical distribution of Italian Jewry. Ever since the expulsions of 1492 and 1541 Italian Jewish life had been confined to the north of the country; south of Rome there was only the barest handful of Jews, with a community of a few hundred in Naples and a nominal one of very recent establishment at Palermo where the Allied military authorities had abrogated the racial laws as early as 12 July.[1] Southern Italy was liberated by the Anglo-Americans before the end of 1943, and while defending it Kesselring's forces were too fully occupied with military matters to devote much attention to the racial question. Hence the foreign Jews interned at Alberobello, Ateleta, Campagna, Ferramonti Tarsia, and elsewhere in the south were freed after little further suffering. The community of Naples likewise underwent no great molestation before the city was captured by British troops on 1 October. But the expected Allied landings in the Gulf of Genoa (which would have made a rapid German retreat inevitable) unfortunately failed to materialize, with the result that the area of Jewish settlement from Rome northwards, including the capital, remained under the complete control of the Germans until June 1944. It remains to add that until the announcement of the Italian armistice all German plans had been made on the assumption that Kesselring's troops would be withdrawn to the north as quickly as possible—if only because their communications, if they remained in the south, would be at the mercy of their equivocal allies. As late as 10 September Goebbels wrote in his diary: 'Naturally we shall not be able to hold Southern Italy. We must withdraw northwards beyond Rome.'[2] In the second half of September, however, the complete success of Operation 'Axis'—the speedy collapse of all Italian resistance to their former comrades-in-arms and the ponderous slowness of the Allied advance on Naples—caused the Führer to change his mind. It was this accident of politics and strategy which spelt the death-warrant for several thousand Jews.

[1] Roth, *History of the Jews*, p. 542; S. Della Pergola, 'The Geography of Italian Jews; Countrywide Patterns', in E. Toaff (ed.), *Studi sull'Ebraismo italiano in memoria di Cecil Roth*, Rome, 1974, pp. 99-100.
[2] G. A. Shepperd, *The Italian Campaign 1943-1945. A Political and Military Re-assessment*, London, 1968, pp. 137-56, 389-90; M. Howard, *Grand Strategy*, *IV*, London, 1972, pp. 515-38, 602-13; Goebbels, *Tagebücher*, p. 395.

Second, Hitler's decision, taken immediately after the *coup d'état* of 25 July, to rescue the imprisoned Duce and restore him to power. Most of the Führer's advisers were opposed to such a course. The German military chiefs were in favour of outright military occupation. Mackensen reported that the Fascist Party had 'disappeared from the stage unsung and unheard', adding that the Fascist leaders, in dealing a political death-blow to Mussolini, had unwittingly 'committed suicide'. Rudolf Likus, an intimate of Ribbentrop's, affirmed that in view of the general mood of the Italian people 'any attempt to reinstate the Duce by force would, at least in the present phase, enjoy no prospect of success'. Herbert Kappler, the German police attaché in Rome, warned Himmler that Fascism was dead and could not be revived. Even Goebbels was doubtful whether the Duce was capable of playing a useful role; the elimination of Fascism (he argued) would enable Germany to annex the South Tyrol and Venetia, whereas a 'régime under the leadership of the Duce would presumably fall heir to all the rights and duties incident to the Three-Power Pact'.[1] But Hitler brushed all these objections aside, insisting that there was no one behind Badoglio 'except Jews and riffraff' and that hence the restoration of Fascism was a practical proposition—Nazism was, after all, the German variant of Fascism, and the Führer was obsessed by the idea that the collapse of the kindred system might set an unfortunate example before his subjects. On 12 September Mussolini was rescued by German glider troops and flown to Hitler's headquarters at Rastenburg; on 15 September it was announced that he had 'resumed the supreme direction of Fascism in Italy'; and on 23 September the composition of the new Fascist administration was made public. If the setting-up of the 'Italian Social Republic' had enabled Mussolini to recover some measure of independence, it might have saved the Jews from a great tragedy, given the Duce's aversion to the German method of solving the Jewish problem. But since he was now virtually a prisoner of the Germans, his reinstatement had the effect of

[1] Deakin, op. cit., pp. 492–7; GFM/133/I/72502–6 (Mackensen to Wilhelmstrasse, 27 July 1943); GFM/146/129360–69 (memorandum by Likus, 13 Aug. 1943, submitted to Hitler on 15 Aug.); von Plehwe, *Schicksalsstunden in Rom*, pp. 120–1, 169; Goebbels, *Tagebücher*, pp. 413–14 (entry for 13 Sept. 1943).

facilitating the implementation of the 'final solution' in Italy.[1]

Third, Hitler's change of mind with regard to the projected occupation of the Vatican City. After the *coup d'état* of 25 July his first thought had been to stage a second putsch and to capture the new government by force. And when asked if the exits of the Vatican should be blocked, he had answered that he would 'go right into the Vatican': 'Do you think the Vatican embarrasses me? We'll take that over right away.' Subsequently, however, under pressure from Ribbentrop and Goebbels, he had agreed to spare the Holy See. On 11 September Goebbels noted in his diary: 'The Vatican has inquired of our Ambassador whether its rights would be safeguarded in the event of our occupying Rome. The Führer has sent an affirmative reply.'[2] Of all the decisions taken by Hitler after the Italian 'betrayal', this was the only one which benefited the Jews, for it enabled the Church to save a not inconsiderable number of Jewish lives.

Even before the 'liberation' of his brother dictator, Hitler had taken steps 'to wipe the slate clean in Italy', ordering the setting-up of a political or military system which would take effective control of the country and which would bring under its wing any future Fascist administration. Dr. Rudolf Rahn, Mackensen's successor in Rome, had become plenipotentiary of the Greater German Reich. Obergruppenführer (SS Lieutenant-General) Karl Wolff, hitherto chief of Himmler's personal staff, had been appointed commander of the SS in Italy and 'security adviser' to the projected Fascist puppet government. The two border provinces of Venezia Giulia and Alto Adige had been placed under two German Gauleiters, Friedrich Rainer at Trieste and Franz Hofer at Innsbruck. For the rest, Italy had been divided into two zones, operational and occupied, the former coming under Kesselring's Army Group South and the latter under Rommel's Army Group B.[3]

---

[1] Heiber (ed.), *Hitlers Lagebesprechungen*, p. 369; Schröder, op. cit., pp. 320–5; Goebbels, *Tagebücher* p. 418; *O.O.* xxxii. 231.

[2] *Hitlers Lagebesprechungen*, p. 329; Goebbels, *Tagebücher*, pp. 373, 406: cf. also Rahn, *Ruheloses Leben*, pp. 232–3.

[3] Directive of 10 Sept. 1943 (GFM/131/III/72072–75); E. Collotti, *L'amministrazione tedesca dell'Italia occupata 1943–1945*, Milan, 1963, pp. 221–3, 407–9; cf. also IFZ/ZS 126 I (testimony of General H. Röttiger, 26 June 1952). On Wolff's 'moderation' (because of his conviction that Germany had lost the war), see Weizsäcker's deposition of 19 April 1949 (IFZ/ZS 528) and YVS/TRO–10/639/*Strafsache gegen Karl Wolff*, p. 313; cf. also Moellhausen, *La carta perdente*, pp. 280–2.

When the Duce arrived at Rastenburg on 14 September, the Führer received him with warmth. The next day, however, he told him bluntly that his policy of non-intervention in Italian domestic matters had been a fatal mistake. On 17 September Goebbels noted in his diary that Hitler had lost his illusions about his erstwhile Italian mentor: 'Obviously sentimental, emotional considerations no longer influence him'. And on 23 September, after an intimate talk with his master, he recorded that the latter had no intention of making 'the personality of the Duce the corner-stone of our relations with Italy':

> The Duce's personality did not impress him as powerfully this time as at their earlier meetings. The main reason may be that the Duce now came to the Führer without any power and that the Führer accordingly looked at him somewhat more critically. The Duce has not drawn the moral conclusions from Italy's catastrophe which the Führer expected. He was naturally overjoyed to see the Führer and to be fully at liberty again. But the Führer expected that the first thing the Duce would do would be to wreak full vengeance on his betrayers. He gave no such indication, however, which showed his real limitations. He is not a revolutionary like the Führer or Stalin ... The Führer now realizes that Italy never was a Power, is no power to-day and will not be a Power in the future ... He now demands territorial safeguards to prevent any further crisis.

On the same occasion Hitler told his Propaganda Minister that Edda Ciano (whom he accused of 'exerting an unwholesome influence' on her father) was probably Jewish on her mother's side: 'The Führer ... is convinced that territorial guarantees alone can give us some sort of security with reference to Italy if the Duce, after all his bitter experiences, again places himself in the hands of his daughter Edda.'[1]

Preziosi (who had by now become Hitler's *homme de confiance*) did his best to pour oil on the flames, deploring the Duce's failure to eliminate the Jews from Italian life and denouncing the 'Jew-lovers' in the new Fascist Cabinet, with special reference to Buffarini (the new Minister of the Interior) and Pavolini (the new Party Secretary). On 23 September he drafted a letter to Ribbentrop in which he accused Buffarini of sabotaging the racial laws he was supposed to administer. On 9 October he handed the draft to Ribbentrop's second-in-command, Baron

[1] *The Goebbels Diaries*, p. 519; Goebbels, *Tagebücher*, pp. 434–7.

Gustav Adolf von Steengracht, and told him that Mussolini was surrounded by traitors, adding that 'the only one who could break this circle was the Führer'.[1] On 30 October he initiated an anti-Jewish campaign in Hitler's paper; simultaneously he lashed out at the 'Jew-lovers' of Salò in a series of Italian-language broadcasts over Munich radio. And on 18 November he paid a visit to Goebbels who noted in his diary that Preziosi's account of the situation in Italy 'gave much food for thought. He even criticized the Duce very severely and blamed him for not having hewn to the line in his treatment of Jews and Masons. That, he said, was the reason for his fall'. Subsequently Preziosi submitted to Goebbels several exposés about Mussolini and his entourage which the latter found 'very depressing': 'Despite his grave debacle the Duce has learned nothing. He is still surrounded by traitors, former Freemasons and Jew-lovers who give him entirely wrong advice ... It is nauseating to read these reports. The Duce has learned nothing and forgotten nothing.'[2]

Hitler was impressed by Preziosi's reports, given his spiritual affinity with the dean of Italian Jew-baiters; and Ribbentrop, though more sceptical, ordered Rahn 'to keep an eye on Buffarini'. Rahn himself was inclined to think that Buffarini might indeed be 'planning treachery', but other German observers in Italy dismissed Preziosi as an ideological crank who need not be taken seriously. On 16 December Mussolini's German A.D.C., Colonel Johann Jandl, advised Berlin that Preziosi's friend Canevari—an untrustworthy intriguer who had been expelled from the Royal Army and was now Secretary-General of the Fascist War Office—hoped to effect a 'big ministerial reshuffle' with Preziosi's help and that Preziosi himself, in a talk with Rahn, had pressed for the dismissal of Buffarini, Pavolini, and Tullio Tamburini (the new Chief of Police), on top of which he maintained that 'another great betrayal' was being hatched 'in the Duce's immediate circle'.

---

[1] Note by Hilger, 12 Oct. 1943 (GFM/132/123679–81). Ironically, the only member of the new Cabinet to enjoy Preziosi's 'complete confidence' was Marshal Graziani who claimed descent from a Jewish banker named Baruch (*Processo Graziani*, I, Rome, 1948, p. 49).

[2] G. Preziosi, 'Die geheimen Mächte in Italien. Zur Vorgeschichte des Badoglio-Verrats'. *V.B.*, 30 and 31 Oct. 1943; id., 'Zur Vorgeschichte des Badoglio-Verrats. Folgen der ungelösten Judenfrage in Italien', *V.B.*, 14 and 15 Nov. 1943; Anfuso, *Da Palazzo Venezia al Lago di Garda*, p. 348; *The Goebbels Diaries*, pp. 586, 609–10.

Jandl thought that 'we ought to be sceptical about wholesale accusations of this kind'; to claim that one could not trust anyone at all in Italy was 'to throw out the baby with the bath-water'. For the rest, 'Buffarini's type, his reassuring, conciliatory, pacifying manner, suits the Duce who considers him useful for maintaining his internal balance of power.' Jandl's dispatch appears to have had the desired effect, for soon after the Wilhelmstrasse reached the conclusion that the charges against Buffarini were unfounded, and the 'Buffarini affair' was closed for a space.[1]

Undeterred by this set-back, Preziosi (who, after a brief visit to Italy, returned to Germany in December) continued to denounce the 'Jew-lovers' in Mussolini's entourage over Munich radio. And on 31 January 1944 he sent the Duce a twelve-page memorandum on the Jewish peril in which he called for the 'total elimination' of Jews, 'half-breeds', and 'Jew-tainted' Gentiles from Italian life, affirming that no one 'with a single drop of Jewish blood in his veins' could possibly be loyal to the Rome–Berlin Axis. A copy of this document was transmitted to the Führer. Mussolini was furious; speaking to Count Serafino Mazzolini, the new *de facto* head of the Foreign Ministry, he described Preziosi as a 'repulsive creature, a real figure of an unfrocked priest'. There was, however, nothing he could do about Preziosi's underhand activities in Germany, given the latter's 'special relationship' with Hitler; he decided, therefore, to bring him under control by making him a member of his administration. On 15 March he appointed him 'Inspector-General of the Race, directly subordinate to the Duce'; and on 18 April he had his Council of Ministers ratify the appointment. Preziosi took advantage of his promotion to step up his vendetta against the 'Jew-lovers' of Salò and to devise a new racial code modelled on the Nuremberg laws. But while calling for a drastic anti-Jewish purge, he never went so far as to advocate a policy of extermination; nor did he approve of 'illegal' German interference in Italian domestic affairs.[2]

---

[1] Hilger to Steengracht, 15 Oct. 1943 (GFM/131/70868); Rahn to Ribbentrop, 16 Nov. 1943 (GFM/131/I/71100); Deakin, pp. 621–3.
[2] Preziosi to Mussolini, 31 Jan. 31 1944 (IC/Job 331/95–106); Tamaro, *Due anni di storia*, II, 370; G. Dolfin, *Con Mussolini nella tragedia*, Milan, 1950, pp. 264–9; *O.O.* xxxii. 76; Buffarini Guidi, *La vera verità*, pp. 53–62. On the genesis of Preziosi's appointment to the

Prior to Preziosi's return to Italy, Mussolini's puppet government had issued a series of 'moderate' anti-Jewish decrees with the object of taking the wind out of the sails of the Germans and restoring a measure of Italian sovereignty. On 14 November 1943 the Fascist Party Congress at Verona had endorsed a manifesto which defined the Jews of Italy as 'aliens', to be regarded as 'enemy nationals' for the duration of the war. On 30 November Buffarini had ordered the arrest and internment of all Jews resident in the Salò Republic ('even if exempted and irrespective of citizenship') and the immediate confiscation of their property 'for the benefit of the indigent refugees from enemy air attacks'. On the following day this order had been broadcast over the radio, with the result that thousands of Jews went into hiding or fled the country. (According to E. F. Moellhausen, Rahn's second-in-command in Rome, this was precisely what the 'Jew-lover' Buffarini had hoped to achieve.) On 10 December Tamburini had instructed the heads of all provinces to exempt certain categories of Jews from internment, including the aged, the sick, the 'Aryanized', and those with Aryan spouses. On 4 January 1944 a decree law had been promulgated, prohibiting Jews from owning shares or land and ordering the sequestration of their wealth, including liquid assets and real estate. On 20 January Buffarini had protested to the Germans against the 'illegal' deportation of Italian Jews to the East (in addition to which he requested the commandants of concentration camps not to hand over Jewish internees to the SS); and on 19 March he had asked the heads of provinces not to deprive the Jews of all their means of livelihood, the order of 30 November and the decree law of 4 January notwithstanding.[1] As an extension of this policy of shielding Jews from the *furor teutonicus*, the Italian Embassy in Berlin had repeatedly intervened on behalf of deported Italian Jews, naturally with inconclusive

---

post of 'Inspector-General of the Race', cf. Preziosi to Steengracht, 8 Mar. 1944 (GFM/131/II/71698–99); on Preziosi's advocacy of Italian Nuremberg laws on the German model, cf. his memorandum of 10 April 1944 (IC/Job 325/110865); on his opposition to 'illegal' German measures, see below, pp. 381, 385; on his opposition to German policy in the border provinces, see BA/K/EAP 161-b-12/239/*Akten Reichsführer SS/Persönlicher Stab* (Renato Ricci to Himmler, 10 Sept. 1943).

[1] Buffarini Guidi, op. cit., pp. 48–50; De Felice, *Storia degli ebrei italiani*, pp. 434–8; Moellhausen, op. cit., pp. 317–18.

results.[1] The expropriation of Jewish wealth was undoubtedly dictated by the poor financial condition of the 'Italian Social Republic'—between December 1943 and March 1945 sequestration was to yield a sum of well over two billion lire.[2]

If the 'Jew-lovers' of Salò had been masters in their own house, no Italian Jew would have perished in the Holocaust. Hitler, however, was determined that his Italian jackal should not regain any measure of independence; nor had he any intention of respecting Fascist laws designed to save Jews from the death camps. Immediately after the Italian armistice he began to extend the 'final solution' to Italy, without even waiting for the restoration of the Fascist regime. On 12 September—fifteen days before Mussolini's new Cabinet held its first meeting—Kappler, by now head of the Gestapo in Rome, received a telephone call from Rastenburg, informing him that Himmler wanted to proceed with a round-up and deportation of the Roman Jews. And on 23 September—the day the Salò Republic came into being—Kaltenbrunner's office sent a circular to all its branches, specifying that 'in agreement with the Foreign Ministry' Jews of Italian nationality could now be included in the racial measures. It remains to add that within a few days of the Italian surrender SS detachments carried out a pogrom in the summer resorts around Lago Maggiore—the first since the age of the Ghetto.[3]

[1] Verbal note of Italian Embassy in Berlin to Wilhelmstrasse, 8 Nov. 1943 (GFM/4668/346049); Police d'Israël, Quartier général 6-ème bureau, Adolf Eichmann, iii, Jerusalem, 1961, pp. 1692–4 (case of Bernardo Taubert); Anfuso (Berlin) to Republican Foreign Ministry, 20 June 1944 (IC/Job 325/110897–98/1).

[2] De Felice, *Storia degli ebrei italiani*, pp. 437, 592–3.

[3] Between 15 and 24 Sept. 1943, 49 Jews were butchered by members of the *Leibstandarte Adolf Hitler*—16 at Meina, 15 at Baveno, 9 at Arona, 4 at Stresa, 3 at Mergozzo, and 2 at Orta (Giuliana Donati, 'Eccidi di Ebrei in Italia', *Ebrei in Italia: deportazione, resistenza*, ed. Centro di Documentazione Ebraica Contemporanea, Florence, 1975, p. 31; CDEC/5D/Eccidi/Lago Maggiore/Testimony G. Capotossi (June 1945)); cf. also L. Gasparotto, *Diario di un deputato. Cinquant'anni di vita politica italiana*, Milan, 1945, pp. 350–355. At Merano 25 Jews were arrested between 16 and 18 September and deported to Auschwitz via Reichenau (*Deportazione degli ebrei dall'Italia. Ricerca condotta da Giuliana Donati*, Centro di Documentazione Ebraica Contemporanea, Milan, 1975, p. 1). On the telephone call from Rastenburg, see M. Tagliacozzo, 'La Comunità di Roma sotto l'incubo della svastica. La grande razzia del 16 ottobre 1943', *Gli ebrei in Italia durante il fascismo, iii* (Quaderni del Centro di Documentazione Ebraica Contemporanea), Milan, 1963, p. 9; on Kaltenbrunner's circular, YVS/NG-2652-H. Tagliacozzo's paper is part of an as yet unpublished monograph on Roman Jewry under the German occupation; cf. also M. Tagliacozzo, 'Le responsabilità di Kappler nella tragedia degli ebrei di Roma', *Scritti in memoria di Attilio Milano*, Milan–Rome, 1970, pp. 389–414; id., 'Ha-matsod ha-gadol al yehudei Roma b'yom 16 b'oktober 1943', *Scritti in memoria di Enzo Sereni*, Jerusalem, 1970, pp. 252–80.

The telephone call from Rastenburg was followed by a secret cable which read: 'Recent Italian events impose an immediate solution to the Jewish problem in the territories recently occupied by the armed forces of the Reich. The Reichsführer SS therefore requests Obersturmbannführer Kappler to take without delay all preliminary measures necessary to ensure the swiftness and secrecy of the operation to be carried out in the territory of the city of Rome. Immediate further orders will follow.'[1]

Kappler was a rabid Jew-hater. As recently as 3 July he had sent Kaltenbrunner a report on an imaginary 'Jewish espionage centre' in Rome.[2] But he was no more happy about the idea of deporting the Roman Jews than about the 'liberation' of Mussolini (which, as we have seen, he had vainly tried to prevent). He felt this new order was 'yet another gross political stupidity' (*eine neue grosse politische Dummheit*). The Italian Jews, besides being few in number, 'had not as in Germany grown rich off the backs of the people'; nor was there any marked racial difference between Jews and Gentiles in Italy. The Jews of Rome, as far as he knew, were orderly and passive—perhaps the least dangerous element of the population, despite any connection they might have with the 'international Jewish conspiracy' in which Kappler blindly believed.[3]

Hitler and Himmler, however, were determined to impose their anti-Jewish obsession on the German-occupied part of Italy, no matter what Kappler's views on the subject. On 24 September—the day after the setting-up of the new Fascist regime—Himmler's office in Berlin dispatched a top secret message to Kappler, calling for a 'final solution' to the Jewish problem in Rome; all Jews, regardless of age, sex, citizenship, and state of health, were to be arrested and sent to the Reich 'for liquidation'. Somewhat ambiguous in that it did not set a date for the planned operation, the message continued:

---

[1] Tagliacozzo, 'La Comunità di Roma sotto l'incubo della svastica', p. 9.
[2] R. A. Graham, 'Spie naziste attorno al Vaticano durante la seconda guerra mondiale', *La Civiltà Cattolica* (3 Jan. 1970), 25.
[3] Transcript of sworn testimony of Herbert Kappler, taken at the military prison at Gaeta, 27 June 1961 (quoted in R. Katz, *Black Sabbath. A Journey through a Crime against Humanity*, Toronto, 1969, pp. 48–9). The Military Tribunal of Rome which sentenced Kappler to life imprisonment on 20 July 1948 concurred with his contention that he had opposed Himmler's plan for the immediate deportation of the Roman Jews (Tribunale Militare di Roma, *Processa Kappler, Sentenza No. 631. N. 6003/45*).

It is known that this nucleus of Jews has actively collaborated with the Badoglio movement [*sic*], and therefore its speedy removal will represent, among other things, a necessary security measure guaranteeing the indispensable tranquillity in the immediate rear of the Southern front. The success of this undertaking is to be ensured by means of a surprise action, and for this reason it is absolutely necessary to suspend the application of any anti-Jewish measures in the nature of individual acts in order not to arouse any suspicions among the population of an imminent *Judenaktion.*[1]

Though marked 'strictly confidential and personal', the above dispatch was read by the military commandant of Rome, General Rainer Stahel, who at once contacted Consul Moellhausen (then in charge of the German Embassy) and told him that he did not want to be mixed up in this kind of *Schweinerei.* The Consul (a non-Nazi whose Italian lady friend was hiding a family of Jews in her home with his approval) agreed that the planned operation was objectionable on both political and moral grounds; and on 26 September he took up the matter with Kappler, asking him if he would co-operate in obstructing Himmler's order and adding that in Tunisia Rahn had succeeded in saving the Jews from deportation by persuading the military to mobilize them for forced labour. Kappler replied that he had no authority to cancel an order from the Reichsführer; he was, however, willing to put the matter before Kesselring who might be assumed to share Moellhausen's views on the subject, having favourably responded to Rahn's intervention on behalf of the Tunisian Jews in 1942. The two then called upon the Field-Marshal who told them that he could not give his approval to the projected *Judenaktion,* being unable to spare a single soldier for the purpose. If, however, Berlin considered it necessary to do something about the Jewish question in the area under his jurisdiction, he would favour using Jewish labour for fortification work around Rome.[2]

Moellhausen thought he had won a battle. What he did not know was that Kappler, prior to their meeting that morning, had decided on a 'final solution' of his own—the imposition of a levy of fifty kilogrammes weight of gold on the Roman Jewish community, to be paid within thirty-six hours. Jews, in Kappler's

[1] Tagliacozzo, 'La Comunità di Roma', pp. 9–10.
[2] Ibid., pp. 10–12; Moellhausen, pp. 112–15; S. Bertoldi, *I tedeschi in Italia*, Milan, 1964, p. 222; Moellhausen to Ribbentrop, 7 Oct. 1943 (GFM/132/123599).

view, had but a single weapon—money; from which it followed that the best way of dealing with the 'menace' was not to deport them but to deprive them of their riches.

On his return from Kesselring's headquarters, Kappler had a meeting with two leading Jews, Dante Almansi and Ugo Foà, in his office at the German Embassy. Foà (President of the Jewish Community of Rome since 1938) later recalled that the German at first assumed a rather courteous demeanour, regretting any inconvenience he might have caused. After a few minutes, however, his tone changed and he came to the point:

You and your co-religionists are Italian citizens, but that is of little importance to me. We Germans regard you only as Jews and as such our enemies. Rather, to be more precise, we regard you as a distinct group, but not wholly apart from the worst of the enemies against whom we are fighting. And we will treat you as such. However, it is not your lives or the lives of your children that we will take—if you fulfil our demands. It is your gold we want in order to provide new arms for our country. Within 36 hours you will have to pay 50 kg. If you pay, no harm will come to you. If not, 200 of your Jews will be arrested and deported to Germany, where they will be sent to the Russian border or otherwise rendered innocuous.[1]

When asked whether by 'Jews' he meant only persons inscribed in the Jewish Community, Kappler replied that he considered anyone with a drop of Jewish blood in his veins ('inscribed or not, baptized or mixed') as a Jew and hence an enemy of the Reich. And when his interlocutors wanted to know if the ransom could be paid in Italian lire, he answered that he would not know what to do with their money ('I can print as much as I want of it'). On the other hand, he was willing to be flexible on the time-limit, first setting it to expire at 11 a.m. on Tuesday, 28 September, then rounding it off at noon. In conclusion he again warned the two presidents that failure to pay would have dire consequences for Roman Jewry: 'Mind you, I have already

[1] 'Relazione del Presidente della comunità Israelitica di Roma, Ugo Foa, circa le misure razziali adottate in Roma dopo l'8 settembre 1943 (date dell'armistizio Badoglio) a diretta opera delle autorità tedesche di occupazione, Roma, 15 Novembre 1943', in L. Morpurgo, *Caccia all'uomo! Pagine di diario 1938–1944*, Rome, 1946, pp. 113–14; CDEC/13B/Roma/D. Almansi, 'Prima relazione al governo italiano circa le persecuzioni nazi-fasciate degli ebrei in Roma (settembre 1943–giugno 1944), U.C.I.I., Rome, 1944. Kappler himself affirmed at his trial that the Jews' weapons 'were not firearms but money and gold and, as all enemies had to be stripped of their weapons, so they too had to be relieved of their arms' (*Processo Kappler, Sentenza No. 631*).

carried out several operations of this kind, and I have always brought them to a successful conclusion. Only once did I fail, but that time several hundred of your brethren paid with their lives.'[1]

After the meeting Almansi and Foà addressed an appeal for help to Epifanio Pennetta, Chief of the Rome Police, who replied that he was 'not in the picture' and that their troubles were 'no concern of his'. Next they raised the matter with two of Pennetta's subordinates, pointing out that extortion by a foreign Power on Italian soil constituted a violation of Italy's sovereignty and that there was every reason for the Duce himself to be alerted. But although the two police officers showed more understanding than their chief (one of them even agreed to notify all his colleagues in the *Questura*), they were equally powerless to intervene. 'Evidently', Foà later commented, 'there was nothing our authorities could do in the face of Teutonic insolence.'[2]

The only recourse now left to the two presidents was to inform their fellow Jews and to ask them 'to offer such objects of gold as might be in their possession'.[3]

On Monday morning, 27 September, a meeting of Jewish leaders was held in Foà's office at the main synagogue in Rome. Foà told them what had taken place the day before at the German Embassy, after which it was decided to set up a collection centre in the boardroom of the synagogue, to entrust Renzo Levi, the President of DELASEM (the Committee for Aid to Jewish Emigrants) with the task of directing the operation and to ask the Vatican for a loan. At 2 p.m. the Pope was approached through an intermediary; and at 4 p.m. he replied that he was ready to lend the Jewish Community any amount of gold they might need. By then, however, the collection campaign had very largely reached its goal; nor did the news of the Vatican's 'noble gesture' (as Foà was to call it) have the effect of slowing the flow of donations. Not only Jews (who felt their lives to be at stake) came forward with offerings but also 'a great many Catholics, including not a few priests'—a fact which made a deep impression on the Jewish leaders.[4] The Gentiles seemed uncertain as to

[1] Morpurgo, op. cit., p. 114. Despite his assertion to the contrary, Kappler had no previous experience in persecuting Jews, having served as police attaché in Rome since January 1939 (URO, *Judenverfolgung in Italien*, p. 221).

[2] Morpurgo, pp. 114–15.

[3] Ibid., p. 115; CDEC/13B/D. Almansi.

[4] Morpurgo, pp. 115–16; Katz, op. cit., pp. 79–88.

whether their gold would be welcome. In the words of a Jewish eye-witness: 'Circumspectly, as if fearing a refusal, as if afraid of offering gold to the rich Jews, some "Aryans" presented themselves. They entered that place adjacent to the synagogue full of embarrassment, not knowing if they should take off their hats or keep their heads covered, according to the well-known Jewish custom. Almost humbly they asked if they too could— well, if it would be all right for them to . . . Unfortunately, they did not leave their names.'[1]

On the following morning the fifty-kilogramme mark was reached before the time-limit set by Kappler had expired; whereupon Foà (who feared that the Germans might later deny ever having received the blood-money) sent a message to Pennetta, containing a summary of the account he had given him orally the day before and a request to provide a police escort for the transport of the gold to the German Embassy. As he was later to explain, he did this with the dual purpose of having 'incontrovertible proof of the payment' and of furnishing the Italian authorities with an 'official documentation of the incredible extortion that was taking place in Rome at the hands of foreigners and of the damage suffered . . . by a considerable number of good Italian citizens'. Pennetta agreed to Foà's request; and in the early afternoon a Fascist police escort arrived at the synagogue, Kappler meanwhile having extended the deadline until 4 p.m.[2]

Before handing over the gold to the Germans, the Jewish leaders made a final attempt to obtain at least a measure of relief from the Fascist authorities. On Tuesday morning Foà requested Luciano Morpurgo, a well-known Jewish writer and publisher with 'Fascist merits', to raise the matter with some of his highly placed Aryan friends. Morpurgo thereupon contacted General Giuseppe Boriani, President of the Italian Red Cross, and told him that fifty kilogrammes of gold ought to be donated to the victims of Allied bombings in Italy ('We Italian Jews would be happy and proud to offer our gold . . . in the same manner as our fathers and brothers gave their lives on all the fields of battle'). Boriani replied that he himself could do nothing but that it might be worth Morpurgo's while to try his luck at the

[1] G. Debenedetti, *16 ottobre 1943*, 2nd edn., Milan, 1959, p. 20.
[2] Morpugo, p. 116.

headquarters of the Republican Fascist Party. The latter agreed and went to see the Party Secretary who was a personal friend of his. But Pavolini was out and Morpurgo, after talking to one of his aides, concluded that the Party was as helpless in the face of German insolence as the Red Cross.[1]

At 4 p.m. the gold was duly delivered to the Gestapo, and the Jews of Rome heaved a sigh of relief. The relaxation of tension, however, was short-lived. The very next morning, 29 September, a party of SS men, led by Kappler's intelligence officer, called on Foà and ordered him to accompany them to the synagogue where they were about to conduct a search of the premises. Foà was outraged (all the more so because the intruders failed to exhibit 'any decree or ordinance from the superior German authorities') but had to obey. Contrary to their hopes, the Germans found neither incriminating equipment nor compromising documents; but since the files of Jewish names and addresses fell into their hands, they had every reason to consider the operation a success.[2]

On the following day—the last of September and the first of the Jewish New Year—Germans of a different kind presented themselves at the synagogue: two Orientalists, one of them a professor of Hebrew, who wanted to have a look at the Community's libraries, the Biblioteca Comunale (which had a unique collection of books and documents on Judaism and early Christianity) and the Biblioteca del Collegio Rabbinico. On 1 October the two German visitors (who turned out to be members of the Einsatzstab Rosenberg) called on President Foà and informed him of their desire to browse among the books. (That same day Foà had a highly unpleasant encounter with two SS officers who were seeking further information about the finances and holdings of the Community's wealthiest members.) On 2 October the two Einsatzstab officers broke into the abandoned apartment of Israel Zolli, the Chief Rabbi of Rome, where they confiscated books and papers—the first German assault on the property of an individual Jew. And on 11 October another member of the Einsatzstab Rosenberg, a lieutenant with an escort of SS men, appeared at the synagogue in order to examine the libraries. In the words of a noted Jewish writer:

[1] Ibid., pp. 97–9.
[2] Ibid., pp. 118–20.

While his men began to rifle through the library of the Rabbinical College and that of the Community, the officer, with . . . hands like fine embroidery, touched, caressed, and fondled the papyri and the incunabula, turned the pages of manuscripts and rare editions and leafed through membranaceous codices and palimpsests. The varying attention of his touch, the differing caution of his gestures were at once proportionate to the volume's worth. Most of these works were written in obscure alphabets. But in opening their pages, the officer's eyes would fix on them, widening and brightening, in the same way as some readers who are particularly familiar with a subject know where to find the desired part . . . In those refined hands, as if under keen and bloodless torture, a kind of very subtle sadism, the ancient books had spoken. Later it was learnt that the officer . . . was a distinguished student of paleography and Semitic philology.[1]

On leaving the library, the lieutenant informed Rosina Sorani, an employee of the Community, that the books were under sequestration and must not be removed, adding that in the event of non-compliance she would be shot. Miss Sorani told Foà who in turn contacted Almansi (the man responsible for the administration of the libraries under article 36 of the Jewish Community Law). The two presidents decided to address a letter of protest to the competent Italian authorities, stressing the immense value of the libraries, the confiscation of which would be a loss to Italy as well as to the Jewish Community. As might be expected, there was no response. 'Not one of the authorities', as Foà put it later, 'budged an inch or even acknowledged receipt of those anguished appeals which should have sounded the alarm-bell for whoever took to heart the patrimony of Italian culture.' On 14 October Rosenberg's experts returned to remove the books, emptying the Biblioteca Comunale entirely and the Biblioteca del Collegio Rabbinico partially, after which one of them thanked Miss Sorani for her 'help'. Foà was shaken. 'By now', he wrote, 'the continuous presence of German officers, their armed escorts, and the invariable accompaniment of demands and repetitious ultimatums, was spreading ever more oppressively in the offices of the Community; and from those offices it overflowed into the midst of the entire Jewish population of Rome. All the Roman Jews by now felt themselves abandoned, without any defence and at the mercy of an enemy devoid of

---

[1] Ibid., pp. 121–4; Katz, pp. 118–23; Debenedetti, op. cit., pp. 26–7.

both scruples and compassion.' Even so, they found it impossible to believe that in eternal Rome 'Hitler's gangsters would dare to repeat the incredible slaughter to which their brethren in Poland and Germany, in Holland and Belgium had already fallen victim'.[1]

It was a vain illusion. While the Einsatzstab officers were sacking the Jewish libraries, Eichmann was preparing to extend the 'final solution' to Rome. Kappler, for his part, was still opposed to the planned operation, considering it technically difficult as well as politically unwise. For one thing (he argued in his reports to Berlin), he did not have enough SS police in Rome to bring off the round-up; for another, there was reason to fear that the Gentile population of Rome would adopt a hostile attitude in the event of a *Judenaktion*, and the possibility of passive, or even active, resistance on the part of the Aryan Romans could by no means be ruled out.[2]

It may be useful at this stage to deal briefly with a subject which has given rise to a great deal of controversy since the war—the alleged failure of the Jewish community leaders to react promptly and effectively to the German danger. The first to promote this notion was the late Chief Rabbi of Rome, Israel (later Eugenio) Zolli, who claims to have urged his co-religionists to disperse themselves within the city and the surrounding villages immediately after the entry of the Germans. In his memoirs, published nine years after the fall of Fascism, Zolli tells us that, but for the rejection of his advice by President Foà, everything might have worked out for the best. A very different view was expressed by Renato J. Almansi, son of Dante Almansi, who wrote in August 1971:

As far as my father was concerned, it was by no means true that he saw no danger ahead. Efficiently and tempestively he put the Union's money and important papers in a safe place . . . I was told several times by my mother that throughout that whole period he very often repeated to her the sentence, 'the circle is getting tighter' (*Il cerchio si stringe*). Certainly, like all other Roman Jews, he must have had some hope that the worst could be averted and that Italian moderation and the vicinity of the Pope might exert some beneficial influence, but this certainly did not influence his actions. As a practical man who was in the habit of

---

[1] Debenedetti, pp. 122–4; Katz, pp. 123–5.
[2] Tagliacozzo, 'La Comunità di Roma', p. 19.

thinking things through, he had clearly realized how powerless he actually was and what difficulties any such attempt (at the dispersal of the Roman Jews, M. M.) would have met in actual practice in September 1943. The truth is that until the deportations actually started the practical and psychological circumstances for a successful dispersal of the Jews of Rome just did not exist . . . Rabbi Zolli (does not seem) to have given thought to the fact that it is enormously difficult for people to make the truly heroic decision to move from their homes, leaving behind most of their possessions towards uncertain surroundings and a dark future, unless it is an absolute matter of life or death. (In fact, some even refused to do so after the start of the deportations.) Besides, where could they have gone? An outlying village would have offered no real safety, as it is just in small places that the stranger (*forestiero*), is immediately noticed. In a village, as in Rome itself, the Jews thus displaced would not have been able to get a place of their own under a new name, had they been lucky enough to find one, because of the lack of forged papers and ration cards. My father, even with his excellent connections with the Underground (*Resistenza*), was not able to get any until the middle of November. The only possibility for the Jews was to be concealed by friendly Christians. But how many could reasonably be able to summon the courage to ask for shelter when no actual immediate need was apparent, particularly at that time, when everyone's life in Rome—Jew and Gentile alike—was beset by the most horrible difficulties, deprivations and fears? And how many, among the Gentiles, at that time and under those circumstances, would have found it possible to shelter and feed them, even if animated by the best intentions and the greatest compassion?

Once the deportations began the situation changed dramatically. The hunted Jew, fearing for his life, was able to find the courage and the moral justification to ask for shelter and the Gentile unhesitatingly and generously helped him. The very fact that the Germans started the deportations and were not able to get all the Jews at one time, enabled most of those who were not immediately caught to survive.[1]

Eichmann, for his part, had every reason to be pleased with the refusal of the Roman Jews to leave their homes until it was too late. He was, however, displeased with Kappler, who continued to express doubts about the wisdom of the projected round-up. When his attention was drawn to Kappler's objections, he responded by calling in one of the ablest and most experienced

---

[1] 'Dante Almansi', pp. 35–7; id., 'Mio padre, Dante Almansi', *La Rassegna Mensile di Israel*, xlii (May–June 1976), 251–2. For Zolli's version, cf. E. Zolli, *Before the Dawn*, New York, 1954, pp. 140–55.

of his aides, 30-year-old Hauptsturmführer (SS Captain) Theodor Dannecker, who had previously distinguished himself as *Juden-referent* in Paris and *Judenberater* in Sofia. At the beginning of October Dannecker arrived in Rome at the head of an Einsatzkommando (execution team) composed of forty-four armed SS men, including fourteen officers and N.C.O.s. Kappler later recalled that the young captain presented himself at the German Embassy armed with a document empowering him to deport the Jews of Rome—'a definitive authorization, containing an order to the local police commands to furnish all aid requested by Dannecker', signed by Gestapo Chief Heinrich Müller.

Kappler realized that his attempts at obstructing the Reichs-führer's deportation order had failed. Even so, he continued to raise objections. 'I told (Dannecker)', he later recounted, 'that first of all I had no men who could be placed at his disposal. When he asked me for topographical information . . . I said that none of the men in my command knew the city well enough.' If the captain was in need of help, he had better go to the Questura and see Raffaele Alianello, the liaison officer between the German and Italian police forces in Rome. Kappler subsequently claimed that he furnished this information 'in the certainty that through the Italian police the news would be leaked'. On the other hand, he saw no point in withholding the list of Jewish names and addresses which had been confiscated by his men a few days earlier.[1]

Kappler was not the only German representative in Rome to worry about the possible effects of the projected *Judenrazzia*. Others were Weizsäcker (Ambassador to the Holy See since 31 March), Albrecht von Kessel (Weizsäcker's closest aide who, after the Italian surrender, had urged the Jews through a Swiss friend to go into hiding), Stahel (who insisted that before any *Judenaktion* in his zone of command the Wilhelmstrasse would have to give its blessing), and Moellhausen (who was still at a loss to explain why his earlier plotting with Kappler had ended in failure). Weizsäcker and Kessel felt that Moellhausen (who, in the absence of Rahn, was the chief representative of the Reich in German-occupied Rome) was the one who ought to intervene.

[1] Tagliacozzo, 'La Comunità di Roma', pp. 19–20; Kappler's testimony of 27 June 1961 (see above, p. 353, n. 3); Kappler's testimony of 1 June 1948 (*Processo Kappler*); Katz, pp. 125–9. On Dannecker, see Reitlinger, *The Final Solution*, pp. 79, 329, 332–9, 381, 410.

The Consul concurred with this view, and on 6 October he sent the following cable (marked 'very very urgent') to the 'Reich Foreign Minister personally' which was received in Berlin at 1.30 p.m.: '*Obersturmbannführer* Kappler has received orders from Berlin to arrest the eight thousand [*sic*] Jews resident in Rome and transport them to Northern Italy [*sic*] where they are to be liquidated (*wo sie liquidiert werden sollen*). The Commandant of Rome, General Stahel, informs me that he will permit this action only on approval of the Herr Reich Minister of Foreign Affairs. In my personal view it would be better business to employ the Jews for fortification work, as was done in Tunis and, together with Kappler, I will propose this to Field-Marshal Kesselring [*sic*]. Please advise.'[1]

On the following day the Consul dispatched another 'very very urgent' message to 'the Herr Reich Minister personally' which arrived at the Wilhelmstrasse at 10.05 a.m.: 'Field-Marshal Kesselring had asked *Obersturmbannführer* Kappler to postpone the planned *Judenaktion* for the time being. But if something has to be done, he would prefer to use the able-bodied Jews of Rome for fortification work near here.'[2]

Once again Moellhausen thought he had won a battle. As he puts it in his memoirs, he wrote the above 'with the conviction that I was giving good news—above all because all responsibility had been assumed by Kesselring, and the Ministry of Foreign Affairs would have nothing to fear'. He was, however, speedily undeceived. Ribbentrop, when informed of the Consul's cables, regarded them as anything but 'good news'. Indeed, he was upset—both because a subordinate of his had used the word 'liquidate' in an official document addressed to him personally and because he feared that Moellhausen's meddling would antagonize the Reichsführung SS (as in fact it did). To extricate himself from a tricky position, he ordered that Rahn and Moellhausen be notified 'not to interfere'. On 9 October the following 'very urgent' telegram was dispatched to the Consul by Eberhard von Thadden of Inland II, the German Affairs Department of the Wilhelmstrasse: 'On the basis of the Führer's

---

[1] Moellhausen to Ribbentrop, 6 Oct. 1943 (GFM/132/123580). Why Moellhausen said that he was about to propose something which had in fact been proposed ten days earlier is not clear.

[2] See above, p. 354 n. 2.

instructions, the 8,000 Jews resident in Rome are to be taken to Mauthausen as hostages [*sic*]. The Reich Foreign Minister asks you not to interfere in any way in this affair and to leave it to the SS. Please inform Rahn.'[1]

A few hours later a second message was sent which brought the matter to a close: 'The Herr Reich Minister of Foreign Affairs insists that you keep out of all questions concerning Jews. Such questions, in accordance with an agreement between the Foreign Ministry and the Reich Main Security Office, are within the exclusive competence of the SS, and any further interference in these questions could cause serious difficulties for the Ministry of Foreign Affairs.'[2]

It was evident that Ribbentrop and his aides were unwilling to risk a clash with Himmler, whatever their views on the imminent *Judenrazzia*. Moellhausen now decided to bring the Vatican into the picture. He passed on Thadden's telegrams to Weizsäcker's Embassy which in turn informed the Holy See. If the Jews of Rome were to be saved, the Holy Father might have to break the silence which he had hitherto maintained.

Up to the Italian surrender Vatican aid to persecuted Jews in Italy had been largely confined to co-operation with DELASEM.[3] But as soon as Weizsäcker informed the Curia of Hitler's decision to respect and safeguard the extra-territorial status of the Vatican City and its multitude of enclaves, Pius XII personally ordered the clergy to open these sanctuaries to all non-Aryans in need of refuge. Weizsäcker approved and initiated efforts to guarantee the inviolability of these islands of safety. At the same time, however, he urged the Pontiff to refrain from public statements which might give offence to the rulers of the Third Reich: 'I spoke very confidentially to Montini (the future Pope Paul VI) and advised him that any protest by the pope would only result in the deportations being really carried out in a thoroughgoing fashion. I know how our people react in these matters. Montini,

---

[1] Moellhausen, p. 116; Sonnleithner to Ribbentrop's Bureau, 9 Oct. 1943 (GFM/132/123642); Thadden to Moellhausen, 9 October 1943 (IFZ/NG-5027).
[2] IFZ/NG-5027.
[3] R. Leiber, 'Pio XII e gli ebrei di Roma 1943–1944', *La Civiltà Cattolica* (4 Mar. 1961), 451–3; *Aperçu sur l'œuvre du Bureau d'informations vatican 1939–1946*, Vatican City, 1948, pp. 65–6.

incidentally, saw the point.'[1] So did Pius XII who refused to break his silence even when Dannecker's men rounded up Jews right under his windows. It remains to add that the open-door policy of the Holy See saved the lives of nearly 5,000 Jewish Romans. According to Michael Tagliacozzo, the foremost authority on the subject, 477 were sheltered in the Vatican and its enclaves, while another 4,238 found refuge in the numerous monasteries and convents of Rome.[2]

While Weizsäcker and Kessel were trying to find a way of saving the Roman Jews and averting a fresh crisis in German–Vatican relations, Dannecker was busy completing the preparations for the planned deportations. Finally, on 16 October—a Sabbath and the blackest day in the long history of Roman Jewry—the signal was given at 5.30 a.m. and the *Judenrazzia* began. Wherever Jews lived in Rome, they were brutally seized, regardless of age, sex, and state of health, and taken to the Collegio Militare (where Kappler was to be tried as a war criminal four years later); thence, after two days, they were shipped off to the killing centre of Auschwitz. A Gentile Italian eyewitness subsequently recorded that it 'all seemed like a scene out of hell': 'The children were crying. Everywhere you could hear pleas for help and cries of distress . . . I could not understand why these innocent creatures should be considered a danger to Germany. I was terrified, but I kept watching the scene, perhaps with an unconscious hope of somehow being able to help the victims. Suddenly a German N.C.O. came up to me and told me to be off, accompanying his words with a persuasive push. There was nothing I could do but leave the place.'[3]

A few hours after Dannecker had struck, Albrecht von Kessel contacted Legation Secretary Gerhard R. Gumpert (who, in the absence of Moellhausen, was in charge of the German Embassy in Rome) and asked him to take the matter up with Berlin. Gumpert replied that he could not act without the backing of the

---

[1] A. Giovanetti, *Roma città aperta*, Milan, 1962, p. 179; L. E. Hill (ed.), *Die Weizsäcker-Papiere 1933–1950*, Berlin, 1974, p. 354; id., 'The Vatican Embassy of Ernst von Weizsäcker, 1943–1945,' *The Journal of Modern History*, xxxix (June 1967), 149; *Actes et documents du Saint Siège*, ix: Notes du Cardinal Maglione, 16 Oct. 1943, pp. 505–6.

[2] Memorandum on 'Ebrei rifugiati nelle zone extraterritoriali del Vaticano', addressed to the writer (16 June 1975).

[3] Morpurgo, pp. 124–9; Debenedetti, pp. 34–64; Tagliacozzo, 'La Comunità di Roma sotto l'incubo della svastica', pp. 21–37; Katz, pp. 175–294.

Holy See, whereupon Kessel called on Father Pankratius Pfeiffer (better known as Padre Pancrazio), a Bavarian, who served as Pius XII's liaison officer with the German occupation authorities. Pfeiffer put the matter before the Pope who promptly agreed to intervene within the limits of the policy of silence. An official protest being considered undesirable, it was decided to address an unofficial appeal to Stahel (who had just enabled Dannecker to carry out the *Judenrazzia* by placing three companies of SS Police at his disposal). The prelate chosen to sign it was Bishop Alois Hudal, Rector of the German Catholic Church in Rome, an ardent German nationalist who had expressed qualified approval of Hitler's Nuremburg laws in 1937.[1]

The person of the signatory having been agreed upon, a letter of protest was drafted by Gumpert, prepared for Hudal's signature by Kessel, and delivered to Stahel by his fellow Bavarian, Pfeiffer, at 5 p.m., three hours after the completion of the round-up. It read:

I must speak to you of a matter of great urgency. A high Vatican dignitary in the immediate circle of the Holy Father has just informed me that this morning a series of arrests of Jews of Italian nationality has been initiated. In the interests of the good relations which have existed until now between the Vatican and the German High Command— above all thanks to the political wisdom and magnanimity of Your Excellency which will one day go down in the history of Rome—I earnestly request that you order the immediate suspension of these arrests both in Rome and its vicinity. Otherwise I fear that the Pope will take a public stand against this action which would undoubtedly be used by the anti-German propagandists as a weapon against us.[2]

Stahel (who did not wish to be mixed up in a conflict between the Curia and the Reich) handed the letter to Gumpert who in turn passed it on to Berlin. A day later Weizsäcker expressed support of Gumpert's appeal in the following dispatch to the Wilhelmstrasse:

With regard to Bishop Hudal's letter ... I can confirm that this represents the Vatican's reaction to the deportation of the Jews of Rome. The Curia is particularly upset (*betroffen*) because the action took

[1] Moellhausen, pp. 118–19; Katz, pp. 198–203; IFZ/NG-315; A. Hudal, *Die Grundlagen des Nationalsozialismus*, Leipzig–Vienna, 1937, pp. 75, 85, 86–8; id., *Römische Tagebücher. Lebensbeichte eines alten Bischofs*, Graz–Stuttgart, 1976.
[2] IFZ/NG-5027.

place, in a manner of speaking, under the Pope's own windows. The reaction could be muffled somewhat if the Jews were to be used for labour service here . . . The people hostile to us in Rome are using this affair as a means of forcing the Vatican from its reserve. People say that when similar incidents took place in French cities, the bishops there took a firm stand. The Pope, as supreme head of the Church and Bishop of Rome, cannot be more reticent than they. People are also drawing a parallel between the stronger character of Pius XI and that of the present Pope. Enemy propaganda abroad will certainly view this event in the same way in order to disturb the friendly [*sic*] relations between the Curia and ourselves.[1]

Even before the above last-minute appeal was sent off to Berlin, the Gestapo in Rome had prepared the following report on the round-up of the Jews, presumably written by Dannecker, signed by Kappler, and addressed to Obergruppenführer Karl Wolff:

Judenaktion according to plan worked out in this office exploiting all possibilities was today initiated and completed. Put into action were all available forces of the Security- and Order Police (*Sicherheits- und Ordnungspolizei*). Participation of the Italian Police in the affair was not possible, given their unreliability . . . Blocking off entire streets was not practicable considering the character of the Open City and also the insufficient aggregate of only 365 German police. Nevertheless during the action, which lasted from 5.30 a.m. to 2 p.m., 1,259 persons were arrested in Jewish homes and brought to a central collection point at a military college here. After the release of the half-breeds, the foreigners (incl. one citizen of the Vatican City), the members of mixed marriages (incl. the Jewish partners), the Aryan domestics and subtenants, there remained in custody 1,007 Jews. Deportation set for Monday, 10/18 at 9 a.m.

The report then went on to sum up the impact of the *Razzia* on the native population:

The behaviour of the Italian people was outright passive resistance which in many individual cases amounted to active assistance. In one case, for example, the police came upon the home of a Fascist in a black shirt and with identity papers which without doubt had already been used one hour earlier in a Jewish home by someone claiming them as his own. As the German police were breaking into some homes, attempts to hide Jews were observed, and it is believed that in many

[1] Ibid.

cases they were successful. The anti-Semitic section of the population was nowhere to be seen during the action, only a great mass of people who in some individual cases even tried to cut off the police from the Jews. In no case was there any need to use fire-arms.

Commenting on the above in a routine report to the Reichsführung SS, Kappler gave it as his opinion that the situation was 'in general unchanged'.[1]

All observers are agreed that the round-up made a deep impression on the Romans. In the words of one writer, this 'was the city's first view of persecution with its robes down, and though there had been racial laws for five years, no one ever thought what lay underneath looked like this. Rome was horrified. Many non-Jews found a sudden need or desire to express their disbelief in the concept of racial differences and in the idea that Jews were in some way inferior to Aryans, that is, themselves.'[2] *L'Italia Libera,* an underground newspaper, gave expression to the general feeling of revulsion in an article from which the following is worth quoting:

The Germans during the night and all day long went around Rome seizing Italians for their furnaces. The Germans would like us to believe that these people are in some way alien to us, that they are of another race. But we feel them as part of our flesh and blood. They have always lived, fought, and suffered with us. Not only able-bodied men, but old people, children, women, and babies were crowded into covered trucks and taken away to meet their fate. There is not a single heart that does not shudder (*frema*) at the thought of what that fate might be . . . We do not hate anymore; we are horrified. Not until Europe is freed of this nightmare, can there be any hope for peace.[3]

On Sunday, 17 October, people began making inquiries at the Italian Red Cross, the local authorities, and the Vatican, whereupon General Boriani went to see Stahel in order to find out what was going on. Unsuccessful there, he called on the Gestapo, only to be told—apparently by Kappler himself—that

---

[1] IFZ/NO-2427 (17–18 Oct. 1943); IFZ/NO-315. According to Katz, over 1,060 Roman Jews were listed for departure on the Rome–Auschwitz train (op. cit., p. 212); according to Giuliana Donati, at least 1,035 were actually deported (*Deportazione degli ebrei dall'Italia,* p. 1).

[2] Katz, p. 220.

[3] *L'Italia Libera,* 17 Oct. 1943. It is worth noting that the editor of the paper was a Russian-born Jew, Leone Ginzburg.

it was 'useless to concern oneself, useless to inquire: this was a matter which concerned only the Germans and no one else'.[1]

The Vatican, according to one source, was in touch with Stahel's office through Hudal who learnt from the General himself that 'in view of the special character of Rome', the Reichsführer SS had ordered Kappler to call off the operation.[2] Subsequently, it was claimed by defenders of Vatican policy (though never by the Curia itself) that the Holy Father's intervention had induced the Germans to stop the arrests. In reality, Hudal's appeal to Stahel had no such effect. For one thing, there was never any intention of continuing the round-up after 16 October, mainly because it was technically impossible to extend any such operation after it had run its natural course. For another, Himmler could not have ordered Kappler to call off the *Razzia* for the simple reason that he had not yet received any information on the subject. As a matter of fact, no order to stop the arrests was ever given, and indeed one to the contrary was later issued.[3]

On Monday morning, 18 October, the Jews in the Collegio Militare were taken to the railway station in trucks, and at 2.5 p.m. the train with its cargo of human misery left for Auschwitz where all but sixteen of the deportees met their end.[4]

On Tuesday, 19 October, Thadden passed on Gumpert's and Weizsäcker's telegrams to Ribbentrop who replied through an aide that he would consider the matter at some later date. On the same day Rahn rebuked Moellhausen for having intervened in the Jewish issue on his own initiative: 'You should have reported to me, and I would have tried to arrange something with Wolff. You have created chaos and ruined everything.'[5]

The Wilhelmstrasse did not act on Gumpert's and Weizsäcker's cables until 23 October, by which time most of the deportees from Rome had been turned to smoke. Eichmann later testified at his trial in Jerusalem that Thadden had sent him a memorandum on the subject, pointing out that in Weizsäcker's

---

[1] Tagliacozzo, 'La Comunità di Roma', p. 34 (based on testimonies of Italian officers who took refuge in the Lateran Church after Badoglio's surrender).
[2] P. Duclos, *Le Vatican et la seconde guerre mondiale. Action doctrinale et diplomatique en faveur de la paix,* Paris, 1955, p. 190.
[3] IFZ/NO-315 (entry for 17 Oct. 1943); Katz, pp. 225–6.
[4] *Deportazione degli ebrei dall'Italia,* p. 1.
[5] Moellhausen, p. 119; on Wolff's attitude see above, p. 347 n. 3.

opinion the reaction of the Holy See might be 'somewhat dampened' if the Roman Jews were to be employed for labour service in Italy. Eichmann promptly transmitted the document to Heinrich Müller, 'asking him, as usual, to indicate to me what was to be done'.[1] No reply from Müller has ever been found.

In Rome Pope Pius XII maintained his silence in accordance with Weizsäcker's advice. His disapproval of the German action, however, found expression in a semi-official communiqué (published in the Vatican organ on 25–6 October) which was to give rise to considerable controversy after the war and from which the following is worth quoting:

Persistent and pitiful echoes of calamities which, as a result of the prolongation of the present conflict do not cease to accumulate, continue more than ever to reach the Holy Father. As is well known, the August Pontiff, after having vainly tried to prevent the outbreak of the war by striving to dissuade the Rulers of the peoples from having recourse to force of arms . . . has not desisted for one moment from employing all the means in His power to alleviate the suffering which, whatever form it may take, is the consequence of this cruel conflagration. With the augmentation (*accrescersi*) of so much evil, the universal and paternal charity of the Supreme Pontiff has become, it might be said, ever more active; it knows neither boundaries nor nationality, neither religion nor race (*stirpe*). This manifold and ceaseless activity on the part of Pius XII has intensified even more in recent times in view of the increased suffering of so many unfortunates. Such blessed activity . . . can achieve even greater results in the future and hasten the day on which the shining glow of peace will return to the earth.[2]

Commenting on the above in a dispatch to the Wilhelmstrasse on 28 October, Weizsäcker claimed that Pius XII had done everything in his power to avert a fresh crisis between the Holy See and the Reich:

Although under pressure from all sides, the Pope has not allowed himself to be drawn into any demonstrative censure of the deportation of the Jews of Rome. Although he must expect that such an attitude will be resented by our enemies and exploited by the Protestant circles in the Anglo-Saxon countries for the purpose of propaganda against Catholicism, he has done all he could in this delicate matter not to

[1] Thadden to Eichmann, 23 Oct. 1943 (GFM/4353/E421509-10); Eichmann's testimony of 3 July 1961 (*Bezirksgericht Jerusalem/Strafakt 40/61/Der Generalstaatsanwalt des Staates Israel gegen Adolf, Sohn des Karl Adolf Eichmann*, Bd. xi, Jerusalem, 1961, session 84, p. 01).
[2] 'La carità del Santo Padre', *L'Osservatore Romano*, 25–6 Oct. 1943.

strain relations with the German Government and German circles in Rome. As there is probably no reason to expect further German actions against the Roman Jews, we may consider that a question so disturbing to German-Vatican relations has been liquidated. In any case, an indication of this state of affairs can be seen in the Vatican's attitude. *L'Osservatore Romano*, in its issue of October 25–26, has in fact given prominence to a semi-official communiqué on the Pope's charitable activities. This communiqué, written in the Vatican's distinctive style, that is, very tortuous and obscure (*reichlich gewunden und unklar*), declares that all men, without distinction of nationality, *race (Rasse)*, or religion, benefit from the Pope's paternal solicitude. The varied and continued activities of Pius XII have lately increased even further because of the greater sufferings of so many unfortunates. There is no reason whatever to object to the terms of this message . . . as only a very few people will recognize in it a special allusion to the Jewish question.[1]

Critics of Vatican policy have generally taken Weizsäcker's praise of the 'tortuous and obscure' papal communiqué at face value; the opposite view has been expressed by the editor of the Weizsäcker Papers, Leonidas E. Hill, who claims that the above report was a deliberate attempt to mislead and calm Berlin about the import of the Pope's 'oblique' message. Weizsäcker knew he was lying when he assured his superiors that 'only a very few people' would recognize the allusion to Dannecker's *Razzia*; but such a lie 'fitted in with his diplomacy'. To prove his thesis, Hill points out that 'even vague statements' by the head of Catholicism 'were taken very seriously indeed in Berlin' and that Weizsäcker himself had reacted sharply to the Pope's 'tortuous and obscure' pronouncements on previous occasions. In January 1940, for instance, he had written to Bergen that the Pontiff 'has made stinging references to us in various utterances, particularly in the encyclical *Summi Pontificatus* and in his Christmas address . . . If the Vatican describes these demonstrations as general and not directed against anyone in particular, we are of the opinion that this is correct in form only. The Vatican, it is true, used general terms, but it is quite clear who was meant on each occasion.'[2]

While Weizsäcker was reassuring the Wilhelmstrasse, Settimio Sorani (brother of Rosina and executive secretary of DELASEM)

---

[1] IFZ/NG-5027.
[2] Hill, 'The Vatican Embassy of Ernst von Weizsäcker', 150–1; cf. *ND*/NG-4603 (Weizsäcker to Bergen, 25 Jan. 1940).

made a vain attempt to deliver to Pius XII an appeal from the Jewish Community for papal intervention on behalf of the Jewish deportees from Rome. When he arrived at the home of the intermediary (a Yugoslav diplomat who had agreed to pass on his message to the Pope), he was promptly arrested by Kappler's men, with the result that the document never reached its destination. Fortunately, he was released ten days later, thanks to his false identity papers.[1]

When, at the beginning of December, the Vatican organ attacked Fascist racial policy, deploring Buffarini's decree of 30 November, Weizsäcker again hastened to reassure Berlin, affirming that these comments were 'not official', not having been broadcast by the Vatican radio. In the ensuing months the Jew-hunt was stepped up, despite Stahel's assurances to Mgr. Hudal. Pius XII, continuing acts of charity, maintained his silence, while *L'Osservatore Romano* went on deploring the persecution in 'vague terms'.[2]

Before leaving the subject of Vatican policy, it may be well to deal briefly with the conflict of opinion to which the silence of Pius XII gave rise. Albrecht von Kessel affirmed after the war that Hitler continued to toy with the idea of occupying the Vatican and deporting the Pope to Greater Germany from September 1943 until June 1944, i.e. until the capture of Rome by American troops. If the Holy Father had resisted arrest (as he was apparently determined to do), he might even have been 'shot while trying to escape'. A 'flaming protest' by the Pope would not only have been unsuccessful in halting the machinery of destruction but might have caused a great deal of additional damage—to the thousands of Jews hidden in the Vatican and the monasteries, to the *Mischlinge*, the Church, the territorial integrity of the Vatican City, and—last but not least—to the Catholics in all of German-occupied Europe.[3] Nor were these the only reasons for the Pontiff's silence in the face of crime. As Father Leiber, one of the late Pope's secretaries, pointed out in 1963, Pius XII could not choose sides in a conflict between the two arch-enemies

[1] S. Sorani, 'Come sono riuscito a imbrogliare la "Gestapo" ', in Morpurgo, pp. 248–58.
[2] Weizsäcker to Wilhelmstrasse, 3 Dec. 1943 (PA/Pol. III/22). On the continuation of the Jew-hunt in Rome, cf. Comunità Israelitica di Roma, *Ottobre 1943: cronaca di un'infamia*, Rome, 1961, p. 29.
[3] A. von Kessel, 'Der Papst und die Juden', in Raddatz (ed.), *Summa iniuria oder Durfte der Papst schweigen?*, pp. 169–70.

of the Church, Hitler and Stalin. While refusing to bless Hitler's anti-Bolshevik crusade, he could not desire a Bolshevik victory over the West.[1]

Critics of Vatican policy have levelled four main charges at Pius XII. According to Reitlinger, the Pope's failure to protest against the massacres was motivated, not by 'Christian prudence', but by 'un-Christian cowardice' (i.e. fear of arrest and deportation). According to Lewy and De Felice, anti-Jewish prejudice prevented him viewing the plight of the Jews with a real sense of urgency and moral outrage. According to Hochhuth and others, he could have saved numerous lives (if not put a stop to the mass murders), had he chosen to take a public stand on the 'final solution' and had he confronted the Germans with the threats of an interdict or the excommunication of Hitler and the other renegade Catholics within the German ruling clan. As examples of the effectiveness of public protests Hochhuth cited the resolute reaction of the German Episcopate to Hitler's eugenic policies (which forced the dictator to abandon his euthanasia programme) and the forceful intervention of the Papal Nuncios in Slovakia, Hungary, and Romania on behalf of the Jews (which led to temporary suspension of the deportations). At the very least (Hochhuth argued), a public denunciation of the massacres by the head of Catholicism, broadcast widely over the Vatican radio and read from the pulpits by his bishops, would have revealed to Jews and Gentiles alike what 'resettlement' in the East entailed. Pius XII would have been believed, whereas the broadcasts of the Allies were often shrugged off as 'atrocity propaganda'. Many of the deportees who were taken in by the German tales about 'resettlement' and 'labour service' might thus have been warned and given an impetus to escape. Many more Catholics and other non-Jews might have sheltered Jews, and many more Jewish lives might have been saved.[2]

[1] Leiber, 'Der Papst und die Verfolgung der Juden', pp. 103–4.
[2] Reitlinger op. cit., p. 380 ('plain physical fear'); Lewy *The Catholic Church and Nazi Germany*, p. 305: R. De Felice, 'La chiesa cattolica e il problems ebraico durante gli anni dell'antisemitismo fascista', *La Rassegna Mensile di Israel*, xxiii (Jan. 1957), 23–35; id. *Storia degli ebrei italiani*, p. 466. On the intervention of the Papal Nuncios, see F. Cavalli, 'La Santa Sede contro le deportazioni degli ebrei dalla Slovacchia durante la seconda guerra mondiale', *La Civiltà Cattolica* (1 July 1961), 3–18; A. Martini, 'La Santa Sede e gli ebrei della Romania durante la seconda guerra mondiale', *La Civiltà Cattolica* (26 Aug. 1961), 449–63; Hilberg, *The Destruction of the European Jews*, p. 539; Livia Rothkirchen, *Khurban yehudei Slovakia. Te-ur histori b'te-udoth*, Jerusalem, 1961, pp. 131 3; id., 'Vatican

According to Cardinal Tisserant and other loyal Catholics, Pius XII failed to provide moral leadership for his flock. In his above-quoted letter to the Archbishop of Paris, Tisserant complained that 'our superiors do not want to understand the real nature of this conflict', adding that he had vainly pleaded with the Pontiff to issue an encyclical on the duty of the individual to follow the dictates of his conscience rather than blindly execute all orders, no matter how criminal.[1] Three years later Father Alfred Delp, a Jesuit and a member of the German Resistance, told a gathering of Bavarian clergymen that the Church's silence on the horrors perpetrated in the East was endangering its moral prestige. After the war a forthright American Catholic made the same point: 'The problem is whether the Church, in its dealings with the Nazis, compromised its absolute spiritual essence; whether, faced with an absolute evil such as the Germans posed, it was right to think of "reasons of state".'[2]

The first of the above charges—that of 'un-Christian cowardice—is obviously unfounded. As Ciano noted in his diary, the Pope 'is even ready to be deported to a concentration camp but will do nothing against his conscience'.[3] The second charge— that of 'anti-Jewish prejudice'—is based mainly on the fact that in 1941 the Holy See failed to object to the 'Jewish statutes' introduced by the Vichy Government. But while it is true that the Vatican did not consider 'defensive' measures against Jews in conflict with Catholic teaching, it is equally true that Pius XII was profoundly shocked at Hitler's method of solving the Jewish problem. In 1964 it was revealed by Pirro Scavizzi (a military chaplain who repeatedly accompanied an Italian hospital-train to the German-occupied East) that the Pontiff, on being informed

---

Policy and the Jewish Problem in "Independent" Slovakia', *Yad Vashem Studies,* xi (1967), 27–53; J. S. Conway, 'The Churches, the Slovak State and the Jews 1939–1945', *Slavonic and East European Review,* lii (Jan. 1974), 85–112.

[1] See above, p. 247 n. 2.

[2] Lewy, op. cit., p. 307; J. L. Featherstone, 'Did the Church Fail?' *Commonweal,* lxxix (28 Feb. 1964), 650.

[3] Ciano, *Diario,* i, 264 (entry for 13 May 1940); cf. note by Montini (Pius XII–Alfieri, 13 May 1940): 'L'Ambasciatore ha lasciato capire lo stato di grande tensione e nervosismo che regna negli ambienti fascisti, e non ha nemmeno escluso che posse accadere qualche cosa di grave. Al che il Santo Padre si è mostrato molto tranquillo e sereno, osservando di non avere alcun timore di finire, se sarà il caso, in un campo di concentramento o in mani ostili' (*Actes et documents du Saint Siegè et la Guerre en Europe,* i, 454).

of the mass murders, 'cried like a child'.[1] The third charge—that a forceful public stand by the Pope would have saved 'numerous lives'—raises a host of complex problems. Even if we reject Kessel's contention that a 'flaming protest' would only have made matters worse, it does not necessarily follow that Pius XII would have done well to break his silence. In the words of Guenter Lewy, himself a severe critic of the Catholic Church:

Whether a Papal decree of excommunication against Hitler would have dissuaded the Führer from carrying out his plan to destroy the Jews is very doubtful. A revocation of the Concordat by the Holy See would have bothered Hitler still less. However, a flaming protest against the massacre of the Jews, coupled with the imposition of the interdict upon all of Germany or the excommunication of all Catholics in any way involved with the apparatus of the Final Solution, would have been a far more formidable and effective weapon. It certainly would have warned many who were deceived by the Germans' promises of good treatment. Yet this was precisely the kind of action which the Pope could not take without risking the allegiance of the German Catholics. Given the indifference of the German population toward the fate of the Jews, and the highly ambivalent attitude of the German hierarchy toward Nazi anti-Semitism, a forceful stand by the Supreme Pontiff on the Jewish question might well have led to a large-scale desertion from the Church ... The Pope knew that the German Catholics were not prepared to suffer martyrdom for their Church; still less were they willing to incur the wrath of their Nazi rulers for the sake of the Jews whom their own bishops for years had castigated as a harmful influence in German life ... Once the inability of the Pope to move the masses of the faithful into a decisive struggle against the Nazis is accepted as a fact, there is thus some basis for the contention that a public protest, along with any good that would have come of it, might have made some things worse.[2]

Elsewhere in his book Lewy pointed out that there was no real parallel between resistance to the euthanasia programme and resistance to the 'final solution'. The murder of the innocent sick shocked the Germans because the victims were flesh of their flesh; the murder of the Jews, on the other hand, 'did not give rise to similar humane feelings'. Lewy might have added that the 'final solution' was a major plank in Hitler's programme, while

[1] *Actes et documents du Saint Siège,* viii, 669; cf. H. Stehle, *Die Ostpolitik des Vatikans,* Munich, 1975, p. 239.
[2] Lewy, pp. 303–4.

the killing of the mentally infirm was very much a secondary issue.[1]

Lewy also challenged the comparison drawn by Hochhuth between the intervention of Mgr. Giuseppe Burzio, the Papal Chargé d'Affaires in Slovakia (which led to a temporary suspension of the deportations) and the silence of the Pope on the *Judenaktion* in Rome. For one thing (he argued), the case of Slovakia was a special one, the head of the Slovak Quisling regime being a Catholic priest. For another, Eichmann's emissary in Bratislava had instructions to avoid 'political complications'— in spite of which the deportations were resumed in the autumn of 1944.[2] It remains to add that in Hungary it was not the Papal Nuncio who persuaded the Nazis to release some of the deportees in August and October 1944 but the representatives of the Jewish Rescue Committee in Budapest. And while the Nuncios were dealing with reluctant satellites who resented German interference in the domestic affairs of their countries, a public condemnation of the 'final solution' by the Pontiff would have constituted a direct challenge to the arch Jew-baiter in Berlin.[3]

The fourth charge—that the Pope failed to offer unequivocal moral guidance to his flock—has been raised repeatedly by those within the Church who felt that, in the face of a monstrous evil, it was wrong to be guided by 'reasons of state'. In his encyclical *Summi Pontificatus* Pius XII affirmed his duty 'to testify to the truth with Apostolic firmness': 'In the fulfilment of this Our duty We shall not let Ourselves be influenced by earthly considerations nor be held back by mistrust or opposition, by rebuffs or lack of appreciation of Our words.'[4] There is, however, little evidence of 'Apostolic firmness' in the Pontiff's reaction to the massacre of the Jews; nor is it easy to resist the impression that 'earthly considerations' played a prominent part in his decision to maintain his silence in the face of an upsurge of barbarism. In the words of L. E. Hill: 'In the extraordinary circumstances of

[1] Ibid., pp. 265–7.

[2] Ibid., p. 300; Hilberg, op. cit., pp. 469–70. Contrary to Lewy's assumption, the President of Slovakia (Mgr. Josef Tiso) was by no means more responsive to Vatican appeals than Horthy or Antonescu (Rothkirchen, 'Vatican policy and the Jewish Problem in "Independent" Slovakia,' 39, 40, 50).

[3] A. Biss, 'Einstellung der Deportationen in Ungarn', in F. J. Raddatz (ed.), *Summa iniuria oder Durfte der Papst schweigen?*, pp. 179–80.

[4] Quoted in Lewy, p. 306.

1943–45 the Papacy was faced with difficult choices. Nevertheless, its moral powers seem to have been unduly dulled by fear of Bolshevism and an unwillingness to antagonize any of the major Powers . . . The cautious, realistic and unimaginative diplomacy of the Papacy suffers when measured against the highest standards of the Church.' But whatever our views on the Pope's performance as a moral teacher, we cannot but agree with Albrecht von Kessel that 'no one should expect his neighbour, in the biblical sense of the term, to become a martyr'.[1]

In sum, Pius XII was a diplomat who thought it his duty to keep silent *ad maiora mala vitanda* (to avoid greater evils). His critics may be right in affirming that, in failing to speak out, he missed an opportunity for regaining stature; but they are wrong in accusing him of 'un-Christian cowardice' or indifference to human suffering. If he was guilty of an error of judgement, it does not follow that his silence was due to unworthy motives; nor is it likely that in 1943 a 'flaming protest' would have saved the life of a single Jew. Kessel put the point well when he wrote:

All we could do . . . was to warn the Vatican, the Curia, and the Pope himself against rash utterances and actions. To offer any opinion on a question of martyrdom would have been entirely out of place for us Germans whose Head of State was a criminal . . . But would it not have been better from the point of view of human dignity, of Christendom and the Catholic Church, if Pius XII had assumed the martyr's crown, even without achieving any practical results, in the spirit of, let us say, Hans and Sophie Scholl in Munich? Perhaps such a politically senseless sacrifice might have sown seeds that would be yielding the rich harvest which we miss today. Pius XII . . . was a great personality. But I was convinced then and am still convinced today that he almost broke down under the conflicts of conscience. I know that day by day, week by week, month by month he struggled to find the right answer. No one could relieve him of the responsibility for this answer. But who can now maintain . . . that he found the wrong answer when he avoided martyrdom? And who dares, if the answer was indeed the wrong one, to cast the first stone?[2]

[1] Hill, 'The Vatican Embassy of Ernst von Weizsäcker', 158; von Kessel, op. cit., p. 170.
[2] Von Kessel, ibid. On the need for silence *ad maiora mala vitanda*, see Pius XII to Bishop Konrad von Preysing, 30 Apr. 1943 (*Actes et documents du Saint Siège*, ii, 324) and A. Martini, ' "Il Vicario". Una tragedia cristiana?', *La Civiltà Cattolica* (18 May 1963), 324. In his letter to Preysing the Pontiff also expressed his sympathy for the persecuted Jews: 'Es hat Uns . . . getröstet zu hören, dass die Katholiken, gerade auch die Berliner Katholiken, den sogenannten Nichtariern in ihrer Bedrängnis viel Liebe entgegengebracht haben', *Actes et documents*, p. 323.

Dannecker's *Razzia* horrified the Curia, the Catholic clergy, and the overwhelming majority of the Italian people, including even staunch Fascists. Himmler and his aides, on the other hand, were displeased to learn from Kappler that for every Roman Jew seized by the SS, eleven others had escaped. They were equally dissatisfied with Dannecker's subsequent operations all over Northern Italy which resulted in the deportation of another 2,000 Jews.[1] At the beginning of December Kaltenbrunner's office notified Horst Wagner, Luther's successor as head of Inland II, that 'the round-ups in Italy ordered by the Reichsführer SS have so far yielded no result worthy of mention (*bisher zu keinem nennenswerten Ergebnis geführt*)', Italian sabotage having enabled a majority of the potential victims to go underground in time. But since the forces at Dannecker's disposal were quite insufficient for the remaining task, he would have no choice but to enlist the aid of the Republican Fascists, unreliable though they were.[2]

Dannecker was recalled to Berlin where, on 4 December, he took part in a conference on the Italian Jewish problem at the Foreign Ministry, the other participants being Sturmbannführer Friedrich R. Bosshammer, Eichman's expert on Italian affairs, and Eberhard von Thadden of Inland II. Bosshammer proposed that the Italians be congratulated on their decision to intern the Jews, adding that Berlin should press for the handing-over of the internees to the Einsatzkommando Italien. Thadden approved of the first proposal but objected strongly to the second, arguing that a demand for the surrender of the Jews to the SS would probably give rise to a great deal of friction; Buffarini's order would be carried out with greater facility if internment in Italy were made to appear as the 'final solution' and not as a prelude to deportation. In other words, the Jews and their Italian protectors should be lulled into a false sense of security, after which the Gestapo would strike. Bosshammer and Dannecker agreed, whereupon Inland II drafted a detailed memorandum for Ribbentrop from which the following is worth quoting:

With the forces at our disposal it is impossible to carry out a thorough

---

[1] On Fascist disapproval of the *Razzia*, see Tamaro, *Due anni di storia*, ii. 239–40; Pini and Susmel, *Mussolini. L'uomo e l'opera*, iv. 349; M. Caudana and A. Assante, *Dal regno del Sud al vento del Nord*, i, Rome, 1963 pp. 349–50. On Himmler's and Eichmann's disappointment, see YVS/TR-10/754a/*Anklageschrift in der Strafsache gegen Friedrich Bosshammer*, p. 263.

[2] Memorandum by Wagner, 4 Dec. 1943 (YVS/NG-5026).

search of all the ... Italian communities. Since in the meantime the
Italian government has enacted a law providing for the segregation of
all Jews in concentration camps, Group Inland II, in agreement with
the Reich Main Security Office, proposes: that Ambassador Rahn be
instructed to convey to the Fascist Government the satisfaction of the
German Government with this law which is vitally necessary for
security reasons; that (the Italians) be asked to speed up the
implementation of this law and the setting-up of concentration camps
in Northern Italy so as to enable us to remove unreliable elements from
the operational zones ... and that they be informed of the German
Government's readiness to supply them with experienced advisers for
this purpose. In this way it would be possible for us to integrate
(*einbauen*) what is now the *Einsatzkommando* into the government
agencies, to supervise the actual enforcement of this law and to harness
the entire executive apparatus of the Fascist Government to the
implementation of the anti-Jewish measures.

As for shipment to the East, Inland II was of the opinion that
this subject had better not be raised with the philo-Semitic
Italians for the time being: 'The Reich Main Security Office has
no objection to the tactical procedure proposed by *Inland II*.'[1]

Five days later Ribbentrop replied through Gustav Hilger, a
member of his personal staff, that he was in complete agreement
with the above proposals.[2] And another five days later the
Wilhelmstrasse advised Kaltenbrunner's office that Rahn had
been instructed to express the Reich Government's approval of
the new racial law and to press for its speedy implementation. As
for the surrender of the Jews to the SS, it would be better not to
rush matters. As had been pointed out to Bosshammer and
Dannecker on 4 December, 'the Foreign Ministry is inclined to
assume on the basis of its experience that an immediate demand
for the handing over of these Jews would gravely endanger the
success of the segregation measures ... In view of the lack of zeal
which the Italian authorities have shown in carrying out the
anti-Jewish measures decreed by the Duce in recent months, the
Foreign Ministry considers it urgently desirable that the
implementation of these measures should henceforth be super-
vised by German officials.' The Wilhelmstrasse concluded with
the request that the Einsatzkommando Italien be informed of the

[1] Ibid., cf. *Anklageschrift*, pp. 265–7.
[2] Hilger to Inland II, 9 Dec. 1943 (YVS/NG-5026).

above and that Dannecker be instructed to establish co-operation with Rahn or one of his aides.[1]

Dannecker had meanwhile returned to Italy, ostensibly in order to initiate the 'requisite measures' in accordance with the decisions reached on 4 December, in reality in order to extend the 'final solution' to Mussolini's Social Republic without delay. As early as 10 December the SS in Italy began to give orders to the local police which ran counter to both existing Fascist legislation and the proposals approved by the German Foreign Minister. And on 20 December the head of the Security Service (SD) at Bologna issued the following instructions to the Chief of the Bologna Police:

With reference to our conversation of 10 December 1943, I request the handing over to me of the Jews arrested in accordance with the Italian decree (of November 30) in the following cases: 1) Pure Jews (*Volljuden*) with Jewish spouses; in such cases the whole family is to be arrested and handed over to me, irrespective of age or state of health ... 2) Pure Jews who are nationals of Enemy States are likewise to be handed over to me ... 3) Under German law a Jew is defined as a person, at least three of whose grandparents were of pure Jewish stock or who, although born of mixed marriage, professes the Jewish religion; hence you are to arrest and hand over to me also those persons of the Jewish race who are exempt or are considered Aryans for the purposes of the Italian laws hitherto in force. I request that the Jews arrested in virtue of this directive be reported to me on the first and the fifteenth of each month. The evacuation of the arrested persons will be carried out by my office (*Dienststelle*), in agreement with the office of the commander of the Security Police and the SD in Italy.[2]

On the same day a similar letter was dispatched to the Police Chief of Modena, while in Milan the SS requested the Italian police to arrest and surrender to them all those Jews under seventy years of age who had hitherto been exempt or privileged, including even 'half-breeds' and invalids. Yielding to German pressure, the 'Jew-lover' Tamburini dispatched the following cable to the heads of all provinces on 22 January 1944: 'You should make suitable arrangements with the local German authorities to whom the dispositions made by order of the Duce have been explained stop. Consequently cause to be sent to the

[1] YVS/TR-10/754b/*Strafsache gegen Friedrich Bosshammer*, pp. 14–15.
[2] Ibid., pp. 19–21.

concentration camp all Jews even if hitherto exempt or privileged stop. Communicate arrangements reached stop. Tamburini, Chief of Police'.[1]

Emboldened by Italian subservience, the Germans decided to step up the pressure. On 27 January the head of the SD in Milan went so far as to order the Police Chief of Varese to arrest even sick Jews over seventy and to hand them over to him within two days.[2]

The activities initiated by Dannecker on his return to Italy led to the arrest and deportation of at least another 700 Jews. On 30 January yet another convoy—the sixth since the Italian surrender—departed for Auschwitz, by which time the young SS captain had been recalled to Berlin and replaced by Eichmann's adviser on Italian affairs, Bosshammer, who was appointed Judenreferent for Italy and charged with the task of directing 'the fight against the Jews on Italian soil'. Bosshammer arrived in Italy at the end of January and installed himself at Verona (where the Einsatzkommando Italien was now stationed). On 31 January he inspected the convoy of Jews which had left Milan on the previous day, after which he reported to his nominal superior, Brigadeführer (SS Brigadier) Wilhelm Harster, commander of the SD in the Italian Social Republic.[3]

In the ensuing weeks Bosshammer established contact with the Aussenkommandos of the SD all over Republican Italy 'in order to prepare the ground for the "final solution" '. Subsequently, he also called on Preziosi, by now Inspector-General of the Race, in order to discuss 'the anti-Jewish measures to be carried out in Italy'. At Bosshammer's trial after the war it was revealed that Preziosi had stressed the need for acting legally and that the Judenreferent had expressed agreement, assuring his interlocutor that Jews with Aryan spouses would under no circumstances be deported to Germany or to the Eastern territories.[4]

Even before the above meeting, however, it had become evident to all concerned that Bosshammer had no intention whatever of respecting Fascist laws designed to prevent him from making Italy *judenrein*; nor did he feel bound by the

[1] C. E. Heathcote Smith (Rome) to Sir Herbert Emerson (Director, Inter-Governmental Committee on Refugees, London), 18 July 1944 (PRO/F.O. 371/WR435/42843).
[2] *Strafsache gegen Friedrich Bosshammer*, p. 22.
[3] Ibid., p. 23.
[4] Ibid., pp. 24–5.

decisions reached at the Wilhelmstrasse on 4 December. As early as 28 February 1944 an official of the Ministry of the Interior in Genoa reported to Buffarini that the new Judenreferent had taken a series of anti-Jewish measures which went counter to existing legislation:

The direct intervention of the German police ... which acted quite independently and without the co-operation of the local authorities led to the arrest of numerous Jewish men and women, including members of mixed families, who were immediately evacuated from the city and who have not been heard of since. The *Questura* arrested numerous Jews who were interned in the concentration camp of Chiavari; there, too, the German police intervened, removing many Jews, especially males, and we have no idea where they were sent and what happened to them. Their next of kin and other relatives are making inquiries, but we are in no position to enlighten them, not having received any information about the fate of the deportees from the Germans ... Numerous are the cases in which coercive measures against persons and property have been taken in defiance of the orders issued by the Ministry of the Interior. We know of many families where the Jewish partner has been arrested and deported, leaving his Aryan wife and his Catholic children behind in misery and distress. They are asking for news and aid which we are in no position to give and for decisions in their favour which it is difficult and in many cases impossible for us to make. In carrying out the racial policy, the German police do not apply any of the exemptions decreed by the Ministry of the Interior, taking measures which are not brought to our notice until the cases come up for examination in a different context ... Finally, it is imperative to remove the impression now spreading in circles close to the Jews that all the Jews and half-breeds so far deported have been killed ... In these circumstances you may recognize, Excellency, what form the racial policy is likely to assume ... and if it lies in your power, do try to intervene and help us.[1]

On 7 March Buffarini (who presumably shared his subordinate's resentment at the high-handed behaviour of the SS) responded to the above appeal by issuing a fresh decree on the racial issue which was immediately passed on to all German *Dienststellen* in the Fascist Social Republic and from which the following is worth quoting:

In connexion with the relevant communication received from the Directorate-General of Demography and Race and with reference to the telegraphic circular of January 22, it is hereby reaffirmed that

[1] Ibid., pp. 25–6.

persons of *pure Jewish stock,* whether of Italian or foreign citizenship, are to be sent to concentration camps, *with the exception of old people over 70 years of age and invalids.* Jewish members of mixed families, including foreign Jews with Aryan wives . . . *will continue to be exempted from this measure.* Also exempt are all those who . . . are not considered members of the Jewish race for the purposes of the law of July 13, 1939–XVII, No. 1204 [*sic*], which is still in force.[1]

Bosshammer's reaction to this half-hearted challenge took the form of a countermand addressed to his subordinates which the latter duly passed on to the competent Italian authorities. On 4 April, for instance, the SD at Bologna sent the following circular letter to the police chiefs of Bologna, Forlí, Ravenna, Ferrara, Modena, Parma, Reggio Emilia, and Piacenza:

My previous directives regarding the treatment of Jews resident or imprisoned on Italian soil are herewith modified as follows:

1) All arrested Jews who are not married to Aryan women . . . are to be sent to the concentration camp at Fossoli di Carpi,[2] (regardless) of nationality, age or state of health. 2) Under German law the following are considered Jews: a) persons who have at least three grandparents of pure Jewish stock; b) half-Jews (with two grandparents of Jewish race), provided they are members of the Jewish religious community or married to a pure Jew or a pure Jewess; c) persons who do not belong to the Jewish race but who have identified themselves with Judaism by joining the Jewish religious community. 3) No account is to be taken of the current religious beliefs of the Jews in question. Thus a pure Jew, even if a baptized Catholic of lifelong standing, is a Jew just the same . . . 4) Exempted Jews who are enjoying a privileged position under the Italian laws hitherto in force are likewise to be arrested and to be treated as pure Jews in accordance with German racial law. 5) The exemptions hitherto granted to Jewish nationals of neutral or friendly States are to be revoked. 6) All those arrested, including all their next of kin, are to be transferred to the concentration camp at Fossoli di Carpi without delay. *Each week the number of those arrested is to be reported to me by telephone or cable until Friday at the latest* . . . This is to be followed by a written report containing all the relevant particulars . . . 7) Half-breeds, i.e. half-Jews (with at least two Jewish grandparents) and quarter-Jews (with at least one Jewish grandparent) are not to be arrested within the framework of this operation. To the extent,

[1] Ibid., pp. 26–7. For Law No. 1024 see above, p. 254 and p. 255 n. 1.

[2] The camp at Fossoli di Carpi (near Modena) had originally been set up for British and Maltese prisoners of war; it was taken over by the SS at the end of February or the beginning of March 1944 (Strafsache gegen Friedrich Bosshammer, p. 303).

however, that they are considered pure Jews for the purposes of the Italian racial laws [*sic*], they may be treated accordingly. Should any half-breeds of German nationality be among those arrested, you should inform me in writing without delay . . . 8) Pure Jews married to Aryans . . . are to be placed under the strictest surveillance. *If there is the faintest suspicion that they are engaged in political or criminal activities, they are to be arrested at once*[1] . . . 11) You are requested to entrust a very senior official . . . with the implementation of the anti-Jewish measures. In addition, I would ask the chiefs of police to deal with this matter personally as far as possible, given its importance . . .

In conclusion I would point out that this communication is to be treated as 'secret' and that the chiefs of police should *personally keep it under lock and key*. Its transmission to subordinate offices (*Dienststellen*) is inadmissible.[2]

As a result of the above directive, the 'final solution' was extended to all those Jews with Aryan spouses who had the misfortune to fall into German hands, Bosshammer's solemn promise to Preziosi notwithstanding. The Italians, for their part, went on protesting against these violations of the Fascist race laws. On 10 April the Head of Verona Province wrote to Harster at the request of the local chief of police, pointing out that one of the Jewish internees at Fossoli, Volterra, should never have been arrested, being married to an Aryan woman. Harster passed the letter on to Bosshammer who left it unanswered.[3] On 13 April the Chief of the Modena Police informed the Italian commandant at Fossoli di Carpi that another Jewish internee with a Gentile wife, Bassi, should be permitted to rejoin his family in Milan, 'provided the German *Dienststelle* at the camp had no objection'. The camp commandant replied on 3 June that the local German representative had brought the matter to the notice of his superior but that the latter had made no reply.[4] On 27 May the Chief of the Modena Police drew the attention of the camp commandant to the case of the Jew Levi whose Aryan spouse had appealed to the Questura of Milan to secure his release. The commandant replied on 3 June that Mrs. Levi's appeal had been

[1] Our italics.
[2] *Strafsache gegen Friedrich Bosshammer*, pp. 27–30.
[3] Ibid., p. 32. Volterra was deported to Auschwitz on 1 August 1944, where he met his end.
[4] Ibid., pp. 32–3. Bassi was shipped off to Auschwitz on 1 August 1944; unlike Volterra, however, he survived the war.

duly passed on to Bosshammer's office by the local German *Dienststelle* but that so far no reply had been vouchsafed to him.[1]

Undeterred by these rebuffs, the Questore of Modena advised the camp commandant on 5 June that the Ministry of the Interior had ordered the release of the Jew Alces Piazza who was likewise married to a Gentile woman. The commandant replied on 12 June that he would be pleased to comply with the Ministry's order as soon as Bosshammer's consent had been obtained; but since all communications to the Judenreferent had so far remained unanswered, Piazza would have to stay at Fossoli di Carpi until further notice.[2]

On 14 June the Questura of Modena informed the commandant of Fossoli that the Questura of Milan would welcome the release of Vitta Zelman of Trieste, the Jewish wife of an Italian Gentile, 'provided the local German authorities were agreeable'. This letter was duly passed on to the Sturmbannführer by his representative at the camp, Untersturmführer (SS Second Lieutenant) Karl Titho. Again there was no reply.[3]

Finally, on 24 July, even Preziosi felt compelled to enter a protest against Bosshammer's high-handed methods, pointing out in a letter to the Head of Verona Province that the Jewish lawyer Jenna (who had been arrested by the SS at Verona sixteen days earlier) should be set at liberty forthwith, being married to a woman of Aryan race. Despite his 'special relationship' with Hitler, however, the dean of Italian Jew-baiters was as powerless to restrain Eichmann's Judenreferent as the 'Jew-lover' Buffarini. When, at the end of July or the beginning of August, Mrs. Jenna turned up at Bosshammer's office to plead the cause of her husband, the latter responded by giving her a violent push and telling her to be off. And instead of releasing Jenna in accordance with Preziosi's request, he had him transferred to the concentration camp at Gries near Bolzano whence he was shipped off to Auschwitz for extermination on 24 October 1944.[4]

---

[1] Ibid., p. 33. Levi was sent to Auschwitz on 1 August 1944; he died at Dachau in December.

[2] Ibid., pp. 33–4. Piazza, too, was deported to Auschwitz on 1 August 1944; he returned home after the war.

[3] Ibid., p. 34. Vitta Zelman (later Belfiore) was deported to Auschwitz on 1 August 1944; she survived the war and testified at Bosshammer's trial.

[4] Ibid., pp. 34–5. Jenna was killed at Auschwitz.

Not content with extending the 'final solution' to the Jewish members of mixed marriages, Eichmann's emissary launched an all-out offensive against the aged and the sick of Jewish race. In March 1944 the Aussenkommando of the SD at Bologna informed the local Questore that Jewish invalids or half-breeds should be sent to the camp at Fossoli whenever possible. And in May the same Aussenkommando requested eight Italian questori on Bosshammer's orders to comb 'all hospitals, lunatic asylums, and monasteries for Jews or half-breeds'. As a result, hundreds of men and women who had hitherto been considered exempt were arrested and added to the pathetic convoys, including even nonagenarians and mental patients. Of twenty-eight Jews who arrived at Fossoli on 26 May, nineteen were over seventy, twelve were over eighty, and one, Elena Servi, was in her ninetieth year.[1]

At his trial after the war, Bosshammer maintained that he had been opposed to the mass murders but had favoured evacuation to the East for 'security reasons'. It is safe to assume, however, that security reasons played no part in his decision to deport the inmates of mental hospitals and homes for the aged; nor was he under any pressure to send Jews with Aryan spouses to their death. His real motive was presumably the desire to impress his superiors with big figures. As has been noted, Dannecker had achieved 'no result worthy of mention' and been recalled. Bosshammer was determined to succeed where his predecessor had failed, even if it meant exceeding his instructions.[2]

With all his anti-Jewish zeal, however, Eichmann's Juden-referent could not alter the fact that the conditions for a radical solution of the Jewish question did not exist in Republican Italy. For one thing, most of the potential victims had gone into hiding long before his arrival. For another, they could count on the sympathy of the Italian masses and the active help of the Catholic clergy. Opposition to the 'final solution' was widespread even among the Fascist officials who were supposed to co-operate in the implementation of the racial measures. Worst of all, there were quite a few Germans in the Italian Social Republic— diplomats and scholars, soldiers and policemen—who joined

---

[1] Giuliana Donati, 'Elenco cronologico dei convogli di Ebrei deportati dall'Italia', *Ebrei in Italia: deportazione, resistenza*, p. 23.
[2] *Strafsache gegen Friedrich Bosshammer*, pp. 6, 31, 68.

with the Italians in sabotaging the anti-Jewish policy. The following extracts from the diary of Bernard Berenson, the celebrated Jewish humanist and art historian in Florence, throw light on the manifold problems Bosshammer had to face:

November 4th, 1943; ... With the Nazi occupation, Jews naturally feared the worst and took to the *macchia* (bush). As many as ten or twelve are hiding in a villa near Siena. One great landed proprietor, brother and cousin of officers high in army and navy, has been flitting from hole to hole, and at last has decided to take shelter in the small apartment of a friend in the heart of Florence ... It was said that the Fascist prefect, the moment he was installed, warned Jews to leave their homes and go into niding.

December 2nd: ... It seems that the prefect is beside himself, threatens to resign if the execution (of Buffarini's order to arrest and intern the Jews) is insisted on.

January 25th, 1944: ... I am seeing friends who, unlike myself, have no drop of Jewish blood to taint their veins. They are at least as horrified over the treatment of Jews as I am, and can get it as little out of their minds ... The other day a parish priest of this diocese was arrested for harbouring a Jew. The Cardinal of Florence intervened, declaring that he himself was the culprit and requesting to be jailed in place of the priest; which, of course, resulted in the liberation of the prisoner.

September 1945: ... (The Italian people's) sympathies for suffering, whether physical or moral, are wide and warm ... Nowhere else have I encountered like generosity and self sacrifice. Marchese and Marchesa Serlupi Crescenzi were little more than acquaintances when they offered me shelter at serious risk to their peace of mind, and even to their personal safety. They took me in, and treated me not as a refugee ... but as if it made them happy to have me, to serve me, to see to my every comfort ... Unforgettable proofs of friendship were given me by the German Consul, Gerhard Wolf, and by the assistant chief, now chief of police, Virgilio Soldani Benzi. Both of them not only knew where I was but spread the semi-official declaration that I had gone to Portugal. Hundreds of persons could have known and some did know my *macchia* ... Despite alarms and excursions, nobody in any situation gave me away. I learned afterwards that some friends deliberately avoided finding out where I was, not to run the risk of betraying it under torture.[1]

[1] B. Berenson, *Rumor and Reflection*, New York, 1952, pp. 143, 163, 218, 443. On Consul Wolf's opposition to the anti-Jewish excesses, cf. Wolf to Rahn, 6 Nov. 1943 (GFM/131/I/71042). It is worth noting that even SS officers joined with the Italians in sabotaging the anti-Jewish policy. One of these was Sturmbannführer Herbert Herbst,

Several hundred Jews managed to make their way over the mountain passes into Switzerland—a fact which prompted the SS to have a *Sperrzone* (prohibited area) established on the Italo-Swiss border in June 1944.[1] The vast majority, however, went underground in the half of Italy under the German heel. Between 2,000 and 3,000 joined the Italian Resistance, and seven of these (Eugenio Calò, Eugenio Colorni, Eugenio Curiel, Sergio Forti, Mario Jacchia, Rita Rosani, and Ildebrando Vivanti) were posthumously awarded the Gold Medal, the highest Italian decoration for valour. Many others took refuge in monasteries and convents all over the Fascist Social Republic, yet others moved to country places (where they could pass themselves off as Aryan refugees from the Southern provinces) or hid in the homes of Gentile friends. Fascist officials helped by urging the Jews to abandon their houses, by supplying them with false identity papers, or by destroying the police files on non-Aryans; while banks and similar institutions assisted by suppressing or delaying information about Jewish holdings.[2] And although the corporate life of Italian Jewry was ostensibly suspended, DELASEM succeeded in maintaining its activity on behalf of native and foreign Jews right up to the end of the German occupation, largely owing to the co-operation of self-sacrificing monks and priests, such as Père Benoît-Marie (better known as Padre Maria Benedetto) in Rome, Don Francesco Repetto in Genoa, and Don Paolo Liggeri in Milan.[3]

Italian sabotage was not the only obstacle to a drastic solution of the Jewish problem in Italy. An additional stumbling-block was the intervention of allied and neutral governments on behalf of their Jewish nationals which prompted Berlin to advise the Fascist Foreign Ministry on 11 May that Jews of Turkish,

---

Bosshammer's predecessor as head of the Aussenkommando at Padua (*Strafsache gegen Friedrich Bosshammer*, pp. 58, 60).

[1] Rahn (Fasano) to Wilhelmstrasse, 2 Sept. 1944 (YVS/K207003). In Switzerland the Italian-Jewish refugees were aided by the Italian colony at Lausanne and by the Aid Committee for Italian Political and Racial Deportees, of which Angelo Donati had meanwhile become a member (I. Silone, 'Le "Nuove edizioni di Capolago" e gli anni della guerra', in *Egidio Reale e il suo tempo*, Florence, 1961, pp. 162–5).

[2] For details, see, e.g., B. Coccani, *Mussolini, Hitler, Tito alle porte orientali d'Italia*, Bologna, 1948, pp. 170–6; Strazzera-Perniciani, *Umanità ed eroismo nella vita segreta di Regina Coeli, passim*; De Felice, *Storia degli ebrei italiani*, pp. 448, 460–2. Gherardi Bon, *La persecuzione antiebraica*, p. 245.

[3] De Felice, *Storia degli ebrei italiani*, pp. 468–9, 615–16.

Spanish, Portuguese, Swiss, Swedish, and Finnish citizenship should be allowed to return to their countries of origin 'within a reasonable space of time'. On 23 May Mazzolini informed Preziosi that the Duce was in favour of repatriation, there being no reason why he should be more severe on the foreign Jews than his German master; on 30 May Preziosi expressed 'agreement in principle'; and on 29 July Inland II notified the German Embassy in Ankara that the Reich had no objection to the repatriation of Turkish Jews resident in the Italian Republic.[1]

At the trial of Eichmann after the war, it was stated by a Jewish lady witness from Florence that 'every Italian Jew who survived owed his life to the Italians'. But while it is true that at least four-fifths of the Jews living in Italy succeeded in eluding the grasp of the SS and that most of these were saved by Italian Aryans of all classes, it is no less true that such successes as Bosshammer was able to achieve were largely due to (willing or unwilling) Italian collaborators. Thousand of Jews were arrested and interned by the Fascist police to be deported and killed by Himmler's myrmidons. Others were denounced by the local agents and spies of the Gestapo; as Bernard Berenson noted in his diary on 25 January 1944, 'forty new agents were appointed in Bologna to ferret out Jews still in hiding'. Yet others were tracked down by Fascist action squads, headed by notorious thugs and Jew-baiters who took advantage of the German occupation to do their worst. Not a few Jews had their hiding-places betrayed by Italian civilians who were actuated either by racial prejudice or by greed for gain (the Germans having offered rewards for the denunciation of Jews). There were even a few renegade Jews who made common cause with the enemies of their people, the most notorious being Celeste di Porto (nicknamed the 'Black Panther') who turned over dozens of her fellow Jews to the Italian SS for 5,000 lire each.[2]

[1] IC/Job 325/110868—71 (German memorandum transmitted by Reichert, 11 May 1944); 110876—77 (Mazzolini to Preziosi, 23 May 1944; 110879/2 (Preziosi to Foreign Ministry, 30 May 1944); Inland II to Embassy Ankara, 29 July 1944 (YVS/K207055–57).

[2] For details, see Renata Segre, *Appunti sulle persecuzioni antisemite e sulla vita della comunità israelitiche nell'Italia occupata*, Rome, 1964, pp. 13–14; Tagliacozzo, 'Le responsabilita di Kappler nella tragedia degli ebrei di Roma', pp. 399–403; De Felice, *Storia degli ebrei italiani*, pp. 447–9; cf. also D. Carpi, 'Batei kelleu-makhanoth rikuz b'Italia b'tekufat ha-shoah', *Dappim le-khekker ha-shoah v'ha-mered*, i (1969), 178–93. On Celeste di Porto, see *Pantera nera, la spia di piazza Giudia*, Rome, 1945; on Mauro Grini of Trieste, another

In Rome the new Questore, Pietro Caruso, demonstrated his zeal by launching a Jew-hunt in February which resulted in the capture of several hundred persons.[1] He even disregarded the sanctuary agreement between the Vatican and the Germans, permitting his men on 3 February to raid the Basilica of Saint Paul where they seized six non-Aryans, two of them Swiss citizens.[2] The Holy See reacted sharply and so did the local German representatives, most particularly Weizsäcker and Rahn. Ribbentrop at first disagreed with his diplomats, pointing out that the Pope had refused to recognize the Italian Social Republic and that hence the Lateran treaties were no longer binding on the Fascist Government. On learning, however, that his Spanish colleague had protested to the German Ambassador in Madrid, he changed his mind and requested the Duce through Anfuso to put the brake on his over-zealous underling. Mussolini naturally hastened to comply with Ribbentrop's request, while Buffarini, in a confidential talk with a prelate close to the Holy Father, put the blame for the incident on the Germans.[3]

Prior to Bosshammer's arrival at Verona, at least 3,110 persons of Jewish race were shipped to Auschwitz, 2,224 of whom are known to have perished in the Holocaust.[4] Between February and December 1944 at least another 4,056 were deported to the East on Bosshammer's orders, 2,425 of whom are known to have lost their lives: 141 from Fossoli di Carpi to Bergen-Belsen on 19 February; 650 from Fossoli to Auschwitz on 22 February; 835 from Fossoli, Mantua, and Verona to Auschwitz on 5 April; between 738 and 835 from Fossoli to Auschwitz and Bergen-Belsen on 16 May; 35 from Milan to Bergen-Belsen on 19 May; about 1,000 from Fossoli and Verona to Auschwitz on 26 June; at least 425 from Verona to Buchenwald, Ravensbrück, and Bergen-Belsen on 2 August; at least 150 from Gries near Bolzano to Auschwitz on 24 October (by which time Bosshammer had been transferred to Padua); and at least 80 from Gries to

notorious renegade Jew, Gherardi Bon op. cit., pp. 217–18 and CDEC/13B/ Venezia/ Testimony Laura Jacchia Fano.

[1] It is estimated that after 16 October 1943, another 1,084 Roman Jews were arrested by the Germans and their Italian accomplices (*Ottobre 1943: cronaca di un'infamia*, p. 29). On Caruso, see Zara Algardi, *Il processo Caruso*, Rome, 1945.

[2] M. Tagliacozzo, 'Ebrei rifugiati nelle zone extraterritoriali del Vaticano', p. 2; *Il processo Caruso*, pp. 30–3 (report by Pietro Koch, 4 Feb. 1944).

[3] Moellhausen, pp. 162–5.

[4] *Deportazione degli ebrei dall'Italia*, p. 1.

Ravensbrück and Flossenbürg on 14 December (by which time the Allied forces had liberated almost the whole of Central Italy).[1]

Until July Bosshammer's victims were sent off for extermination in trucks. By the beginning of August, however, they had to be transported in buses and ferried across the River Po in boats, the Italian railway system having been paralysed by Allied air raids. By the end of the year, the deportees had to be shipped to camps in the Reich, Auschwitz being about to be captured by the Russian army.[2]

About 2,700 Italian Jews were deported from areas outside Bosshammer's jurisdiction—837 from Trieste to Auschwitz, Ravensbrück, and Bergen-Belsen where all but 77 met their end; over 1,800 from Rhodes to Auschwitz where 1,622 of them died; and at least 82 from foreign countries under German rule, only 9 of whom survived the war.[3] At least 44 were deported for reasons unconnected with their race; 25 of these are known to have lost their lives. In addition, there were 387 deportees the date of whose departure has not yet been ascertained and 334 of whom are known to have perished.[4]

Between the Italian armistice and the collapse of the Fascist Republic at least 173 Jews were murdered on Italian soil: 49, as we have seen, were massacred by the SS in the summer resorts around Lago Maggiore between 15 and 24 September 1943; 4 were done to death at Intra on 11 October; another 4 were among the eleven persons shot at Ferrara on 15 November as a reprisal for the killing of the Fascist *federale*; 78, including Aldo Finzi, were among the 335 hostages butchered by Kappler's men at the Ardeatine Caves on 24 March 1944 in retaliation for the ambush of an SS detachment in Rome; 3 (youngsters from Florence) were slain by the Germans at Gubbio on 27 March; 7

[1] Ibid.; cf. also 'Elenco cronologico dei convogli di Ebrei deportati dall'Italia', pp. 18–27. At Bosshammer's trial no mention was made of the convoy which left Fossoli for Bergen-Belsen in 19 February 1944, presumably because all the 141 deportees survived the war.
[2] *Strafsache gegen Friedrich Bosshammer*, pp. 374–6; *Anklageschrift*, p. 57. Auschwitz was captured by Russian troops on 27 January 1945.
[3] Giuliana Donati, 'Deportazione da Trieste', *Ebrei in Italia: deportazione, resistenza*, pp. 29–30; *Deportazione degli ebrei dall'Italia*, p. 1; see also G. Botteri and F. Carniel, 'I sopravissuti', *Trieste*, vi (May–June 1959), 9–16 and Gherardi Bon, pp. 212–30. The last convoy of Jews from Trieste departed for Bergen-Belsen on 24 February 1945.
[4] Giuliana Donati, 'Dati sulla persecuzione e sulla deportazione degli Ebrei dall'Italia', pp. 9–11; *Deportazione degli ebrei dall'Italia*, p. 1.

were among the twelve persons cut down by the SS at Pisa on 1 August, including Comm. Giuseppe Pardo Roques, the venerable president of the local Jewish community; 3 (the wife of Robert Einstein, cousin of the world-famous physicist, and her two daughters) were slaughtered by the SS at Rignano on 3 August; 19 (17 of them foreigners) were shot or hanged by SS men at Forlí in the course of September; and 6 (all of them foreigners) were killed by the SS at Cuneo on 26 April 1945, three days before the collapse of Hitler's hold on Italy. In addition, at least 119 persons of Jewish race perished in Italian prisons and internment camps during the twenty months of the German occupation.[1]

At the time of the Italian armistice there were some 44,500 Jews in Italy and Rhodes, about 12,500 of them foreigners. By the end of the war at least 7,682 of these had perished in the Holocaust. Of the 8,369 deportees who have so far been identified, 979 returned home after the war, plus a baby born at Bergen-Belsen. In addition, at least 415 Jews survived imprisonment or detention in Italy proper, including 95 who managed to escape. A few leapt to freedom while on their way to the death camps.[2]

Although over four-fifths of the Jews of Italy survived the Holocaust, Bosshammer's anti-Jewish zeal appears to have made the desired impression in Berlin; for on 1 September 1944 he was awarded a decoration, the War Cross of Merit Second Class with Swords, on the recommendation of his nominal superior, Brigadeführer Wilhelm Harster.[3]

On 4 June 1944, after nearly nine months of anguish, Rome was captured by the American Fifth Army, and the Jewish fugitives came out of their hiding-places. On 5 June the anti-Jewish laws were repealed, and a ceremony was held in the main synagogue, attended by Jewish members of the Allied forces.[4] On 18 July Ancona was liberated, on 19 July Leghorn, and on 4 August Florence. In the ensuing months, however, Kesselring succeeded in slowing down the Allied advance, with the result

---

[1] Donati, 'Eccidi di Ebrei in Italia', pp. 31–3.

[2] Ibid., pp. 10–11, 34; *Deportazione degli ebrei dall'Italia*, p. 1.

[3] *Strafsache gegen Friedrich Bosshammer*, pp. 59–60.

[4] R. Sorani, 'Appunti personali di Rosina Sorani del periodo di occupazione tedesca in Roma' (entry for 5 June 1944), quoted in Katz, p. 299.

that all the major Jewish communities of Northern Italy remained under German rule until April 1945.[1]

On 14 July 1944 C. E. Heathcote Smith, resident representative of the Inter-Governmental Committee on Refugees in Rome, drew attention to the tragic plight of the Italian Jews in a cable to his superior in London. On 15 July he sent a second cable on the subject, a copy of which was transmitted to the Foreign Office by the British High Commissioner in Italy a day later and which is worth quoting at some length:

1. I hold official original of German orders on April 22nd . . . for the removal northwards into German concentration camps of all internees except Belgian Norwegian etc. but including Jews of all nationalities, presumably Italians also . . . 43 British Jews were thus suddenly removed in April to a German camp near Modena (Fossoli di Carpi, M. M.)

2. Evidence scarcely less memorable discloses the monstrous fact that many (Jews) are deported to Germany and liquidated. From Italy alone this fate must have overtaken thousands of men, women and children. Clearly this bestial carnage should be stopped forthwith if this can be achieved without injury to the war effort of the Allies.

3. . . . It is estimated that there should have been 16,000 to 20,000 internees in Northern Italy but what with large scale repatriation of Yugoslavs and deportations of Jews and others, those alive there today may be only 8 or 9 thousand including all Christians and an outside maximum of 5,000 foreign Jews. To these 5,000 foreign Jews should be added the 20,000 [*sic*] Italian Jews whom Fascist laws have rendered stateless.

4. Could President Roosevelt following on his initiative for the 1,000 stateless now being shipped to United States be approached to intervene, using the Pope as intermediary if thought advisable. It is suggested that he would invite the Axis to deliver all internees and notably all stateless persons held in Republican Italy to a named port in the North Adriatic. There a mercy ship would be sent to collect them, and this ship could carry on a shuttle service to a near-by port in liberated Italy until all had been removed to safety. As for their eventual disposal, many thousands could be kept in Italy and if United States did not see fit to harbour any then huge camps in Algeria could be made available if required . . .

6. . . . This suggestion of mercy ships is not original but never before has there been such urgency nor so high a probability of success. The

[1] For details, see Shepperd, *The Italian Campaign*, pp. 297–349; B. H. Liddell Hart, *History of the Second World War*, London, 1970, pp. 523–42.

German policy of deportation is well established and total deportation may be carried out if we do not move quickly. On the other hand never before has Germany herself proclaimed so emphatically that she is now on the defensive and hard pressed. She may therefore welcome the opportunity of performing this comparitively small act of decent behaviour which will saddle the Allies with several more thousand mouths to feed . . .

8. . . . . It is suggested that invitation should be merely courteous and direct and that only after eventual rejection should threat be used but that Germany should be informed from the outset that we hold the names of the majority of those interned in Italy.

9. I have discussed the mercy ship suggestion with Mr. Myron Taylor, American Ambassador at the Vatican, who I understand is cabling direct to the President on this matter to endeavour to enlist his support.[1]

On 18 July, in a lengthy dispatch to the Director of the Inter-Governmental Committee on Refugees, Heathcote Smith submitted documentary evidence of 'forcible removal of Foreign Civilian Internees in German Concentration Camps in the North', including Tamburini's above-quoted telegram of 22 January 1944, and a letter dated 4 May 1944 from the Head of Macerata Province to the Ministry of the Interior at Valdagno, stating that all internees of enemy nationality as well as Jews of every nationality had been arrested and transported to Fossoli di Carpi 'in agreement with the German SS Command here'. A copy of Tamburini's cable had also been received at the Ministry of the Interior in Rome where it provoked a negative reaction: 'Here in Rome, the Head of the division of secret affairs for foreigners in the Ministry decided that the order was difficult of fulfilment, as it went counter to existing legislation. He decided to sit on the telegram.' Heathcote Smith concluded by again stressing the extreme urgency of the problem: 'One thing stands out clear and that is that the Civilian Internees moved Northwards are living in much more imminent danger now than they did prior to April 1944, and that unless some measures are found to keep them in Italy, their fate may be that already reserved by the Germans for the countless tens of thousands of their victims.'[2]

[1] Heathcote Smith to Inter-Governmental Committee on Refugees, 15 July 1944 (PRO/F.O.371/WR260/428422). The British High Commissioner was Sir Noel Charles.
[2] See above, p. 381 n. 1.

As might be expected, Pius XII was eager to co-operate in the endeavour to save Jewish lives, all the more so perhaps because he was keenly aware of the bad impression which his policy of silence had made on Western opinion. On 5 August Heathcote Smith reported to his chief that Myron Taylor had already taken up the matter with the Pontiff and that he himself had had a highly satisfactory audience with the Holy Father on 2 August:

The Pope will, as though coming from himself, request the German Ambassador to make earnest endeavour to stay all further deportations and to communicate to His Holiness probable numbers of Jews and others in North Italy still awaiting deportation including possibly Italian Jews. He will further suggest that the Axis should permit these people eventually to reach some haven of refuge . . .

The Pope declared that neither history nor his conscience would forgive him if he made no effort to save at this psychological juncture further threatened lives . . . He would do his best to pave the way and gain time for any steps the American and British Governments might initiate in regard to internees in Europe . . . Under Secretary of State of the Vatican said the Papal Nuncio in Switzerland reported on July 31st recent murder by the Axis of fifty Jewish internees in German concentration camp near Modena.[1]

Pius XII was as good as his word. But the Germans, hard pressed though they were, ignored the Pontiff's appeal. On 26 August Heathcote Smith cabled to his chief:

Under Secretary of State Tardini informs me that the Vatican has received no reply from the German side but he will now urge the Pope to repeat the request with the utmost emphasis. He revealed that the Papal Nuncio in Berlin is most passive, ineffective and elderly and that the German Minister (*sic*) at the Vatican had almost no influence... The Papal Nuncio also had telegraphed August 23rd that all young

[1] PRO/F.O.371/WR583/42843. Heathcote Smith's sense of urgency was not shared at the Foreign Office: 'It is clear that Heathcote Smith is not too well informed of the problems facing us at present. We are confronted with the likelihood of a substantial influx of refugees from the Balkans; also considerable difficulties are being encountered in connection with arrangements for medical personnel and supplies. The military authorities are not likely to agree to the maintenance of many thousands of refugees in Italy until these problems can be resolved' (Foreign Office to Inter-Governmental Committee on Refugees, 11 Aug. 1944, quoted in cable from Winant to Hull, 14 Aug. 1944, *FRUS 1944*, i. 1124). In his reply to Winant on 23 August, Hull deplored the British attitude: 'Strongly felt that every effort should be made to effect rescue of Jews still alive in Northern Italy, even though real possibility thereof may be non-existent. Also agree with statement attributed to Pope that if this attempt was not made neither history nor our conscience would forgive us' (ibid., p. 1132).

people of Jewish race had been deported to Germany from concentration camps (*sic*) at Fossoli near Modena. He will endeavour to ascertain whether 'young people' includes women.[1]

Berlin did not react to the Pontiff's appeal until September and then only in order to point out that the Italian Social Republic was a sovereign State and that the problem of the Jewish internees in Italy was an Italian domestic affair in which Germans had no business to interfere. On 9 September Sir Francis Osborne (who had taken up the matter with the Curia at the request of the British High Commissioner in Rome) reported to the Foreign Office that the issue had by now reached deadlock, the German government having replied to the Pope that the question of refugees in Northern Italy was "one affecting the Fascist Republican Government" and that, as the Holy See had no relations with this government, Pius XII had no "*locus standi* for intervention in the matter"[2]).

It was evident that, even at this juncture, the Germans were not interested in the opportunity of performing a "small act of decent behaviour"; nor were the Allies prepared to go beyond a "courteous invitation" to stay the deportations. Nothing remained to the Jews and their well-wishers but to wait for the liberation of Northern Italy. As we now know, they had to wait until a few days before the end of the war.

While the Germans and their Italian accomplices were hunting down Jews throughout the Salò Republic, Mussolini (by now installed as puppet dictator in a villa near Gargnano on Lake Garda) was having second thoughts about the wisdom of the racial policy he had initiated in 1938. Speaking to Bruno Spampanato in December 1943, he claimed that his brand of racialism had nothing whatever to do with Hitler's anti-Semitic folly:

I have practised racialism since 1922 but a racialism of my own. The health, the conservation of the race, its betterment, the fight against tuberculosis, mass sport, children to camps—that was racialism as I understood it. But there was also a moral racialism that I advocated, the pride in belonging to this millenarian race born between the snows of the Alps and the fire of Etna. Our racialism with respect to the outside world? The elevation of Italian prestige, of the genius of our civilization.

[1] Heathcote Smith to Sir Herbert Emerson, 26 Aug. 1944 (PRO/F.O.371/WR893/42843).
[2] PRO/F.O.371/WR1078/42843.

In July 1938 the Duce had boasted of being the principal, if not the sole, author of the Race Manifesto. In December 1943, however, he told Spampanato that the Manifesto was a "piece of pseudo-scientific rubbish (*astruseria scientifica*) concocted by certain scholars and journalists":

The Manifesto of the Race could have been avoided... It is a long way from anything I have said, written or signed on the subject. I suggest you look at the back issues of *Il Popolo d'Italia*. I have always considered the Italian people an admirable product of diverse ethnic fusions on the basis of geographical, economic, and especially spiritual unity. It is the spirit which has put our culture on the by-ways of the world; members of different races have been the bearers of one and the same splendid civilization. That is why I am opposed to Rosenberg's myth.

In July 1938 Mussolini had denied that he was aping 'anyone or anything'. In December 1943, however, he frankly admitted to Spampanato that the 'Manifesto of the Race' was nothing but 'a ponderous German treatise translated into bad Italian'.[1]

Speaking to Serafino Mazzolini on 12 January 1944—the day after the execution of Ciano and four other members of the Grand Council who had voted for Grandi's motion—the Duce lashed out at the Fascist thugs who were co-operating with the SS in the Jew-hunt, saying that they would suffer the same fate as the 'traitors' of 25 July. About the same time he told Augusto Liverani, his Minister of Transport and Communications, that he now agreed with Nino d'Aroma who in 1938 had made a vain attempt to dissuade him from importing the German racial theories into Italy.[2]

Speaking to Dr. Georg Zachariae, his German medical adviser, in February 1944, Mussolini declared that he was 'not an anti-Semite' and that Hitler's treatment of the Jews 'did not redound to Germany's honour'. And while reiterating his charges against Jewish high finance, he denied the existence of a Jewish problem in Italy.[3]

In his public utterances the Fascist leader naturally continued to pay lip-service to the anti-Jewish cause; but he did so as rarely and as briefly as possible. Between September 1943 and April 1945 he made only one single reference to the Jewish peril in a

[1] Spampanato, *Contromemoriale*, ii. 130–2.
[2] Tamaro, *Due anni di storia*, ii. 370; d'Aroma, *Mussolini segreto*, pp. 289–90.
[3] G. Zachariae, *Mussolini si confessa*, Milan, 1948, pp. 169–70.

public speech—on 14 October 1944 at Gargnano when he denounced the 'voracity of Jewish capitalism which is aiming at . . . the scientific exploitation of the world'. During the same period he mentioned the Jews only seven times in the ninety-nine articles he wrote for the *Corrispondenza Repubblicana.* On 3 November 1943 he accused the Minister of the Royal Household, Duke Pietro d'Acquarone, of having unleashed 'Masonic-Jewish scoundrelism' against the Fascist regime; on 17 November he referred to America as the 'levy of Israel'; on 27 December he charged the Jews with a desire for 'integral, spiteful vengeance' against the Third Reich; on 9 February 1944 he branded as criminals the American pilots who were waging war against defenceless civilians in accordance with 'Talmudic doctrine'; on 5 June he let fly at the 'anti-national forces enslaved to Jewish-Masonic interests'; and on 18 February 1945, commenting on the meeting of the Big Three at Yalta, he lashed out at Stalin's 'Jewish-inspired ferocity', at the devilish anti-German plot hatched by 'the Jew Morgenthau', and at the unholy alliance between 'Jewish capitalism' and 'Jewish Bolshevism'.[1] In his conversations with Rahn, however, he made no secret of his aversion for Preziosi and his repugnance to the racial measures that were being carried out in the part of Italy under his nominal rule.[2]

In his memoirs of 1942–3, published in *Il Corriere della Sera* between 24 June and 18 July 1944, the Duce devoted no more than four sentences to the 'Jewish aspect' of the Italian tragedy. In the opening chapter ('From El Alamein to the Mareth Line') he accused Gaullist France ('the France of the Jews, Freemasons, and Bolsheviks') of having 'opened the door of the Mediterranean to America'. In the chapter on the monarchy ('The Drama of the Dyarchy') he poked fun at the monarchist brand of republicanism ('represented by the Jew Salvatore Barzilai'), at the King (the 'honorary brother' of the Jews), and at the Crown Prince (who had had a Jewish tutor, Vittorio Polacco). Unlike Preziosi and other Fascist scribes, however, he made no mention of the 'Jewish

[1] *O.O.* xxxii. 115, 264, 284, 311, 371, 451, 452.
[2] Speaking to Rahn on 23 October 1943, Mussolini praised Preziosi as a 'loyal friend' and an 'expert on the Masonic–Jewish question', adding, however, that he had no intention of entrusting him with any political mission (GFM/131/70839x); in a subsequent talk he made it clear that he disapproved of Preziosi's anti-Jewish crusade (Rahn, op. cit., p. 245).

war' and no attempt to put the blame for the fall of Fascism on the Jews.[1]

Anti-Semitism did not figure in any of the confidential utterances Mussolini is recorded as having made during the last two months of his life—to Madeleine Mollier, wife of the German press attaché, at the beginning of March 1945, to the journalist Ivanoe Fossani on 20 March, to the Prefect Gioacchino Nicoletti on 18 April, and to the journalist Gian Gaetano Cabella on 20 April. We are left with the impression that he did not regard the Jewish question as an essential concern for Fascism.[2]

It now remains to deal briefly with the Duce's vain attempts to restore a measure of sovereignty to the Fascist Republic and to assess their bearings on the Jewish issue.

Within a few days of his return from Munich it became clear to Mussolini that the Germans now regarded Italy as conquered as well as occupied territory and that he himself had been reduced to the role of political figurehead. On 26 September 1943 he gave vent to his resentment in a private talk with Rahn, deploring 'the diverse unsystematic ways in which Germany was interfering in every department of public life' and adding that it would be 'meaningless to set up a government that did not govern, to lay down regulations without having the means to enforce them, and to reorganize an administration which no longer had anything left to administer . . . He regarded it as the task of the new Italian Government to maintain law and order in the rear of the German armed forces, and he would ask that at the earliest opportunity he should once again be granted the necessary means for doing so.'[3]

On 27 September, after the first meeting of his new Cabinet, the Duce drafted a letter to Hitler to plead again for an end to German meddling in Italian internal affairs:

The Republican Government which I have the honour to lead has only one desire and aim—to see that Italy resumes her place in the war as soon as possible. But to reach this supreme result, it is essential for the

[1] *O.O.* xxxiv. 305, 408, 410. Needless to say, Mussolini continued to attack the Jews in his correspondence with German anti-Semites. In a letter to the German translator of his memoirs, for instance, he wrote that the Allies would lose the war because they were guided by an 'essentially Jewish' conception of life (G. Bocca, *La repubblica di Mussolini*, Rome–Bari 1977, pp. 203–4).

[2] *O.O.* xxxii. 157–61, 168–82, 186–90, 190–201.

[3] Rahn to Wilhelmstrasse, 26 Sept. 1943 (GFM/132/123328–32).

German military authorities to confine their activity to the military sphere only and, for all the rest, to allow the Italian civil authorities to function . . . If this is not accomplished, both Italian and world opinion will judge this government incapable of functioning, and the government itself will fall into discredit and, even more, into ridicule. I am sure, Führer, that you will realize the importance of the points which I have put to you.[1]

To this appeal Hitler made no reply. Undeterred, Mussolini took advantage of the impending departure of Graziani for Germany to send him a second message on 4 October:

It is my duty, Führer, to indicate to you the obstacles to the reorganization of Italian life . . . The German military commands issue a continuous stream of orders on matters concerning civilian life . . . The Italian civil authorities are ignored, and the population has the impression that the Fascist Republican Government has absolutely no authority even in matters totally extraneous to the military sphere . . . I also have the duty to tell you that the nomination of a High Commissioner at Innsbruck for the provinces of Bolzano, Trent, and Belluno has created a painful impression throughout Italy . . . The only person who is going to profit by this will be the traitor Badoglio.[2]

Again there was no reply. But the Duce was not prepared to resign himself to the part of figurehead which his German master had assigned to him, impotent though he was. Throughout the twenty months of the German occupation he went on protesting against the violations of Italian sovereignty—against the *de facto* annexation of the Alto Adige and the Venezia Giulia, against the establishment of military government in Upper Italy, against German sabotage of his social policy, against the meddling of German 'experts' and 'advisers' in every detail of internal administration, against the misconduct of the German military, and—last but not least—against the excesses of the SS.[3]

In his talks with Rahn and Wolff the Duce repeated with

[1] Spampanato, op. cit. iii. 260.

[2] *O.O.* xxxii. 205-7.

[3] For details, see Rahn to Ribbentrop, 10 Oct. 1943 (GFM/132/123646); IC/*Segretaria particolare del Duce*/Job 162/047427–29; M. Toscano, 'La controversia tra Salò e Berlino per l'occupazione nazista e per le decisioni annessionistiche di Hitler dell'Alto Adige e del Trentino nei documenti diplomatici della Repubblica Sociale Italiana', *Storia e Politica*, vi. (Jan.–Mar. 1967), 1–59; K. Stuhlpfarrer, *Die Operationszonen 'Alpenvorland' und 'Adriatisches Küstenland' 1943–1945*, Vienna, 1969; Buffarini Guidi, op. cit., pp. 160–76; De Felice, *Il problema dell'Alto Adige nei rapporti italo-tedeschi dall'Anschluss alla fine della seconda guerra mondiale*, Bologna, 1973, pp. 69–96.

wearisome insistence that German disregard of Italian rights and susceptibilities was harmful to the common cause. And in a letter to the former, dated 17 August 1944, he wrote that it was 'necessary to give the twenty-two million Italians of the Po Valley the impression that there is a Republic, a government; and that such government is considered as an ally and its territory not as *war-booty*, twelve months after it has been officially recognized by the Reich. We must not give the least justification to those who regard us—in so far as we are your allies—as traitors.'[1]

In his conversations with members of his entourage Mussolini continually gave vent to his resentment against the German occupiers. On 12 November 1943 he said to his private secretary, Giovanni Dolfin, that it was 'useless for these people (the Germans) to persist in calling us allies' and that 'none of us' would ever assist in the 'gradual enslavement of our country'. On 12 January, in his above-mentioned talk with Mazzolini, he blamed the Germans for the death of Ciano. On 31 August he told his Cabinet in 'accents of deep bitterness' that he had had enough of German meddling: 'Either the government will be placed in a position to function, or it will resign'. On 27 September he spoke to the Japanese Ambassador, Shiurukuro Hidaki, of 'the tragic situation facing Italy as a result of German lack of comprehension'. On 17 February 1945 he informed his *chef de cabinet* at the Foreign Ministry, Alberto Mellini, that relations with the German authorities were 'not working out at all' and that rather than submit to further humiliations he would withdraw from public life. And on 18 April, in his conversation with Nicoletti, he blamed the German leaders for the loss of the war.[2]

Mussolini's 'deep bitterness' was shared by all his collaborators, not least by those who, like Mazzolini and Anfuso, remained 'pro-German' to the end.

At the beginning of November 1943 Vittorio Mussolini went to Berlin to plead his father's cause. In a talk with Steengracht on 3 November he pointed out that the conduct of the Germans in

[1] Deakin, pp. 670–2, 676, 679–80, 731–2; for Mussolini's letter of 17 Aug. 1944, cf. Kirkpatrick, *Mussolini*, pp. 603–4

[2] Dolfin, op. cit., pp. 89–90; Tamaro, *Due anni di storia*, ii. 370; iii. 270–1; A. Mellini Ponce de Leon, *Guerra diplomatica a Salò*, Bologna, 1950, pp. 69–72; *O.O.* xxxii. 190.

Italy was calculated to create the impression that the Duce was 'a mere executive organ of the German Government'. For example, the Duce had nominated prefects only to be overridden; he had no channel of communication with the prefectures except through German army links; the Italian security organs had no weapons; the Fascist newspaper in Brescia had been confiscated by the German authorities; and the South Tyrol had been virtually incorporated into the Reich. All this, Vittorio said, 'weighed heavily on his father, whom he had left in a very depressed state of mind'.[1]

On 10 May 1944 an Italian Foreign Office minute addressed to Rahn drew attention to the harm the German occupation was doing to the common cause:

As a result of the Armistice between the Badoglio Government and the Allied Powers, the German Armed Forces in Italy found themselves in a situation which justifiably gave them the appearance of occupying troops in enemy territory ... On 25 September 1943, however, with the birth of the new Italian Republican State, recognized by the Government of the Reich and considered to be the continuation of Italy as a member of the Tripartite Pact, the juridical and actual situation underwent a substantial change: the territory of the Italian Social Republic lost its character of enemy territory ... In regard to the above the Ministry of Foreign Affairs points out that nevertheless there has been no modification since 25 September 1943 in the relations between the German Armed Forces and the National Republican State ... The Ministry for Foreign Affairs has the honour to stress the following considerations with regard to this situation: while on the one hand this attitude on the part of the German Military Authorities is in sharp contrast with the new situation created on 25 September 1943, on the other, the continued exercise by the Germans of the rights of an occupying power not only deprives the Italians of the concrete means of reconstituting their Armed Forces, but ... removes the very foundation of such reconstitution ... It would therefore seem to be to our common interest, both for general political purposes and in order to allow of the reconstitution of the Italian military instrument, that the present state of affairs should be modified.[2]

By the end of June even Graziani (the only member of Mussolini's Cabinet to enjoy the confidence of Preziosi) had lost faith in the Axis alliance. In a long memorandum addressed to

---

[1] Minute by Hencke, 3 Nov. 1943 (GFM/131/I/71009–21).
[2] IC/RSI/Min. Affari Esteri/Job 16/0070072/–74.

the Duce he went so far as to claim that, as a result of German misrule, the Fascist Social Republic was on the verge of collapse: 'Although everyone recognized the absolute right of Germany, after the betrayal of 8 September, to secure the position of her armies at the front, it is equally deplorable that after more than nine months of countless proofs of absolute loyalty on the part of the Italian Social Republic the regime of military occupation has become even more oppressive and extended to every sector of national life. Everyone is convinced that the government counts for nothing and that the Germans are the real masters.'

The sending of men to Germany ('the most unpopular aspect of life in Italy today') had the effect of driving tens of thousands of Italians into the ranks of the partisans and of undermining the political and military structure of the Fascist State: 'In practice the government of the Italian Social Republic controls, and that only up to a point, the stretch of plain astride both banks of the Po. All the rest is virtually in the hands of the so-called rebels who are supported by large sections of the population . . . All our 'peripheral' organizations have been destroyed. The local centres and the countryside lack today any element of force which can carry out the orders of the government and make them respected.'[1]

Hitler, for his part, had no intention of ceasing interference in Italian domestic affairs, whatever the effect on the Fascist administration. He saw no virtue in an Italian army or in according any liberty to the ramshackle Salò Republic. In November 1943 he told Otto Abetz that his friendship for Italy had been 'a great mistake'. And in December, when asked by his military advisers for his views on the constitution of an Italian Fascist army, he replied disdainfully: 'Germany is no longer interested in an Italian army because her relations with Italy are too strained as the result of the events of last September *and are bound to remain so.* The organizing of Italian military units would therefore demand the greatest caution and watchfulness.'[2]

At the Klessheim Conference (22–3 April, 1944) Hitler complained bitterly that he had based his plans on the personality of Mussolini, only to find that both the man and his regime had

[1] *Processo Graziani*, ii. 31–3.
[2] O. Abetz, *Das offene Problem*, Cologne, 1951, p. 266; *Führer Conferences on Naval Affairs (Brassey's Naval Annual)*, London–New York 1948, p. 109, 19–20 Dec. 1943).

vanished overnight. On the same occasion he argued that he could not afford to stop interfering until the Fascist system had been strengthened—to which the Duce might have retorted that it was precisely German meddling which effectively impeded any strengthening of the system.[1] Finally, on 17 February 1945, in one of the monologues recorded by Martin Bormann, he stated that his policy of non-intervention in Italian internal affairs had been a fatal error on his part:

Out of gratitude (for I shall never forget the attitude adopted by the Duce at the time of the Anschluss) I have always abstained from criticizing or passing judgement on Italy. I have on the contrary always been at great pains to treat her as an equal. Unfortunately, the laws of nature have shown that it is a mistake to treat as equals those who are not your equals . . . Neither my personal affection for the Duce nor my instinctive feelings of friendship for the Italian people have changed. But I do blame myself for not having listened to the voice of reason which bade me to be ruthless in my friendship for Italy . . . Life does not forgive weakness.[2]

For all his bitterness, however, Hitler was still anxious to keep up appearances. He therefore assured the Italians that all his measures were designed 'for and not against the Duce', that 'not a single square yard' of Italian territory had been annexed, that he would do his best to fulfil all Italian wishes, and that he continued to regard Mussolini as his 'best and possibly only friend'. And while these fair words bore little relation to the truth, they provided the Duce with a peg on which to hang his ceaseless complaints about German violations of Italian sovereignty.[3]

Hitler's refusal to permit the creation of an independent Italian State with its own armed forces affected the Jewish issue in a variety of ways. On the one hand, it enabled the SS to

[1] A. Hillgruber (ed.), *Staatsmänner und Diplomaten bei Hitler. Vertrauliche Aufzeichnungen über Unterredungen mit Vertretern des Auslandes, ii: 1942–1944*, Frankfurt/Main, 1970, pp. 406–438. The Jews were mentioned three times in the course of the conversations. Graziani informed the Führer that 'Freemasons and Jews' were being eliminated from the Italian officer corps (p. 411); Hitler told the Duce that the days of the 'Jewish democracies' were numbered (p. 422) and that the war was being waged against the 'international Jewish gang' (p. 438).
[2] H. Trevor-Roper (ed.), *The Testament of Adolf Hitler. The Hitler–Bormann Documents, February–April 1945*, London, 1961, pp. 74–5.
[3] GFM/131/I/71020; Anfuso, op. cit., 378, 487–93; De Felice, *Il problema dell'Alto Adige*, pp. 75–80; Moellhausen, p. 275.

include the Italian Jews in their 'resettlement' programme and to thwart Buffarini's attempts to remove the racial question from German hands. On the other, it fatally weakened the Fascist administration on whose co-operation the success of the Jew-hunt depended. When Buffarini ordered the internment of the Jews, it seemed to Bosshammer that the 'final solution' of the Italian Jewish problem was within easy reach. Eight months later he had to inform Berlin that the liquidation of Italian Jewry was no longer a practical proposition, given the progressive disintegration of the Fascist Social Republic and the growing partisan threat.[1]

Italian resistance to the 'final solution' took the form of unofficial sabotage and futile complaints about German violations of the Fascist race laws. In addition, there were repeated attempts to liquidate the Fascist bands which co-operated with the SS in the Jew-hunt (in October 1944 Pietro Koch, one of the worst of Kappler's protégés, was arrested and imprisoned on Mussolini's orders) as well as ceaseless protests by the Duce and his Ministers against the sequestration of Jewish property by the German authorities in the border provinces.[2] In February 1945 the 'Jewish problem' cropped up in a new and unexpected form when the SS arrested a member of Mussolini's entourage, the Questore Eugenio Apollonio, accusing him of being 'half-Jewish and about to intrigue against the Germans'. The Duce was furious and threatened to resign. But when his German guardians refused to give way, he thought it wiser not to insist.[3]

While the SS were rounding up and deporting the Jews, Preziosi was busy devising Nuremberg laws on the German model with the object of eliminating 'Jewish blood' from Italian public life. On 15 May 1944 he submitted a draft to Mussolini which provoked a violent reaction from Buffarini who (in a memorandum dated 17 May) denounced Preziosi's racial theories as politically harmful and scientifically untenable. On 18 May

[1] *Anklageschrift in der Strafsache gegen Friedrich Bosshammer*, p. 381.
[2] *Il processo Caruso*, p. 41; Buffarini Guidi, pp. 125–7; P. Pisenti, *Una repubblica necessaria (R.S.I.)*, Rome, 1977, pp. 83–7; IC/Job 325/110911 (10 Feb. 1944); 110913 (14 Feb. 1944); 110921–22 (11 Apr. 1944); 110923–24 (16 Apr. 1944); 110931–32 (10 July 1944); 110946–47 (16 Sept. 1944); 110949 (4 Oct. 1944); 110958–59 (9 Feb. 1945); 110961 (30 Mar. 1945); 110962 (21 Apr. 1945).
[3] Mellini, op. cit., pp. 70–100; G. Pini, *Itinerario tragico (1943–1945)*, Milan, 1950, pp. 248–51.

the Duce informed Preziosi that he agreed with his Minister of the Interior. As a result, no new anti-Jewish law was passed by the Fascist Cabinet until 16 April 1945, by which time the Italian Social Republic had all but ceased to exist.[1]

Six days earlier—on 9 April—the Allied armies had at long last resumed their offensive in Upper Italy. They were aided by the Italian partisans who took over the major Northern Italian cities—Genoa (26 April), Milan (26 April), and Turin (28 April). While his soldiers in Italy were withdrawing to the Po, Hitler gave vent to his hatred of the Jews in a last lunatic message to Mussolini:

The struggle for existence or non-existence has reached its climax. Using huge forces and materials, Bolshevism and Judaism have engaged themselves up to the hilt to assemble their destructive forces on German territory, to precipitate our continent into chaos. Nevertheless, with their obstinate scorn of death, the German people and all the others who are animated by the same sentiments will fling themselves to the rescue, however hard the struggle, and with their incomparable heroism will change the course of the war at this historic moment which will decide the fate of Europe for centuries to come.[2]

The above telegram reached Milan on 24 April and was published in the papers the following morning. On 26 April Giovanni Preziosi committed suicide. On 28 April Mussolini and his mistress were caught by partisans and shot near the shores of Lake Como. On 29 April their bodies were hung up on a gibbet in Milan where the Duce had proclaimed the Rome–Berlin Axis on 1 November 1936. On the same day, at 2 p.m., German envoys at Caserta signed a document providing for the unconditional surrender of all Axis troops in Italy by 2 May.[3]

The nightmare was over. But Italian Jewry had suffered a blow from which it has not yet recovered.

---

[1] Buffarini Guidi, pp. 53–9; De Felice, *Storia degli ebrei italiani*, pp. 443–47. On the anti-Jewish law of April 1945, cf. IC/Job 325/110907.

[2] Tamaro, *Due anni di storia*, iii. 514.

[3] On Preziosi's end, see *Il Meridiano d'Italia* (31 May 1959), 14–15; on Mussolini's, ibid. 2–11; Deakin, pp. 814–17; on the surrender of the Axis forces in Italy, Shepperd, op. cit., pp. 351–69; *Kriegstagebuch des Oberkommandos der Wehrmacht*, iv/2, ed. P. E. Schramm, Frankfurt/Main, 1961, pp. 1662–6.

XI Epilogue

ALTHOUGH THE Fascist seizure of power caused a good deal of uneasiness in Jewish circles, few students of Italian Fascism alluded to a Jewish problem in Italy before the birth of the Axis. Robert Michels, the noted sociologist, warned of a possible clash between Fascists and Jews in an article published at the end of 1922. Bolton King, a leading authority on the Risorgimento, charged the Fascists with hatred of 'Protestants and Jews' in a book published in 1931.[1] But these were the exceptions which prove the rule.

After 1929 the Italian anti-Fascists began to worry about the honeymoon between the Duce and the Jews. In September 1931 Carlo Sforza, the former Italian Foreign Minister, expressed the hope that the Jews would refuse to play the Fascist game, despite Mussolini's repeated professions of philo-Semitism and anti-racialism: 'Les israélites ne doivent pas combattre seulement pour les causes juives. Ils ne doivent pas faire le jeu de leurs ennemis en considérant leurs problèmes comme séparés des autres problèmes de liberté'.[2] On the eve of the Ethiopian campaign the attitude of the Jews of Italy was described by Gaetano Salvemini as 'even more servile and abject' than that of their Catholic compatriots.[3] And as late as 1937 Giuseppe Antonio Borgese lashed out at the Jewish intellectuals ('novelists and moralists of international renown') who were betraying the cause of Italian liberty because the Fascist dictator had so far refrained from persecuting their co-religionists in Italy: 'If the Jews are allowed a decent or at least a bearable life in Rome or Vienna, why bother about Italy? "We cannot refuse our gratitude to Mussolini", thus spake one of them.'[4]

The Duce's declaration of war on the Jews took most students of Fascism by surprise. So acute an observer of the Italian scene as D. A. Binchy wrote in November 1939:

[1] R. Michels, 'Der Aufstieg des Faschismus', *Neue Zürcher Zeitung*, 29 Dec. 1922; Bolton King, *Fascism in Italy*, London, 1931, pp. 48–9.
[2] Quoted in De Felice, *Storia degli ebrei italiani*, p. 119.
[3] *Giustizia e Libertà*, 15 Aug. 1935.
[4] Borgese, *Goliath*, pp. 341–2.

Of all the bewildering inconsistencies which (Mussolini's) policy has shown, the jump from extreme philo-Semitism to extreme anti-Semitism was at once the most sudden and the most difficult to explain. Nobody had spoken more contemptuously of Hitler's pseudo-science than he ... But perhaps the most curious evidence of the suddenness of the Duce's 'conversion' is furnished by the Fascist Encyclopaedia, so often glorified as the greatest intellectual achievement of the régime: the admirably balanced article on 'Anti-Semitism' (iii. 127) is from the pen of a Jewish scholar, while that on 'Race' (xxviii. 910) roundly declares: 'There is no Italian race, but rather an Italian people and nation'. In face of such signal marks of benevolence, it was no wonder that the Jewish press in Italy and abroad hailed Mussolini as a very paragon of dictators.[1]

There were some observers who found the Duce's inconsistencies less bewildering and less difficult to explain than Binchy. In April 1937 Neville Laski was told by an unnamed Italian that Mussolini was neither a Jew-lover nor a Jew-hater but purely and simply an opportunist, 'willing, on purely material grounds, to have one policy today and another tomorrow, as he may conceive such policy to be productive of most material results for himself, Italy and his ambitions. If philo-semitism pays, he is philo-semitic; if anti-semitism pays, he is quite willing equally to be an anti-semite.'[2] Commenting on Laski's report, the British press attaché in Rome pointed out that certain expressions of anti-Jewish prejudice had always occurred in Italy in times of crisis, even prior to the rise of Fascism.[3]

Mussolini's break with the Jews gave rise to a debate over the origins and nature of Fascist racialism. Some critics agreed with Binchy that it was a sudden reversal of traditional Fascist policy; others pointed out that Fascism had been tinged with anti-Semitism from its very inception; yet others stressed the importance of pre-Fascist (clerical and nationalist) anti-Judaism and anti-Zionism.[4] The Fascists, for their part, insisted that their leader had been a consistent racialist since 1919; and the Duce himself reminded his lieutenants that he 'had spoken of the

---

[1] Binchy, *Church and State*, pp. 610–11.

[2] Laski to Vansittart, 7 Apr. 1937 (see above, p. 111 and n. 3).

[3] McClure to Foreign Office, 11 May 1937 (see above, p. 8 and n. 1).

[4] See above, pp. 120–127. On pre-Fascist anti-Semitism, cf. G. Valabrega, 'Il fascismo e gli ebrei: appunti per un consuntivo storiografico', in S. Fontana (ed.), *Il fascismo e le autonomie locali*, Bologna, 1973, pp. 401–26; id., *Ebrei, fascismo, sionismo*, Urbino, 1974; U. Caffaz, *L'antisemitismo italiano sotto il fascismo*, Florence, 1975, pp. 2, 31.

Aryan race in 1921 and after that always of race'.[1] It was noted with interest that the racial laws, in addition to alienating the Church and public opinion, were causing heart-searchings even among committed supporters of the Fascist regime. Ezio Garibaldi publicly attacked Interlandi. Alfredo Goffredo, Mussolini's former *chef de cabinet,* openly protested against the publication of the *Protocols of the Elders of Zion.* Mino Somenzi, a friend of Marinetti's, denounced anti-Semitism as a side-tracking stunt, while Gioacchino Volpe, the leading historian of the Fascist movement, frankly deplored the importation of the German racial theories into Italy.[2] Camillo Pellizzi, a Fascist propagandist in London, wrote in 1939: 'Every Italian is willing to recognize that, whatever the merits of the present legislation from a general point of view, individual cases of law-abiding and patriotic Jews who feel very hurt by the present anti-Jewish laws are not infrequent and deserve sympathy; Italy is not and never will be a country for pogroms.'[3]

After Mussolini's downfall, the former Fascist hierarchs generally maintained an embarrassed silence, except those who, like Acerbo and Federzoni, had opposed the racial laws. The neo-Fascist apologists generally admitted that the persecution of the Jews had been a deplorable error. According to Attilio Tamaro, Mussolini's conversion to racialism marked 'the beginning of the crisis of Fascism'. According to Giorgio Pini, the race laws were 'repugnant to the Italian temperament'; worse still, they undermined the respect for law and order, with unfortunate results. According to Luigi Villari, the anti-Jewish measures antagonized Mussolini's friends as well as his enemies: 'While the existence of a Jewish problem demanding some solution was generally admitted [*sic*], the measures enacted by the Italian Government did not help to solve it, but they brought much odium on Mussolini and on Italy in general. They undoubtedly constituted one of the chief mistakes of the Duce,

---

[1] *O. O.* xxix. 190. On 3 April 1921 Mussolini had spoken of 'our Aryan and Mediterranean stock' (*O. O.* xvi. 239).

[2] See above, p. 194 and p. 194 n. 1; E. Garibaldi, 'Discorso di attualità', loc. cit., pp. 39–47; G. Volpe, *Storia del movimento fascista,* Milan, 1939, pp. 239–40; see also U. Ojetti, *I taccuini 1914–1943,* Florence, 1954, p. 495: 'What saddens me most, is the appearance of copying, or rather obeying the Germans in everything: the Roman step, the persecution of the Jews. There is no better way of making Germany unpopular.'

[3] Pellizzi, *Italy,* p. 194.

inasmuch as they were unnecessary and aroused a wide measure of disapproval even among many loyal Fascists. Their effect abroad was equally deplorable, even among persons who were not prejudicially hostile to Italy, to Fascism or to Mussolini personally.'[1] Even those who defended the Duce's racial policy, such as Julius Evola and Giorgio Pisanò, did so rather half-heartedly, stressing the profound difference between the German and Italian approaches to the Jewish problem.[2]

Meanwhile the debate over Mussolini's racialist aberration was being resumed by the scholars. Most of the explanations offered revolved either round the Axis alliance or round the conquest of Ethiopia. At least two writers thought that racial anti-Semitism was a logical development of the Fascist creed, while a third reached the startling conclusion that the 'Manifesto of the Race' was not an imitation of Nazi doctrine but rather 'a refutation thereof', i.e. a counterblast to Hitler's Nordic heresy with its anti-Italian implications.[3]

Thirty years after the fall of Fascism it is generally recognized that the decision to import racialism into Italy was Mussolini's, not Hitler's. But the motive or combination of motives which prompted the Duce to persecute the Jews is still the subject of controversy. Was racial anti-Semitism inherent in Fascist doctrine? Or was it a tactical move caused by a shift in the European balance of power? Was it the African war which made the Fascist dictator 'Jew-conscious' as well as race-conscious? Or was it only after the forging of the Rome–Berlin Axis that he felt the need to place the Jewish problem 'squarely on the racial plane'? These are some of the questions which remain fundamentally open.

If the analysis of Fascist theory and practice presented in the foregoing pages is correct, the following conclusions emerge:

1. Although there was friction between Fascists and Jews from the very outset, mainly because of Fascist suspicions of Jewish 'separatism' and 'internationalism', there was no attempt on the

---

[1] Tamaro, *Due anni di storia*, iii, 311; Pini and Susmel, *Mussolini*, iv. 1–2; Villari, *Italian Foreign Policy under Mussolini*, p. 202. On 6 August 1938 Pini claimed in *Il Popolo d'Italia* that Mussolini had been a consistent racialist since 1919; after the war, however, he admitted that Fascist racialism was a 'last-minute improvisation' (*Mussolini*, iii. 420).

[2] Evola, *Il cammino del Cinabro*, pp. 158–9; id., *Gli uomini e le rovine*, 3rd edn., Rome, 1972, pp. 185–207; G. Pisanò, *Mussolini e gli ebrei*, Milan, 1967, *passim*.

[3] See above, pp. 123–25 and p. 124 n. 2.

part of the Fascist regime to create a Jewish problem in Italy until Mussolini decided to throw in his lot with Hitler. No Fascist leader, not even Farinacci, was allowed to attack the Jews in public before the birth of the Axis.

2. Until 1937 the Duce's approach to the racial issue was not merely different from the Führer's but diametrically opposed to it; according to Fascist doctrine, all persons born in Italy were Italians, irrespective of race or creed, and intermarriage between Jews and Gentiles was not only permitted but welcomed. Even Preziosi called for the 'Fascistization' of the Jews, not for their elimination from Italian life, until the growing exigencies of the Axis alliance forced him to change his mind.[1]

3. There was a strong element of continuity in Mussolini's thought on the Jewish issue, his sudden change of front notwithstanding. Throughout his career he both attacked and defended the Jews. As early as 1917 he identified the Bolshevik Revolution with the 'synagogue'; but as late as 1944 he insisted that he was 'not an anti-Semite'. As early as 1919 he accused the Jews of plotting against the 'Aryan race'; but as late as 1944 he denied the existence of a Jewish problem in Italy. As early as 1921 he referred to the Italian people as 'this our Aryan and Mediterranean stock (*stirpe*)'; but as late as 1944 he deplored Hitler's racialist aberrations, with special reference to the 'final solution'.

4. Prior to the *rapprochement* between Rome and Berlin the term 'race' was synonymous with 'people' and 'nation' in Italy; Mussolini's earlier references to the *razza italiana*, therefore, had no anti-Jewish implications. After his break with the Jews, however, the Duce found it expedient to recall his previous utterances on the 'Italian race' in order to defend himself against the well-founded charge of mimicry.

5. The totalitarian pretensions of Fascism affected Italian Jewry in two diametrically opposed ways. On the one hand, Mussolini's success in imposing totalitarian rule paved the way for the establishment of cordial relations between the regime and the Jews; on the other, the Fascist urge for regimentation and centralization greatly facilitated the subsequent switch from

[1] G. Preziosi, 'Fatti e commenti', *La Vita Italiana*, xliii. (May 1934), 629; for Preziosi's conversion to racialism, see 'Fra coloro che son sospesi', *La Vita Italiana*, xlix. (June 1937), 659–67.

philo-Semitism to anti-Semitism. And while no thought of racial persecution can have been in the minds of those who framed the laws on the Italian Jewish Communities in 1930 and 1931, their rigid organization of Italian Jewry under the control of the State was to be singularly helpful to the Fascist leaders in the policy of social and economic segregation which they embarked on a few years later.[1] The Fascist drive for monolithic unity ('everything within the State, nothing outside the State, nothing against the State') was a potential threat to the Jews from the very beginning (a fact which was well understood by the Jewish leaders). Even so, no appreciable anti-Semitism developed until Italy became a pawn of the Reich.[2]

6. In 1933 and 1934 Mussolini tried to win laurels as a mediator between Hitler and the Jews. In the light of the evidence now available it is clear that even after the forging of the Axis he would have preferred the role of mediator to that of persecutor. His decision to persecute the Jews, therefore, was a symptom of his decline.

7. Racial anti-Semitism was neither a logical development of the Fascist creed nor a logical extension of the ban on miscegenation in Africa. It was, however, a logical consequence of Mussolini's Axis policy. It was inherent in Fascism because and in so far as the Pact of Steel was inherent in the Fascist pursuit of empire.[3]

8. The 'Manifesto of the Race' was neither an original Italian creation nor a slavish imitation of the German model but an unsuccessful attempt to adapt the German racial theories to Italian conditions. The subsequent evolution of the racial question in Italy reflected the conflicting pressures to which Mussolini was subject. On the one hand, he wanted to convince

---

[1] This was rightly stressed by Binchy (op. cit., p. 606).

[2] On Fascist totalitarianism, see M. Jänicke, *Totalitäre Herrschaft*, Berlin, 1971, pp. 20–36. Many scholars hold that Fascism was not truly totalitarian (A. Aquarone, *L'organizzazione dello stato totalitario*, Turin, 1965, pp. 290–1; De Felice, *Mussolini il fascista*, ii. 9; L. Schapiro, *Totalitarianism*, London, 1972, p. 113; D. Fisichella, *Analisi del totalitarismo*, Messina–Florence 1976, pp. 215–26). The fact remains, however, that Fascism made an all-embracing claim on the individual which was potentially dangerous to the Jews.

[3] Most students of Fascism are of the opinion that the Axis pact was implicit in the affinities of the two systems and the parallelism of their policies (Namier, *Europe in Decay*, p. 129; Mack Smith, *Italy*, p. 447; Siebert, *Italiens Weg*, pp. 6, 46, 58; G. Rumi, 'Tendenze e caratteri degli studi sulla politica estera fascista', *Nuova Rivista Storica*, li. Jan.–Apr. 1967, 158; K. D. Bracher, *Die deutsche Diktatur*, Cologne–Berlin, 1969, p. 331; Petersen, *Hitler–Mussolini*, p. 502).

the Germans of his loyalty; on the other, he wanted to impress Italian and Western opinion with his 'magnanimity' and avoid a clash with the Church. As a result he fell between two stools. He may well have been sincere when he told Ciano that his racial policy signified 'discrimination, not persecution'. Once unleashed, however, the campaign against the Jews inevitably acquired a momentum of its own, and the dictator neither would nor could control it.

9. The severity of the racial laws was tempered by corruption and inefficiency, by the philo-Semitism of the Italian masses, by the Italian capacity for compromise and *combinazione,* and—last but not least—by the growing anti-Axis feeling within the Italian ruling class. Italian opposition to the 'final solution' was in part a spontaneous reaction to German barbarism, in part a symptom of the widespread dissatisfaction with the Duce's Axis policy, and in part a manifestation of Fascist resistance to German encroachments on Italian sovereignty. Some of the credit for this resistance must go to Mussolini.

10. Hitler was determined to impose his racial obsession on the whole of Europe, including Italy. Until Mussolini's downfall, however, he was not prepared to stake relations with Rome on a question of extending the 'final solution' to the Italian sphere of influence. He was pleased with the Duce's conversion to racialism because it reinforced the myth of 'Axis unity' and put an end to Germany's ideological isolation as an anti-Semitic Power. Unlike Himmler and his Jewish affairs experts, however, he took little or no interest in the details of Fascist racial policy until Mussolini's regime was on the verge of collapse.

11. After the Italian armistice, the part of Italy under German control was treated as conquered as well as occupied territory. The writ of the Fascist puppet government did not run beyond the road-blocks of Gargnano. Mussolini's attempts to remove the Jewish question from German hands were therefore doomed to failure from the start. His internment order, though designed to protect the Jews, had the effect of facilitating the task of Eichmann's emissaries; so had his decision to denationalize his Jewish subjects and declare them to be 'enemy nationals' for the duration of the war. A good deal has been written about the Duce's efforts to save the Jews from the gas chambers. But while it is true that Mussolini was too much of an Italian to approve of

the 'final solution', it is no less true that he and his henchmen helped to create the conditions in which the Holocaust became possible. In the words of Piero Caleffi, an Italian Jew who was both a veteran anti-Fascist and a survivor of a German concentration camp: 'Consciously or not, the Fascists had been the originators (*anticipatori*) of the extermination camps.'[1]

12. Although over four-fifths of the Jews of Italy survived the war, Italian Jewry suffered a blow from which it is unlikely to recover in the foreseeable future. Thousands had abandoned the Community, and some 6,000 had emigrated; many of those who remained were physically and spiritually broken. The habit of Jewish life had been interrupted, and in many places its setting had disappeared. Thirty years after the fall of Fascism Italian Jewry is still only a shadow of its former self.

---

[1] P. Caleffi, *Si fa presto a dire fame*, Milan–Rome, 1955, p. 135. On the after-effects of Fascist racialism, see A. M. di Nola, *Antisemitismo in Italia 1962/1972*, Florence, 1973.

Appendix I   The Anti-Jewish Press
             Polemics of 1933–1934

ACCORDING TO Renzo De Felice (*Storia degli ebrei italiani,* pp. 122, 141–143), the anti-Jewish press campaign of 1933–4 'originated outside Mussolini's entourage', among Fascist extremists who disapproved of the dictator's philo-Semitic policy. This astounding assertion is based partly on the wholly unfounded assumption that the leader of this campaign, Telesio Interlandi, was 'almost certainly' in German pay (pp. 122, 142). In reality Interlandi was Mussolini's confidant and unofficial mouthpiece, in close personal touch with the dictator (IC/Job 331/35; ASMEI/Segreteria generale/Pacco 89/Udienze). The *Tevere* was financed, not by the Germans, but by Mussolini's Press Bureau and by the Directorate of the Fascist party (ACS/Segreteria particolare del Duce/Carteggio riservato/busta 51 H/R). The role of the paper was accurately described by Adrian Lyttelton who wrote (*The Seizure of Power,* p. 400):

Il Tevere . . . performed a special function of some interest. It was inspired directly by Mussolini and it was encouraged to air themes and views (e.g. anti-semitism) on which he did not wish to commit himself officially. He spoke with two voices, cautious, official, opportunistic in the *Popolo d'Italia* and the rest of the obedient flock marshalled by the Press Office: extremist, unrestrained and speculative in *Il Tevere.* He regarded *Il Tevere* as his own personal, unofficial organ, just as the *Popolo d'Italia* was his official one, and for this reason its opinions had always to be treated with respect by the other papers. The role of *Il Tevere* in cultural questions was particularly important; a writer condemned in its columns as lacking the true Fascist spirit was in serious trouble. This type of informal control exercised through *Il Tevere* (and to a lesser degree some of the other extremist papers) was of great importance in creating a climate of anxiety in which journalists wrote only what they knew to be safe.

We may note in passing that the importance of the *Tevere* was stressed by foreign observers long before Hitler's rise to power. The Rome correspondent of the *Manchester Guardian* wrote as early as 15 February 1927 (in the first of two articles on the 'Intellectuals of Fascism'): 'The "Tevere" seems to be far nearer to the spirit of Mussolini and far more accurate in its prophecies of his future conduct than the heavy ex-liberal organs with their elaborate and often hypocritical translations of the Duce's "dynamism" into terms acceptable to the static middle classes.'

De Felice further contends that by 1934 an anti-Semitic pressure group had emerged, 'with which the (Fascist) Party, for better or worse, had to reckon' (p. 149). He is, however, quite unable to name the members of this alleged pressure group. It is worth noting in this connection that both Farinacci and Preziosi expressed disapproval of Hitler's racialism and his persecution of 'Jews as such' during the period under review (see, for example, G. Preziosi, 'Attenti!', *La Vita Italiana*, xlii (Nov. 1933), 600; id., 'Risposta agli "italiani di religione ebraica"', *La Vita Italiana*, xliii (June 1934), 754; id., 'Manicomio razzista', *La Vita Italiana*, xlv (Jan. 1935), 97–8; R. Farinacci 'Risposta ai signori dell'Israel"', *Il Regime Fascista* (18 Apr. 1934). And it is also worth noting that there is no reference to an anti-Semitic pressure group in any of the German diplomatic records at our disposal. As late as August 1938 the German press attaché in Rome informed the Reich Propaganda Ministry that the Italian anti-Semites were men of little account and that their influence on Mussolini was slight (see above, p. 109).

De Felice also maintains that 'direct Nazi interference' was a not inconsiderable factor in the anti-Jewish campaign, pointing out that Hitler covered Italy with a network of agents and that National Socialist elements staged anti-Semitic incidents at Merano in July 1933 (pp. 133–4, 141–2). He fails to add, however, that the Italian authorities reacted violently to German attempts at interference. On 18 February 1934 the Ortsgruppenleiter of Trieste, Berger, was arrested by the Italian police (see Hassell's dispatch of 22 February, BA/K/R43 II/1448), and in the following month the National Socialist party organization in Italy was temporarily dissolved on Mussolini's orders (Pini and Susmel, *Mussolini*, iii. 302). By the beginning of 1935 things had come to such a pass that a young German tourist in the South Tyrol was arrested and expelled for no other reason than that he was a member of the National Socialist Party (Windels to Wilhelmstrasse, 1 Feb. 1935, GFM/8968H/E629605). The German Ambassador dismissed the anti-Jewish polemics in the Fascist press as a domestic affair of minor significance (to which he and his collaborators were entirely extraneous), pointing out that Italy had no 'Jewish problem' in the German sense of the term and that hence there was no parallel whatever between Interlandi's attacks on 'unassimilated' and 'disloyal' Jewish elements and Hitler's all-out attack on the whole Jewish race (Hassell to Wilhelmstrasse, 8 Feb. 1934, GFM/L1027/L301082–3).

To be sure, some of Mussolini's henchmen were more eager for an accord with Hitler during the period of Italo–German tension than the dictator himself. One of these was Francesco Giunta, a former Party Secretary, who began to press for close collaboration between Rome and Berlin as early as December 1934 (de Felice, *Mussolini il duce*, i. pp. 729–30). Another was Count Galeazzo Ciano, the Duce's son-in-law and, since August 1933, his Press Chief who, in his talks with the German Ambassador, repeatedly criticized the Jews of Vienna and Trieste for trying to 'sow discord' between Germany and Italy (Hassell's memorandum of 9 June 1934, GFM/5257H/E315514–15). A third was Ciano's friend Dino Alfieri, President of the Società Italiana Autori ed Editori and future Ambassador in Berlin, who had a secret meeting with Hitler in the summer of 1934 when the Italo–German quarrel over Austria was at its height (GFM/3236H/D700758–62). Hitler subsequently praised him for having 'put Mussolini on his guard against the intrigues and false friendship of the French and their Italian friends' (*Hitlers Tischgespräche im Führerhauptquartier 1941–1942*, p. 264; cf. also IFZ/ED 83/1/Goebbels–Kriegstagebuch I/31, entry for 14 Feb. 1942). There is, however, no evidence that either Ciano or Alfieri aimed at creating a Jewish problem in Italy for the sake of friendship with Hitler during the period under consideration. Ciano, as we know from his diary, was opposed to the adoption of anti-Jewish measures in Italy as late as February 1938 (*1937–1938 Diario*, p. 107).

Nor is there any evidence that the 'massive influx' of Jewish refugees from Germany, to which De Felice refers on p. 122 of his book, was a factor in the Fascist press campaign against the Jews. For one thing, Italy gave asylum to no more than 500 refugees from Germany in 1933 (see report by J. G. MacDonald, High Commissioner of the League of Nations, *New York Times* of 26 Dec. 1933). For another, the anti-Jewish polemics were directed, not against the handful of refugees, but against the old-established Italian Jews, presumably with the aim of placating Hitler and accelerating the *Gleichschaltung* of Italian Jewry. The arrival of German–Jewish physicians, scientists, and merchants in Italy was bound to give rise to occasional friction (see McClure's memorandum of 11 May 1937, PRO/F.O. 371/21182/R3585/2476/22/p. 6), but it had no bearing on the Duce's decision to administer an unofficial rebuke to his Jewish subjects.

Finally, in evaluating the apparent contrast between Mussolini's philo-Semitic policy and the anti-Semitic campaign waged by some of his underlings, it should be borne in mind that most of the anti-Jewish arguments used by Interlandi, Farinacci, and 'Farinata' recur in the Duce's anonymous articles and in his private utterances (cf. *O.O.* xxvi. 309; d'Aroma, *Mussolini segreto*, p. 86).

Appendix II   The 'ras' of Cremona

ROBERTO FARINACCI (1892–1945) was a lifelong intransigent—recalcitrant schoolboy, rabble-rousing journalist, anticlerical firebrand, Fascist Party Secretary after the Matteotti affair, champion of the Rome–Berlin Axis, and leader of the anti-Semitic faction in the Fascist Party. In 1926 he undertook the defence of Amerigo Dumini, leader of the gang that kidnapped and murdered Matteotti.

After his dismissal from the post of Party Secretary on 30 March 1926, Farinacci was temporarily ousted from the Fascist Grand Council and subjected to various forms of petty persecution (De Felice, *Mussolini il fascista*, ii. 185–6, 512–14; Fornari, *Mussolini's Gadfly*, pp. 176, 185). In 1934, however, Farinacci's enthusiastic support for the projected African venture enabled him to regain the confidence of his master and to stage a political come-back; there was a reconciliation between the two men, followed by Farinacci's readmission to the Grand Council (*O.O.* xxvi. 360; xxvii. 21–2; Fornari, op. cit., pp. 156–7). Once the Fascist dictator decided to embark on a pro-German and anti-Jewish policy, Farinacci, as the 'arche-typal Fascist' and the 'only genuine National Socialist of the Revolution', predictably became its principal mouthpiece (Fornari, pp. xi, 179; Deakin, *The Brutal Friendship*, p. 112). On 3 March 1937 Mussolini informed Giorgio Pini that the *ras* of Cremona had come back into favour: 'Farinacci ora è in linea' (*Filo diretto con Palazzo Venezia*, p. 88); simultaneously he dispatched Farinacci on a personal mission to General Franco, introducing him as 'one of the pioneers of Fascism' (IC/Job 122/033899).

In 1941 Mussolini told his biographer that Farinacci had been converted to anti-Semitism by Preziosi whose periodical had become the monthly magazine of *Il Regime Fascista* in 1931 (De Begnac, *Palazzo Venezia*, p. 643). There is ample evidence, however, that Farinacci's approach to the racial issue differed radically from Preziosi's; while the latter, a renegade priest and a doctrinaire fanatic, believed in the *Protocols of the Elders of Zion,* the former, a power-addict and a cynic, regarded Fascist racial policy as little more than a useful piece of pro-German tactics (De Felice, *Storia degli ebrei italiani*, pp. 241–2; Fornari, pp. 176, 185; U. Alfassio Grimaldi and G. Bozzetti, *Farinacci il più fascista*, Milan, 1972, pp. 167–8, 240). Three weeks after the publication of the 'Race Manifesto', Farinacci made it clear in a note to Mussolini that he did not believe in the racial theories on which the anti-Jewish policy was allegedly based (Farinacci to Mussolini, 5 Aug. 1938, IC/Segretaria particolare del Duce/Job 122/033909).

Farinacci subsequently claimed in an interview with the editor of

Himmler's paper that he had pursued 'a clear anti-Semitic line' since 1921, citing his campaign against Toeplitz as evidence ('Unterredung mit Farinacci', *Das Schwarze Korps*, 15 Sept. 1938); he might have added that in 1932 he had gone so far as to reproach Hitler for his alleged failure to combat 'Jewish power' ('Fascismo e nazional-socialismo', *La Vita Italiana*, xl (15 Sept. 1932), 250). But while it is true that Farinacci used anti-Semitic slurs as part of his slander technique as early as the 1920s, it is no less true that his attitude towards the Jews was as inconsistent and contradictory as Mussolini's. As has been noted in Appendix I, he was opposed to German racialism until the birth of the Axis; in 1934 he also criticized Mosley for copying anti-Semitism and other German aberrations (*Il Regime Fascista*, 2 Nov. 1934). In 1939 he was forced to admit the truth of the charge made against him by the Bishop of Lugano that the editorial staff of his paper had included a Jew down to the beginning of the racial campaign (*Il Regime Fascista*, 22 Jan. 1939). And as late as 1944, while calling for unconditional loyalty to the Axis, he defended the fifty odd 'Semites' of Cremona against the *furor teutonicus*, urging them to go into hiding before the Germans could arrest them (Alfassio Grimaldi and Bozzetti, op. cit., p. 240).

There is some evidence that Farinacci, like Buffarini and other high-ranking Fascist dignitaries, was involved in the 'Aryanization' racket which sprang up soon after the enactment of the anti-Jewish laws (see, for example, police report of 29 Jan. 1942, IC/Segreteria particolare del Duce/Job 122/033994). Shortly after Mussolini's 'resignation' and Farinacci's flight to Germany, the King of Italy told Ambassador von Mackensen that Farinacci, while posing as an arch Jew-baiter, had enriched himself by obtaining *brevetti di arianesimo* for Jews who were willing and able to buy them (Mackensen to Ribbentrop personally, 4 Aug. 1943, GFM/133/II/72767–70: 'Farinacci habe mit seiner Broschüre [*sic*] die Juden bekämpft, sich aber nicht geniert, als Anwalt gern jene Prozesse zu übernehmen und erfolgreich durchzuführen, in denen Juden sich an ihn wandten, um durch den Nachweis, dass ihr Vater nicht ihr Vater gewesen sei, sich der Judengesetzgebung zu entziehen').

Despite his fascination with National Socialism (which had succeeded in establishing the kind of totalitarian regime he had always envisaged as the true goal of Fascism), Farinacci was by no means uncritical of the German leaders. In March 1943 he urged Hitler to call off his crusade against the Christian Churches; and in the following month he affirmed in a note to the Duce that the Germans, though 'strong in war', were 'still novices in politics': 'come ti ho detto a voce, mi convinco sempre più che i Tedeschi in guerra sono forti, ma in politica dei novizi' (Farinacci to Mussolini, 23 Apr. 1943, IC/Segreteria particolare del Duce/Job 114/031581; cf. also Fornari, pp. 167, 192).

Appendix III   Mussolini and Léon Blum

MUSSOLINI WAS not alone in placing the blame for his disastrous alliance with Hitler on Blum. Similar charges were made by various Italophile French personages, including Pierre Laval, Joseph Caillaux, and Count Charles de Chambrun. Caillaux, a former President of France, wrote after World War II: 'M. Léon Blum avait négligé les intérêts de la France. J'explique: au commencement de 1937, M. Mussolini lui fit savoir que M. Hitler lui offrait une alliance totale mais "que cela lui ripugnait" [sic] et qu'il n'y souscrirait pas si nous voulions bien lui tendre la main. Tout en reconnaissant que la proposition du dictateur italien s'alliait à l'intérêt de la patrie, M. Léon Blum déclina l'offre, parce que, dit-il, son parti le lui interdisait. Il sacrifiait ainsi la France, à une idéologie, il jetait, en pleine connaissance de cause, l'Italie dans les bras de l'Allemagne' (*Memoires*, iii: *clairvoyance et force d'âme dans les épreuves (1912–1940)*, Paris, 1947, p. 241). This corresponds in large measure to Ciano's diary note for 12 May 1938: 'God knows how hard I have worked to prevent the alliance with Berlin which is burdensome (*ingombrante*) for the present and worrying for the future. But I have come to think that French pettiness will render my efforts vain and that before long a new document will be signed in the halls of the Wilhelmstrasse. Mussolini has made up his mind' (*1937–1938 Diario*, p. 171).

Franklin D. Laurens (*France and the Italo–Ethiopian Crisis*, pp. 354–6) likewise charges Blum with failure to conciliate Mussolini but partly contradicts himself by stressing the Duce's own intransigence:

The French attitude towards the Italian conquest and annexation of Ethiopia was conditioned by the fact that all major policy decisions had to be made with a view to satisfying Premier-designate Blum. Otherwise, these decisions might soon be reversed. Sarraut, Flandin and Paul-Boncour apparently still hoped that France might make her peace with Italy and induce the latter to co-operate against the ambitions of Hitler. With this in mind, they suggested to Blum that he join them in a proposal that sanctions be lifted immediately. Had he accepted, they probably would have pressed also for French recognition of Italy's annexation of Ethiopia. But Blum demurred, expressing his belief that there was not the slightest chance of bringing about a *rapprochement* with Italy and making it clear that no deal with Italy on sanctions or recognition of the conquest would be binding on his government. Consequently, the Sarraut government made no further attempt to revoke sanctions ... On May 11 the statesmen of Europe once more converged upon Geneva, this time for the 92nd session of the Council. Paul-Boncour told reporters in Geneva that day that he hoped to postpone Council discussion of the Italo–Ethiopian dispute until mid-

June. He boasted to the newsmen that France prided herself on having kept Italy in the League, and laughingly told them that he had advised Aloisi to ride around the block while the Ethiopian delegate addressed the Council. But the Italian delegate disregarded this friendly advice and attended the Council meeting that afternoon to insist that, since the Ethiopian state had ceased to exist, the dispute should be excluded from the agenda. The other members of the council disagreed, however, and as a result, Aloisi withdrew from the meeting . . . During the second half of May, French diplomacy was more or less paralyzed by the fact that Blum would not assume office until after June 1 . . . Franco-Italian relations worsened temporarily during this same period. On 20 May the Italian government declared that the few (150) French troops acting as railway guards in Ethiopia must be withdrawn immediately. Rome also stated on that date that trade between Ethiopia and the 'sanctionist' states was thereafter forbidden. Both of these actions naturally perturbed French policymakers, as did an Italian order a few days later for the expulsion of the eighty-four year old Mgr. Jarosseau, Vicar Apostolic at Harar. Even more serious was the warning delivered to General Gamelin by the Italian military attaché in Paris to the effect that, unless sanctions were soon lifted, the Franco–Italian military agreement might be repudiated by Italy.

On 22 June 1936, eighteen days after Blum's advent to power, the Duce let it be known through a French intermediary, Senator Jean-Louis Malvy, that if France were willing to take the lead at Geneva in proposing the removal of the sanctions, the two countries might be able to resume their friendship (*DDF*, 2e série ii. 513–14; E. Bonnefous, *Histoire politique de la Troisième République*, vi, Paris, 1965, pp. 410–11). Blum did not respond to this gesture because he believed that it would not be possible to keep Hitler and Mussolini apart: 'Sooner or later their policies would converge' (Earl of Avon, *Facing the Dictators*, p. 382). He was confirmed in this belief when, on 11 July, Mussolini acquiesced in the signing of an Austro–German agreement which paved the way for the Anschluss (*Les événements survenus en France de 1933 à 1945: Temoignages et documents recueillis par la commission d'Enquête Parlementaire*, i, Paris, 1947, p. 125). Two weeks later Italy's intervention in the Spanish Civil War afforded final proof of Mussolini's Mediterranean ambitions and cemented the friendship between the Duce and the Führer.

On 31 December 1936 Mussolini denounced the 'Jewish Blum government' in the columns of *Il Popolo d'Italia* (see above, p. 116). A few days later, however, he advised Blum through Vittorio Cerruti, his 'Jew-tainted' Ambassador in Paris, that he 'detested' Hitler—Cerruti used the term 'répulsion insurmontable'—and sincerely desired the restoration of close relations (*une union étroite*) with France. If France would cease to involve herself on the side of the Spanish Republic, the Duce could obtain for her the friendship and goodwill of General Franco. Blum replied that he too desired improved relations with

Rome, but that Italy would have to honour the non-intervention agreement she had signed. Subsequently, he declared that he regarded Mussolini's proposition as a *ruse de guerre*, i.e. an attempt to facilitate the victory of Fascism in Spain(*Les Événements*, i, 220; Bonnefous, op. cit., p. 403).

Yet another episode which infuriated the Duce and his French supporters was Blum's decision to remove the Italophile French Ambassador in Rome, Count Charles Pineton de Chambrun, who had reached retirement age. Mussolini reacted by announcing that Chambrun's successor would have to be accredited to Victor Emanuel III as King of Italy *and* Emperor of Ethiopia. As a result, France had no ambassador at the Pallazo Farnese from October 1936 to October 1938—the years of the Spanish Civil War, the Austrian crisis, and the Munich crisis. When Chambrun deplored the unfriendly turn in Franco–Italian relations in a talk with Blum, the latter allegedly replied: 'You forget that I was a friend of Matteotti's' (C. de Chambrun, *Traditions et souvenirs*, Paris, 1952, pp. 227–8).

Mussolini's French admirers never forgave Blum. Neither did Mussolini himself who reiterated as late as April 1945—a few days before his inglorious end—that it was Blum's failure to respond to his advances which had driven him into Hitler's arms (E. Susmel, *Mussolini e il suo tempo*, Milan, 1950, p. 335). In the light of the evidence now available, however, it is impossible to believe that a more positive response on the part of Blum would have changed the course of events. Two accords with Britain (the Gentlemen's Agreement and the Easter Pact) did not prevent the Italian dictator from declaring war on that country in June 1940; on the other hand, the Steel Pact of May 1939 did not prevent him from remaining neutral when war broke out three months later. Blum's refusal to send an ambassador to Rome may have been a tactical error; but, as his American biographer rightly affirms, 'it would be fatuous to conclude that cordial relations with Italy would have resulted from a different attitude' (J. Colton, *Léon Blum. Humanist in Politics*, New York, 1966, p. 223). Blum felt a personal aversion for Mussolini whom he regarded as the 'assassin of Matteotti' ('Les Deux Augures', *Le Populaire*, 5 Jan. 1935). But he rejected the idea of an ideological crusade against Fascism. In 1933 he had endorsed Mussolini's Four-Power Pact ('La France et les dictatures', *Le Populaire*, 14 June 1933); and in 1935 he had even supported the ill-starred Laval–Mussolini agreement ('Est-ce Mussolini? Est-ce Pierre Laval?', *Le Populaire*, 27 Aug. 1935). Once in power, he joined the British in calling for the dropping of sanctions (Salvemini, *Prelude to World War II*, pp. 462–4). Mussolini's decision to join forces with Hitler was motivated, not by Western hostility to Fascism, but by his conviction that the days of the 'decadent plutocracies' were numbered; and he was confirmed in this conviction by the social unrest which erupted in France on 14 May 1936, three weeks before the advent of the Popular Front Government (see his statement to Bertrand de Jouvenel of 3 June 1936, *DDF*, 2e série ii, 432–3). Laurens admits as much when he states on p. 381 of his book that Mussolini went over to Hitler's camp because he considered France 'done for' and hence incapable of standing up to Germany. Colton makes the same point: 'Nothing that Blum could have done in 1936 and 1937 would have stayed Mussolini's dagger in June 1940' (op. cit., p. 223).

Appendix IV   Pius XII and
The Third Reich

EUGENIO PACELLI (1876–1958) was Papal Nuncio in Berlin from 1920 to 1929 and Cardinal Secretary of State from February 1930 to March 1939. On 2 March 1939 he succeeded to the Papal tiara and took the name of Pius XII.

Rolf Hochhuth, in his controversial play *Der Stellvertreter*, depicts Pius XII as an unprincipled politician, possessed of 'aristocratic coolness' and eyes having an 'icy glow', who stood by passively while millions of Jews were being murdered. A very different picture was drawn by Sir Francis Osborne, a non-Catholic British diplomat, who was in close touch with the Pontiff for over ten years:

As British Minister to the Holy See from 1936 to 1947 and, in that capacity, His Holiness's enforced guest in the Vatican City from June 1940 . . . to the autumn of 1944, I had exceptional opportunities of getting to know Pius XII and to appreciate his qualities. And, first of all, I must emphatically declare that, so far from being a cool (which, I suppose, implies cold-blooded and inhumane) diplomatist, Pius XII was the most warmly humane, kindly, generous, sympathetic (and, incidentally, saintly) character that it has been my privilege to meet in the course of a long life. I know that his sensitive nature was acutely and incessantly alive to the tragic volume of human suffering caused by the War and, without the slightest doubt, he would have been ready and glad to give his life to redeem humanity from its consequences. And this quite irrespective of nationality or Faith. But what could he effectively do? (letter to *The Times*, 20 May 1963).

Pius XII loved Germany in which he had spent nine happy years; but there is no evidence whatever that pro-German feeling warped his judgement. Those who accuse him of 'trusting' Hitler or of underestimating the magnitude of the German peril would do well to read the following report by the Chargé d'Affaires at the British Legation to the Holy See, written less than seven months after Hitler's rise to power (Kirkpatrick to Vansittart, 19 Aug. 1933, *DBFP*, 2nd Ser. v. 524–5):

I called on the Cardinal Secretary of State and took the opportunity afforded by a long conversation to ask him what he thought of recent events in Germany. His Eminence was extremely frank and made no effort to conceal his disgust at the proceedings of Herr Hitler's Government. The Vatican usually profess to see both sides of any political question, but on this occasion there was no word of palliation or excuse. As regards the German treatment of Austria, the Cardinal said that . . . the Germans were determined to pursue their present policy and would not be restrained by anything short of force. Cardinal Pacelli equally deplored the action of the German Government at home, their persecution of the Jews, their proceedings against political opponents, the reign of terror to which the whole nation was subjected. I said to His Eminence that I had heard the opinion expressed in Italy and elsewhere that these events were but manifestations of the revolutionary spirit. With the passage of time and the responsibilities of office Herr Hitler would settle down, temper the zeal of his supporters and revert to more normal methods of government. The Cardinal replied with emphasis that he saw no ground for such easy optimism. It seemed to him that there was no indication of any modification of the internal policy of the German Government. These reflections on the iniquity of Germany led the Cardinal to explain apologetically how it was that he had signed a concordat with such people. A pistol, he said, had been pointed at his head and he had had no alternative. The German Government had offered him concessions, concessions, it must be admitted, wider than any previous German Government would have agreed to, and he had to choose between an agreement on their lines and the virtual elimination of the Catholic Church in the Reich. Not only that, but he was given no more than a week to make up his mind. In a matter of such importance he would have liked more time, but it was a case of then or never. He wished me to know the facts so as to be able to appreciate the dilemma of the Vatican. The Church ... had no political axe to grind. They were outside the political arena. But the spiritual welfare of 20 million Catholic souls in Germany was at stake and that was the first and, indeed, the only consideration. If the German Government violated the concordat—and they were certain to do so—the Vatican would have a treaty on which to base a protest.

As Cardinal Secretary of State, Pacelli played a major part in the campaign against German racialism. On 11 July 1937 he denounced the pagan cult of the race in a public speech at Lisieux which provoked a sharp reaction from the Reich Ministry of Ecclesisatical Affairs (ADAP, Serie D i. 808, Muhs to Wilhelmstrasse, 6 Aug. 1937: 'Den Erklärungen des Kardinalstaatssekretärs Pacelli, sein Besuch in Frankreich habe keinerlei politische Zwecke verfolgt, steht die Tatsache entgegen, dass er in seiner Ansprache am 11. Juli in Lisieux mit einer unverkennbaren Spitze gegen Deutschland von einer Nation Sprach, die "von schlechten Hirten zur Vergötzung der Rasse verleitet werden sollte", ein Wort, das im Volksfront-Frankreich und in der deutsch-feindlichen Welt sehr wohl verstanden wurde'). Mussolini keenly resented the Pope's attitude. Speaking to Nino d'Aroma in October 1944, he denounced Pius XII as a renegade Italian who had sided with the enemies of his country: 'Tra due opposte parti che combattono, il Pacelli s'è assunto la tremenda responsabilità storica di trascinare tutte le forze, le tradizioni della Chiesa nel campo anglo-americano' (N. d'Aroma, *Mussolini segreto*, p. 308). Mussolini's resentment was shared by certain pro-Axis prelates, most particularly by Bishop Alois Hudal, Rector of the German Church in Rome, who made several vain attempts to bring about a *modus vivendi* between the Holy See and the Third Reich (A. Hudal, *Römische Tagebücher. Lebensbeichte eines alten Bischofs,* pp. 13–20, 107–51, 191–262).

In conclusion we cannot but agree with Guenter Lewy (*The Catholic Church and Nazi Germany,* p. 268) that Hochhuth, in attacking Pius XII, 'has personalized a problem which cannot adequately be understood in terms of personalities. The attitude of the Roman Catholic Church toward National Socialist anti-Semitism must be seen in the context of the still partially unresolved 2,000-year-old conflict between Church and Synagogue.'

A Note on the Sources

THIS BOOK has grown out of an introduction to a batch of unpublished German records on Fascist racial policy. The original intention was to supplement a series of articles on Italian Jewry under Fascism which I had published in Israel and Italy between 1960 and 1966. But the more I delved into the newly available documents, the more I came to realize that there was room for a more ambitious undertaking.

The German Foreign Ministry files consulted at the Foreign Office Library in London cover every aspect of German–Italian relations during the period under review, including Nazi–Fascist contacts prior to Hitler's rise to power, the genesis of the Axis alliance and the Steel Pact, Axis policy in the Arab world, the origins and nature of Fascist racialism, co-operation between German and Italian 'racial experts', and Italian resistance to the 'final solution' of the Jewish question in Axis-occupied Europe. Additional unpublished German material on some of these subjects has been acquired from the Political Archives in Bonn, the Federal Archives in Coblenz, the Central Archives at Potsdam, and the Yad Vashem Archives in Jerusalem.

Microfilms from the Main Archives of the Nazi party have been consulted at the Wiener Library in London; they include memorandums and correspondence on Nazi–Fascist relations before Hitler's accession to the chancellorship.

A visit to the German Federal Republic in 1968 gave me an opportunity of examining previously untapped sources at the Munich Institute of Contemporary History and the Military Archives at Freiburg im Breisgau, including the unpublished sections of the Goebbels Diaries, the Himmler files, testimonies of protagonists, and intelligence reports on the military crisis of the Axis.

Unpublished Nuremberg documents relating to the theme of this book have been consulted at the Wiener Library, the Munich Institute of Contemporary History, and the Yad Vashem Archives.

The newly available British documents at the Public Record Office in London (Cabinet Minutes, dispatches of diplomats, Foreign Office memorandums, and secret correspondence) cover the whole period under review and throw light on most of the issues discussed in this work, including Italian policy towards Zionism, Anglo-Italian rivalry in the Middle East and the Mediterranean, the evolution of the racial question in Italy, and the implementation of the 'final solution' in the German-occupied Fascist Republic.

I have made ample use of the Italian Collection at St. Antony's College, Oxford, which consists of voluminous files from Mussolini's private secretariat and from various Italian ministries. It contains such valuable items as Major Renzetti's reports on Hitler, Anfuso's dispatches from Berlin, correspondence between the Duce and the Führer, letters from Farinacci, Interlandi, and Preziosi to Mussolini, police reports on various Fascist personages, and a wealth of material on various aspects of the racial persecutions in Italy. I have also made a detailed study of the Italian materials deposited at the Yad Vashem Archives, including the files of the Jewish Community in Rome and records on Fascist racial policy from the Central Archives of the Italian State and the Historical Archives of the Italian Foreign Ministry. Additional Italian documents (some of them of great value) have been obtained from the Archives of the Union of Italian Jewish Communities in Rome and from the Jewish Documentation Centre in Milan. Dr. Jens Petersen of the German Historical Institute in Rome was good enough to communicate to me the contents of some of the Grandi Papers and of reports by Fascist agents on their contacts with Julius Streicher and other German anti-Semites during the Ethiopian campaign.

In tracing the evolution of Fascist policy towards Zionism I have drawn extensively on original documents from the Weizmann Archives at Rehovoth and the Central Zionist Archives in Jerusalem. For the Italo–German controversy over policy towards the Arab world I have relied largely on unpublished German files consulted at the Yad Vashem Archives. My account of the Holocaust in the part of Italy under the German heel is based partly on the proceedings of the Kappler and Bosshammer trials which are likewise available at the Yad Vashem Archives. Lists of deportees from the Fascist Social Republic have been kindly furnished by the archivist of the Jewish Documentation Centre.

The published documentary collections constitute an additional source of the highest value. The diplomatic documents are generally, though not invariably, reliable. The records of the various transactions, whether they be Anglo–Italian, Franco–Italian, or Italo–German, are in substantial agreement, having for the most part been written not by the principals, but by officials trained to make accurate reports. The Vatican documents on World War II (of which nine volumes have so far been published) are indispensable to the student of the Jewish tragedy in Europe, and so are the published Nuremberg documents (also nine volumes), the proceedings of the Eichmann trial, and the various documentary collections on Jews under Fascist rule (Molho,

Poliakov, and Sabille, United Restitution Organization). Other important sources are the writings and speeches of Hitler and Mussolini, the published correspondence between Hitler and Mussolini, the Ciano Papers, the records of Hitler's military conferences, the war diaries of the German High Command, and the Weizsäcker Papers.

Newspapers and periodicals have been consulted at the Wiener Library, the British Museum, and the Royal Institute of International Affairs in London; at the Italian department of the University of Reading; at the Institute of Contemporary History in Munich and the Military Archives at Freiburg im Breisgau; and at the Hebrew University Library, the Yad Vashem Library, the Central Zionist Archives, and the Central Archives for the History of the Jewish People in Jerusalem. Photostatic copies of certain articles in Italian Fascist newspapers have been kindly furnished by Dr. Karl-Egon Lönne, formerly of the German Historical Institute in Rome.

To verify and amplify the primary sources I have discussed the subject of this book with a number of surviving witnesses. I have also drawn on the testimonies deposited at the Yad Vashem Archives which were obtained by Signora Fanny Minerbi, one-time representative of the Yad Vashem Institute in Rome. Valuable though this 'interrogatory evidence' undoubtedly is, I have used it circumspectly unless I have been able to check the post-war testimony with contemporary documents.

Diaries and memoirs, like post-war testimonies of surviving participants, have to be used with care. Some of the diaries were almost certainly touched up, and memoirs born of defeat seldom make pleasant reading. The least suspect of the diaries are those of the professional diplomats, some of which (Aloisi, Cadogan, Hassell) are of outstanding importance. Bernard Berenson's *Rumor and Reflection* is a first-rate source for the twenty-two months from Mussolini's 'resignation' to the final collapse of the Fascist Republic. The Ciano Diaries are full of contradictions but invaluable as a portrait of the author and his master. So are the Goebbels Diaries. Of the many memoirs cited in this study the most revealing (if not the most reliable) are generally those of the leading protagonists. Giacomo Acerbo's *Fra due plotoni di esecuzione* and Giuseppe Bottai's *Vent'anni e un giorno* are the most serious attempts made to date by Fascist hierarchs to analyse critically, after defeat, the historical experience of Fascism. The memoirs of Dino Alfieri, Filippo Anfuso, and Giuseppe Bastianini, though necessarily suspect, are of value in throwing light on the profound conflict of interest between the two Axis partners. Guariglia's

Ricordi, though full of inaccuracies, contain some valuable information on Fascist policy towards Zionism. Of the other memoirs consulted I have found the following most useful: Carl J. Burckhardt's *Meine Danziger Mission*; Roberto Cantalupo's *Fu la Spagna*; Nino d'Aroma's *Mussolini segreto*; Yvon De Begnac's *Palazzo Venezia*; Anthony Eden's *Facing the Dictators*; Luigi Federzoni's *Italia di ieri per la storia di domani*; André François-Poncet's *Au Palais Farnèse*; Nahum Goldmann's *Memories*; Fritz Grobba's *Männer und Mächte im Orient*; Michele Lanza's *Berlino. Ambasciata d'Italia*; Guido Leto's *OVRA*; Kurt G. W. Lüdecke's *I Knew Hitler*; Massimo Magistrati's *Il prologo del dramma*; the same author's *L'Italia a Berlino*; Alberto Mellini's *Guerra diplomatica a Salò*; Eitel Friedrich Moellhausen's *La carta perdente*; Luciano Morpurgo's *Caccia all'uomo!*; William Phillips's *Ventures in Diplomacy*; Giorgio Pini's *Filo diretto con Palazzo Venezia*; Friedrich-Karl von Plehwe's *Schicksalsstunden in Rom*; Rudolf Rahn's *Ruheloses Leben*; Enno von Rintelen's *Mussolini als Bundesgenosse*; Cesare Rossi's *Mussolini com'era*; Paul Schmidt's *Statist auf diplomatischer Bühne*; Carmine Senise's *Quando ero capo della polizia*; Bruno Spampanato's *Contromemoriale*; Alberto Theodoli's *A cavallo di due secoli*; Chaim Weizmann's *Trial and Error*; and Sumner Welles's *The Time for Decision.*

Most of the secondary works I have cited contain or make use of original material. I have learned much from the writings of other scholars. Among them I should like to mention in particular Paolo Alatri's *Le origini del fascismo*; Daniel A. Binchy's *Church and State in Fascist Italy*; Alan Bullock's *Hitler*; Giampiero Carocci's *La politica estera dell'Italia fascista*; Alan Cassels's *Mussolini's Early Diplomacy*; Frederick William Deakin's *Brutal Friendship*; Renzo De Felice's *Storia degli ebrei italiani sotto il fascismo*; Manfred Funke's *Sanktionen und Kanonen*; Sir Ivone Kirkpatrick's *Mussolini*; Adrian Lyttelton's *The Seizure of Power*; Denis Mack Smith's *Italy*; Attilio Milano's *Storia degli ebrei in Italia*; Jens Petersen's *Die Entstehung der Achse Berlin–Rom*; Cecil Roth's *The History of the Jews of Italy*; Gaetano Salvemini's *Scritti sul fascismo*; Christopher Seton-Watson's *Italy from Liberalism to Fascism*; Ferdinand Siebert's *Italiens Weg in den Zweiten Weltkrieg*; Mario Toscano's *Le origini diplomatiche del Patto d'Acciaio*; and Elizabeth Wiskemann's *The Rome–Berlin Axis.* For the demography of Italian Jewry I have largely relied on the writings of Roberto Bachi and his two gifted pupils, Sergio Della Pergola and E. Franco Sabatello. For Fascist policy towards Zionism I have made much use of Daniel Carpi's 'The Political Activity of Chaim Weizmann in Italy' and Gabriel Cohen's 'Mussolini, Italian Policy and Palestine'. I am indebted to Renato Almansi's notes on his late father, Dante Almansi, for stimulating me to re-examine the whole of the documentary evidence for the period from the fall of Mussolini to the deportation of the Jews of Rome. The painstaking researches of Giuliana Donati, Silva Gherardi Bon, Liliana Picciotto-Fargion, Eloisa Ravenna, and Michael Tagliacozzo have enabled me to provide a fuller and more accurate account of the Holocaust in German-occupied Italy. My assessment of the military operations and their impact on the fate of Italian Jewry is based partly on the works of Michael E. Howard and Lieutenant-Colonel G. A. Shepperd. My other debts, too numerous to acknowledge here, have been indicated in the footnotes and the bibliography.

Bibliography

I WRITINGS AND SPEECHES OF HITLER AND MUSSOLINI

BAYNES, N. H. (ed), *The Speeches of Adolf Hitler*, i–ii: *April 1922–August 1939*, London–New York–Toronto, 1942
DOMARUS, M. (ed.), *Hitler. Reden und Proklamationen*, i: *1932–1938*; ii: *1939–1945*, Würzburg, 1962–3.
HITLER, A., *Mein Kampf*, 15th edn., Munich, 1932.
MUSSOLINI, B., *Scritti e discorsi*, i–xii, Milan, 1934–40.
—— *Opera Omnia di Benito Mussolini*, i–xxxvi, ed. E. and D. Susmel, Florence, 1951–63.
PICKER, H., *Hitlers Tischgespräche im Führerhauptquartier 1941–1942*, ed. P. E. Schramm, A. Hillgruber, and M. Vogt, Stuttgart, 1963.
PREISS, H. (ed.), *Adolf Hitler in Franken*, Nuremberg, 1939.
—— Reden des Führers am Parteitag Grossdeutschland 1938, Munich, 1938.
TREVOR-ROPER, H. R. (ed.), *Hitler's Table Talk 1941–44*, London, 1953.
—— (ed.), *The Testament of Adolf Hitler. The Hitler–Bormann Documents, February–April 1945*, London, 1961.
WEINBERG, G. (ed.)., *Hitlers Zweites Buch. Ein Dokument aus dem Jahre 1928*, Stuttgart, 1961.

II. UNPUBLISHED DOCUMENTS

(a) *Archivio Centrale dello Stato Italiano, Rome*

Min. Int./Dir. gen. PS, Div. affari gen. e ris. (1923)/bb. 21 e 22 (H. Esser, visit to Italy, 1923).
Segreteria particolare del Duce/Cart. ris., b. 51 H/R (Mussolini–Interlandi).
Carte Grandi/fasc. 6/sottofasc. 1 (Grandi–Schubert, 15 Mar. 1932, contents of document kindly communicated by J. Petersen, Rome).
Min. Cultura Popolare/b. 324/Movimento fascista in Germania (contacts between Fascist agents and German anti-Semites, Sept.–Oct. 1935, contents of documents kindly communicated by J. Petersen).
Min. Cultura Popolare /b. 325/Antikomintern (contacts between Fascist agents and German anti-Semites, Dec. 1935, contents of documents kindly communicated by J. Petersen).
Rilevazione sugli ebrei del 22 agosto 1938/Min. Int./Dir. gen. Demografia e Razza/cart. 14/fasc. 47 (Jewish census on 'racial' basis).

(*b*)   *Archivio Storico Ministero Affari Esteri, Rome*

Segreteria generale—Pacco 89/Udienze (Mussolini–Interlandi).
Palestina, p. 5, 1933/Colloquio fra il Capo del Governo e il Signor
Weitzemann (*sic*) (memorandum by F. Suvich).
Italia/p. 57/1938 (Ciano on racial policy, 26 July 1938).

(*c*)   *Archivio Unione Comunità Israelitiche Italiane, Rome*

1938/Ministeri/Min. Int./Dir. gen. Demografia e Razza (conversation
on racial policy between unnamed Italian Jew and unnamed Fascist
deputy, undated and unsigned).
1938/Ministeri/Min. Educ. Naz. (Ascoli–Bottai, 7 Oct. and 16 Nov.
1938).
1938/Capo del Governo (Jarach to Sebastiani and Mussolini, 30 Oct.
1938).
1939/Ministeri/Min. Int./Div. Culti (Union to Montecchi, 21 Feb.
1939).
1939/Ministeri/Min. Int./Dir. gen. Demografia e Razza (Ascoli–Le
Pera, 16 Sept. 1939).
1939/Ministeri/Min. Int. (Union to Minister of Interior, 20 Sept. 1939).
1940/Ministeri/Min. Int. (Almansi to Ministry of Interior, 10 Mar.
1940).
1943/Abolizione decreti razziali (circular by Almansi, 31 Aug. 1943;
Union to Rabbi of Turin, 3 Sept. 1943).
1944/Leggi razziali/Vittime (list of Jews shot at Ardeatine Caves, 24
Mar. 1944; list of racial laws, 1938 to 1944).

(*d*)   *Bundesarchiv, Coblenz*

R 43/I 80 (Nord–Südkorrespondenz, 1928).
R 43/II/1465 (Hassell on Germany's withdrawal from League of
Nations, 14 and 20 Oct. 1933).
R 43/II/1448 (Hassell on Berger, 22 Feb. 1943; Mussolini–Sven von
Müller, 9 July 1935).
R 43/II/1440a (Tisserant to Suhard, 11 June 1940).
EAP 161-b-12/239 (Himmler files, Ricci to Himmler, 10 Sept. 1943).

(*e*)   *Bundesarchiv-Militärarchiv, Freiburg i. Br.*

H 27/13 (General H. Fischer on Ciano, 12 June 1936).
OKW/1041 (intelligence reports on Italian crisis, Oct. 1942–May
1943).
III M/1000/39–50 (diary of German naval staff, 1 Oct. 1942–31 Oct.
1943).
OKW 1482 (Operations 'Alaric' and Axis, 1943).

434 Bibliography

(*f*) *Centro di Documentazione Ebraica Contemporanea, Milan*

5A/Persecuzione e sterminio in Italia, nei paesi occupati e nelle colonie/Testimonianza M. Tagliati, Apr. 1958.

5D/Eccidi/Lago Maggiore/Dichiarazione del capo guardia G. Capotossi (guigno 1945).

5D/Eccidi/Lago Maggiore/Diario di Beki Behar Ottolenghi.

13B/Vicissitudini delle singole comunità/Roma/D. Almansi, 'Prima relazione al governo italiano circa le persecuzioni nazi–fasciste degli ebrei in Roma (settembre 1943–giugno 1944)', U.C.II, Rome, 1944.

13B/Vicissitudini delle singole comunità/Roma/U. Foà, 'Appunti circa il salvataggio dalla rapina tedesca degli arredi sacri della Comunità israelitica di Roma', Nov. 1950.

13B/Vicissitudini delle singole comunità/Venezia/Relazione Laura Jacchia Fano/'Fine degli ebrei degenti nei vari ospedali, manicome, ospizi di uomini, case di salute per vecchi (1944–45)'.

13B/Vicissitudini delle singole comunità/A. Wachsberger, 'Les déportations des juifs italiens', Dec. 1950.

(*g*) *Central Zionist Archives, Jerusalem*

File Z4/2136 (Beilinson on Vatican opposition to Zionism, 7 Dec. 1921; Lattes to Zionist Executive, 7 Dec. 1922; Lattes and Beilinson on meeting with Mussolini, 20 Dec. 1922; Italian Zionist Federation to Weizmann, 13 Feb. 1923; to Zionist Executive, 6 May 1923, 22 May 1924).

File Z4/2571 (reports on Vatican hostility to Zionism and its effect on Mussolini, 24 Oct. and 14 Nov. 1924).

File Z4/2571 (H. Kohn on position of Jews in Italy, 24 May 1926).

File Z4/3238/I (Jacobson in Italy, 29 May–14 June 1927).

File 1325/Political Department (Jacobson–Mussolini, 6 June 1927).

File Z4/3238/III (Lattes on anti-Zionist polemics in *Popolo di Roma*, 27 Dec. 1928).

File Z4/10347/I (Kisch on Fascist complaints about Zionism, 10 Jan. 1929).

File Z4/17049 (Weizmann to Mussolini, 17 June 1933; Goldmann on conversation with Ciucci, 3 Mar. 1938).

File Z4/10347/I (Jacobson on Weizmann–Mussolini meeting of 17 Feb. 1934).

File Z4/17049 (L. Kohn on Weizmann–Mussolini meeting, 23 Feb. 1934; Weizmann to Mussolini, 13 June 1934).

File Z4/3238/II (Goldmann on Zionism in Italy, 12 July 1934; Nahon to Jacobson on same subject, 18 July 1934).

File Z4/17123 (Theodoli to Weizmann, 31 July 1934).

File S25/1322 (Goldmann to Ben Gurion, 15 June 1936; Goldmann–

Bibliography   435

Theodoli, 3–4 May 1937; Goldmann–Ciano, 4 May 1937; Goldmann–
Bova Scoppa, 10 Sept.1937; Weizmann–Goldmann–Bova Scoppa, 14
Sept. 1937).

(h) *Deutsches Zentralarchiv, Potsdam*

60952 (Neurath to Dieckhoff on intervention in Spain, 24 and 27 Aug.
1936).
60975–78 (Ribbentrop, 1934–7).

(i) *Foreign Office Library, London*

L232/L067418–559 (Reich Chancellory, Italy, 1919–33).
K529/K151910–152843 (German Embassy Rome, reports, 1921–
1932).
K548/K154780–846 (Mussolini in Germany, 1922).
291/183720–839 (Munich Putsch and trial, 1923–4).
5272H/K326331–63 (Italian money for Hitler, 1923–9).
L1703/L501419–804 (Nazi–Fascist relations, 1923–32).
K428/K123452–998 (German–Italian relations, 1923–32).
K31/K003412–41 (Nazism, Fascism, and kindred movements, 1925–
1932).
5739/H029681–030438 (exchange visits between Rome and Berlin,
1925–36).
8067H/E579249–53 (Italy and National Socialism, 1933).
L1027/L301081–85 (Fascism and Jewish question, 1933–4).
8949H/E627783–87 (Italy and National Socialism, 1934).
5257H/E315503–15 (Hitler–Mussolini meeting, 1934).
8032H/E577821–36 (Italian press, 1934).
4680H/E224542–225003 (German Embassy Rome, reports, 1935–6).
8039H/E578217–29 (Italo–German co-operation against Bolshevism,
1935–8).
43/28659–29197 (Ribbentrop, 1935–9).
803/274827–979 (Bureau Ribbentrop, Likus on Ciano, Italian situation,
1935–41).
2390/D499888–954 (anti-Bolshevism, 1935–44).
3175H/D682369–848 (German Embassy Rome, reports, 1936).
3236H/0700758–62 (Hitler–Alfieri, 3 Aug. 1936).
348/III/201759–863/2 (Ciano's visit to Germany, Oct. 1936).
1500/370359–495 (German–Italian relations, 1936–7).
7196H/E529610–31 (press and propaganda, 1936–7).
3153/D665852–937 (Italy, racial and national problems, 1936–8).
7433H/E539945–540074 (Rosenberg, 1936–40).
325/194321–475 (Mussolini's visit to Germany, Sept. 1937).
1519/373079–3156 (German–Italian relations, 1937–9).

119/118762–119444 (Foreign Organization of National Socialist Party, Italy, 1937–40).

348/II/201482–758 (Hitler's visit to Italy, May 1938).

2172/47261–338 (Fascism and racial question, 1938).

33/25312–20 (Mackensen on Chamberlain–Mussolini meeting, 12 and 13 Jan. 1939).

100/65439–42 (Himmler to Bocchini on anti-Italian incidents, 28 Sept. 1939).

B14/B001879–2522 (German–Italian relations, May–Dec. 1940).

2191/472706–844 (Fascism and racial question, 1940–2).

B13/B001292–1867/4 (German–Italian relations, 1941).

1517/372603–3009 (German–Italian relations, Aug.–Nov. 1941).

2281/482484–86 (Alfieri on anti-Italian feeling in Germany, 19 Oct. 1941).

1206/331837–332115 (German–Italian relations, Dec. 1941–Feb. 1942).

1210/332233–361 (German–Italian relations, Mar.–May 1942).

133/73161–525 (German–Italian relations, June–Aug. 1942).

F19427–34 (Hitler to Mussolini, 4 Aug. 1942).

F19407–12 (Hitler to Mussolini, 21 Oct. 1942).

F15222–90030 (Göring–Mussolini, 23 Oct. 1942).

138/77158–682 (Bureau Ribbentrop, reports by Likus, June 1942–July 1943).

5602H/E401490–611 (Jews under Italian rule, Sept. 1942–Mar. 1943).

132/123744–124143 (German–Italian relations, Jan.–Mar. 1943).

1045/311326–37 (Ciano and Italian diplomats with Jewish wives, May–June 1943).

133/I/72331–702 (German–Italian relations, July 1943).

133/II/72703–73160 (German–Italian relations, Aug. 1943).

146/129360–69 (Likus on fall of Mussolini, 13 Aug. 1943).

131/III/71921–72330 (German–Italian relations, 1–22 Sept 1943).

132/123253–743 (German–Italian relations, 23 Sept.–15 Oct. 1943).

131/I/70851–71332 (German–Italian relations, 16 Oct.–31 Dec. 1943).

131/II/71333–920 (German–Italian relations, Jan.–Apr. 1944).

(*j*) *Italian Collection, St. Antony's College, Oxford*

Job 1/00039–46 (Mussolini's secret speech of 5 Feb. 1939).

Job 16/006968–70072 (Anfuso's dispatches from Berlin, 1943–4; Fascist Social Republic, German occupation).

Job 20/009430–544 (Renzetti, 1933–5).

Job 28/013262–89 (Fascist propaganda in Palestine, 1938–42).

Job 29/013506–89 (Fascist propaganda in Arab countries, 1937–41).

Job 33/016879–989 (papers concerning Emil Ludwig, 1931–2).

Job 35/017699–825 (Fascist movements abroad, 1934).

Job 53/026223–701 (Farinacci–Mussolini, Farinacci–Franco, Farinacci–Hitler, Grand Council, corruption in application of racial laws).

Job 54/026756–779 (Grandi–Mussolini, 1926–39).

Job 103/028031–44 (Interlandi to Mussolini, 1943–5).

Job 109/029683–A (Edda Mussolini and 'young Pacifici', 15 Sept. 1929).

Job 114/031394–677 (Farinacci, Finzi, Interlandi).

Job 122/033851–34221 (Farinacci, Jole Foà).

Job 123/034231–80 (Farinacci to Mussolini, 1923–35).

Job 129/035467–98 (police reports on Balbo, 1931–9; Eden's 'Jewish origin').

Job 160/046585–93 (Jewish 'Fascists of the first hour').

Job 162/047380–465 (Italian Social Republic, social policy).

Job 170/050243–50, 52–78 (Renzetti, 1931–3).

Job 261/072743–68 (Guido Jung).

Job 263/2/074978–75002 (Fascist racial policy).

Job 286/087159–74/2 (Bastianini, Fascism abroad).

Job 287/087718–93 (Gravelli, Fascist International).

Job 289/088463–658 (Preziosi, 1922–45; Fascist racial policy).

Job 302/095985–97/2 (Fascist Arabic-language broadcasts, 1944).

Job 321/106976–107930 (Italian Foreign Ministry reports, 1935–8, 1941).

Job 325/110824–963 (Italian Social Republic, racial persecutions, 1943–5).

Job 330/113305–6 (Biseo to Farinacci, 8 Oct. 1926).

Job 331/35, 94–106 (Mussolini to Farinacci, 1925; Preziosi to Mussolini, 31 Jan. 1944).

(*k*)   *Institut für Zeitgeschichte, Munich*

F34/1–2 (diary of General N. von Vormann, Aug.–Sept. 1939).

ED83/1–2 (unpublished sections of Goebbels's war diary, 1942–3).

RF1230 (Röthke to Eichmann, 6 Mar. 1943).

NO–315 (extracts from war diary of General R. Stahel, 23 Sept.–31 Oct. 1943).

NG–5027 (exchange of telegrams and letters on deportation of Roman Jews, 6 Oct.–16 Nov. 1943).

NO–2427 (Kappler on deportation of Roman Jews, 17–18 Oct. 1943).

MA–654/1619–48 (German military measures in Italy, July–Oct. 1943).

ZS 29 (A. Dresler on Hitler, 6 June 1951).

ZS 126/I (General H. Röttiger on military and civil authorities in German-occupied Italy, 24 June 1952).

ZS 528 (Weizsäcker on Karl Wolff, 19 Apr. 1949).
ZS 918 (interrogation of Prince of Hesse, 6 May 1947).
ZS 1030 (interrogation of Hermann Esser, 6 Dec. 1946).
ZS 1546 (Baron Gustav Adolf von Steengracht).
ZS 1596 (Consul-General Walther Wüster).

(*l*)   *Hauptarchiv der NSDAP, Wiener Library, London*

Reel 52/Folder 1225 (testimony of Franz Thanner on Göring's flight to
Italy, 1 Feb. 1934, 15 Feb. 1935).
Reel 78/Folder 1575 (H. Reupke to E. Röhm on Fascist militia, 30 Oct.
1931; circular by A. Dresler on Nazi–Fascist contacts, 25 Feb. 1932;
undated and unsigned memorandum on Nazi–Fascist relations, found
at Brown House on 7 June 1932; Röhm on misconduct of Party
members in Italy, 20 Oct. 1932).

(*m*)   *Politisches Archiv, Bonn*

II/Pol.29/1–6/Nationalsozialismus, Faschismus und ähnliche Bestre-
bungen (National Socialism, Fascism, and kindred movements).
AA/Chef AO/Schriftwechsel betr. Landesgruppe Italian 1932 (Foreign
Organization of National Socialist Party, activities in Italy 1932).
Abt.II/Polit. Beziehungen Italiens zu Deutschland/4 (Hassell to
Neurath, 1933).
Inl.II/g82/Italien/Polizei-Attaché/I/1939–1945 (Kappler, 1939–45).
Inl.I/Partei/Italien/Baron Julius Evola/1941–1942 (Evola's activities in
Germany, 1941–2).
RAM/34/43/Schmidt-Niederschriften (minutes by Paul Schmidt,
1942–3).
Inl.II/g395/Italien/Berichte und Meldungen zur Entwicklung der Lage
in Italien/2/Januar–August 1943 (situation in Italy, Jan.–Aug. 1943).
Inl.II/g396/Italien/Berichte und Meldungen zur Entwicklung der Lage
in Italien/3/September–Dezember 1943 (situation in Italy, Sept.–Dec.
1943).
Pol.3/22/Vatikan (Weizsäcker to Wilhelmstrasse, 3 Dec. 1943).

(*n*)   *Public Record Office, London*

F.O.371/8993/E371/53/65/20 (Graham on Weizmann–Mussolini meet-
ing, 5 Jan. 1923).
F.O.371/12960/C5033/4353/22 (Chamberlain–Bordonaro on danger
of Fascist revisionism, 28 June 1928).
F.O.371/14422/C3869/22 (Rumbold on Theodor Wolff–Mussolini, 12
May 1930).
F.O.371/15979/202–203/C611/321/22 (Ogilvie-Forbes on Vatican sup-
port for Mussolini, 19 Jan. 1932).

F.O.371/15979/205–207/C1377/321/22 (Ogilvie-Forbes on Mussolini's visit to Pius XI, 12 Feb. 1932).

F.O.371/15979/C2509/327/22 (Graham–Grandi, 24 Mar. 1932).

F.O.371/15987/C6572/6225/22 (Graham on Grandi, 27 July 1932).

F.O.371/15986/C6633/2868/22 (Graham–Mussolini, 28 July 1932).

F.O.371/16720/410 (Graham–Mussolini on Jews in Germany, 3 Apr. 1933).

F.O.371/16932/E7823/6438/31 (Drummond–Theodoli on Zionism, 13 Dec. 1933).

F.O.371/17876/E1279/96/31 (Drummond on Mussolini and Zionism, 19 Feb. 1934).

Cab.24/259, C.P. 13 (36) (The German Danger. A collection of reports from H. M. Embassy in Berlin, 1933–5).

F.O.371/19480/R6285/72/3 (O'Malley on Italian weakness, 18 Nov. 1935).

F.O.371/20411/R3159/226/22 (Vansittart on need for collaboration with Italy, 2 June 1936).

F.O.371/R3302/341/22 (Drummond on Italo–German *rapprochement*, 5 June 1936).

F.O.371/19983/6948/106–7 (Italian support for Jewish State, 15 July 1936).

F.O.371/19983/6948/241–48 (Italian intrigues in Middle East, 21 Aug. 1936).

F.O.371/R2476/2476/22 (Laski on position of Jews in Italy, 7 Apr. 1937).

F.O.371/21182/R3585/2476/22 (McClure on position of Jews in Italy, 11 May 1937).

F.O.371/20786/E5489/145/65 (Italian intrigues in Middle East, 17 Sept. 1937).

F.O.371/20786/E6999/145/65 (Italian intrigues in Middle East, 19 Nov. 1937).

F.O.371/21659/22 (Cadogan on Italy and 'German menace', 14 Oct. 1938).

F.O.371/23799/R10/10/22 (Perth on Fascist racial policy, 27 Dec. 1938).

Cab.23/97/4–9 (Cabinet meeting of 18 Jan. 1939).

F.O.371/23799/R573/10/22 (Osborne on controversy between Church and State over Fascist racial laws, 18 Jan. 1939).

F.O.371/23799/R751/10/22 (McFaydean on position of Jews in Italy, 25 Jan. 1939).

Cab.23/98/73–86 (Cabinet meeting of 20 Mar. 1939).

F.O.800/316 (Halifax Papers, Halifax to Chamberlain, 19 Aug. 1939).

Cab.23/100/441–57 (Cabinet meeting of 1 Sept. 1939).

F.O.371/22949/7670/157–72 (Weizmann to Butler, 19 Oct. 1939).

F.O.371/25238/737/38/48 (Scrivener to Palazzo Chigi on Jewish immigration to Palestine, 10 Jan. 1940).

F.O.371/25239/2633/38/48 (Scrivener–Rabbi Prato, 10 Feb. 1940).

F.O.371/36015/2955/52/17 (differences between treatment of Jews by Germans and Italians in France, 1943).

F.O.371/12641/49/48 (Osborne on evacuation of Jews from Italy, 24 Aug. and 9 Sept. 1943).

F.O.371/WR260/428422 (Heathcote Smith on deportation of Jews from German-occupied Italy, 15 July 1944).

F.O.371/WR435/42843 (Heathcote Smith on internment and deportation of Jews in Italy, 18 July 1944).

F.O.371/WR583/42843 (Heathcote Smith on audience with Pius XII, 15 Aug. 1944).

F.O.371/WR893/42843 (Heathcote Smith on Vatican intervention in favour of Jews, 26 Aug. 1944).

F.O.371/WR1078/42843 (Osborne on failure of Vatican intervention, 9 Sept. 1944).

(*o*)   *Weizmann Archives, Rehovoth*

Weizmann Diary (Weizmann–Mussolini meeting, entry for 3 Jan. 1923).

Lattes (Rome) to Weizmann (Cairo), 20 Apr. 1933.

Palazzo Chigi to Weizmann, 25 Apr. 1933.

Weizmann to Mussolini, 15 June 1933 (draft).

Weizmann to Mussolini, 17 June 1933.

Weizmann (London) to Nahon (Milan), 24 July 1933.

Nahon (Milan) to Weizmann (London), 27 July 1933.

Lattes (Rome) to Weizmann (Merano), 18 Sept. 1933.

Weizmann to Lattes, 4 Dec. 1933.

Weizmann (London) to Nahon (Milan), 21 Jan. 1934.

Palazzo Chigi to Weizmann, 16 Feb. 1934

Weizmann–Mussolini meeting of 17 Feb. 1934 (memorandum by Jacobson).

Drummond (Rome) to Weizmann (Jerusalem), 8 Mar. 1934.

Weizmann to Theodoli, 28 May 1934.

(*p*)   *Yad Vashem Archives, Jerusalem*

JM/1687/1–3/Archivio Comunità israelitica di Roma/Relazioni con le Autorità (Jewish Community Rome, relations with authorities, 1919–40).

JM/1688/1–3/Comunità israelitica di Roma/Correspondenze con la Prefettura (Jewish Community Rome, correspondence with Prefecture, 1934–43).

JW/1689/1–3/Assistenza profughi Germania e Comitato ricerche deportati (aid to refugees from Germany, deportations).

L319798–802/P03/L450 (German Consulate-General Jerusalem on Italian intrigues in Palestine, 7 June 1935).

K394442–43/Pal.465/2 (Grobba on Arab hostility to Italy, 30 May 1936).

Archivio Centrale dello Stato/JM/2792/1/Demografia e razza (Fascist racial policy, 1938–43).

1691/1–3/Italia–Roma/Persecuzioni razziali (racial persecutions in Italy, 1938–45).

Archivio Ministero Affari esteri/JM/2840/Italia, Francia, Croazia (Jews under Italian rule, 1939–43).

481571–74/1269B/4 (Weizsäcker on need for Italo–German co-operation in Arab matters, 9 Sept. 1940).

481604/1269B/4 (Grobba on Arab hostility to Italy, 30 Sept. 1940).

481622–23/1269B/4 (German Embassy Rome on Italo–Arab relations, 15 Nov. 1940).

Archivio Centrale dello Stato/JM/2917/1–4/Persecuzioni (racial persecutions, collaboration between German and Italian police forces, 1941–4).

482025–26/1269B/4 (Hentig on Mufti's relations with Rome, anti-Italian feeling in Arab world, need for Italo–German co-operation in Arab matters, 21 Feb. 1941).

261123/2258/4 (German Embassy Rome on Arab hostility to Italy, 6 Aug. 1942).

261155–60/2258/4 (Mufti on his support for Rome–Berlin Axis, 10 Aug. 1942).

K206733–35 (Doertenbach on conversation with Preziosi, 2 Feb. 1943).

K206729–30 (Mackensen on Preziosi, 15 Feb. 1943).

K206728 (Mackensen on anti-Jewish propaganda in Italy, 12 Mar. 1943).

K206769–72 (Thadden on plans for anti-Jewish International, 11 May 1943).

K206919 (Thadden on Kube and 'final solution', 15 May 1943).

K206912 (Günther on pro-Jewish Italian diplomats in Bucharest, 19 May 1943).

K206741–43 (Thadden to Himmler on Italian resistance to 'final solution', 8 June 1943).

371616–28/Pol.7/340 (Prüfer on Arab hostility to Italy, 17 July 1943).

NG–2652–H (circular by Kaltenbrunner's office on 'final solution' in German-occupied countries, 23 Sept. 1943).

NG–5026 (Wagner and Hilger on Jewish question in Italy, 4 and 9 Dec. 1943).

K207055–57 (Wilhelmstrasse to Embassy Ankara on repatriation of Turkish Jews in Italy, 29 July 1944).

K207003 (Rahn on flight of Italian Jews to Switzerland, 2 Sept. 1944). TRO–10/639 (trial of Karl Wolff). TRO–10/754a–b (trial of Friedrich R. Bosshammer). Testimonies of participants (General Giorgio Liuzzi, 8 Feb. 1960; General Ivo Levi, Apr. 1960; Senator Ferruccio Parri, Sept. 1960; Senator Emilio Lussu, 20 Jan. 1961).

III.   PUBLISHED DOCUMENTS

(a)   *Nuremberg Trials*

The Trial of the Major War Criminals before the International Military Tribunal. Proceedings, i–xxiii; *Documents in Evidence*, xxiv–xlii, Nuremberg, 1947–9.

(b)   *Official Collections of Diplomatic Documents*

Actes et documents du Saint Siège relatifs à la Seconde Guerre Mondiale, i–ix, ed. P. Blet, R. A. Graham, A. Martini, B. Schneider, Vatican City, 1965–75.

Akten zur Deutschen Auswärtigen Politik, Serie B: *1925–1933*, i–vii, Göttingen, 1966–74; Serie C: *1933–1937*, i–iii, Göttingen, 1971–3; Serie D: *1937–1945*, i–xiii, Baden-Baden, Bonn, Frankfurt/Main, and Göttingen, 1950–70; Serie E: *1941–1945*, i–iii, Göttingen, 1969–74; English trans. of Serie C: *Documents on German Foreign Policy*, Series C, i–v, London, 1957–66.

Documents on British Foreign Policy 1919–1939, 1st Series: *1919–1929*, i–viii, London, 1947–58; 2nd Series: *1930–1937*, i–xii, London, 1947–1972; 3rd Series: *1938–1939*, iii–vii, London, 1950–4.

Documenti diplomatici italiani 1861–1943, 6ª serie 1, Rome, 1956; 7ª serie: *1922–1935*, i–viii, Rome, 1953–72; 8ª serie: *1935–1939*, xii–xiii, Rome, 1952–3; 9ª serie: *1939–1943*, i–v, Rome, 1954–65.

Documents diplomatiques français 1932–1939. 1re série: *1932–1935*, i–vi, Paris, 1964–72; 2e série: *1936–1939*, i–viii, Paris, 1963–73.

Foreign Relations of the United States. Diplomatic Papers 1933–1945, Washington, 1950–67.

MOSCA, R. (ed.), *L'Europa verso la catastrofe. 184 colloqui di Mussolini, Franco, Chamberlain, Sumner Welles, Rustu Aras, Stoiadinovic, Göring, Zog, François-Poncet, ecc., raccolti da Galeazzo Ciano*, i: *1936–1938*; ii: *1939–1942*, Milan, 1964.

Bibliography

(c)   Other Documentary Material

ALGARDI, Z., *Il processo Caruso*, Rome, 1945.

Aperçu sur l'œuvre du Bureau d'information vatican 1939–1946, Vatican City, 1946.

Bezirksgericht Jerusalem/Strafakt 40/61/Der Generalstaatsanwalt des Staates Israel gegen Adolf, Sohn des Karl Adolf Eichmann, i–xiv, Jerusalem, 1961.

BUFFARINI GUIDI, G., *La vera verità. I documenti dell'archivio segreto del ministro degli Interni Guido Buffarini Guidi dal 1938 al 1945*, Milan, 1970.

COLLOTTI, E., 'I rapporti italo–tedeschi dopo 18 settembre in due recenti raccolte di fonti tedesche', *Studi Storici*, iii (Oct.–Dec. 1962), 856–73.

——, 'Documenti sull'attività del Sicherheitsdienst nell'Italia occupata', *Il Movimento di Liberazione in Italia*, 83 (Apr.–June 1966), 38–77.

DEL BUONO, O. (ed.), *Eia, Eia, Eia, Alalà! La stampa italiana sotto il fascismo 1919/1943*, Milan, 1971.

DEL VECCHIO, G., *Una nuova persecuzione di un perseguitato; documenti*, Rome, 1945.

FLORA, F., *Stampe dell'era fascista*, Rome, 1945.

FRIEDLANDER, S., *Pie XII et le IIIe Reich. Documents*, Paris, 1964.

Führer Conferences on Naval Affairs (Brassey's Naval Annual), London–New York, 1948, pp. 25–496.

Geheimer Briefwechsel Mussolini–Dollfuss, ed. K.-H. Sailer, Vienna, 1949.

GIOVANETTI, A. (ed.), *Il Vaticano e la guerra. Note storiche*, Vatican City, 1960.

——, *Roma città aperta*, Milan, 1962.

HEIBER, H. (ed.), 'Aus den Akten des Gauleiters Kube', *VJZG* 4 (Jan. 1956), 67–92.

——, *Hitlers Lagebesprechungen. Die Protokollfragmente seiner militärischen Konferenzen 1942–1945*, Stuttgart, 1962.

——, *Goebbels–Reden*, i–ii, Düsseldorf, 1971.

HILL, L. E. (ed.), *Die Weizsäcker-Papiere 1933–1950*, Berlin, 1974.

HILLGRUBER, A. (ed.), *Staatsmänner und Diplomaten bei Hitler. Vertrauliche Aufzeichnungen über Unterredungen mit Vertretern des Auslandes*, i: *1939–1941*; ii: *1942–1944*, Frankfurt/Main, 1967–70.

Hitler e Mussolini. Lettere e documenti, Milan–Rome, 1946.

HUBATSCH, W. (ed.), *Hitlers Weisungen für die Kriegsführung 1939–1945. Dokumente des Oberkommandos der Wehrmacht*, Frankfurt/Main, 1962.

HUDAL, A. C., *Römische Tagebücher. Lebensbeichte eines alten Bischofs*, Graz–Stuttgart, 1976.

Il processo Roatta: i documenti, Rome, 1945

KRAUSNICK, H. (ed.), 'Himmler über seinen Besuch bei Mussolini vom 11.–14. Oktober 1942', *VJZG* 4 (Oct. 1956), 423–6.

Kriegstagebuch des Oberkommandos der Wehrmacht (Wehrmachtführungsstab) 1940–1945, i–iv, ed. P. E. Schramm, Frankfurt/Main, 1961–5.

Le Livre jaune français. Documents diplomatiques, 1938–1939, Ministère des Affaires Étrangères, Paris, 1939.

LUDLOW, P. (ed.), 'Dokumentation. Papst Pius XII., die britische Regierung und die deutsche Opposition im Winter 1939/1940', *VJZG* 22 (July 1974), 299–341.

MATTEINI, C. (ed.), *Ordini alla stampa*, Rome, 1945.

MICHAELIS, M., 'La prima missione del Principe d'Assia presso Mussolini (agosto '36)', *Nuova Rivista Storica*, lv, (May–Aug. 1971), 367–70.

——, 'I nuclei nazisti in Italian e la loro funzione nei rapporti tra fascismo e nazismo nel 1932. La Landesgruppe Italien del partito nazionalsocialista tedesco alla luce di alcuni documenti inediti', *Nuova Rivista Storica*, lvii, (May–Aug. 1973), 422–38.

MOLHO, M. (ed.), *Communauté israélite de Thessalonique. In Memoriam. Hommage aux victimes juives des Nazis à Grèce*, 2nd edn., Thessalonica, 1973.

POLIAKOV, L. and J. Sabille, *Jews under the Italian Occupation*, Paris, 1955.

——, *Gli ebrei sotto l'occupazione italiana*, Milan, 1956.

POLICE D'ISRAËL, Quartier général 6-ème bureau, *Adolf Eichmann*, i–vi, Jerusalem, 1961.

Processo Graziani, i–iii, Rome, 1948.

Relazione sull'opera svolta dal Ministero degli Affari Esteri per la tutela delle comunità ebraiche (1938–1943), Rome, n. d. (1945?).

ROBERTSON, E., 'Zur Wiederbesetzung des Rheinlandes 1936', *VJZG* 10 (Apr. 1962), 178–205.

ROSSI, E., *Documenti sulle origini e gli sviluppi della questione araba 1875–1944*, Rome, 1944.

SCOPPOLA, P., *La chiesa e il fascismo. Documenti e interpretazioni*, Bari, 1976.

SIMONE, M. DI (ed.), *P.N.F. Pagine eroiche della rivoluzione fascista*, Milan, 1925.

STADERINI, T., *Legislazione per la difesa della razza*, 3rd edn., Rome, 1940

TOSCANO, M., 'La controversia tra Salò e Berlino per l'occupazione nazista e per le decisioni annessionistiche di Hitler dell'Alto Adige e del Trentino nei documenti diplomatici della Repubblica Sociale Italiana', *Storia e Politica* vi (Jan.–Mar. 1967), 1–59.

TRIBUNALE MILITARE DI ROMA, *Processo Kappler. Sentenza No. 631, N.6003/45.*

UNITED RESTITUTION ORGANIZATION, *Dokumente über Methoden der Judenverfolgung im Ausland,* Frankfurt/Main, 1959.

——, *Judenverfolgung in Italien, den italienisch besetzten Gebieten und in Nordafrika. Dokumentensammlung vorgelegt von der United Restitution Organization,* Frankfurt/Main, 1962.

WEIZMANN, C., *American Addresses,* New York, 1923.

ZUCÀRO, D. (ed.), *Lettere all 'O.V.R.A. di Pitigrilli,* Florence, 1961.

IV. DIARIES AND MEMOIRS

ABETZ, O., *Das offene Problem. Ein Rückblick auf zwei Jahrzehnte deutscher Frankreichpolitik,* Cologne, 1951.

ACERBO, G., *Fra due plotoni di esecuzione. Avvenimenti e problemi dell'epoca fascista,* Bologna, 1968.

ALFIERI, D., *Due dittatori di fronte,* Milan, 1948.

ALLASON, B., *Memorie di un'antifascista,* Florence, 1946.

ALOISI, P., *Journal (25 juillet 1932–14 juin 1936),* Paris, 1957.

ANFUSO, F., *Da Palazzo Venezia al Lago di Garda,* Bologna, 1957.

AVON, EARL OF (Anthony Eden), *The Eden Memoirs. Facing the Dictators,* London, 1962.

BADOGLIO, P., *L'Italia nella seconda guerra mondiale,* Milan, 1946.

BASTIANINI, G., *Uomini, cose, fatti. Memorie di un ambasciatore,* Milan 1959.

BERENSON, B., *Rumor and Reflection,* New York, 1952.

BOTTAI, G., *Vent'anni e un giorno (24 luglio 1943),* Milan, 1949.

BRÜNING, H., *Memoiren 1918–1934,* Stuttgart, 1970.

BURCKHARDT, C. J., *Meine Danziger Mission 1937–1939,* Munich, 1960.

CALEFFI, P., *Si fa presto a dire fame,* Milan–Rome, 1955.

CANTALUPO, R., *Fu la Spagna. Ambasciata presso Franco febbraio–aprile 1937,* Milan, 1948.

CARBONI, G., *Memorie segrete 1935–1948. 'Più che il dovere',* Florence, 1955.

CAVALLERO, U., *Comando supremo. Diario 1940–43 del capo di S.M.G.,* Bologna, 1948.

CAVIGLIA, E., *Diario (aprile 1925–marzo 1945),* Rome, 1952.

CERRUTI, E., *Visti da vicino,* Milan, 1951.

CHARLES-ROUX, F., *Huit ans au Vatican 1932–1940,* Paris, 1947.

CHURCHILL, W. S., *The Second World War,* i–vi, London–Boston, 1948–1954.

CIANO, E., *My Truth. As told to Albert Zarca,* London, 1977.

CIANO, G., *Diario,* i: *1939–1940*; ii: *1941–1943,* Milan, 1946: 6th edn. 1950.

——, *1937–1938 Diario,* Bologna, 1948.

D'AROMA, N., *Mussolini segreto*, Bologna, 1958.

DILKS, D. (ed.), *The Diaries of Sir Alexander Cadogan 1938–1945*, London, 1971.

DOLFIN, G., *Con Mussolini nella tragedia. Diario del capo della segreteria particolare del Duce 1943–44*, Milan, 1950.

DOLLMANN, E., *Roma nazista*, Milan, 1949 and 1951.

EVOLA, J. C., *Il cammino del Cinabro*, 2nd edn., Milan, 1972.

FEDERZONI, L., *Italia di ieri per la storia di domani*, Milan, 1967.

FRANÇOIS-PONCET, A., *Au Palais Farnèse. Souvenirs d'une ambassade à Rome*, Paris, 1961.

FRANK, H., *Im Angesicht des Galgens*, 2nd edn., Neuhaus b. Schliersee, 1955.

FRASSATI, L., *Il destino passa per Varsavia*, Bologna, 1949.

GAFENCU, G., *Derniers jours de l'Europe. Un Voyage diplomatique en 1939*, Paris, 1946.

GASPAROTTO, L., *Diario di un deputato. Cinquant'anni di vita politica italiana*, Milan, 1945.

GOEBBELS, J., *Vom Kaiserhof zur Reichskanzlei*, 31st edn., Munich, 1941
———, *Tagebücher aus den Jahren 1942–43*, ed. L. Lochner, Zurich, 1948.

GOLDMANN, N., *Memories. The Autobiography of Nahum Goldmann*, London, 1970.

GORLA, G., *L'Italia nella seconda guerra mondiale. Diario di un milanese, ministro del Re nel governo di Mussolini*, Milan, 1959.

GROBBA, F., *Männer und Mächte im Orient; 25 Jahre diplomatische Tätigkeit im Orient*, Göttingen, 1967.

GUARIGLIA, R., *Ricordi (1922–1946)*, Naples, 1949.

GUARNERI, F., *Battaglie economiche tra le due grandi guerre*, i–ii, Milan, 1953.

HALDER, F., *Kriegstagebuch. Tägliche Aufzeichnungen des Chefs des Generalstabes des Heeres 1938–1942*, i–iii, ed. H.-A. Jacobsen, Stuttgart, 1962–4.

HASSELL, U. VON, *Vom anderen Deutschland. Aus den nachgelassenen Tagebüchern 1938–1944*, Zurich, 1946.

HERZL, T., *Tagebücher*, iii (Gesammelte Zionistische Schriften, iv), Tel Aviv, 1934.

HOROWITZ, D., *State in the Making*, New York, 1950.

HOSSBACH, F., *Zwischen Wehrmacht und Hitler*, 2nd edn., Göttingen, 1965.

KÁLLAY, N., *Hungarian Premier. A Personal Account of a Nation's Struggle in the Second World War*, London–New York, 1954.

KERSTEN, F., *The Kersten Memoirs 1940–1945*, London, 1956.

KESSELRING, A., *Soldat bis zum letzten Tag*, Bonn, 1953.

KISCH, F. H., *Palestine Diary*, London, 1938.

KORDT, E., *Nicht aus den Akten. Die Wilhelmstrasse in Frieden und Krieg. Erlebnisse, Begegnungen und Eindrücke 1928–1945*, Stuttgart, 1950

LETO, G., *OVRA. Fascismo-antifascismo*, 2nd edn., Bologna, 1952

LÜDECKE, K. G. W., *I Knew Hitler. The Story of a Nazi Who Escaped the Blood Purge*, New York, 1937; London, 1938.

MAGISTRATI, M., 'La Germania e l'impresa italiana in Etiopia', *Rivista di Studi Politici Internazionali*, xvii (Oct.–Dec. 1950), 563–606.

——, *L'Italia a Berlino (1937–1939)*, Milan, 1956.

——, *Il prologo del dramma. Berlino 1934–1937*, Milan, 1971.

MELLINI PONCE DE LEON, A., *Guerra diplomatica a Salò (ottobre 1943–aprile 1945)*, Bologna, 1950.

MOELLHAUSEN, E. F., *La carta perdente. Memorie diplomatiche (25 luglio 1943–2 maggio 1945)*, 2nd edn., Rome, 1948.

MORPURGO, L., *Caccia all'uomo! Pagine di diario 1938–1944*, Rome, 1946.

MOSLEY, Sir O., *My Life*, London, 1968.

MÜLLER, J., *Bis zur letzten Konsequenz. Ein Leben für Frieden und Freiheit*, Munich, 1975.

MUSSOLINI, E., *Mio fratello Benito*, Florence, 1957.

MUSSOLINI, V., *Vita con mio padre*, Milan, 1957.

OJETTI, U., *I taccuini 1914–1943*, Florence, 1954.

PHILLIPS, W., *Ventures in Diplomacy*, London, 1955.

PINI, G., *Filo diretto con Palazzo Venezia*, Bologna, 1950.

——, *Itinerario tragico (1943–1945)*, Milan, 1950.

PLEHWE, F.-K. VON, *Schicksalsstunden in Rom. Ende eines Bündnisses*, Berlin, 1967.

PRATO, D., *Dal Pergamo della Comunità di Roma*, Rome, 1950.

QUARONI, P., *Valigia diplomatica*, Milan, 1956.

RAFANELLI, L., *Una donna e Mussolini*, Milan, 1946.

RAHN, R., *Ruheloses Leben. Aufzeichnungen und Erinnerungen*, Düsseldorf, 1949.

RINTELEN, E. VON, *Mussolini als Bundesgenosse. Erinnerungen des deutschen Militärattachés in Rom 1936–1943*, Tübingen–Stuttgart, 1951.

ROCCA, M., *Come il fascismo devenne una dittatura*, Milan, 1952.

ROSENBERG, A., *Letzte Aufzeichnungen. Ideale und Idole der nationalsozialistischen Revolution*, Göttingen, 1955.

——, *Das politische Tagebuch Alfred Rosenbergs, 1934–35 und 1939–40*, ed. H.-G. Seraphim, Göttingen, 1956.

ROSSI, C., *Mussolini com'era*, Rome, 1947.

——, *Trentatre vicende mussoliniane*, Milan, 1958.

SCHELLENBERG, W., *The Schellenberg Memoirs*, London, 1956.

SCHMIDT, P., *Statist auf diplomatischer Bühne 1923–1945*, Bonn, 1952.

SCORZA, C., *La notte del Gran Consiglio*, 2nd edn., Milan, 1969.

SENISE, C., *Quando ero capo della polizia 1940–1943*, Rome, 1946.
SIMONI, L. (Michael Lanza), *Berlino. Ambasciata d'Italia 1939–1943*, Rome, 1946.
SPAMPANATO, B., *Contromemoriale*, i–iii, Rome, 1951–2.
STARHEMBERG, E. R. VON, *Between Hitler and Mussolini*, London–New York, 1942.
STRAZZERA-PERNICIANI, A., *Umanità ed eroismo nella vita segreta di Regina Coeli—Roma 1943–1944*, Rome, 1959
THEODOLI, A.. *A cavallo di due secoli*, Rome, 1950.
VARÈ, D., *The two Impostors*, London, 1949.
WARD PRICE, G., *I Know these Dictators*, London, 1937.
WEIZMANN, C., *Trial and Error*, London, 1949.
WEIZSÄCKER, E. VON, *Erinnerungen*, Munich, 1950.
ZACHARIAE, G., *Mussolini si confessa*, Milan, 1948.
ZANGRANDI, R., *Il lungo viaggio attraverso il fascismo*, 3rd edn., Milan, 1962.
ZOLLI, E., *Before the Dawn*, New York, 1954.

V. SECONDARY WORKS

ACERBO, G., *I fondamenti della dottrina fascista della razza*, Rome, 1940.
ALATRI, P., 'Un tentativo di mediazione tra Hitler e Pio XI', *Ulisse*, iv (autumn 1953), 134–47.
——, *Le origini del fascismo*, 3rd edn., Rome, 1962.
ALFASSIO GRIMALDI, U. and G. BOZZETTI, *Farinacci il più fascista*, Milan, 1972.
ALMANSI, R. J., 'Mio Padre, Dante Almansi', *La Rassegna Mensile di Israel*, xlii (May–June 1976), 234–55.
ANCHIERI, E., 'Les Rapports italo–allemands pendant l'ère nazi-fasciste', *Revue d'Histoire de la Deuxième Guerre Mondiale*, vii (Apr. 1957), 1–23.
ANDRÉ, G., 'la politica estera del governo fascista durante la seconda guerra mondiale', in R. de Felice (ed.), *L'Italia fra tedeschi e alleati. La politica estera fascista e la seconda guerra mondiale*, Bologna, 1973.
AQUARONE, A., *L'organizzazione dello stato totalitario*, Turin, 1965
BACHI, R., *la demografia degli ebrei italiani negli ultimi cento anni* (Atti del Congresso internazionale di studi sulla popolazione), Rome, 1931.
——, 'La demografia dell'ebraismo italiano prima dell'emancipazione', *Scritti in onore di Dante Lattes*, Città di Castello, 1938, pp. 256–320.
——, 'Ha-hitpathut ha-demografit shel yehudei Italia mi–1600 ad 1937', *Scritti in memoria di Sally Mayer*, Jerusalem, 1956, pp. 52–76.
——, 'The Demographic Development of Italian Jewry from the

Seventeenth Century', *Jewish Journal of Sociology*, iv (Dec. 1962), 172–191.

BARTH, H., *Romanische Köpfe*, Berlin, 1938.

HAUMGART, W., 'Zur Ansprache Hitlers vor den Führern der Wehrmacht am 22. August 1939', *VJZG* 16 (Apr. 1968), 120–49.

BEDARIDA, G., *Ebrei d'Italia*, Leghorn, 1950.

BELLOTTI, F., *La repubblica di Mussolini. 26 luglio 1943–25 aprile 1945*, Milan, 1947.

BIANCHI, G., *25 luglio. Crollo di un regime*, Milan, 1963.

BINCHY, D. A., *Church and State in Fascist Italy*, Oxford, 1941 and 1970.

BOCCA, G., *La repubblica di Mussolini*, Rome–Bari, 1977.

BODENSIECK, H., 'Prag und die jüdische Frage nach München', *VJZG* 9 (July 1961), 249–61.

BODRERO, E. (ed.), *Inchiesta sulla massoneria*, Rome, 1925.

BORGESE, G. A., *Goliath. The March of Fascism*, London, 1938.

BRACHER, K. D., *Die deutsche Diktatur. Entstehung, Struktur, Folgen des Nationalsozialismus*, Cologne–Berlin, 1969, 5th edn., 1976.

BROSZAT, M., 'Das Dritte Reich und die rumänische Judenpolitik', *Gutachten des Instituts für Zeitgeschichte*, Stuttgart, 1958, pp. 102–83.

BULLOCK, A., *Hitler. A Study in Tyranny*, rev. edn., Harmondsworth, 1962

CAFFAZ, U., *L'antisemitismo italiano sotto il fascismo*, Florence, 1975.

CANEVARI, E., *La guerra italiana. Retroscena della disfatta*, i–ii, Rome, 1948–9.

CAPASSO, A., *Idee chiare sul razzismo*, Rome, 1942.

CAROCCI, G., *La politica estera dell'Italia fascista (1925–1928)*, Bari, 1969.

CARPI, D., 'The Catholic Church and Italian Jewry under the Fascists (to the Death of Pius XI)', *Yad Vashem Studies*, iv (1960), 43–56.

——, 'Il problema ebraico nella politica italiana fra le due guerre mondiali', *Rivista di Studi Politici Internazionali*, xxiii (Jan.–Mar. 1961), 46–50.

——, 'Batei kelleh u-mahanot rikuz b'Italia b'tekufat ha-shoah', *Dappim l'hekker hashoah v'ha-mered*, i (1969), 178–93.

——, 'P'iluto ha-medinit shel Weizmann b'Italia ba-shanim 1923–1934', *Ha-Zionut. M'assef l'toldoth ha-tenuah ha-zionit v'ha-yishuv ha-yehudi b'Eretz Yisrael*, ii, Tel Aviv, 1971, pp. 169–207.

——, 'Ma'asseh ha-hatzalah shel yehudim b'ezor ha-kibbush ha-italki b'Kroatia', in *Nissiyonot u-f'ulot hatzalah b'tekufat ha-shoah*, ed. Y. Gutman, Jerusalem, 1976.

CARPI, L., *Come e dove rinacque la marina d'Israele. La scuola marittima del Bethar a Civitavecchia*, Rome, 1967.

CASSELS, A., 'Mussolini and German Nationalism, 1922–1925', *Journal of Modern History*, xxxv (June 1963), 137–57.

——, *Mussolini's Early Diplomacy, 1922–1927*, Princeton, 1970.

CAUDANA, M. and A. ASSANTE, *Dal regno del Sud al vento del Nord*, i–ii, Rome, 1963.

CAVALLI, F., 'Pio XII visto da vicino', *La Civiltà Cattolica*, (16 Apr. 1960), 163–72.

——, 'La Santa Sede contro le deportazioni degli ebrei dalla Slovacchia durante la seconda guerra mondiale', *La Civiltà Cattolica*, (1 July 1961), 3–18.

CHABOD, F., *L'Italia contemporanea (1918–1948)*, 4th edn., Turin, 1961.

CIANFARRA, C. M., *The Vatican and the War*, New York, 1945.

CLIADAKIS, H., 'Neutrality and War in Italian Policy 1939–1940', *Journal of Contemporary History*, 9 (July 1974), 171–90.

COCEANI, B., *Mussolini, Hitler, Tito alle porte orientali d'Italia*, Bologna, 1948.

COGNI, G., *Il razzismo*, Milan 1936; 2nd edn., 1937.

——, *I valori della stirpe italiani. Appendice di Hans F. K. Günther*, Milan, 1937.

COHEN, G., 'Ra-ayon halukat Eretz Yisrael u-medina yehudit 1933–1935 (b'magaei Italia, memshelet Britannia, ha-tenuah ha-zionit v'ha-manhigut ha-aravit)', *Ha-Zionut*, iii, Tel Aviv, 1973, pp. 346–417.

COHEN, I., 'The Jews in Italy', *Political Quarterly* (July–Sept. 1939), 405–18.

COLLOTTI, E., *L'amministrazione tedesca dell'Italia occupata 1943–1945*, Milan, 1963.

COLTON, J., *Léon Blum. Humanist in Politics*, New York, 1966.

CONWAY, J. S., 'The Churches, the Slovak State and the Jews 1939–1945', *Slavonic and East European Review*, lii (Jan. 1974), 85–112.

D'AMOJA, F., *La politica estera dell'impero. Storia della politica estera fascista dalla conquista dell'Etiopia all'Anschluss*, 2nd edn., Padua, 1967.

D'AROMA, N., *Vent'anni insieme. Vittorio Emanuele e Mussolini*, Bologna, 1957.

——, *Hitler. Rapporto a Mussolini*, Rome, 1974.

DEAKIN, F. W., *The Brutal Friendship. Hitler, Mussolini and the Fall of Italian Fascism*, London, 1962.

DE BEGNAC, Y., *Palazzo Venezia. Storia di un regime*, Rome, 1950.

DEBENEDETTI, G., *16 ottobre 1943*, 2nd edn., Milan, 1959.

DE FELICE, R., 'La Chiesa cattolica e il problema ebraico durante gli anni dell'antisemitismo fascista', *La Rassegna mensile di Israel*, xxiii (Jan. 1957), 23–35.

——, *Storia degli ebrei italiani sotto il fascismo*, Turin, 1961; 3rd edn. 1972.

——, 'Giovanni Preziosi e le origini del fascismo', *Rivista Storica del Socialismo*, 17 (Sept.–Dec. 1962), 493–555.

——, 'Per una storia del problema ebraico in Italia alla fine del xviii secolo e all'inizio del xix. La prima emancipazione (1792–1814)', *Italia giacobina*, Naples, 1965, pp. 317–96.

——, *Mussolini il fascista*, i: *La conquista del potere 1921–1925*; ii: *L'organizzazione dello stato fascista 1925–1929*, Turin, 1966–8.

——, *Le interpretazioni del fascismo*, Bari, 1969; 4th edn. 1974.

——, 'Alcuni osservazioni sulla politica estera mussoliniana', in id. (ed.), *L'Italia fratedeschi e alleati*, Bologna, 1973, pp. 57–74.

——, *Il problema dell'Alto Adige nei rapporti italo–tedeschi dall'Anschluss alla fine della seconda guerra mondiale*, Bologna, 1973.

——, *Mussolini il duce*, i: *Gli anni del consenso 1929–1936*, Turin, 1974.

——, *Intervista sul fascismo*, ed. M. A. Ledeen, Bari, 1975.

——, *Mussolini e Hitler. I rapporti segreti 1922–1933*, Florence, 1975.

DELLA PERGOLA, S., *Jewish and Mixed Marriages in Milan 1901–1968*, Jerusalem, 1972.

——, 'Indagine statistica sugli ebrei in Italia, I. Condizioni e prospettive demografiche delle Comunità', *La Rassegna Mensile di Israel*, xxxiv (Oct. 1968), 572–81.

——, 'Ha-demografia shel yehudei Italia', Jerusalem, 1972 (doctoral dissertation).

——, 'A Note on Marriage Trends among Jews in Italy', *Jewish Journal of Sociology*, xiv (Dec. 1972), 197–205.

——, 'The Geography of Italian Jews: Countrywide patterns', in E. Toaff (ed.), *Studi sull'Ebraismo italiano in memoria di Cecil Roth*, Rome, 1974, pp. 93–128.

DEL BOCA, A. and M. GIOVANNA, *I 'figli del sole'. Mezzo secolo di nazifascismo nel mondo*, Milan, 1965.

DELZELL, C. F., *Mussolini's Enemies. The Italian Anti-Fascist Resistance*, Princeton, 1961.

——, 'The Italian Anti-Fascist Resistance in Retrospect: Three Decades of Historiography', *Journal of Modern History*, xlvii (Mar. 1975), 66–96.

DI NOLA, A. M. (with E. Melani and F. M. Ferro), *Antisemitismo in Italia 1962/1972*, Florence, 1973.

DI NOLFO, E., *Mussolini e la politica estera italiana (1919–1933)*, Padua, 1960.

DONATI, G., 'Persecuzione e deportazione degli Ebrei dall'Italia durante la dominazione nazifascista', *Ebrei in italia: deportazione, resistenza*, ed. CDEC, Florence, 1975, pp. 9–34.

——, *Deportazione degli ebrei dall'Italia. Ricerca condotta da Giuliana Donati*, CDEC, Milan, 1975.

DONOSTI, M. (Mario Luciolli), *Mussolini e l'Europa. La politica estera fascista*, Rome, 1945.

DRAENGER, J., *Nahoum Goldmann*, i–ii, Paris, 1956.

DRESLER, A., *Mussolini*, Leipzig, 1924.
——, *Die Presse im faschistischen Italien*, Essen, 1939.
——, *Benito Mussolini*, Leipzig, 1940.
DUCLOS, P., *Le Vatican et la seconde guerre mondiale. Action doctrinale et diplomatique en favour de la paix*, Paris, 1955.
ESCO FOUNDATION, *Palestine. A Study of Jewish, Arab and British Policies*, i–ii, New Haven–London, 1947.
ESSER, H., *Die jüdische Weltpest*, rev. edn., Munich 1939.
EVOLA, J. C., *Il mito del sangue*, Milan, 1937.
——, *Sintesi della dottrina della razza*, Milan, 1941.
——, *Il fascismo. Saggio di una analisi critica dal punto di vista della Destra*, Rome, 1964; 2nd edn. 1970.
——, *Gli uomini e le rovine*, 3rd edn., Rome, 1972.
FALDELLA, E., *L'Italia e la seconda guerra mondiale*, 2nd edn., Bologna, 1960.
FARGION, L., 'La partecipazione ebraica alla resistenza', *Ebrei in italia: deportazione, resistenza*, ed. CDEC, Florence, 1975, pp. 43–53.
FARINACCI, R., *Storia della rivoluzione fascista*, i–iii, Cremona, 1937–9 (the real author of the book was one of Farinacci's collaborators, Giorgio Masi).
——, *Realtà storiche*, Cremona, 1939.
FISICHELLA, D., *Analisi del totalitarismo*, Messina–Florence, 1976.
FORMIGGINI, G., *Stella d'Italia, stella di David; gli ebrei dal risorgimento alla Resistenza*, Milan, 1970.
FORNARI, H., *Mussolini's Gadfly. Roberto Farinacci*, Nashville, 1971.
FRANZI, L., *Fase attuale del razzismo tedesco*, Rome, 1939.
FREDRIGOTTI, G., 'Der Faschismus und seine falschen Freunde', *Der Weltkampf*, i (Sept. 1924), 18–21.
FRIEDMAN, I., *The Question of Palestine 1914–1918. British–Jewish–Arab Relations*, London, 1973.
FUNKE, M., *Sanktionen und Kanonen. Hitler, Mussolini und der internationale Abessinienkonflikt*, Düsseldorf, 1970; 2nd edn. 1971.
——, 'Hitler und Mussolini. Anatomische Anmerkung zum 40. Jahrestag der "Achsen"–Allianz', *Aus Politik und Zeitgeschichte. Beilage zur Wochenzeitung Das Parlament*, B43/76 (23 Oct. 1976).
——, (ed.), *Hitler, Deutschland und die Mächte. Materialien zur Aussenpolitik des Dritten Reiches*, Düsseldorf, 1976.
GARIBALDI, E., *L'Italia e i problemi della pace*, 3rd edn., Rome, 1939.
GAROSCI, A., *La vita di Carlo Rosselli*, i–ii, Rome–Florence–Milan, n.d. (1946?).
——, *Storie dei fuorusciti*, Bari, 1953.
GEHL, J., *Austria, Germany and the Anschluss, 1931–1938*, London, 1963.

GERMINO, D. L., *The Italian Fascist Party in Power. A Study in Totalitarian Rule*, Minneapolis, 1959.

GHERARDI BON, S., *La persecuzione antiebraica a Trieste (1938–1945)*, Udine, 1972.

GIGLI, G., *La seconda guerra mondiale*, 2nd edn., Bari, 1964.

GOLDMAN, A. L., 'Sir Robert Vansittart's Search for Italian Cooperation against Hitler, 1933–6', *Journal of Contemporary History*, ix (July 1974), 93–130.

GRAHAM, R. A., 'Spie naziste attorno al Vaticano durante la seconda guerra mondiale', *La Civiltà Cattolica* (3 Jan. 1970), 21–31.

GREGOR, A. J., *The Ideology of Fascism. The Rationale of Totalitarianism*, New York, 1969.

HALPERN, I., *Tehiat ha-yama'ut ha-ivrit*, Tel Aviv, 5721 (1961).

HECKER, H. (ed.), *Praktische Fragen des Entschädigungsrechts—Judenverfolgungen im Ausland*, Hamburg, 1958.

HEIBER, H., 'Die deutsche Beeinflussung der Rassenpolitik des faschistischen Italien bis 1943', *Gutachten des Instituts für Zeitgeschichte*, ii, Stuttgart, 1966, pp. 80–92.

HEIDEN, K., *One Man against Europe*, Harmondsworth, 1939.

——, *Der Fuehrer. Hitler's Rise to Power*, London, 1967 (preface by A. Bullock).

HILBERG, R., *The Destruction of the European Jews*, 2nd edn., Chicago, 1967.

HILL, L. E., 'The Vatican Embassy of Ernst von Weizsäcker 1943–1945', *Journal of Modern History*, xxxix (June 1967), 138–59.

HILLGRUBER, A., *Hitlers Strategie. Politik und Kriegsführung 1940–1941*, Frankfurt/Main, 1965.

——, 'Grundzüge der nationalsozialistischen Aussenpolitik', *Saeculum*, xxiv (1973), 328–45.

HOEPKE, K.-P., *Die deutsche Rechte und der italienische Faschismus. Ein Beitrag zum Selbstverständnis und zur Politik von Gruppen und Verbänden der deutschen Rechten*, Düsseldorf, 1968.

HOWARD, M. E., *Grand Strategy*, iv: *August 1942–September 1943*, London, 1972.

HUDAL, A., *Die Grundlagen des Nationalsozialismus. Eine ideengeschichtliche Untersuchung*, Leipzig–Vienna, 1937.

INTERLANDI, T., *Contra Judaeos*, Rome–Milan, 1938.

JACOBSON, H.-A., *Nationalsozialistische Aussenpolitik 1933–1938*, Frankfurt/Main–Berlin, 1968.

JACOMONI DI SAN SAVINO, F., *La politica dell'Italia in Albania*, Bologna, 1965.

JÄNICKE, M., *Totalitäre Herrschaft. Anatomie eines politischen Begriffes*, Berlin, 1971.

JANSSEN, G., *Das Ministerium Speer. Deutschlands Rüstung im Krieg*, Frankfurt/Main–Berlin, 1968

KALK, I., 'I campi di concentramento italiani per ebrei profughi: Ferramonti Tarsia (Calabria)', *Gli Ebrei in Italia durante il fascismo*, i (Quaderni della Federazione Giovanile Ebraica d'Italia), Turin, 1961, pp. 63–71.

KATZ, R., *Black Sabbath. A Journey through a Crime against Humanity*, Toronto, 1969.

KESSEL, A. VON, 'Der Papst und die Juden', in F. J. Raddatz (ed.), *Summa iniuria oder Durfte der Papst schweigen?*, Hamburg, 1963, pp. 167–171.

KHADDURI, M., *Independent Iraq 1932–1958*, 2nd edn., London–New York–Karachi, 1960.

KIRKPATRICK, Sir I., *Mussolini. Study of a Demagogue*, London, 1964.

KLEINLERER, E. D., 'A year of Racialism in Italy', *Contemporary Jewish Record*, ii (July–Aug. 1939), 30–43.

KORDT, E., *Wahn und Wirklichkeit. Die Aussenpolitik des Dritten Reiches*, Stuttgart, 1947.

KUBOVY, A. L., 'The Silence of Pope Pius XII and the Beginnings of the "Jewish Document"', *Yad Vashem Studies*, xi (1967), 7–25.

KÜHNL, R., *Die nationalsozialistische Linke*, Meisenheim/Glan, 1966.

LANDRA, G., 'Die wissenschaftliche und politische Begründung der Rassenfrage in Italien', *Nationalsozialistische Monatshefte*, 10 (Apr. 1939), 296–306.

LA PIANA, G., 'The Political Heritage of Pius XII', *Foreign Affairs*, xviii (Apr. 1940), 486–506.

LAPIDE, P. E., *The Last Three Popes and the Jews*, London, 1967.

LAQUEUR, W., *A History of Zionism*, London, 1972.

LAURENS, F. D., *France and the Italo–Ethiopian Crisis 1935–1936*, The Hague, 1967.

LEDEEN, M. A., *Universal Fascism. The Theory and Practice of the Fascist International, 1928–1936*, New York, 1972.

——, 'La "Questione ebraica" nell'Italia fascista', *Nuova Antologia*, cix (Feb. 1974), 185–201.

——, 'The Evolution of Italian Fascist Antisemitism', *Jewish Social Studies*, xxxvii (Jan. 1975), 3–17.

——, *D'Annunzio a Fiume*, Bari, 1975.

——, 'Nota al saggio di Renato J. Almansi', *La Rassegna Mensile di Israel*, xlii (May–June 1976), 256–8.

LEERS, J. VON, *Die Verbrechernatur der Juden*, Berlin, 1944.

LEIBER, R., 'Pio XII e gli ebrei di Roma 1943–1944', *La Civiltà Cattolica* (4 Mar. 1961), 449–58.

——, '*Der Papst und die Verfolgung der Juden*', in F. J. *Raddatz (ed.), Summa iniuria oder Durfte der Papst schweigen?*, Hamburg, 1963, pp. 101–107.

LEONI, E., *Mistica del razzismo fascista*, Padua, 1941.

LEVI, A., *Noi ebrei. In risposta a Paolo Orano*, Rome, 1937.

LEVI, L., 'Antifascismo e Sionismo: convergenze e contrasti (note e ricordi sui "fermi" e sui fermenti torinesi del 1934)', *Gli Ebrei in Italia durante il fascismo*, i (Quaderni della Federazione Giovanile Ebraica d'Italia), Turin, 1961, pp. 49–62.

LEWY, G., *The Catholic Church and Nazi Germany*, New York–Toronto, 1964.

LIDDELL HART, B. H., *History of the Second World War*, London, 1970.

LIVI, L., *Gli ebrei alla luce della statistica*, i: *Caratteristiche antropologiche e patologiche e individualità etnica*; ii: *evoluzione demografica, economica e sociale*, Florence, 1918–20.

LUDWIG, E., *Colloqui con Mussolini*, 2nd edn., Milan, 1950.

LYTTELTON, A., 'Fascism in Italy: The Second Wave', *Journal of Contemporary History*, i (Jan. 1966), 75–100.

——, *The Seizure of Power. Fascism in Italy 1919–1929*, London, 1973.

MACK SMITH, D., *Italy. A Modern History*, 2nd edn., Ann Arbor–London, 1969.

——, *Le guerre del Duce*, Bari, 1976.

——, *Mussolini's Roman Empire*, London–New York, 1976.

MANUEL, F. E., 'The Palestine Question in Italian Diplomacy 1917–1920', *Journal of Modern History*, xxvii (Sept. 1955), 263–80.

MARTINI, A., 'La Santa Sede e gli ebrei della Romania durante la seconda guerra mondiale', *La Civiltà Cattolica (26 Aug. 1961), 449–63*.

——, '"Il Vicario". Una tragedia cristiana?', *La Civiltà Cattolica* (18 May 1963), 313–25.

——, *Studi sulla questione romana e la Conciliazione*, Rome, 1963.

MAZZEI, V., *Razza e nazione*, Rome, 1942.

MAZZETTI, R., *L'antiebraismo nella cultura italiana da 1700 al 1900. Antologia storica*, Modena, 1939.

——, *Orientamenti antiebraici della vita e della cultura italiana. Saggi di storia religiosa politica e letteraria*, Modena, 1939.

MALETTI, V., *Die faschistische Revolution*, Munich, 1931 (preface by A. Hitler).

MELLINI PONCE DE LEON, A., *L'Italia entra in guerra. Gli eventi diplomatici dal 10 gennaio al 10 giugno 1940*, Bologna, 1963.

MICHAELIS, M., 'On the Jewish Question in Fascist Italy. The Attitude of the Fascist Regime to the Jews in Italy', *Yad Vashem Studies*, iv (1960), 7–41.

——, 'I rapporti italo–tedeschi e il problema degli ebrei in Italia (1922–

1938)', *Rivista di Studi Politici Internazionali*, xxviii (Apr.–June 1961), 238–82.

——, 'Appunti bibliografici sulla persecuzione antisemita', *Gli Ebrei in Italia durante il fascismo*, ii (Quaderni del Centro di Documentazione Ebraica Contemporanea), Milan, 1962, pp. 45–54.

——, 'Gli ebrei italiani sotto il regime fascista dalla marcia su Roma alla caduta del fascismo (1922–1945)', *La Rassegna Mensile di Israel*, xxviii (May 1962), 211–29; (June–July 1962), 262–83; (Aug. 1962), 350–68; (Oct. 1962), 451–65; xxix (Jan.–Feb. 1963), 18–41; (July–Aug. 1963), 291–308; xxx (Jan. 1964), 3–23; (June–July 1964), 247–260; xxxii (Jan. 1966), 15–37.

——, 'I rapporti tra fascismo e nazismo prima dell'avvento di Hitler al potere (1922–1933). I: 1922–1928', *Rivista Storica Italiana*, lxxxv (Sept. 1973), 544–600.

——, 'Ricordo di Dante Lattes', *La Rassegna Mensile di Israel*, xli (Nov.–Dec. 1975), 489–501.

——, 'The "Duce" and the Jews. An Assessment of the Literature on Italian Jewry under Fascism (1922–1945)', *Yad Vashem Studies*, xi (1976), 7–32.

——, 'Il conte Galeazzo Ciano di Cortellazzo quale antesignano dell'asse Roma–Berlino. La linea "germanofila" di Ciano dal 1934 al 1936 alla luce di alcuni documenti inediti', *Nuova Rivista Storica*, lxi (Jan.–Apr. 1977), 116–49.

——, 'Riflessioni sulla recente storia dell'Ebraismo italiano', *La Rassegna Mensile di Israel*, xliii (May–June 1977), 191–211.

MILANO, A., *Storia degli ebrei italiani nel Levante*, Florence, 1949.

——, *Bibliotheca historica italo–judaica*, Florence, 1954; supplement 1964.

——, *Storia degli ebrei in Italia*, Turin, 1963.

MINERBI, S. I., *L'Italie et la Palestine (1914–1920)*, Paris, 1970.

——, 'Gli ultimi due incontri Weizmann–Mussolini (1933–1934)', *Storia Contemporanea*, v (Sept.–Dec. 1974), 431–77.

MINNEY, R. J., *The Private Private Papers of Hore-Belisha*, London, 1960.

MOMIGLIANO, E., *Storia tragica e grottesca del razzismo fascista*, Milan, 1946.

MONELLI, P., *Mussolini piccolo borghese*, Milan, 1950 and 1954.

MÜNZ, M., *Die Verantwortlichkeit für die Judenverfolgungen im Ausland während der nationalsozialistischen Herrschaft*, Frankfurt/Main, 1958.

NAHON, U., 'Rapporto confidenziale all 'Esecutivo Sionistico, giugno 1937', in D. Carpi, A. Milano, and A. Rofé (eds.), *Scritti in memoria di Leone Carpi*, Jerusalem, 1967, pp. 261–84.

——, 'Il viaggio di Sokolow a Roma nel 1917', *La Rassegna Mensile di Israel*, xxxiv (May 1968), 262–74.

——, 'Gli echi della Dichiarazione Balfour in Italia e la Dichiarazione

Imperiali del maggio 1918', *La Rassegna Mensile di Israel*, xxxiv (June 1968), 334–50.
——, 'La polemica antisionista del "Popolo di Roma" nel 1928', in D. Carpi, A. Milano, and U. Nahon (eds), *Scritti in memoria di Enzo Sereni. Saggi sull'Ebraismo romano*, Jerusalem, 1970, pp. 216–53.
NAMIER, L. B., *Diplomatic Prelude 1938–1939*, London, 1948.
——, *Europe in Decay. A Study in Disintegration 1936–1940*, London, 1950.
NOLTE, E., *Der Faschismus in seiner Epoche. Die Action Française, der italienische Faschismus, der Nationalsozialismus*, Munich, 1963.
NORTHEDGE, F. S., *The Troubled Giant. Britain among the Great Powers 1916–1939*, London, 1966.
ORANO, P., *Gli ebrei in Italia*, Rome 1937.
——, (ed.), *Inchiesta sulla razza*, Rome, 1939.
OVAZZA, E., *Sionismo bifronte*, Rome, 1935.
——, *Il problema ebraico. Risposta a Paolo Orano*, Rome, 1938.
PAPA, E. R., *Storia di due manifesti*, Milan, 1958.
PASTORELLI, P., 'La politica estera fascista dalla fine del conflitto etiopico alla seconda guerra mondiale', in R. de Felice (ed.), *L'Italia fra tedeschi e alleati. La politica estera fascista e la seconda guerra mondiale*, Bologna, 1973.
PELLICANI, A., *Il Papa di tutti. La Chiesa cattolica, il fascismo e il razzismo 1929–1945*, Milan, 1964.
PELLIZZI, C., *Italy*, London, 1939.
PERTICONE, G., *La politica italiana nell'ultimo trentennio*, i–iii, Rome 1945–1947.
PESE, W. W., 'Hitler und Italien 1920–1926', *VJZG* 3 (Apr. 1955), 113–26.
PETERSEN, J., 'Deutschland und Italien im Sommer 1935. Der Wechsel des italienischen Botschafters in Berlin', *Geschichte in Wissenschaft und Unterricht*, xx (June 1969), 330–41.
——, 'Italien in der aussenpolitischen Konzeption Hitlers', in K. Jürgensen and R. Hansen, *Historisch-politische Streiflichter. Geschichtliche Beiträge zur Gegenwart*, Neumünster, 1971, pp. 206–20.
——, *Hitler–Mussolini. Die Entstehung der Achse Berlin–Rome 1933–1936*, Tübingen, 1973 (revised Italian edition: *Hitler e Mussolini. La difficile alleanza*, Bari, 1975).
——, 'Gesellschaftssystem, Ideologie und Interesse in der Aussenpolitik des faschistischen Italien', *Quellen und Forschungen aus italienischen Archiven und Bibliotheken*, liv (1974), 428–70.
——, 'Die Aussenpolitik des faschistischen Italien als historiographisches Problem', *VJZG* 22 (Oct. 1974), 417–57.
——, 'La nascita del concetto di "Stato totalitario" in Italia', *Annali dell'Istituto Storico Italo–Germanico in Trento*, i (1975), 143–68.

——, 'Der italienische Faschismus zwischen politischer Polemik und historischer Analyse', *Geschichte in Wissenschaft und Unterricht*, xxvii (May 1976), 257–72.

——, 'Der italienische Faschismus aus der Sicht der Weimarer Republik. Einige deutsche Interpretationen', *Quellen und Forschungen aus italienischen Archiven und Bibliotheken*, lv–lvi (1976), 315–60.

PIERI, P. and ROCHAT, G., *Pietro Badoglio*, Turin, 1974.

PINCHERLE, A., 'In margine alla storia degli ebrei italiani', *Nuova Rivista Storica*, xlvi (Sept.–Dec. 1962), 599–602.

PINI, G. and D. SUSMEL, *Mussolini. L'uomo e l'opera*, i–iv, 3rd edn., Florence, 1963.

PISANÒ, G., *Mussolini e gli ebrei*, Milan, 1967.

PISENTI, P., *Una repubblica necessaria (R.S.I.)*, Rome, 1977.

PRETI, L., *I miti dell'impero e della razza nell'Italia degli anni '30*, Rome, 1965.

——, *Impero fascista, africani ed ebrei*, Milan, 1968.

PREZIOSI, G., *Come il giudaismo ha preparato la guerra*, 2nd edn., Rome, 1940.

——, *Giudaismo, bolscevismo, plutocrazia, massoneria*, Milan, 1941; 3rd edn. 1944.

REITLINGER, G., *The Final Solution. The Attempt to Exterminate the Jews of Europe 1939–1945*, London, 1953, rev. edn. 1968.

RINTELEN, E. von, 'Mussolinis Parallelkrieg im Jahre 1940', *Wehrwissenschaftliche Rundschau*, 12 (Jan. 1962), 16–38.

ROCHAT, G., *Militari e politici nella preparazione della campagna d'Etiopia. Studi e documenti 1932–1936*, Milan, 1971.

——, 'Mussolini, chef de guerre (1940–1943)', *Revue d'Histoire de la Deuxième Guerre Mondiale*, xxv (Oct. 1975), 43–66.

ROMANO, G., 'La persecuzione e le deportzioni degli ebrei di Roma e d'Italia nelle opere di scrittori ebrei', *Scritti in memoria di Enzo Sereni*, Jerusalem, 1970, pp. 314–39.

ROSEN, E. R., 'Mussolini und Deutschland 1922–1923', *VJZG* 5 (Jan. 1957), 17–41.

——, 'Die deutsche Rechte und das faschistische Italien', *Zeitschrift für Politik*, N. F. viii (1961), 334–8.

ROSENBERG, A., *Der Zukunftsweg einer deutschen Aussenpolitik*, Munich, 1927.

——, *Der Mythus des 20. Jahrhunderts*, Munich, 1930; 3rd edn. 1940.

——, *Müssen weltanschauliche Kämpfe staatliche Feindschaften ergeben? Vortrag auf dem Empfang am 7. Februar 1939 für die Diplomaten und die ausländische Presse*, Munich, 1939.

ROSSI, E., *Il manganello e l'aspersorio*, Florence, 1958.

——, *Padroni del vapore e fascismo*, Bari, 1966.

Rossi, M., 'Emancipation of the Jews in Italy', *Jewish Social Studies*, xv (Apr. 1953), 113–34.

Roth, C., *The History of the Jews of Italy*, Philadelphia, 1946.

Rothkirchen, L., *Khurban yehudei Slovakia. Te-ur histori b'te-udot*, Jerusalem, 1961.

——, 'Vatican Policy and the Jewish Problem in "Independent" Slovakia', *Yad Vashem Studies*, xi (1967), 27–53.

Rubin, E., *Mussolini: Raciste et antisemite*, Paris, 1938.

——, *140 Jewish Marshals, Generals and Admirals*, London, 1952.

Rumi, G., 'Tendenze e caratteri degli studi sulla politica estera fascista (1945–1966), *Nuova Rivista Storica*, li (Jan.–Apr. 1967), 149–68.

——, *Alle origini della politica estera fascista (1918–1923)*, Bari, 1968; 2nd edn. 1973.

Sabatello, E. F., 'L'indagine statistica sugli ebrei in Italia II. Caratteristiche professionali e sociali delle Comunità', *La Rassegna Mensile di Israel*, xxxiv (Nov. 1968), 626–37.

——, 'Aspetti economici ed ecologici dell'Ebraismo ramano prima, durante e dopo le leggi razziali (1928–1965)', *Scritti in memoria di Enzo Sereni*, Jerusalem, 1970, pp. 254–92.

——, 'Ha-megamot ha-hevratiot v'ha-mikzoiot shel yehudei Italia 1870–1970', Jerusalem, 1972 (doctoral dissertation).

——, 'Il censimento degli ebrei del 1938 (note metodologiche sulla sua preparazione, la sua realizzazione ed i suoi risultati)', *La Rassegna Mensile di Israel*, xlii (Jan.–Feb. 1976), 25–55.

Salvatorelli, L. and G. Mira, *Storia d'Italia nel periodo fascista*, 5th edn., Turin, 1964.

Salvemini, G., *The Fascist Dictatorship in Italy*, London, 1928.

——, (with G. La Piana), *What to do with Italy*, New York, 1943.

——, *Mussolini diplomatico*, Bari, 1952.

——, *Prelude to World War II*, London, 1953.

——, *Scritti sul fascismo*, i–ii (*Opere di G. Salvemini*, vi), ed. R. Vivarelli, N. Valeri, and A. Merola, Milan, 1961–6.

——, *Preludio alla seconda guerra mondiale* (*Opere di G. Salvemini*, iii), ed. A. Torre, Milan, 1967.

Sannes, H. W. J., *Onze Joden en Duitschland's Greep naar de Wereldmacht*, Amsterdam, 1946.

Santarelli, E., *Storia del movimento e del regime fascista*, i–ii, Rome, 1967.

——, *Ricerche sul fascismo*, Urbino, 1971.

Santin, A., *Trieste 1943–1945*, Udine, 1963.

Schapiro, L., *Totalitarianism*, London, 1972.

Schieder, W., 'Fascismo e nazionalsocialismo, profilo d'uno studio strutturale comparativo', *Nuova Rivista Storica*, liv (Jan.–Apr. 1970), 114–24.

SCHRÖDER, J., _Italiens Kriegsaustritt 1943. Die deutschen Gegenmassnahmen im italienischen Raum: Fall 'Alarich' und 'Achse'_, Göttingen–Zurich–Frankfurt, 1969.

SCHUBERT, G., _Anfänge nationalsozialistischer Aussenpolitik_, Cologne, 1963.

SEGRE, R., _Appunti sulle persecuzioni antisemite e sulla vita delle comunità israelitiche nell'Italia occupata_, Rome, 1964.

SEGRE AMAR, S., 'Sopra alcune inesatezze storiche intorno alle passate vicende degli ebrei d'Italia', _La Rassegna Mensile di Israel_, xxvii (May 1961), 236–8.

——, 'Sui "fatti" di Torino del 1934 Sion Segre Amar ci ha scritto . . .', _Gli Ebrei in Italia durante il fascismo_, ii (Quaderni del Centro di Documentazione Ebraica Contemporanea), Milan, 1962, pp. 125–34.

SERRA, E., 'I rapporti italo–tedeschi durante la non belligeranza dell'Italia', _Rassegna di Politica e di Storia_, i (Jan. 1955), 8–15.

SETON-WATSON, C., _Italy from Liberalism to Fascism 1870–1925_, London, 1967.

SHEPPERD, G. A., _The Italian Campaign 1943–1945. A Political and Military Re-assessment_, London, 1968.

SIEBERT, F., _Italiens Weg in den Zweiten Weltkrieg_, Frankfurt/Main–Bonn, 1962.

SPINOSA, A., 'Le persecuzioni razziali in Italia', _Il Ponte_, viii (July 1952), 964–78; (Aug. 1952), 1078–96; (Nov. 1952), 1604–22; ix (July 1953), 950–68.

STARR, J., 'Italy's Antisemites', _Jewish Social Studies_, i (Jan. 1939), 105–124.

STEHLE, H., _Die Ostpolitik des Vatikans_, Munich, 1975.

STUHLPFARRER, K., _Die Operationszonen 'Alpenvorland' und 'Adriatisches Küstenland' 1943–1945_, Vienna, 1969.

SUSMEL, D., _Vita sbagliata di Galeazzo Ciano_, Milan, 1962.

SUSMEL, E., _Mussolini e il suo tempo_, Milan, 1950.

SUSTER, R., _La Germania repubblicana_, Milan, 1923 (preface by B. Mussolini).

TAGLIACOZZO, M., 'La Comunità di Roma sotto l'incubo della svastica. La grande razzia del 16 ottobre 1943', _Gli ebrei in italia durante il fascismo_, iii (Quaderni del Centro di Documentazione Ebraica Contemporanea), Milan, 1963, pp. 8–37.

——, 'Le responsabilità di Kappler nella tragedia degli ebrei di Roma', _Scritti in memoria di Attilio Milano_, ed. Y. Colombo, U. Nahon, and G. Romano, Milan–Rome, 1970, pp. 389–414.

——, 'Ha-matsod ha-gadol al yehudei Roma b'yom 16 b'oktober 1943', _Scritti in memoria di Enzo Sereni_, Jerusalem, 1970, pp. 252–80.

TAMARO, A., _Due anni di storia 1943–1945_, i–iii, Rome, 1948–50.

——, _Venti anni di storia 1922–1943_, i–iii, Rome, 1953–4.

TASCA, A., *Nascita e avvento del fascismo*, Florence, 1950 and 1963.

THOMAS, H., *The Spanish Civil War*, London, 1961, 2nd edn. 1976.

TOEPLITZ, I., *Il banchiere*, Milan, 1963.

TOSCANO, M., *Le origini diplomatiche del Patto d'Acciaio*, 2nd edn., Florence, 1956.

——, 'Eden a Roma alla vigilia del conflitto italo–etiopico (con documenti inediti)', *Pagine di storia diplomatica contemporanea*, ii, Milan, 1963, pp. 133–59.

——, 'Origini e vicende diplomatiche della seconda guerra mondiale', *Pagine di storia diplomatica contemporanea*, ii, Milan, 1963, pp. 89–132.

——, 'Problemi particolari della storia della seconda guerra mondiale', *Pagine di storia diplomatica contemporanea*, ii, Milan, 1963, pp. 75–87.

——, 'L'asse Roma–Berlino—Il patto anticomintern—La guerra civile in Spagna—L'Anschluss—Monaco', in *La politica estera italiana dal 1914 al 1943*, Turin, 1963, pp. 188–230.

——, *Storia diplomatica della questione dell'Alto Adige*, Bari, 1967, 2nd edn. 1968.

TREVOR-ROPER, H. R., 'Hitlers Kriegsziele', *VJZG* 8 (Apr. 1960), 121–33.

VALABREGA, G., 'Il fascismo e gli ebrei: appunti per un consuntivo storiografico', in S. Fontana (ed.), *Il fascismo e le autonomie locali*, Bologna, 1973, pp. 401–26.

——, *Ebrei, fascismo, sionismo*, Urbino, 1974.

VAN CREVELD, M., *Hitler's Stategy 1940–1941. The Balkan Clue*, Cambridge, 1973.

——, 'Beyond the Finzi-Contini Garden. Mussolini's "Fascist Racism"', *Encounter*, xlii (Feb. 1974), 42–7.

VAUSSARD, M., *Histoire de l'Italie contemporaine*, Paris, 1950.

VENERUSO, D., 'Il fascismo internazionale (1919–1938)', in S. Fontana (ed.), *Il fascismo e le autonomie locali*, Bologna, 1973, pp. 23–72.

VILLARI, L., 'Luigi Luzzatti', in *Twelve Jews*, ed. H. Bolitho, London, 1934, pp. 123–52.

——, *Storia diplomatica del conflitto italo–etiopico*, Bologna, 1943.

——, *Affari esteri 1943–1945*, Rome, 1948.

——, *Italian Foreign Policy under Mussolini*, New York, 1956.

VOLLI, G., *Breve storia degli ebrei d'Italia*, Milan, 1961.

VOLPE, G., *Storia del movimento fascista*, Milan, 1939

WATT, D. C., 'The Anglo–German Naval Agreement of 1935: An Interim Judgment', *Journal of Modern History*, xxviii (June 1956), 155–175.

——, 'An Earlier Model for the Pact of Steel. The Draft Treaties Exchanged between Germany and Italy during Hitler's Visit to Rome in May 1938', *International Affairs*, 33 (Apr. 1957), 185–97.

——, 'The Rome–Berlin Axis, 1936–1940. Myth and Reality', *Review of Politics*, xxii (Oct. 1960), 519–43.

WEBSTER, R. A., *The Cross and the Fasces. Christian Democracy and Fascism in Italy*, Stanford, 1960.

WEINBERG, G. L., *The Foreign Policy of Hitler's Germany. Diplomatic Revolution in Europe, 1933–36*, Chicago–London, 1970.

WIEDEN, K. VON, 'Was wir vom Faschismus wissen müssen', *National-sozialistische Monatshefte*, 3 (May 1932), 223–7.

WIRSING, G., *Engländer, Juden, Araber in Palästina*, Jena, 1938.

WISCHNITZER, M., *To Dwell in Safety. The Story of Jewish Migration since 1800*, Philadelphia, 1948.

WISKEMANN, E., *The Rome–Berlin Axis. A Study of the Relations between Hitler and Mussolini*, London, 1949; 3rd rev. edn. 1969.

——, *Fascism in Italy. Its Development and Influence*, London, 1969.

WULF, J., 'Juden in Finnland', *Aus Politik und Zeitgeschichte Beilage zur Wochenzeitung Das Parlament*, B16/59(15 Apr. 1959), 161–8.

ZANGRANDI, R., *1943: 25 luglio–8 settembre*, Milan, 1964.

Index

Note: The following were not indexed as they appear throughout the book: Anti-Fascism, Anti-Fascist(s), anti-Semite, anti-Semitism, Fascism, Germany, Hitler, Italy, Jews, Mussolini, National Socialism, National-Socialist, Nazi, Third Reich.

Abetz, Otto, 305, 315–17, 403
Abyssinia, see Ethiopia
Acerbo, Giacomo, 37, 283, 324–7, 409
D'Acquarone, Duke Pietro, 398
Addis Ababa, 89, 97, 99, 115, 198
Adriatic, 218, 221, 299, 393
Aegean Islands, 169, 344
Africa, 6, 77, 82–4, 94, 102, 115–17, 119, 126, 128–9, 139, 164, 171, 195, 200, 209, 215, 297–9, 305, 316–18, 330, 338, 342–4, 410, 412
Agenzia Stefani, 70
Ahram, 135
Alatri, Paolo, 242
Albania, 215, 221, 231, 266, 294, 344
Alberobello, 345
Albert, King of the Belgians, 289
Alessi, Rino, 140
Alfieri, Dino, 108, 116, 131, 161, 177–8, 185, 229, 279, 289–90, 296, 301–2, 316, 333, 337, 417
Algeria, 299, 343, 393
Alianello, Raffaele, 362
Allason, Barbara, 149
Almagià, David, 287
Almagià, Roberto, 289
Almansi, Dante, 286, 302, 355–6, 359, 360
Almansi, Dr. Renato J., 360
Aloisi, Baron Pompeo, 67, 68, 91, 115, 421
Alpenzeitung, 50
Alpes-Maritimes, Department of, 306, 322
Alps, The, 29, 39, 77, 119, 396
Altenburg, Günther, 312, 314
Alto Adige, 16, 21–2, 41, 44–6, 48, 50, 145, 347, 400
Ambrosio, General Vittorio, 308, 338
America, see United States
American (Jewish) Joint Distribution Committee, 204
Amhara, 181
Ancona, 293, 392
Anfuso, Filippo, 133, 147, 277, 341, 390, 401
Angelis, Mariano de, 84
Angriff, Der, 127
Ankara, 389
Annecy, 307
Anti-Comintern Pact, 95, 139
Anti-Europa, 47

Aosta, Emanuele Filiberto, Duke of, 195
Apollonio, Eugenio, 405
Aprilia, 151
Aras, Tewfik Rüstü, 73
Arbe, Island of, 305
Ardeatine Caves, 391
Arditi, 37
Arias, Gino, 52
Arrow Cross, 156
Asquith, Henry Herbert, 34
Asti, 333
Ateleta, 345
Athens, 311–12, 314
Attolico, Bernardo, 97, 155, 213, 217, 221, 223, 224, 260–3, 266, 269, 272, 281
Augustus Caesar, 53, 77
Auschwitz, 307, 365, 369, 381, 390–1
Austria, 7, 58, 61, 67, 68, 74, 76–8, 94, 99, 133, 136, 143, 186, 219, 223, 246, 249, 253, 417, 421
Avanti, 10
Azione Coloniale, 90

Bab-el-Mandeb, 144
Badoglio, Marshal Pietro, 115, 120–1, 295, 311, 333, 340–1, 342–4, 346, 354, 400, 402
Balabanoff, Angelica, 11
Balbo, Marshal Italo, 185, 189, 205, 282, 302
Baldwin, Stanley (Earl Baldwin of Bewdley), 204
Balfour, Arthur James, Earl of, 34, 84
Balfour Declaration, 14–15
Balkans, 93, 218–19, 221, 278, 296–7, 337
Baltic, 280, 320
Banca Commerciale Italiana, 7, 18, 38–9
Banque France-Italie, 309
Bari, 76, 98, 101, 167
Barilli, Manlio, 95
Barone-Russo, Giacomo, 22
Barzilai, Salvatore, 398
Basse-Alpes, Department of, 322
Bassi, Ugo, 384
Bastianini, Giuseppe, 44, 308, 331
Batault, Georges, 91–2
Bauer, SS-Hauptscharführer Helmut, 310
Bavaria, 17, 20

Bedarida, Guido, 24
Beilinson, Moshe, 24
Belgium, 279, 290, 320, 360
Belluno, Province of, 400
Ben Avi, Ittamar, 86
Benedetto, Padre Maria (Père Benôit-
  Marie), 388
Ben Gurion, David, 87–8
Berchtesgaden, 142, 264
Berenson, Bernard, 387, 389
Bergen, Diego von, 251–3, 371
Bergen-Belsen, 390–2
Berger, Ortsgruppenleiter in Trieste, 416
Berlin, 15–16, 18, 22, 45, 58, 61, 63, 65–7,
  69, 73, 77–8, 81, 93–5, 98, 101–2, 113,
  121, 125, 128–9, 131, 144, 146, 153–4,
  158–60, 164, 177, 181, 189, 193, 197,
  213, 216–17, 219–21, 223, 225–6, 229,
  235, 241–2, 253, 259, 263, 270, 274,
  278–9, 282, 286, 290, 294, 296–8, 300,
  302, 308–9, 314–15, 317–20, 322–6, 328,
  333–4, 341, 349, 351, 353–4, 360, 363,
  365–7, 371–2, 376, 378, 381, 388, 395–
  6, 401, 405, 411, 416–17, 420
Berliner Tageblatt, 7, 48
Berne, 323
Binchy, D. A., 244, 407-8
Bismarck, Otto von (1815–98), 96
Bismarck, Prince Otto von, 304, 314, 320,
  329, 334
Bissolati, Leonida, 10
Blum, Léon, 97, 114, 119, 132, 135, 420–3
Board of Deputies of British Jews, 111, 204
Bocchini, Arturo, 92, 102, 129–30, 283,
  286
Bohemia, 217, 332
Bolaffi, Gino, 11
Bologna, 257, 380, 383, 386, 389
Bolshevik Revolution, 6, 8, 12, 411
Bolshevism, 6, 8, 12–13, 23, 32, 34, 44, 96,
  101–2, 107–8, 119, 122–3, 125, 166, 180,
  214, 242, 246, 250, 279–82, 377, 398,
  406
Bolzano, 50, 385, 390, 400
Bonnefous, E., 421–2
Bonomi, Ivanoe, 10, 344
Borelli, Aldo, 182
Borgese, Giuseppe Antonio, 11, 407
Boriani, General Giuseppe, 357, 368
Bormann, Martin, 340, 404
Bosshammer, SS-Sturmbannführer Fried-
  rich Robert, 378–9, 381, 383–7, 389–92,
  405
Boston, 282
Bottai, Giuseppe, 170, 178, 188, 258, 273,
  341
Bozzetti, G., 418
Brand, Heinrich, 54
Bratislava, 376
Brazil, 200, 202, 239

Brenner, 22, 41, 44, 78, 82, 93, 96, 144,
  225, 263, 267, 281, 285, 296
Brescia, 402
Brindisi, 334
Britain, 7, 2–5, 57, 70, 77, 81, 84, 86–9, 91,
  94, 97–8, 123, 133, 148, 179, 184, 193–4,
  202–4, 231, 233, 262, 268–70, 273, 280,
  283, 285, 295–7, 323, 338, 422
British Union of Fascists, 159
Brussels, 320
Bucharest, 157
Buchenwald, 390
Budapest, 376
Buffarini-Guidi, Guido, 136, 178, 234,
  255–6, 274–5, 341, 348–51, 372, 378,
  382, 385, 387, 390, 405, 419
Bulgaria, 311–12, 332, 338
Burzio, Mgr. Giuseppe, 376
Bülow-Schwante, Vicco von, 138

Cabella, Gian Gaetano, 399
Cabrini, Angelo, 10
Cadogan, Sir Alexander, 203
Caesar, Gaius Julius, 53, 77, 300
Caillaux, Joseph, 420
Cairo, 88–9
Caleffi, Piero, 414
Calò, Eugenio, 388
Camicia Rossa, 117
Campagna, 345
Canevari, Emilio, 283, 349
Caporetto, 7
Carasso, Effendi, 7
Carlà, Colonel Vincenzo, 331
Carpi, Daniel, 241–2
Caruso, Pietro, 390
Casati, Count Alessandro, 184
Caserta, 406
Castellino, Nicolò, 137
Catholic Herald, 238
Cavellero, General (later Marshal) Ugo,
  226
Caviglia, Marshal Enrico, 289
Cavour, Camillo Benso Di, 96
Cerruti, Vittorio, 49, 59, 78, 95, 121, 421
Chamberlain, Arthur Neville, 193, 201–4,
  208–9, 221, 231–3, 268, 272
Chamberlain, Houston Stewart, 35–6
Chambrun, Count Charles de Pineton de,
  73, 420, 422
Chiavari, 382
Chvalkovsky, František, K., 157
Cianetti, Tullio, 134–5
Ciano di Cortellazzo (Mussolini), Countess
  Edda, 130–1, 348
Ciano di Cortellazzo, Count Galeazzo, 95,
  99, 101–2, 111, 113, 115, 131, 133, 136–
  7, 140–7, 151–2, 154, 158–9, 178, 180–
  1, 183–6, 188–90, 193, 195, 197, 199–
  204, 212–14, 217–18, 220–5, 232–4,

Ciano di Cortellazzo (*contd.*)
251–4, 259–69, 271–4, 276–7, 279–80,
282, 285, 288–90, 296, 298–9, 301–2,
304, 312, 314, 318–19, 323–4, 329, 332,
374, 397, 401, 413, 416–17
Codreanu, Corneliu Zelea, 156
Cogni, Giulio, 116, 127, 176, 187
Cohen, Israel, 243
Col d'Echerle, 11
Colorni, Eugenio, 388
Colton, J., 422–3
Comité des Délégations Juives, 65
Como, Lake, 406
Coppola, Francesco, 11
Corriere della Sera, Il, 55, 182, 398
Corriere Italiano, 23, 36
Corrispondenza Repubblicana, 398
Corsica, 215
Coselschi, Eugenio, 62, 86, 129
Cosenza, 292
Cosmelli, Count, Counsellor at German
Embassy, 301
Côte d'Azur, 309–10
Cermona, the ras of, *see* Farinacci, Roberto
Cremona, Paul, 180
Cresenzi, Marchese and Marchesa Serlupi,
387
Crete, 311
Croatia, 299, 304–5, 331–2
Croce, Benedetto, 4
Csáky, Count István, 157
Cuneo, 392
Curiel, Eugenio, 388
Curzon, Lord George Nathaniel, 25
Cyprus, 215
Cyrenaica, 25, 293
Czechoslovakia, 147, 157, 179, 189, 212,
219, 223, 320

D'Acquarone, Duke Pietro, 398
Daily Graphic, 7
Daily Mail, 97
Daily Telegraph, The, 7, 98
Daladier, Edouard, 192, 232
Dalmatia, 344
Dannecker, SS-Hauptsturmführer, Theo-
dor, 362, 365–7, 371, 378–81, 386
D'Annunzio, Gabriele, Prince of Monte-
nevoso, 37, 172, 256
Danube Basin, 77, 193, 219
Dante, Alighieri, 300
Danzig, 260–2, 265, 267, 271
D'Aroma, Nino, 78, 397, 417, 425
Dava, 114
Deakin, F. W., 418
De Begnac, Yuon, 39, 125
De Bono, Marshal Emilio, 189
De Felice, Renzo, 127, 373, 415–17, 418
DELASEM (Committee For Aid to Jewish
Emigrants), 356, 364, 371, 388

Delp, Father Alfred, 374
Denmark, 287, 290
De Stefani, Alberto, 39, 189
Deutsch-Völkische Freiheits-Partei, 17
De Vecchi di Val Cismon, Count Cesare
Maria, 134
Del Vecchio, Giorgio, 52, 228, 254
Difesa della Razza, La, 118, 165, 329
Dinale, Ottavio ('Farinata'), 59
Di Porto, Celeste (the 'Black Panther'),
389
Dizengoff, Meir, 86
Doar Hayom, 86–7
Dolfin, Giovanni, 401
Dollfuss, Engelbert, 61, 67–8, 75–6, 81
Dollmann, SS-Obersturmbannführer
(later Standartenführer) Eugen, 160–1
Donati, Angelo, 309–10, 342–4
Dordona, Captain, 88
Dresler, Adolf, 37, 95
Dugdale, Blanche, C., 84
Dumini, Amerigo, 418
Durham, Bishop of, 241

East Africa, *see* Africa
Eastern Europe, *see* Europe
Eden, Anthony (Earl of Avon), 90, 97–8,
183, 421
Egypt, 88, 97, 295, 297
Ehrt, Adolf, 95
Eichmann, Adolf, 306–7, 309, 314, 321,
360–1, 369–70, 376, 381, 385–6, 389,
413
Einstein, Robert, 392
Eisenhower, Dwight, D., 311
El Alamein, 398
England, *see* Britain
Esser, Hermann, 155
Ethiopia, 78, 80, 82, 85, 88–91, 99–102,
115, 171–2, 174, 195–6, 198, 200, 208,
215, 248, 282, 407, 410, 420–1
Etna, 396
Europe, 12–13, 34, 43, 47, 58, 75, 77, 93,
96, 98, 107, 109, 115, 123, 126, 144, 157,
164, 179–80, 186, 198, 208–10, 213–14,
217, 219–20, 222, 231–2, 258, 260–1,
265, 267, 273, 278, 280, 294, 300, 303,
318–21, 335, 368, 395, 406, 413
Evian Conference, 208
Evola, Baron Julius C., 137, 187, 328–30,
410

Facta, Luigi, 19
Faitlovich, Dr. Jacques, 86
Falashas, 85, 100
Farinacci, Roberto (the ras of Cremona),
36, 39, 45, 52, 59, 63, 101, 108–12, 121–
2, 127, 132–4, 137, 139, 149, 165, 178,
180, 183, 185, 188, 240–1, 243–5, 256,
276, 283–4, 286, 289, 291, 293, 325, 329,
333, 339–41, 411, 416–17, 418–19

'Farinata' (Ottavio Dinale), 59, 417
Farnesi, Mario, 336
Federzoni, Luigi, 27, 189, 323, 409
Feltre, 333, 339–40
Ferramonti Tarsia, 292, 345
Ferrara, 293, 383, 391
Fiamma Nera, La, 37
Finland, 179, 279
Finzi, Aldo, 21 37, 51, 391
Fischer, Professor Eugen, 325–7
Fiume, 172, 256
Flandin, Pierre Etienne, 420
Fleischhauer, Lt.-Col. Ulrich, 19
Florence, 8, 95, 147–8, 211, 257, 283, 286,
    293–4, 326, 387, 389, 391–2
Flossenburg, 391
Foà, Carlo, 52
Foà, Jole, 180
Faò, Ugo, 355–60
Forlí, 154, 383, 392
Fornari, Harry, 121–2, 188, 418
Forti, Sergio, 388
Fossani, Ivanoe, 128, 399
Fossoli di Carpi, 383–6, 390, 393–4, 396
France, 7, 16, 27, 70, 72, 77, 79, 81, 91, 93,
    97, 114, 133, 159, 176, 179, 184, 193–4,
    197, 209, 215–16, 218, 222, 224, 231–2,
    262, 269–70, 273, 280, 283, 285, 294–5,
    305–11, 320, 322, 331, 335, 337, 342–4,
    398, 421
Franco, y Bahamonde, General Francisco,
    183, 221, 259–60, 418, 421
François-Poncet, André, 285
Franconia, 94
Frank, Hans, 44, 95, 130, 132–3
Frankfurter, Felix, 34
Frankfurter Zeitung, 7
Fredrigotti, Giuseppe, 36
French North Africa, 101, 215, 316
Frercks, Dr. Rudolf, 161, 175–8
Friedlander, Shaul, 242
Fuschl, 262–3

Gafencu, Grigore, 157
Galicia, 321
Garda, Lake, 37, 396
Gargnano, 396, 398
Garibaldi, Ezio, 117, 137, 409
Gayda, Virginio, 286
Geloso, General Carlo, 312–14
Geneva, 64, 70, 90, 96, 110
Genoa, 257, 292–3, 345, 382, 388, 406
Gerarchia, 52, 85, 87
Germino, Dante L., 123–4, 188
Ghigi, Pellegrino, 312
Gibraltar, 144, 215
Giolitti, Giovanni, 34
Giornale di Genova, 113
Giornale d'Italia, 33, 91, 152, 286
Giunta, Francesco, 416

Giuriati, Giovanni, 48
Giustiniani, Marchese, Cultural Attaché
    in Berlin, 177
Givat Brenner, 27
Glaser (Milan Nazi), 55
Goebbels, Paul Joseph, 50, 107–8, 127,
    132, 190, 260, 335–6, 340, 345, 347–9
Goffredo, Alfredo, 409
Gojjam area (Abyssinia), 88
Goldbeck, Kreisleiter of Recklinghausen,
    301
Goldmann, Dr. Nahum, 65–72, 77–8, 87,
    136, 228
Göring, Hermann Wilhelm, 44–5, 63, 74,
    134, 156, 222–3, 261
Graham, Sir Ronald, 25, 72–4
Gramsci, Antonio, 4
Grandi, Dino, 32, 48, 85, 97–8, 142, 145,
    333, 338, 341, 397
'Grand Mufti' of Jerusalem (Hadj Amin
    El-Husseini), 298
Gravelli, Asvero, 47
Graziani, Rodolfo, Marshal, 115, 400, 402
Great Britain, *see* Britain
Greece, 231, 296–7, 311–16, 338, 344
Grego, Adriano, 113
Gregor, A. James, 127–8
Gries, 385, 390–1
Grimaldi, Alfassio V., 418–19
Gringorie, 91
Gross, Dr. Walter, 149–50, 175, 229, 286,
    302, 324, 326, 328–30
Gualtieri, General Carlo Avarna di, 309
Guariglia, Raffaele, 32, 86
Guarneri, Felice, 137
Gubbio, 391
Guggenheim (family), 13
Gumpert, Gerhard R., 365–6, 369
Günther, Hans F. K., 116

Habsburg, 42, 219
Hague, The, 320
Haile Selassie, 93
Halifax, Lord Edward, 201–2, 271–2
Harster, SS-Brigadeführer Wilhelm, 381,
    384, 392
Hassell, Ulrich von, 74, 91, 94, 96, 99, 158,
    182, 416–17
Hasson, Ines, 315
Haute-Savoie, Department of, 322
Heathcote Smith, Sir Clifford E., 393–395
Heiden, Konrad, 122–3
Herzl, Theodor, 3
Hess, Rudolf, 54, 182, 229
Hesse, Prince Philip of, 100, 133, 285
Heydrich, Reinhard, 219, 301
Hidaki, Shiurukuro, 401
Hildebrandt, Dr. Phillipp, 138
Hilger, Gustav, 379
Hill, Leonidas E., 371, 376

Himmler, Heinrich, 102, 129–30, 154, 160–61, 182, 219, 229, 240, 252, 278, 306, 308, 315, 321, 334–35, 339, 346–7, 352–4, 364, 369, 378, 389, 413, 419
Hindenburg und Beneckendorff, Field-Marshal Paul von, 12
Hochhuth, Rolf, 373, 376, 424, 426
Hofer, Franz, 347
Hohenzollern, 17
Holland, 156, 209, 279, 290, 320, 360
Holy See, *see* Vatican
Hore-Belisha, Leslie, 145, 283
Hudal, Bishop Alois, 366, 369, 372, 425–6
Hull, Cordell, 211
Hungary, 156, 198–9, 210, 234, 259–60, 321, 332, 338, 373, 376

Impero, L', 37
Imredy, Béla, 154
Indian Ocean, 215
Informazione Diplomatica, 141–2, 166–7
Innsbruck, 326, 347, 400
Inter-Governmental Committee on Political Refugees, 198–201, 207–8, 210–11, 393–4
Interlandi, Telesio, 51–2, 58, 90, 114, 117, 135, 137, 156, 165, 167, 176, 187, 235, 241, 325, 329, 341, 409, 415, 417
Intra, 391
Intransigeant, L', 98
Ionian Islands, 311, 315
Iraq, 88
Iron Guard, 156
Isère, Department of, 310
Israel, 26, 29, 34, 136
Israel (people of), 115, 286, 398
Istria, 344
Italia Liberia, L', 368
Italia che scrive, L', 326
Italian Nationalist Association, 7
Italian Red Cross, 357–8, 368
Italian Refugee Committee, 211
Italian Socialist Party, 7, 10
Italian Socialist Republic, 346, 352, 380, 382, 386, 396, 402–3, 405–6. *See also* The Salò Rep.
Italy–Palestine Committee, 30
Italian Zionist Federation, 28, 31, 61, 82

Jabotinsky, Vladimir Zeev, 86
Jacchia, Mario, 388
Japan, 159, 213, 224, 226, 259–60
Jandl, Colonel Johann, 349–50
Jarach, Ermanno, 11
Jarach, Federico, 63, 110, 136
Jaroseau, Mgr. André, 421
Jenna, Advocate, Jewish internee, 385
Jenna, (Mrs.) (Aryan wife of above), 385
Jerusalem, 84, 369
Jesi, Lieutenant Bruno, 282

Jewish Agency, 84, 86–7, 123
Jewish Relief Committee, 277–8, 293
Jewish Rescue Committee in Budapest, 376
Jewish Telegraphic Agency, 134, 227
Jodl, General Alfred, 339
Jona, Elio, 11
Jouvenel, Bertrand de, 423
Jubaland, 195
Jüdische Rundschau, 122
Jung, Guido, 5, 29, 52

Kahn, Otto Herman, 33, 40
Kállay, Nicholas (Miklós), 331
Kaltenbrunner, SS-Obergruppenführer Dr. Ernst, 309, 314, 321, 352–3, 378–9
Kamenev, Lev, 12
Kánya, Kálmán, 154
Kappler, SS-Obersturmbannführer Herbert, 345, 352–5, 357–8, 360–3, 365, 367–9, 372, 378, 391, 405
Kasche, Siegfried, 305
Keitel, Field-Marshal Wilhelm, 222, 296
Kenya, 144, 198
Kessel, Abrecht von, 362, 365–6, 372, 375, 377
Kesselring, Field-Marshal Albert, 344–5, 347, 354–5, 363, 392
King, Bolton, 407
Kirkpatrick, Sir Ivone, 127, 424
Kisch, Colonel Frederick Herman, 34
Kleinlerer, Eduard David, 227, 229, 238, 256
Klessheim, 293, 403
Knochen, SS-Standartenführer Dr. Helmut, 160, 306–7, 309, 322
Koch, Pietro, 405
Kohn, Dr. Leo, 86–7
Kordt, Erich, 147
Kornicker, Kurt, 122–3

Lampedusa, 338
Landra, Dr. Guido, 118, 161, 175–8, 229, 286, 324, 328
Landsberg, 43
La Piana, Giorgio, 241
Larissa, 314
Laski, Neville, 111–12, 116, 204, 210, 243, 408
Lateran Treaties, 30, 245, 390
Lattes, Dante Abramo, 24, 31, 61, 84–5, 110, 112, 136, 247
Laurens, Franklin D., 420, 423
Laval, Pierre, 77, 81, 420, 422
League of German Nationalist Jews, 16
League of Nations, 67–8, 74, 80, 82, 91, 94, 96
Ledeen, Michael A., 124
Leghorn, 257, 293, 392
Leiber, Father Robert, 372

Leipzig, 144
Lenin, Vladimir Ilich, 12–13, 34
Le Pera, Dr. Antonio, 149–50, 161, 165,
    171, 175–6, 341
Levant, 5
Levi, Jewish internee, 384
Levi, (Mrs.) (Aryan wife of above), 384
Levi, Renzo, 356
Lewy, Guenter, 242, 373, 375–6, 426
Libya, 6–7, 11, 135, 169, 215, 218, 292–3,
    297
Liggeri, Don Paolo, 388
Likus, SS-Oberführer Rudolf, 346
Lipari Islands, 27
Lisieux, 425
Litvinov, Maxim, 281
Liuzzi, Alberto, 52
Liverani, Augusto, 397
Locarno, Treaty of, 96, 98
Lombard invasion, 152
London, 13, 38, 84–5, 139, 142, 193, 203,
    218, 220–1, 231, 246, 271–2, 322, 344,
    393, 409
Longo, Guido, 90
Loraine, Sir Percy, 232, 285
Lospinoso, Guido, 308–11
Löhr, General Alexander, 312
Lublin, 280
Ludendorff, General Erich, 20, 45, 49
Ludwig (Cohn), Emil, 28, 41, 48, 51
Lugano, Bishop of, 419
Luzzatti, Luigi, 5, 228
Luther, Franz Julius Martin, 304, 317–18,
    378
Lüdecke, Kurt George Wilhelm, 20–3, 43,
    45
Lyon, 307
Lyttelton, Adrian, 415

McClure, Sir William Kidston, 6, 8, 122–
    3, 417
MacDonald, James G., 417
Macerata Province, 394
McFadyean, Sir Andrew, 204–10
Mackensen, General Hans Georg von,
    160–1, 171, 173–5, 195, 199, 217–19,
    233, 268, 270, 273, 279, 301, 304, 307–8,
    314, 317, 319–20, 327, 329, 331, 336,
    340, 346–7, 419
Madrid, 260, 390
Maggiore, Lago, 352, 391
Magistrati, Count Massimo, 132, 158, 233,
    262–3
'Maître' Salem, 7
Malta, 215
Malvy, Jean-Louis, 421
Manacorda, Guido, 95, 129
Manchester Guardian, 415
Manin, Daniele, 35
Mantua, 390

March on Rome, 6, 8, 11, 16, 23–4, 29, 43,
    48, 51, 55, 134, 162, 165, 171, 247, 256
Mareth Line, 398
Margulies, Samuel Hirsch, 31, 115
Marinetti, Filippo Tommaso, 409
Marqui, Count Pietro, 305
Marseilles, 310–11
Massaua, 115
Matin, Le, 97
Matteotti, Giacomo, 36, 39, 119, 172, 256,
    418, 422
Mauthausen, 364
Mazzolini, Count Serafino, 350, 389, 397,
    401
Mediterranean, 8, 32, 88, 98, 111, 119,
    122–3, 145–6, 184, 215, 218–21, 231,
    296–7, 299, 337, 339, 398, 421
Mégève, 310
Mein Kampf, 41, 76, 179
Mellini Ponce di Leon, Count Alberto, 401
Merano, 45, 416
Messagero, Il, 261
Messedaglia, Senator Luigi, 294
Michelangelo, Buonarotti, 300
Michels, Robert, 407
Middle East, 14, 87, 89, 98, 298
Migiurtinia, 181, 195
Milan, 9, 20, 31, 77, 96, 149, 182, 204, 223,
    240, 257–8, 292–3, 328, 380–1, 384–5,
    388, 390, 406, 422
Mira, Giovanni, 60
Modena, 380, 383–5, 393, 395–6
Modigliani, Giuseppe Emanuele, 7, 10, 12
Moellhausen, Eitel Friedrich 351, 354,
    362–5, 369
Mollier, Dr. Hans, 161, 163–9, 175, 187
Mollier, Madeleine, 399
Mondolfo, Bruno, 11
Montefiore, Dr. Claud G., 84
Montenegro, 331
Montini, Mgr. Giovanni Battista, see Pope
    Paul VI
Montreux, 61, 86
Morgenthau, Henry, 398
Morning Post, 97
Morocco, 299, 343
Morpurgo, Luciano, 357–8
Mortara, Lodovico, 37
Moscow, 27, 107–8, 184, 260, 263, 267–8,
    278–9, 281
Mosley, Sir Oswald Ernan, 61, 75, 91, 156,
    419
Mostar, 304
Muhs, 425
Munich, 18, 22–3, 44–5, 81, 121, 156, 158,
    177, 194–5, 201, 215, 217, 233–4, 262,
    264, 273, 295, 334, 349–50, 377, 399,
    422
Mussert, Anton Adrian, 61, 156
Mussolini, (Mancini) Edvige, 183

Mussolini, Vittorio, 189, 401–2
Muti, Ettore, 285
Müller, Heinrich, 306–9, 322, 362, 370
Müller, Dr. Sven von, 95

Nahon, Dr. Umberto, 136
Naples, 145, 147, 286, 345
Naumann, Dr. Max, 16
Neue Freie Presse, 7
Neumann, Heinrich von, 143
Neurath, Baron Konstantin von, 23, 99, 133
New York, 13
New York Times, 98, 417
Nice, 311, 344
Nicoletti, Gioacchini, 399, 401
Nietzsche, Frederich Wilhelm, 10
Nile Delta, 298
NKVD, 148
Nord-Süd Korrespondenz, 45
Norway, 287, 290
Nostra Bandiera, Le, 60, 101
Nuremberg, 107–10, 122, 126–7, 132–3, 135, 149, 171, 173, 175, 191, 234, 254, 335, 350, 366, 405

Orano, Paolo, 111–14, 136
Orgesch Organisation Escherich, 15
Orsini Baroni, Luca, 49
Orvieto, Angiolo, 84–5
Osborne, Sir Francis d'Arcy Godolphin, 342–4, 396, 424
Osservatore Romano, 254, 288–90, 371–2
Ottolenghi, General Giuseppe, 5
Ovazza, Ettore, 112, 114

Pacelli, Eugenio, *see* Pope Pius XII
Pacifici, Alfonso, 55
Padova (Padua), 259, 294, 390
Padre Pancrazio, *see* Pfeiffer, Father Pankratius
Palermo, 345
Palestine, 8, 13–14, 16, 25–6, 30–1, 79, 83–9, 97–8, 101, 123, 141, 144, 172, 174, 195, 231, 259, 277, 298
Pantelleria, Island of, 338
Pariani, General Alberto, 222
Parini, Piero, 132
Paris, 64, 97–8, 114, 159, 164, 197, 220, 231, 246, 271, 276, 306, 309, 315, 318, 320, 322, 362, 374
Parma, 383
Paul, Prince Regent of Yugoslavia, 218, 231
Paul-Boncour, Joseph, 420
Pavelič, Ante, 304
Pavolini, Alessandro, 329, 348–9, 358
Pellizi, Camillo, 409
Pennetta, Epifanio, 356–7

Perth, Earl of (Sir Eric Drummond), 180, 193
Perugia, 112
Peterich, Dr. Eckart, 326–7
Petrograd, 12
Pfeiffer, Father Pankratius (Padre Pancrazio), 366
Phillips, William, 137, 147, 196–9, 208, 211–13, 227, 231, 277–8, 282
Piacenza, 383
Piazza, Alces, 385
Piccoli, Il, 137
Piedmont, 333
Pietrabissa, Italian diplomat, 324
Pietromarchi, Count Luca, 324
Pignatti Morano di Custoza, Count Bonifacio, 253
Pini, Giorgio, 113–14, 116, 121, 136, 409, 418
Pirow, Oswald, 157
Pirzio, Biroli, General Alessandro, 331
Pisa, 287, 392
Pisanò, Giorgio, 410
Pistillo, Gaetano, 90
Pittalis, Francesco, 81
Plessen, Baron Johann von, 161–3, 326, 330
Po, 391, 401, 403, 406
Prodrecca, Guido, 10
Poincaré, Raymond, 25
Polacco, Vittorio, 398
Poland, 44, 70, 110, 206, 210, 222–4, 226, 231, 233, 259, 261–5, 267–9, 272–3, 277, 279–80, 282, 284, 287, 303–4, 312, 320–1, 332, 360
Polish Corridor, 77
Ponte Tresa, 60
Pontremoli, Giuseppe, 11
Pope Benedict XV, 14,
Pope Paul VI, 364
Pope Pius XI, 53, 128, 146, 153–4, 165, 181, 235–45, 247–8, 250–1, 367
Pope Pius XII, 238, 242, 247, 250-4, 288–9, 356, 360, 364, 367, 370–7, 390, 393, 395–6
Pope, Generoso, 137
Popolo d'Italia, Il, 11–12, 52, 55, 57, 59, 74, 112–13, 115, 149, 287, 397, 415, 421
Popolo di Roma, 30, 134
Populaire, Le, 422
Portugal, 387
Prague, 192, 217–18, 220–21, 224, 231, 249, 260, 301, 320
Prato, David, 136
Preziosi, Giovanni, 18–20, 37–39, 49, 51–2, 74, 90, 134, 137, 140, 159, 161, 165, 183, 187, 293–4, 324–6, 328, 333, 336, 340–1, 348–51, 381, 384–5, 389, 398, 402, 405–6, 411, 416, 418
Primo de Riveria, General Miguel, 47

Prittwitz und Gaffron, Baron Friedrich
  Wilhelm von, 23
Prontocols of the Elders of Zion, 8–9, 85, 409,
  418
Prussia, 75
Pugliese, General Emanuele, 182

Quadrivio, Il, 117, 138, 140, 241
Quisling, Vidkun, 376

Rafanelli, Leda, 11
Rahn, Dr. Rudolf, 347, 349, 354, 362, 369,
  379–80, 390, 398–400, 402
Rainer, Friedrich, 347
Rapallo treaty, 16
Rastenburg, 346, 348, 352–3
Rathenau, Walther, 15–17
Rati, Achille, *see* Pope Pius XI
Rauff, SS-Obersturmbannführer Walter,
  159
Ravenna, 257, 383
Ravenna, Felice di Leone, 110–11, 133,
  136
Ravensbrück, 390–1
Recklinghausen, 301
Reggio Emilia, 383
Regime Fascista, Il, 59, 90, 108, 110, 113,
  256, 416, 418–19
Reitlinger, Gerald, 373
Renzetti, Major Giuseppe, 48–9, 235, 324
Repetto, Don Francesco, 388
Resto de Carlino, Il, 257, 283
Revisionist Zionist Party, 86
Revue Hébdomadaire, La, 91–2
Rhine, 41, 77
Rhineland, 96, 100
Rhodes, 134, 311, 391–2
Ribbentrop, Joachim von, 139, 147, 151,
  155, 158–9, 193, 197, 214, 219, 221,
  223–4, 225–6, 233, 252–3, 260–4, 266–
  7, 281, 285, 296, 298, 301–2, 304–5, 307,
  314–15, 317, 319, 324, 330–1, 335–6,
  346–9, 363–4, 369, 378–9, 390, 419
Ribière, Prefect, 306
Riccardi, Raffaello, 340
Ricci, Renato, 95, 129, 340
Riccio, Vicenzo, 19
Rignano, 392
Rintelen, General Enno von, 158, 300
Roatta, General Mario, 263, 305
Robotti, General Mario, 331
Rocco, Alfredo, 324
Romania, 156–7, 186, 198–9, 206, 210,
  231, 296, 318, 332, 338, 373
Romanini, Alfredo, 101
Rome, 3, 19, 22–25, 27, 33, 38, 40, 44, 61,
  65–7, 75–7, 81, 93, 94–5, 97–8, 101, 113,
  122, 129, 132, 134–41, 144–7, 149, 158–
  61, 170–1, 175–7, 179, 181, 184, 190,
  193, 196, 201, 204, 207–8, 211–13, 219,

222–3, 226–7, 230, 238–9, 241, 251, 257,
  259–60, 263, 265, 269, 271–2, 274, 276,
  278, 287–9, 293–4, 298, 304–5, 308–18,
  321–3, 325–7, 331, 333–4, 336, 340,
  344–7, 351–72, 376, 388, 390–2, 394,
  407–8, 411, 421–2, 425
Rome–Berlin Axis, 19, 27, 100–1, 113,
  122, 128, 164, 179, 184–5, 215, 230, 240,
  246, 249–50, 254, 308, 350, 406, 410,
  418
Rommel, Field-Marshal Erwin, 298, 337,
  344, 347
Roosevelt, Franklin Delano, 183, 195–9,
  201–2, 208–9, 227, 231, 246, 278, 285,
  393
Roques, Comm. Giuseppe Pardo, 392
Rosani, Rita, 388
Rosenberg, Alfred, 36, 38–42, 52, 229,
  328, 397
Rossi, Ernesto, 241
Rosso-Longhi, Italian diplomat, 324
Rossoni, Edmondo, 95
Roth, Cecil, 3, 243
Rothschild (family) Misspelt by Mussolini
  as Rotschild, 13
Röthke, SS-Obersturmführer Heinz, 307,
  309–11, 315, 322
Rublee, George, 203
Russia, 16, 34, 93, 107, 110, 179–80, 198,
  200, 202, 224, 268–9, 280–1, 296–7, 300,
  338
Russian Revolution, *see* Bolshevik
  Revolution
Rust, Bernhard, 325

Saar, 68
Sacerdoti, Dr. Angelo, 24, 28, 33, 63–6, 70,
  72
Salò Republic, 349–52, 396, 403. *See also*
  Italian Social Republic
Salonica, 7, 311–15
Salvatorelli, Luigi, 60, 142
Salvemini, Gaetano, 79, 120, 241, 407, 422
Salvotti, Baron Troilo de, 134
Salzburg, 262, 264, 267, 323
Sapuppo, Giuseppe, 324
Sardinia, 291
Sarfatti, Cesare, 11
Sarfatti, Margherita, 11, 21, 31, 52, 141,
  181
Sarfatti, Roberto, 11–12
Sarraut, Albert Pierre, 420
Savoie, Department of, 310, 322
Scavizzi, Pirro, 374
Schanzer, Carlo, 15
Schellenberg, Walter, 309
Schiff, Jacob, 33
Schleier, Rudolf, 322
Schmidt, Paul, 130, 147, 269
Scholl, Hans, 377

Scholl, Sophie, 377
Schuschnigg, Dr. Kurt von, 35, 68, 96, 135–6
Schwarze Korps, Das, 154, 419
Schyff (Schiff family) Misspelt by Mussolini, 13
Senise, Carmine, 308
Sereni, Enzo, 27
Servi, Elena, 386
Sforza, Carlo, 407
Sharett (Shertok), Moshe, 84, 87
Sicily, 291, 338
Siena, 387
Sinigaglia, Duilio, 11
Slovakia, 332, 373, 376
Smith, Sir Grafton Elliot, 76
Sofia, 362
Sokolov, Nahum, 32, 62
Soldani Benzi, Virgilio, 387
Somaliland, 181
Somenzi, Mino, 409
Sonnino, Baron Sidney, 5, 15, 228
Sorani, Rosina, 359, 371
Sorani, Settimio, 371
South Tyrol, 15–16, 21–3, 37–8, 41–3, 46, 74, 76, 144–5, 259, 265, 279, 293, 299–300, 346, 402, 416
Soviet Revolution, see Bolshevik Revolution
Spain, 3, 5, 88, 99–102, 107, 111, 119, 122–3, 132, 193, 221, 246, 259–60, 262, 279, 297, 421–2
Spampanato, Bruno, 396–7
Speer, Albert, 344
Spinosa, Antonio, 242
Spirit and Blood, 328
Stahel, General Rainer, 354, 362, 366, 368–9, 372
Stalin, Josif Vissarionovitch, 148, 268, 279, 281, 348, 398
Stampa, La, 34
Starace, Achille, 27, 124, 165, 176, 178, 185, 188, 279
Starhemberg, Ernst Rüdiger von, 30, 35, 56, 61, 75
Starr, Joshua, 122–3
Stato Corporativo, 52
Steengracht von Moyland, Baron Gustav Adolf von, 316, 323, 349, 401
Stevens, Colonel Harold, 338
Strasser, Gregor, 39, 54
Strasser, Otto, 39
Strautz, Felix Ritter von, 161, 170–1
Streicher, Julius, 94–5, 128, 135, 155
Stresa, 81–2, 93–4, 96–97, 99, 144–5
Stresemann, Gustav, 15, 23, 38
Strunk, Roland, 95, 129
Stürmer, Der, 128, 155
Sudan, 215
Suez, 215

Suñer, Ramón Serrano, 259
Susmel, E., 422
Suvich, Baron Fulvio, 67, 74, 85, 150–1, 186
Svevo, Italo (Ettore Schmitz), 282
Switzerland, 321, 323, 388, 395
Syria, 88
Szálasi, Ferenc, 156

Tablet, The, 238
Tacchi-Venturi, Father Pietro, 91, 181, 329
Tagliacozzo, Michael, 365
Tagliacozzo, Dr. Pio, 238
Tamaro, Attilio, 409
Tamburini, Tullio, 349, 351, 380–1, 394
Tana, Lake, 282
Taranto Harbour, 296
Tardini, Mgr. Domenico, 395
Taylor, Myron, 210–12, 394–5
Tedeschi, Corrado, 85–7
Teheran, 148
Tel-Aviv, 86
Tevere, Il, 49, 59, 62, 79, 86, 117, 135, 138, 140, 276, 325, 415
Thadden, Eberhard von, 363–4, 369, 378
Theodoli, Marquis Alberto, 87–8
Theresienstadt, 334
Thrace, 311
Times, The, 85, 322, 424
Tisserant, Cardinal Eugène, 374
Titho, SS-Untersturmführer Karl, 385
Toeplitz, Giuseppe, 38–40
Tokyo, 193, 197
Torrès, Maurice, 31
Toscano, Mario, 192, 225
Trentino, 10, 400
Treves, Claudio, 7, 10, 31
Trieste, 145, 150, 154, 174, 257, 282–3, 287–8, 300, 331, 336, 344, 347, 385, 391, 416–17
Tripiccione, General, 313
Tripoli, 25, 38, 88, 135, 138
Trotsky, Lev Davidovich, 12, 34
Tunis (ia), 14, 159, 176, 215, 316–18, 335, 343, 354, 363
Turati, Augusto, 48
Turati, Filippo, 8
Turin, 60, 67, 70, 149, 257–8, 286, 293–4
Turkey, 6–7, 232, 311

Ufficio studi sulla razza, 176
Umberto, Crown Prince, 398
Union of Italian-Jewish Communities, 53, 63, 84, 100, 110, 136, 257, 286, 303, 360
United Kingdom, see England
United Restitution Organization, 121
United States, 18, 33, 150, 180, 196–202, 204, 209, 231–2, 241, 277, 280, 288, 338, 393, 398

U.S.S.R., *see* Russia

Valdagno, 394
Vansittart, Sir Robert (later Lord), 112, 424
Var, Department of, 322
Varè, Daniele, 35
Varese, 381
Vatican, 14, 30, 53, 146, 181, 197, 226, 235–8, 241–3, 245–54, 288–90, 323, 342, 347, 356, 362, 364–75, 377, 390, 394–6, 424–6
Vecchio-Verderame, Angelo, 50
Venice, 69, 108, 132, 300, 344, 346–7
Verona, 351, 381, 384–5, 390
Versailles, Treaty of, 16, 21, 70, 272
Vichy, 297, 305, 309, 316, 322, 342, 344, 374
Vienna, 67, 143, 205, 217, 229, 260, 334, 407, 417
Villari, Luigi, 5–6, 123, 409
Virgil (Publius Naso), 77
Visco, Sabato, 328
Vita Italiana, La, 18, 37, 138, 283, 294, 325, 416, 419
Viterbo, 257
Vitetti, Leonardo, 235, 264, 323–4
Vittorio Emmanuele III, 3, 100, 130, 153–4, 182–3, 185, 193, 258–9, 268, 274, 285, 288, 338, 341, 344, 398, 419, 422
Vittorio Veneto, 289
Vivanti, Ildebrando, 388
Volpe, Gioacchino, 409
Volpi di Misurata, Count Giuseppe, 38–9, 188
Volterra, Jewish internee, 384
Völkischer Beobachter, 36, 159

Wagner, Horst, 378
Wagner, Richard, 329
Warburg family (Misspelt by Mussolini as Warnberg), 13
Warsaw, 223, 260, 322
Washington D.C., 323
Webster, Richard A., 241

Weimar Republic, 15, 17, 38, 43, 45–6
Weizmann, Dr. Chaim, 3, 25–8, 63–5, 69, 78–80, 84–5, 87, 89, 276, 278
Weizsäcker, Baron Ernst von, 260, 301–2, 316–17, 362, 364–6, 369–72, 390
Welles, Sumner, 285
Weltdienst, 19
Weltkampf, 36
Wenner, SS-Hauptsturmführer Eugene, 160
Wille und Macht, 134
Windels, German diplomat, 416
Wirth, Karl Joseph, 15
Wittelsbach (dynasty), 17
Woermann, Ernst, 302, 317
Wolf, Gerhard, 387
Wolf, Lucien, 7
Wolff, SS-Obergruppenführer Karl, 347, 367, 369. 400
Wolff, Theodor, 47
World Jewish Congress, 65, 68, 111
World War I, 5, 7, 14, 16, 18, 169
World War II, 123, 126, 161, 179, 190, 226, 233, 247, 272
World Zionist Organization, 25, 71
Wulle, Reinhold, 17–18
Wüster, Walther, 326

Yalta, 398
Yugoslavia, 218, 222, 265, 296, 344

Zachariae, Dr. Georg, 397
Zeitschel, SS-Sturmbannführer Dr. Carltheo, 159, 161
Zelman, Vitta, 385
Zevi Guido, 136
Zinoviev, Grigori, 12
Zionism, Zionist(s), 6, 8, 13–14, 24–8, 30–2, 34–5, 65, 68, 71, 78–80, 81, 83–7, 89–90, 94, 101, 110–12, 114, 119, 123, 125, 134, 136, 138, 142, 243, 257, 259, 291, 408
Zolli, Israel (later Eugenio), 358, 360–1
Zweig, Stefan, 79